AF906230

Counter-Terrorism and International Law

The International Law of Peace and Security
Series Editor: Professor Nigel D. White

Titles in the Series:

The Use of Force in International Law
Tarcisio Gazzini and Nikolaos Tsagourias

Arms Control Law
Daniel H. Joyner

Post-Conflict Rebuilding and International Law
Ray Murphy

Counter-Terrorism and International Law
Katja L.H. Samuel and Nigel D. White

Counter-Terrorism and International Law

Edited by

Katja L.H. Samuel

Nottingham University, UK

Nigel D. White

Nottingham University, UK

Routledge
Taylor & Francis Group
LONDON AND NEW YORK

First published 2012 by Ashgate Publishing

Published 2016 by Routledge
2 Park Square, Milton Park, Abingdon, Oxon OX14 4RN
711 Third Avenue, New York, NY 10017, USA

First issued in paperback 2017

Routledge is an imprint of the Taylor & Francis Group, an informa business

British Library Cataloguing in Publication Data
Counter-terrorism and international law. – (The
international law of peace and security)
1. Terrorism–Prevention–Law and legislation.
2. Terrorism–Prevention–International cooperation.
3. Terrorism.
I. Series II. Samuel, Katja L. H. III. White, N. D., 1961–
345'.02–dc22

Library of Congress Control Number: 2011930004

ISBN 13: 978-1-138-11083-0 (pbk)
ISBN 13: 978-0-7546-2947-4 (hbk)

Contents

PART V INTERNATIONAL INSTITUTIONAL APPROACHES

PART VI STATE RESPONSES

PART VII JUDICIAL RESPONSES

PART VIII AN EMERGING FRAMEWORK?

Acknowledgements

The editor and publishers wish to thank the following for permission to use copyright material.

American Society of International Law for the essays: Ruth Wedgewood (2002), 'Al Qaeda, Terrorism and Military Commissions', *American Journal of International Law*, **96**, pp. 328–37; Harold Hongju Koh (2002), 'The Case against Military Commissions', *American Journal of International Law*, **96**, pp. 337–44.

Cambridge University Press for the essays: Jörg Friedrichs (2006), 'Defining the International Public Enemy: The Political Struggle behind the Legal Debate on International Terrorism', *Leiden Journal of International Law*, **19**, pp. 69–91. Copyright © 2006 Foundation of the Leiden Journal of International Law; Luis Miguel Hinojosa Martínez (2008), 'The Legislative Role of the Security Council in its Fight against Terrorism: Legal, Political and Practical Limits', *International and Comparative Law Quarterly*, **57**, pp. 333–59; Johan Steyn (2004), 'Guantanamo Bay: The Legal Black Hole', *International and Comparative Law Quarterly*, **53**, pp. 1–15; Paul James Cardwell, Duncan French and Nigel White (2009), 'Decisions of International Courts and Tribunals: Yassin Abdullah Kadi', *International and Comparative Law Quarterly*, **58**, pp. 229–40; Helen Duffy (2008), 'Human Rights Litigation and the "War on Terror"', *International Review of the Red Cross*, **90**, pp. 573–97.

Case Western Reserve University/School of Law for the essays: Mary Ellen O'Connell (2004), 'The Legal Case against the Global War on Terror', *Case Western Reserve Journal of International Law*, **36**, pp. 349–57; John P. McLoughlin, Gregory P. Noone and Diana C. Noone (2009), 'Security Detention, Terrorism and the Prevention Imperative', *Case Western Reserve Journal of International Law*, **40**, pp. 463–505.

Hart Publishing Limited for the essay: Adam Roberts (2008), 'Countering Terrorism: A Historical Perspective', in A. Bianchi and A. Keller (eds), *Counterterrorism: Democracy's Challenge*, Oxford: Hart, pp. 3–41.

Harvard University Law School for the essay: M. Cherif Bassiouni (2002), 'Legal Control of International Terrorism: A Policy-Oriented Assessment', *Harvard International Law Journal*, **43**, pp. 83–103.

North Carolina Journal of International Law and Commercial Regulation for the essay: Ingrid Detter Frankopan (2008), 'Extraordinary Rendition and the Law of War', *North Carolina Journal of International Law and Commercial Regulation*, **33**, pp. 657–92.

Oxford University Press for the essays: Antonio Cassese (2006), 'The Multifaceted Criminal Notion of Terrorism in International Law', *Journal of International Criminal Justice*, **4**, pp. 933–58. Copyright © 2006 Oxford University Press; Ben Saul (2005), 'Definition of "Terrorism" in the UN Security Council: 1985–2004', *Chinese Journal of International Law*,

4, pp. 141–66. Copyright © 2005 Ben Saul; Kimmo Nuotio (2006), 'Terrorism as a Catalyst for the Emergence, Harmonization and Reform of Criminal Law', *Journal of International Criminal Justice*, **4**, pp. 998–1016. Copyright © 2005 Oxford University Press; Noëlle Quénivet (2006), 'You are the Weakest Link and We Will Help You! The Comprehensive Strategy of the United Nations to Fight Terrorism', *Journal of Conflict and Security Law*, **11**, pp. 371–97. Copyright © 2006 Noëlle Quénivet; Helen Keller and Andreas Fischer (2009), 'The UN Anti-terror Sanctions Regime under Pressure', *Human Rights Law Review*, **9**, pp. 257–66. Copyright © 2009 Oxford University Press; Rene Bruin and Kees Wouters (2003), 'Terrorism and the Non-derogability of *Non-refoulement*', *International Journal of Refugee Law*, **15**, pp. 5–29. Copyright © 2003 Oxford University Press; Eric Rosand (2006), 'The UN-Led Multilateral Institutional Response to Jihadist Terrorism: Is a Global Counterterrorism Body Needed?', *Journal of Conflict and Security Law*, **11**, pp. 399–427. Copyright © 2006 Eric Rosand; David Kretzmer (2005), 'Targeted Killing of Suspected Terrorists: Extra-Judicial Executions or Legitimate Means of Defence?', *European Journal of International Law*, **16**, pp. 171–212. Copyright © 2005 Oxford University Press;

Texas International Law Journal for the essay: Daniel Moeckli (2008), 'The Emergence of Terrorism as a Distinct Category of International Law', *Texas International Law Journal*, **44**, pp. 157–83.

Every effort has been made to trace all the copyright holders, but if any have been inadvertently overlooked the publishers will be pleased to make the necessary arrangement at the first opportunity.

Series Preface

The essays collected in the four volumes of this reprint series, The International Law of Peace and Security, focus on a number of facets of international law concerned with peace and security. Clearly there are existing volumes in the Library of Essays on International Law (series editor Robert McCorquodale) that are essential reading for anyone interested in this area of international law, primarily *Collective Security Law*, edited by Nigel White, and *International Peacekeeping*, edited by Boris Kondoch. However, the aim of this series is not simply to develop and deepen the reader's understanding of international law in the area of peace and security, but to introduce new areas and concepts, namely the international laws that purport to govern and regulate arms control, counter-terrorism, the use of force, and peace-building. The focus will be on peace and security rather than on conflict, as the law of armed conflict has already been covered in the aforementioned series, in *Humanitarian Law* edited by Judith Gardam.

The international laws in the area of peace and security are essentially different from those that apply in conflicts – basically, the difference is between the law of peace and the law of war. Simply put, the law of war is concerned with regulating warfare – its means, methods, and issues of targeting and protecting persons – thereby upholding principles of humanity while recognizing the dictates of military necessity. The law of peace and security is about preventing conflicts and wars, and is increasingly concerned with rebuilding a situation of peace and security on the other side of the conflict following a ceasefire and peace agreement. Of course, it is not always possible to maintain a clear line between the *jus ad bellum*, *jus in bello* and *jus post bellum* – an issue raised by the controversial 'war on terror', but coming through more practically in specific instances such as the application of international humanitarian law to peacekeepers. In addition, the series only considers issues of international criminal justice when analysing the rebuilding of a post-conflict state or as an element of counter-terrorism, thus giving rise to little overlap with the collection in the aforementioned series, *The International Criminal Court* edited by Olympia Bekou and Robert Cryer.

The focus of these four volumes is essentially on the law of peace, more specifically those laws and legal regimes that underpin peace by means of controlling the spread of dangerous weapons and by limiting the occasions when states can use force on the international stage, or restoring it when that peace has been broken. In times of peace the main fear is of sudden attacks, possibly by the use of WMD or by terrorists, signifying that arms control law, the law regulating the use of force and anti-terrorist laws are all potentially applicable. In post-conflict situations, peace is being restored usually with the involvement of international actors, which raises a whole host of legal issues, including the applicability of human rights law within the unstable post-conflict state and the principles governing international intervention and involvement. The presence of the UN Security Council, as principal international guarantor and guardian of peace and security, in each of the four volumes is not only illustrative of the unifying theme of peace and security, but also raises concerns and issues about the central role of this most political of bodies in this area of law.

In considering the four volumes in this series individually, it can be seen that the volume edited by Dan Joyner – *Arms Control Law* – is a pretty unique collection of secondary sources collected from both legal and non-legal areas. The essays in this collection review and analyse the major arms control treaties and institutions including the Security Council. The contribution of arms control law to international peace and security is a key theme.

In *The Use of Force and International Law*, Tarcisio Gazzini and Nikolaos Tsagourias have carefully selected essays from a vast range of literature to reflect the debates and controversies of this most fundamental, but much contested, area. The rules on when states and organizations can use or authorize the use of force is not only confined to the primary international treaty governing peace and security – the UN Charter – but also includes different viewpoints on controversial (customary) exceptions such as humanitarian intervention, as well as the more recent debates on the responsibility to protect. All this again requires attention to be given to the Security Council.

In *Counter-Terrorism and International Law*, Katja Samuel and Nigel White consider the problem of international terrorism (embodied in the struggle to define it) and the range of responses crafted by states and international organizations in order to try to respond to it, ranging from declaring 'war' to consensual cooperative criminal justice-type measures. The role of the Security Council in developing the legal regimes here, by use for example of targeted sanctions, is considered against the backdrop of existing conventions and practices. The contribution of these measures to the goals of peace and security embodied in the UN Charter is central to this collection.

Finally, *Post-Conflict Rebuilding and International Law*, edited by Ray Murphy, comprises an interesting collection of essays illustrating the phenomenon of rebuilding peace within different regions, followed by a consideration of the general normative framework including the arguments for and against recognizing (the need for) a *jus post bellum*. The essays review and analyse various types, stages and institutions involved in post-conflict peace-building from an international law perspective. They include discussion of rebuilding and peace operations (a much wider concept than peacekeeping operations), electoral support, humanitarian assistance and rule-of-law capacity-building. Post-conflict accountability mechanisms (amnesties, truth commissions, criminal tribunals) and their contribution to peace-building, as well as the wider restoration of peace and security, are also covered. Because this area is new and still developing there will be a need to identify the applicable principles of international law (for example, human rights including economic, social and cultural rights and the right of self-determination, but also the right to security), and the possible development of a *jus post bellum*, but Ray Murphy identifies a number of other challenges to this most difficult of tasks – rebuilding peace.

Each volume of collected essays is of immense value in itself, but each is also supplemented by an introduction by the volume editors and a selected bibliography, both of which add considerably to the usefulness of the collections to the reader.

NIGEL D. WHITE
Series Editor
University of Nottingham

Introduction

History

'The word "terrorism", like many abstract political terms, is confusing, dangerous and indispensable'. So begins Adam Roberts' supremely balanced essay, 'Countering Terrorism: A Historical Perspective', which opens this volume (p. 5). Terrorism is something more than a criminal act or acts, it is something directed at civilians and against the very fabric of society more generally – 'violence intended to spread terror' (p. 5). Although the current forms of international terrorism in terms of ruthlessness and coverage are new, Roberts warns us not to forget the lessons of past episodes of terrorism and counter-terrorism, episodes from which he draws a number of propositions. For instance, he points to the EOKA insurgency in Cyprus to show that sometimes the terrorist is not seeking to defeat establishment forces in battle, but is seeking to provoke disproportionate suppression which results in killing innocents as well as terrorists, thus bringing further recruits to the terrorist cause. Terrorist blows followed by establishment counter-blows often lead to an escalating cycle of violence that is very difficult to break (Farer, 2002). Terrorism and counter-terrorism become endemic, thus making it difficult to eradicate terrorism completely even though peace may appear in some instances to have been achieved, either by negotiations (as in Northern Ireland) or by force of arms (as in Sri Lanka).

The history of causes of terrorism and the memory of the atrocities committed by both sides are not easily forgotten, as the reprise of the Bloody Sunday Inquiry shows us (Irwin, 1999). Ending terrorism is particularly difficult if the underlying causes of terrorism are not addressed: as Roberts states, 'To say that a movement responds to real grievances – as for example over Palestine – is not to say that it is justified in resorting to terror, but it is to say that the terrorist movement reflects larger concerns in society that need to be addressed in some way' (p. 20).

Roberts stresses that effective counter-terrorism responses do not have to disregard national and international legal standards. Although new forms of warfare may lead to question marks over the applicability of certain aspects of international humanitarian law, '[u]nderstandable doubt over the formal applicability of some provisions of existing law should not be turned into a licence to flout basic norms' (p. 21). It seems that these lessons and others, expertly drawn out by Roberts, were not remembered at the outset of the 'war on terror' declared by President Bush after the attacks of 9/11 in 2001. Roberts is entirely correct in his analysis that this declaration was not simply rhetorical flourish by a shocked and wounded president, but was the start of a multifaceted campaign that included major military operations (in Afghanistan and Iraq) intended somehow to result in victory over the terrorists. Roberts is scathing about the historical evidence for a military strategy (propounded by both the USA and the UK) that takes the fight to the terrorist-enemy in faraway lands, which in part is a recipe for the revival of imperialism. He cautions against such disproportionate responses but does not rule out the use of military force where necessary and advocates actions taken within a legal framework to diminish terrorism, 'including arrests, trials and a willingness to take military action where appropriate' (p. 41). The aim should not be the 'capture of every last terrorist leader, but their relegation to a status of near-irrelevance as life moves on, long-standing grievances are addressed and peoples can see that a grim terrorist war of attrition is achieving little and damaging their own societies' (p. 41). There can be no better introduction to the essays collected together in this volume.

Defining Terrorism

No collection on counter-terrorism and international law would be complete without consideration of the absence of a universal definition of terrorism, which continues to elude the international community despite over 70 years of efforts to agree on one (Saul, 2006). In Chapter 2, 'The Multifaceted Criminal Notion of Terrorism in International Law', Antonio Cassese argues that the necessary substantive (objective and subjective) elements for three classes of criminal conduct, which may incorporate terrorist offences, already exist within international law. The first is a generally accepted definition of terrorism as a peacetime international crime which has developed within customary international law[1] and which may be attributed to factors such as: the strength of universal public opinion against terrorist activities which has existed over many years; the resultant national and regional legislative efforts and jurisprudential developments; and other international responses, such as the passing of UN General Assembly resolutions on a range of terrorism-related issues.[2]

A second class of offences relates to war crimes committed during an armed conflict, whether of an international or non-international character. Not only has terrorism been proscribed by international humanitarian law, but it has also been criminalized (both directly and indirectly) by the statutes and jurisprudence of existing international courts and tribunals. However, this class of offence is much narrower than that arising under the international law of peace because it is effectively limited to the prohibited conduct being perpetrated against civilians and protected persons not participating directly in the hostilities, and civilian objects. The third class of offences is where significant terrorist acts may be prosecuted as crimes against humanity, whether perpetrated in times of peace or armed conflict, which was one way in which the terrorist attacks on the USA on 11 September 2001 (9/11) might have been responded to (Lawless, 2007–08).

One of the primary obstacles to agreeing a universal definition of terrorism remains disagreement as to whether or not those engaged in armed self-determination struggles should be criminalized and included within the scope of anti-terrorism instruments together

---

1 For alternative views see, for example, Scharf (2004); Di Filippo (2008); Saul (2009, pp. 163, 184, 172).

2 See, for example, UNGA Res. 65/34, 6 December 2010 (measures to eliminate international terrorism); UNGA Res. 65/221, 21 December 2010 (protection of human rights and fundamental freedoms while countering terrorism); UNGA Res. 51/210, 17 December 1996 (establishment of Ad Hoc Committee); and UNGA Res. 60/288, 8 September 2006 (adoption of the UN Global Counter-Terrorism Strategy).

with other non-state actors classified as being terrorist in nature; or whether they should be exempted due to the nature of their struggles, not least the pursuit of self-determination as a fundamental human right. At present, a definitional impasse persists in the negotiations of the UN draft Comprehensive Convention on Terrorism due to the insistence of the state members of the Organization of the Islamic Conference that those engaged in self-determination struggles be excluded from its scope under Article 18 (now 20) of the draft Convention.[3] Whilst such a stance is undoubtedly influenced by ideological and political factors, some commentators – most notably Cassese – suggest that the normative effect of UN General Assembly resolutions especially[4] is such that '... although they [that is, self-determination movements] do not possess a *legal right* to enforce their substantive right to self-determination by resort to war, [they] nevertheless have a *legal licence* to do so ... legal rules take these wars into account, without however upgrading them to the status of manifestations of *jus ad bellum* proper' (Cassese, 1995, pp. 153–54). Not all commentators agree with such a position. For example, in contrast, Halberstam (2003) argues that the UN's current position is an unequivocal condemnation of any terrorist acts as criminal and unjustifiable regardless of who perpetrated them or the underlying motivations. Such a wide spectrum of disagreement is unlikely to be resolved any time soon.

However, there is another important and less frequently discussed source of definitional political tension, which is the primary focus of Jörg Friedrichs' analysis in Chapter 3. Like Cassese, Friedrichs attributes the absence of a universal definition to political, rather than substantive, obstacles. However, he attributes these primarily to Western hegemonic agendas – especially those of the USA, assisted by the UK – seeking to project power globally under the auspices of the 'war on terror' rather than to historic, entrenched positions between primarily non-aligned and Western states especially on the issue of national liberation struggles. In particular, Friedrichs argues that any achievement of a universal definition would be contrary to the interests and agendas of such governments:

> It is precisely the absence of a legal definition of terrorism that makes it possible for the hegemonic power (read 'United States') and its followers to determine the international public enemy on a case-by-case basis. A legal definition would serve as a limitation to this discretional power. (p. 73)

As Friedrichs concludes,

> From the standpoint of the less powerful ... it is precisely the absence of a legal definition which is dangerous. A reasonably clear and legally binding definition of terrorism would work as an insurance against the tendency of the hegemonic power to determine the international public enemy at its own discretion. There are certainly common enemies of all states, such as al Qaeda, and these should definitely be covered by the definition of terrorism. (p. 91)

In addition to leaving weaker states more vulnerable, the absence of a universal definition of terrorism also has significant implications in terms of counter-terrorist cooperation,

---

3 See UN Doc. A/57/37 (2002), at 17; Hmoud (2006); and Gioia (2006).

4 For example, the Declaration on the Granting of Independence to Colonial Countries and Peoples in 1960, UNGA Res. 1514 (XV), 14 December 1960.

the effectiveness of which is pivotal to the success of international efforts to counter this transnational threat.[5] In his essay, 'Definition of "Terrorism" in the UN Security Council: 1985–2004' (Chapter 4), besides describing and contrasting the significantly different approaches of the UN Security Council to terrorist issues prior to and following the 9/11 terrorist attacks, Ben Saul examines some of its legislative efforts to strengthen the legal framework, including as a means to strengthen interstate cooperation. In particular, Saul examines the impact of UN Security Council Resolution 1373, which required UN member states to legislate on a range of terrorist activities.[6] This obligation was helpful in the sense that it required all UN member states to address any gaps within their existing domestic criminal frameworks in relation to such offences. However, in the absence of a working definition of terrorism – which was not introduced until Security Council Resolution 1566 some three years later, after which time most states had carried out the necessary reforms[7] – it also permitted states to define terrorism unilaterally, according to their own criteria and '"geared towards their own interests"' (Guillaume, quoted by Saul at p. 115). Consequently, the diversity and inconsistency of domestic definitions and legislation introduced often poses obstacles to, rather than strengthens, international cooperation. As Saul observes,

> The absence of a definition is not merely of theoretical interest, because the terms 'terrorism' and 'terrorist' have operative legal significance in Res 1373, triggering obligations to criminalize financing of *terrorism*; suppress *terrorist* groups; deny refugee status to *terrorists*; prevent the movement of *terrorists*; bring *terrorists* to justice; and, vitally, establish *terrorist acts* as serious domestic crimes. (pp. 113–14)

Criminal Justice Approach

One final observation made by Saul refers to a recurring tension throughout this collection, namely whether particular counter-terrorist responses should fall within the criminal justice or existing armed conflict approaches, or whether a new 'war paradigm' is emerging under the global 'war on terror'. With respect to the former approach, as Saul notes, this was the immediate, instinctive response of the Security Council to the 9/11 attacks:

> Most Council members did not immediately conceptualize 11 September as an armed attack, instead invoking a criminal law paradigm by speaking of *bringing the perpetrators to justice* or referring to *crimes* rather than acts of war. It was only later that explicit claims of armed attack and self-defence were articulated, which soon gained acceptance. (p. 109)

---

5 See, for example, United Nations (2004, paras 17, 24); and the Council of Europe's Parliamentary Assembly, Resolution 1258 (2001), adopted 26 September 2001, para. 7.

6 UNSC Res. 1373, 28 September 2001, para. 2 (e).

7 UNSC Res. 1566, 8 October 2004, para. 3. See also UNGA Res. 49/60, 9 December 1994, para. 3.

Certainly, despite the responses and rhetoric associated with the 'war on terror', there is general consensus that the criminal justice approach should be the norm and the armed conflict approach exceptional, with every effort being made to strengthen the existing legal framework. This is exemplified in the requirement on states under Security Council Resolution 1373 to ratify UN anti-terrorism conventions, and is an underlying principle of the UN Global Counter-Terrorist Strategy which emphasizes 'the rule of law, respect for human rights, and effective criminal justice systems, which constitute the fundamental basis of our common fight against terrorism'.[8]

However, despite the importance of the international legal framework, it suffers from a number of inherent weaknesses in addition to the absence of a universal definition. M. Cherif Bassiouni, in 'Legal Control of International Terrorism' (Chapter 5) focuses on one of these, namely the counter-terrorist implications of the absence of coherent legislative policy on international criminal law. For example, he identifies the narrowness of current legislative approaches to tackling terrorism in which 'the term "international terrorism" has come to exclude the activities of state actors and even insurgent and revolutionary groups. Instead it is applied to small, ideologically motivated groups' (p. 126). This is despite the fact that the other two categories also continue to pose a threat, demonstrated by the fact that some states – currently Cuba, Iran, Syria and Sudan – remain categorized by the US as perpetrators of direct or indirect acts of terrorism (US Department of State, n.d.), and insurgency persists in some parts of the world, often with devastating consequences, as is the case in Iraq. Whilst some of the specific criminal activities of these two categories of actors do fall within the scope of other instruments,[9] it is not a comprehensive or easily enforceable framework. Nor are all criminal acts which may potentially be committed by any of these three groups currently included within the existing legal framework. For example, although a nuclear suppression convention now exists, significant gaps remain with respect to the utilization of chemical or biological weapons for terrorist purposes. In addition there are significant problems with enforcement, especially at the national level, even where no normative gaps exist within the international criminal law framework. Bassiouni concludes that '[i]nternational criminal law, therefore, suffers from both substantive and enforcement deficiencies, leading to a substantial lack in deterrence' (p. 131) and describes current policy approaches as being '*ad hoc* and discretionary … [with] no international initiative to systematize, update, integrate, or even harmonize these international norms' (p. 142).

Consequently, Bassiouni is a strong advocate for the adoption of 'a comprehensive convention on terrorism that is, as much as is possible, value-neutral, encompassing all actors, and covering all modalities and techniques of terror-violence' (p. 141). This picks up a central concern of Kimmo Nuotio, the author of the next essay, 'Terrorism as a Catalyst for the Emergence, Harmonization and Reform of Criminal Law' (Chapter 6): namely, how the criminal justice approach may be strengthened through the harmonization of criminal law measures at the national, regional and international levels, not least to address some of the cooperative challenges arising from the definitional differences and discrepancies referred to

---

8 UN Global Counter-Terrorism Strategy, Action Plan: Pillar IV, para. 5.

9 For example, Rome Statute of the International Criminal Court 1998; UN Convention against Torture and Other Cruel, Inhuman or Degrading Treatment or Punishment 1984 ; Geneva Conventions 1949, and Additional Protocols 1977.

already. However, Nuotio identifies a number of core challenges to achieving this in practice. One is that 'many domestic criminal justice systems tend to treat terrorist offences in a manner that conforms with their domestic criminal codes', with the consequence that any 'effort to "harmonize" domestic definitions of terrorist offences across various states is likely to fail' (p. 148). Nevertheless, he believes that it is essential for 'each state to revise its definitions of offences in such a way as to cover the areas of action that the internationally binding agreements have deemed worth including in a definition of terrorism' (p. 148).

Another important difficulty discussed by Nuotio relates to the conceptual differences which exist between national and international legislative approaches:

> Terrorism as a national problem could be dealt with according to the paradigm of criminal law, that is, as an ordinary crime. International terrorism is more difficult to place within conventional paradigms. Despite the rhetoric, it is relatively clear that terrorist acts carried out by non-state actors are not acts of war in a proper sense. Such terrorist acts are basically not considered violations of international law. For that reason, the international community has sought to handle terrorism as a crime problem. (p. 149)

A further challenge he identifies is how to establish the right balance in harmonizing national criminal justice approaches, such that they are neither too rigid nor too broad in the offences that they encompass. Finally, where states legislate due to external political pressures, he is concerned about the resultant quality of the law produced, with the possibility that '[a]n apparent success in the short term might prove to be a failure in the long term.' (p. 159)

Other commentators have identified further challenges to efforts to harmonize the existing legal framework. Nuotio identifies one of these as domestic resistance to any such attempts that is fuelled by 'the need to preserve the coherence of domestic legal order and its principles and traditions of criminal justice' (p. 159), especially on issues of national security which many states believe remains their national preserve and sole responsibility. Consequently, as Grief notes in the context of the EU, 'the security imperative both unites Member States in common cause and provokes controversy' (Grief, 2007, p. 752). Other hurdles to harmonization include differing priorities; this is illustrated by the anti-terrorism focus of Association of Southeast Asian Nations which is on strengthening practical, rather than legislative, measures of cooperation (Saul, 2008, p. 111). As Nuotio concludes, for such reasons 'the real merits of harmonization of terrorist laws are, at present, very difficult to assess' (p. 159).

The importance of having an effective international criminal law framework – including through the ratification, implementation, and enforcement of UN anti-terrorism treaties – could not be more starkly highlighted than by the need to prevent access to nuclear materials and the subsequent employment of a nuclear device by terrorist actors. These are the issues explored by Christopher Joyner in 'Countering Nuclear Terrorism' (Chapter 7) with respect to the most recent treaty, the International Convention for the Suppression of Acts of Nuclear Terrorism 2005 (hereafter Nuclear Terrorism Convention), which was negotiated while the events of the 9/11 terrorist attacks were still very fresh in everyone's mind. The Nuclear Terrorism Convention reflects many of the law-making features of more recent anti-terrorism instruments, especially (including in terms of how it is structured) in the criminalization of particular acts considered to be 'terrorist' and its provisions on extradition. Indeed, many of its provisions mirror, or are similar to, those of the International Convention for the Suppression of Terrorist Bombings 1997. It also experienced recurring difficulties during its negotiations, such as disagreement on both its scope and exceptions, especially with respect to acts of state terrorism (which are excluded due to ongoing legal debates regarding a state's use of nuclear weapons) and exemption of military activities and personnel (its scope is therefore limited to acts perpetrated against civilians), on the basis that the use of armed force remains governed by international humanitarian law (see, for example, Lambert, 1990; Verwey, 1981; Bantekas, 2003; Bassiouni, 2001, 2003).

Furthermore, the Nuclear Terrorism Convention was innovative in a number of ways. Significantly, Article 2 established a new crime of 'nuclear terrorism' under international law, namely where a person unlawfully acquires nuclear materials, damages a nuclear facility, or participates in the planning or execution of such acts. In addition, the Convention, in Article 7, places significant importance on strengthening effective practical cooperation between states to detect, prevent, suppress and investigate offences of nuclear terrorism, especially through the sharing of information and intelligence. However, Joyner identifies two key challenges common to the effectiveness of any anti-terrorism instrument as part of multilateral cooperation. The first relates to potential issues of consistency of approach and harmonization. In particular, '[w]hile the agreement requires that specific prohibitions be legislated into the domestic law of party states, it also leaves significant latitude to governments in implementing their own international obligations' (p. 186). The second relates to the importance of adopting cohesive strategy and policy approaches. As Joyner notes,

> ... [the] promulgation of multilateral conventions to counter acts of terrorism is not sufficient to prevent or deter their perpetration. An instrument's fundamental value lies in its being an integral component of a broader, more comprehensive coordinated strategy to combat terrorism ... If it is to be effective, the CNT [Nuclear Terrorism Convention] must depend on the governments of states parties to respect, abide by, and enforce its provisions. (pp. 190–91)

War on Terror

When the USA declared war on terrorism after 9/11 the intention, though not thought out with any precision or foresight, was that the attacks on the USA meant that a new form of warfare needed addressing whereby, as Mary O'Connell neatly puts it in 'The Legal Case against the Global War on Terror' (Chapter 8), '[t]he war attaches to individuals not to situations of armed hostilities' (p. 196) as required by the Geneva Conventions. The USA's intent to view the war on terror in legal, and not just rhetorical, sense was demonstrated by the Bush administration's claims to three types of privilege under the laws of war: 'the right to declare individuals "enemy combatants" if they are suspected of terrorism; the right to target and kill individuals wherever they are if they are suspected terrorists; and the right to search ships and seize cargoes suspected of carrying weapons or material for terrorists' (p. 197). To treat terrorists as combatants rather than criminals is directly contrary to the lessons of history that Adam Roberts rightly instructs us to learn from: historically governments – for example, the British government in countering the IRA – has been very reluctant to inflate the importance of terrorists' campaigns by seeing them as military campaigns and thereby giving the combatants legitimacy and encouraging support for them. Once a global war is recognized, military forces from countries engaged in counter-terrorist operations are legitimate targets, and, bearing in mind that in previous campaigns NATO states have viewed TV stations, railway bridges and power stations to be legitimate targets in military campaigns in Yugoslavia and Iraq (Benvenuti, 2001), then the war on terror potentially backfires on those prosecuting it.

The war on terror, if accepted as a legitimate legal concept, also breaks down the division between the *jus in bello* and the *jus ad bellum*. A continuing war on terror, once embarked upon, would mean that it is no longer necessary to gauge military actions under the *jus ad bellum*, which requires armed attacks to trigger the right of self-defence, or threats to the peace for Security Council-authorized action; instead, we simply judge all military actions under the *jus in bello*, which essentially accepts the reality of the use of force and tries to regulate its extremes. This is perhaps the most invidious aspect of the war on terror: the prohibition on the use of force contained in the UN Charter – one of the most significant developments of the twentieth century – is effectively bypassed. Although there has been little academic support for the global war on terror and, with the end of the Bush administration in the USA and the Blair government in the UK, the rhetoric has been turned down, the fact is that enemy combatants are still being held at Guantanamo Bay in Cuba, that unmanned drones are being used against individuals suspected of being terrorists, and ships are being searched on the basis of carrying cargoes believed to be destined for terrorists (Guilfoyle, 2007).

In 'Targeted Killing of Suspected Terrorists: Extra-Judicial Executions or Legitimate Means of Self-Defence?' (Chapter 9), David Kretzmer shows why it is impossible to completely dismiss the armed conflict approach to countering terrorism. By focusing on targeted killings, Kretzmer unpicks the problems of applying the alternative (and overlapping) regimes of international humanitarian law or human rights law to terrorism. His contention is essentially that the modern form of international terrorism is a new security phenomenon and therefore cannot be viewed strictly as either a pernicious form of criminal activity leading to a law-enforcement approach or an armed conflict involving combatants from two opposing sides to which the laws of war apply. The concern should be to identify standards that should prevent governments from adopting disproportionate counter-terrorism responses that violate the standards of humanity and protection found in both codes of law.

Human rights law protects the right to life but recognizes that it might be taken by the state in certain circumstances, as established in 1996 by the European Court of Human Rights in the *McCann* case, when the Court found that the shooting of three IRA terrorists in Gibraltar by British special forces was not a violation of the right to life under the European Convention, because they genuinely believed that the detonation of a bomb was imminent unless lethal force was used.[10] Furthermore, although a human rights approach is based on suspected criminals being arrested and tried with due process guarantees, this only fully works when the terrorists are apprehended within the arresting state and does not extend easily to situations in which the terrorists are based in another country that is unwilling or unable to apprehend the terrorists and either prosecute them or extradite them. Thus, it is Kretzmer's contention that, under human rights law, targeted killings are necessarily an arbitrary deprivation of the

10 *McCann* v. *UK* (1996) 21 EHRR 97.

right to life. However, '[w]hen the terror is intense, organized and protracted, the appropriate model should be the armed conflict model, which is not based on notions of imminent danger from the specific person targeted, but on notions of the danger posed by the group to which the person belongs' (p. 217). The problem then becomes one of the inability of international humanitarian law to address a conflict between a victim state and an international terrorist group. Since terrorists do not normally meet the conditions necessary to achieve combatant status in an international armed conflict, they are viewed by international humanitarian law as civilians who lose their protected status when they take a direct part in hostilities. Thereby 'terrorists enjoy the best of both worlds – they can remain civilians most of the time and only endanger their protection as civilians while actually in the process of carrying out the terrorist attack' (p. 227). This means that governments can only target individuals when launching or preparing to launch a terrorist attack; they cannot target terrorist groups per se. However, Kretzmer suggests that it may be possible to classify an armed conflict with a terrorist group as a non-international armed conflict, allowing the state to 'enjoy almost unlimited power to target persons it claims to be active members of that group' (p. 236). Thus, international humanitarian law's regulation of armed conflict is either very strict or very loose, resulting in claims and counter-claims about the nature of the conflict. In a valiant attempt to solve these problems, Kretzmer arguably comes back to the view that it is permissible to apply the classical *jus ad bellum* standard of force when there is a 'necessity of self-defence, instant, overwhelming, leaving no choice of means, and no moment for deliberation' (p. 82) as formulated by the UK following the *Caroline* incident of 1837 (see Jennings, 1938).

International Institutional Responses

Terrorism has transcended national boundaries and barriers, necessitating a counter-terrorist strategy that attempts not only to coordinate the efforts of states and their national criminal systems, but also to coordinate enforcement measures that might be taken against terrorists and rogue states that support them, and capacity-building measures for those states that are unable to tackle them effectively. Although regional systems of counter-terrorism have developed (see, for example, Warbrick, 2004; Scalabrino, 2004; Maged, 2003), tackling international terrorism ultimately requires the development of an effective and legitimate UN strategy. In her essay 'You are the Weakest Link and We Will Help You!' (Chapter 10) Noëlle Quénivet traces the development of the UN's strategy against the background of a radical post-9/11 move away from the post-Cold War consensus on international cooperation using myriad suppression conventions towards using military force to combat terrorism. Quénivet points out that:

> ... the inability of States to combat national and/or international terrorism through an array of criminal laws and through traditional institutions such as the police and criminal courts led some of them to look for short cuts and for a quick fix especially when the terrorists attack was carried out abroad or seemed to have been planned abroad. (p. 255)

Such divergence in state practice would seem to make the achievement of a unifying strategy very difficult, if not impossible. However, although the Security Council came close to endorsing the use of force against Afghanistan in 2001,[11] it has not clearly authorized the use of force against terrorists as a collective security action under Chapter VII of the UN Charter. Thus, although international terrorism is deemed by the Security Council as a threat to international peace and security (Saul, 2006, p. 46), it may be possible to achieve a strategy that unifies both the General Assembly, with its concentration on both the causes of terrorism and capacity-building in weaker states, and the Security Council, with its focus on non-forcible enforcement action. Nevertheless, as Quénivet points out, given that both organs 'have different visions of what "peace" and "collective security" are as well as how terrorism should be combated' (p. 263), achieving a common strategy even within the UN is difficult enough let alone persuading states (which tend to opt for the quiet life and go along with the consensus in the UN) to take measures against terrorism.

Quénivet traces the possible consensus through various documents including the High-Level Panel Report (United Nations, 2004), the Secretary General's report, *In Larger Freedom* (United Nations, 2005), and the 2005 World Summit Outcome Document.[12] Unfortunately, the essay was published before the UN General Assembly adopted by consensus the UN's Global Counter-Terrorism Strategy in September 2006,[13] but the reader will be able to judge whether the shortcomings identified by Quénivet are overcome by the Strategy. It is worth noting, however, that the body of the UN's Strategy contains a recognition of the causes of terrorism, including a recognition that the 'peaceful resolution of such [prolonged and unresolved] conflicts would contribute to strengthening the global fight against terrorism', a clear reference to the need to resolve the Palestinian question. The Strategy develops many of the measures contained in the 1994 General Assembly Declaration on Measures to Eliminate International Terrorism, adopted by consensus in 1994,[14] but also takes account of Security Council resolutions and mechanisms including the Counter-Terrorism Committee established by the Security Council to ensure the implementation of Security Council Resolution 1373 (although it calls on it to work with states at their request), and the 1267 Committee established for the purpose of targeting sanctions against members of the Taliban and Al Qaeda (although it calls on it to ensure fair and transparent procedures). This amounts to a general recognition by the Assembly of the Security Council's actions in this area, but also represents an attempt to balance those actions with human rights protection and to emphasize traditional principles such as state consent. The movement of the membership towards the Security Council's anti-terrorist regime is made clearer in a later Assembly resolution, again adopted by consensus,[15] which reminds states of their obligations under relevant treaties but also under Security Council resolutions including 1373, 'to ensure that perpetrators of terrorist acts are brought to justice'.

Luis Miguel Hinojosa Martinez, in 'The Legislative Role of the Security Council in its Fight against Terrorism' (Chapter 11), considers the development of UNSC powers in the area

---

11 UNSC Res. 1368, 12 September 2001.

12 UNGA Res. 60/1, 24 October 2005.

13 UNGA Res. 60/288, 20 September 2006.

14 UNGA Res. 49/60, 9 December 1994.

15 UNGA Res. 61/40, 18 December 2006.

of counter-terrorism. Martinez is not convinced by those who argue that the Security Council has no legislative competence (see, for example, Happold, 2003), nor is he convinced that such competence is discretionary and unregulated. In a footnote, he cites the statement of the President of the Security Council in explanation of the adoption of Resolution 1540 in 2004, which addressed the spread of WMD and the danger that they could end up in the hands of terrorists:

> … there was a gap in international law pertaining to non-State actors. So, either new international law should be created, either waiting for customary international law to develop, or by negotiating a treaty or convention. Both took a long time, and everyone felt that there was an 'imminent threat', which had to be addressed and which could not wait for the usual way. (p. 278, fn. 3)

For Martinez, this encapsulates the Security Council's role and restricts its legislative competence to filling in gaps in the legal frameworks governing terrorism, since, as well as the purposes and principles of the UN Charter, general principles of international law also bind the Security Council, signifying that it should not attempt to override them. Using its exceptional powers to tackle specific threats to the peace, the Security Council is empowered to override conflicting treaty obligations, but only when its actions are 'indispensable for safeguarding international security' (p. 292). This soundly argued approach reduces the extent of application of the so-called supremacy clause contained in Article 103 of the UN Charter (see further Liivoja, 2008). Furthermore, Martinez rightly identifies that state consent is still central to any form of law-making within the international legal order, where even legislative acts of an executive organ can only work if supported by the general membership and, furthermore, may be viewed as legally problematic if the membership were not consulted (which is now the norm in the case of such general Security Council resolutions).

While Martinez's analysis may be a sobering reminder to advocates of a more active and aggressive Security Council, the essay by Helen Keller and Andreas Fischer on targeted sanctions, 'The UN Anti-Terror Sanctions Regime under Pressure' (Chapter 12), illustrates the legal problems created by the Security Council's coercive measures when the Council comes into conflict with the fundamental rights of the individual guaranteed by international law. While targeted or smart sanctions directed against suspected members of the Taliban and Al Qaeda and their supporters constitute specific measures to combat terrorism and therefore seem to be more centrally executive,[16] their impact on the lives of those targeted individuals and their families is debilitating, not only preventing access to finances but also preventing free movement and, by dint of listing on publicly available blacklists, constituting an invasion of their privacy. Like administrative detention for suspected terrorists, these may be justified as preventive measures but their impact is punitive, arguably being a criminal form of sanction that has bypassed normal due process and fair-trial guarantees.

Keller and Fischer focus on the *Sayadi* case decided by the Human Rights Committee in 2008, in which the Human Rights Committee upheld the targeted individual's complaint that his freedom of movement and his right to privacy had been violated, but dismissed his contention that his fair-trial rights were breached by Belgium's implementation of its obligations under

[16] UNSC Res. 1267, 15 October 1999; SC Res. 1333, 19 December 2000; SC Res. 1390, 16 January 2002.

Security Council resolutions on the grounds that the sanctions were administrative and not criminal in nature. Although this aspect of the opinion can be criticized, the finding that a state's implementation of Security Council obligations has to comply with human rights is an important one – indeed, one that has been recognized by the Council itself.[17] An important human right is that of access to remedies (see Francioni, 2003), and if the Security Council does not provide for judicial remedies at UN level for those who believe they have been wrongly listed, individuals will continue to seek redress before national courts, and before international and regional human rights bodies.[18] The issue of judicial redress is returned to later in this collection, but it is worth noting at this stage that the Security Council's creation, first of a focal point for individual complaints[19] and then of an ombudsperson to review such complaints and make recommendations to the UNSC,[20] falls short of granting judicial redress and therefore will not prevent further claims being made before the courts.

State Responses

This collection considers the counter-terrorist responses of states, which raise many important rule-of-law challenges and tensions, especially with respect to international human rights and refugee law. The spectrum of issues, arising out of both the criminal justice and armed conflict approaches, incorporates: the capture and treatment of persons suspected or convicted of terrorist offences; their right to a fair trial; forms of detention; *non-refoulement* and the utilization of diplomatic assurances; special investigation techniques; the employment of torture, degrading or inhumane treatment – for example, in the course of an investigation; extraordinary rendition; issues of extraterritoriality; and discriminatory responses. As the breadth of these issues precludes their full inclusion here, four prominent examples have been selected, which clearly illustrate significant, recurring security imperative themes and their associated challenges to the rule-of-law framework.

The first relates to what John McLoughlin, Gregory Noone and Diana Noone describe in their essay, 'Security Detention, Terrorism and the Prevention Imperative' (Chapter 13), as:

> … a new dominant security imperative: prevention of terrorist attacks against [states'] homelands and national interests. In succinct terms, the prevention imperative posits that the U.S. will engage all elements of national power (legal, economic, diplomatic, financial, military, intelligence, and information) to neutralize the threat posed by al Qaeda and other non-state actors. (p. 318)

Although the essay focuses on how this imperative is being worked out in the form of preventive detention, its wider themes, related tensions and justifications are of more general potential application to any state's counter-terrorist responses. Certainly, in terms of strengthening the existing legal framework, a primary concern remains that any notion of dominance may result

---

[17] UNSC Res. 1546, 20 January 2003.

[18] See, for example, *HM Treasury* v. *Mohamed Jabar Ahmed and Others* [2010] UKSC 2.

[19] UNSC Res. 1730, 19 December 2006.

[20] UNSC Res. 1904, 17 December 2009.

in national security needs and interests prevailing over anything perceived to be threatening them, the consequences of which are often detrimental to the applicable legal principles.

More specifically:

> Preventive detention refers to the detention or confinement of a person believed to pose a threat to national security or to public safety and order, or a person whose presence at a public proceeding is required but cannot be guaranteed. The purpose of the detention is avoidance of the potential danger or absence rather than the punishment of a criminal offense. (p. 330)

The legality of such a concept and its boundaries are complex. First, they straddle different national (and often constitutional) as well as international standards and requirements (especially those of human rights and international humanitarian law in times of armed conflict). In addition, the concept of preventive detention is not prohibited per se, provided that the necessary substantive and procedural safeguards are in place and adequately justified. However, the mere fact that such a concept has been resorted to – and some even suggest that the notion of preventive detention be more formally adopted in order to ensure that the necessary safeguards are in place – points to another legal issue of wider relevance, namely '[t]he pressure on traditional doctrines to accommodate the challenges of modern international terrorism [which] tends to skew those doctrines in disturbing ways' (p. 358; see also (Dickinson, 2001–02).

The seminal lecture given by Lord Johan Steyn in 2003, 'Guantanamo Bay: The Legal Black Hole', reproduced here as Chapter 14, examines how such pressures and their related strains on the applicable legal framework – not least in terms of concerted policy decisions to create lacunae within it – have been played out in relation to the detention of non-US nationals at the Guantanamo Bay detention facility. Lord Steyn focuses on the relationship between the executive and judicial branches of government, especially the critical role of the judiciary in checking any excessive responses of the executive to perceived threats to national security, which are usually to the detriment of fundamental rights and freedoms (see further de Londras and Davis, 2010; Tomkins, 2010). In particular, Lord Steyn is concerned 'that unchecked abuse of power begets ever-greater abuse of power' (p. 362), describing how history has the ability to repeat itself, not least in terms of temptations to erode the rule of law under the auspices of national security interests. However, he is deeply troubled that the judiciary is often unduly deferential in its approaches to reviewing the employment of disproportionate executive powers relating to security matters, which he illustrates through the early jurisprudence of the US courts to reviewing the status and rights of Guantanamo Bay detainees. Lord Steyn further considers some of the negative consequences of such policies and treatment which have deliberately undermined the rule of law, including the likely mistreatment of US soldiers if captured during future conflicts and the contradictory message given to authoritarian and repressive regimes with poor human rights records. Overall, he advocates the importance of liberal democracies adhering to and protecting their cherished values, even if it means that they are constrained in the measures that they can employ in their counter-terrorist responses.

The essay by Rene Bruin and Kees Wouters, 'Terrorism and the Non-derogability of *Non-refoulement*' (Chapter 15), considers what has become another prominent source of security imperative versus rule-of-law tensions – namely, the international refugee law principle of *non-refoulement* which prohibits the forced return of a refugee deemed to be a security threat to their country of origin if there is a significant risk that they would be mistreated or even killed. The issues represented here are part of a broader discourse of concerns regarding the growing trend to misuse immigration and refugee law for national security purposes. More specifically, due to the relationship of *non-refoulement* with other key rule-of-law principles in a counter-terrorist context – especially the right to liberty and the prohibition against torture, degrading or inhumane treatment – this principle has come to lie at the heart of many of the legal and practical challenges currently facing governments engaged in counter-terrorism measures.

Governments have responded to these challenges in a number of ways. One approach, considered by the authors, is the attempt by governments to balance the requirements of national security with the protection of fundamental, especially non-derogable, rights such as the prohibition against torture, which was the core issue in *Suresh* v. *Canada*.[21] In this case, the Canadian Supreme Court adopted a broad approach to determining what may constitute a national security threat, coupled with noticeable deference to the executive, although on the facts they were satisfied that the applicant did indeed face a significant risk of torture if returned under the principle of *non-refoulement*. However, it highlights concerns regarding any notion, and related slippery slope, of states adopting such balancing tests with fundamental human rights protections.

Another well-documented approach has been that of the UK government in relation to the 'Belmarsh detainees' who faced a recurring conundrum attributable to the principle of *non-refoulement*. The detainees were non-UK nationals[22] who were considered by the executive to pose a continuing national security threat, making their release undesirable. However, under the requirements of *non-refoulement*, they could not be returned to their country of origin.[23] The UK responded in three ways. The first was to detain such persons indefinitely without charge or trial under the Anti-Terrorism, Crime and Security Act 2001, Part 4 (sections 21–23, no longer in force). However, following the successful challenge of this approach in the case of *A* v. *Secretary of State for the Home Department*[24] – in which the UK House of Lords on a 8–1 majority held that such detentions were incompatible with, *inter alia*, the right to liberty as articulated under Article 5 of the European Convention on Human Rights 1950 – they resorted to a second, equally controversial method, namely the imposition of control orders which prescribe measures such as curfews and other restrictions on freedom of movement.[25] However, these have raised other significant human rights-related challenges, including with respect to the right to liberty, fair trial and private and family life in related determinations.[26]

---

21 *Suresh* v. *Canada*, Judgment 11 January 2002, Supreme Court of Canada, 2002 SCC 1, File no. 27790. See also Okafor and Okoronkwo (2003).

22 On the potentially discriminatory implications of such selections see Moeckli (2006).

23 On such tensions see further, for example, Elliott (2010).

24 [2004] UKHL 56; [2005] 2 AC 68; confirmed by the Grand Chamber ECtHR in *A* v. *UK* (2009) ECtHR 3455/05, (2009) 26 BHRC 1.

25 Tomkins (2010, p. 550), referring to *Secretary of State for the Home Department* v. *MB* (2008) 1 AC 440, 24.

26 For example, *Secretary of State for the Home Department* v. *MB* (n. 49); *Secretary of State for the Home Department* v. *AP* [2010] UKSC 24 (SC); Elliott (2010); and Walker (2010).

Indeed, the adoption of a system of control orders has been described as resulting 'in exceptional measures, restraints of liberty outside the criminal justice system, being normalised by its broader application' (Tham, 2010, p. 101). The third, equally controversial, approach has been to seek diplomatic assurances from the receiving states, although both the exact legal nature and practical effectiveness of these remain controversial and unclear (Satterthwaite, 2007, pp. 1379–86; Tooze, 2010).

As Bruin and Wouters point out – specifically on the issue of refugees, but the application is wider – the protection of individuals is not synonymous with their impunity:

> Asylum law is not meant to be an escape route to avoid prosecution. Not only should States take responsibility whenever an individual is in need of protection, but they also should hold individuals criminally accountable for their acts. The current measures proposed by States neglect both international responsibilities. (p. 401)

The final significant and equally controversial example of state practice included here is that of extraordinary rendition, namely the transfer of persons to other jurisdictions with which they normally have no connections, usually for the purpose of carrying out acts which would be prohibited in the requesting state, in particular obtaining intelligence through coercive interrogation techniques amounting to torture – measures which equate to 'torture by proxy' (see further Sadat, 2007; Sands, 2006; Lavers, 2007). Driven by perceived, self-justified, security imperative agendas, the related practices have represented deliberate policy choices by certain states to (attempt to) circumvent their existing international obligations,[27] including those of the rule-of-law framework in which lawful and legitimate counter-terrorist responses should take place. Ingrid Frankopan's essay, 'Extraordinary Rendition and the Law of War' (Chapter 16), gives a comprehensive overview of the central themes and issues.

One significant issue that has arisen in relation to these practices is the lack of any, or sufficient, oversight of detainees and their treatment. This has often been attributable to the fact that they are 'ghost detainees' and are therefore not officially registered as being within the custody or control of a particular state and/or they are held in unregistered detention facilities, often known as 'black sites' (p. 421). This has led for calls – for example, in the Marty Report Parliamentary Assembly, (2007) – for increased democratic oversight of such practices. Indeed, non-judicial forms of oversight – which also include oversight by civil society and investigative journalism – have often done more to increase the accountabilty of those governments engaged or collaborating in such practices than the courts, not least due to the significant practical and legal obstacles which can exist in any attempt to bring a successful civil or criminal case against those responsible (Duffy, Chapter 18, this volume; Laflin, 2000). Ultimately, as Frankopan notes, the extraterritorial nature of certain international law obligations – such as, the prohibition of torture, which is a norm of *jus cogens* – is such that the '[d]elegation of interrogation procedures to another state can thus not rid a state of its responsibility for torture if it arranges flights to areas outside its own territory' (p. 437).

However, despite increased judicial and non-judicial measures to ensure greater accountability of governmental practices, the use by some states of evidence which has most

[27] For example, those under Article 7 of the International Covenant on Civil and Political Rights 1966.

likely been the product of torture by a third party – whether or not in the course of extraordinary rendition – has not been ruled out all together. Rather, for example, the UK House of Lords, in the case of *A and Others (Appellants) (FC)* v. *Secretary of the Home Department*,[28] whilst condemning 'torture and its fruits' which could not be relied on in evidence during court proceedings (para. 51), nevertheless stated that such information could be used operationally by the police because 'it would be ludicrous for them to disregard information [about a ticking bomb] if it had been procured by torture' (para. 68).

Judicial Responses

Many of the essays included in this collection have included references to, and analysis of, the role of courts – national (for example, the US Supreme Court in the *Hamdi* and *Rasul* cases),[29] regional (for example, the European Court of Human Rights in the *McCann* case and the European Court of Justice in the *Kadi* case) and international (the International Court of Justice in the *Wall* opinion of 2004 and the Human Rights Committee in the *Sayadi* case) – but it is essential in a collection on counter-terrorism and international law to consider the responses of the courts to counter-terrorist actions that breach international norms.

Much criticism can be levelled at the *Kadi* judgment of the European Court of Justice in 2008,[30] on the basis that its dualist approach, arguably, failed to uphold the supremacy of international law. What is at issue in targeted sanctions, however, is not the supremacy of international law per se, but rather the supremacy of Security Council obligations over human rights obligations that are found not only in international law, but often also in regional systems and national public law systems. In the case analysis of *Kadi* by Paul Cardwell, Duncan French and Nigel White (Chapter 17), the authors argue that although the Court was very careful to confine its decision to obligations upon states to protect the fundamental rights of individuals in the European legal order, it is in fact possible to see the Court's decision as upholding human rights which the Security Council is obliged to respect, and which states must take into account when implementing obligations derived from Security Council resolutions. Although the Court found that Kadi's fundamental rights to property and due process had been violated, it allowed the European institutions to modify its regulations in order to comply with the judgment.

The grudging unwillingness of executive bodies (at all levels) to accept the judgments of Courts in counter-terrorism cases is highlighted more fully in the excellent review of the role of Courts in the war on terror, 'Human Rights Litigation and the "War on Terror"', by Helen Duffy (Chapter 18). An obstructive executive can find sympathy from a judiciary reluctant to step into issues of national security. In the litigation concerning detainees held at Guantanamo Bay it took until 2008 for the US Supreme Court to decide that detainees had the constitutional privilege of habeas corpus.[31] Despite this decision, hundreds of

28 (Conjoined Appeals) [2005] UKHL 71.

29 *Hamdi* v. *Rumsfeld*, 124 S. Ct 2633 (2004); *Rasul* v. *Bush*, 124 S. Ct 2686 (2005).

30 *Yassin Abdullah Kadi and Al Barakaat International Foundation* v. *Council and Commission* (Joint Cases C-402/05P and C-415/05P), European Court of Justice, Judgment of 3 September 2008.

31 *Boumediene* v. *Bush* 553 US (2008).

detainees remain at Guantanamo, only a minority of which are headed for trial before the military commissions or before US criminal courts. In the UK, the House of Lords found that administrative detention at Belmarsh prison was a violation of the rights to liberty and non-discrimination,[32] a judgment met by a more positive response from the British government, although the control orders that replaced detention have amounted in a number of instances to *de facto* detention and have been subject to further challenge.

While the US government (incorrectly) refused to recognize that its human rights obligations extended extraterritorially to Guantanamo Bay and other places of detention outside the USA, the UK government did accept this after the case of *Al-Skeini*.[33] However, the House of Lords did accept the government's argument that the UK's human rights obligations did not extend outside places of detention or similar bases, resulting in a bizarre distinction between detainees abused in a UK detention facility in Basra, where human rights law applies, and those who may be detained or seized on the streets of Basra and subject to abuse where, according to the UK government and judiciary, human rights law does not apply. When this is combined with the decision in *Al-Jedda*,[34] in which the Court accepted the government's contention that the right to liberty of detainees in Iraq was overridden by obligations created by a Security Council resolution, then we seem to have a situation where human rights are only applicable in limited circumstances in countries where UK troops are present and active.

Duffy analyses these and many other cases and shows that the courts do perform a vital role in trying to restore the democratic legitimacy in countries where the executives have gone too far in eroding basic liberties, although their record is variable. When judicial protection of the rights of suspected terrorists has been criticized as transferring power from the executive to the judiciary, the correct response is that the transfer of power is a limited one and it is not from the executive to the judiciary but from the executive to the individual, since the individual is seeking redress before the courts from executive action (detention, rendition, interrogation and so on) which is designed to place the individual outside the reach of the law (p. 477).

Of course, the involvement of courts in counter-terrorism is not just to provide some redress from ill-conceived and illegal executive action; in fact, the main function of courts lies at the opposite end of the spectrum, as fora for the prosecution of individuals charged with terrorist offences according to the law. As an extreme form of criminal behaviour, terrorism and terrorist trials are difficult processes, where public pressure for conviction, the fear of retribution, the fear of the suspected terrorists being freed for lack of admissible evidence, and the reluctance to give terrorists the oxygen of publicity that public trials provide can gain lead to executive interference in the criminal process. In the UK, the trial of suspected terrorists in Northern Ireland before the so-called 'Diplock Courts' without juries was one example (Rasnic, 1999), while the military commissions in Guantanamo are a more extreme instance. Nevertheless, if the events of 9/11 have sparked a war on terror then, as Ruth Wedgewood argues in 'Al Qaeda, Terrorism and Military Commissions' (Chapter 19), those commissions are a justifiable response in the extreme security situation we find ourselves in. On the other hand, Harold Koh, in 'The Case against Military Commissions' (Chapter 20) is critical of such

32 *A and Others* v. *Secretary of State for the Home Department* [2004] UKHL 56.

33 *Al-Skeini* v. *Secretary of State for Defence* [2004] UKHL 26.

34 *R (Al-Jedda)* v. *Secretary of State for Defence* [2007] UKHL 58.

executive-style judicial bodies which may not even provide the same guarantees of justice as the normal courts martial provided by US military justice. Moreover, he points to the ordinary US criminal justice system as not only being adequate for the purpose of trying high-profile cases but more importantly as presenting a far more legitimate response to the terrorist threat.

An Emerging Framework?

The final two selected essays examine whether or not a distinct counter-terrorism framework is emerging, both normatively and institutionally. Daniel Moeckli, in his essay 'The Emergence of Terrorism as a Distinct Category of International Law' (Chapter 21), focuses on the former – namely, whether a separate corpus of counter-terrorism law is developing – by examining the effects of the significant volume of international norms, procedures and institutions on counter-terrorism which have been appearing and developing, often at a fast pace, especially since the 9/11 terrorist attacks. In particular, he argues that '[t]errorism law, it seems, is going through the same process as human rights law, trade law, space law, or environmental law in earlier years' (p. 500). He concludes that:

> ... a considerable body of norms, institutions, and mechanisms specifically designed to deal with terrorism has emerged over the last few years and continues to grow. This body has the most important characteristics of a special legal regime: it appears as an interrelated cluster of primary rules on a limited problem, namely terrorism, together with rules for the administration of those primary rules. (pp. 509–10)

In addition to considering different explanations for the development of a special legal regime, Moeckli further reflects upon its counter-terrorism relevance and implications. He is concerned especially that:

> [u]nder the special treatment model, the starting point of any legal analysis of terrorism is that what is offered by general international law is inadequate to deal with this exceptional phenomenon, and so special rules, bodies, and mechanisms – a fresh legal approach – are required. The result is a self-perpetuating circle of assertions of the exceptional nature of contemporary international terrorism and the need for a resolute legal response in the form of unprecedented special measures. (p. 520)

Whilst Moeckli is correct in suggesting that such an approach can sometimes obscure, rather than clarify, the application of existing legal principles, especially in times of actual or perceived crisis, such a regime nevertheless also has the potential to strengthen the existing legal framework, not least in terms of filling normative lacunae and clarifying the interpretation of key principles underpinning criminal justice and armed conflict approaches. He concludes that:

> ... [it is] too soon to speak of a coherent 'self-contained' regime of substantive 'international anti-terrorism law,' given the disparate and contradictory ways in which terrorism is approached in

different areas of law, the lack of procedural clarity surrounding counter-terrorism efforts, and the absence of any global institutions for coordinating counter-terrorism responses. Terrorism is thick with law; coherence is lacking. (Moeckli, pp. 182–3).

Finally, Eric Rosand's essay, 'The UN-Led Multilateral Institutional Response to Jihadist Terrorism' (Chapter 22) is concerned with how the cohesiveness and effectiveness of multilateral cooperation may be maintained and strengthened –a critical factor in countering the current transnational threat posed by jihadist terrorism, the associated complexities of which require 'comprehensive, multifaceted response at the global, regional and local levels' (p. 530). In particular, he is concerned that '[t]o be effective, responses must be enduring and sustainable and must include a significant non-military component' (pp. 530–31), because 'the extent that the global counterterrorism campaign succeeds in crippling al-Qaeda's global network and its ability to conduct massive attacks or leads to further decentralisation of al-Qaeda ... the more difficult it will be to maintain the international coalition' (p. 531), especially in the absence of the adhesiveness that a universal definition of terrorism could provide. Coupled with this are other challenges such as: keeping the South fully engaged in a phenomenon largely perceived as being a Western priority; a range of operational, administrative deficiencies in capacity, attributable to such factors as resource constraints and/or lack of political will; and the requirement for increased capacity-building, especially in terms of law enforcement.

Rosand does a brief survey of existing regional and UN institutional bodies and legal frameworks through which multilateral cooperation should take place, highlighting many of the current inherent weaknesses. He concludes that they are often attributable more to 'political reactions rather than strategic decisions with corresponding achievable technical objectives', which has led to 'a general lack of sustained attention from politicians and senior government officials ... failed to inspire the confidence of national technical experts ...[and resulted in] duplication of efforts, overlapping mandates and lack of co-ordination at the international, regional and sub-regional levels – all of which have limited the different bodies' overall contribution to the global non-military counterterrorism effort' (p. 534). However, objectives such as capacity-building of weaker and even rogue states are premised on an assumption of their consent and compliance, which may not always be forthcoming. Consequently, Rosand proposes the establishment of a multilateral body which is independent of, yet related to, the UN, which would be better equipped to address many of the identified weaknesses.

References

Bantekas, I. (2003), 'The International Law of Terrorist Financing', *American Journal of International Law*, **97**, pp. 315–33.

Bassiouni, M.C. (ed.) (2001), *International Terrorism: Multilateral Conventions (1937-2001)*, Ardsley, NY: Transnational Publishers.

Benvenuti, P. (2001), 'The ICTY Prosecutor and the Review of the NATO Bombing against the Federal Republic of Yugoslavia', *European Journal of International Law*, **12**, pp. 503–29.

Cassese, A. (1995), *Self-Determination of Peoples: A Legal Reappraisal*, Cambridge: Cambridge University Press.

de Londras, F. and Davis, F.F. (2010), 'Controlling the Executive in Times of Terrorism: Competing Perspective on Effective Oversight Mechanisms', *Oxford Journal Legal Studies*, **30**, pp. 19–47.

Dickinson, L.A. (2001–02), 'Using Legal Process to Fight Terrorism: Detentions, Military Commissions, International Tribunals, and the Rule of Law', *Southern California Law Review*, **75**, pp. 1407–92.

Di Filippo, M. (2008), 'Terrorist Crimes and International Co-operation: Critical Remarks on the Definition and Inclusion of Terrorism in the Category of International Crimes', *European Journal of International Law*, **19**, pp. 533–70.

Elliott, M. (2010), 'The "War on Terror", UK Style: The Detention and Deportation of Suspected Terrorists', *International Journal of Constitutional Law*, **8**, pp. 131–45.

Farer, T.J. (2002), 'Beyond the Charter Frame: Unilateralism or Condominium?', *American Journal of International Law*, **96**, pp. 359–64.

Francioni, F. (ed.) (2003), *Access to Justice as a Human Right*, Oxford: Oxford University Press.

Gioia, A. (2006), 'The UN Conventions on the Prevention and Suppression of International Terrorism', in G. Nesi (ed.), *International Cooperation in Counter-terrorism: The United Nations and Regional Organizations in the Fight against Terrorism*, Aldershot: Ashgate, pp. 3–23.

Grief, N. (2007), 'EU Law and Security', *European Law Review*, **32**, pp. 752–65.

Guilfoyle, D. (2007), 'Maritime Interdiction of Weapons of Mass Destruction', *Journal of Conflict and Security Law*, **12**, pp. 1–36.

Halberstam, M. (2003), 'The Evolution of the United Nations Position on Terrorism: From Exempting National Liberation Movements to Criminalizing Terrorism Wherever and by Whomever Committed', *Columbia Journal of Transnational Law*, **41**, pp. 573–84

Happold, M. (2003), 'Security Council Resolution 1373 and the Constitution of the United Nations', *Leiden Journal of International Law*, **16**, pp. 593–610.

Hmoud, M. (2006), 'Negotiating the Draft Comprehensive Convention on International Terrorism', *Journal of International Criminal Justice*, **4**, pp. 1031–43.

International Bar Association (2003), *International Terrorism: Legal Challenges and Responses,* Herndon, VA: Transnational Publishers.

Irwin, E. (1999), 'Prospects for Justice: The Procedural Aspects of the Right to Life under the European Convention on Human Rights and Its Application to Investigations of Northern Ireland's Bloody Sunday', *Fordham International Law Journal*, **22**, pp. 1822–59.

Jennings, R.Y. (1938), 'The Caroline and McLeod Cases', *American Journal of International Law*, **32**, pp. 82–89.

Laflin, M.M. (2000), 'Kidnapped Terrorists: Bringing International Criminals to Justice through Irregular Rendition and other Quasi-Legal Options', *Journal of Legislation*, **26**, pp. 315–35.

Lambert, J.J. (1990), *Terrorism and Hostages in International Law: A Commentary on the Hostages Convention 1979*, Cambridge: Grotius.

Lavers, T. (2007), 'Extraordinary Rendition and the Self-Defense Justification: Time to Face the Music', *Michigan State Journal of International Law*, **16**, pp. 385–410.

Lawless, M. (2007–08), 'Terrorism: An International Crime?', *International Journal*, **63**, pp. 139–59.

Liivoja, R. (2008), 'The Scope of the Supremacy Clause of the United Nations Charter', *International and Comparative Law Quarterly*, **57**, pp. 583–612.

Maged, A.L. (2003), 'International Legal Cooperation: An Essential Tool in the War Against Terrorism', in W.P. Heere (ed.), *Terrorism and the Military: International Legal Implications*, The Hague: TMC Asser Press, pp. 157–80.

Moeckli, D. (2006), 'The Selective "War on Terror": Executive Detention of Foreign Nationals and the Principle of Non-Discrimination', *Brooklyn Journal of International Law*, **31**, pp. 495–534.

Okafor, O.C. and Okoronkwo, P.L. (2003), 'Re-configuring Non-Refoulement? The Suresh Decision, "Security Relativism", and the International Human Rights Imperative', *International Journal of Refugee Law*, **15**, pp. 30–67.

Parliamentary Assembly of the Council of Europe (2007), '[Alleged] Secret Detentions and Illegal [Unlawful Inter-state] Transfers of Detainees Involving Council of Europe Member States: Second Report', Rapporteur Dick Marty, 11 June, at: http://assembly.coe.int/Documents/WorkingDocs/Doc07/edoc11302.pdf (accessed 19 November 2010).

Rasnic, C.D. (1999), 'Northern Ireland's Criminal Trials Without Jury: The Diplock Experiment', *Annual Survey of International and Comparative Law*, **5**, pp. 239–56.

Sadat, L.N. (2007), 'Extraordinary Rendition, Torture, and other Nightmares from the War on Terror', *George Washington Law Review*, **75**, pp. 1200–48.

Sands, P. (2006), 'International Rule of Law: Extraordinary Rendition, Complicity and its Consequences', *European Human Rights Law Review*, **11**, pp. 408–21.

Satterthwaite, M.L. (2007), 'Rendered Meaningless: Extraordinary Rendition and the Rule of Law', *George Washington Law Review*, **75**, pp. 1333–1420.

Saul, B. (2006), *Defining Terrorism in International Law*, Oxford: Oxford University Press.

Saul, B. (2008), 'Branding Enemies: Regional Legal Responses to Terrorism in Asia', Sydney Law School, Legal Studies Research Paper No 08/127, *Asia-Pacific Yearbook of International Law*, pp. 110–34.

Saul, B. (2009), 'The Emerging International Law of Terrorism', *Indian Yearbook of International Law and Policy*, pp. 163–92.

Scalabrino, M. (2004), 'Fighting Against Terrorism: The Latin American Response', in A. Bianchi (ed.), *Enforcing International Law Norms against Terrorism*, Oxford: Hart, pp. 163–210.

Scharf, M.P. (2004), 'Defining Terrorism as the Peacetime Equivalent of War Crimes: Problems and Prospects', *Case Western Reserve Journal of International Law*, **36**, pp. 359–74.

Shelton, D. (2005), *Remedies in International Human Rights Law*, Oxford: Oxford University Press.

Tham, J-C. (2010), 'Parliamentary Deliberation and the National Security Executive: The Case of Control Orders', *Public Law*, pp. 79–110.

Tomkins, A. (2010), 'National Security and the Role of the Court: A Changed Landscape?', *Law Quarterly Review*, **126**, pp. 543–67.

Tooze J. (2010), 'Deportation with Assurance: the Approach of the UK Courts', *Public Law,* p. 362

United Nations (2004), *A More Secure World: Our Shared Responsibility. Report of the High-Level Panel on Threats, Challenges and Change*, UN Doc A/59/565. Available at: http://www.un.org/secureworld/report2.pdf.

United Nations (2005), *In Larger Freedom: Towards Security, Development and Human Rights for All. Report of the Secretary-General of the United Nations*, Available at: http://www.un.org/largerfreedom.

US Department of State (n.d.), 'Sponsors of State Terrorism', at: http://www.state.gov/s/ct/c14151.htm (accessed 19 November 2010).

Verwey, W.D. (1981), 'The International Hostages Convention and National Liberation Movements', *American Journal of International Law*, **75**, pp. 69–92.

Walker, C. (2010), 'The Threat of Terrorism and the Fate of Control Orders', *Public Law*, pp. 4–17.
Warbrick, C. (2004), 'The European Response to Terrorism in an Age of Human Rights', *European Journal of International Law*, **15**, pp. 989–1018.

Bibliography

Ackerman, B. (2006), *Before the Next Attack: Preserving Civil Liberties in an Age of Terrorism*, New Haven, CT: Yale University Press.
Bassiouni, M.C. (ed.) (2002), *International Terrorism: A Compilation of UN Documents (1972-2001)*, Vols 1 and 2, Ardsley, NY: Transnational Publishers.
Bassiouni, M.C. (ed.) (2001), *International Terrorism: Multilateral Conventions (1937–2001)*, Ardsley, NY: Transnational Publishers.
Bianchi, A. (ed.) (2004), *Enforcing International Law Norms against Terrorism*, Oxford: Hart.
Bianchi, A. and Keller, A. (eds) (2008), *Counterterrorism: Democracy's Challenge*, Oxford: Hart.
Duffy, H. (2005), *The 'War on Terror' and the Framework of International Law*, Cambridge: Cambridge University Press.
Eden, P. and O'Donnell, T. (eds) (2004), *11 September 2001: A Turning Point in International and Domestic Law*, Ardsley, NY: Transnational Publishers.
Gross, O. and Aoláin, F. Ní (2006), *Law in Times of Crisis*, Cambridge: Cambridge University Press.
Guiora, A.N. (2007), *Global Perspectives on Counterterrorism*, Riverwood, IL: Aspen.
Heere, W. (ed.) (2003), *Terrorism and the Military: International Legal Implications*, The Hague: TMC Asser Press.
Higgins, R. and Flory, M. (eds) (1997), *Terrorism and International Law*, London: Routledge.
International Bar Association (2003), *International Terrorism: Legal Challenges and Responses*, Ardsley, NY: Transnational Publishers.
Melzer, N. (2009), *Targeted Killing in International Law*, Oxford: Oxford University Press.
Moeckli, D. (2008), *Human Rights and Non-discrimination in the 'War on Terror'*, Oxford: Oxford University Press.
Nesi, G. (ed.) (2006), *International Cooperation in Counter-Terrorism*, Aldershot: Ashgate.
Paust, J.J. (2007), *Beyond the Law: The Bush Administration's Unlawful Response in the War on Terror*, Cambridge: Cambridge University Press.
Posner, E.A. and Vermeule, A. (2007), *Terror in the Balance: Security, Liberty and the Courts*, Oxford: Oxford University Press.
Ramraj, V., Hor, M. and Roach, K. (eds) (2005), *Global Anti-Terrorism Law and Policy*, Cambridge: Cambridge University Press.
Saul, B. (2006), *Defining Terrorism in International Law*, Oxford: Oxford University Press.
Saul, B. (2010), *Documents in International Law: Terrorism*, Oxford: Hart.
Sterba, J. (ed.) (2003), *Terrorism and International Justice*, Oxford: Oxford University Press.
van Krieken, P.J. (2002), *Terrorism and the International Legal Order*, The Hague: TMC Asser Press.
Wilson, R.A. (ed.) (2005), *Human Rights in the 'War on Terror'*, Cambridge: Cambridge University Press.
Zegveld, L. (2002), *The Accountability of Armed Opposition Groups in International Law*, Cambridge: Cambridge University Press.

Part I
History

[1]

*Countering Terrorism: A Historical Perspective**

ADAM ROBERTS

WHAT CONCLUSIONS CAN be drawn from the long history of terrorist and counterterrorist campaigns? And what directions does this history suggest for the ongoing international campaign against terrorism? Today's international terrorism has assumed organisational forms and means of operating that are historically new. The shadowy entities labelled 'Al Qaeda' are different from earlier terrorist movements in the extremism of their aims and in the far-flung, co-ordinated and ruthless character of their operations. No less novel is the contemporary US and international campaign against international terrorism. And yet, despite all the unprecedented aspects of this conflict, there are dangers in neglecting the history of terrorism and counterterrorism. These dangers include the repetition of mistakes made in earlier eras. The long and tangled history of terrorism and counterterrorism suggests a number of conclusions about the nature of terrorist and counterterrorist campaigns that need to be taken into account in policy-making.

This survey has three sections. *Section I* glances at the history of attempts at defining terrorism. It notes not only the unavoidable difficulties in international discussions of this topic, but also the degree of progress that there has been in defining and prohibiting terrorism. Above all, this section is a warning against over-simple use of this necessary but troublesome term. *Section II* is about the history of terrorism and counterterrorism, seeking to distil some general conclusions about a phenomenon that is always, in reality, deeply rooted in time, place and circumstance. It indicates how debates on terrorism and counterterrorism

* This text is an extensively revised, expanded and updated version of the author's article 'The "War on Terror" in Historical Perspective', which appeared in (Summer 2005) 47(2) *Survival* (London), 101–30.

have often lacked an all-important historical dimension. It offers some inevitably simplified propositions derived from the history of terrorist campaigns, starting with the critical issue of whether terrorism is properly seen as an external threat to democracies. *Section III* is about the 'war on terror' itself, looking particularly at the marshalling of international support for it, and at the emphasis on military intervention that has been part of that war. In the conclusions, six main lines of criticism of the US-led campaign are advanced. This Section suggests that the US doctrine on the 'war on terror' is vulnerable to the charge that it takes too little account of the history of the subject. There is a need to articulate what might be called a British (or, more ambitiously, a European) perspective on terrorism and counterterrorism – one that is more historically informed, encompassing certain elements distinctive from the US doctrine.

Before proceeding, it is necessary to say a brief word about the difficult topic of the causes of terrorism. In most areas of life – including crime, sickness and war – it is possible to discuss causes without inviting the degree of controversy that arises in the case of terrorism. Unfortunately, discussion of the 'causes of terrorism' has become emotionally charged. The principal reason for this sorry state of affairs is that any discussion of causes is easily interpreted as amounting to a justification of terrorism.

The demonstrable historical fact is that terrorist campaigns have arisen in response to several types of situation. They have had as stated purposes the overthrowing of what are perceived as autocratic regimes, including that of the Tsars in Russia in the nineteenth century. They have arisen, even in democracies such as Spain, Sri Lanka and the United Kingdom, as a response to one part of a population's alleged dominance over another. They have also frequently arisen in response to colonial rule, and to foreign occupation. The common thread in the growth of suicide bombing since the attack on the US Embassy in Beirut in 1983 is not just religious extremism but the presence of foreign military occupation. As Robert Pape has written, 'the close association between foreign military occupations and the growth of suicide terrorist movements in the occupied regions should give pause to those who favor solutions that involve conquering countries in order to transform their political systems'.[1] This clear view, that terrorist campaigns are a response to particular types of situation, does not mean that such campaigns are either inevitable or justified. Even in the most difficult circumstances there are moral and strategic choices, and it is far from self-evident that terrorism

[1] R Pape, 'The Strategic Logic of Suicide Terrorism' (August 2003) 97(3) *American Political Science Review* 357.

has superior claims over other forms of action. The attempt to define terrorism arises in part from a desire to underline this point.

I. DEFINING 'TERRORISM'

The word 'terrorism', like many abstract political terms, is confusing, dangerous and indispensable. Confusing, because it means very different things to different people, and its meaning has also changed greatly over time. Dangerous, because it easily becomes an instrument of propaganda, and a means of avoiding thinking about the many forms and causes of political violence. Indispensable, because there is a real phenomenon out there that poses a threat to many societies.

A case can be made that a better generic term to cover the phenomenon under discussion would be 'political violence'. It is less emotion-laden, less condemnatory and certainly wider in scope than 'terrorism'. Yet there is a continuing need for a term that distinguishes some forms of political violence from others. Violence used or threatened by those manning an insurrectionary barricade, or defending an area from police or army incursion, is hardly in itself terrorism. By contrast, violence intended to spread terror much more generally, especially when involving attacks on civilians and/or based on the idea of violence as transforming the political landscape, is a distinct category. In short, and despite a large area of debatable borderland between the two, terrorism can in principle be distinguished from certain other forms of political violence.

The problem of defining 'terrorism' is similar to that of defining many other political abstract terms, such as 'imperialism' and 'war': the core meaning may be clear enough, and it may be possible to secure agreement that certain cases fit that meaning. At the edges, however, there is often scope for genuine debate about whether particular acts, or types of action, really deserve to be included in the category.

Even within certain countries there can be different legal definitions of terrorism. For example, different US government agencies have had different understandings of the term, and this has sometimes complicated intra-governmental cooperation. That there should be international disagreement on the meaning of the term is not surprising: what is remarkable is that there has been significant progress towards a definition.

There are traps in most attempted definitions of terrorism, and in the uses made of the term. The most serious is that the label 'terrorist' has sometimes been applied to the activities of movements which, even if they did resort to violence, had serious claims to political legitimacy, and also exercised care and restraint in their choice of methods. Famously, in

1987–88 the UK and US governments labelled the African National Congress of South Africa 'terrorist': a shallow and silly attribution even at the time, let alone in light of Nelson Mandela's later emergence as statesman.

In certain circumstances, the repeated use of the term 'terrorist' to describe a particular class of adversaries can conceal rather than clarify key aspects of the political environment. In particular, the description of a group as 'terrorist' may obscure the fact that its opponents also use terror; and it may also obscure the fact that the so-called terrorist group has a moral, political and economic basis for its power, and does not rely exclusively on terror to maintain its influence. For example, in the 1960s many writers and journalists freely used the word 'terrorist' to describe a member of the Vietcong, the military arm of the National Liberation Front of South Vietnam. The Vietcong did undoubtedly use the weapon of terror ruthlessly and systematically against the South Vietnamese population. However, serious studies suggested that terror was not on its own an adequate basis of control: a sense of the moral justice of the cause was also present. The two factors were mutually reinforcing – and this helped to explain the capacity of the Vietcong to endure.[2]

The problem of defining 'terrorism' is especially difficult as it is generally seen as a pejorative term: all diplomatic attempts to define it have been combined with attempts to prohibit it. This brief exploration of the difficult issue of definition looks at international negotiations on the topic, especially those within a UN framework; and it then offers a short working definition indicating how the term is used in this chapter.

A. Negotiating towards a Definition

The UN General Assembly, which has addressed the problem of terrorism since the early 1970s, has adopted 13 treaties prohibiting particular terrorist acts from air piracy to acts involving nuclear reactors; but it has been able to reach only a limited measure of agreement on a general definition of terrorism.[3] The General Assembly's ad hoc committee on terrorism, established in 1996, has not yet been able to agree all parts of a definition which would form part of the draft comprehensive convention. One problem has been that many post-colonial states in the General

[2] This is the conclusion, for example, of two exceptionally thorough and impressive US studies of the Vietcong published during the war: D Pike, *Vietcong: The Organization and Techniques of the National Liberation Front of South Vietnam* (Cambridge, MA, MIT Press, 1966); and N Leites, *The Vietcong Style of Politics*, Rand Memorandum RM-5487-1-ISA/ARPA (Santa Monica, CA, Rand, 1969).

[3] For information on the wide range of General Assembly activities on terrorism, see the UN website at <http://www.un.org/terrorism/ga.html>.

Assembly claim origins in national liberation struggles that colonial powers called terrorist campaigns. Such states have been at the forefront of demands to incorporate in any text defining terrorism a pledge to address the root causes of terrorism – which seemed to the United States and others as a backdoor justification of terrorism. There have been parallel difficulties in working out an acceptable generic distinction between terrorists and freedom fighters. Yet there has been some modest progress towards a definition of terrorism.

Partly this has been due to the focus on a particular aspect of contemporary terrorism – the fact that it often involves deliberate attacks on civilians. Progress has been made in the UN Security Council – where there has been less concern than in the General Assembly about referring to the root causes. A Security Council resolution in October 2004, after condemning 'all acts of terrorism regardless of their motivation', came close to a definition of terrorism when it stated that the Council:

> *Recalls* that criminal acts, including against civilians, committed with the intent to cause death or serious bodily injury, or taking of hostages, with the purpose to provoke a state of terror in the general public or in a group of persons or particular persons, intimidate a population or compel a government or an international organization to do or to abstain from doing any act, which constitute offences within the scope of and as defined in the international conventions and protocols relating to terrorism , are under no circumstances justifiable by considerations of a political, philosophical, ideological, racial, ethnic, religious or other similar nature, and *calls upon* all States to prevent such acts and, if not prevented, to ensure that such acts are punished by penalties consistent with their grave nature.[4]

Similarly, the UN High-level Panel on Threats, Challenges and Change, which issued its report in December 2004, focused on civilians in its suggested definition of terrorism:

> any action, in addition to actions already specified by the existing conventions on aspects of terrorism, the Geneva Conventions and Security Council resolution 1566 (2004), that is intended to cause death or serious bodily harm to civilians or non-combatants, when the purpose of such an act, by its nature or context, is to intimidate a population, or to compel a Government or an international organization to do or to abstain from doing any act.[5]

A limitation of both these definitions put forward in 2004 (and especially of the second one) should be noted. The emphasis being largely on the threat to civilians or non-combatants, they might appear not to encompass certain acts such as attacks on armed peacekeeping forces, attacks

[4] SC Res 1566 of 8 October 2004, operative para 3.

[5] UN High-level Panel on Threats, Challenges and Change, *A More Secure World: Our Shared Responsibility*, UN doc A/59/565, 2 December 2004, para 164(d).

on police or armed forces, or assassinations of heads of state or government. They might not include the attack on the Pentagon on 11 September 2001, but for the fact that it involved the hijacking of a civilian airliner.

The UN General Assembly's World Summit Outcome document of September 2005 condemned 'terrorism in all its forms and manifestations, committed by whomever, wherever, and for whatever purposes'.[6] However, this document did not attempt to define terrorism. Subsequently, in September 2006, the General Assembly approved a resolution entitled 'UN Global Counter-terrorism Strategy' the preamble of which contained some elements of a definition when it reaffirmed 'that acts, methods and practices of terrorism in all its forms and manifestations are activities aimed at the destruction of human rights, fundamental freedoms and democracy, threatening territorial integrity, security of States and destabilizing legitimately constituted Governments'. The document promised support for a future comprehensive convention on international terrorism, which would contain a legal definition.[7] Then in December 2006, in much the same vein, the General Assembly passed a resolution on 'Measures to Eliminate International Terrorism' in which it stated that the General Assembly:

> *Reiterates* that criminal acts intended or calculated to provoke a state of terror in the general public, a group of persons or particular persons for political purposes are in any circumstances unjustifiable, whatever the considerations of a political, philosophical, ideological, racial, ethnic, religious or other nature that may be invoked to justify them.[8]

The 2005 Council of Europe Convention on the Prevention of Terrorism defines terrorism in a similar fashion in a preambular clause:

> Recalling that acts of terrorism have the purpose by their nature or context to seriously intimidate a population or unduly compel a government or an international organisation to perform or abstain from performing any act or seriously destabilise or destroy the fundamental political, constitutional, economic or social structures of a country or an international organisation;

In sum, although there is agreement on elements of a definition, there is as yet no agreement on a formal legal definition. This is why the nearest things there are to a definition tend to be found in preambular clauses, where their incompleteness is less worrisome than it would be if they

[6] GA Res 60/1 of 16 September 2005, '2005 World Summit Outcome', UN doc A/Res./60/1 of 24 October 2005, para 81.

[7] GA Res 60/288 of 8 September 2006.

[8] GA Res 61/40 of 4 December 2006.

were presented as a formal definition. It is also why it has been easier to draw up conventions prohibiting specific terrorist acts than to prohibit terrorism in general.

B. Defining 'Terrorist Acts'

A category that is easier to define than the grand abstraction of terrorism is *terrorist acts*. While still surrounded by a dense thicket of thorny problems, this term has the merit of keeping the focus on specific types of action. It encompasses certain violent acts that can be judged to be unlawful by well-established criteria. The category of 'terrorist acts' can encompass actions that contravene any or all of the following bodies of law:

- certain national laws relating to terrorism;
- regional international agreements on terrorism. Examples include the 2005 Council of Europe Convention on the Prevention of Terrorism;
- global international agreements on terrorism – that is, the 13 conventions approved by the UN General Assembly prohibiting particular terrorist acts;
- the basic principles and specific provisions of the laws of war. However, the question of whether this body of law is formally applicable to particular terrorist acts would depend on whether the acts concerned are part of an ongoing armed conflict (and, if so, on whether the conflict is international or non-international in character).

On the basis of criteria contained in such bodies of law it is possible, at least sometimes, to draw a distinction between prohibited acts and other types and forms of armed resistance. That is why the adage 'one man's terrorist is another man's freedom fighter', while it contains more than a grain of truth (especially that the same act can be seen differently by different people), is too simple: it reflects a lack of awareness that there are some established criteria for distinguishing between the two.

C. Towards a Provisional Definition of 'Terrorism'

A feature of several of the UN attempts at definition is the implication that terrorism is essentially a non-state or even anti-state activity, aimed at undermining governments and/or international organisations. This approach may be unavoidable in the process of narrowing down a broad subject into a specific criminalisation of particular activities. It reflects the fact that, being a form of action in which individuals and small groups can engage, terrorism has often been a weapon of non-state bodies, from anarchists in the nineteenth century to Al Qaeda in the twenty-first. Moreover, the terrorism of non-state groups is of special concern to governments because it threatens their monopoly of the instruments of violence and coercion within a state. This is a perfectly legitimate concern, which many citizens share: to have more than one wielder of violence within a state can be a recipe for anarchy and civil war. Thus it is not surprising that some attempts at definition focus on terrorism's non-state character.

However, many states have also used terror – whether against their own population, expatriates whom they wish to silence or foreign adversaries. While it would be wrong to characterise all state coercion as terrorism, there have been instances in which states have resorted to terrorism through their own armed services, police forces and other state agents, or by secretly supporting non-state terrorist groups. Sometimes they have used *agents provocateurs* to discredit their opponents by falsely attributing terrorist acts to them. A serious definition of terrorism needs to take account of this fact.

In light of the multi-faceted nature of past uses of terrorism, and the many ways in which terrorism overlaps with and shades into other activities, this survey suggests a broad definition – and one that is certainly not definitive granted the controversies that necessarily surround the subject. 'Terrorism' is used here mainly to refer to: *the systematic use of violence and threats of violence – often but not exclusively by non-state groups, and generally clandestine in its organisation and modes of action – designed to cause dislocation, consternation, and submission on the part of a target population, government or international organisation*. This is no more than a provisional working definition indicating how the term is used in this chapter. It is offered because of the continuing absence of an authoritative international definition. In what follows, the focus is mainly on the terrorism of non-state groups.

II. HISTORY OF TERRORISM AND COUNTER-TERRORISM

A. Denial of History

Since 11 September 2001, statements by the principal Western leaders on the subject of the 'war on terror' have contained few references to the previous experience of governments in tackling terrorist threats, or to the ways in which certain international wars of the twentieth century were sparked off by concerns about terrorism. This appears to be true also of their inner deliberations, as revealed by Bob Woodward, Seymour Hersh and others. In particular, Woodward's *Plan of Attack* shows that there was little reference to historical precedents in the two years of decision-making leading up to the invasion of Iraq. An honourable exception occurred when Secretary of State Colin Powell, at a planning meeting on Iraq, asked sarcastically: 'Are we going to be off-loading at Gallipoli?'.[9]

General Bernard Montgomery's first rule of warfare was 'Don't march on Moscow.'[10] Regarding terrorism and counterterrorism there is no such straightforward rule. The history of these matters repays study, not because it offers a single recipe for action, but rather because it enriches our understanding of a peculiarly complex subject. It indicates a range of possibilities for addressing it, and a number of hazards to avoid. Historians are neither agreed nor infallible in addressing this subject, any more than are my own colleagues in the field of international relations. A profession that encompasses both Professor Sir Michael Howard and Professor Bernard Lewis is not about to reach a unanimous party line on a subject as contentious as what to do about terrorism.

Yet it remains odd that since 2001 much writing on terror, particularly in the United States, has tended to neglect the long history of terrorism and counterterrorism. This is true even of historians and historically informed writers: some, such as John Gaddis and Walter Mead, have written books about the war on terror that contain much important insight into US history and the US role in the world, but say almost nothing about the history of terror and counterterror.[11] On the other hand, since 2001 there has been a good deal of writing touching on the history of these matters. A few works have covered only the last few decades.[12] Some works, however, have taken into account experiences of terrorism and counterterrorism from the nineteenth century to the twenty-first – an excellent example being that of Michael Ignatieff.[13]

[9] Bob Woodward, *Plan of Attack* (New York, Simon & Schuster, 2004) 324.

[10] General Bernard Montgomery said of US policy in Vietnam: 'The US has broken the second rule of war. That is, don't go fighting with your land army on the mainland of Asia. Rule One is don't march on Moscow. I developed these two rules myself': A Chalfont, *Montgomery of Alamein* (London, Weidenfeld & Nicolson, [1976]) 318.

[11] JL Gaddis, *Surprise, Security, and the American Experience* (Cambridge, MA, Harvard University Press, 2004); and WR Mead, *Power, Terror, Peace, and War: America's Grand Strategy in a World at Risk* (New York, Alfred A Knopf, 2004). See also JL Gaddis, 'And Now This: Lessons from the Old Era for the New One', in S Talbott and N Chanda (eds), *The Age of Terror: America and the World After September 11* (Oxford, Perseus Press, 2001) 1–22.

[12] B Maxwell, *Terrorism: A Documentary History* (Washington DC, CQ Press, [2003]). The documents in this book cover only a 30-year period, 'from 1972, when international terrorism bust into the public consciousness with live TV pictures of Palestinian terrorists holding Israeli athletes hostage at the Munich Olympics'. In some countries the public was aware of terrorism decades, or even centuries, earlier.

[13] M Ignatieff, *The Lesser Evil: Political Ethics in an Age of Terror* (Edinburgh, Edinburgh University Press, 2004).

In practice, the response of each country to the 'war on terror' has been deeply influenced by its own particular experience of terrorism and counterterrorism. In the United Kingdom there has been frequent reference to the experience of countering terrorism in Northern Ireland. British Ministers and officials, however, have refrained from pointing out bluntly, and in public, that almost everything about the language and manner in which terror in Northern Ireland has been opposed, and about the attempts at underwriting its end through mediation and even negotiation, has been very different from the US approach to the 'war on terror'. Partly, of course, this is because the problems faced have been different: the Irish Republican Army (IRA) is far removed from Al Qaeda in ideology, in political goals and in methods. Yet the British may have been too reticent about their experience of terrorism.

The tendency to approach terrorism without benefit of history has, itself, a long history. Political debates about terrorism have perennially been ahistorical. Both terrorists and their adversaries tend to talk and write publicly about their campaigns with little reference to the centuries-long history of terrorism and counterterrorism. This is not to say that they do not articulate a view of history more generally. Terrorists, for example, often focus on deep resentments based on perceptions of alien domination of the societies they claim to defend. When terrorists have put pen to paper, either at the time of their activism or subsequently, they have sometimes shown considerable awareness of international developments and the history of their own and earlier epochs.[14] At the same time, the long and tangled history of both terrorism and counterterrorism is frequently airbrushed out of the picture. The publicly articulated world-view of terrorists and their adversaries is often a world of moral and political absolutes, in which terrorism, or the war against it, is seen as an essentially new means of ridding the world of a unique and evil scourge. On both sides, the favoured form of argument is phrased in terms of morality – and a relatively simple morality at that, in which the adversary's actions are seen as such a serious threat as to create an overwhelming necessity for the use of counter-violence.

Many specialists in counter-insurgency have seen their subject more as a struggle of light versus darkness than as a common and recurrent theme of history. A fine example of such an ahistorical approach to the subject is the French group of theorists writing in the 1950s and early 1960s about *la guerre révolutionnaire*. These theorists denied the complexities – especially the mixture of material, moral and ideological factors – that are keys to understanding why and how terrorist movements come

[14] See eg D Rapoport, 'The International World as Some Terrorists Have Seen It: A Look at a Century of Memoirs' (December 1987) 10(4) *The Journal of Strategic Studies* 32–58.

into existence. Colonel Lacheroy, a leading figure in this group and head of the French Army's *Service d'Action Psychologique*, famously stated: 'In the beginning there is nothing.'[15] Terrorism was seen as having been introduced deliberately into a peaceful society by an omnipresent outside force – namely international communism. It is a demonological vision of a cosmic struggle in which the actual history of particular countries and ways of thinking has little or no place. These French theories – no doubt because they date from a period of failed military campaigns, attempted military *coups d'état*, systematic use of torture against insurgents, and a generally disastrous period in French history – are now almost entirely forgotten, even in France itself. They are also ignored in the United States, even though they, and the events with which they are connected, provide object-lessons in how not to conduct a counterterrorist campaign.

If terrorists and counter-terrorists have often forgotten history, history has not entirely forgotten them. Many historians have written subtly and interestingly about the evolution of terrorism (which, like so much else, has significant European as well as extra-European origins), about its ever-changing philosophy, about its sociology and its consequences. Those historians who have combined historical analysis of terrorism with advocacy have tended to favour a tough line against terrorism, but biased more towards a strong police response than towards military interventions.[16]

In present circumstances there are powerful reasons to buttress the claim that the threat faced is totally new, and needs to be tackled in new ways. Today's terrorist incidents can involve a combination of elements, many of which are new: elaborate planning carried out far from the location of the attack; a suicide mission; an assault on a nuclear-armed power; the destruction of major buildings and the killing of hundreds or even thousands of people, usually civilians. Such an attack may be on behalf of a movement many of whose demands are probably unachievable and certainly non-negotiable. Something new is undoubtedly happening, whether at the World Trade Center in Manhattan or at Beslan in North Ossetia. The difference between the scale of carnage now and what

[15] Col C Lacheroy, 'La Guerre Révolutionnaire', Talk given on 2 July 1957, reprinted in *La Défense Nationale* (Paris, 1958) 322, cited in P Paret, *French Revolutionary Warfare from Indochina to Algeria: The Analysis of a Political and Military Doctrine* (London, Pall Mall Press, 1964) 15. Paret comments that 'nothing', in this case, means 'the secure existence of the *status quo*'.

[16] See eg W Laqueur, *The Age of Terrorism* (London, Weidenfeld & Nicolson, 1987). See also M Howard, 'What's in a Name? How to Fight Terrorism' (January/February 2002) *Foreign Affairs* 9–13.

resulted from earlier phases of terrorism brings to mind the grim biblical statement that is inscribed on the Machine Gun Corps monument in London:

> Saul hath slain his thousands
>
> but David his tens of thousands.[17]

So sharp is the distinction from earlier eras that, from today's grim perspective, it would be easy to implore earlier terrorists: 'Come back: all is forgiven.' Former terrorists themselves, in the manner of old soldiers, have often deplored the terrible things that later generations of terrorists did, and the impurity of their motivations.[18] Because the changes have been so great, it would also be easy to brush aside earlier historical experience of terrorism on the grounds of diminished relevance – and this indeed appears to have happened in much contemporary analysis. It is a huge mistake.

B. Ten Propositions based on Earlier Campaigns

At the risk of over-simplification, the following ten propositions can be drawn from the long history of terrorism, and action against it. These propositions all have a bearing on the conduct of, and language regarding, today's international campaign against terrorism.

1. The Relation between Terrorism and Democracy is Complex

Terrorism has long been seen as a threat to democracies. The illustration below, from a novel published in 1893, shows this view of the threat more eloquently than any words can.

[17] Monument 'erected to commemorate the glorious heroes of the Machine Gun Corps who Fell in the Great War (1914–1918)', Hyde Park Corner, London. As the monument's inscription notes, the Machine Gun Corps was formed on 14 October 1915, and its last unit was disbanded on 15 July 1922. The quotation is from I Samuel 18: 7.

[18] A good example is Ratko Parezanin, a member of the Young Bosnia movement in 1914 and a friend of Gavril Princip, the assassin of Archduke Ferdinand in 1914. Parezanin's memoirs, published in 1974, are mentioned below, n 20.

SHELLING THE HOUSES OF PARLIAMENT

Source: E Douglas Fawcett, Hartmann the Anarchist: or, The Doom of the Great City (London, Edward Arnold, 1893) frontispiece.[19]

This vision of the mother of parliaments going down shows just how enduring is the image of terrorism as a threat to democracy. In recent years this tradition of thought has continued, with many seeing contemporary terrorist campaigns as part of a totalitarian attack on the whole idea of democracy. Many, too, have seen democracy as constituting the antidote or prophylactic for terrorism. The historical record suggests that the connections between democracy and terrorism are more complex.

The proposition that democracies are attacked simply because they are democracies has obvious strengths. It is usually associated with the idea that the ideologues leading terrorist campaigns see democracy as their enemy because their whole scheme is about imposing a vision upon society. There is also an argument that democracies are attacked because

[19] Also shown in B Porter, 'Oo Let 'Em In? Asylum Seekers and Terrorists in Britain, 1850–1914', in R Louis (ed), *Yet More Adventures with Britannia* (London, IB Tauris, 2005) 21. This shows the Attila, an airship (or 'aëronef') with powerful engines and a 'projecting aëroplane', shelling the Houses of Parliament at an imagined future date in 1920. When it was published, flight was still in its infancy. The first powered heavier-than-air aeroplane flight would be 10 years later, by Orville and Wilbur Wright on 17 December 1903, at Kitty Hawk.

they represent an easier target than autocracies – their very liberalism being used against them. Yet there are other explanations for the occurrence of terrorist attacks in democracies. In particular, because they have a free press, democracies give far more publicity to terrorists than do more autocratic systems of government; and they may also offer them easier chances to gather like-minded people together to initiate a campaign. There is a long history of violent campaigns of various kinds, including terrorist struggles, being supported in democratic countries while having as their main targets governments elsewhere: this is part of the explanation of why London came to be seen by nineteenth-century autocrats as a haven for terrorists – a precursor of its twenty-first century characterisation as 'Londonistan'.

The vision of democracies as simply the innocent victims of terrorism also falls foul of other historical considerations. It risks leaving out of the picture some grievance-based elements in the politics of terrorism. The involvements of democratic states in what are perceived as oppressive policies at home or abroad, including supporting military occupations, are frequently cited as supposed 'justifications' of terrorism. Moreover, the process of democratisation within a hitherto non-democratic society – whether it is brought about by intervening forces or purely domestic ones – can be deeply disruptive and may provoke a violent, even terrorist, response from sections of the population whose rights or privileges appear to be threatened. The nervousness of a large ethnic minority about dominance by a local majority is part of the explanation of why terrorist campaigns have developed and have proved persistent in a number of democratic political systems, including Northern Ireland for well over a generation from 1971, and Sri Lanka from 1983. Not only did they originate within formal democracies, but for long periods both rebellions received significant assistance from ethnic kin support groups in well-established Western democracies – the United States in the case of Northern Ireland, and the United Kingdom and Canada in the case of Sri Lanka.

None of this challenges the view that in the long run a mature and inclusive democracy, recognising rights of minorities, may be an effective means of reducing the likelihood of terrorism. What is called into question is the frequently asserted assumption that democracy in all its forms is the enemy of terrorism.

2. *Terrorist Action often has Unintended Consequences*

Most terrorist movements and individuals have notions of change with two main strands: (1) a spectacular act of violence will transform the political landscape, particularly by mobilising and radicalising the dormant masses; (2) a long terrorist campaign will wear down the adversary, leading to demoralisation, doubt and withdrawal. These are the terrorist equivalents of *blitzkrieg* and war of attrition, and just as conventional warfare often has unintended consequences, so does terrorism.

There is no doubt that some terrorist campaigns have achieved significant objectives. Certain temporary international presences have proved vulnerable to terrorist campaigns, including especially those of overstretched colonial powers, and, more recently, of international bodies such as the United Nations. One common consequence of a sustained terrorist campaign in a particular area is that it is bad for tourism – especially when, as has happened in several attacks in the past decade, from Egypt to Indonesia, it is the tourists themselves who are targets. Yet only rarely has the discouragement of tourism been the principal goal of a terrorist movement.

Other consequences of terrorist campaigns are much more unpredictable. For example, political assassinations have very seldom had the effects for which the terrorists hoped, and more often have led to a strengthening of the regime against which they were fighting. An exhaustive study concentrating particularly on the effects of 56 assassinations of heads of government or state in the period 1919–68 concluded:

> We are dismayed by the high incidence of assassination indicated by our collected data ... We are also surprised by the fact that the impact of any single assassination, even of a chief executive or dictator, normally tends to be low.[20]

Sometimes terrorist actions lead to major consequences that are different from what the terrorists anticipated. They may lead to vigorous political or military campaigns against the terrorists, and even to the outbreak of international wars, as in Europe in 1914. According to a friend who was close to him, Gavril Princip, the 19-year-old Bosnian Serb student who killed Archduke Ferdinand in Sarajevo in June 1914, had no idea that the result of the assassination would be war, let alone world war.[21]

In some cases terrorist action has been so callous that it has aroused antagonism even among the population that has some sympathy with, even involvement in, the terrorist cause. For example, in August 1949, when communist terrorists in the Philippines murdered the popular widow of President Quezon, for the first time there was widespread

[20] MC Havens, C Leiden and K Schmitt, *The Politics of Assassination* (Engelwood Cliffs, NJ, Prentice-Hall, [1970]) 153.

[21] See the remarkable and detailed memoir by a fellow-student in the Young Bosnia movement who was a friend of Princip, Ratko Parezanin, *Mlada Bosna I prvi svetski rat* [*Young Bosnia and the First World War*] (Munich, Iskra, 1974). The book was published on the sixtieth anniversary of the Sarajevo assassination. A useful short report is I Macdonald, 'Sarajevo: When a Teenager with a Gun Sent the World to War', *The Times* (London), 28 June 1974, 18.

popular wrath against the insurgents.[22] Such actions can contribute to the isolation of terrorist groups. Indeed, the terrorist dream of awakening the masses through their actions has almost never worked in the way in which terrorists have perennially hoped.

Sometimes terrorists may secretly intend what appear to be unintended and even unwelcome consequences. A terrorist leader may seek to provoke a repressive response from the adversary's regime, thus exposing its supposedly true nature – the iron fist inside the velvet glove. As Lawrence Durrell wrote in *Bitter Lemons*, his rich and subtle account of the Eoka insurgency in Cyprus:

> [H]is primary objective is not battle. It is to bring down upon the community in general a reprisal for his wrongs, in the hope that the fury and resentment roused by punishment meted out to the innocent will gradually swell the ranks of those from whom he will draw further recruits.[23]

In some cases an aim may be to provoke not just government repression, but foreign military intervention. The possibility that these may be prime terrorist aims confirms the need for caution in crafting a counterterrorist policy.

3. Terrorism's Tendency to become Endemic

One of the most pernicious aspects of terrorism is its capacity to become endemic in particular regions, cultures and societies. Because of its unofficial and clandestine character, and because of the extreme bitterness it engenders within and between communities, it becomes a habit much more easily than does regular state-based warfare. The experience of terrorism suggests that, after it has been taken up in one cause, it gets adopted by others, and by splinter groups; and that it is difficult to reach a definitive end to terrorist activities. Started by the Right, it gets taken up the Left, or vice versa. Started by nationalists, it may get taken up by so-called religious fundamentalists. Started by the Stern Gang, it gets taken up by the PLO. Started by the high-minded, it gets taken up by criminals, drug-smugglers and Mafiosi. Moreover, it can be difficult to call off terrorist struggles. A hard-core splinter group within a movement may refuse all compromise; and may be able to continue the struggle because the decentralised nature of terrorist organisation and action makes that easy.

This view of terrorism as damaging to the societies in which it takes place is confirmed by the history of the Middle East, Latin America, the

[22] R Asprey, *War in the Shadows: The Guerrilla in History* (London, Macdonald and Jane's, 1976) 811; drawing on ND Valeriano and CTR Bohannan, *Counter-Guerrilla Operations: The Philippine Experience* (New York, Praeger, 1962).

[23] L Durrell, *Bitter Lemons* (London, Faber & Faber, 1956) 216.

Balkans and Ireland over the past two centuries. It forms an important buttress to moral condemnations of terrorism. An understanding of its destructive character within the societies that produce terrorist movements – which are of course the very societies that they purport to save – provides a better basis for securing international action against terrorism than do certain views of terrorism that focus on it as a threat principally to the democratic states of the West in general, or indeed to the United States in particular.

4. Capacity of Counterterrorism to Achieve Results

Contrary to myth, counterterrorist activities and policies can sometimes succeed – at least in the sense of contributing to a reduction or ending of the activities of terrorists without yielding power to them. For example, the forces opposed to terrorists/guerrillas were successful in this sense in the Huk Rebellion in the Philippines in 1946–54; in the long-running Malayan 'emergency' of 1948–60; and against the 'Red Brigades' that were active in Italy and Germany in the early 1970s. Arguably, they had a measure of success in the troubles in Northern Ireland over three decades from 1969.

Perhaps 95 per cent of the important action in any campaign against terrorism consists of intelligence and police work: identifying suspects, infiltrating movements, collaborating with police forces in other countries, gathering evidence for trials and so on. This underlying truth is far from being denied by President Bush or other leading figures involved in the 'war on terror'. However, their rhetoric, being much more that of open war and of victory, has sometimes obscured this basic fact.

5. Need to Address Underlying Grievances

While there is no simple formula for how terrorism can be undermined or defeated, the process often, perhaps even generally, requires action that is sensitive to the political environment. Where counterterrorist strategies have succeeded, success has often been in combination with a political package that either responded to certain terrorist demands while rejecting others, or undercut the terrorists by reducing their pool of political support, or both. In Malaya, for example, the promise, and the actuality, of unqualified national independence was crucial to containing the terrorist threat.

Apropos the 'war on terror', John Gaddis has reminded us that during the Cold War it was perfectly well accepted that there was a need to address social issues on which Communist propaganda played:

> With the rehabilitation of Germany and Japan after World War II, together with the Marshall Plan, we fought the conditions that made the Soviet alternative attractive even as we sought to contain the Soviets themselves.[24]

It is sometimes suggested that making changes that respond in some way to terrorist demands constitutes appeasement, or at least implies recognition that a campaign of terrorism is justified. Such a suggestion is flawed. To say that a movement responds to real grievances – as for example over Palestine – is not to say that it is justified in resorting to terror, but it is to say that the terrorist movement reflects larger concerns in society that need to be addressed in some way. The exact way in which they are addressed may not be the way the movement is demanding. To refuse all changes on an issue because a terrorist movement has embraced that issue is actually to allow terrorists to dictate the political agenda.

6. Respect for a Legal Framework

Respect for law has been an important element in many operations against terrorists. One of the key figures involved in the Malayan campaign in the 1950s, Sir Robert Thompson, distilling five basic principles of counter-insurgency from this and other cases, wrote of the crucial importance of operating within a properly functioning domestic legal framework:

> The government must function in accordance with law.
>
> There is a very strong temptation in dealing both with terrorism and with guerrilla actions for government forces to act outside the law, the excuses being that the processes of law are too cumbersome, that the normal safeguards in the law for the individual are not designed for an insurgency and that a terrorist deserves to be treated as an outlaw anyway. Not only is this morally wrong, but, over a period, it will create more practical difficulties for a government than it solves.[25]

It is not only national legal standards that are important, but also international standards, including those embodied in the laws of war. A perception that the states involved in a coalition are observing basic international standards may contribute to public support for military operations within the member states; support (or at least tacit consent) from other states for coalition operations; and avoidance of disputes within and between coalition member states. In short, there can be strong

[24] Gaddis, 'And Now This', n 11 above at 20.

[25] R Thompson, *Defeating Communist Insurgency: Experiences from Malaya and Vietnam* (London, Chatto & Windus, 1966) 52. From 1957 to 1961 the author was successively Deputy Secretary and Secretary for Defence in Malaya. As his and other accounts make clear, in the course of the Malayan Emergency there were certain derogations from human rights standards, including detentions and compulsory relocations of villages.

prudential considerations (not necessarily dependent on reciprocity in observance of the law by all the parties to a war) that militate in favour of observing the laws of war.

There are some well-known difficulties in applying the laws of war to terrorist and counterterrorist activities. Most terrorists do not conform to the well-known requirements for the status of lawful belligerent, entitled to full prisoner-of-war (PoW) status. Further, few states could accept application of the law if it meant that all terrorists were deemed to be legitimate belligerents on a par with the regular uniformed forces of a government. However, application of the law does not require acceptance of either of these doubtful propositions. Rather it means recognition that, even in a war against ruthless terrorists, the observance of certain restraints may be legally obligatory and politically desirable – especially as regards treatment of detainees. Understandable doubt over the formal applicability of some provisions of existing law should not be turned into a licence to flout basic norms.[26]

7. Treatment of Detainees

The treatment of detainees is an issue of crucial importance in the history of terrorism and counterterrorism. Indeed, the defining moment in the birth of modern terrorism was an event in Russia in 1878 in response to the flogging of a political prisoner. This was what led a young woman, Vera Zasulich, to shoot and seriously wound General Trepov, the Police Chief of St Petersburg who had had the prisoner flogged.[27] Walter Laqueur has said of this event: 'Only in 1878, after Vera Zasulich's shooting of General Trepov, the governor of the Russian capital, did terrorism as a doctrine, the Russian version of "propaganda by the deed", finally emerge.'[28] Likewise, torture meted out in Egyptian jails from Nasser's time onwards has often been cited as part of the explanation for the emergence of radical purportedly Islamic terrorism.

When fighting an unseen and vicious enemy, who may have many secret sympathisers, all societies encounter difficulties. In such circumstances, most states, even democratic ones, resort to some form of detention without trial. This is an understandable and even necessary response, but it involves huge risks. First, there is a risk of arresting and

[26] For a fuller account, see A Roberts, 'The Laws of War in the War on Terror', in P Wilson (ed), *International Law and the War on Terrorism*, US Naval War College, International Law Studies, vol 79 (Newport, RI, Naval War College, 2003) 175–230.

[27] R Gaucher, *The Terrorists: From Tsarist Russia to the OAS*, trs Paula Spurlin (London, Secker & Warburg, 1968) 10–11.

[28] Laqueur, *Age of Terrorism*, n 16 above at 33.

convicting the wrong people; and second, the maltreatment of detainees. Both tend to create martyrs and to give nourishment to the terrorist campaign.

The United Kingdom's long engagement against terrorism in Northern Ireland from 1969 onwards affords ample evidence for both these propositions, and it also points in the direction of a possible solution. This was one of many conflicts in which those deemed to be 'terrorists' were aware of the value, including propaganda value, of making claims to PoW status and publicising claims of ill-treatment. While denying that there was an armed conflict, whether international or otherwise, and strongly resisting any granting of PoW status to detainees and convicted prisoners, the United Kingdom did slowly come to accept that they had a distinct status, and that international standards had to apply to their treatment. After initially using methods that were legally questionable and highly controversial, from March 1972 onwards the United Kingdom adopted a different approach, in effect applying basic legal principles derived from the laws of war. This helped in the long and difficult process of taking some of the political sting out of the emotionally charged issue of treatment of detainees.[29]

The treatment of detainees and prisoners has been one of the major failures of the 'war on terror' ever since it began in late 2001. In January 2002 US Secretary of Defense Donald Rumsfeld infamously said of the prisoners in Guantanamo:

> I do not feel even the slightest concern over their treatment. They are being treated vastly better than they treated anybody else over the last several years and vastly better than was their circumstance when they were found.[30]

Needless to say, this and similar remarks were widely broadcast on radio and TV stations critical of the United States. The episodes of maltreatment and torture in Iraq since April 2003 have reinforced the damage. Those who suggest that humane treatment is a relatively unimportant issue – and those far fewer individuals who argue that torturing prisoners is a way to combat terrorism – do need to address the criticism that ill-treatment and torture have in the past provided purported justifications for the resort to terrorism, and also discredited the anti-terrorist cause.

[29] The key document in this process was Lord Gardiner's minority report in *Report of the Committee of Privy Counsellors Appointed to Consider Authorized Procedures for the Interrogation of Persons Suspected of Terrorism*, Cmnd 4901 (London, HMSO, March 1972). His minority report was accepted by the government, as announced by Prime Minister Edward Heath in the House of Commons on 2 March 1972: *Hansard*, House of Commons, 2 March 1972, cols 743–4.

[30] Donald Rumsfeld roundtable with radio media, 15 January 2002, available at <http://www.defenselink.mil /transcripts/2002/t01152002_t0115sdr.html>.

8. Evil versus Error

In the history of both terrorism and counterterrorism there has long been a temptation to depict the adversary as evil. In terrorist movements, many otherwise decent and serious individuals have been seduced by the simple and attractive notion of the power of the deed: that a cleansing act of violence can rid the world of uniquely evil forces. This belief of many terrorists that their goals will be achieved by spectacular acts of violence is the central error of their philosophy.

In counterterrorist operations, the depiction of the adversary as evil, while it may faithfully reflect understandable feelings in a society under terrorist assault, poses severe practical problems. One hazard of treating terrorism as a problem of evil is that many people in the population from whom the terrorists come will know that such an explanation is too simple. They will have a broader idea of the mixture of characteristic traits that can make a terrorist: idealism, self-sacrifice, naiveté, hope, despair, ignorance, short-sightedness, thuggishness, hatred, sadism, cleverness and stupidity. The population may have sympathy with the cause for which the terrorists stand but not with the method. If the terrorist group is described as simply 'evil', the population will therefore be further alienated from the anti-terrorist cause, which they will see as depending on a caricature that they do not recognise.

In the struggle against terrorism, it may be most useful to conceive of terrorism as a problem not so much of extreme evil (although it may involve that), but rather of dangerously wrong conduct and ideas. The difference in approach – the view of terrorism more as a dangerous idea and as morally reprehensible than as absolute evil – has significant implications for how terrorist campaigns may be opposed, and how they may end.[31]

9. Similarities between Terrorists and Some of their Opponents

A student of the history of terrorism cannot help being struck by certain similarities between terrorists and at least some of their opponents. Both share not only a vision of the world as a struggle of good versus evil, but also a belief that particular new weapons and tactics now give an opportunity to strike directly at the heart of the adversary's power. Russian terrorists in the nineteenth century believed that their new and

[31] The problematic character of defining the 'war on terror' as one of good versus evil is recognized in Talbott and Chanda, *The Age of Terror*, n 11 above at xiv.

quite accurate weapons – the pistol, the rifle and the bomb – could enable them to attack the source of all evil (namely the Tsar) directly and with limited side-effects.[32]

The similarity between so-called terrorists and their adversaries was noted by Régis Debray in his little-known novel *Undesirable Alien*. In this remarkably unsentimental view of his fellow revolutionaries in Latin America, he mocks his comrades in the struggle for having a taste for cowboy films, and suggests that red revolutionaries may be propounding nothing more than the ideology of the American western.[33] Sadly, events have moved on since then, and it is the Hollywood disaster movie that is emulated by Osama bin Laden and his colleagues.[34] The general philosophy of radical Islam also has Californian roots due to the presence there in the 1950s of its founding father, Sayyid Qutb.[35]

In the 'war on terror', a vision of clean and well-targeted war against dictatorial regimes has informed much US policy-making. As George Bush put it in his infamous (because premature) 'Mission Accomplished' speech on 1 May 2003:

> In the images of falling statues, we have witnessed the arrival of a new era. For a hundred of years of war, culminating in the nuclear age, military technology was designed and deployed to inflict casualties on an ever-growing scale. In defeating Nazi Germany and Imperial Japan, Allied forces destroyed entire cities, while enemy leaders who started the conflict were safe until the final days. Military power was used to end a regime by breaking a nation.
>
> Today, we have the greater power to free a nation by breaking a dangerous and aggressive regime. With new tactics and precision weapons, we can achieve military objectives without directing violence against civilians. No device of man can remove the tragedy from war; yet it is a great moral advance when the guilty have far more to fear from war than the innocent.[36]

[32] Laqueur, *Age of Terrorism*, n 16 above at 36–8.

[33] R Debray, *Undesirable Alien*, trs Rosemary Sheed (London, Allen Lane, 1978) 121, 123 and 172; first published as *L'Indésirable* (Paris, Editions du Seuil, 1975).

[34] This may be literally true, although reports of information by detainees given during interrogation need to be treated with extreme caution. According to numerous reports, Abu Zubaydah (a Palestinian captured in Pakistan in 2002 who was allegedly Osama bin Laden's chief of operations) told his interrogators in Guantanamo that terrorists might be taking clues from the film *Godzilla*, which had been remade in 1998 and showed a monster attack on Brooklyn Bridge and the Statue of Liberty: T Maier, 'Has FBI Cried Wolf Too Often?' *Insight on the News*, 5 August 2002, available at <http://www.insightmag.com/news/2002/08/26>.

[35] On possible connections between southern California and religious radicalism see the brief references in M Ruthven, *Fundamentalism: The Search for Meaning* (Oxford, Oxford University Press, 2004) 10 and 38. Sayyid Qutb (1906–66), when he was in California in the 1950s, was deeply influenced by the Western culture that he opposed as degenerate and corrupt.

[36] President George W Bush, Remarks from the *USS Abraham Lincoln* at sea off the coast of San Diego, California, 1 May 2003.

Countering Terrorism: A Historical Perspective 25

This vision of the 2003 Iraq War as a more or less clinical excision of an evil regime looks to have been a desert mirage – just as many terrorist visions of achieving change through violence have also led to disappointment.

10. How Past Terrorist Campaigns Ended

A decisive result is seldom encountered in counterterrorist struggles. There is a need for much broader understanding, based on historical evidence, of how terrorist campaigns do in fact end.[37] The processes – some of them deeply flawed – by which terrorist campaigns end usually include debilitating losses to the terrorist movement caused by military action, arrests and trials. However, they can also involve any or all of the following five elements:

First, *awareness on the part of terrorist movements that they are being defeated politically, or at least are not making gains*. The actions of terrorists usually fail to arouse the masses: indeed, they frequently cause antagonism in the very population whose support is sought. Such failures can often lead to defections and splits, and to a political decision by all or part of a terrorist movement or its political allies to move to a different phase of struggle or of political action. For example, on 1 October 1951 the Malayan Communist Party formally decided to end the armed struggle – an important moment in the long process of the winding-down of the terrorist campaign that had started in 1948. A more indecisive indication of the end of a campaign occurred in Spain in 2004–7. In November 2004 it was reported that six senior members of the Basque separatist group ETA had called on the organisation from their prison cells to lay down its arms. In their letter they stated: 'Our political-military strategy has been overcome by repression … It is not a question of fixing the rear-view mirror or a burst tyre. It is the motor that does not work.' This letter was 'the closest ETA members had come to recognising that, after more than 30 years in which it has killed more than 800 people, the group is facing defeat'.[38] On 24 March 2006 ETA announced a 'permanent ceasefire' to end its campaign of violence, but on 6 June 2007 it declared this ceasefire over: this is a typical example of the twists and turns that are often involved in the ending, or otherwise, of terrorist campaigns.

[37] A useful distillation of conclusions on how terrorist campaigns end may be found in A Guelke, *The Age of Terrorism and the International Political System* (London, IB Tauris, 1995) 180–81. See also A Kurth Cronin, *How Terrorism Ends: Lessons from the Decline and Demise of Terrorist Campaigns* (Princeton, NJ, Princeton University Press, forthcoming, late 2008).

[38] G Tremlett, 'Old Guard Urges End to Eta Terror', *The Guardian* (London), 3 November 2004, 15.

Second, *recognition by governments which organised or assisted terrorism that they must renounce this method of pursuing a cause.* Such recognition may sometimes (as in the case of Libya in 2003) be coupled with compensation to the families of victims of terrorist acts.

Third, *the amelioration of conditions in order to weaken the strength and legitimacy of the terrorist movement's support.* Such amelioration is something in which Messianic terrorists have no interest. It may include a change in the political context, which sidesteps some of the issues that provided grist to the mill of the terrorist movement, provides new opportunities for pursuing its aims in a different manner, or emphasises a new range of attainable goals of general appeal, for example in the field of human rights.

Fourth, *the holding of genuine multi-party elections.* Democratic procedures, especially where there are safeguards for minorities, can undercut terrorist claims to speak for a specific nation or section of society.

Fifth, *a shared awareness of stalemate, giving both sides a possible incentive to reach a negotiated or tacit settlement involving mutual concessions.* This may encompass a recognition by its adversaries that the terrorist movement, however criminal its actions, did represent a serious cause and constituency – leading to a reluctant acceptance that certain concessions should be made to some positions held by terrorists.

Sometimes terrorist campaigns wind down rather than end. They may degenerate into mafia-like activities, including kidnappings for ransom, drug trafficking and bank robberies. Or a few terrorist leaders, hidden in a jungle or a city, maintain their faith, even continue to plot or to detonate the occasional bomb, but lose completely their following and their impact.[39]

In some cases the combatants, or at least a proportion of them, may be retrained. This happened in Guatemala following the civil war of the 1980s and 1990s. The former Marxist guerrillas, who had been called terrorists by their enemies, received extensive retraining at a centre in Quetzaltenango. When I visited it in 1997, the work of the centre, supported mainly by European funds, appeared to be effective, the main concern being whether there would be jobs for the suitably retrained guerrillas.

A general conclusion follows: that terrorist campaigns, while they may go on for a long time, do eventually end; and do so not because every last terrorist is captured or killed, or because they are comprehensively

[39] In 1987, nearly 40 years after the declaration of a state of emergency in Malaya, and over 35 years after the Malayan Communist Party had publicly announced its decision to end the armed struggle, some 600 guerrillas laid down their arms and started a new life as farmers in southern Thailand. M Fathers, 'Communist "Bandits" Lay Down Arms in Malaysia' *The Independent* (London), 8 June 1987.

defeated in military operations, or because there is a clear victory, but rather because terrorism is seen for what it is: a highly problematic means of bringing about change. It cannot be the sole basis for a movement, it often damages the very people in whose name it is waged, and it may burn itself out or backfire on its own authors.

III. THE 'WAR ON TERROR'

The major pronouncements of what has been variously termed in official US speeches the 'war against terrorism' and the 'war on terror' have been self-consciously historic in character; they have enunciated historically novel and ambitious goals; but have contained only limited reference to the history of terrorism and counterterrorism. In his address to Congress nine days after the destruction of the Twin Towers in New York, President George W Bush stated:

> Our war on terror begins with al Qaeda, but it does not end there. It will not end until every terrorist group of global reach has been found, stopped and defeated ...
>
> Americans are asking: 'How will we fight and win this war?' We will direct every resource at our command – every means of diplomacy, every tool of intelligence, every instrument of law enforcement, every financial influence, and every necessary weapon of war – to the disruption and to the defeat of the global terror network.[40]

At the end of September 2001 President Bush added, in a radio address:

> Our war on terror will be much broader than the battlefields and beachheads of the past. This war will be fought wherever terrorists hide, or run, or plan. Some victories will be won outside of public view, in tragedies avoided and threats eliminated. Other victories will be clear to all.[41]

The term 'war' is not being used here in a purely rhetorical sense, as in the 'war on drugs' or 'war on poverty'. It has such a rhetorical side, but is being used to describe a notably broad and multi-faceted overall campaign of a type that is essentially new, and that includes major military operations (starting with Afghanistan) as one important aspect. In respect of both aspects of the war – the visible and the invisible – what is sought is 'victory'.

[40] President George W Bush, Speech to Congress, 20 September 2001.
[41] President George W Bush, 'Radio Address to the Nation', 29 September 2001, available at <http://www.whitehouse.gov/news/releases/2001/09/>.

The most important subsequent articulation of the 'war on terror' was the February 2003 White House document, *National Strategy for Combating Terrorism*. This began by emphasising the unique nature of the current threat:

> The struggle against international terrorism is different from any other war in our history. We will not triumph solely or even primarily through military might. We must fight terrorist networks, and all those who support their efforts to spread fear around the world, using every instrument of national power – diplomatic, economic, law enforcement, financial, information, intelligence, and military.[42]

The oft-repeated claim of uniqueness has provided a justification for much of the rhetoric and strategic direction of the 'war on terror', and has provided, too, an implied justification for making little more than ritual reference to earlier history. However, the February 2003 document did contain at least a nod to history: 'Americans know that terrorism did not begin on September 11, 2001.' It continued: 'For decades, the United States and our friends abroad have waged the long struggle against the terrorist menace. We have learned much from these efforts.' In particular, past successes in destroying or neutralising various movements that had been active in the 1970s and 1980s 'provide valuable lessons for the future'.[43], the document was unclear about exactly what terrorist movements were being referred to, and about what lessons had been learned.

Subsequent articulations of US doctrine offered little further reference to the history of terrorism and counterterrorism.[44] The most extraordinary omission in most US statements in the 'war on terror', at least up to 2006, is the lack of reference to the existing US counter-insurgency doctrine, and the reluctance to embrace it even when faced with an insurgency in Iraq. By contrast, the UK military view tends to be that counter-insurgency doctrine is a principal basis of addressing terrorism.

Has the international campaign against terrorism achieved the historically unique breadth of international support that Bush has sought? It was framed from the start as a campaign on a broad front, involving a large number of countries – but at the same time it was always as a US-led operation. Bush's words in his 20 September 2001 speech reflected this duality:

[42] The White House, *National Strategy for Combating Terrorism* (Washington, DC, February 2003) at 1.

[43] *Ibid* at 5.

[44] See eg the subsequent version of The White House, *National Strategy for Combating Terrorism* (Washington, DC, September 2006).

> Every nation, in every region, now has a decision to make. Either you are with us, or you are with the terrorists. From this day forward, any nation that continues to harbor or support terrorism will be regarded by the United States as a hostile regime.[45]

In 2001–02 the variety and extent of international support for the campaign against terrorism was remarkable. As the US State Department pointed out in March 2002, 136 countries offered some form of military assistance, 46 multilateral organisations issued declarations of support, and three treaty bodies (NATO, the OAS and ANZUS) invoked their collective defence treaty obligations with the United States.[46]

Despite the extensive evidence of international support, including in such delicate matters as sharing intelligence and cooperation between police forces, the idea that the 'war on terror' was a universal project, in which all states could join the United States, ran into trouble. First was the awkward and unavoidable fact that different countries see the world differently. Many had doubts about a war on terror that relied so extensively on military force and did not, at least in its early stages, address underlying grievances with the same level of determination. Second, there was a major difficulty in the particular way in which the US leadership in this struggle was presented. Many were antagonised by the blunt and US-centred approach of: 'Either you are with us, or you are with the terrorists.' Third, several NATO members were offended by aspects of US policy: in 2001, the apparent lack of US response to NATO's unprecedented invocation of Article V, bringing collective self-defence into play; from 2001 onwards, growing concern about the US handling of questions regarding the status and treatment of detainees; and from 2003 onwards, increasing dissatisfaction with US policy on Iraq.

A. Can Military Interventions be Effective against Terrorism?

In countries faced with terrorist attacks, there are often strong reasons for attacking terrorism at what is seen as its source. A state that allows terrorists to organise on its territory to wage operations elsewhere is naturally the object of suspicion, and may well be thought to deserve whatever it gets. Yet in the 'war on terror' the question of military intervention has proved extremely divisive.

[45] President George W Bush, Address to a Joint Session of Congress and the American People, Washington, DC, 20 September 2001. The peroration added that 'God is not neutral'.

[46] US State Department, 'Boucher Summarizes International Support for War on Terrorism', 1 March 2002; cited in M Sheehan, 'Diplomacy', in A Kurth Cronin and J Ludes (eds), *Attacking Terrorism: Elements of a Grand Strategy* (Washington, DC, Georgetown University Press, 2004) 107.

Counterterrorist operations, when taking the form of open war and a conventional military response, have often led to tragedy. The First World War began when the assassination of Archduke Ferdinand in Sarajevo in June 1914 by a young Serbian nationalist led to an Austrian determination to root out the 'hornet's nest' that was Serbia. Similarly, Israel's disastrous intervention in Lebanon in 1982 was explicitly a response to a persistent and intense pattern of terrorist attacks on Israeli and Jewish targets not only in Israel but also internationally.

It is not surprising, therefore, that historians have generally been sceptical about waging war as a response to terrorist acts. However, they tend to be admirably discriminate: more sceptical than dogmatic. Two or three months after 11 September 2001, the American historian Paul Schroeder wrote:

> Three lessons emerge from reasoning by historical analogy from the early summer of 1914 to the late summer of 2001. The first is that a great power must avoid giving terrorists the war they want, but that the great power does not want. The second is that a great power must reckon the effects of its actions not only on its immediate circumstances, but also with regard to the larger structure of international politics in which it clearly has a significant stake. The third is that a great power must beware the risks of victory as well as the dangers of defeat. If it is not careful and wise, the United States could find itself enmeshed even deeper in the Middle East and Southwest Asia than it is today, and risk generating greater prospective dangers in the process of containing smaller near-term ones.[47]

He drew a crucial distinction between Afghanistan, where the war had a legitimate objective and was widely understood internationally, and other possible target countries, including Iraq.[48] Within 18 months of this warning, the United States was deeply involved in Iraq in exactly the way he had feared, with no prospect of an early exit. He was right that the two cases, and the nature of the US involvements in them, were very different, both in the justifiability of the intervention and in the consequences that followed.

1. *Afghanistan: War and its Aftermath*

The first major engagement of the 'war on terror', *Operation Enduring Freedom*, which encompassed the US-led coalition military operations in and around Afghanistan that began on 7 October 2001, was widely

[47] P Schroeder, 'The Risks of Victory: An Historian's Provocation' (Winter 2001–2) 66 *The National Interest* (Washington, DC) at 22.

[48] *Ibid* at 28–9. See also his article warning against the likely effects of an attack in the Middle East, 'Iraq: The Case Against Preemptive War' (October 2002) 8(20) *The American Conservative*, available at <http://www.amconmag.com/10_21/iraq.html>.

viewed as a justifiable use of force – a term greatly preferable to the more familiar term 'just war'. It had a great deal of diplomatic support, and received significant legitimation from resolutions passed at the United Nations.[49] There appeared to be no other means of stopping the activities of Al Qaeda, protected as they were by the Taliban regime. The war did result in a victory – at least of sorts. By the end of the year, the Taliban regime had gone, replaced by the Afghan Interim Authority, and then in June 2002 by the Afghan Transitional Government. Between January 2002 and mid-2007, according to the UN High Commissioner for Refugees (UNHCR), more than 4.8 million refugees have returned to Afghanistan (mainly from Pakistan and Iran), and in addition another half million internally displaced have returned to their homes. This is an astonishing achievement. Afghanistan has been UNHCR's largest repatriation operation worldwide for five consecutive years.[50] Although the return of refugees was not the main objective of the campaign – and the capture of the main Al Qaeda leaders, which was an objective, was *not* achieved – this huge refugee return was evidence that the 'war on terror' could achieve at least some positive effects, by helping to depose a reactionary, oppressive and thoroughly dangerous regime. The remarkably successful presidential election on 9 October 2004 provided a further small sign of progress in post-war Afghanistan.

On the first day of the US bombing campaign in Afghanistan, Donald Rumsfeld said of the Taliban: 'Ultimately they're going to collapse from within. That is what will constitute victory.'[51] That is what happened in November and December 2001. Some were critical of the fact that the main achievement was regime change. Richard Clarke, the White House counterterrorism specialist, criticised the otherwise successful handling of the Afghan war on the grounds that 'we treated the war as a regime change rather than as a search-and-destroy against terrorists'.[52]

[49] While no UN Security Council resolution specifically authorised the US-led military operations in Afghanistan, several resolutions passed both before and after 11 September 2001 provided a significant degree of support for such action. Resolution 1189 of 13 August 1998 had emphasised the responsibility of Afghanistan to stop terrorist activities on its territory. Resolution 1368 of 12 September 2001 recognised 'the inherent right of individual or collective self-defence in accordance with the Charter', condemned the attacks of the previous day, and stated that the Council 'regards such acts, like any act of international terrorism, as a threat to international peace and security'. It also expressed the Council's 'readiness to take all necessary steps to respond to the terrorist attacks of 11 September 2001, and to combat all forms of terrorism'. These key points were reiterated in Resolution 1373 of 28 September 2001, which additionally placed numerous requirements on all states to bring the problem of terrorism under control.

[50] See <ww.unhcr.org/afghan.html>, visited 8 August 2007.

[51] Rumsfeld, cited in news report by B Knowlton, *International Herald Tribune* (London), 8 October 2001, 1.

[52] R Clarke, *Against All Enemies: Inside America's War on Terror* (London, Simon & Schuster UK, 2004) 274.

Three unique facts enabled the Afghan campaign to succeed: (1) the Taliban regime was weak both within Afghanistan and internationally; (2) the fanatical character of the bombing of the World Trade Centre, and the persuasive evidence of links to Afghanistan, contributed to the Taliban's loss of allies, especially Pakistan, and also meant that the world accepted the legitimate element of self-defence in the US-led campaign; and (3) the role on the ground of the US-supported forces of the Northern Alliance enabled the US-led bombing campaign to be effective rather than merely punitive, and then provided a basis for post-war administration.

In respect of Afghanistan some historians doubted whether any positive result could be achieved in the US-led campaign in late 2001. They could and in some cases did point out, very reasonably, that Afghanistan is not a country in which foreign armed forces have ever had a happy time; that there is good reason to be cautious about the prospects of changing Afghanistan's violent political culture; and that there are problems in waging a bombing campaign against so devious and elusive a target as a terrorist movement.

Sir Michael Howard, former Regius Professor of History at Oxford, criticised the Afghan war during its opening phase, when its main aspect was bombing rather than support for ground forces. In a lecture in London on 30 October 2001 (and subsequently published in *Foreign Affairs*) he said that it would be 'like trying to eradicate cancer cells with a blow-torch'.[53] Three months later, in a thoughtful reappraisal, he said: 'I got it wrong, and I apologize.'[54] Yet in a broader sense he did not get it entirely wrong. Historians have good reasons to be sceptical about the efficacy of military interventions as a response to terrorist campaigns. Howard's vivid image of hazardous use of the blow-torch may fit other cases, including Iraq since 2003, better than it fitted Afghanistan. Moreover, by 2007 Afghanistan itself was the scene of a growing insurgency movement in the South that threatened to undo some of the achievements of the period since the 2001 intervention.

2. *Iraq: War and its Aftermath*

The Iraq war of 2003 provides a very different context for exploring the question of whether invasion of states believed to assist terrorism is an effective way to achieve the aims of a counterterrorist policy. The rhetoric

[53] M Howard, Lecture in London on 30 October 2001, reported in T Branigan, 'Al-Qaida is Winning War, Allies Warned', *The Guardian* (London), 31 October 2001. The lecture was the basis of M Howard, 'What's in a Name?', n 16 above.

[54] His reappraisal was in 'September 11 and After: Reflections on the War Against Terrorism', Lecture at University College London, 29 January 2002.

of the 'war on terror', with its emphasis on open war, may be part of the explanation of the US-led assault on Iraq in 2003. In his television address of 17 March 2003 presenting Saddam Hussein with an ultimatum to get out of Iraq within 48 hours, President Bush included the statement that Iraq had 'aided, trained and harbored terrorists, including operatives of al-Qaeda'.[55] Yet in reality Iraq's links to Al Qaeda up to March 2003 appear to have been very limited. There were some Iraqi connections with terrorists, especially those involved in the Arab–Israel conflict, but Iraq does not appear to have had any significant part in the ruthless campaign of international terrorist attacks for which Al Qaeda had been seen as responsible. Within the US government, there was already in early 2003 some official awareness that the accusation of the link between Iraq and al-Qaeda was weak. When on 20 March 2003 the US government gave to the UN Security Council a letter containing its justification for attacking Iraq, the letter dealt exclusively with Iraq's non-compliance with a range of UN Security Council resolutions on weapons issues. Terrorism was not even mentioned.[56]

Against this background, it is peculiar that the US government called the war in Iraq part of the 'war on terror', and issued medals for both the Afghanistan and Iraq campaigns which are called 'the Global War on Terrorism Expeditionary Medal' (for those who served in Afghanistan or Iraq) and 'the Global War on Terrorism Service Medal' (for those whose service was elsewhere). Naturally, critics objected that the administration was 'subtly using the single campaign medal to buttress its contention that the war in Iraq was undertaken as part of the worldwide battle against al Qaeda and other Islamic extremists'.[57]

Overall, the Iraq war has done more harm than good to the US and UK efforts to combat terrorism. The principal criticisms of the use of force in Iraq are that certain of the stated grounds for going to war (especially violations of the UN resolutions on disarmament) have proved to be weak; that the planning for the aftermath of war was so feeble; that the results of the war have proved so violent; and that a perception has arisen that Western countries seek to force Muslim populations into a single, externally imposed political template: a perception that damages efforts at coalition building.[58] Historians were right to warn, as Professor

[55] President George W Bush, Speech from the White House, 17 March 2003.

[56] The stated reason for going to war in March 2003 was 'Iraq's continued material breaches of its disarmament obligations under relevant Security Council resolutions': Letter dated 20 March 2003 from the Permanent Representative of the USA, John Negroponte, to the President of the UN Security Council.

[57] V Loeb, 'Medals Couple Two Conflicts: Critics Seek Separate Awards for Afghanistan, Iraq Fighting' *Washington Post*, 6 January 2004.

[58] J Stevenson, *Counter-Terrorism: Containment and Beyond,* IISS Adelphi Paper 367 (Oxford, Oxford University Press, October 2004) 108–13.

Michael Howard did in interviews in March 2003, that Iraq might be easy to defeat in a military campaign, but would be difficult to occupy and administer. At least in terms of the struggle against terrorism, the results so far of the Iraq war appear to be distressingly negative. There is much force in the criticism of Robert Tucker and David Hendrickson:

> The pattern of the first Iraq war, in which an overwhelming victory set aside the reservations of most skeptics, has failed to emerge in the aftermath of the second. If anything, skepticism has deepened.[59]

The presence and role of foreign (mainly US) armed forces in Iraq is regularly cited as justification for terrorist bombings, kidnappings and executions there, and also in other countries. Critics seized on this point. As Richard Clarke argued, Bush 'launched an unnecessary and costly war in Iraq that strengthened the fundamentalist, radical Islamic terrorist movement worldwide'.[60]

There are, to be sure, grounds for questioning the generally negative picture of the results of the Iraq war. Within Iraq, the removal from office of Saddam Hussein was widely welcomed, and some still retain the hope that a stable democratic order can emerge slowly from the twisted wreckage of his brutal regime. The elections in January 2005, with participation of close to 60 per cent of those entitled to vote, strengthened hopes that something could be salvaged from the country's disasters. Outside Iraq, the war may have helped to induce an element of prudence in the conduct of policy of some governments.

One possible case is Libya. In December 2003 Colonel Gaddafi made his decision to bring Libya in from the cold, confirming his renunciation both of terrorism and of ambitions to develop nuclear weapons. Whether his decision owed anything to the Iraq war is debated. Although the process which bore fruit in December had begun long before the initiation of hostilities in Iraq in March 2003, it is possible that seeing a fellow Arab leader unceremoniously deposed may have helped to concentrate Gaddafi's mind. At the very least the Iraq war did not foreclose a highly significant policy development in Libya. That is a small and somewhat speculative consolation for a war whose effects have been so overwhelmingly negative.

3. *UK and US Doctrine on Military Intervention*

The sobering consequences of the 2003 intervention in Iraq suggest a need to revisit the argument that attack is the best form of defence – an

[59] R Tucker and D Hendrickson, 'The Sources of American Legitimacy' (November/ December 2004) 83(6) *Foreign Affairs* 18.

[60] Clarke, *Against All Enemies*, n 52 above at x.

argument that had been expressed in two key documents of the 'war on terror', both issued in 2002. The UK *Strategic Defence Review: A New Chapter* said: 'Experience shows that it is better where possible, to engage an enemy at longer range, before they get the opportunity to mount an assault on the UK.'[61] There has never been any indication that this statement was based on consideration of any actual cases. As for the US government, *The National Security Strategy of the United States* commits it to attack terrorist organisations by 'convincing or compelling states to accept their sovereign responsibilities'.[62] The implication here is that states will not get rid of terrorists on their soil, the United States will do it for them. The argument is buttressed by the more fundamental ideas that lack of democracy is a principal cause of terrorism, and that a forcible intervention could lead to the growth of a stable democratic system.

In addition to the questions about the circumstances in which democracy can be imposed from outside, there are three serious grounds of criticism of the proposition that terrorism should be attacked at source rather than warded off defensively.

First, *it is a false choice*. However desirable it may be to engage the enemy at longer range, there is no substitute for defensive anti-terrorist and counterterrorist activities. Granted the imperfections of intelligence, the multiplicity of possible sources of attack, and the hazards of taking military action against sovereign states, it may not always be possible, or sensible, to attack terrorism at its source. Meanwhile, much can be done at home to reduce the risk of terrorist attack. The astonishing casualness of US airport security before 11 September 2001 illustrates the point.

Second, *the history of counterterrorist operations suggests no such simple conclusion*. True, some counterterrorist operations have involved military action in states perceived to be the sources of, or providers of support to, terrorist movements. However, by no means all have been successful. Furthermore, many counterterrorist campaigns have been effectively conducted with only limited capacity to engage the enemy at longer range. For example, the UK and Malayan governments had to engage in the long struggle against terrorism without attacking the People's Republic of China (PRC), despite the fact that the PRC was aiding and abetting the Communist Terrorist movement in Malaya from 1949 onwards. Similarly, the UK government had to deal with terrorism in Northern Ireland without resorting to military action in the Republic of Ireland,

[61] UK Ministry of Defence, *The Strategic Defence Review: A New Chapter*, Cm 5566, vols I and II (London, HMSO, July 2002) vol I at 9.

[62] The White House, *The National Security Strategy of the United States of America* (Washington, DC, September 2002) at 6.

despite claims that the Provisional IRA was deriving benefit from resources and support there – not to mention from communities in the United States.

Third, *it is a recipe for a revival of imperialism*. Military intervention in states in order to eliminate the sources of terrorism must inevitably mean, in many cases, exercising external domination for a period of decades. This was the pattern of much European colonialism in the nineteenth century, including in Egypt. By a perverse paradox, external control, intended to stop terrorism in its tracks, frequently has the effect of provoking it and providing a ready-made justification for it.

Paul Schroeder has argued persuasively that the United States can legitimately and sensibly aim to exercise hegemony, but it is ill advised to lunge, on the basis of blinkered historical ignorance, into the mirage of empire. His conclusion is that America's leaders, because they are ignorant of the past, are actually stumbling backwards into it:

What they are now attempting therefore is not a bold, untried American experiment in creating a brave new world, but a revival of a type of nineteenth and early-twentieth century imperialism that could succeed for a time then (with ultimately devastating consequences) only because of conditions long since vanished and now impossible to imagine reproducing. Launched now, this venture will fail and is already failing. Its advocates illustrate the dictum that those unwilling to learn from history are doomed to repeat it.[63]

Any assessment of the US and UK doctrines of intervention in response to terrorism has to differentiate between cases. On both legal and prudential grounds, there was a stronger case for intervention in Afghanistan than in Iraq. In particular, there was a real chance of reducing by such means Afghanistan's involvement in terrorism. Any assessment must also be provisional, as eventual outcomes will necessarily affect judgements of the interventions. However, what is clear is that there was a curious and historically uninformed optimism about the Iraq venture, which led to a lack of planning for those traditional consequences of distant empires – military occupation and counter-insurgency.

[63] P Schroeder, 'The Mirage of Empire Versus the Promise of Hegemony', in P Schroeder, *Systems, Stability and Statecraft: Essays on the International History of Modern Europe*, D Wetzel, R Jervis and J Levy (eds) (New York and Basingstoke, Palgrave Macmillan, 2004) 305.

B. How is the 'War on Terror' supposed to End?

1. The Bush Administration's Vision

The advocates of the 'war on terror' offer a limited vision of how the war might end. The focus is more on victory than other visions of possible endings, but it is victory of a special kind. Some elements of it were outlined in the White House *National Security Strategy* document of September 2002[64]; and they were further elaborated in the White House doctrinal statement of February 2003:

> Victory against terrorism will not occur as a single, defining moment. It will not be marked by the likes of the surrender ceremony on the deck of the USS Missouri that ended World War II. However, through the sustained effort to compress the scope and capability of terrorist organizations, isolate them regionally, and destroy them within state borders, the United States and its friends and allies will secure a world in which our children can live free from fear and where the threat of terrorist attacks does not define our daily lives.
>
> Victory, therefore, will be secured only as long as the United States and the international community maintain their vigilance and work tirelessly to prevent terrorists from inflicting horrors like those of September 11, 2001.[65]

In his State of the Union address on 3 February 2005, President Bush, while referring to the importance of 'eliminating the conditions that feed radicalism and ideologies of murder', reiterated the key central conception of offensive action as the main way to defeat terrorism: 'Our country is still the target of terrorists who want to kill many, and intimidate us all – and we will stay on the offensive against them, until the fight is won.'

Such glimpses of how victory might come about are essentially schematic and prescriptive rather than historical. They have an abstract and euphemistic quality. Because they leave little room for complexity, they have enabled some individuals to focus on the idea of destruction more than other possible mechanisms. When Timothy Garton Ash asked a very high US administration official how the 'war on terror' would end, he received the answer: 'With the elimination of the terrorists.'[66]

Such simple prescriptive views of how a terrorist campaign should end are also to be found in a book by two supporters of the Bush administration, David Frum and Richard Perle. Published in 2003, *An End to Evil: How to Win the War on Terror* is modestly described by its authors as 'a

[64] The White House, *National Security Strategy of the United States*, 2002 version, at 5–7.

[65] The White House, *National Strategy for Combating Terrorism*, 2003 version, at 12. This was the text under the heading 'Victory in the War against Terror'.

[66] This *answer* was given by a senior administration official in Washington, DC, on 10 December 2002, as reported in T Garton Ash, *Free World: Why a Crisis of the West Reveals the Opportunity of our Time* (London and New York, Allen Lane, 2004) 126.

manual for victory'.[67] This paean of praise for Bush's anti-terrorist policy is also a diatribe against all those allies and bureaucrats who fail to support it properly: 'While our enemies plot, our allies dither and carp, and much of our government remains ominously unready for the fight.'[68] What does it say about how terrorist campaigns end? Virtually nothing. In true American fashion, this is a 'How to' book which is full of hectoring instruction but which gives no clue about how terrorist campaigns actually end.

2. *UK Policy to Eliminate Terrorism as a Force in International Affairs*

On the ending of terrorist campaigns, UK policy is subtly different from that of the United States. It is also flawed, but in a different way. The key UK statement of doctrine about terrorism, published in July 2002, *The Strategic Defence Review: A New Chapter*, says that the goal of the government's efforts is 'to eliminate terrorism as a force in international affairs'.[69] This is a carefully thought-out phrase, and of course it is properly recognised that 'countering terrorism is usually a long-term business requiring the roots and causes to be addressed as well as the symptoms'.[70] Nonetheless, there are two main disadvantages to proclaiming as a goal 'the elimination of terrorism as a force in international affairs'.

First, *terrorism is notoriously difficult to 'eliminate'*. The proclamation of this goal is not only unrealistic, but it also undermines one of the strongest arguments against terrorism – namely that, once started, it easily becomes endemic. The unofficial, decentralised, and hydra-headed character of terrorism provides the main explanation for the difficulty of eliminating it.

Second, *if 'elimination' is the proclaimed goal, then every subsequent terrorist incident represents a victory for the terrorists*. The United Kingdom faced this problem in Northern Ireland. A number of government pronouncements in the 1970s and early 1980s had indicated the United Kingdom's aim was the complete ending of terrorist activity. Thereafter, every terrorist assault, including the IRA's mainland campaign, had a possible added bonus of 'proving' that the government had failed to achieve its proclaimed goal. Eventually the United Kingdom's aims were restated in more modest terms as being the reduction of terrorist activities: this was

67 D Frum and R Perle, *An End to Evil: How to Win the War on Terror* (New York, Random House, [2003]) 9.

68 *Ibid* at 4.

69 UK Ministry of Defence, *New Chapter*, n 61 above, vol I, at 4 and 7.

70 *Ibid* at 10.

accepted by the public with remarkably little complaint, and may have helped in the slow winding-down of the conflict in Northern Ireland.

C. Six Lines of Criticism of the 'War on Terror'

Any conclusions about how a historical perspective may affect views of the 'war on terror' must begin by acknowledging that this extraordinary 'war' is unique in having achieved something, however incomplete, in military operations in Afghanistan; in having put the full weight and ingenuity of the United States into the struggle; and in having involved a remarkable degree of international collaboration, some of which has survived the fall-out over Iraq. This struggle is not a single campaign, but is highly variegated. The responses to certain events, such as the Bali, Madrid and London bombings, have been much less military in character than the responses to other outrages. There has been slowly growing recognition that the war on terror involves not just a battle of arms, but a 'battle of ideas'.[71] The overall verdict is not entirely negative.

Yet, against a background of the long historical record of the subject, six main lines of criticism of the US-led international campaign arise.

First, the title and language of the so-called 'war on terror' is misleading. It conjures up the image and expectation of open war being a major and recurrent part of the action against international terrorist movements; and it suggests the unrealisable aim of the complete elimination of terrorist movements. There is a need for words to describe the overall policy with regard to terrorism that convey toughness but do not rely so heavily on the imagery of war. The core idea has to be a vigorous and sustained countering of terrorist threats, involving action at many levels, and aimed at achieving a significant reduction and marginalisation of terrorist activities. A better term, more accurate if less dramatic, would be 'international campaign against terrorism'. It may not be too late to use this term in at least partial substitution for 'war on terror'.

Second, the 'war on terror' risks becoming an exercise in latter-day imperialism. There is a need for intervention in certain societies, but it needs to be handled with extraordinary skill and care. The risk of stumbling into a colonial role is especially great because in US political culture there is a caricatured vision of European colonialism of the nineteenth and twentieth centuries. In consequence it is believed, erroneously, that nothing the United States does today could remotely resemble such deplorable European practices. Yet to many the similarities are all

[71] The phrase 'battle of ideas' is used six times in the September 2006 version of the White House document *National Strategy for Combating Terrorism*. In the 2003 version it had not appeared at all.

too real. The irony of the situation is that foreign rule, especially foreign military occupation, is notoriously a producer of terrorist movements.

Third, some official statements made in the course of the 'war on terror' have inadvertently credited terrorist movements with a greater capacity to achieve intended results than can be justified on the basis of the record. For example, in several passages the UK *Strategic Defence Review* states or implies that international terrorist attacks have 'the potential for strategic effect'.[72] This phrase is used for a good reason – to avoid implying that it is essential to tackle absolutely all terrorist movements everywhere simultaneously and with equal vigour – but it is flawed. It ignores the important distinction between *intended* and *actual* strategic effect. Although terrorist actions frequently have major effects, they are seldom those that the terrorists intended. It does not make sense to give terrorists more credit than they deserve for the size and capacity of their organisations, for the accuracy of their political calculations or for the effectiveness of their actions.

Fourth, the history of counterterrorist operations in the twentieth century suggests that in the long struggle against terrorism, four assets are important:

(1) public confidence in official decision-making;
(2) public confidence in the intelligence on which that decision-making is based;
(3) an understanding that operations are conducted with respect for a framework of law;
(4) a willingness to address some of the problems that have contributed to the emergence of terrorism.

Tragically, all of these assets risk being undermined by many events connected with the 'war on terror', especially the 2003 intervention in Iraq and the subsequent insurgency.

Fifth, the torture and ill-treatment of detainees, of which there has been much evidence in the war on terror, is, to quote Talleyrand, worse than a crime: it is a mistake. Guantanamo and Abu Ghraib have provided propaganda gifts to adversaries.

Sixth, the international campaign against terrorism stands in need of a more realistic vision of how terrorist campaigns end than the simple picture of the elimination or incarceration of terrorists.

On the basis of the historical record, some positive recommendations can be advanced about the most appropriate basic aims and character of the international campaign against terrorism. The struggle should be presented, not just as a fight against evil or as a defence of free societies,

[72] UK Ministry of Defence, *New Chapter*, n 61 above, vol I, at 7.

but also as a fight against tragically erroneous ideas. It should be seen as a means of ensuring that the societies from whence terrorism comes do not succumb to endemic violence. An important aim must be not the capture of every last terrorist leader, but their relegation to a status of near-irrelevance as life moves on, long-standing grievances are addressed and peoples can see that a grim terrorist war of attrition is achieving little and damaging their own societies. It needs to encompass close attention to after-care in societies that have been torn apart by terrorism.

The problem of terrorism can diminish over time. Such diminution will require continued resolution and toughness, including arrests, trials and a willingness to take military action where appropriate. It will also require a patient and more prudent approach that would mark a departure from certain major aspects of what we have seen so far in the 'war on terror'. Above all, the international campaign against terrorism needs to take account of the long history of terror and counterterror – and of the way historians have understood it.

Part II
Defining Terrorism

[2]

The Multifaceted Criminal Notion of Terrorism in International Law

Antonio Cassese*

Abstract

Contrary to what many believe, a generally accepted definition of terrorism as an international crime in time of peace does exist. This definition has evolved in the international community at the level of customary law. However, there is still disagreement over whether the definition may also be applied in time of armed conflict, the issue in dispute being in particular whether acts performed by 'freedom fighters' in wars of national liberation may (or should) constitute an exception to the definition. As a consequence of disagreement on terrorism in armed conflict, states have so far been unable to lay down a general definition of the whole phenomenon of terrorism in a general treaty. The fact, however, remains that under current customary international rules terrorism occurring in a time of peace and which is international in nature (i.e. not limited to the territory of a state and showing transnational connections) may, depending on the circumstances, constitute a discrete international crime, or a crime against humanity. In time of armed conflict, terrorism (i.e. attacks on persons not taking an active part in armed hostilities, with a view to spreading terror among the civilian population) currently amounts to a specific war crime (crime of terror). In time of armed conflict, terrorist acts may also amount to crimes against humanity (if part of a widespread or systematic attack on the civilian population). The objective and subjective elements of each of these three classes of criminal conduct are set out in the article on the basis of existing international law. While in the view of the author, the current legal regulation of terrorism is thus sufficiently clear, the fact remains that states are politically and ideologically divided on whether the actions of 'freedoms fighters' involving attacks on civilians should be defined as terrorist or instead lawful. In this contentious area three divergent political trends are emerging in the world community: (i) to sic et simpliciter *exempt freedom fighters' actions from the category of terrorism, without however specifying what law would regulate their actions or whether such actions are in any case always lawful; (ii) to exclude attacks against civilians in armed conflict from the legal regulation of the international rules on terrorism and thus*

* Professor of international law, University of Florence; member of the Board of Editors. [cassesea@tin.it]

934 *JICJ* **4** (2006), 933–958

assign such legal regulation to international humanitarian law solely; (iii) to combine the application of both international norms on terrorism and international humanitarian law to actions in armed conflict, classifying as terrorist (not as war crimes) attacks on civilians carried out in the course of such conflicts with a view to spreading fear.

1. Introduction: the Problem

The need for a generally accepted definition of international terrorism is self-evident. Each state, in passing legislation on the matter, may and does of course define terrorism as it pleases. However, terrorism is a phenomenon that very often affects multiple states, which are all compelled to cooperate to repress it. Hence, however imperfect and incomplete, a common working definition is necessary so that all states concerned may agree on the target of their repressive action: how can states work together for the arrest, detention or extradition of alleged terrorists, if they do not move from the same notion? In particular, if some states assert that certain categories of persons who engage in conduct that normally would fall under the definition of terrorism must nevertheless not be classified as terrorists on some ideological or political grounds, how can cooperation be smoothly carried out between these states and others taking a different legal view?

The legally binding Framework Decision on the European Arrest Warrant that the Council of the European Union (EU) passed on 13 June 2002 (and which entered into force on 1 January 2004) is a telling instance of this need for cooperation. The Decision provides that terrorism is one of the offences for which arrest warrants can be issued in one of the Member States of the EU and expeditiously executed in another Member State (see Article 2(2)). Clearly, as far as terrorism is concerned, the Decision can be easily implemented as among Member States of the EU only because on the very same day the EU Council also adopted a legally binding Framework Decision on Combating Terrorism,[1] which in Article 1 contained a detailed definition of terrorist offences.[2]

1 Pursuant to Art. 11(1) of the Decision Member States of the European Union 'shall take the necessary measures to comply with this Framework Decision by 31 December 2002'.

2 Art. 2 of the Decision stipulates as follows: 'Each Member State shall take the necessary measures to ensure that the intentional acts referred to below in points (a) to (i), as (*sic*) defined as offences under national law, which, given their nature or context, may seriously damage a country or an international organisation where committed with the aim of:
— seriously intimidating a population, or
— unduly compelling a Government or international organisation to perform or abstain from performing any act, or
— seriously destabilising or destroying the fundamental political, constitutional, economic or social structures of a country or an international organisation, shall be deemed to be terrorist offences:
(a) attacks upon a person's life which may cause death; (b) attacks upon the physical integrity of

It is common knowledge that interminable polemical arguments were exchanged between states in the 1970s through the 1990s over what should be meant by terrorism. The bone of contention was two-fold: could 'freedom fighters' engaged in national liberation movements be classified as terrorists? Should the working out of international rules on terrorism be made contingent upon delving into the root causes of this phenomenon?[3] Many states asserted that as long as no agreement was reached on these two contentious issues, no consent could evolve on the very notion of terrorism either.

As a consequence, *treaty rules* laying down a comprehensive definition have not yet been agreed upon. However, over the years, under the strong pressure of public opinion and also in order to come to grips with the spreading of terrorism everywhere, in fact widespread consensus on a generally acceptable definition of terrorism has evolved in the world community, so much so that the contention can be made — based on the arguments I shall set forth subsequently — that indeed a *customary rule* on the objective and subjective elements of the crime of international terrorism in time of peace has evolved. The requisite practice (*usus*) lies in, or results from, the converging adoption of national laws, the handing down of judgments by national courts, the passing of UN General Assembly resolutions, as well as the ratification of international conventions by a great number of states (such ratifications showing the attitude of states on the matter). In contrast, disagreement continues to exist on a possible *exception* to such definition: whether to exempt *in time of armed conflict* from the scope of the definition acts that, although objectively and subjectively falling within its purview, according to a number of states are nevertheless *legitimized* in law by their being performed by 'freedom fighters' engaged in liberation wars.

It would appear that generally speaking the question of investigating the historical, social and economic causes of terrorism has instead been put on

a person; (c) kidnapping or hostage taking; (d) causing extensive destruction to a Government or public facility, a transport system, an infrastructure facility, including an information system, a fixed platform located on the continental shelf, a public place or private property likely to endanger human life or result in major economic loss; (e) seizure of aircraft, ships or other means of public or goods transport; (f) manufacture, possession, acquisition, transport, supply or use of weapons, explosives or of nuclear, biological or chemical weapons, as well as research into, and development of, biological and chemical weapons; (g) release of dangerous substances, or causing fires, floods or explosions the effect of which is to endanger human life; (h) interfering with or disrupting the supply of water, power or any other fundamental natural resource the effect of which is to endanger human life; (i) threatening to commit any of the acts listed in (a) to (h).'

3 On this issue see, for instance, § 9 of the UN GA Res. 40/61, adopted on 9 December 1985 or § 8 of Res. 42/159, adopted on 7 December 1987. See also the statement the delegate of Ghana made on 6 February 1986 in the Security Council ('...the international community, including the [Security] Council, must summon the necessary political will to delve into the reasons why the frustrations of dispossessed Palestinians are vented in this manner. A glib condemnation of terrorism alone, without a scientific and impartial study of its origins will not, we are afraid, eradicate the phenomenon'.) (S/PV.2655/Corr.1, 18 February 1986)

936 *JICJ* **4** (2006), 933–958

the backburner, although very recently the UN Secretary-General has again drawn attention to the need to 'address conditions conducive to exploitation by terrorists'.[4]

2. The Current International Legal Framework

A. *Factors Pointing to a Generally Agreed Definition of International (or Transnational) Terrorism in Time of Peace*

As emphasized above, many factors point to the formation of substantial consensus on a definition of terrorism in time of peace. First, the Conventions on terrorism adopted by the Arab League, the Organization of African Union (OAU) and the Conference of Islamic States, while providing in terms for the aforementioned exception, nevertheless lay down a definition that is to a large extent in line with that enshrined in other international instruments.[5] Secondly, both the 1999 UN Convention for the Suppression of the Financing of

4 See his Report to the General Assembly of 27 April 2006 (A/60/825), *Uniting against Terrorism: Recommendations for a Global Counter-Terrorism Strategy*, at §§ 20–37.

5 Art. 1(2) of the Arab Convention for the Suppression of Terrorism, of 22 April 1998, defines terrorism as 'Any act or threat of violence, whatever its motives or purposes, that occurs in the advancement of an individual or collective criminal agenda and seeking to sow panic among people, causing fear by harming them, or placing their lives, liberty or security in danger, or seeking to cause damage to the environment or to public or private installations or property, or to [sic] occupying to seizing them, or seeking to jeopardize a natural resources [sic].' (Text online: www.al-bab.com/arab/docs/league/terrorism98.htm; visited 30 August 2006.)
Art. 1(2) of the Convention of the Organization of the Islamic Conference on Combating International Terrorism, of 1 July 1999, provides that '"Terrorism" means any act of violence or threat thereof notwithstanding its motives or intentions perpetrated to carry out an individual or collective criminal plan with the aim of terrorising people or threatening to harm them or imperilling their lives, honour, freedoms, security or rights or exposing the environment or any facility or public or private property to hazards or occupying or seizing them, or endangering a national resource, or international facilities, or threatening the stability, territorial integrity, political unity or sovereignty of independent States.' (Text online: www.oic-un.org/26icfm/c.html; visited 26 July 2006.) Article 1(3) of the OAU Convention on the Prevention and Combating of Terrorism of 14 July 1999 provides that: '"Terrorist act" means:
(a) any act which is a violation of the criminal laws of a State Party and which may endanger the life, physical integrity or freedom of, or cause serious injury or death to, any person, any number or group of persons or causes or may cause damage to public or private property, natural resources, environmental or cultural heritage and is calculated or intended to: (i) intimidate, put in fear, force, coerce or induce any government, body, institution, the general public or any segment thereof, to do or abstain from doing any act, or to adopt or abandon a particular standpoint, or to act according to certain principles; or (ii) disrupt any public service, the delivery of any essential service to the public or to create a public emergency; or (iii) create general insurrection in a State.
(b) any promotion, sponsoring, contribution to, command, aid, incitement, encouragement, attempt, threat, conspiracy, organizing, or procurement or any person, with the intent to commit any act referred to in paragraph (a) (i) to (iii).'

Terrorism[6] and various UN General Assembly resolutions contain a similar notion,[7] which is also shared in the Draft Comprehensive Convention on Terrorism that is still being negotiated.[8] Thirdly, most national laws,[9] as well as national case law, take the same approach.[10]

What are the elements of this definition on which there is general consent? They are as follows: broadly speaking, terrorism consists of (i) acts normally criminalized under any national penal system, or assistance in the commission of such acts whenever they are performed in time of peace; those acts must be (ii) intended to provoke a state of terror in the population or to coerce a state or an international organization to take some sort of action, and finally (iii) are politically or ideologically motivated, i.e. are not based on the pursuit of private ends.

These are the rough elements of a generally accepted definition. Let us consider how they can be translated into a rigorous articulation within international law. Thereafter, it will be appropriate briefly to look at the contentious *exception*.

6 Art. 2(1)(b) provides that terrorism is 'Any ... act intended to cause death or serious bodily injury to a civilian, or to any other person not taking an active part in the hostilities in a situation of armed conflict, when the purpose of such act, by its nature or context, is to intimidate a population, or to compel a government or an international organization to do or to abstain from doing an act.' So far 134 states are parties to the Convention.

7 Since 1994, the UN General Assembly has adopted resolutions including the following proposition: 'Criminal acts intended or calculated to provoke a state of terror in the general public, a group of persons or particular persons for political purposes are in any circumstance unjustifiable, whatever the considerations of a political, philosophical, ideological, racial, ethnic, religious or any other nature that may be invoked to justify them.' See § 3 of the Declaration on Measures to Eliminate International Terrorism, annexed to Res. 49/10 adopted on 9 December 1994; § 2 of the subsequent resolutions 50/53 (11 December 1995), 51/110 (17 December 1996), 52/165 (15 December 1997), 53/108 (8 December 1998), 54/110 (9 December 1999), 55/158 (12 December 2000), 56/88 (12 December 2001), 57/27 (19 November 2002), 58/81 (9 December 2003), 69/46 (16 December 2004).

8 See Art. 2, in Report of the Ad Hoc Committee established by General Assembly Resolution 51/210 of 17 December 1996, Sixth Session (28 January–1 February 2002), A/57/37, Annex II (at 6).

9 For instance, see the US Iran and Libya Sanction Act of 1996 (Public Law 104-172, 5 August 1996); the US Antiterrorism and Effective Death Penalty Act of 1996; the UK Terrorism Act 2000, Section 1; Art. 83.01(1) of the Canadian Criminal Code (which defines terrorism as a criminal offence that is committed '(A) in whole or in part for a political, religious or ideological purpose, objective or cause, and (B) in whole or in part with the intention of intimidating the public, or a segment of the public, with regard to its security, including its economic security, or compelling a person, a government or a domestic or an international organization to do or to refrain from doing any act, whether the public or the person, government or organization is inside or outside Canada'. See also Art. 15 of the Italian law: Executive Decree (*decreto legge*) no. 144 of 27 July 2005, passed as Law no. 155 on 31 July 2005), which adds Art. 270 *sexies* to the provisions of the Italian Criminal Code.

10 See for instance the decision of the Supreme Court of Canada in *Suresh* (judgment of 11 January 2002, online at www.scc-csc.gc.ca; visited 5 October 2006), where the Court held that the definition of terrorism laid down in Art. 2(1)(b) of the UN Convention for the Suppression of Financing of Terrorism 'catches the essence of what the world understands by "terrorism"' (§ 98; see also § 93).

938 *JICJ* **4** (2006), 933–958

B. *The Ingredients of International Terrorism as a Discrete International Crime in Time of Peace*

1. *The Objective Element*

A first element of international terrorism (as distinguished from, i.e. not necessarily coinciding with terrorism under national legislation) relates to *conduct*. The terrorist act must lie in conduct that is *already criminalized* under any national body of criminal law: murder, mass killing, serious bodily harm, kidnapping, bombing, hijacking and so on. This conduct may, however, be in some exceptional instances, lawful per se: for instance, financing of an organization. It becomes criminal if the conduct has the requisite connection to terrorism, for example, if the organization to which money is provided or channelled, or on whose behalf it is collected, is terrorist in nature. In that case, the character of the organization makes the otherwise lawful action tainted with criminality.

Furthermore, the conduct must be *transnational* in nature, that is, not limited to the territory of one state with no foreign elements or links whatsoever (in which case it would exclusively fall under the domestic criminal system of that state). The transnational nature of international terrorism is pithily caught in Article 3 of the Convention for the Suppression of the Financing of Terrorism ('This Convention shall not apply where the offence is committed within a single State, the alleged offender is a national of that State and is present in the territory of that State and no other State has a basis . . . to exercise jurisdiction . . .').

As for the *victims* of criminal conduct, they may embrace both private individuals or the civilian population at large and also state officials including members of state enforcement agencies.

2. *The Subjective Element*

A second element characterizing terrorism concerns the *purpose* of the act. A number of international instruments and national laws provide that the objective pursued by terrorists may be *either* to spread terror among the population *or* to compel a government or an international organization to perform or abstain from performing an act.[11] Other instruments also envisage a third possible objective: to destabilize or destroy the structure of a country.[12]

11 See for instance § 3 of Security Council Res. 1566, adopted on 4 October 2004; Art. 83.01(1)(B) of the Canadian Criminal Code.

12 See, for instance, Art. 1(2) of the 1999 Convention of the Organization of the Islamic Conference on Combating International Terrorism; Art. 1 of the EU Framework Decision on Combating Terrorism (which refers to the aim of 'seriously destabilising or destroying the fundamental political, constitutional, economic or social structures of a country or an international organization').

One can understand that, both for descriptive purposes and also in order to cover the whole range of possible criminal actions, these treaties, laws or other legal instruments enumerate a wide set of terrorist aims. In addition, expressly contemplating various alternative purposes pursued by terrorists may prove useful to prosecutors and other enforcement agencies when the demands of terrorist groups are not clear or are not made with regard to a specific terrorist attack; in these cases, in order to classify the conduct as terrorist, it may suffice to determine that at least the immediate aim of terrorists was to spread panic among the population. This, indeed, may greatly facilitate the action of prosecutors in applying national laws against terrorism. However, close scrutiny and legal logic demonstrate that, in fact, the *primary goal* of terrorists is always that of coercing a public (or private) institution to take a certain course of action. The spreading of deep fear or anxiety is only *a means* for compelling a government or another institution to do (or not to do) something; it is never an end in itself. Also the destabilization of the political structure of a state is a means of making the incumbent government take a certain course of action. To be sure, in some instances the terrorists' goal is not set forth in so many words either before or after the terrorist action. For instance, the 11 September attack on the Twin Towers and the Pentagon was not accompanied by demands of the terrorist organization that had planned the attack. Yet, even in these cases, the murder, bombing or kidnapping are not made for their own sake; it is instrumental in inducing a public or private authority to do or refrain from doing something. In the 11 September case, the attack was clearly intended to prompt the US government to change its overall policy in the Middle East, in particular, by pulling out its military forces there and reversing its policy vis-à-vis Israel.

Hence, it can be said that ultimately terrorism always pursues one primary and essential purpose, that of coercing a public authority (a government or an international organization) or a transnational private organization (for instance, a multinational corporation) to take (or refrain from taking) a specific action or a certain policy. This is the hallmark of any terrorist action.

The purpose in question can be attained through *two possible modalities*. First, by spreading fear or anxiety among civilians (for instance, by blowing up a theatre, kidnapping civilians or planting a bomb in a train, in a bus or in a public place such as a school, a museum or a bank). Clearly, the aim of terrorists is to induce the scared population to put pressure on the government authorities. Secondly, the purpose may be achieved by engaging in criminal conduct against a public institution (e.g. blowing up, or threatening to blow up, the premises of Parliament, the Ministry of Defence or a foreign embassy) or else against a leading personality of a public or private authority (for instance, the head of government, a foreign ambassador, the president of a multinational corporation and so on).

Another element unique to terrorism regards *motive*. The criminal conduct must not be taken for a personal end (for instance, gain, revenge or personal hatred). It must be based on political, ideological or religious motivations. Motive is important because it serves to differentiate terrorism as a

940 *JICJ* **4** (2006), 933–958

manifestation of *collective criminality* from criminal offences (murder, kidnapping and so on) that are instead indicative of *individual criminality*. Terrorist acts are normally performed by groups or organizations, or by individuals acting on their behalf or somehow linked to them. A terrorist act, for instance the blowing up of a disco, may surely be performed by a single individual not belonging to any group or organization. However, that act is terrorist if the agent was moved by a collective set of ideas or tenets (a political platform, an ideology or a body of religious principles), thereby subjectively identifying himself with a group or organization intent on taking similar actions. It is this factor that transforms the murderous action of an individual into a terrorist act.

Let us now translate the above into rigorous legal language. It can be said that for terrorism to materialize two subjective elements (*mens rea*) are required. First, the subjective element (*intent*) proper to any underlying criminal offence: the requisite psychological element of murder, wounding, kidnapping, hijacking and so on (*dolus generalis*). Second, the *specific intent* of compelling a public or a prominent private authority to take, or refrain from taking, an action (*dolus specialis*).

Motive in criminal law is normally immaterial ('an actor's ultimate reason for acting may not bear on his liability'[13]), although it sometimes is taken into account under some specific conditions in a few national legal systems.[14] Motive exceptionally becomes relevant here: as noted earlier, criminal conduct must be inspired by non-personal inducements. Hence, if it is proved that a criminal action (for instance, blowing up a building) has been motivated by non-ideological or non-political or non-religious considerations, the act can no longer be defined as international terrorism, although it may of course fall under a broader notion of terrorism upheld in the state where the act has been accomplished. This, for instance, holds true for cases similar to an American criminal act that lacks, however, the transnational element proper to international terrorism: Timothy McVeigh's blowing up in 1995 of a public building in Oklahoma City, with the consequent death of 168 persons. Reportedly that action was carried out in revenge for the killing, by the FBI,

13 G.P. Fletcher, *Rethinking Criminal Law* (reprint, Oxford: Oxford University Press, 2000), at 452.

14 For instance, according to the penal provisions applying in Italy before 1981, voluntary murder of either a female spouse, daughter or sister (guilty of having unlawful sexual intercourse with another person) or of their sexual partner, perpetrated in an outburst of anger caused by the offence to the perpetrator's honour or to the 'family honour', was punished with a much lighter penalty (3–7 years' imprisonment) than any ordinary murder (not less than 20 years' imprisonment). See Art. 587 of the 1930 Italian Criminal Code, repealed by the Italian Law no. 442 of 5 August 1981.

At present, political motives are taken into account for the purpose of defining a crime as political and consequently attributing jurisdiction over such crime to Italian courts. Under Art. 8 of the Italian Criminal Code a national or a foreigner committing a crime abroad may be brought to trial before an Italian court if, among other things, the crime was 'determined, in whole or in part, by political motives'.

of members of a religious sect at Waco, Texas. Similarly, if bandits break into a bank, kill some clients and take others hostage for the purpose of escaping unharmed with the loot, this action cannot be classified as terrorism, although the killing and hostage-taking are also intended to spark terror among civilians and compel the authorities to do or not to do something. Here the essential element of ideological or political motive is lacking. Consequently, the offence is one of armed robbery aggravated by murder and hostage-taking, not terrorism. Let us take another example, namely the episode at the Los Angeles International airport (where on 4 July 2002 an Egyptian fired at and killed some tourists who were about to take a plane bound for Israel, and was eventually shot down by enforcement officers). To determine whether this was a terrorist act or simply murder, one ought to inquire into the possible motives of the killer; in that case, these motives could have been inferred from his life, his possible statements, his criminal record, any links he might have had with terrorist groups and so on.

Let me add that of course, motive by itself may not suffice for the classification of a criminal act as terrorist. To clarify this point I shall give an example (although it again relates to terrorist groups that were not involved in transnational terrorism, it may nevertheless be useful for illustration purposes). In the 1970s, some terrorist groups in Italy and Germany (respectively the Red Brigades and the Rote Armee Fraktion) carried out armed robberies against banks to replenish the organization's funds. Here the motive of the criminal act was not personal (to acquire a private gain), but collective (to boost the organization's cash). Yet, the action was not terrorist in nature, but an ordinary criminal offence, because another crucial element proper to terrorism was lacking (the purpose of compelling through criminal conduct an authority to take a certain stand). This conclusion does not exclude however that individual national criminal systems may consider that, since the aforementioned acts were performed to support a terrorist organization, the crimes involved must be characterized as terrorist at least for such purposes as jurisdiction, the use of special investigative methods and so on.

The legal relevance of motive for determining whether one is faced with a terrorist offence does undoubtedly pose serious problems for any prosecutorial agency or criminal court. It may admittedly prove hard to find the reasons that inspired the agent, and to disentangle the specific basis for his action from the intricacies of his possible motivations. In particular, it may be laborious to establish whether he acted out of political, ideological or religious motivations. In addition to this factual difficulty, it may also be difficult to decide in a particular instance whether a set of ideas or aspirations make up a political credo, an ideology or a religion. One easy way out could consist of ascertaining whether the agent only acted out of strictly personal reasons, in which case one could rule out that his acts be termed terrorist. Admittedly, the question is complicated and may give rise to much controversy. The fact remains, however, that the nature of motive is taken into account by international rules as one of the discriminating factors in this matter.

942 JICJ 4 (2006), 933–958

C. *Specific Sub-categories of International Terrorism as a Discrete International Crime*

It is common knowledge that at the time when ideological clashes mired the international discussion on terrorism, preventing the achievement of general consensus on the matter, in order to break the deadlock states opted for the passing of international conventions on specific categories of conduct. They thus agreed upon a string of conventions through which they imposed on contracting parties the obligation to make punishable and to prosecute in their domestic legal orders certain classes of actions. These actions were defined in each convention by indicating the principal outward elements of the offence. The conventions refrained from terming the conduct terrorist and did not point to the purpose of the conduct or motive of the perpetrators either. Instead, they confined themselves to setting out the *objective elements* of prohibited conduct.

This applies to (i) acts that, whether or not they are offences under national law, may or do jeopardize the safety of aircraft, or of persons or property therein or which jeopardize good order and discipline aboard;[15] (ii) unlawful taking control, by force or threat thereof or by any other form of intimidation, of an aircraft in flight;[16] (iii) acts of violence against persons on board an aircraft in flight or against the aircraft;[17] (iv) murder and other violent acts against internationally protected persons or their official premises, private accommodation or means of transport;[18] (v) unlawful possession, use, transfer or theft of nuclear material as well as threat to use it;[19] (vi) taking control of a ship by force or threat thereof or any other form of intimidation or acts of violence against persons aboard or against the ship;[20] (vii) taking control over a fixed platform by force or threat thereof or any other form of intimidation, or acts of violence against persons on board or against the platform;[21] (viii) acts of violence against persons at an airport serving international civil aviation or against the facilities of the airport;[22] (ix) the manufacture, or the movement into or out of a territory, of unmarked plastic explosives;[23] (x) the delivery,

15 Art. 1(b) of the 1963 Tokyo Convention on Offences and Certain Other Acts Committed on Board Aircraft.

16 Art. 1(a) of the 1970 Hague Convention for the Suppression of Unlawful Seizure of Aircraft.

17 Art. 1(1) of the 1971 Montreal Convention for the Suppression of Unlawful Acts against the Safety of Civil Aviation.

18 Art. 2(1) of the 1973 Convention on the Prevention and Punishment of Crimes against Internationally Protected Persons, Including Diplomatic Agents.

19 Art. 7 of the 1979 Vienna Convention on the Physical Protection of Nuclear Material.

20 Art. 3(1) of the 1988 Rome Convention for the Suppression of Unlawful Acts against the Safety of Maritime Navigation.

21 Art. 2 of the 1988 Rome Protocol for the Suppression of Unlawful Acts against the Safety of Fixed Platforms Located on the Continental Shelf.

22 Art. II of the 1988 Montreal Protocol for the Suppression of Unlawful Acts of Violence at Airports Serving International Civil Aviation.

23 Arts II and III of the 1991 Montreal Convention on the Marking of Plastic Explosives for the Purpose of Detection.

placing, discharging or detonation of explosive or other lethal device in a place of public use, a state or government facility, a public transportation system or an infrastructure facility.[24]

Other Conventions, instead, besides setting out the objective elements of criminal conduct, also place emphasis on the *purpose* pursued by the perpetrators. This holds true for the 1979 Montreal Convention against the Taking of Hostages, as well as the 1999 Convention for the Suppression of the Financing of Terrorism. Both Conventions characterize the terrorist actions they deal with as intended to compel a state or an international organization to do or to abstain from doing any act; in addition the latter Convention contemplates the purpose of intimidating a population.[25]

It is warranted to contend that for the whole range of aforementioned conduct the hallmarks of international terrorism as a discrete crime in time of peace, outlined above, were considered *implicit* in the banning of such conduct. Indeed, the primary purpose of those conventions was to put a stop to terrorist conduct belonging to each category of action banned by the conventions and increasingly ubiquitous when the conventions were drafted.

Nevertheless, as the classes of actions prohibited by the aforementioned first 10 conventions are very broad, one cannot exclude from the scope of such conventions conduct that, although clearly banned by them, does not fall under the category of terrorism for lack of the requisite elements. For instance, the hijacking of a plane by a robber that aims at obtaining a huge sum of money as a ransom or the release of some fellow criminals in exchange for saving the passengers, plainly falls under the 1970 Hague Convention, without however constituting an act of international terrorism proper.

D. *International Terrorism in Armed Conflict: a Sub-category of War Crimes*

At present, both international humanitarian law and international criminal law already cover acts of terrorism performed during an international or internal armed conflict.

24 Art. 2(1) of the 1998 International Convention for the Suppression of Terrorist Bombings.

25 Art. 1(1) of the Convention on the Taking of Hostages provides that 'Any person who seizes or detains or threatens to kill, to injure or to continue to detain another person (hereinafter referred to as the "hostage") in order to compel a third party, namely a State, an international intergovernmental organization, a natural or juridical person, or a group of persons, to do or abstain from doing any act as an explicit or implicit condition for the release of the hostage commits the offence of taking hostages ("hostage-taking") within the meaning of this Convention.'

Art. 2(1)(b) of the Convention on the Financing of Terrorism provides that a person commits an offence within the meaning of the Convention if that person provides or collects funds to carry out among other things any act 'intended to cause death or serious bodily injury to a civilian, to any other person not taking an active part in the hostilities in a situation of armed conflict, when the purpose of such act, by its nature or context, is to intimidate a population, or to compel a government or an international organization to do or to abstain from doing any act'.

944 JICJ 4 (2006), 933–958

One question with which we should deal at the outset is that of so-called *state terrorism*. It is claimed that in time of war attacks carried out by a belligerent against the enemy civilian population may amount to state terrorism. This is primarily a political or ideological catchword without legal value (except when referring to possible instances of state responsibility for serious violations of international law, as we shall soon see). In legal terms those attacks, if they are deliberate and only target civilians, amount to a grave breach of international humanitarian law; if they target instead the enemy combatant but cause incidental damage to civilians, they may be regarded as unlawful if the damage to civilians is disproportionate.[26] As we shall soon see, terrorist acts performed by states in time of war can only occur when a belligerent engages in unlawful attacks on civilians intended to spread terror; their planners or perpetrators may consequently be punished for war crimes of terrorism.

Let us now move to the crucial question of terrorist acts performed by combatants (be they members of the armed forces of a state, or rebels or guerrillas, or members of the armed forces of a non-state entity).

International rules indisputably ban terrorism in time of armed conflict. Article 33(1) of the Fourth Geneva Convention of 1949 prohibits 'all measures . . . of terrorism' against civilians. Although the provision was primarily calculated to forestall terrorism by Occupying Powers or, more generally, by belligerents,[27] terrorist acts are also prohibited if perpetrated by civilians or organized groups in occupied territories or in the territory of a party to the conflict. Thus Article 33(1) is a provision of general purport, applicable in any situation (whether terrorism is resorted to in the territory of one of the belligerents, in the combat area or in an occupied territory).

A similar provision is contained in the Second Additional Protocol of 1977. Article 4(2)(d) prohibits 'acts of terrorism' against 'all persons who do not take a direct part or have ceased to take part in hostilities, whether or not their liberty has been restricted' [Article 4(1)].

The two Protocols also spell out the general prohibition of terrorism. Article 51(2) of the First Protocol prohibits 'acts or threats of violence the primary purpose of which is to spread terror among the civilian population'. Article 13(2) of the Second Protocol repeats word for word this prohibition.

26 See for instance: UK Ministry of Defence, *The Manual of the Law of Armed Conflict* (Oxford: Oxford University Press, 2004), §§ 5.32–5.33.5; J.-M. Hanckaerts and L. Doswald-Beck, *Customary International Humanitarian Law*, vol. 1 (Cambridge: Cambridge University Press, 2005), at 46–76; A. Cassese, *International Law* (2nd edn., Oxford: Oxford University Press, 2005), at 415–423.

27 According to the ICRC Commentary, Art. 33(1) was aimed primarily aimed at forestalling a common practice, that of belligerents resorting to 'intimidatory measures to terrorise the population' with a view to preventing hostile acts (see ICRC, *Commentary, Fourth Geneva Convention* (Geneva, ICRC, 1958), at 225–226).

It can be safely contended that all these provisions reflect, or at least have turned into customary law.[28]

Thus, international humanitarian law proscribes terrorism both in international and internal armed conflicts. The question, however, arises of whether, in addition to addressing its prohibition to states, international customary and treaty law also *criminalize* terrorism in armed conflict. An International Criminal Tribunal for the former Yugoslavia (ICTY) Trial Chamber convincingly proved in 2003 in *Galić* that already in 1992 (when the facts at issue in that case occurred) a serious violation of the prohibition against terrorizing the civilian population entailed, at least under treaty law, the individual criminal responsibility of the person breaching the rule.[29]

Contrary to this holding, one could object that the Statute of the International Criminal Court (ICC), which carefully and extensively lists in Article 8 the various classes of war crimes, fails to mention resort to terror against civilians. This argument would not, however, be compelling. Indeed, the various provisions of the ICC Statute are not intended to codify existing customary rules; this is borne out by Article 10 of the Statute ('Nothing in this Part shall be interpreted as limiting or prejudicing in any way existing or developing rules of international law for purposes other than this Statute'), as well as by the fact that some specific provisions of the Statute concerning the crimes over which the Court has jurisdiction go beyond customary or previous treaty rules, whereas others only partially take account of customary law.[30]

Support for the criminalization of terrorist acts in the course of armed conflict can be found in various normative developments. The relevant provisions of the Statutes of the ICTR and the Special Court for Sierra Leone, in granting these two criminal tribunals jurisdiction over violations of international

28 In its Decision on Interlocutory Appeal issued on 22 November 2002, the ICTY Appeals Chamber in *Strugar and others* (IT-01-42-AR72) held that 'the principles prohibiting attacks on civilians and unlawful attacks on civilian objects stated in Articles 51 and 52 of Additional Protocol 1 and Article 13 of Additional Protocol II are principles of customary international law' (§ 10).
It is notable that in 1977, at the close of the Geneva Diplomatic Conference on the Reaffirmation of International Humanitarian Law, the United Kingdom stated that Art. 51(2) was 'a valuable reaffirmation of existing customary rules of international law designed to protect civilians (CDDH, *Official records*, vol. VI, at 164, § 119). The 2004 British *Manual of the Law of Armed Conflict* referring to the prohibition of 'terror attacks', seems clearly based on the assumption that this rule is general in nature (see UK Ministry of Defence, *The Manual of the Law of Armed Conflict*, *supra* note 26, § 5.21.1).
The important research work undertaken by the ICRC on customary law also concludes that a customary rule has evolved on this matter (see Henckaerts and Doswald-Beck, *supra* note 26, at 8).

29 ICTY, Judgment, *Galić* (IT-98-29-T), Trial Chamber, 5 December 2003, §§ 113–129. It would seem, however, that the Trial Chamber's finding that the prohibition of terror in armed conflict was criminalized was essentially limited to the case at issue and to the accused standing trial. In addition, the Trial Chamber left open the question of the possible criminalization of terror under customary international law (see § 138).

30 See A. Cassese, *International Criminal Law* (Oxford: Oxford University Press, 2003), at 59–62, 93–94, 107–108.

946 *JICJ* **4** (2006), 933–958

rules of humanitarian law, include 'acts of terrorism'.[31] This proves that the drafters of those Statutes considered that such acts may amount to war crimes. Also the 1996 ILC Draft Code of Crimes against Peace and Security of Mankind takes the view that 'acts of terrorism' committed in internal conflicts constitute war crimes. Furthermore, it seems significant that Article 2(1)(b) of the 1999 Convention of the Financing of Terrorism explicitly refers to 'a situation of armed conflict', thus implying that terrorist acts can be committed in such a 'situation'. Of course the Convention is only binding on the contracting parties. Nevertheless, so far the Convention has been ratified or acceded to by 153 states (only three of which have entered reservation to the relevant treaty stipulation);[32] the provision at issue is, therefore, indicative of the generally held view that terrorism is also criminalized in time of armed conflict.

In sum, attacks on civilians and other 'protected persons' in the course of an armed conflict, aiming at spreading terror, may amount to war crimes (although not to grave breaches of the Geneva Conventions,[33] with the consequence that the Geneva provisions on mandatory universal jurisdiction over such crimes do not apply, such universal jurisdiction being simply authorized by the Geneva Conventions[34]).

What are the *constitutive elements* of terrorism as a war crime?

It would seem that in humanitarian law terrorism as a war crime has a narrower scope than the notion contemplated by the whole body of general international law of peace. First of all, the *prohibited conduct* arguably consists of any *violent action* or *threat* of such action *against* civilians or other persons not taking a direct part in armed hostilities (wounded, shipwrecked, prisoners of war). It can be inferred both from the whole spirit and purpose of international humanitarian law and also from the wording of Articles 4(1) and (2)(d) of the Second Additional Protocol (a rule that, it is submitted, codifies a general principle applicable to any armed conflict)[35] that attacks on combatants not

31 Art. 4(d) of the 1994 Statute of the ICTR provides that the Tribunal has jurisdiction over violations of common Art. 3 of the Geneva Conventions and the Second Additional Protocol and explicitly provides for jurisdiction over 'acts of terrorism'. Article 3(d) of the 2000 Statute of the Special Court for Sierra Leone grants the Court jurisdiction over 'acts of terrorism'.

32 See above, 2.A.

33 The relevant provisions of the 1949 Geneva Conventions (Arts 50/51/130/147) do not include 'acts or measures of terrorism' among the offences amounting to grave breaches.

34 As rightly held, with regard to the war crime of torture in armed conflict, by The Hague District Court in the *Afghani* cases (judgments of 9 February 2006). The Court rightly emphasized the importance of the common provision of the Conventions (Arts 49(3); 50(3); 129(3); 146(3)) stipulating that 'Each High Contracting Party shall take measures necessary for the suppression of all acts contrary to the provisions of the present Convention other than the grave breaches defined in the following Article.'

35 This provision is simply an expansion and elaboration of common Art. 3 of the four Geneva Conventions of 1949, which the International Court of Justice stated in 1986 in *Nicaragua (merits)* constitutes 'a minimum yardstick' applicable to any armed conflict (at § 218). For the state practice and the practice of international organizations that can corroborate the proposition set out above in the text, see the wealth of material collected in Henckaerts and Doswald-Beck, *supra* note 26, at 306–83. See also the *Report of the International Commission of Inquiry on Darfur*, UN Doc. S/2005/60 (25 January 2005), at §§ 154–167.

being actively engaged in armed hostilities can also amount to terrorism: for instance, attacks (or threats of attack) on officers attending a mass or praying in a mosque, a church or a synagogue, or military personnel taking their children to the movie. This proposition is borne out by the aforementioned Article 2(1)(b) of the Convention for the Suppression of the Financing of Terrorism, which includes among the possible victims of terrorist acts in time of armed conflict 'any other persons [than civilians] not taking an active part in the hostilities'.

The violent action or threat thereof can also be directed against a civilian object, even if it is empty (for instance, a square, a private building as a theatre), as long as the goal pursued in taking such an action is that of terrorizing the population. As rightly noted by the 2004 British Manual of the Law of Armed Conflict, the rule prohibiting terror attacks 'would apply, for instance, to car bombs installed in busy shopping streets, even if no civilians are killed or injured by them, their object being to create panic among the population'.[36] As for threats, again the British Manual rightly pointed out that 'threats of violence would include, for example, threat to annihilate the enemy's civilian population'.[37] In contrast, the prohibition on terror does not cover terror caused as a by-product of attacks on military objectives 'or as a result of genuine warning of impending attacks on such objectives'.[38]

We can thus move to the *subjective element* of the action or threat of action. Articles 51(2) of the First Protocol and 13(2) of the Second Protocol, which, as I stated earlier, can be taken to spell out in many respects the terse content of other provisions on humanitarian law on terrorism, make it clear that terrorist acts in armed conflict are acts calculated to 'spread terror' among the civilian population or other protected persons. Here, then, the purpose of coercing a public (or private) authority to take a certain course of action disappears or, at least, wanes. The only conspicuous purpose appears to be that of terrorizing the enemy. In other words, in international humanitarian law, terrorist acts are acts performed within the framework of the general goal of defeating the enemy. Their ultimate purpose is to contribute to the war effort. Instead of simply attacking civilians, a belligerent carries out actions (for instance, random killing of persons passing through a bridge, or haphazard blowing up of civilian installations, or systematic shelling of an empty place in a populated area) designed to beget profound insecurity and anxiety in the population (and consequently in the enemy belligerent).

36 *The Manual of the Law of Armed Conflict*, *supra* note 26, at §5.21.1.

37 *Ibid.*

38 See M. Bothe, K.-J. Partsch and W.A. Solf, *New Rules for the Victims of Armed Conflicts: Commentary on the Two 1977 Protocols Additional to the Geneva Conventions of 1949* (The Hague, Boston, London: M. Nijhoff Publishers, 1982), at 301; *The Manual of the Law of Armed Conflict*, *supra* note 26, at § 5.21.1.

948 *JICJ* **4** (2006), 933–958

It is thus clear that also in time of armed conflict international criminal law requires *intent*, with the consequence that, as rightly emphasized in *Galić*, simple *dolus eventualis* or recklessness must be ruled out.[39]

In addition, *motive* becomes immaterial in terrorist acts as war crimes. In time of armed conflict, actions designed to spread terror in the enemy are always 'public' in nature and any personal motives (for instance, desire for revenge, racial or ethnic hatred, anger and so on) of the officer or the leader of an armed group ordering such acts does not acquire any legal relevance.

In sum, during an armed conflict, belligerent acts of terrorism, being prohibited and criminalized, are covered both by international *humanitarian* law and international *criminal* law. They may also be covered by rules on terrorism as a discrete crime to the extent that a state fighting terrorism is bound by an international convention on terrorism that addresses terrorism both in time of peace and in time of war. In this event, there would be a *two-fold legal characterization* of the same conduct or the *combined simultaneous application of two different bodies of law* to the same conduct. A case in point is the Convention on the Financing of Terrorism. If a state is party to such convention, it may apply its provisions to the financing of terrorist acts performed or planned in a foreign country where an armed conflict is underway. It would consequently punish the financing of violent acts abroad directed against persons not taking an active part in armed hostilities, whereas, it would not consider unlawful the financing of groups solely aimed at attacking enemy armed forces in the foreign country concerned.

E. International Terrorism as a Sub-category of Crimes against Humanity

Can terrorist acts amount to crimes against humanity? Yes, subject to a number of conditions.

First of all, it can be inferred from the relevant international rules and case law on crimes against humanity that terrorist acts may fall under this category of crimes, *whether they are perpetrated in time of war or peace*. Furthermore, they must cause (or consist of) the following *conduct:* (i) murder, or (ii) great suffering, or (iii) serious injury to body or to mental or physical health, or else take the form of (iv) torture, (v) rape or even (vi) enforced disappearance of persons (namely, 'arrest, detention or abduction of persons by, or with the authorization, support or acquiescence of, a state or a political organization, followed by a refusal to acknowledge that deprivation of freedom or to give information on the fate or whereabouts of those persons, with the

39 The Trial Chamber noted that 'the Prosecution is required to prove not only that the Accused accepted the likelihood that terror would result from the illegal acts — or, in other words, that he was aware of the possibility that terror would result — but that that was the result which he specifically intended. The crime of terror is a specific-intent crime'(§ 136).

intention of removing them from the protection of the law for a prolonged period of time'[40]).

Terrorist acts must also meet the basic requirements of the category of crimes under discussion. Consequently (i) terrorist action must be part of a widespread or systematic attack against a civilian population; (ii) the perpetrator, in addition to *mens rea* required for the underlying offence (murder, torture, etc.) must also have *knowledge* that his action is part of a widespread or systematic attack.

It would seem that, as in the case of terrorism as a discrete crime, also when terrorist acts are such as to amount to crimes against humanity, the *victims* may embrace both civilians and state officials including members of armed forces. Admittedly, the Statutes of international criminal tribunals, in granting jurisdiction to these tribunals over crimes against humanity, stipulate that the victims of such crimes must be civilian. However, this limitation cannot be found in customary international law, which to my mind provides instead that crimes against humanity may also be perpetrated against military personnel and members of other enforcement agencies.[41] Generally speaking, it would be contrary to the whole spirit and logic of modern international human rights law and humanitarian law to limit to civilians (especially in time of peace) the international protection of individuals against horrendous and large-scale atrocities. This, I believe, also holds true for terrorism as a crime against humanity. For instance, it would not make sense to suggest that the 11 September 2001 attacks against the Twin Towers in New York, housing almost exclusively civilians, amounted to a crime against humanity, whereas the crashing of a civilian aircraft into the Pentagon in Washington D.C. constituted a different category of crime because the victims were not civilians but primarily state officials (mostly even military personnel) at work.

In the case of terrorist acts, what matters from the point of view of law is not so much the sheltering of civilians from becoming the target of grave crimes. What is crucial is to avoid (and punish) criminal action, whomever its victims, taken to compel a public or private entity to do or not to do something. In a way, the victims play almost a secondary role in the criminalization of conduct. What clearly emerges from current international law is that the widespread or systematic attack required as the necessary *context* of a crime against humanity must be one that targets the civilian population. This is only logical, for a widespread or systematic attack against members of armed forces in time of *peace* would simply constitute part and parcel of

40 This is the definition of 'enforced disappearance of persons' set out in Art. 7(2)(i) ICCSt., which can be taken to be declaratory of existing rule of customary international law banning and criminalizing that offence. See also the International Convention for the Protection of All Persons from Enforced Disappearances, recently adopted by the UN Human Rights Council. It applies in all circumstances (see http://daccessdds.un.org/doc/UNDOC/LTD/G06/125/78/PDF/G0612578.pdf?OpenElement; visited 5 October 2006).

41 See Cassese, *supra* note 30, at 85–91.

950 JICJ 4 (2006), 933–958

an armed conflict (internal if the attackers are within the territory, international if they come from outside); in time of *war*, depending upon the circumstances that attack could, or could not, amount to a string of large-scale breaches of humanitarian law. If, instead, a widespread or systematic attack is undertaken against the civilian population, for such atrocities to amount to a crime against humanity, one set of atrocities (for instance, torture, rape or other inhumane acts of similar gravity) may also be directed against military personnel.

Let me give some examples. If in time of peace a group of terrorists, in addition to conducting attacks on civilians, engages in atrocities against military or police personnel such as bombing barracks, blowing up police stations, destroying a major building of the defence ministry, or else kidnaps servicemen and subjects them to torture or rape, these acts (murder, imprisonment, torture, rape and so on) should be classified as crimes against humanity. Similarly, if in time of armed conflict an armed group or organization (or even a state), besides indiscriminately and violently attacking on a large scale civilians and other persons not taking an active part in hostilities, captures, rapes or tortures enemy combatants for the purpose of spreading terror among the enemy belligerent or to obtain from him the release of imprisoned members of the group, organization (or state), these acts, which normally would be classified as war crimes, may acquire the magnitude of a crime against humanity.

It is clear from what I have just pointed out that, in addition to the aforementioned objective elements, it is also necessary for the author of terrorist acts to entertain the *specific intent* required for terrorism as a discrete crime, namely, the purpose of compelling a public or private authority to take, or refrain from taking, a certain course of action, a purpose that may be achieved by either generating fear and anxiety among the public or by other criminal actions (see above).

In sum, terrorism as a crime against humanity substantially constitutes an *aggravated form* of terrorism as a discrete crime.

3. The Current Controversy over Acts of Freedom Fighters in Armed Conflict

A. The Principal Bone of Contention

So far I have set out what I consider to be the international legal regulation of the various categories of terrorism: terrorism as a discrete crime and as a subcategory of war crimes or of crimes against humanity. I must now tackle the major political and legal issue currently dividing the international community: whether 'freedom fighters' involved in armed conflict against a foreign belligerent, a national authority allegedly oppressing them or an occupying power may be exempt from criminal responsibility when they engage in acts that would normally (under the definitions suggested above) be termed terrorist.

For many years, this exception has been propounded in rather ambiguous terms. The Arab, OAU and Islamic Conventions generically refer to struggles for self-determination and against foreign occupation and aggression.[42] The scope and purport of this exception are not clear. In particular, it is not clear whether these Conventions intend to refer to the whole set of armed actions undertaken by liberation movements, and thus exempt them from the label of terrorism, or whether instead they more specifically aim at removing the characterization of terrorism from those acts performed by members of liberation movements that are directed against civilians and calculated to spread terror or fear. It would seem that no state practice or official statements are available that cast light on this issue.

B. *The Three Different Attitudes Emerging among States*

Be that as it may, recently the stand of many Arab or Islamic countries seems to have changed.[43] *Three different positions* of states and other authorities may be identified, positions that do not necessarily exclude one another, and in some instances overlap.

The first is that of states stubbornly insisting on any act by peoples or organizations engaged in wars of self-determination being *exempt from the*

42 The 1998 Arab Convention for the Suppression of Terrorism provides in Art. 2(a) that 'All cases of struggle by whatever means, including armed struggle, against foreign occupation and aggression for liberation and self-determination, in accordance with principles of international law, shall not be regarded as an offence. This provision shall not apply to any act prejudicing the territorial integrity of any Arab State.'

Art. 3(1) of the 1999 OAU Convention on the Prevention and Combating of Terrorism provides that 'Notwithstanding the provisions of Article 1 [defining terrorism] the struggle waged by peoples in accordance with the principles of international law for their liberation or self-determination, including armed struggle against colonialism, aggression and domination by foreign forces shall not be considered as terrorist acts.'

Art. 2(a) of the 1999 Convention of the Organization of the Islamic Conference on Combating International Terrorism stipulates that 'Peoples' struggle including armed struggle against foreign occupation, aggression, colonialism, and hegemony, aimed at liberation and self-determination in accordance with the principles of international law shall not be considered a terrorist crime.'

The same notions are restated in other documents. See for instance the Kuala Lumpur Declaration on International terrorism adopted on 1–3 April 2002 at the Extraordinary session of the Islamic Conference of Foreign Ministers on Terrorism (§§ 8–11; and see also § 3 of the Plan of Action adopted by the same Conference; online: www.oic-oci.org/English/fm/11.extraordinary/declaration.htm; visited 5 October 2006). See also the Final Document of the Thirteenth Conference of Heads of State or Government of the Non-Aligned Countries (Kuala Lumpur, 20–25 February 2003), §§ 106–108 and 115 (in UN Doc. A/57/759 or S/2003/332). See also the Declaration of the Second High-Level Intergovernmental Meeting on the Prevention and Combating of Terrorism in Africa (Algiers, 13-14 October 2004), at preambular paragraph 3.

43 See in this special issue the contribution by M. Hmoud.

952 *JICJ* **4** (2006), 933–958

label of terrorism (even when they engage in attacks against civilians). These states, however, *do not clarify what law would govern such acts* or whether, and more simply, these acts should be held to be *authorized* under international law. This stand was taken, for instance, by Pakistan in 2002 when acceding to the 1997 Convention for the Suppression of Terrorist Bombing. The Convention excludes from its scope activities of armed forces, including freedom fighters, in armed conflict, keeping such activities subject to the legal regulation of international humanitarian law. Pakistan entered a reservation[44] that can be held to be at least ambiguous. A very similar position is taken by other states, which purport to exclude the application of *anti-terrorist conventions* to armed conflict, without, however, clarifying whether the use of force by freedom fighters against civilians in such conflicts must be covered by international humanitarian law. This stand was taken by Egypt, Jordan and Syria in the reservation they made in 2003–2005 when ratifying, or acceding to, the Convention for the Suppression of the Financing of Terrorism.[45]

The second position is that of states or authorities which hold that, while any act performed by freedom fighters in wars of national liberation is

44 That Convention stipulates in Art. 19(2) that 'The activities of armed forces during an armed conflict, as those terms are understood under international humanitarian law, which are governed by that law, are not governed by this Convention, and the activities undertaken by military forces of a State in the exercise of their official duties, inasmuch as they are governed by other rules of international law, are not governed by this Convention.'
In 2002 Pakistan, in acceding to the Convention, made the following reservation: 'The Government of the Islamic Republic of Pakistan declares that nothing in this Convention shall be applicable to struggles, including armed struggles, for the realization of the right to self-determination launched against any alien or foreign occupation or domination, in accordance with the rules of international law. This interpretation is consistent with Article 53 of the Vienna Convention on the Law of Treaties 1969, which provides that an agreement or treaty concluded in conflict with an existing *jus cogens* or preemptory norm of international law is void, and the right to self-determination is universally recognized as a *jus cogens*' (www.coe.int/t/E/Legal.affairs/Legal.co-operation/Public.international.law/Texts.&.Documents/2003/CAHDI%20.2003.%202E.pdfI; visited 5 October 2006). This reservation was rejected by many States Parties as inconsistent with the object and purpose of the Convention. These states declared that they nevertheless did not consider their objection as preventing the entry into force of the Convention between themselves and Pakistan (see *ibid.*).

45 Art. 2(1)(b) provides that terrorist acts are, in addition to those prohibited by some specific conventions on terrorism, 'Any other act intended to cause death or serious bodily injury to a civilian, or to any other person not taking an active part in the hostilities in a situation of armed conflict, when the purpose of such act, by its nature or context, is to intimidate a population, or to compel a government or an international organization to do or to abstain from doing any act.'
Egypt, Jordan and Syria made a reservation to the effect that they did not consider 'acts of national resistance in all its forms, including armed resistance against foreign occupation and aggression with a view to liberation and self-determination, as terrorist acts within the meaning of Article 2(1)(b)'. Many other states objected, considering the reservation contrary to the object and purpose of the Convention, but nevertheless held that their objection did not preclude the entry into force of the Convention between the objecting and reserving state (see www.untreaty.un.org/ENGLISH/bible/englishinternet bible/partI/chapterXVIII/treaty1; visited 5 October 2006).

not covered at all by the body of international law on terrorism, it remains nevertheless *governed by the international humanitarian law of armed conflict*. It would seem that this view was implicitly taken by the Secretary-General of the Arab League, Mr Amre Moussa. On at least two occasions, he clearly asserted that the legitimacy of the Palestinian struggle for self-determination did not imply that innocent civilians (be they Palestinian or Israeli) might be attacked.[46] By this he clearly meant to say that Palestinians legitimately fighting in the occupied territories against the foreign Occupant were not allowed by international law deliberately to attack civilians. Similarly, the Member States of the Islamic Conference participating in the UN negotiations for the elaboration of a Comprehensive Convention on Terrorism have proposed a draft provision encapsulating the famous exception to the notion of terrorism. However, this time the proposal spells out the hitherto ambiguous formula used by Arab and Islamic countries.[47] It is now specified that actions undertaken in the course of an armed conflict 'including in situations of foreign occupation' are not covered by the Convention, hence may not be classified as

46 See the interview given by the Secretary-General on 30 July 2002 in French [online at: www.arableagueonline.org/arableague/english/details.en.jsp?art_id=1262&leve; visited 5 October 2006: '*La situation au Moyen-Orient, ou entre Israël et la Palestine, ce n'est pas le terrorisme face à une campagne de lutte contre le terrorisme. C'est un cas d'occupation militaire étrangère et de résistance à l'occupation. Tant qu'il y aura occupation, il y aura résistance. Cela dit, je ne défends ni ne soutiens l'implication de civils innocents israéliens et palestiniens dans le conflit*' (at 1); '*il s'agit de l'occupation militaire d'un territoire étranger: cela ne justifie pas le terrorisme, mais cela justifie la résistance. Lorsque les Israéliens affirment que tuer un soldat israélien dans les Territoire occupés, c'est du terrorisme, c'est un non-sens. Si l'on suit cette logique, alors toute la résistance française était un mouvement terroriste*' (at 3)]. See also the speech made by Mr Moussa at the 2004 Ambrosetti Conference: '. . .we DO condemn any action, any crime that results in killing innocent people, children or women or men, be that in Israel or in Egypt, or in Algeria, or in Palestine, or in Russia, or in Colombia or in the United States or in Spain'. (*ibid.*, at 1)

47 See the text of Art. 18 proposed by the Member States of the Organization of the Islamic Conference: 'Nothing in this Convention shall affect other rights, obligations and responsibilities of States, peoples and individuals under international law, in particular the purposes and principles of the Charter of the United Nations, and international humanitarian law.
1. The activities of the parties during an armed conflict, including in situations of foreign occupation, as those terms are understood under international humanitarian law, which are governed by that law, are not governed by this Convention.
2. The activities undertaken by the military forces of a State in the exercise of their official duties, inasmuch as they are in conformity with international law, are not governed by this Convention.
3. Nothing in this article condones or makes lawful otherwise unlawful acts, nor precludes prosecution under other laws.' This text is reproduced in the UN Doc. A/57/37 (2002), at 17.
The provision proposed by the Coordinator corresponding to §1 speaks of 'the activities of armed forces during an armed conflict'. It would seem that the expression 'armed forces' must be taken to cover all the combatants of any party to the conflict, that is, not only the armed forces of states, but also the organized armed groups of rebels or insurgents or non-state groups or organizations. This view is also taken by the Milan Court of Assize in its judgment of 9 May 2005 in *Bouyahia Hamadi Ben Abdlaziz and others* (transcript, on file with the author, at 26).

'terrorist acts'. Nevertheless — and here comes the novelty — it is now added that those actions remain covered by other rules of international law (in particular, humanitarian law). It logically follows that, if such actions are contrary to those rules, their authors may be prosecuted under other relevant rules of international law. Translated into 'contemporary' terms, this means that, for instance, Palestinians' deliberate attacks on Israeli civilians in the West Bank (occupied territory), while they could not be termed as terrorist acts, would amount to war crimes, in particular to 'crimes the primary purpose of which is to spread terror among the civilian population'; their perpetrators would be liable to be punished under national and international law for such crimes. If this is so, it becomes clear that now the intent of Islamic states is simply to remove the label of 'terrorism' from any action of 'freedom fighters' contrary to international law. The fact remains, however, that even those states now concede — or, at least, it would seem so — that the authors of those actions may be prosecuted and punished for their criminal conduct. The diplomatic contention then boils down to an *essentially ideological dispute* over how to further term an act that is undisputedly criminal: as a *terrorist* act or as a *war crime* (intended to spread terror)? This difference in ideology and social psychology is not, however, the end of the matter. For, classifying an act as terrorist may trigger the use by the relevant national police of a set of investigative powers normally not authorized for any ordinary crime or for any war crime. It follows that, if agreement emerges on assigning acts performed by freedom fighters in armed conflict to the regulation of international humanitarian law alone, the whole range of investigative powers and consequent measures accruing to enforcement agencies may no longer be applied with regard to them.

Be that as it may, it bears stressing that a trend towards removing actions undertaken in armed conflict from the ambit of the legal regulation of terrorism and leaving such actions under the legal commands of humanitarian law can also be seen in Western countries. This is, for instance, apparent in both the Framework Decision of the EU on terrorism[48] and in a text supported by the Western group for inclusion in the Comprehensive Convention on Terrorism.[49]

48 §11 of the preamble of this Decision states that 'Actions by armed forces during periods of armed conflict, which are governed by international humanitarian law within the meaning of these terms under that law, and, inasmuch as they are governed by other rules of international law, actions by the armed forces of a State in the exercise of their official duties are not governed by this Framework Decision.'

49 Art. 18(2) of the draft proposed by the Coordinator of the UN Ad Hoc Committee established by GA Res. 51/210 (1996), to a large extent inspired by Western countries, stipulates that 'The activities of armed forces during an armed conflict, as those terms are understood under international humanitarian law, which are governed by that law, are not governed by this Convention.' (see UN Doc. A/57/37 (2002), at 17).
To my mind the expression 'armed forces' used in this provision should be construed liberally, as referring to all those groups of combatants that fight for each of the parties to the conflict. It, thus, also includes armed groups of rebels or organized groups fighting on behalf of a non-state entity opposing belligerent occupation.

A third, middle of the road position, has also emerged, which combines the application of international rules on terrorism with international humanitarian law. This view is enshrined in the UN Convention for the Suppression of the Financing of Terrorism[50] and is shared by 150 out of the 153 current parties to the Convention. The same view is laid down in Canadian legislation on terrorism[51] and has also been put forward by some Italian courts,[52] as well as the Israeli Foreign Minister.[53] It would seem plausible to contend that this stand is shared by the UN Secretary-General.[54] The supporters of this position hold that attacks by freedom fighters and other combatants in armed conflict, if directed at military personnel and objectives in keeping with international humanitarian law, are lawful and may not be termed terrorism. If instead they target civilians, they amount to terrorist acts (not, therefore, to war crimes)

50 See the text of Art. 2(1)(b) of this Convention reproduced *supra*, note 45.

51 Art. 83.01(1)(E) of the Canadian Criminal Code provides that terrorism 'does not include an act or omission that is committed during an armed conflict and that, at the time and in the place of its commission, is in accordance with customary international law or conventional international law applicable to the conflict, or the activities undertaken by military forces of a state in the exercise of their official duties, to the extent that those activities are governed by other rules of international law'.

52 See the decision of 24 January 2005 of the Milan Judge (*Giudice dell'Udienza Preliminare*) Clementina Forleo in the *Bouyahia Maher Ben Abdelaziz and others* case (transcript, on file with the author, at 52–64). The Judge held that the raising of funds and forging of documents by a group of Muslim foreigners in Milan in February–March 2003 was aimed at supporting guerrilla fighters in Iraq; however, the prosecution had been unable to prove that the activity of those who would have benefited in Iraq from the funds and the forged documents would carry out actions directed against civilians; hence the actions could not be classified as terrorist, for they were probably directed against military personnel or military objectives. See also the decision of the same judge, acting as *Giudice delle indagini preliminari*, delivered the same day, in *Drissi and Hamraqui* (typescript, at 9–13).
The same view was set out, even more clearly and with a more compelling legal reasoning, by the Milan Court of Assize, in its decision of 9 May 2005, *supra* note 47 (at 15–26 of the typescript) and by Appellate Court of Assizes, in its decision in the same case of 28 November 2005 (at 35–74 of the typescript of the decision). In contrast, other judges excluded the possibility of considering under certain conditions actions by organized groups as lawful if not aimed at attacking civilians. See, for instance, the decision of the Brescia *Giudice delle Indagini preliminari* in *Hamraoui and Drissi* (decision of 31 January 2005, at 12–16 of the typescript).

53 On 11 April 2006, Israeli Foreign Minister Tzipi Livni stated in an interview on US television network ABC that 'Somebody who is fighting against Israeli soldiers is an enemy and we fight back, but I believe that this [does] not [fall] under the definition, if the target is a soldier.' (http://news.yahoo.com/s/afp/20060411/wl_mideast_afp/mideastisraelpalestinianattack; visited 5 October 2006). In a later interview with Israeli public radio, Ms Livni, who is also justice minister, said that a distinction should be made between militants who attack soldiers and those who target civilians (*ibid.*).

54 In his aforementioned Report to the General Assembly, of 27 April 2006 (see *supra* note 4), the Secretary-General wrote the following: 'In order to constrict the pool of those who may resort to terrorism, we must make absolutely clear that no cause, no matter how just, can excuse terrorism. This includes the legitimate struggle of peoples for self-determination. Even this fundamental right defined in the Charter of the United Nations does not excuse deliberately killing or maiming civilians and non-combatants' (at § 10).

956 JICJ 4 (2006), 933–958

if their purpose is to terrorize civilians. Thus the conduct of hostilities is not left to the exclusive legal dominion of international humanitarian law. Principles and rules on terrorism reach out to armed conflict, in that they apply to acts that are not consonant with international humanitarian law.

C. *Major Implications of the Three Positions*

So far, no consensus has been attained in the international community on any of the three positions outlined above. However, it would seem that the second and third positions are broadly shared by many states. Current negotiations in New York at the UN on the Comprehensive Convention on terrorism show that the second position is gradually mustering increasing support. On the other hand, the third position is shared, as pointed out above, by the 150 States Parties to the Convention on the Financing of Terrorism which all support, at least with regard to the specific but important issue of financing of terrorism, the blending and simultaneous application of norms on terrorism and humanitarian law.

The difference between the two positions is fairly clear. The second position (that emerging in New York in the current negotiations) postulates a *rigid dichotomy* between two bodies of law (terrorism norms and humanitarian law) to the effect that in time of armed conflict terrorism norms stop applying and humanitarian law takes over. The third position is instead grounded on the notion that the two bodies of law can be *combined and applied simultaneously*.

As noted earlier, at first sight, there is no major difference in practical terms between the two positions. Attacks by belligerents (whether or not they are lawful combatants) on civilians or civilian objects in time of armed conflict (including in occupied territory) are in any case criminalized. They are criminalized either as *terrorist offences* or as *war crimes* (or even, whenever the aim of the attack was to spread terror, as war crimes of terror). There is however a two-fold difference. First, the extent of the powers of investigation and collection of evidence granted to criminal investigators is different. In the event of those offences being classified as acts of terrorism, those powers are much broader. Secondly, preparatory acts may be criminalized in the case of terrorism, which normally are not, if the actual offence amounts to a war crime. A good illustration of the last point may be found in the Italian case referred to above: according to Italian courts, the collection of funds and forging of documents in a place (*in casu*: Italy) other than that of perpetration (*in casu*: Iraq) are not terrorist acts when the beneficiaries of those acts are not planning or executing terrorist attacks on civilians in an armed conflict abroad; they are either common offences (forging of documents) or lawful acts (collecting funds). If, instead, the combatants at issue use the funds and documents to attack civilians, these attacks are terrorist and the financing and forging are classified as pertaining to terrorism, hence trigger the broader investigative power (and the heavier penalties) proper to terrorism.

Clearly, it follows from this argument that in contrast, were attacks on civilians in Iraq simply classified as war crimes, such preparatory acts as raising funds abroad would not be criminalized at all.

4. Summing up and Conclusion

I have tried above to distinguish between the current legal regulation of international terrorism that can be found in international law, and the political controversy underway on whether actions by some classes of individuals ('freedom fighters') engaged in armed conflict should constitute an exception to that definition.

My conclusion is that indeed international law defines and regulates international terrorism. International terrorism as a discrete international crime perpetrated *in time of peace* exhibits the following requisites: (i) is an action normally criminalized in national legal systems; (ii) is transnational in character, i.e. not limited in its action or implications to one country alone; (iii) is carried out for the purpose of coercing a state, or international organization to do or refrain from doing something; (iv) uses for this purpose two possible modalities: either spreading terror among civilians or attacking public or eminent private institutions or their representatives; and (v) is not motivated by personal gain but by ideological or political aspirations.

In time of peace, international terrorism may also exhibit the hallmarks of a crime against humanity. This happens when it is part of a widespread or systematic attack against civilians (although terrorist conduct as such may be taken against state officials or even combatants) and in addition takes the shape of certain categories of criminal conduct (murder, causing great suffering or serious injury to body or to mental or physical health, torture, rape or enforced disappearance).

In time of armed conflict, terrorism is criminalized when it consists of violent action (or even threat of such action) taken (i) against civilians or any other person not taking an active part in armed hostilities, and (ii) has as its primary purpose the spreading terror among the civilian population.

At present it is this legal classification relating to the use of terror in time of armed conflict that poses most problems at the political level and has indeed become the political albatross for final agreement on a treaty definition of terrorism. The classification is in fact *rejected* by some states (see *supra*, the reference to the first of the three political positions emerging in the international community on the matter). These states, while in fact opposing the application of some general and treaty rules of humanitarian law, do not propose any alternative to the simple violation of (or disregard for) existing law. Other states are, instead, prepared to accept that classification subject, however, to the condition that the same acts covered by international humanitarian law not also be classified as terrorism under general or treaty rules on terrorism (see *supra*, the reference to the second political stand, taken

958 *JICJ* **4** (2006), 933–958

by many states and other authorities), or be classified as such with a limited interference of rules on terrorism in time of peace (see *supra*, at § 9 the reference to the third position taken by states).

Time and the upshot of ongoing diplomatic negotiations will tell us which of these three stands will prevail. Admittedly scholars should not have a say on this matter. It is, however, warranted to suggest that the whole thrust of current international law would tip the balance in favour of the third position: it is the only stand that would fully safeguard the concerns of civilians while furthering the interest of a sweeping eradication of terror through criminalization of acts aimed at promoting and financing terrorist action. Let me add that one ought not to exclude that, on account of the current discussions on terrorist conduct by 'freedom fighters', the evolution of the legal regulation of terrorism in time of armed conflict might lead to the formation of a distinct category of *warlike terrorist acts*. In other words, a process could take place similar to that leading to the formation within the broad category of crimes against humanity, of the class of genocide. Genocide, initially a sub-category of crimes against humanity, gradually became a discrete class of international crimes, with distinct requisites different from those of the 'parent class' of crimes against humanity. Similarly, terrorism in time of armed conflict, currently a sub-category of war crimes, might gradually become a discrete class of international crimes as a result of the combined application of humanitarian law and general norms on terrorism.

[3]

Defining the International Public Enemy: The Political Struggle behind the Legal Debate on International Terrorism

JÖRG FRIEDRICHS*

Abstract

Who shall have the power to define international terrorism? To answer this question, which means determining the international public enemy, is an eminently political task. According to Carl Schmitt, politics is essentially about determining the public enemy. When it comes to a situation of emergency, whoever is in the position to distinguish friend from enemy holds ultimate power. While Schmitt was still thinking primarily in terms of the nation-state, the determination of the public enemy has now become an international issue. To demonstrate this point, this article examines the political struggle behind the legal debate on the definition of international terrorism. This is done by comparing two debates on international terrorism, one held in the 1970s and the other in the 2000s. Both these debates had, and still have, their institutional locus in the UN General Assembly and its Legal Committee. In the 1970s the non-aligned countries tried to challenge the discretion of the West in determining the international public enemy. In the 2000s the incumbent regimes of the Third World agree with Western states that terrorism is a common threat. The main cleavage is now between the leading Western powers that would like to determine the public enemy on a case-by-case basis (the United States and the United Kingdom), and the status quo states that would like to tie these hegemonic powers by a legal definition. It is precisely the absence of such a legal definition that makes it possible for the hegemonic powers and their followers to determine the international public enemy on a case-by-case basis. A legal definition would increase the coherence of the international coalition against terrorism and serve as a limitation on the discretionary power of the hegemonic states.

Key words

Carl Schmitt; Comprehensive Convention on International Terrorism; definition of terrorism; terrorism; United Nations

Who shall have the power to define terrorism? Who will distinguish it from other forms of political violence? Who is going to tell a terrorist from a freedom fighter?

To answer these questions is an eminently political task. It is tantamount to deciding who is with 'us' and who is against 'us', or in other words it means

---

* Research Associate, School of Humanities and Social Sciences, International University Bremen, j.friedrichs@iu-bremen.de. Research on this article was carried out in a project on the internationalization of the monopoly of the legitimate use of force, within a collaborative research centre on the transformation of statehood. The research project is based at the International University Bremen, Germany, and is directed by Markus Jachtenfuchs. Funding by the Deutsche Forschungsgemeinschaft is gratefully acknowledged. Thanks are due to those who have collaborated on empirical research: Eva Herschinger, Christiane Kasack, Holger Stritzel, and Dana Trif; to those who have provided valuable comments: Alessandro Colombo, Bibi van Ginkel, and the anonymous reviewers of the *Leiden Journal of International Law*; and above all to Raphael Muturi for having contributed to an earlier version of the paper.

determining the international public enemy. According to Carl Schmitt, 'The specific political distinction to which political actions and motives can be reduced is that between friend and enemy'.[1] The person, group or institution that has the authority to draw this distinction holds the key to sovereign power. Writing in the early 1930s, Schmitt was thinking primarily about the nation-state of his time and its leaders. But the moment has come to apply Schmitt's ideas to the international realm, given the fact that the determination of the international public enemy (read 'terrorist'), whether by definition or on a case-by-case basis, is a matter of worldwide concern.

It is precisely the absence of a legal definition of terrorism that makes it possible for the hegemonic power (read 'United States') and its followers to determine the international public enemy on a case-by-case basis. A legal definition would serve as a limitation to this discretional power. Especially from the viewpoint of those continental European states that do not share the US approach to the 'war on terror', it would be highly desirable if international law became a restraint on the power of the Anglo-Saxon hegemon.

On the surface, the definition of terrorism may be a matter of debate among legal experts in bodies such as the Sixth Committee of the UN General Assembly, the International Law Commission, or the International Law Association. But as soon as one looks behind the technicalities of these reputedly legal debates, it becomes clear that the problem is at the centre of a political maelstrom. Moreover, experience has shown that, as long as states do not agree on who the international public enemy is, it does not help very much to vest the problem in a legal cloak. In the present article I will therefore try to examine the political struggle behind the legal debate on international terrorism.

The first section starts with a general overview of the efforts undertaken at the UN against international terrorism, followed by a brief outline of the two debates as they unfolded in the 1970s and again in the 2000s. In the second section I compare the positions taken by the four major European powers (Britain, France, Germany, and Italy) in either debate. On this basis, the third section analyses the political struggle that is lying behind the legal debate on international terrorism. This leads me, in the conclusion, to the formulation of some policy suggestions. The suggestions are particularly, but not exclusively, directed to the conservative states representing 'old Europe'.

1. The UN and international terrorism

After a series of terrorist attacks in 1972, most prominently on the Olympic village in Munich, the quest for a common understanding of international terrorism took centre stage at the UN, namely the General Assembly and its Legal Committee. It soon became apparent that due to profound political disagreements no consensus

---

1. C. Schmitt, *Der Begriff des Politischen* (1932), translated by G. Schwab under the title *The Concept of the Political* (1996), 26.

could be reached. During the 1980s and 1990s the quest for a common understanding of international terrorism was therefore left aside, and a more pragmatic approach held sway. Over the last few decades, this approach has led to more than a dozen conventions against particular manifestations of international terrorism. Nevertheless, in the absence of an overarching legal framework these conventions do not agglomerate into a coherent whole. While affording some help in dealing with international terrorism, they do not provide guidance on how to tackle the threat of new kinds of violence against innocent victims. It is therefore not surprising that the quest for a common understanding of terrorism has returned to the agenda of the United Nations.[2]

In international as well as in domestic politics, the fight against terrorism tends to follow the 'politics of the latest outrage'.[3] Domestic laws and international conventions are mostly discussed, and eventually agreed upon, after major events. This pattern can be detected from the very first and inconclusive attempt to set up a comprehensive convention on international terrorism. That attempt was undertaken by the League of Nations between 1934 and 1937, after the assassination of the Yugoslav King Alexander and the French foreign minister.[4] The same pattern could again be observed in the 1970s. After a series of terrorist attacks in the early 1970s, international terrorism became a topic on the UN agenda. Eventually the debate ended in failure, in 1979. Another round of the debate is now under way. It had a difficult start in 2000. After the outrage of 11 September 2001, the debate started to become more lively. But although there has been considerable progress in recent years no final agreement has yet been reached on the legal project of a comprehensive anti-terrorist convention.

It is cold comfort that there are by now more than a dozen UN conventions against particular manifestations of terrorism such as skyjacking, assaults on diplomats, hostage taking, and so forth. Despite the obvious usefulness of these instruments, they do not lead significantly closer to a shared understanding of the problem. In most cases the word 'terrorism' is not even used, let alone defined, in these instruments. This is unfortunate, since the lack of consensus about the political and legal boundaries of the phenomenon can undermine international coalitions. The predetermined breaking point for any anti-terrorist coalition is disagreement about the essence of the phenomenon. Ever since decolonization, there has been disagreement as to whether international terrorism covers activities by national liberation movements on the one hand, and certain acts of state-committed and state-sponsored political violence on the other. In the 1970s, states such as Algeria, Libya, and Syria struggled to exempt national liberation movements from the definition of terrorism. At least in part, this is still true after the terrorist attacks on the World Trade Center of 11 September 2001. For example, there is still some disagreement

2. M. J. Peterson, 'Using the General Assembly', in J. Boulden and T. G. Weiss (eds.), *Terrorism and the UN: Before and After September 11* (2004), 173.
3. P. Wilkinson, *Terrorism Versus Democracy: The Liberal State Response* (2000), 197.
4. M. D. Dubin, *International Terrorism: Two League of Nations Conventions* (1991).

as to whether the violent actors in Palestine and Chechnya are terrorists or, rather, freedom fighters.

1.1. The first debate (1972–9)

In September 1972, when the world was outraged by the terrorist attacks on the Olympic village in Munich, West Germany was not yet a member of the United Nations. Israel, as the country representing the victims, did not refer the issue to the Security Council. UN Secretary-General Kurt Waldheim, however, placed international terrorism on the agenda of the General Assembly. The initiative was welcomed by a majority of Western countries including West Germany, Israel, and the United States, while most Arab and African countries had serious misgivings.[5]

Only a few days after the initiative of the Secretary-General, the United States submitted a draft Convention for the Prevention and Punishment of Certain Acts of International Terrorism.[6] The US draft was explicitly and deliberately limited to certain acts of international terrorism and did not suggest any legal definition of the phenomenon. It was clearly not intended to provide a comprehensive convention on terrorism. Nevertheless, the US initiative faced stout opposition from the Non-Aligned Group, spearheaded by Algeria. Many Arab and African countries argued that it would be appropriate first to discuss the root causes of terrorism before suggesting repressive measures. Moreover the non-aligned countries, many of which were themselves the offspring of national liberation movements, suspected that the US draft was intended to outlaw their brethren fighting against colonialism and oppression. Against this, the non-aligned countries maintained that 'state terrorism' was actually the most harmful and deadly form of terrorism. These allegations were not very much to the point if one considers the letter of the US draft, which took a relatively moderate and pragmatic stance. But whether justified or not, the fierce opposition of the non-aligned phalanx ultimately scuttled the US draft in the General Assembly.[7]

Instead of the US draft, at the instigation of Algeria and other states of the Non-Aligned Group (and against the vote of the United States) the General Assembly adopted a resolution to establish an Ad Hoc Committee on International Terrorism.[8] Despite the affinity of this resolution with the requests of the non-aligned states, the United States and many other Western countries nevertheless were ready to engage in the deliberations of the Ad Hoc Committee on International Terrorism. As could have been expected, its main problem was to find a common understanding of international terrorism. At its first round of meetings in 1973, the Ad Hoc Committee

5. Italian Diplomatic Archives, *Telegrams to and from New York* (1972).
6. UN Doc. A/C.6/L.850 (25 Sept. 1972): draft convention.
7. Department of State, 'U.S. Votes against U.N. General Assembly Resolution Calling for Study of Terrorism', *Department of State Bulletin*, 22 Jan. 1973, 81; L. Hoffacker, 'The U.S. Government Response to Terrorism: A Global Approach', in M. Cherif Bassiouni (ed.), *International Terrorism and Political Crimes* (1975), 537; E. N. Evans, 'American Policy Response to International Terrorism: Problems of Deterrence', in M. H. Livingston (ed.), *International Terrorism in the Contemporary World* (1978), 376.
8. UN Doc. A/RES/3034 (18 Dec. 1972): GA resolution.

did not reach any substantive consensus on the definition of international terrorism and could only restate 'the diversity of existing views on the various aspects of the subject submitted for consideration'.[9] Although the Ad Hoc Committee was reconvened in 1977 and 1979, it finally had to be suspended without any tangible results due to a blatant lack of political consensus.[10]

Disagreement among the states represented on the Ad Hoc Committee started with the apparently innocuous question of if and when concrete measures should be taken against international terrorism. The non-aligned states held that first it was necessary to study the underlying causes of terrorism, and that only after understanding the legitimate reasons behind the grievances raised by international terrorists would it make sense to take practical steps. In this spirit, the Algerian delegation not only pinpointed certain root causes of international terrorism, but also suggested that terrorism sometimes could be justified. 'Violence becomes terrorism, when situations which lead to violence are exacerbated.'[11] Terrorism was considered as the inevitable consequence of fundamental freedoms being violated, and accordingly was a cause for sympathy rather than retribution. Against these and similar arguments, the United States and other Western states protested that in their domestic legislation states did not wait for the underlying causes of crime to be identified before enacting penal laws against criminals.[12]

Another bone of contention was whether international terrorism had to be condemned regardless of motive, or whether certain causes such as national emancipation struggles could justify the political use of violent means. Again, on behalf of the Non-Aligned Group the Algerian delegation was very outspoken on that point: a distinction should be made between 'heinous terrorism' and 'terrorism that was political in origin and purpose'.[13] The Western response was somewhat ambiguous. On the one hand, most delegations were paying lip service to the 'legitimate' claims of national liberation movements. On the other hand, they insisted that the end could never justify the means; that is, violence against innocent people could not be condoned under any circumstances.[14]

Finally, the Non-Aligned Group was adamant on the inclusion of state terrorism under the Ad Hoc Committee's mandate. Acts of violence by colonial, racist,

9. UN Doc. A/9028 (1973): report of the Ad Hoc Committee.
10. UN Docs. A/32/37 (28 April 1977); A/34/37 (17 April 1979); A/AC.160/SR.11–19 (1979): reports and summary records of the Ad Hoc Committee. See also T. M. Franck and B. B. Lockwood, 'Preliminary Thoughts towards an International Convention on Terrorism', (1974) 68 (1) AJIL 69; J. Dugard, 'International Terrorism: Problems of Definition', (1974) 50 (1) *International Affairs* 67; J. Dugard, 'International Terrorism and the Just War', in D. C. Rapoport and Y. Alexander (eds.), *The Morality of Terrorism: Religious and Secular Justifications* (1982), 77; F. Hoveyda, 'The Problem of International Terrorism at the United Nations', (1977) 1 (1) *Terrorism: An International Journal* 71; G. Levitt, 'Is "Terrorism" Worth Defining?', (1986) 13 *Ohio Northern University Law Review* 97; J. F. Murphy, 'United Nations Proposals on the Control and Repression of Terrorism', in Bassiouni, *supra* note 7, at 493; J. F. Murphy, 'Defining International Terrorism: A Way Out of the Quagmire', in *Israel Yearbook on Human Rights 19* (1989), 13; J. Toman, 'Developing an International Policy Against Terrorism', in S. Flood (ed.), *International Terrorism: Policy Implications* (1991), 111.
11. UN Doc. A/9028 (1973): report of the Ad Hoc Committee, annex 7b.
12. UN Doc. A/C.6/SR.1355–1374 (November 1972): verbatim records of the Sixth Committee.
13. UN Doc. A/32/37 (28 April 1977): report of the Ad Hoc Committee, 14.
14. UN Docs. A/AC.160/1 (16 May 1973); A/AC.160/1/Add.1 (12 June 1973); A/AC.160/2 (22 June 1973): observations of states and analytical study by the Secretary-General.

and alien regimes, they maintained, constituted 'the cruellest and most pernicious form' of international terrorism and therefore had to be given the highest priority during the deliberations.[15] Against this, Western states insisted that in international law there already existed appropriate provisions to restrain state violence, for example the Geneva conventions and the convention against genocide. While rejecting the inclusion of state-perpetrated terrorism, however, some Western states paradoxically supported the inclusion of state-supported terrorism under the convention. To cover up these and similar inconsistencies, some Western states (most prominently the United States and the United Kingdom) opposed a definition of terrorism as being counter-productive and called for practical measures instead.

1.2. The second debate (2000–5)

The debate in the 1970s was the last serious attempt to reach a common understanding of international terrorism for many years to come. Only in January 1997 did the General Assembly again establish an Ad Hoc Committee on International Terrorism.[16] The committee, which is supported by a Working Group, has the mandate of drafting appropriate instruments against international terrorism. The Ad Hoc Committee and the Working Group meet once a year, in spring and autumn respectively. Late in 1999, the General Assembly called upon the Ad Hoc Committee and the Working Group to deal with a comprehensive convention on international terrorism.[17] Since 2000, discussions have been taking place on the basis of a draft submitted by India.[18]

Already in 1999 the United Nations had adopted a convention on the financing of terrorism. This convention contains, for the first time, an embryonic definition. Building on this precedent, Article 2 of the Draft Comprehensive Convention on International Terrorism in its present version contains a relatively broad definition of international terrorism. According to this definition, serious offences against persons or heavy damage to private or public property qualify as offences within the meaning of the Convention 'when the purpose of the conduct, by its nature or context, is to intimidate a population, or to compel a Government or an international organization to do or abstain from doing any act'.[19] Although the word

15. UN Doc. A/32/37 (28 April 1977): report of the Ad Hoc Committee, at 14.
16. UN Doc. A/RES/51/210 (16 Jan. 1997): GA resolution. This is an exception to the rule that debates on terrorism follow major events. Already in the second half of the 1980s and the first half of the 1990s, there had been inconclusive attempts by some states of the Third World, namely Syria and Algeria, to revitalize the item in the General Assembly. B. T. van Ginkel, 'The United Nations: Towards a Comprehensive Convention on Combating Terrorism', in M. van Leeuwen (ed.), *Confronting Terrorism: European Experiences, Threat Perceptions and Policies* (2003), 207, at 214–16. In 1996/1997 the return of the issue to the agenda of the Sixth Committee was provoked by discussions about whether or not to include terrorism in the mandate of the International Criminal Court. In 1998 the terrorist attacks on the US embassies in Nairobi and Dar es Salaam may have played a catalytic role in convincing member states of the urgency of the problem.
17. UN Doc. A/RES/54/110 (2 Feb. 2000): GA resolution.
18. UN Doc. A/C.6/55/1 (28 Aug. 2000): revised draft convention; cf. UN Doc. A/C.6/51/6 (11 Nov. 1996): original version.
19. UN Doc. A/59/894 (12 Aug. 2005): letter containing Draft Comprehensive Convention on International Terrorism, 9.

'terrorism' is used only in the title and in the preamble of the draft, the definition in Article 2 is clearly meant to be a definition of international terrorism. It would be a decisive breakthrough for international law if the UN were to succeed in writing a legal definition of international terrorism into the comprehensive convention.

Initially the bargaining positions were similar to those familiar from the 1970s. Thus many Third World states insisted that terrorism be clearly distinguished from acts of legitimate self-defence by national liberation movements.[20] Most notably, the 56 members of the Organization of the Islamic Conference (OIC) demanded the exemption of national liberation movements from the reach of the convention.[21] 'People's struggle including armed struggle against foreign occupation, aggression, colonialism, and hegemony, aimed at liberation and self-determination in accordance with the principles of international law shall not be considered a terrorist crime'.[22] The countries of the OIC were calling for a binding legal definition of international terrorism along these lines, which was rejected by the majority of Western countries.

Despite these apparent continuities, on closer examination it turns out that there is a significant departure from the traditional view of Arab countries that state terrorism is the most harmful and deadly form of terrorism and therefore must fall under a comprehensive convention on international terrorism. Of course this view was initially brought to the negotiation table and is still being reiterated in certain contexts, especially with hindsight to Israel.[23] But the exclusion of state terrorism has now become negotiable under the condition that political violence by liberation movements be exempted as well. Thus in January 2002 the OIC group rejected a proposal to exempt the activities of armed forces during an armed conflict. According to the OIC, the exemption of state terrorism is acceptable but should be expanded to cover all parties during an armed conflict, whether regular forces or national liberation movements.[24] The discussions are still going on, and according to the reports issued over the last five years some substantial progress has been made. However, the decisive breakthrough has still not occurred.[25]

The most important bone of contention has been draft Article 18 (now Art. 20), of which there were two versions on the table. The so-called version of the co-ordinator was very clear in the exemption of the 'activities of armed forces', but it remained a bit nebulous as to whether this would cover the activities of parties to a conflict other than regular troops. To avoid this kind of ambiguity, the alternative version of the OIC asserted that 'the parties during an armed conflict, including in situations

20. UN Doc. GA/L/3008 (4 Oct. 1996): press release.
21. OIC Resolution No. 64/27-P (June 2000).
22. Malaysia on behalf of the OIC Group, in UN Doc. A/C.6/55/L.2 (19 Oct. 2000): report of the Working Group, 38.
23. E.g. UN Doc. A/57/730-S/2003/178 (13 Feb. 2003): verbal note by Syria.
24. L/2993 (1 Feb. 2002): press release.
25. Reports of the Ad Hoc Committee: UN Docs. A/56/37 (27 April 2001); A/57/37 (21 Feb. 2002); A/58/37 (25 April 2003); A/59/37 (22 July 2004); A/60/37 (18 May 2005). Reports of the Working Group: UN Docs. A/C.6/55/L.2 (19 Oct. 2000); A/C.6/56/L.9 (29 Oct. 2001); A/C.6/57/L.9 (16 Oct. 2002); A/C.6/58/L.10 (10 Oct. 2003); A/C.6/59/L.10 (8 Oct. 2004); A/C.6/60/L.6 (14 Oct. 2005).

of foreign occupation', were to be exempt from the provisions of the convention.[26] At least in situations of armed conflict, this would have led to an explicit exemption of both state terrorism and national liberation movements from the remit of the comprehensive convention. For the members of the OIC, maintaining the distinction between freedom fighters and terrorists was a strategic objective that superseded earlier efforts at delegitimizing so-called state terrorism. Due to the uncompromising stance of both sides, the two conflicting versions of Article 18 (recently renamed as Article 20, and complemented by a new preambulary paragraph) were still the main problem after a consolidated version of the draft was transmitted, in August 2005, to the 60th General Assembly of the United Nations.[27]

Another interesting development could be observed with regard to the traditional claim that before taking specific measures it is necessary to study the underlying causes of international terrorism. While an OIC resolution from 2000 still alluded to the 'underlying causes' argument,[28] and while the Islamic states periodically repeat this argument and demand a high-level conference to discuss the problems connected with international terrorism, the question of the causes underlying terrorism no longer seems to pose any serious obstacle to the conclusion of a comprehensive convention.

A recent report has made explicit another concern that was looming over the last few years: 'A point was made against the unilateral practices of certain States which were considered contrary to the norms of international law and to the purposes and principles of the Charter of the United Nations'. While there is no explicit naming of these 'certain States', it is remarkable in itself to find this articulation of uneasiness with the conduct of the 'war on terror' in an official UN document.[29]

All these difficulties notwithstanding, there seems to be considerable progress in comparison with the situation in the 1970s. However, this is not to deny that the discussions illustrate once more how difficult it is to agree on the conceptual boundaries of terrorism, let alone reach a legal definition of the term. In the first weeks after 11 September, a breakthrough seemed in sight. But although disagreement could quickly be limited to only one article (Article 18 on the exemption of state terrorism and/or national liberation movements, in combination with Article 2 on the legal definition of international terrorism), the attempt to reach a comprehensive convention was weakened once more by the mutually exclusive claims of certain Western countries and certain states of the Third World.[30]

After the terrorist attacks in London in July 2005, Washington and London suddenly tried to break free from deadlock and joined the Secretary-General in

26. UN Doc. A/57/37 (11 Feb. 2002): report of the Ad Hoc Committee, 17.
27. UN Doc. A/59/894 (12 Aug. 2005): letter containing Draft Comprehensive Convention on International Terrorism; cf. A/C.6/60/L.6 (14 Oct. 2005): report of the Working Group; for the predictably negative OIC reaction see UN Docs. A/C.6/60/3 (5 Oct. 2005) and A/C.6/60/SR.3 (24 Oct. 2005), 6; for recent amendments proposed by the Friends of the Chairman see UN Docs. A/C.6/60/INF/1 (20 Oct 2005); A/C.6/INF/2 (20 Oct. 2005); A/C.6/60/SR.10 (31 Oct. 2005).
28. OIC Resolution No. 64/27-P (June 2000); a more recent formulation of the OIC position can be found in UN Doc. A/60/440-S/2005/658 (19 Oct. 2005), 15.
29. UN Doc. A/59/37 (2 July 2004): report of the Ad Hoc Committee, 6.
30. K. Wiesbrock, 'Wer ist Terrorist?', (2002) 50 (2) *Vereinte Nationen* 72.

calling for an instant solution to the problem of defining terrorism.[31] The plan was to condemn terrorism in all its manifestations, amounting to the 'deliberate and unlawful targeting and killing' of civilians, since this could not be 'justified or legitimised by any cause or grievance'.[32] This would have included attacks on civilians by national liberation movements. In the absence of an exemption for national liberation movements, however, it is hardly surprising that the attempt to reach a breakthrough at the UN's 60th anniversary meeting in September 2005 failed due to the resistance of the Arab and Middle Eastern countries that were wary of the Palestinian liberation struggle being outlawed.[33]

Despite the inevitable failure of this manoeuvre, at the time of writing, in December 2005, the attempt to conclude a comprehensive convention on international terrorism is being passed to the 61st UN Plenary Assembly in 2006. After more than five years, it will be necessary either to abandon the project of a comprehensive convention altogether, or to compromise on the pending issue of an exemption clause for liberation movements.

1.3. Change and continuities

Cynics stick with great relish to the cliché that 'your' terrorist may be 'my' freedom fighter. And indeed, if one looks at the debate held in the 1970s about international terrorism, this does not seem to be far off the mark. States tended to favour those concepts of terrorism that subsumed their political enemies, while opposing concepts that might have stigmatized their political friends. Since it was impossible to reach agreement on these and similar issues, the international community had to limit itself to conventions against particular manifestations of terrorism. The word 'terrorism' normally did not even appear in the main text of these sector-specific conventions, although it was sometimes used in the title and preamble. In none of these early conventions was there any explicit attempt to define terrorism. The focus was on specific criminal acts, and the political intent of the perpetrators was set aside. Thereby it was possible to avoid conflicts over basic definitional principles, permitting textual agreement to be reached.

Although it should be appreciated that the 'piecemeal' approach has slowly contributed, by way of induction, to the emergence of a common understanding of terrorism, the fundamental legal and political problem remains unsolved. While new categories of conduct are always subject to coverage in subsequent instruments, the international fight against terrorism remains inherently reactive and potentially controversial. A comprehensive approach to international terrorism is therefore still an important desideratum.

---

31. 'World Leaders Seek Terror Definition', *New York Sun*, 8 July 2005; State Department Press Release, 20 July 2005, 'United States Urges Completion of Terrorism Convention'.
32. The US and British initiative was in part prepared by Security Council resolution UN Doc. S/2000/792 (8 Oct. 2004) and, in particular, by the elements for a definition suggested in the report of the High-Level Panel on Threats, Challenges and Change: UN Doc. A/59/565 (2 Dec. 2004), 49.
33. 'UN Struggles to Agree on Definition of Terrorism', Agence France-Presse, 12 Sept. 2005; 'The Obstacles that Block the Way to a Watertight Definition of Terrorism', *Herald*, 17 Sept. 2005; 'A Reckless Salesman: Blair's Approach to Terrorism Will Not Suit All Members', *Financial Times*, 19 Sept. 2005. Cf. A/RES/60/1 (24 Oct. 2005), 22.

After an interruption lasting more than twenty years there now exists another attempt to reach a common understanding of international terrorism. It seems that positions are much less erratic now than they were in the 1970s. Despite the inconclusive attempt to reach a consensus in the immediate aftermath of 11 September (and again after the London terrorist attacks in July 2005), it should be appreciated that the Islamic countries are less adamant now than was the Non-Aligned Group in the 1970s. Whereas the Non-Aligned Group categorically demanded the inclusion of state terrorism in the definition of terrorism, the OIC group has come to accept its exemption. Moreover, the members of the OIC group are no longer making the drawing up of a comprehensive convention conditional on a study of the underlying causes. However, they are still adamant on the exemption of all parties during an armed conflict, 'including in situations of foreign occupation'. This is the last substantive obstacle to an agreement on the legal definition of international terrorism, and thereby to the conclusion of a comprehensive convention.[34]

It is sometimes maintained that 11 September has completely changed the terms of the debate on terrorism. But this is at best a half-truth. Although the political context of the debate has changed considerably, the debate in the 2000s seems to reproduce many arguments that are familiar from the 1970s.[35] There are both continuities and change. While some familiar arguments are still assiduously repeated, other important cleavages from the 1970s are obsolete.

This can be explained by a number of contextual differences and similarities underlying the two debates. The most important factor concerns power and ideology, namely the question of who defends and who challenges the political status quo. In the 1970s, the Western states played the role of status quo powers challenged by the Third World, with the communist bloc somewhere in between.[36] The maintenance of political violence used by national liberation movements in general, and by the Palestine Liberation Organization (PLO) in particular, was in the real or perceived interest of many Third World regimes.[37] Therefore these regimes demanded the exemption of national liberation movements from the definition of international terrorism, and called for the inclusion of state terrorism instead; moreover, they asked that the causes of terrorism be analysed prior to measures being taken against it. Unsurprisingly the Western status quo powers were not willing to accommodate the claims of the Non-Aligned Group, and the quest for a common understanding of international terrorism was doomed to failure.

By the 2000s the situation has changed significantly. There are still many European and Asian powers interested in the status quo, but the Third World movement is

34. Rowe in UN Doc. A/C.6/57/L.9 (16 Oct. 2002): report of the Working Group, Annex ii.

35. Cf. Ginkel, *supra* note 16; C. Walter, 'Defining Terrorism in National and International Law', in C. Walter, S. Vöneky, V. Röben, et al. (eds.), *Terrorism as a Challenge for National and International Law: Security versus Liberty?* (2004), 23.

36. V. Abellán Honrubia, 'El terrorismo internacional', (1975) 28 *Revista Española de Derecho Internacional* 33; S. J. Rosen and R. Frank, 'Measures against International Terrorism', in D. Carlton and C. Schaerf (eds.), *International Terrorism and World Society* (1975), 60; I. Blishchenko and N. Zhdanov, *Terrorism and International Law* (1984), 208–31.

37. L. Migliorino, 'International Terrorism in the United Nations Debates', in *Italian Yearbook of International Law* (1976), II, 102; L. Migliorino, 'Il terrorismo internazionale nei dibattiti alle Nazioni Unite', in L. Bonanate (ed.), *Dimensioni del Terrorismo Politico: Aspetti Interni e Internazionali, Politici e Giuridici* (1979), 255.

virtually dead. The Arab and Muslim states are losing ground at the regional and global level. Accordingly their stance has become more defensive, and their demands more moderate. As we have seen, they have come to accept the exemption of state terrorism from the reach of the convention, and they have dropped their claim that the causes of terrorism must be analysed prior to taking practical measures (while still asking for the exemption of all parties during an armed conflict, 'including in situations of foreign occupation'). Since this is not too far from what many Western states are demanding, one would expect that an agreement on some sort of compromise should be possible. Such a coming together of occidental and oriental countries could be greatly facilitated by the fact that Islamic terrorists are the enemies not only of Western civilization, but of the incumbent regimes in the Muslim world as well.

The crux, however, is that in the 2000s the United States no longer behaves like a status quo power. Mainly under the banner of the 'war against terrorism', the United States is projecting its own power all over the world. In Afghanistan the United States has created a situation of foreign occupation and has become party to an armed conflict. Together with a small number of other states, the United States has furthermore occupied Iraq and thereby created a fait accompli in the Gulf region. In such a situation, it has clear advantages for the hegemonic power to determine on a case-by-case basis who is a terrorist and who is not. For example, it is difficult to imagine that the United States will deny itself the possibility of stigmatizing its political opponents in Afghanistan and Iraq as 'terrorists'.

As long as this situation persists, the United States can hardly accept the OIC version of the exemption clause in the Draft Comprehensive Convention, which exempts all parties to an armed conflict, 'including in situations of foreign occupation'. Or, in other words, for the comprehensive convention on international terrorism to be concluded, the United States would have to accept or at least to respect sovereign equality again.

2. The positions of the major European states

Let us now consider the positions of the major European states. The analysis is limited to the largest and most important west European countries: France, Germany, Italy, and the United Kingdom. For the sake of comparison, the analysis covers only the three most controversial topics that were debated during both periods: (i) the quest for a definition of international terrorism; (ii) the need to study its underlying causes; and (iii) the inclusion or exclusion of national liberation movements. A careful comparative analysis of the political preferences of these four European countries will shed further light on the political struggle underlying the legal debate on international terrorism.

2.1. The first debate (1972–9)

When the new item was placed on the UN agenda in September 1972, all Western countries welcomed the initiative. However, after the topic was used by the non-aligned countries for propaganda purposes, reactions differed.

Against all odds,[38] the United Kingdom was initially very interested in the topic. The main reason was that a strong condemnation of terrorism would have helped to criminalize external support for the IRA (Irish Republican Army) in Northern Ireland. As one official in the Foreign Office put it, the objective was to have 'a periodic stick with which to beat the Irish Government'. On the other hand, Britain did not want to jeopardize its relationships with the Arab world. Accordingly, the Egyptian foreign minister was reassured that the United Kingdom wanted terrorism to be dealt with as an international problem and not as particular Arab problem. At the same time, Britain was careful not to provoke international debate on the 'underlying causes' of terrorism in Northern Ireland. The objective was rather to demonstrate the lack of effective action by the Republic of Ireland against IRA cross-border terrorist activity. Furthermore, there were clear normative limits to Britain's readiness to accept special treatment for national liberation movements: 'Freedom fighting with propaganda is one thing; with bombs another'.[39]

In any case, Britain's flirtation with the topic completely evaporated when the non-aligned countries started using the UN as a propaganda platform. From then on, the United Kingdom worked for a 'decent burial' of the item.[40] Britain torpedoed all attempts by the Non-Aligned Group to exclude national liberation movements from the definition of international terrorism and to include state terrorism instead. The bottom line of the British position was that 'the main immediate objective should be to devise concrete, agreed measures to prevent senseless acts of violence which maimed or killed innocent victims'.[41] At this point Britain opposed a formal definition of international terrorism altogether, and preferred defining the international public enemy on an ad hoc basis. The study of underlying causes, important as this might be, should not be allowed to hamper the adoption of immediate measures. The United Kingdom maintained this pragmatic approach, according to which it was better to devise conventions against specific manifestations of international terrorism than to insist on the ambitious objective of a comprehensive convention, until the debate was ended in 1979.[42]

The French case is interesting because Paris considered international terrorism to be a moral ill and agreed with the non-aligned countries that the problem should

38. In the 1930s the United Kingdom had been unenthusiastic about, if not highly critical of, plans for a comprehensive convention against international terrorism. British National Archives, *Terrorism: Committee for International Repression* (1937), CO 323/1466/11; *Diplomatic Conference, November 1937: Correspondence, Reservations on Particular Provisions of the Terrorism Convention* (1937), HO 189/7; *Convention for the Prevention and Punishment of Terrorism and Convention for the Establishment of International Criminal Court: Draft Report* (1937), HO 189/8.

39. British National Archives, *Motion for Recommendation on International Terrorism* (1972), FCO 41/938; *Reports of the 6th Committee at 27th United Nations General Assembly* (1972), FCO 58/667; *Measures to Combat Terrorism Including Hijacking* (1972), FCO 14/1078. The quotations are from *Motion for Recommendation on International Terrorism* (undated document) and *Measures to Combat Terrorism Including Hijacking* (19 Oct. 1972); see also Freeland in UN Docs. A/C.6/SR.1359 (15 Nov. 1972) and A/C.6/SR.1390 (11 Dec. 1972).

40. British National Archives, *Measures to Combat Terrorism* (1973), FCO 76/633.

41. Freeland in UN Doc. A/C.6/SR.1310 (25 Sept. 1972).

42. Douglas-Home in UN Doc. A/PV.2042 (27 Sept. 1972); Crowe in UN Doc. A/PV.2114 (18 Dec. 1972); cf. UN Docs. A/AC.160/1 (16 May 1973), A/9028 (1973), 28; Fifoot in UN Docs. A/C.6/SR.1581 (4 Dec. 1975), A/32/37 (28 April 1977), 33–34, A/C.6/32/SR.58 (29 Nov. 1977), A/AC.160/SR.15 (28 March 1979); cf. UN Doc. A/34/37 (17 April 1979), 26–27. Britain took a similar position at the Council of Europe: British National Archives, *Council of Europe: Consultative Assembly Recommendation 684 on International Terrorism* (1973), FCO 41/1085.

be legally defined.[43] On such normative grounds the French Ministry of Justice submitted a proposal for the definition of terrorism.[44] France had also suggested to the Secretary-General that the agenda item should be amended to 'international terrorism', adding a qualifying epithet and thereby assuaging the concerns of some African and Arab delegations.[45] Although it is difficult to imagine that France would have accepted measures that would have seriously infringed national sovereignty, Paris saw it as a moral duty vis-à-vis the international community to bridge the gap between extreme positions and help find an adequate legal response.

Unlike its fellow Western democracies France believed in the moral axiom that 'the phenomenon of terrorism could not be dealt with unless its causes were eliminated'.[46] Moreover, France was apparently convinced that a legal definition of terrorism was the best way to legitimize the international fight against terrorism. Only on the exclusion of national liberation movement from the definition of terrorism was the French delegate a little more hesitant, although not entirely opposed.[47] The insistence on the underlying causes of terrorism was probably a tribute to the former French colonies. France had a national interest in maintaining a large sphere of influence in the Third World, most notably in the Arab countries, and an accommodating stance on terrorism furthered this interest.

In any event, France shared the conviction of many states that the fight against terrorism needed the support of all countries, that is, had to be universal in order to be effective. Paris believed that international interests would be best served by a universal agreement and that there was no reasonable alternative to the UN as the legitimate geographical framework. Accordingly, France insisted that the UN, rather than the European Economic Community (EEC) or the Council of Europe, was the proper place to devise a comprehensive strategy against terrorism.[48] It was relatively safe for France to take such a conciliatory stance, since the Ad Hoc Committee was used as a talking shop by the newly independent countries of the Third World. This situation engendered so much disagreement that the debate was never going to reach the point where a serious commitment would have become necessary.

---

43. French Diplomatic Archives, *Note pour la Direction des Nations Unies et Organisations Internationales: Terrorisme international, 19 juin 1973*, in NUOI 1409: 1970–1973; d'Haussy in UN Doc. A/32/37 (28 April 1977), 20; cf. UN Doc. A/9028 (1973), 21.
44. UN Doc. A/9028 (1973), 21: 'A heinous act of barbarism committed in the territory of a third State by a foreigner against a person possessing a nationality other than that of the offender for the purpose of exerting pressure in a conflict not strictly internal in nature'.
45. French Diplomatic Archives, *Télégrammes de M. de Guiringaud, Représentant de la France auprès des Nations Unies: 19 Sept. 1972, 24 Sept. 1972, 03 Oct. 1972*, in NUOI 1409: 1970–1973. During the 1970s, France considered international terrorism to be less of a danger to French territory than a problem in the international sphere. P. G. Czerny, 'France: Non-terrorism and the Politics of Repressive Tolerance', in J. Lodge (ed.), *Terrorism: A Challenge to the State* (1981), 91.
46. Guiringaud in UN Doc. A/BUR/SR.201 (21 Sept. 1972); d'Haussy in UN Doc. A/AC.160/SR.14 (26 March 1979).
47. French Diplomatic Archives, *Rapport sur l'Assemblée des Nations Unies 1972*, in NUOI 1409: 1970–1973; d'Haussy in UN Docs. A/AC.160/SR.10 (30 March 1977) and A/AC.160/SR.19 (13 April 1979). France did not address the problem of state terrorism.
48. Bessou in UN Doc. A/C.6/SR.1360 (15 Nov. 1972); French Diplomatic Archives, *Note pour la Direction des Affaires Politiques: 51ème session du Comité des Ministres du Conseil de l'Europe, 12 décembre 1972*, in NUOI 1409: 1970–1973; Council of Europe, CM (74) PV.2, 1974, 19; d'Haussy in UN Doc. A/32/37 (28 April 1977), 20.

It was therefore easy for France to lend moral support to the Ad Hoc Committee, although Paris was not particularly satisfied with its work.[49] First, everyone should have an opportunity to present his ideas and opinions; then the debate should move on to study the problem of the underlying causes; subsequently there should be an attempt to formulate a definition; 'after that, it would be much easier to consider measures to combat international terrorism'.[50] This attitude must have further contributed to the slow pace of the work in the Ad Hoc Committee, and France did not stress a need to speed up the process. All in all one gets the impression that, while formally courting the favour of the non-aligned countries, in reality France was not entirely unhappy that the Ad Hoc Committee on International Terrorism had become a propaganda platform.

Italy, meanwhile, tried to take on itself the role of honest broker.[51] This was mainly due to the fact that Italy at the time was pursuing a 'global peace strategy' for the Middle East. The idea was that the only way towards an enduring end to political violence in Palestine was a comprehensive approach that took into account the political, social, and economic grievances of the Third World in general and of the Palestinian people in particular.[52] At the same time, Italy's role as honest broker was also in the national interest, since it was warmly welcomed by the US delegation that had found itself in an impasse, and since successful mediation would have increased Italy's diplomatic prestige. Accordingly, the Italian delegation at the United Nations called persistently for a compromise that should meet with as wide an international approval as possible.[53] The Foreign Ministry in Rome even went as far as to stress that 'any action regarding the problem of international terrorism can only be effective if it is undertaken on a global scale'.[54]

Although Italy saw itself as a mediator between the conflicting parties, it also had its own preferences on the most important substantive points.[55] For example, Rome recognized the importance of studying the underlying causes of terrorism, although this should not be allowed to become an obstacle to the goal of adopting concrete measures. Moreover, Rome was in favour of safeguards for national liberation movements, instead of criminalizing their members as international terrorists. But, of course, Italy emphasized that atrocities could not be condoned, however politically motivated they might be. Furthermore, Italy recommended that the phenomenon of 'state terrorism' should not be dealt with under the label of international terrorism but rather under the rubric of human rights.[56] As far as possible, Italy would

---

49. France kept a certain critical distance from the Ad Hoc Committee and usually abstained from voting.
50. Lennuyeux-Comnenk in UN Doc. A/AC.160/SR.12 (28 March 1979).
51. Italian Diplomatic Archives (1972), *supra* note 5; Italian Diplomatic Archives, *Telegrams to and from New York* (1973); cf. L. Migliorino, 'L'Italia e il terrorismo internazionale', in L. Bonanate (ed.), *Dimensioni del Terrorismo Politico: Aspetti Interni e Internazionali, Politici e Giuridici* (1979), 313.
52. G. Medici, Italian Foreign Minister, in Italian Senate, Plenary Assembly, 6 Oct. 1972.
53. Migliuolo in UN Doc. A/C.6/SR.1389 (11 Dec. 1972); cf. Italy's initial refusal to deal with the problem at the Council of Europe: CM (74) PV.2, 1974.
54. Italian Diplomatic Archives, *Telegrams to and from New York* (1974), 20 Jan. 1974.
55. Italy sponsored a compromise proposal, which eventually failed in 1972: UN Docs. A/C.6/L.879 (27 Nov. 1972); C.6/L.879/Rev.1 (8 Dec. 1972); Migliuolo in UN Docs. A/C.6/SR.1389 (11 Dec. 1972); A/AC.160/1 (16 May 1973), 14–16.
56. Vinci in UN Doc. A/C.6/SR.1386 (8 Dec. 1972); Danovi in UN Doc. A/32/37 (28 April 1977), 22–23; Forlani in UN Doc. A/31/PV.13 (1 Oct. 1976); Bosco in UN Doc. A/C.6/32/SR.58 (28 April 1977).

also have preferred to avoid the 'thorny problem' of finding a legal definition of international terrorism.[57]

After the kidnapping of the former Italian Prime Minister Aldo Moro in 1978, Italy became more pragmatic and called vociferously for concrete measures against terrorism.[58] Nevertheless, the senior Italian politician Giulio Andreotti continued to draw a distinction between terrorists and freedom fighters,[59] and even in 1986 – seven years after the demise of the Ad Hoc Committee – the Italian Minister of Defence kept calling for the adoption of a comprehensive convention on international terrorism.[60]

It is somewhat ironic that West Germany, the country struck by the Munich terrorist assault, was not yet a member of the United Nations when the item of international terrorism was put on the agenda. At an EEC meeting in September 1972 the West German Foreign Minister asked the UN delegations of the nine EEC member states to seize the General Assembly of the necessity of an international convention against terrorism in all its forms.[61] When West Germany finally became a UN member, in 1973, the country formally disclosed its position.[62] But since it had no delegate on the Ad Hoc Committee on International Terrorism, Bonn continued to keep a relatively low profile.

In any event, West Germany declared that concrete measures against terrorism were more important than a study of its underlying causes, and that national liberation struggles were no excuse for committing terrorist acts.[63] Internal documents, however, reveal that West Germany tried to keep neutral on the question of whether there was an overlap between national liberation movements and terrorism. Interestingly, it wanted the political use of violence to be proscribed not only for non-state actors but also for states. Since the lowest common denominator at the United Nations was too low for a comprehensive agreement on terrorism to be reached, Germany had a preference for the more exclusive multilateral fora in Europe. Even NATO was deemed more suitable than the UN for reaching the desired agreement on terrorism.[64]

Already in 1973 West Germany had declared its conviction that the best way to achieve a convention on international terrorism was pragmatically to cover particular aspects of the phenomenon.[65] From 1976 onwards, then, Germany focused on its own political project, the draft International Convention against the Taking of Hostages.[66] According to a chief officer from the Ministry of Justice, Germany's

57. Italian Diplomatic Archives, *Telegrams to and from New York* (1973), 9 May 1973.
58. Serafini in UN Doc. A/AC.160/SR.16 (22 March 1979); given this pragmatic turn, it is quite surprising that Italy was now in favour of defining terrorism (ibid.; but cf. also Serafini in UN Doc. A/C.6/34/SR.9 (3 Oct. 1979)).
59. G. Andreotti, 'Considerazioni sul terrorismo', in M. Galleni (ed.), *Rapporto sul terrorismo* (1981), 545, at 552.
60. G. Spadolini, 'Una alleanza antiterrorismo fra Ovest, Est e non allineati', interview in *Corriere della Sera*, 28 Sept. 1986.
61. British National Archives, *Reports of the 6th Committee, supra* note 39.
62. UN Doc. A/AC.160/1 (16 May 1973), 10–11.
63. Busse in UN Doc. A/C.6/SR.1581 (4 Dec. 1975); Bracklo in UN Doc. A/C.6/SR.1521 (9 Dec. 1974).
64. German Federal Archive, *Vereinte Nationen: Internationales Übereinkommen vom 18. Dezember 1979 gegen Terrorismus*, B 141/57349, vol. 4.
65. Paper 'Unsere Position zum TOP Terrorismus', ibid. There are no explicit statements on whether Germany thought it desirable or not to define international terrorism.
66. Genscher in UN Doc. A/31/242 (28 Sept. 1976).

initiative was a reaction to the failure of previous attempts to reach a comprehensive agreement.[67] It was basically due to this failure that Germany had come to the conclusion that concrete measures against certain manifestations of terrorism were better than endless discussions about its essence and underlying causes.

2.2. The second debate (2000–5)

In recent decades the member states of the European Union are often represented at the UN by the country holding the EU presidency. For example, Italy declared in late 2003 on behalf of the European Union: 'With regard, in particular, to the draft Comprehensive Convention on International Terrorism, submitted by India, we reiterate that its scope should be to provide added value in relation to pre-existing specific Conventions by filling the gaps of unregulated issues'.[68] At the same time the member states of the European Union are free to formulate their own policy statements whenever they deem it appropriate.

The most important problem with EU presidency statements is that they usually represent the lowest common denominator among member states. They tend to paper over substantial differences between individual bargaining positions. It is therefore better to analyse the statements of the delegates of the most important member states than EU presidency statements.

The United Kingdom tends to oppose a definition of terrorism at the UN, although it is one of the few European countries where terrorism was legally defined before 11 September. The British permanent representative at the UN said in October 2001,

> There is common ground amongst us all on what constitutes terrorism. What looks, smells and kills like terrorism is terrorism. ... But there are also wars and armed struggles where actions can be characterized, for metaphorical and rhetorical force, as terrorist. This is a highly controversial and subjective area, on which, because of the legitimate spectrum of viewpoints within the United Nations membership, we will never reach full consensus ... Our job now is to confront and eradicate terrorism pure and simple: the use of violence without honour, discrimination or regard for human decency.[69]

Since the terrorist attacks of September 2001, the United Kingdom has two alternative outlets for its initiatives against terrorism. On the one hand is the General Assembly and its Sixth Committee. On the other hand, the United Kingdom has a permanent seat on the Security Council and its Counter Terrorism Committee (CTC). Between these two options, the United Kingdom clearly prefers the pragmatic approach of the Security Council to the legalist approach of the General Assembly. In 2003 the UK delegates even kept absent from the meetings of the Ad

67. E. Corves, 'International Co-operation in the Field of International Political Terrorism', (1978) 1 (2) *Terrorism: An International Journal* 199, at 210; cf. R. Lagoni, 'Die Vereinten Nationen und der internationale Terrorismus', in M. Funke (ed.), *Terrorismus: Untersuchungen zur Struktur und Strategie revolutionärer Gewaltpolitik* (1977), 259, at 268–71.
68. Nesi, EU Presidency Statement, 'Measures to Eliminate International Terrorism', Sixth Committee, 15 Oct. 2003 (http://www.europa-eu-un.org, retrieved 30 July 2004).
69. Greenstock in UN Doc. A/56/PV.12 (1 Oct. 2001).

Hoc Committee.[70] As Sir Jeremy Greenstock, then chairman of the CTC, put it in early 2002, 'the General Assembly is 189 equal voices and votes, with no party discipline and no particular leadership, and it is chaos most of the time in terms of getting collective answers'.[71] This explains the predilection of the United Kingdom to use its permanent seat on the UN Security Council rather than its voice in the General Assembly. Indeed, Greenstock used all his influence to keep the CTC as operational as possible and to prevent it from being dragged into debates on the legal definition of terrorism and its causes and on the legitimacy of political violence by national liberation movements.[72] In the General Assembly and its Sixth Committee the United Kingdom hardly spoke at all on the comprehensive convention on international terrorism.[73]

As has already been mentioned, after the terrorist attack in London in July 2005 Britain apparently reversed its stance on the definition of terrorism. After this dreadful event, the United Kingdom suddenly started to call for a comprehensive convention, including an unequivocal definition and condemnation of terrorism.[74] However, Britain was not at all ready to compromise with the Muslim world on an exemption clause for national liberation movements. Accordingly, what seemed to be a revolution in the British bargaining position may also be seen as a tactical move against the effort to achieve an internationally agreed definition of terrorism. After the failure of this adventurous episode, Prime Minister Tony Blair's official spokesman argued that what mattered most was not a 'perfect' definition of terrorism but the practical measures taken to combat it.[75] One may indeed wonder whether the British–US initiative was really intended to solve the problem of a consensus definition of international terrorism, or whether it was not rather meant to raise the stakes so high that the entire project would fail altogether. Given the general stance of the United Kingdom (and the United States) over the last five years, the latter hypothesis is more plausible.

The French position, in contrast, has been distinguished right from the start by a repeated insistence that a comprehensive convention on terrorism is necessary.[76] Although it is likely that France desires a legal definition of international terrorism, the problem is not directly addressed. France has also remained remarkably silent on the question of whether national liberation movements should be exempted from the application of the convention. However, Paris consistently stresses the point that it is necessary to analyse the underlying causes of terrorism and not just

70. See UN Doc. A/AC/252/2003/INF/1 (18 June 2003).
71. Merill House conversation, 27 Feb. 2002, Carnegie Council on Ethics and International Affairs (http://www.cceia.org/, retrieved 2 Aug. 2004).
72. I. Williams, 'Abbringen, Verweigerung, Zusammenarbeit: der Ausschuss des Sicherheitsrats zur Bekämpfung des Terrorismus', (2002) 50 (6) *Vereinte Nationen* 213; R. Mani, 'The Root Causes of Terrorism and Conflict Prevention', in Boulden and Weiss, *supra* note 2, at 219.
73. Only once, on 12 Nov. 2001, did the UK Foreign Secretary Jack Straw declare to the Security Council that the United Kingdom would 'continue to work to complete the comprehensive convention on terrorism', while at the same time stressing the paramount importance of taking concrete measures (S/PV.4413).
74. Cf. note 31 *supra*; on the British position see 'London Attacks Should Spur New Efforts toward Terrorism Convention, Diplomats Say', Associated Press, 8 July 2005; 'British Diplomats Push Annan for a "No Excuses" Definition of Terrorism', *Sunday Telegraph*, 24 July 2004.
75. 'Blair Frustrated as UN Fails to Agree on Anti-terror Action', *Independent*, 15 Sept. 2005.
76. Levitte in UN Doc. S/PV.4242 (6 Dec. 2000); Villepin in UN Doc. S/PV.4688 (20 Jan. 2003).

to take practical steps against it. Take for example the following statement by a former French foreign minister:

> We are waging a merciless fight against terrorism. Let us at the same time address its roots. That means putting an end to situations that terrorists exploit; giving the world's excluded hope again; restoring dignity to those peoples deprived of it; and ensuring that dialogue and co-operation among civilizations, cultures and religions prevail, rather than conflict and intolerance.[77]

In comparison with the French position, the German stance is even bolder.[78] Not only does Berlin explicitly support the effort to reach a comprehensive convention on international terrorism and stress the necessity to analyse 'the full range of causes and circumstances that permit such hatred and violence to grow';[79] the German Foreign Ministry also declares, and this goes beyond the political rhetoric from the Quai d'Orsay, that it would like to see a universally binding legal definition of terrorism.[80] If it were only up to Berlin, the Comprehensive Convention would cover national liberation movements.[81] The rationale of the German position was neatly put by the foreign minister:

> What we need is a system of global co-operative security. Asymmetrical conflicts in particular must be countered with an international system of sanctions and verification mechanisms. It is the United Nations that provides us with the appropriate framework for that.[82]

Italy has kept a relatively low profile, not only in comparison with the strong attitudes of Britain, France, and Germany, but also in comparison with its own active role in the 1970s. It seems that the Italian delegates in New York, although generally sympathetic to the project of a comprehensive convention, have hardly made any substantial contributions to the debate.[83] It is therefore impossible to reconstruct the details of the Italian position from official UN documents, and, unfortunately, the situation is not much better with regard to official statements by the Italian government.[84] One is therefore forced to turn to more informal sources.[85] According to one interlocutor at the Foreign Ministry in Rome, Italy initially followed the United States in opposing the Comprehensive Convention as drafted by India in 1996.[86] Although Rome is not opposed to a definition of terrorism as such, the source in the Foreign Ministry reveals that Italy considers itself to be a close ally of the United States. Since the United States is a notoriously close ally of Israel, Italy

77. Barnier in UN Doc. A/59/PV.7 (23 Sept. 2004); cf. *inter alia* UN Doc. S/2001/1274 (28 Sept. 2001), 3.
78. Kastrup in UN Docs. A/56/PV.10 (25 Sept. 2001) and A/56/PV.15 (2 Oct. 2001).
79. Fischer in UN Doc. A/56/PV.48 (12 Nov. 2001).
80. Personal communication with a diplomat in the German Foreign Ministry (April 2004); 'Germany Says UN Reform Agenda Falls Short on Disarmament and Terrorism', Agence France-Presse, 15 Sept. 2005.
81. http://www.auswaertiges-amt.de/www/de/aussenpolitik/vn/itb/itb_vn_html, retrieved 8 Aug. 2005.
82. Fischer in UN Doc. S/PV.4688 (20 Jan. 2003).
83. Shortly after 9/11, Italy declared itself in favour of a comprehensive convention; see Ruggiero in UN Doc. A/56/PV.46 (11 Nov. 2001).
84. Foreign Minister Renato Ruggiero made some cursory remarks in the Italian House of Representatives on 9 Oct. 2001; cf. also 'Putin und Berlusconi für Verabschiedung umfassender Konvention gegen Internationalen Terrorismus', *RIA Novosty*, 3 Nov. 2004.
85. Personal communication with a diplomat in the Italian Foreign Office (April 2004).
86. This changed around 2000, after the Indian draft had been rewritten (with strong US involvement).

considers itself as an ally of Israel as well. Still according to the same interlocutor, this is the reason why Rome has for a long time opposed a definition of international terrorism that would have excluded the Palestinian insurrection.[87]

3. The political struggle behind the legal debate

Let us now try and place these findings within the broader conceptual framework. According to Carl Schmitt, politics under extreme conditions is first and foremost about determining and fighting the public enemy.[88] According to such a view, the person or institution able to tell 'us' from 'them' in a state of emergency holds the ultimate sovereign power.[89] This amounts to a sort of litmus test for the true locus of political authority. Of course that is not to deny that in a state of normalcy, that is, most of the time, politics is broadly in line with a civilizing process that delegitimizes the indiscriminate use of violence.[90] But there is another side to the same coin: real or perceived challenges to the civilizing process must be violently suppressed.

As a matter of fact, the Leviathan has always been in the business of suppressing private violence, whether it comes in the shape of individual misdemeanour or organized crime. If this is true about private violence, then it is even truer about political violence in general, and about terrorism in particular. Whereas private violence is a challenge to the state's monopoly of the legitimate use of force and prompts the obligation of the state to uphold law and order, political crime and terrorism are not only a challenge to the monopoly of force but also to the monopoly of the state and its ruling elite to determine the public enemy. Political offenders in general, and terrorists in particular, almost always challenge the state on its own turf by declaring that the incumbent power is the real enemy that must be fought relentlessly for the sake of some higher end, be it anarchy, separatism, communism, or religious rectitude. They thereby challenge the very core of sovereign power: the discretion of the state to determine the public enemy.[91]

This is the main reason why struggles against political violence and terrorism tend to be so acrimonious even when they involve a lesser 'objective' (i.e. statistical) risk to the safety of the individual citizen than other forms of violence. Whenever

87. Nevertheless, Italy accepted an EU compromise proposal that suggested that an explicit reference to the principle of national self-determination should be included in Art. 18 (now 20) of the draft Convention (R. Barberini, 'Alcune osservazioni sul progetto di Convenzione globale contro il terrorismo', (2002) 2 *La Comunità Internazionale* 201, at 208–9); moreover, Italy suggested a 'safeguard clause': whenever the Comprehensive Convention enters into conflict with an existing sector-specific convention, the latter shall continue to apply (ibid., at 203; cf. Vento in UN Doc. A/56/PV.17 (3 Oct. 2001)).

88. C. Schmitt, *Politische Theologie: Vier Kapitel zur Lehre von der Souveränität* (1922), translated by G. Schwab under the title *Political Theology: Four Chapters on the Concept of Sovereignty* (1986); Schmitt, *supra* note 1.

89. There are interesting attempts to construct a political theory of the state of emergency (G. Agamben, *Stato di Eccezione* (2003)). Nevertheless, I do not believe that it is possible to construct such a theory. Although the state of emergency poses a profound challenge to the theory and practice of political and legal order, it can never be an organic part of it. The reason is that any vision of order necessarily derives from the state of normalcy, as endangered as it may be, and not from the state of emergency, as frightening as it may be.

90. N. Elias, *Über den Prozess der Zivilisation* (1939), translated by E. Jephcott under the title *The Civilizing Process* (1994).

91. As the Italian Red Brigades put it, the aim of their fight was to create 'a new legality, a new power' (leaflet distributed in Milan in spring 1970).

the power to determine the public enemy is at stake, there is a tendency for the struggle to become unconditional and for atrocities to take place on both sides. More often than not, such struggles are born out in terms of eschatological 'holy wars' or merciless 'crusades'.

Terrorists challenge by brute force the power of the state to determine the public enemy. This is also the case in situations of civil war and armed conflict, or whenever there is a movement of partisans, rebels, guerrillas, or revolutionary warriors to challenge the incumbent power.[92] Brute force is the hallmark of all these violent entrepreneurs, and more often than not the immediate response of the incumbent power to these challenges is particularly acrimonious and violent.

In less extreme cases, or in concomitance with such a bloody struggle, the fight can also take on a legal dimension. At the international level, for example, this was the case after the Napoleonic wars, when Europe's conservative powers formed a 'Holy Alliance' to determine and suppress the common threat of liberalism and nationalism. Another example is the 1970s. As we have seen, there was a phalanx of African and Arab states who sympathized with the attempt of violent political entrepreneurs to challenge the Western state system in general and states such as Israel and South Africa in particular. Western reactions ranged from denial as in the case of the United States, the United Kingdom, and Germany, to accommodating moves as in the case of France and Italy. Another round in this legal struggle has started in the 2000s, especially after the terrorist attack of 11 September 2001.

As was shown at the end of the first section, there are both important similarities and differences between the debate in the 1970s and that in the 2000s. This becomes even clearer if one moves from an analysis of the general debate to the positions of the major European powers. In either debate, most European countries had (and still have) a stake in defending the status quo. At the same time, there are important divergences due to differences in political context. In the 1970s the status quo was challenged from the bottom, that is, by non-aligned countries that were, at least rhetorically, supporting national liberation movements. In the 2000s, by contrast, the terrorists are mostly isolated from state power. This time the international status quo is rather challenged from the top, namely by the United States and some of its closest allies.

In fact, today there is no revolutionary Third World movement any more. Instead, one challenge comes from violent political entrepreneurs known as Islamic terrorists. Another challenge is posed by the US government, which claims for itself the discretion to determine the international public enemy on a case-by-case basis. The other states are left with the choice of either joining the 'coalition of the willing' and fighting the enemy as determined by the United States, or of running the risk of themselves being associated with the enemy ('either you are with US or you are against

92. Cf. C. Schmitt, *Theorie des Partisanen: Zwischenbemerkungen zum Begriff des Politischen* (1963). All this is not to deny that Schmitt, especially during his flirtation with Nazi power, had a certain contempt for legal norms and celebrated the production of 'concrete orders' by 'decisionist' fiat (C. Schmitt, *Über die Drei Arten des Rechswissenschaftlichen Denkens* (1934)). On the person of Carl Schmitt see the fascinating piece by C. Lindner, 'Himmelsschlachten oder die Heimkehr des Odysseus: Eine Reise zu Carl Schmitt', *Frankfurter Allgemeine Zeitung*, 24 March 2005.

US'). It is easy to understand that, under the immediate impact of 11 September, Western states were more concerned with the challenge posed by the terrorists than with the challenge posed by the United States. Nevertheless, there were differences. Some countries (France, Germany) were just a bit less concerned with international terrorism and a bit less accommodating towards the United States, whereas others (United Kingdom, Italy) tended to bandwagon unconditionally with the hegemonic power in its fight against whomever was declared to be the international public enemy.

By and large, however, the United States has been in a position to determine on a case-by-case basis who the international public enemy (read 'terrorist') happens to be. It therefore came as no surprise that, as far as can be seen from the UN documents, the United States was rather wary of participating in the debates of the Ad Hoc Committee and the Working Group.[93] Since a comprehensive convention with a legal definition of terrorism would have limited the discretion of the United States to determine the international public enemy on a case-by-case basis, the United States has been acting according to an old motto coined by a Roman lawyer: 'omnis definitio in iure periculosa'.[94]

From the standpoint of the less powerful, it is quite to the contrary: it is precisely the absence of a legal definition which is dangerous. A reasonably clear and legally binding definition of terrorism would work as an insurance against the tendency of the hegemonic power to determine the international public enemy at its own discretion. There are certainly common enemies of all states, such as al Qaeda, and these should definitely be covered by the definition of terrorism. At the same time, however, a good definition should prevent the hegemonic power from misusing the label of 'terrorism' as a licence to crack down on its occasional enemies. It is therefore surprising that the major European powers, for a long time, have been keeping such a low profile in the discussions about a comprehensive convention on international terrorism. Maybe this is still due to the experience of the 1970s, when it was rather unpleasant for a Western state to participate in these debates. But the situation has changed, and it would be a gross political mistake for the European powers to neglect the issue.

4. Conclusion

The fight for the power to define the public enemy takes the shape of a permanent eschatological struggle. Its latest manifestation is the fight against Islamic terrorists as *hostes humani generis*. Apart from the atrocity of their deeds, these criminals are posing a challenge to the power of states to tell 'good' from 'evil' at the global level.

93. To the United States, as well as to the United Kingdom, the Security Council and its Counter-Terrorism Committee seem to provide a much more attractive platform than the General Assembly and the Ad Hoc Committee on International Terrorism (Williams, *supra* note 72; C. de Jonge Oudraat, 'The role of the Security Council', in J. Boulden and T. G. Weiss (eds.), *Terrorism and the UN: Before and After September 11* (2004), 151).
94. Any definition in law is dangerous (Iavolenus).

However, the status quo is challenged not only by the terrorists but, although in a somewhat less tangible way, by the leading anti-terrorists as well. If the United States continues to hold the monopoly of determining the international public enemy at its own discretion, this will be a decisive step towards world empire. Most of the present 'friends' of the United States would then turn from allies into vassals, while others might eventually become enemies themselves. The status quo powers must therefore steer their ship between the Scylla of leniency towards terrorist criminals and the Charybdis of excessive accommodation to the hegemonic power. This is definitely not only a legal question but above all a political problem. In the long run, the monopoly of the hegemonic power to determine the international public enemy would pose a higher risk to the political autonomy of the status quo states than the challenge posed by international terrorism, since the six spitting faces of the terrorist Scylla are less likely to lure them than the deep throat of the hegemonic Charybdis that threatens to suck them in.

The world is now at the end of a small hegemonic policy cycle. In the short run, the war on terror created a permanent state of exception (Schmitt's *Ausnahmezustand*) that could rally an ample 'coalition of the willing' around the hegemonic power of the United States. The discretion of defining the international public enemy, be it Osama Bin Laden's al Qaeda or Saddam Hussein's Iraq, engendered a mechanism of 'othering' that initially increased US power. In the medium term, however, the absence of a shared definition of terrorism threatens to undermine the consensus of the international coalition, as can be seen from the campaign against Iraq. Therefore, in the long run, the United States (and its British junior partner) cannot do without a minimum consensus on the definition of the international public enemy, and, interestingly, it is precisely the long-despised UN General Assembly that offers the institutional focal point for such a definition. Insofar as the state of exception is not sustainable in the long run, this is the revenge of the less powerful states. They can now try to drag the hegemonic power into a legal arrangement that is bound to constrain its room for manoeuvre.

It is indeed in the common interest of the Arab states and the European powers to agree on a binding legal definition of terrorism. The current position of the OIC group – to exclude both national liberation movements and state terrorism from the definition – should be acceptable to all those interested in the maintenance of the status quo, especially west European countries but possibly also east European countries, Russia, India, and China. At least as far as western Europe is concerned, national liberation movements have ceased to be a matter of concern many years ago. The times of colonialism and the Cold War are over. The Palestinians have stopped relying on international terrorism and have returned to local campaigning. Where liberation movements are still active they should be dealt with using legal frameworks other than terrorism, such as the Geneva conventions. To meet the imminent challenge, a definition of international terrorism that would rule al Qaeda and other fundamentalist terror organizations in, and the Palestinians and Israelis out, should be acceptable to a wide variety of states.

The familiar policy of the hegemonic power, which tends to determine the international public enemy on a case-by-case basis and thereby not only declares but also reproduces a perpetual *Ausnahmezustand*, is hardly desirable to the status quo states. It is both important and reasonable for them to ensure a legal definition of international terrorism according to which, in order to qualify as an international terrorist, one has to be the enemy of all civilized nations and not just of one or two particular states. This will greatly increase the consensus in the international coalition against terrorism. However, it will depend on the spirit of compromise among all parties concerned whether a comprehensive convention on international terrorism is finally concluded.

[4]

Definition of "Terrorism" in the UN Security Council: 1985–2004

Ben Saul*

Abstract

International debate about the problems of defining terrorism historically centred on the General Assembly. Yet, between 1985 and 2001, the Security Council adopted a range of measures addressing terrorist threats to peace and security, and analysis of the incidents involved reveals much about the Council's understanding of "terrorism". After September 2001, problems of definition became acute, since the Council adopted general legislative measures against terrorism—with serious legal consequences—without defining it. The Council has encouraged States to unilaterally define terrorism in national law, permitting wide and divergent definitions. A non-binding Council definition of late 2004 fails to remedy the serious difficulties caused by the lack of an operative definition in Council practice.

I. Introduction

Within the UN system, the question of terrorism was largely consigned to the General Assembly prior to 2001,[1] reflecting the structural dichotomy between the Assembly as the "soft UN" and the Council as the "hard UN".[2] In particular, international discussion of the complex political and legal problems of defining terrorism has historically been centred on the General Assembly. There has been little scrutiny of the breadth of Council resolutions on terrorism before 11 September 2001,[3] despite the potential importance of Council measures as evidence of customary international norms regulating terrorism. This article charts the

* BA (Hons) LLB (Hons) (Syd) DPhil (Oxon); Lecturer, Faculty of Law, University of New South Wales, Sydney, Australia (email: b.saul@unsw.edu.au).

1 Nicholas Rostow, Before and After: The Changed UN Response to Terrorism since September 11th, 35 Cornell ILJ (2002), 475, 479; Eric Rosand, Security Council Resolution 1373, the Counter-Terrorism Committee, and the Fight Against Terrorism, 97 AJIL (2003), 333, 333.

2 Martti Koskenniemi, The Police in the Temple: Order, Justice and the UN: A Dialectical View, 6 EJIL (1995), 325, 336.

3 David Malone, The Security Council in the Post-Cold War Era: A Study in the Creative Interpretation of the UN Charter, 35 NYU JILP (2003), 487, 501; Chantal de Jonge Oudraat, The Role of the Security Council, in: Jane Boulden and Thomas Weiss (eds.), Terrorism and the UN: Before and After September 11th (2004), 151.

Chinese Journal of International Law (2005), Vol. 4, No. 1, 141–166 doi:10.1093/chinesejil/jmi005

chequered and sometimes contradictory history of Council efforts to confront terrorism before and after 11 September 2001, and evaluates the extent to which Council measures have contributed to the formation of customary norms on the definition of terrorism.

Until late 2001, resolutions did not impose measures against terrorism generally, nor did they define it. However, various resolutions after 1985 designated specific incidents, and types of violence by and against various actors, as terrorism. The first part of this article deductively and incrementally identifies the substantive content of "terrorism" in Council practice, despite the lack of consistency in the identification of terrorist acts.[4] In doing so, it illustrates how the Council has constructed an ad hoc working definition of "terrorism" in its practice over time.

The second part examines radical shifts in the Council's approach after September 2001. Since then, the Council has imposed binding, quasi-legislative measures against terrorism in general,[5] unconnected to specific incidents, and unlimited in time. The Council has also regarded "any" act of terrorism as a threat to peace and security, regardless of its severity, or international effects. Yet, the Council failed to define terrorism until late 2004, despite using it as an operative legal concept with serious consequences for individuals and entities. For three years, States could unilaterally define terrorism and assert universal jurisdiction over it (encouraged by the Counter-Terrorism Committee), despite wide divergences in national definitions. The Council's 2004 definition raises other problems, since it is non-binding (allowing States to preserve unilateral definitions) and potentially conflicts with multilateral treaty negotiations on defining terrorism.

II. Legal implications of Council resolutions

Council resolutions do not create international law, but are normative obligations on Member States under the Charter.[6] The Council is "a political organ having legal consequences",[7] determined by the terms of a resolution, surrounding discussions, the Charter provisions invoked and the circumstances.[8] Resolutions may also assist in interpreting the Charter;[9] evidence general principles of law;[10] or reflect *opinio juris*, "provided that their subject-matter is not restricted to particular circumstances".[11] Even non-binding resolutions

4 Rosalyn Higgins, The General International Law of Terrorism, in Rosalyn Higgins and Maurice Flory (eds), Terrorism and International Law (1997), 13, 19.

5 Jane Stromseth, The Security Council's Counter-Terrorism Role: Continuity and Innovation, 97 ASIL Proc (2003), 41; Paul Szasz, The Security Council Starts Legislating, 96 AJIL (2002), 901; Rosand, above n.1; Stefan Talmon, The Security Council as World Legislature, 99 AJIL (2005), 175, 176–178.

6 Marc Perrin de Brichambaut, The Role of the United Nations Security Council in the International Legal System, in: Michael Byers (ed.), The Role of International Law in International Politics (2001), 268, 268.

7 Ibid., 268.

8 Namibia Advisory Opinion, ICJ Reports (1971), 41.

9 Georg Nolte, The Limits of the Security Council's Powers and its Functions in the International Legal System: Some Reflections, in: Byers (ed.), above n.6, 315, 320, 324.

10 Peter Hulsroj, The Legal Function of the Security Council, 1 Chinese JIL (2002), 59, 70.

11 de Brichambaut, above n.6, 273.

may influence State behaviour.[12] However, given the Council's unrepresentativeness, evidence of more general acceptance is required.[13]

In applying legal rules to specific situations over time, resolutions may have precedential effects in equivalent situations.[14] Precedents are especially important in relation to peace and security because "the body of principles is still so fragmentary and abstract".[15] Caution is, however, warranted, given that the Council is, foremost, a political decision-maker rather than a judicial body applying legal principles.[16]

The Council's presidential statements, adopted by consensus, do not generally create binding obligations on States, although they may bind the Council, its members and the UN Secretariat on organizational and procedural matters.[17] Nonetheless, the terms of statements should be closely examined and they may reinforce and implement binding resolutions.[18]

III. Council resolutions before 1985

Until the 1990s, the Council was reluctant to regard terrorist acts as threats to peace and security, although this was attributable more to Cold War politics than to an absence of terrorist threats. Some of the most flagrant terrorist acts, such as the attack on Israeli athletes at the Munich Olympics in 1972 or the Air France flight hijacked to Entebbe in 1976,[19] failed to produce any action by the Council. In cases involving State violence against civilian aircraft,[20] and non-State aircraft hijacking and hostage-taking,[21] the Council treated such acts within the legal frameworks on the use of force and on international civil aviation, without reference to "terrorism", allowing it to avoid the political and ideological disputes surrounding that term.

The Council's response to the occupation of the US Embassy in Tehran by revolutionary students in November 1979 similarly avoided referring to "terrorism". Instead, a series of

12 Oscar Schachter, The Quasi-Judicial Role of the Security Council and the General Assembly, 58 AJIL (1964), 960, 963.

13 Nolte, above n.9, 325; Vera Gowlland-Debbas, The Functions of the United Nations Security Council in the International Legal System, in: Byers (ed.), above n.6, 277, 300.

14 Schachter, above n.12, 963–4; W. Michael Reisman, The Constitutional Crisis in the United Nations, 87 AJIL (1993), 83, 85; Hulsroj, above n.10, 69; Rosalyn Higgins, The Place of International Law in the Settlement of Disputes by the Security Council, 64 AJIL (1970), 1, 6.

15 Schachter, ibid., 964.

16 Higgins, above n.14, 7.

17 Stefan Talmon, The Statements by the President of the Security Council, 2 Chinese JIL (2003), 419, 449–50.

18 Ibid., 454–8.

19 Francis Boyle, The Entebbe Hostage Crisis, 29 Netherlands ILR (1982), 32.

20 E.g., SC Ress 262 (1968) (Israel attacked Beirut airport); 616 (1988) (US destroyed an Iran Air flight; an ICJ action was discontinued after a settlement: Aerial Incident of 3 July 1988 (Iran v. US) (Order of Discontinuance), 22 February 1996); 1067 (1996) (Cuba shot down two civil aircraft).

21 SC Ress 286 (1970) (appealing for the release of hostages held in hijackings and calling on States to prevent hijackings); 337 (1993) (condemning Israel for forcibly diverting and seizing an Iraqi Airways aircraft from Lebanese air space).

resolutions dealt with the incident within the legal frameworks of diplomatic and consular immunities and State responsibility.[22] The Council's involvement was overtaken by a negotiated settlement in January 1981, resulting in the release of the hostages, and overshadowing Iran's non-compliance with an adverse ICJ judgment of May 1980.[23] Reparations proceedings before the ICJ were discontinued in May 1981 and later dealt with through a bilateral claims process.[24]

IV. Hostage-taking in the 1980s

The first Council resolution to use the term "terrorism" was SC Res 579 of 1985, in response to a spate of terrorist acts in the preceding year.[25] On the day of the Resolution, Palestinian suicide bombers killed 20 people at US and Israeli check-in desks at Rome and Vienna airports. Resolution 579 condemned "all acts of hostage-taking and abduction" as "manifestations of international terrorism".[26] Hostage-taking and abduction (and, impliedly, terrorism) were considered "offences of grave concern to the international community", endangering human rights and friendly relations.[27]

In 1988, SC Res 618 condemned the abduction of a UN military observer in Lebanon and demanded his release.[28] The Council President reported in 1989 that the UN observer "may have been murdered" and called for international action against hostage-taking and abductions as "unlawful, criminal and cruel acts".[29] SC Res 638 was adopted unanimously soon after, condemning hostage-taking and abduction in general and demanding the release of all victims.[30] States were urged to become parties to relevant treaties, and to prevent, prosecute and punish "all acts of hostage-takings and abductions as manifestations of terrorism".[31]

The classification of *all* hostage-takings and abductions as terrorism discounts political motives, an intent to instill fear, or intimidatory or coercive aims, as the defining elements of terrorism. Instead, it is objectively defined by the prohibited *methods* of hostage taking and abduction—even if done for private ends—and despite the political motives underlying the specific incidents that the Council was responding to.

The preamble to Res 638 also stated that such acts were "serious violations" of IHL, indicating that the Council regarded those acts as governed by an existing legal framework when

22 SC Ress 457 (1979) and 461 (1979).

23 Tehran Hostages Case, ICJ Reports (1980), 3.

24 Tehran Hostages case (Order of Discontinuance), 12 May 1981.

25 Including the hijackings of a Kuwaiti aircraft in December 1984; a Jordanian aircraft, a Middle East Airlines flight, and a TWA flight in June 1985; an Egyptair flight in November 1985; the seizure of the Achille Lauro in October 1985; and the seizure of 25 Finnish UN soldiers by the South Lebanon Army in June 1985.

26 SC Res 579 (1985), paras 1 and 5; see also SC Pres Stat (9 October 1985).

27 SC Res 579 (1985), preamble; see also Res 638 (1989), preamble.

28 SC Res 618 (1988), preamble and paras 1–2, respectively.

29 SC Pres Stat (31 July 1989), para. 3.

30 SC Res 638 (1989), paras 1–3.

31 Ibid., paras 4–5.

committed in armed conflict. That is the approach of the 1979 Hostages Convention, which excludes hostage-taking constituting a grave breach of the Geneva Conventions and Protocols.[32] Thus, hostage-taking in armed conflict, including by liberation movements,[33] is treated as a war crime rather than as the general treaty crime of hostage-taking.

There are numerous IHL provisions prohibiting hostage-taking in armed conflict.[34] Traditionally, hostage-taking aimed to intimidate a resisting enemy population, to ensure its obedience and secure control of occupied territory.[35] It was thus a deliberately political use of violence. In contrast, a wider definition is given to the hostage-taking offences in the 1998 Rome Statute, which requires that the

> . . . perpetrator intended to compel a State, an international organization, a natural or legal person or a group of persons to act or refrain from acting as an explicit or implicit condition for the safety or the release of such person or persons.[36]

This definition is similar to that in the 1979 Hostages Convention, suggesting a harmonization of the meaning of hostage-taking in armed conflict and in peacetime. The modern view covers any hostage-taking to obtain a concession or advantage, including for private reasons, such as financial gain.[37] It thus loses some of the specificity of its earlier linkage to explicitly political violence. The modern view is consistent with the Council's approach to regarding *all* hostage-taking as forbidden.

V. Assassination 1989

In 1989, the Council President condemned the assassination of the Lebanese President in Beirut as a "cowardly, criminal and terrorist act" and "an attack upon the unity of Lebanon, the democratic processes and . . . national reconciliation".[38] It is significant that the Council regards assassination as terrorism. To the contrary, some argue that since assassination targets individuals, it is not capable of causing terror generally.[39] Such a conclusion is suspect, because assassination *is* likely to terrify (at least) other politicians, and their

32 1979 International Convention against the Taking of Hostages (adopted 17 December 1979, entered into force 3 June 1983, 1316 UNTS 205), art. 12.

33 Joseph Lambert, Terrorism and Hostages in International Law (1990), 263–98.

34 1949 Geneva Conventions, common art. 3(1)(b); 1949 Fourth Geneva Convention, art. 34; 1977 Protocol II, art. 4(2)(c); 1993 ICTY Statute, art. 2(h); ICTR Statute, art. 4(c); 1998 Rome Statute, art. 8(2)(a)(viii) (international conflicts) and art. 8(2)(c)(iii) (non-international conflicts).

35 Hostages case, 15 Ann Digest (1953), 632, 644; Jean Pictet (ed.), The Geneva Conventions of 12 August 1949: Commentary (1958), 229 (on 1949 Fourth Geneva Convention, art. 34).

36 1998 Rome Statute: Elements of Crimes (2002): common element 3, art. 8(2)(a)(viii) and (c)(iii).

37 Blaškic case, ICTY-95-14-T (3 March 2000), para. 158; Kriangsak Kittichaisaree, International Criminal Law (2001), 154–5.

38 SC Pres Stat (22 November 1989), S/20988.

39 Gilbert Guillaume, Terrorism and International Law, Grotius Lecture, British Institute of International and Comparative Law, London, 13 November 2003, 5; Lambert, above n.33, 18; Alfred Rubin, International Terrorism and International Law, in: Yonah Alexander and Seymour Finger (eds), Terrorism: Interdisciplinary Perspectives (1977), 121, 122.

supporters, who share the victim's political beliefs. While an isolated assassination does not necessarily put the public in fear, it may well have that effect. If prohibiting terrorism aims to protect peaceful, deliberative politics,[40] then assassination will often qualify as terrorism, and is popularly regarded as such.

VI. Plastic explosives 1989

In Res 635 (1989), the Council raised "the implications of acts of terrorism for international security"[41] in the context of detecting plastic explosives. While not naming the incident, the Resolution was prompted by an attack on a civilian aircraft over the Sahara, which killed 400 people.[42] The resolution called on States "to prevent all acts of terrorism" and urged the International Civil Aviation Organization (ICAO) to intensify its efforts to prevent terrorism against civil aviation,[43] particularly the drafting of a treaty on plastic explosives, adopted two years later.[44] The Resolution implies that the unlawful use of plastic explosives may amount to terrorism, suggesting a definition based on prohibited means, rather than political motives, or intimidatory or coercive aims.

VII. Iraq 1991–2004

After the 1991 Gulf War, the "permanent ceasefire" Resolution required Iraq

> . . . to inform the Council that it will not commit or support any act of *international terrorism* or allow any organization directed towards the commission of such acts to operate within its territory and to condemn unequivocally and renounce all acts, methods and practices of *terrorism.*[45]

This obligation was later asserted to constitute a ceasefire condition in the dispute about disarming Iraq from 1991 to 2003.[46] The Council does not specify which Iraqi acts constitute terrorism, and the invasion of Kuwait was a classic case of inter-State aggression. However, the Resolution also invoked the 1979 Hostages Convention and condemned the taking of hostages,[47] some of whom were used as human shields.[48] It is still unclear why the

40 Michael Ignatieff, Human Rights, the Laws of War, and Terrorism, 69 Social Research (2002), 1137, 1157; Ben Saul, 'International Terrorism as a European Crime: The Policy Rationale for Criminalization', 11 European J Crime, Criminal L and Criminal Justice (2003), 323, 333.

41 SC Res 635 (1989), preamble.

42 Lyal Sunga, The Emerging System of International Criminal Law (1997), 197–8.

43 SC Res 635 (1989), paras 2 and 4, respectively.

44 1991 Convention for the Marking of Plastic Explosives for the Purpose of Detection (adopted 1 March 1991, entered into force 21 June 1998, 30 ILM 726).

45 SC Res 687 (1991), para. 32 (emphasis added).

46 See Ben Saul, Legality of the Use of Force against Iraq in 2001, 8 UCLA JIL and Foreign Affairs (2003), 267.

47 SC Res 687 (1991), preamble; see Jordan Paust, Suing Saddam: Private Remedies for War Crimes and Hostage-Taking, 31 Vanderbilt JIL (1991), 351.

48 Others argue that Iraq's destruction of oil wells in retreat from Kuwait amounted to "eco-terrorism" (but it is difficult to see how that alone would terrify a population): Laura Edgerton, Eco-Terrorist Acts during the

Council designated such conduct as terrorism rather than as violations of International Humanitarian Law (IHL), or of obligations concerning hostage-taking or protected persons.

After 11 September 2001, the United States and the United Kingdom sought to prove links between Iraq and the terrorist group, Al-Qaeda, although little evidence of links emerged, even after the overthrow of Saddam Hussein in 2003.[49] This was so despite the aberrant finding of a US judge in 2003, in a civil case for damages, that there was a "conclusive link" between Iraq and Al-Qaeda concerning the 11 September attacks.[50] There was, however, evidence of Iraq funding Palestinian suicide bombings.[51]

Normatively, the resolution is significant because of its binding character under Chapter VII and because it admits not only State-sponsored terrorism, but also direct State terrorism (by requiring Iraq not to "commit" it). It is doubtful whether this description adds anything to the legal framework of States' obligations,[52] since the law on the use of force, non-intervention and State responsibility for transboundary harm by non-State actors already governs international violence by, or supported by, States. There is no evidence that the provision was intended to create individual criminal liability for State terrorism by Iraq, unless it obliquely refers to liability under IHL for acts of terror or spreading terror. No crime of terrorism was included in the 2003 Statute of the Iraqi Special Tribunal for Crimes against Humanity.[53]

After the overthrow of the Iraqi government, the Council shifted its emphasis to non-State terrorism in Iraq. In SC Res 1511, on UN involvement in occupied Iraq, the Council condemned the "terrorist bombings" of the Jordanian and Turkish embassies, UN headquarters in Baghdad, and a mosque in Najaf.[54] It also condemned the murder of a Spanish diplomat and the assassination of an Iraqi leader, and emphasized that those responsible must be brought to justice.[55] The preamble called these "attacks on the people of Iraq, the United Nations, and the international community", and the assassination as an attack on Iraq's future.

Persian Gulf War: Is International Law Sufficient to Hold Iraq Liable?, 22 Georgia JICL (1992), 151; Jesica Seacor, Environmental Terrorism: Lesson from the Oil Fires of Kuwait, 10 American Univ JILP (1994), 481.

49 US Senate (108th Congress) (Select Cttee on Intelligence), Report on the US Intelligence Community's Prewar Intelligence Assessments on Iraq (Washington, DC, 7 July 2004), 346 (concl. 93), 347 (concl. 96), 348 (concl. 97); UK Parliament (Intelligence and Security Cttee), Report on Iraqi Weapons of Mass Destruction: Intelligence and Assessments (HMSO, London, September 2003), 34–5; Report by Privy Counsellors Cttee, Review of Intelligence on Weapons of Mass Destruction (HMSO, London, 14 July 2004), para. 484; Lawrence Freedman, War in Iraq: Selling the Threat, 46 Survival (2004), 7, 18–21.

50 Patricia Hurtado, Baghdad Liable for September 11: judge, Sydney Morning Herald, 9 May 2003 (citing default judgment of January 2003, and damages of US$104 million in May 2003, for Iraq's "material support" to Al-Qaeda); see also Jason Pedigo, Rogue States, Weapons of Mass Destruction, and Terrorism: Was Security Council Approval Necessary for the Invasion of Iraq?, 32 Georgia JICL (2004), 199.

51 Paul McGeough, Saddam Stokes War with Suicide Bomber Cash, Sydney Morning Herald, 26 March 2002.

52 Higgins, above n.4, 20–1.

53 Coalition Provisional Authority, Order No. 49, Delegation of Authority Regarding an Iraqi Special Tribunal, 10 Dec. 2003, annexed Statute, arts 11–14 (crimes within jurisdiction).

54 SC Res 1511 (2003), para. 18. The bombing of UN headquarters was also condemned as a "terrorist attack" "against the international community as a whole" in Pres Stat S/PRST/2003/13 (20 August 2003).

55 SC Res 1511 (2003), para. 18.

148 *CJIL* (2005)

The Resolution emphasized the need for effective Iraqi police and security forces to combat terrorism, and called on States to prevent the transit, arming and financing of terrorists in Iraq.[56] The Resolution does not define terrorism, although the acts that it condemns partly illustrate its conception of terrorism—including attacks on embassies and diplomats, UN premises, political leaders and religious sites—despite most of these acts already being covered by IHL and sectoral treaties.

In SC Res 1546, the Council endorsed the formation of a sovereign interim Iraqi government from 30 June 2004. The Resolution "[c]ondemns all acts of terrorism in Iraq" and refers to States' obligations to prevent "terrorist activities in and from Iraq or against its citizens".[57] The Resolution reaffirmed the authorization of the multinational force established in Res 1511, and gave the force

> ... the authority to take all necessary measures to contribute to the maintenance of security and stability in Iraq ... including by preventing and deterring *terrorism* ....[58]

This is the first Council resolution to give explicit authority to States to use force against "terrorism", albeit limited to a connection with Iraq, and contingent on the (not entirely consensual) "Iraqi request for the continued presence of the multinational force".[59] The Resolution does not define terrorism, implicitly conferring a discretion on the multinational force to determine for itself the meaning of terrorism.

Yet, it is unclear which activities amount to "terrorism" in Iraq. Following the US invasion, a variety of irregular forces continued to resist occupation. Not all of these forces can be characterized as terrorists, since some may qualify as combatants in an international armed conflict—either as irregular forces resisting occupation,[60] or as civilians *levée en masse.* This was implicitly recognized in an amnesty offer to Iraqi insurgents by the incoming Iraqi government.[61] Further, some acts labelled as terrorism by the United States are difficult to accept as such—for instance, given the privatization of military functions, a plot to bomb a civilian passenger airliner, contracted to transport US troops to Iraq,[62] may be a legitimate military action.

It seems unlikely also that the references to terrorism are intended to carefully reflect the limited IHL prohibitions on terror, and the Statute of the Iraqi Special Tribunal does not recognize acts of terror, or spreading terror, as war crimes. Rather, such references derive

56 Ibid., paras 16 and 19; see also SC Res 1546 (2004), para. 17.

57 SC Res 1546 (2004), para. 17.

58 Ibid., para. 10 (emphasis added).

59 Ibid., para.10; see Christopher Le Mon, Legality of a Request by the Interim Iraqi Government for the Continued Presence of United States Military Forces, ASIL Insights, June 2004.

60 Fred Kaplan, This is Not Terrorism, Guardian, 3 April 2003.

61 Rory McCarthy, Suzanne Goldenberg and Nicholas Watt, Amnesty for Iraqi Insurgents, Guardian, 5 July 2004.

62 Thom Shanker, Planes Moving Troops Are in Terrorists' Sights, Says US, Sydney Morning Herald, 14 January 2003.

from earlier unsubstantiated links between Iraq and terrorism, and paradoxically address the appearance of non-State terrorism in Iraq where, pre-invasion, there was none.[63]

VIII. Libya 1992

In 1992, SC Res 731 condemned the destruction of a civil airliner over Lockerbie in Scotland. It deplored Libya's failure to cooperate in establishing responsibility for these "terrorist acts", and urged Libya to help to eliminate "international terrorism".[64] The Resolution implicitly required Libya to surrender two nationals for trial.[65] While terrorism is not defined, it is clear that the Council considers violence against civil aviation (by explosives) to be terrorism, regardless of ulterior motives or aims.

Following non-compliance, SC Res 748 demanded Libyan compliance with requests from France, the United Kingdom and the United States, and imposed aircraft, military and diplomatic sanctions.[66] It also required Libya itself to "cease all forms of terrorist action and all assistance to terrorist groups" and "demonstrate its renunciation of terrorism", and all States to deny freedom of movement to Libyans involved in terrorism.[67] The Resolution did not define terrorism; nor was there any list of terrorist groups.

SC Res 883 also demanded compliance and imposed further financial and aircraft sanctions.[68] Suspension of sanctions was conditioned on Libya surrendering those charged for trial in a UK or US court, satisfaction of French judicial authorities and compliance with earlier resolutions.[69] The preamble noted the Council's determination to bring to justice "those responsible for acts of international terrorism".

In constantly referring to "terrorism", these resolutions avoided invoking the 1971 Montreal Convention, which is evidently an important legal framework governing violence against civil aviation. The deliberate, repeated use of the term suggests that the Council attributed normative importance to it—perhaps because it more fittingly captured the shocking nature of the incident than the more technical law on air safety, or because it supplied a political trigger for Council involvement. Given the suspected responsibility of Libyan officials in the bombing, the Council implicitly accepted that States could perpetrate terrorism.[70]

63 Jeffrey Record, Threat Confusion and its Penalties, 46 Survival (2004), 51, 62; Richard Norton-Taylor, Occupation has Boosted al-Qaida, Says Thinktank, Guardian, 26 May 2004.

64 SC Res 731 (1992), paras 2–3.

65 Reisman, above n.14, 86.

66 SC Res 748 (1992), para. 1 and paras 4–7, respectively. The UK and the US also demanded that Libya disclose all knowledge and evidence of the crime, and pay compensation: US, Statement Regarding the Bombing of Pan Am 103, 27 November 1991, UN Doc. S/23308.

67 SC Res 748 (1992), paras 2 and 6(c), respectively.

68 SC Res 883 (1993), paras 1–7 and 9–10.

69 SC Res 883 (1993), para. 16.

70 Thilo Marauhn, Terrorism: Addendum, in Rudolf Bernhardt (ed.), Encyclopaedia of Public International Law: vol. 4 (2000), 849, 851; Higgins, above n.4, 23.

150 *CJIL* (2005)

The Council's demands conflicted with Libya's attempt to rely on its obligation to prosecute the suspects (as an alternative to extradition, since Libya does not extradite nationals) under the 1971 Montreal Convention. In 1992, the ICJ declined a Libyan request for provisional measures to prevent Libya being forced to transfer the suspects.[71] Since all States are required, under arts 25 and 103 of the Charter, to carry out Council decisions over other treaty obligations, the ICJ found that the treaty rights claimed by Libya were no longer "appropriate for protection" and "would be likely to impair" rights enjoyed by the United Kingdom and the United States in Res 748.[72]

In contrast, at the preliminary objections phase in 1998, the ICJ rejected the argument that Libya's treaty rights could not be exercised because they were superseded by Res 748 and 883.[73] Those Resolutions were adopted after Libya's application was filed in March 1992, and later resolutions could not affect ICJ jurisdiction once established. SC Res 731, adopted before the application, was non-binding and thus did not render the application inadmissible.

The incident was ultimately resolved in a settlement, formalized in SC Res 1192 (1998). Libya handed over two suspects for trial in a Scots law court sitting in the Netherlands.[74] In 2003, Libya accepted responsibility for the acts of Libyan officials, paid compensation, renounced terrorism and committed to cooperation.[75] In SC Res 1506, the Council lifted sanctions and removed the item from its agenda.[76] The ICJ cases were discontinued in

71 Lockerbie (Libya v. UK) (Provisional Measures), ICJ Reports (1992), 3; Lockerbie (Libya v. US) (Provisional Measures), ICJ Reports (1992), 114; Wladyslaw Czaplinski, The Lockerbie Case: Comments, 20 Polish YBIL (1993), 37; Edward McWhinney, The International Court as Emerging Constitutional Court and the Co-Ordinate UN Institutions (especially the Security Council): Implications of the Aerial Incident at Lockerbie, 30 Canadian YBIL (1993), 261; Vera Gowlland-Debbas, The Relationship between the International Court of Justice and the Security Council in the Light of the Lockerbie Case, 88 AJIL (1994), 643; Sami Shubber, The Destruction of Aircraft in Flight over Scotland and Niger: The Question of Jurisdiction and Extradition under International Law, British YBIL (1995), 239.

72 Lockerbie (Libya v. UK) (Provisional Measures), ibid., paras 39–41.

73 Lockerbie (Libya v. UK) (Preliminary Objections), 27 February 1998, paras 38 and 44; see Andreas Paulus, Jurisprudence of the International Court of Justice: Lockerbie Cases, Preliminary Objections, 9 EJIL (1998), 550; Peter Bekker, Questions of Interpretation and Application of the 1971 Montreal Convention Arising from the Aerial Incident at Lockerbie, 92 AJIL (1998), 503.

74 See Netherlands–UK: Agreement between the Government of the Kingdom of The Netherlands and the Government of the United Kingdom of Great Britain and Northern Ireland Concerning a Scottish Trial in The Netherlands, 38 ILM (1999), 926; UK High Court of the Justiciary (Proceedings in the Netherlands) (UN) Order 1998, 38 ILM (1999), 942; The Great Compromise: Where to Convene the Trial of the Suspects Implicated in the Pan Am Flight 103 Bombing over Lockerbie, Scotland, 23 Suffolk Transnational LR (1999), 131; Menno Kamminga, Comment: Trial of Lockerbie Suspects before a Scottish Court in the Netherlands, 45 Netherlands ILR (1998), 417.

75 SC Res 1506 (2003), preamble. Compensation was also subsequently paid for the 1986 bombing of a West Berlin disco: AP, Libya paying out for bombing, Guardian, 4 September 2004; see David Turndorf, The US Raid on Libya: A Forceful Response to Terrorism, 14 Brookings JIL (1988), 187; Wallace Warriner, The Unilateral Use of Coercion under International Law: A Legal Analysis of the United States Raid on Libya on April 14, 1986, 37 Naval LR (1986), 49.

76 SC Res 1506 (2003), paras 1–3.

2003,[77] removing the possibility of ICJ merits review of the legal effects of Council resolutions.[78]

IX. Presidential statements 1992–96

Presidential statements have highlighted the Council's concern at terrorism as a threat to peace and security. In 1992, at the first Council meeting of Heads of State and Government, the Council President expressed "deep concern over acts of international terrorism" and emphasized the need to effectively deal with them.[79] In 1994, the President condemned "terrorist attacks" in Buenos Aires and London, demanded "an immediate end to" such attacks, and stressed the need for cooperation and "to prevent, combat and eliminate all forms of terrorism, which affect the international community as a whole".[80] While terrorism was not defined, the attacks involved killings of civilians by organized groups (such as the IRA) for political purposes.

Similarly, the President condemned a "terrorist attack" in Nordiya, Israel, in 1995, and "terrorist attacks" in Jerusalem and Tel Aviv in 1996, and stated that these acts had "the clear purpose of trying to undermine Middle East peace efforts".[81] While terrorism was not defined, both attacks involved the targeting of civilians for political purposes. Unusually, the Council expressly mentioned the political motives behind the terrorist acts, which were intended to undermine the peace process.

X. Sudan 1996

In SC Res 1044, the Council condemned "the terrorist assassination attempt" on the President of Egypt in Ethiopia in 1995, which violated Ethiopia's sovereignty and integrity, and disturbed regional peace and security.[82] The Resolution called on Sudan to comply with Organization of African Unity (OAU) requests to extradite three suspects to Ethiopia and to "[d]esist from . . . assisting, supporting and facilitating terrorist activities and from giving shelter and sanctuaries to terrorist elements".[83]

Facing non-cooperation, the Council adopted Res 1054 under Chapter VII, which demanded compliance with its earlier requests within two weeks, after which it would

77 Lockerbie (Libya v. UK) (Order of Discontinuance), 10 September 2003; Lockerbie (Libya v. US) (Libya v. UK) (Order of Discontinuance), 10 September 2003.

78 Bernd Martenczuk, The Security Council, the International Court and Judicial Review: What Lessons from Lockerbie?, 10 EJIL (1999), 517, 518; see also Michael Plachta, The Lockerbie Case: The Role of the Security Council in Enforcing the Principle Aut Dedere Aut Judicare, 12 EJIL (2001), 125; Donna Arzt, The Lockerbie "Extradition by Analogy" Agreement: "Exceptional Measure" or Template for Transnational Criminal Justice?, 18 American Univ ILR (2002), 163.

79 SC Pres Stat (31 January 1992), S/23500.

80 SC Pres Stat (29 July 1994), S/PRST/1994/40.

81 SC Pres Stats (30 May 1995), S/PRST/1995/3; (4 March 1996), S/PRST/1996/10.

82 SC Res 1044 (1996), paras 1–2; reiterated in SC Res 1070 (1996), preamble.

83 SC Res 1044 (1996), para. 4(a)–(b).

impose diplomatic sanctions and travel restrictions.[84] In Res 1070, the Council repeated its demands and imposed sanctions on Sudanese aircraft.[85] The Council's management of the incident was interrupted by US air strikes on a pharmaceutical factory in Khartoum,[86] wrongly thought to be producing chemical weapons for terrorist use. Soon after, Sudan expelled Bin Laden. After requests by the OAU, Egypt and Ethiopia, sanctions were finally lifted by Res 1372 (2001).

XI. Kosovo 1998–99

Four resolutions on Kosovo have referred to terrorism, condemning "terrorism in pursuit of political goals by any group or individual, and all external support for such activities in Kosovo, including the supply of arms and training for terrorist activities", as well as its financing.[87] Resolution 1160 characterized terrorism as a non-State activity by condemning "all acts of terrorism by the Kosovo Liberation Army or any other group or individual", while, in contrast, Serbian police violence against civilians was condemned only as "the use of excessive force".[88]

Three resolutions asked Kosovar Albanian leaders alone "to condemn all terrorist action" and stressed that their community should pursue its goals peacefully.[89] One resolution required all States to "prevent arming and training for terrorist activities" in Kosovo, but implicitly recognized underlying causes by stating "that the way to defeat violence and terrorism in Kosovo is for the authorities in Belgrade to offer the Kosovar Albanian community a genuine political process".[90]

SC Res 1244 suggested that State forces may also commit terrorism, by condemning "all terrorist acts by any party".[91] Nonetheless, the Council avoided invoking the IHL of non-international armed conflicts, characterizing the Kosovars as terrorists rather than as belligerent forces in a civil conflict. Even during the NATO bombing of 1999, the Kosovo Liberation Army (KLA) was not recognized as an internal self-determination movement.[92] Yugoslavia even claimed that NATO illegally trained KLA terrorists.[93]

84 SC Res 1054 (1996), paras 1–4.

85 SC Res 1070 (1996), para. 3.

86 Ruth Wedgwood, Responding to Terrorism: The Strikes against Bin Laden, 24 Yale JIL (1999), 559; Leah Campbell, Defending against Terrorism: A Legal Analysis of the Decision to Strike Sudan and Afghanistan, 74 Tulane LR (2000), 1067.

87 Preambles to SC Res 1199 (1998) and 1203 (1998); and 1160 (1998), respectively.

88 SC Res 1160 (1998), preamble.

89 SC Res 1160 (1998), para. 2; 1199 (1998), para. 6; 1203 (1998), para. 10.

90 SC Res 1160 (1998), para. 8 and para. 3, respectively.

91 SC Res 1244 (1999), preamble.

92 Leslie Green, The Contemporary Law of Armed Conflict (2nd ed., 2000), 63.

93 Christine Gray, International Law and the Use of Force (2nd ed., 2004), 42 (argument made in the Legality of the Use of Force (Genocide) cases).

XII. Kenya and Tanzania 1998

In Res 1189, the Council condemned "terrorist bomb attacks" in Kenya and Tanzania, which killed hundreds, injured thousands and caused massive property destruction.[94] It called on all States to assist investigations in Kenya, Tanzania and the United States, "to apprehend the perpetrators of these cowardly criminal acts and to bring them swiftly to justice".[95] More generally, States were called on to prevent terrorism and to prosecute and punish the perpetrators.[96] The Resolution does not define terrorism, but the preamble describes some of its characteristics as "indiscriminate and outrageous" bomb attacks against civilians.

The Resolution did not attribute responsibility for the attacks; nor did it authorize a military response.[97] It is the first resolution to describe terrorism as "criminal". Yet, by mentioning national investigations, it is most likely referring to national crimes or sectoral offences, and not a generic international crime. Still, it is normatively significant that the attacks, which targeted US embassies, were described as terrorism, rather than breaches of the inviolability of diplomatic premises. Without complicity between the host States and terrorists, responsibility could not be attributed to those States, and private groups do not owe obligations of diplomatic protection.

XIII. Afghanistan, Taliban and Al-Qaeda 1998–2004

Soon after, the Council adopted a series of resolutions demanding that the factions in the Afghan conflict, particularly the Taliban, refrain from harbouring, providing sanctuary for and training terrorists, and cooperate in bringing indicted terrorists to justice,[98] including Bin Laden.[99] SC Res 1214 also condemned the Taliban's capture and murder of Iranian diplomats and a journalist as "flagrant violations of international law" (but not as terrorism), and asked the Taliban to investigate and prosecute these crimes and the killings of three UN workers.[100]

SC Res 1267 demanded that the Taliban surrender Bin Laden for trial for the bombings, to a State (such as the United States[101]) where he had been indicted, or would be surrendered or tried.[102] The Taliban had one month to comply, after which aircraft and financial

94 SC Res 1189 (1998), para. 1.

95 Ibid., para. 3.

96 Ibid., para. 5.

97 Adam Roberts, Law and the Use of Force After Iraq, 45 Survival (2003), 31, 37.

98 SC Res 1193 (1998), para. 15; 1214 (1998), para. 13; 1267 (1999), para. 1; 1333 (2000), para. 1, preamble; SC Pres Stats (22 October 1999), S/PRST/1999/29; (7 April 2000), S/PRST/2000/12.

99 SC Res 1267 (1999), preamble; 1333 (1999), preamble.

100 SC Res 1214 (1998), para. 5; 1267 (1999), preamble; 1333 (1999), preamble; SC Pres Stats (22 October 1999), S/PRST/1999/29; (7 April 2000), S/PRST/2000/12.

101 SC Res 1267 (1999), preamble; also SC Res 1333 (2000), preamble; 1390 (2002), preamble; see Efforts to Obtain Custody of Osama Bin Laden, 94 AJIL (2000), 366.

102 SC Res 1267 (1999), para. 2, reiterated in SC Res 1333 (2000), para. 2; see also SC Pres Stats (22 October 1999), S/PRST/1999/29; (7 April 2000), S/PRST/2000/12.

sanctions would be imposed, monitored by a committee.[103] The preamble recalled treaty obligations "to extradite or prosecute terrorists",[104] indicating that sectoral treaties and national law were the appropriate frameworks governing terrorism, particularly given US charges for conspiracy to kill US citizens abroad.

Following non-compliance, later resolutions imposed further military, diplomatic, aircraft and travel sanctions on the Taliban.[105] The most far-reaching provisions require States to freeze the funds and assets of Bin Laden and associated individuals and entities, including Al-Qaeda, as listed by the 1267 Committee.[106] SC Res 1390 extended sanctions beyond Afghan territory after the fall of the Taliban, focusing on the global activities of Bin Laden, Al-Qaeda and "associates".[107] In mid-2004, more than 100 entities were proscribed as associated with Al-Qaeda,[108] including in areas of separatist or religious conflict such as Bosnia, Kosovo, Chechnya, Palestine, North Africa, Sudan, Kurdistan and South East Asia. Despite its sweeping reach, the sanctions regime is not based on a generalized proscription of "terrorists", but on a connection to specific groups, such as the Taliban or Al Qaeda.

Concern has been expressed about the procedural unfairness of the sanctions regime,[109] particularly the low standard of proof in listing individuals and entities, and the lack of a hearing at the listing or delisting stage. While marginal improvements to the standard of proof have been made,[110] the diplomatic protection model underlying the delisting process remains ill-suited to protecting the interests of non-State actors—particularly where political opponents lack effective protection by their State. While the Council has affirmed human rights law in counter-terrorism,[111] it may still suspend non-derogable rights—such as procedural fairness—to maintain security.

103 SC Res 1267 (1999), paras 3 and 6 ("1267 Cttee"), and subject to humanitarian exceptions: para. 4.

104 SC Res 1267 (1999), preamble; 1333 (1999), preamble.

105 SC Res 1333 (2000), paras 5–6 (military), 7–8(a) (diplomatic), 8(b), 11–12 (aircraft), 14 (travel), subject to humanitarian exceptions: paras 11–12; 1452 (2002), paras 1–4. Detailed provisions govern implementation and supervision: SC Res 1333 (2000), paras 15–26; 1363 (2001), paras 1–8; 1388 (2002); 1390 (2002); 1452 (2002); 1455 (2003), paras 1–15; 1526 (2004).

106 SC Res 1333 (2000), paras 8(c) and 16(b).

107 SC Res 1390 (2002), para. 1; Stromseth, above n.5, 42–3; Nico Krisch, The Rise and Fall of Collective Security: Terrorism, US Hegemony, and the Plight of the Security Council, in: Christian Walter et al. (eds), Terrorism as a Challenge for National and International Law (2003), 879, 889.

108 SC (1267 Cttee), Consolidated List of Individuals and Entities Belonging to or Associated with the Taliban and Al-Qaida Organization (3 May 2004).

109 Joan Fitzpatrick, Speaking Law to Power: The War against Terrorism and Human Rights, 14 EJIL (2003), 241, 260–4; Krisch, above n.107, 11–12; E. Miller, The Use of Targeted Sanctions in the Fight against International Terrorism: What about Human Rights?, 97 ASIL Proc (2003), 46, 46, 49–50; Abdirisak Aden v. Commission, Case T-306/01, 10 December 2002.

110 SC Res 1526 (2004), paras 16–18; SC (1267 Cttee), Guidelines of the Cttee for the Conduct of its Work, 7 November 2002, amended 10 April 2003.

111 SC Res 1456 (2003), annexed Decl., para. 6; also 1535 (2004), preamble.

XIV. Terrorist attacks of 11 September 2001

XIV.A. Resolution 1368

The sanctions regime was still in place when the United States was attacked on 11 September 2001. In Res 1368, the next day, under Chapter VII, the Council condemned "in the strongest terms the horrifying terrorist attacks" and regarded "such acts, like any act of international terrorism, as a threat to international peace and security".[112] The attacks involved hijacking of aircraft and their use, or intended use, as weapons against civilian buildings (the World Trade Centre), government offices (the White House and Congress) and military headquarters (the Pentagon). All States were called on to "bring to justice the perpetrators, organizers and sponsors" and hold accountable "those responsible for aiding, supporting or harbouring" them, and to "prevent and suppress terrorist acts".[113]

The preamble recognized "the inherent right of individual or collective self-defence in accordance with the Charter",[114] but it did not explicitly state that the United States had a right of self-defence against the attacks.[115] Indeed, the Council called the attacks a "threat to the peace" rather than an "armed attack".[116] Most Council members did not immediately conceptualize 11 September as an armed attack, instead invoking a criminal law paradigm by speaking of *bringing the perpetrators to justice* or referring to *crimes* rather than acts of war.[117] It was only later that explicit claims of armed attack and self-defence were articulated,[118] which soon gained acceptance.[119]

In spite of expressing "readiness to take all necessary steps to respond to the terrorist attacks ... and to combat all forms of terrorism",[120] the Council did not authorize military action. Instead, the Council deferred to the unilateral, defensive response of a victim State,[121] losing the opportunity to collectively manage the forcible response, including its targets and

112 SC Res 1368 (2001), para. 1; reaffirmed in 1373 (2001), preamble.

113 SC Res 1368 (2001), paras 3–4, respectively.

114 Reaffirmed in SC Res 1373 (2001), preamble.

115 Frederic Mégret, "War"? Legal Semantics and the Move to Violence, 13 EJIL (2002), 361, 374. Self-defence against terrorism is not considered here: see generally Gray, above n.93, 159–94; Thomas Franck, Recourse to Force (2002), 53–68; Michael Byers, Terrorism, the Use of Force and International Law after September 11, 51 ICLQ (2002), 401; Antonio Cassese, Terrorism is Also Disrupting Some Crucial Legal Categories of International Law, 12 EJIL (2001), 993; Wedgwood, above n.86; Oscar Schachter, The Lawful Use of Force by a State against Terrorists in Another Country, 19 IYBHR (1989), 209.

116 Cassese, ibid., 996; Mégret, ibid., 375.

117 SC 56th Sess., 4370th Mtg, Verbatim Record, 12 September 2001, UN Doc. S/PV.4370, 3 (Mauritius), 4 (Tunisia), 5 (Ireland, China, Russia), 6 (Jamaica, Norway).

118 NATO, Press Release 124 (12 September 2001); Elena Katselli and Sangeeta Shah, September 11 and the UK Response, 52 ICLQ (2002), 245, 248; UN Doc. S/2001/947 (7 October 2001) (UK); Conclusions and Plan of Action of the Extraordinary European Council Mtg, 21 September 2001, SN140/01.

119 Eric Myjer and Nigel White, The Twin Towers Attack: An Unlimited Right to Self-Defence?, 7 J Conflict and Security Law (2002), 1, 8–9; Christine Gray, The Use of Force and the International Legal Order, in: Malcolm Evans (ed.), International Law (2003), 589, 604.

120 SC Res 1368 (2001), para. 5; see also 1373 (2001), preamble.

121 Byers, above n.115, 413; Cassese, above n.115, 999–1000; Richard Falk, The Great Terror War (2003), 59.

156 *CJIL* (2005)

duration.[122] This inadvertently encouraged other States to pursue forcible responses to unrelated terrorist problems,[123] despite US double standards in insisting on its exceptional defensive claims.[124]

XIV.B. Resolution 1373

In Res 1373, the Council required States, under Chapter VII, to suppress terrorism, implicitly approving earlier General Assembly recommendations.[125] In a bout of legislative and regulatory activism,[126] States are foremost *required* to prevent, suppress, freeze and criminalize terrorist financing.[127] States must also: (a) refrain from supporting terrorists; (b) prevent terrorist acts; (c) deny safe haven to those who finance, plan, support or commit terrorist acts, or harbour them; and (d) prevent the use of their territory for international terrorism.[128]

Further, States are *required* to (e) bring to justice those who finance, plan, prepare, perpetrate or support terrorist acts, *and establish such terrorist acts as serious criminal offences in domestic laws with proportionate penalties*; (f) assist other States in criminal investigations or proceedings; and (g) prevent the movement of terrorists by controls on borders, documentation and counterfeiting.[129] The Resolution prefers criminal law and regulatory measures over military responses.[130]

Other provisions are framed as *requests* rather than obligations.[131] The Council declared that committing, financing, planning and inciting terrorism are contrary to UN purposes and principles,[132] potentially leading to exclusion from refugee status under the 1951 Refugee Convention.[133] The Council was determined "to take all necessary steps" to

122 Georges Abi-Saab, The Proper Role of International Law in Combating Terrorism, 1 Chinese JIL (2002), 305, 309; Jutta Brunnée, Terrorism and Legal Change: An International Law Lesson, in: Ronald Daniels et al. (eds), The Security of Freedom: Essays on Canada's Anti-Terrorism Bill (2001) 341, 343.

123 Falk, above n.121, 55.

124 Harold Koh, On American Exceptionalism, 55 Stanford LR (2003), 1479, 1487.

125 Szasz, above n.5, 903.

126 Guillaume, above n.39, 8; Krisch, above n.107, 3, 5–6, 13; Rosand, above n.1, 334; Szasz, above n.5, 903; Myjer and White, above n.119, 6.

127 SC Res 1373 (2001), para. 1; see Ilias Bantekas, The International Law of Terrorist Financing, 97 AJIL (2003), 315; Walter Perkel, Money Laundering and Terrorism, 41 American Criminal LR (2004), 183.

128 SC Res 1373 (2001), para. 2.

129 Ibid.

130 Myjer and White, above n.119, 6.

131 SC Res 1373 (2001), paras 3–4: States are called upon to exchange information exchange, cooperate, adopt and implement treaties and resolutions, and deny refugee status and the political offence exception to terrorists. The Council was also concerned about links between terrorism and transnational organized crime, drugs and arms trafficking, money-laundering, and illegal movements of WMDs.

132 SC Res 1373 (2001), para. 5.

133 1951 Convention Relating to the Status of Refugees (adopted 28 July 1951, entered into force 22 April 1954, 189 UNTS 137), art. 1F(c).

implement the Resolution.[134] A Counter-Terrorism Committee (CTC) monitored implementation, including through mandatory State reporting.[135]

As Judge Kooijmans observed in the *Israel Wall Advisory Opinion*, the "completely new element" in these resolutions is classifying "acts of international terrorism, without any further qualification, a threat to international peace and security ... without ascribing these acts of terrorism to a particular State".[136] The general proscription of terrorism eliminates the selectivity in the Council's previous ad hoc approach,[137] which disregarded "the principle of equal treatment".[138]

XIV.C. No definition of terrorism

The quasi-legislative approach, however, creates other problems. Terrorism was not defined in resolutions after 11 September;[139] nor were lists of terrorists established, although the CTC blithely encouraged States to use lists to "eliminate the need for proof of actual involvement" in terrorism.[140] The lack of definition was deliberate, since consensus on Res 1373 depended on avoiding definition.[141] The CTC also decided not to define terrorism, "although its members had a fair idea of what was blatant terrorism".[142] The CTC did not want to interfere in the competence of other UN bodies by judicially or legislatively defining it, or adjudicating on specific acts.[143]

Instead, the CTC proposed an ad hoc approach, deciding whether an act is terrorism "where necessary" and referring political controversies to the Council or other bodies.[144] Its mandate is based on a pragmatic view that terrorism can be combated even without agreement on its criminal wrongfulness in all situations.[145] Res 1373 was, however, drafted partly on the basis that

134 SC Res 1373 (2001), para. 8.

135 Ibid., para. 6 ("CTC"), confirmed and structured in SC Pres Stat (15 April 2002), S/PRST/2002/10; (8 October 2002), S/PRST/2002/26; (17 December 2002), S/PRST/2002/38; (4 April 2003), S/PRST/2003/3; (30 March 2004), S/PRST/2004/8; SC Res 1535 (2004); see Rosand, above n.1, 334–7; Rostow, above n.1, 482; Curtis Ward, Building Capacity to Combat International Terrorism: The Role of the United Nations Security Council, 8 J Conflict and Security L (2003), 289, 298–304; SC, Pres Note, annex: CTC Report on Implementation Problems, 26 January 2004, UN Doc. S/2004/70, 15; UNODC (Terrorism Prevention Branch), Global Programme against Terrorism, Current Developments, Vienna, August 2003; ECOSOC (Commission on Crime Prevention and Criminal Justice), Secretary-General's Report on Strengthening international cooperation and technical assistance in preventing and combating terrorism, 13th Sess., Vienna, 11–20 May 2004, UN Doc. E/CN.15/2004/8 (17 March 2004).

136 Israel Wall Advisory Opinion, ICJ Case 131 (9 July 2004), para. 35 (sep. op. Kooijmans J).

137 See generally Andrea Bianchi, Ad-hocism and the Rule of Law, 13 EJIL (2002), 263, 271–2.

138 Jürgen Habermas, The Inclusion of the Other (2002), 180.

139 Rosand, above n.1, 333, 339–340; Stromseth, above n.5, 44; Rostow, above n.1, 484; Talmon, above n.5, 189.

140 Jeremy Wainwright, CTC Expert Opinion, adopted by CTC, 24 November 2002, para. 8.

141 Loretta Bondi, Legitimacy and Legality: Key Issues in the Fight against Terrorism, Fund for Peace, Washington DC, 11 September 2002, 25.

142 CTC Chair (Ambassador Jeremy Greenstock), Presentation to Symposium: Combating International Terrorism: The Contribution of the United Nations, Vienna, 3–4 June 2002; see also Walter Lacquer, We Can't Define "Terrorism" but We Can Fight It, Wall Street J, 12 July 2002, A12.

143 Greenstock, ibid.

144 Ibid.

145 Rostow, above n.1, 487.

the sectoral treaties provided a framework definition.[146] Even so, the CTC has openly allowed States to unilaterally define terrorist acts.[147] Commonwealth model legislation to implement Res 1373 has defined terrorism by sectoral offences but also generically.[148]

While flexibility in implementation is warranted due to variations in domestic legal systems, this effectively means that each State unilaterally defines terrorism,[149] without any outer legal boundaries set by the international community. Far from urging States to confine overly broad legislation, the CTC has advocated that *domestic* terrorism laws be jurisdictionally widened to cover *international* terrorism,[150] even though some domestic crimes more closely resemble broad national security or public order offences. The absence of a definition also makes it difficult to resolve disputes about whether particular persons or groups qualify as terrorist.[151]

It also raises difficult questions about the scope of the Council's authority, under art. 39 of the Charter, to designate a generalized, indeterminate phenomenon (rather than a specific act or incident, as in past practice[152]) as a threat to peace and security.[153] The Resolution addresses terrorism generally, unconnected to 11 September 2001, and the response is not bound by temporal or geographic limits.[154] While the Council possesses a very wide discretion,[155] its limits remain untested. In the *Namibia Advisory Opinion,* Judge Fitzmaurice has warned of the

> . . . all too great ease with which any acutely controversial international situation can be represented as involving a latent threat to peace and security, even where it is really too remote to genuinely constitute one.[156]

On one view, action against an abstract and non-specific phenomenon,[157] or against distant, speculative or potential threats,[158] may be of questionable validity—quite apart from the

146 Ibid.

147 UNHR Cttee, Press Release HR/CT/630, 27 March 2003 (CTC Expert, Curtis Ward); Ward, above n.135, 294–5.

148 Commonwealth Secretariat, Model Legislative Provisions on Measures to Combat Terrorism, part I.

149 Rosand, above n.1, 339–40; Stromseth, above n.5, 44.

150 Greenstock, above n.142; Walter Gehr, Recurrent Issues: CTC Briefing for Member States, 4 April 2002.

151 Rosand, above n.1, 340.

152 Szasz, above n.5, 901–2; Stromseth, above n.5, 41; de Brichambaut, above n.6, 271, 275; Abi-Saab, above n.122, 310; Nolte, above n.9, 321–4; Derek Bowett, The Impact of Security Council Decisions on Dispute Settlement Procedures, 5 EJIL (1994), 89, 92.

153 Krisch, above n.107.

154 Ibid., 6; Szasz, above n.5, 901; Stromseth, above n.5, 43.

155 Lockerbie, ICJ Reports (1992), 3, 66, 176 (Weeramantry J); Hans Kelsen, The Law of the United Nations (1950), 727; Dapo Akande, The International Court of Justice and the Security Council: Is There Room for Judicial Control of Decisions of the Political Organs of the United Nations?, 46 ICLQ (1997), 309, 314; Gowlland-Debbas, above n.13, 287; Nolte, above n.9, 316; Keith Harper, Does the United Nations Security Council have the Competence to Act as a Court and Legislature?, 27 NYU JILP (1995), 103, 149; Reisman, above n.14, 93; Stromseth, above n.5, 42.

156 Namibia Advisory Opinion, ICJ Reports (1971), 41 (diss. op. Judge Fitzmaurice), para. 116, also para. 112.

157 Abi-Saab, above n.122, 310; de Brichambaut, above n.6, 275; Nolte, above n.9, 321–4; Bowett, above n.152, 92.

158 Namibia, above n.156, 340, para. 34 (Gros J); Kelsen, above n.155, 727–8.

distinct question of whether a judicial body is competent to review Council action.[159] On the other hand, what constitutes a 'threat to the peace' is a continuously evolving and largely political question[160] and, since the early 1990s, the practice of States party to the UN Charter indicates an expanding interpretation of art. 39.[161] The report of the UN High-Level Panel on Threats, Challenges and Change in December 2004 supports the view that in addition to more traditional threats, economic and social threats (including poverty, infectious disease and environmental degradation), terrorism and transnational organized crime threaten security.[162]

The best that can be said is that while terrorism *may* undoubtedly threaten peace and security, in the absence of a definition limited to grave acts of violence with an international dimension, it is very difficult to accept that *every* terrorist act is a threat. It is one thing for the Council to identify particular incidents as terrorist—as with aggression[163]—but quite another matter for it to allow States to arbitrarily do so, in the absence of any "criteria of reference".[164]

The failure to define terrorism has provoked mixed reactions from Council members. Colombia believed that definition was unnecessary, since terrorism was defined in Assembly Res 49/60.[165] Whereas Mauritius did not want to "quibble" about definition,[166] other States have placed more value on it.[167] Syria stated that non-definition had encouraged violations of human rights and IHL, and encouraged "selective accusations of terrorism".[168] Arab and Islamic States have insisted that terrorism be distinguished from self-determination struggles; that "State terrorism" be covered; and that root causes be addressed.[169]

The absence of a definition is not merely of theoretical interest, because the terms "terrorism" and "terrorist" have operative legal significance in Res 1373, triggering obligations to criminalize financing of *terrorism*; suppress *terrorist* groups; deny refugee status to *terrorists*;

159 Akande, above n.155, 325.

160 Talmon, above n.5, 179–181.

161 See, e.g. UN Doc. S/23500 (1992), 3 (referring to non-military threats in the economic, social, humanitarian and ecological fields); Talmon, above n.5, 181.

162 UN High-Level Panel on Threats, Challenges and Change, A More Secure World: Our Shared Responsibility (2004), 2, 21–30, 52–54.

163 Gerald Fitzmaurice, The Definition of Aggression, 1 ICLQ (1952), 137, 143–4.

164 Ian Brownlie, International Law and the Use of Force by States (1963), 356.

165 SC, 4845th mtg, Press Release SC/7900, 16 October 2003.

166 SC, 4413th mtg, Press Release SC/7207, 12 November 2001.

167 SC, 4453rd mtg, Press Release SC/7276, 18 January 2002 (including Syria; Costa Rica for the Rio Group; Morocco for the Arab Group; Qatar for the OIC; Pakistan; Israel); 4512th and 4513th mtgs, Press Release SC/7361, 15 April 2002 (Syria; Malaysia); 4792nd mtg, Press Release SC/7823, 23 July 2003 (Pakistan); 4845th mtg, Press Release SC/7900, 16 October 2003 (Pakistan; Libya; Yemen; Armenia).

168 SC, 4512th and 4513th mtgs, Press Release SC/7361, 15 April 2002.

169 SC, 4453rd mtg, Press Release SC/7276, 18 January 2002 (including Syria; Qatar for the OIC; *cf.* Israel); 4734th mtg, Press Release SC/7718, 4 April 2003 (Pakistan; Syria; 4512th and 4513th mtgs, Press Release SC/7361, 15 April 2002 (Malaysia); 4792nd mtg, Press Release SC/7823, 23 July 2003 (Pakistan); 4845th mtg, Press Release SC/7900, 16 October 2003 (Pakistan; Libya; Yemen).

prevent the movement of *terrorists*; bring *terrorists* to justice; and, vitally, establish *terrorist acts* as serious domestic crimes. Resolutions have also implicitly referred to self-defence against terrorism, so lack of definition allows States to unilaterally target "terrorists" in military operations.[170]

As Amnesty notes, "the terms 'terrorists' and 'terrorist acts' in resolution 1373 are open to widely differing interpretations" and may facilitate rights violations.[171] Analysis of the more than 500 State reports to the CTC reveals that national anti-terrorism laws are widely divergent, with some very broad or vague definitions in play.[172] SC Res 1373 has not produced any consensus definition of terrorism in national laws, nor encouraged harmonization of national definitions. Almost half of States have now enacted special terrorism offences, and almost all are different.[173]

Some States have deployed the international legitimacy conferred by Council authorization to define terrorism to repress or de-legitimize political opponents, and to conflate them with Al-Qaeda. Thus, China bluntly characterizes Uighur separatists in Xinjiang as terrorists;[174] Russia asserts that Chechen rebels are terrorists, even though many are fighting in an internal conflict;[175] and India seldom distinguishes militants from terrorists in Kashmir.[176] In Indonesia, insurgencies in Aceh and West Papua have been described and combated as terrorism, as have a Maoist insurgency in Nepal and an Islamist movement in Morocco.[177] Predictably, Israel has identified Palestinians with Al-Qaeda, with Ariel Sharon calling Arafat "our Bin Laden".[178]

170 US Congress, Authorization for Use of Military Force, Pub L 107-40, 115 Stat. 224 (18 September 2001).

171 Amnesty International, Statement on the Implementation of SC Res 1373, 1 October 2001.

172 See Ben Saul, Unpublished Doctor of Philosophy Thesis: Defining Terrorism in International Law, Faculty of Law, University of Oxford (2004), chapter 3.

173 Ibid.

174 SC, 4688th mtg, Press Release SC/7638, 20 January 2003 (China); Chinese Information Office of State Council, "East Turkistan" Terrorist Forces Cannot Get Away with Impunity, 21 January 2001; Jim Yardley, China puts minorities on terrorist watch list, Sydney Morning Herald, 17 December 2003; Amnesty International, Rights at Risk: Concerns Regarding Security Legislation and Law Enforcement Measures, 18 January 2002, AI Index ACT 30/002/2002, 5; Chien-peng Chung, China's "War on Terror": September 11 and Uighur Separatism, Foreign Affairs (July–August 2002), 8; Rajan Menon, The New Great Game in Central Asia, 45 Survival (2003), 187, 192, 198–9.

175 SC, 4688th mtg, Press Release SC/7638, 20 January 2003 (Russia); Ivanov Denies War in Chechnya, Calls It Fighting with Terrorism, Itar-Tass, 4 March 2004; Struggle in Chechnya: Struggle against International Terrorism, Itar-Tass, 12 November 2002. In 1995, the Russian Constitutional Court Declared that Chechnya Was an Internal Armed Conflict Governed by Protocol II, 17 Human Rights J (1996), 133; Paola Gaeta, The Armed Conflict in Chechnya before the Russian Constitutional Court, 7 EJIL (1996), 563.

176 SC, 4618th mtg, Press Release SC/7522, 4 October 2002 (India).

177 John Aglionby, Jakarta orders attack on Aceh, Guardian, 19 May 2003; ABC TV (Foreign Correspondent), West Papua: Ambushed, 3 August 2004; Randeep Ramesh, Maoists tighten grip on Kathmandu, Guardian, 21 August 2004; Reuters, One Thousand Prisoners Released for Each Tiny Finger, Sydney Morning Herald, 10 May 2003.

178 ABC News, Arafat Accuses Bin Laden of Exploiting Palestinians, 15 December 2002; Dinah Pokempner, Terrorism and Human Rights: The Legal Framework, in: Michael Schmitt and Gian Luca Beruto (eds), Terrorism and International Law (2003), 19, 23.

As a result, the Council has initiated a fight not against terrorism, but "different terrorisms".[179] This devolution of discretionary power is unprincipled and dangerous. Combating terrorism "without defining it remained possible for as long as the word itself was not uttered".[180] In contrast, operatively deploying the term without defining it creates uncertainty and allows States to make "unilateral determinations geared towards their own interests".[181] Few States have objected to Council measures because they align (rather than interfere) with their sovereign interests.[182]

At the same time, by requiring States to criminalize terrorism in domestic law, the Council is substituting itself for—or at least interfering in—conventional law-making processes,[183] particularly given the ongoing negotiation of a UN Draft Comprehensive Convention against terrorism in the General Assembly since 2000.[184] Criminalization of harmful transnational conduct normally takes place in multilateral treaty negotiations—a process marked by broader participation (than 15 unrepresentative Council members)[185] and greater precision (of elements of offences, jurisdictional principles and penalties, which resolutions are silent on). Further, Council negotiations on drafting legislative resolutions are not publicly recorded,[186] in this case creating further uncertainty about the intended meaning of "terrorism".

XV. Terrorist acts 2002–04

From 2002, the Council adopted a series of formulaic resolutions condemning a particular terrorist bomb attack (Bali and Kenya in 2002, Bogota and Istanbul in 2003, and Madrid in 2004), hostage-taking (Moscow in 2002) or missile attack (Kenya).[187] The resolutions regard such acts, "like any act of international terrorism, as a threat to international peace and security", urge States to bring the perpetrators, organizers and sponsors to justice, and express "determination to combat all forms of terrorism".[188]

The Moscow resolution also demanded the release of hostages.[189] That resolution is significant because the Council involved itself in domestic terrorism, and two presidential

179 Walter Laqueur, The New Terrorism: Fanaticism and the Arms of Mass Destruction (2001), 79.

180 Guillaume, above n.39, 4–5.

181 Ibid.; see also Jean-Marc Sorel, Some Questions About the Definition of Terrorism and the Fight against its Financing, 14 AJIL (2003), 365, 370.

182 Krisch, above n.107, 15.

183 Ibid., 6; Rostow, above n.1, 482.

184 UN GAOR (55th Sess.), Ad Hoc Cttee Report (2000), UN Doc. Supp. 37 (A/55/37); see Surya Subedi, The UN Response to International Terrorism in the Aftermath of the Terrorist Attacks in America and the Problem of the Definition of Terrorism in International Law, 4 International Law Forum (2002), 159.

185 *Cf.* Talmon, above n.5, 179 (Council decisions to use force are open to the same criticism, but this is not a basis for opposing Chapter VII actions).

186 Talmon, ibid., 51.

187 SC Res 1438 (2002), para. 1; 1450 (2002), para. 1 (14 votes to 1); 1465 (2003), para. 1; 1516 (2003), para. 1; 1530 (2004), para. 1; 1440 (2002), para. 1, respectively.

188 SC Res 1438 (2002), paras 1 and 3–4; 1440 (2002), paras 1 and 4–5; 1450 (2002), paras 1 and 3–4; 1465 (2003), paras 1 and 3–4; 1516 (2003), paras 1 and 3–4; 1530 (2004), paras 1 and 3–4, respectively.

189 SC Res 1440 (2002), para. 2.

statements have also condemned internal terrorist attacks in Russia connected to the Chechen conflict. The first addressed a "terrorist bomb attack" in Grozny in 2004, which killed the President of the Chechen Republic and others.[190]

The second responded to "the heinous terrorist act" of hostage-taking at a school in Beslan in 2004, and "other terrorist attacks" against "innocent civilians" in Moscow and two Russian airliners.[191] While responsibility was not attributed to Chechen rebels in the statements, investigations later did so. These attacks show how serious acts of domestic terrorism can affect international interests or values, even in the absence of a strict connection to, or impact on, another State.

Only two of the resolutions attribute responsibility for terrorism. Whereas the Kenyan resolution is inconclusive, condemning only "claims of responsibility" by Al-Qaeda in its preamble,[192] the Madrid resolution firmly attributes blame to "the terrorist group ETA" in an operative paragraph.[193] Investigations soon showed that Al-Qaeda was responsible, and the hasty attribution to ETA, on the day of the bombing, was based on erroneous Spanish advice.[194] The Council abandoned its previously cautious approach in a rush to act, making an avoidable mistake, and raising the wider problem of the evidentiary standard used in Council decision-making.[195]

XVI. Terrorism in the Middle East

Despite the prevalence of terrorism in the Middle East for many years, few resolutions have condemned it, due to the political sensitivity of Palestinian self-determination. Only since 2002 have resolutions mentioned terrorism. SC Res 1397, dealing with Israeli–Palestinian violence since the second intifadah from late 2000, demanded the "immediate cessation of ... all acts of terror",[196] reiterated in four later resolutions.[197]

SC Res 1435 called on the Palestinian Authority ("PA") to bring to justice persons responsible for terrorist acts, and condemned "all terrorist attacks against any civilians, including the terrorist bombings in Israel" and "in a Palestinian school in Hebron".[198] SC Res 1402 expressed concern about "suicide bombings" in Israel, which, given the

190 SC Pres Stat (10 May 2004), S/PRST/2004/14.

191 SC Pres Stat (1 September 2004), S/PRST/2004/31.

192 Evidence suggests that Al-Qaeda was indeed responsible: James Risen, US Suspects Qaeda Link to Bombing in Mombasa, NY Times, 30 November 2002.

193 SC Res 1450 (2002), preamble and 1440 (2002), para. 1, respectively.

194 Giles Tremlett, Kofi Annan Calls Aznar Author of his Own Defeat, Guardian, 18 March 2004.

195 See generally Mary Ellen O'Connell, Evidence of Terror, 7 J of Conflict and Security L (2002), 19; Sara Scheideman, Standards of Proof in Forcible Responses to Terrorism, 50 Syracuse LR (2000), 249; After 11 September 2001, the US claimed it had "clear and compelling information" about Al-Qaeda's responsibility: SC, Letter from the US Permanent Representative to the SC President, 7 October 2001, UN Doc. S/2001/946.

196 SC Res 1397 (2002), para. 1.

197 SC Res 1402 (2002), para. 2; 1435 (2002), para. 1; 1515 (2003), preamble; 1544 (2004), preamble.

198 SC Res 1435 (2002), para. 4.

preambular references to terrorism, may be interpreted as terrorism. The Resolution was also concerned about Israel's military attack on Arafat's headquarters, but did not qualify it as terrorism. Likewise, SC Res 1544 refers to housing demolitions and the killing of Palestinian refugees by Israel in Rafah, but does not classify these as terrorism. Further, Res 1435 demanded that Israel cease destroying Palestinian infrastructure in Ramallah and that it withdraw from Palestinian cities, but these acts are not qualified as terrorism.

Most references to terrorism do not ascribe responsibility for it, so it is possible to interpret the condemnation of terrorism as applying equally to Israeli and Palestinian violence against civilians. This even-handed approach is reinforced by the Council's invocation of respect for IHL and the protection of civilians.[199] Only Res 1435 implies that non-State actors are the main perpetrators, when it calls on the PA to bring terrorists to justice. Given the nature of some Palestinian violence, it is likely that the condemnation of terrorism is primarily directed against Palestinians. In contrast, in nearby Lebanon, the Council has avoided mentioning terrorism and instead referred to the activities of "armed militias".[200]

XVII. Thematic resolutions 1999–2004

Since 1999, one binding and three non-binding resolutions have addressed terrorism in general terms, without any link to specific terrorist acts.[201] Reflecting General Assembly resolutions, the Council unequivocally condemned "all acts, methods and practices of terrorism as criminal and unjustifiable, regardless of their motivation, in all their forms and manifestations, wherever and by whomever committed".[202] All resolutions refer to the threat to peace and security posed by terrorism and its danger to life.[203] One resolution states that terrorism endangers human dignity and security, development, global stability, prosperity, and UN purposes and principles.[204]

These resolutions have urged States to prevent and suppress terrorism and its financing; bring perpetrators to justice; deny safe haven by apprehending, prosecuting or extraditing terrorists, and denying them refugee status; exchange information and cooperate; adopt and implement sectoral treaties and Council resolutions; and enhance the United Nations' role.[205] Two resolutions stressed the need to broaden "understanding among civilizations" and address regional conflicts and global development.[206] One resolution warned of global links between terrorism, weapons of mass destruction (WMD) and organized crime.[207]

199 SC Res 1397 (2002), preamble; 1435 (2002), preamble; 1535 (2004), paras 1 and 3; 1544 (2004), para. 3.

200 SC Res 1559 (2004), preamble, para. 3.

201 SC Res 1269 (1999); 1377 (2001), annexed Ministerial Decl.; 1456 (2003), annexed Ministerial Decl.

202 SC Res 1269 (1999), para. 1; 1377 (2001), annexed Decl.; 1456 (2003), annexed Decl., preamble.

203 SC Res 1269 (1999), preamble, paras 1 and 5; 1377 (2001), annexed Decl.; 1456 (2003), annexed Decl., preamble; 1540 (2004), preamble.

204 SC Res 1269 (1999), para. 3; 1377 (2001), annexed Decl.

205 SC Res 1269 (1999); 1377 (2001); 1456 (2003).

206 SC Res 1377 (2001), annexed Decl.; 1456 (2003), annexed Decl., para. 10.

207 SC Res 1456 (2003), annexed Decl., preamble.

164 *CJIL* (2005)

While, in 1999, the Council expressed "its readiness to ... take necessary steps ... to counter terrorist threats",[208] the first three resolutions were non-binding, standard-setting instruments, influenced by Assembly resolutions, and lacking any compliance mechanisms.[209] The first resolution was largely ignored, since many States lacked the technical capacity or political will to take effective action.[210]

SC Res 1540 (2004), however, imposes obligations under Chapter VII to deal with the threat to peace and security posed by links between terrorism, non-State actors and WMD.[211] States must prohibit non-State actors from developing, acquiring, manufacturing, possessing, transporting, transferring or using nuclear, chemical or biological weapons and their means of delivery, "in particular for terrorist purposes".[212] The Resolution establishes detailed control measures and a supervisory committee, and aims not to conflict with specialized WMD treaties and agencies.[213]

Unusually, in a footnote, the Council defines certain concepts for the purpose of the resolution, including "means of delivery", "non-State actor" and "related materials". Such definition is a helpful interpretive device in quasi-legislative resolutions, as long as the definition itself is not too vague,[214] but the device was not used here to define "terrorism". The regime targeting non-State actors is undermined, however, by double standards on the possession and monitoring of nuclear weapons by major nuclear States.[215]

XVIII. A working definition in 2004

Three years after imposing measures against terrorism, the Council adopted a resolution generically defining it. While not expressly framed as a definition, SC Res 1566 of October 2004 recalls that the following acts are never justifiable:

> ... criminal acts, including against civilians, committed with the intent to cause death or serious bodily injury, or taking of hostages, *with the purpose to provoke a state of terror* in the general public or in a group of persons or particular persons, *intimidate a population* or *compel a government or an international organization* to do or to abstain from doing any act, *which constitute offences within the scope of and as defined in the international conventions and protocols* relating to terrorism ....[216]

208 SC Res 1269 (1999), para. 6.

209 Ward, above n.135, 290.

210 Ibid.

211 SC Res 1540 (2004), preamble.

212 Ibid., paras 1–2.

213 Ibid., paras 4–5 (referring to the 1968 Nuclear Non-Proliferation Treaty, 1993 Chemical Weapons Convention, and 1972 Biological and Toxin Weapons Convention; and the IAEA and Organization for the Prohibition of Chemical Weapons).

214 Talmon, above n.5, 190.

215 Dafna Linzer, US backs out of nuclear inspections treaty, Sydney Morning Herald, 2 August 2004.

216 SC Res 1566 (2004), para. 3 (emphasis added).

States were urged to prevent such acts, and punish them "by penalties consistent with their grave nature". The Resolution also created a working group to report on measures that could be imposed on individuals, groups or entities involved in, or associated with, terrorist activities, *other than* those designated by the 1267 committee.[217] The Resolution thus seeks to universalize (in a parallel regime) the proscription model developed by the 1267 Committee for the Taliban and Al-Qaeda. It was based on a Russian proposal to proscribe Chechen terrorists, which was opposed by Arab States objecting to the potential designation of Palestinian groups.[218]

The definition of "terrorism" provides explicit guidance to States (and the working group and CTC) on the meaning of terrorism, and may also exert pressure in the General Assembly to break the impasse on the Draft Comprehensive Convention. It presents a relatively narrow definition, limited to acts constituting sectoral offences (typically serious violence endangering life or property, and requiring an international element), which are *also* intended to create terror, intimidate a population, or coerce a government or organization. It thus combines elements of the definitions in the General Assembly's 1994 Declaration on Measures to Eliminate International Terrorism,[219] and the 1999 Terrorist Financing Convention. It is, however, at variance with the definitions proposed in art. 2(1) of the current Draft Comprehensive Convention and by the UN High-Level Panel in late 2004.[220] While both of those proposals refer to intimidation and coercion (as in SC Res 1566), neither of the proposed definitions covers acts aimed solely to provoke terror.

The definition in Res 1566 does not require a political or other motive, thus encompassing private acts which terrorize, intimidate or coerce. Consequently, some of the distinctiveness of terrorism, as *political* violence, is lost. Pragmatically, the definition may be too little, too late. In the three years to 2004, many States adopted laws implementing their obligations, and it is unlikely that they will further reform their laws to limit "terrorism" in conformity with the Resolution (which merely "recalls" that certain acts are never justified and does not require law reform). As discussed earlier, there are also legitimacy costs in circumventing the treaty process.

XIX. Conclusion

Prior to 1985, the Council refrained from using the term "terrorism", while from 1985 to 2004, it qualified a variety of disparate activities as terrorism, much of it covered by sectoral treaties. In sum, conduct labeled as terrorist includes hostage-taking and hijacking; abduction of UN personnel; unlawful use of plastic explosives; assassination of heads of State or

217 Ibid., para. 9: measures could include prosecution and extradition, asset freezing, and preventing movement and supply of weapons.

218 M. Farley, Chechens in frame as Russia asks UN to redefine terrorism, Sydney Morning Herald, 25–26 September 2004, 20.

219 GA Res 49/60 (1994), annexed Declaration, para. 3.

220 UN High-Level Panel, above n.162, 52; Draft Comprehensive Convention, above n.185.

political leaders; destruction of, or attacks on, civilian aircraft; bombings of embassies and civilians; organized, non-State political violence in peacetime, including attacks on civilian, government and military buildings; and attacks on religious sites in armed conflict. The acts of Al-Qaeda, including its destruction of property,[221] have also been described as terrorist, as has the use of WMD by non-State actors.

It is too soon to judge whether the Council's measures have contributed to customary norms on terrorism. Before 2001, mention of terrorism was limited to specific situations, while generalized references were preambular and contributed marginally to custom formation, although resolutions often invoked customary norms reflected in the 1970 Declaration on Friendly Relations.[222] The frequent designation of terrorism as a threat to peace and security is significant[223] but not evidence of delegated universal jurisdiction.[224] Reference to the obligation to prosecute or extradite terrorists is also deceptive, since many States prosecute terrorism as ordinary crime or sectoral treaty offences. It is still premature to claim universal jurisdiction over terrorism, given the absence of an agreed definition, though its exercise might not give rise to protest.[225]

Mandatory anti-terrorism measures between 2001 and 2004 suffered from lack of definition, but, in late 2004, the Council prospectively defined terrorism as serious (sectoral) criminal violence intended to provoke a state of terror, intimidate a population or compel a government or organization. Following definition, in the long term, Council measures may gradually harmonize national criminal laws, which may, in turn, constitute evidence of State practice and *opinio juris*. Council practice is, however, but one element in the formation of customary norms on terrorism, notwithstanding that the Council has firmly taken hold of the international community's response to the subject. In evaluating custom formation, the position of States in the UN General Assembly and national practice (including domestic implementation and judicial decisions) must also be considered in weighing Council measures.

221 SC Res 1390 (2002), preamble; 1455 (2003), preamble; 1526 (2004), preamble.

222 Preambles to SC Res 748 (1992); 1189 (1998); 1373 (2001), referring to the 1970 Declaration on Principles of International Law concerning Friendly Relations and Cooperation among States in accordance with the Charter of the UN, annexed to GA Res 2625 (XXV) (1970).

223 SC Res 731 (1992); 748 (1992); 1044 (1996); 1054 (1996); 1070 (1996); 1189 (1998); 1193 (1998); 1267 (1999); 1368 (2001); 1373 (2001); 1390 (2002); 1455 (2003); 1511 (2003), 1526 (2004).

224 *Cf.* Robert Kolb, Universal Criminal Jurisdiction in Matters of International Terrorism, 1 Revue Hellenique Droit International (1997), 43, 77.

225 Ibid., 87–8.

Part III
Criminal Justice Approach

[5]

Legal Control of International Terrorism: A Policy-Oriented Assessment

M. Cherif Bassiouni*

I. Introduction

Terrorism has existed, in one form or another, in many societies for as long as history has been recorded. The differences between its various manifestations, however, have been as to methods, means, and weapons. As the means available to inflict significant damage to society improve, the harmful impact of terrorism increases. And as weapons of mass destruction become more accessible, the dangers to the world community increase.

In times of national crisis similar to the one that the United States is experiencing in the wake of the incidents of September 11, renewed interest in the phenomenon of terrorism arises. For many who are just now delving into the subject of terrorism, there is a tendency to rediscover the wheel. The manifestations of terrorism and the means to prevent and control them have long been studied, but governments have tended to ignore the dangers. The lessons of the past, particularly those of Europe and the Middle East from the 1960s onward, have been largely ignored. As a result, we have not recognized the increasing global dimension of this criminal activity. Transnational criminal activity of all kinds (for example, organized crime, drug trafficking, and trafficking of women and children for sexual exploitation) has benefited from the advantages of globalization. States, however, have not foreseen that consequence, and their modalities of interstate cooperation in penal matters have remained fragmented and substantially ineffective.

This Essay assesses substantive international norms and their enforcement, and highlights the weaknesses of the international system's effectiveness in combating transnational crime generally, and terrorism in particular. It starts with defining the phenomenon of terrorism and identifying its characteristics and manifestations, before proceeding into a critical assessment of the modalities of interstate cooperation in penal matters and offering a few recommendations thereto. It is necessarily more a survey than an in-depth study of the questions addressed. Hopefully, however, its contents will prove

* Professor of Law and President, International Human Rights Law Institute, DePaul University; President, International Institute of Higher Studies in Criminal Sciences, Siracusa, Italy; President, International Association of Penal Law, Paris, France.

useful to bring about a better understanding of the phenomenon and how to deal with it in a rational, legal, and effective manner.

II. IDENTIFYING THE PRINCIPAL CHARACTERISTICS OF TERRORISM

A. *Terrorism's Root Causes, Actors, and Strategies*

Terrorism is a strategy of violence designed to instill terror in a segment of society in order to achieve a power-outcome, propagandize a cause, or inflict harm for vengeful political purposes. That strategy is resorted to by state actors either against their own population or against the population of another country. It is also used by non-state actors, such as insurgent or revolutionary groups acting within their own country or in another country. Lastly, it is used by ideologically motivated groups or individuals, acting either inside or outside their country of nationality, whose methods may vary according to their beliefs, goals, and means.

State and non-state actors who commit terrorist acts can be distinguished, inter alia, on the basis of their participants, their goals, their methods, and the means they have at their disposal. But these actors all resort to a strategy of terror-violence in order to achieve goals that include a power-outcome. The quantum or level of violence employed by actors in each category will usually depend on their access to means of terror-inspiring effects, and on whether these effects are likely to cause consequences conducive to attaining the desired power-outcome.

State terrorism is distinguishable from state-sponsored terrorism. In the latter, the actual perpetrators of terrorist acts are non-state actors operating with overt or covert support of a state. The former is carried out by state actors and is usually characterized by extensive, widespread, or systematic use of violence in violation of international humanitarian law and human rights law. It includes genocide,[1] crimes against humanity,[2] war crimes,[3] and

1. Convention on the Prevention and Punishment of the Crime of Genocide, Dec. 9, 1948, 102 Stat. 3045, 78 U.N.T.S. 277 [hereinafter Genocide Convention]. The International Criminal Tribunal for the Former Yugoslavia (ICTY) and the International Criminal Tribunal for Rwanda (ICTR) removed substantive immunity for genocide, crimes against humanity, and war crimes. *See* Statute of the International Criminal Tribunal for the Former Yugoslavia, S.C. Res. 808, U.N. SCOR, 48th Sess., 3217th mtg., Annex, art. 7(2), U.N. Doc. S/RES/808 (1993) [hereinafter ICTY Statute]; Statute of the International Criminal Tribunal for Rwanda, S.C. Res. 955, U.N. SCOR, 49th Sess., 3453d mtg., Annex, art. 6(2), U.N. Doc. S/RES/955 (1994) [hereinafter ICTR Statute]. *See also* Rome Statute of the International Criminal Court, July 17, 1998, U.N. Doc. A/CONF.183/9 (1998) [hereinafter ICC Statute]; M. CHERIF BASSIOUNI, THE STATUTE OF THE INTERNATIONAL CRIMINAL COURT: A DOCUMENTARY HISTORY (1998).

2. Charter of the International Military Tribunal, annexed to Agreement for the Prosecution and Punishment of the Major War Criminals of the European Axis, Aug. 8, 1945, art. 6, 59 Stat. 1544, 82 U.N.T.S. 279 [hereinafter Nuremberg Charter]. *See also* ICTY Statute, *supra* note 1, art. 5; ICTR Statute, *supra* note 1, art. 3; ICC Statute, *supra* note 1, art. 7. *See also* M. CHERIF BASSIOUNI, CRIMES AGAINST HUMANITY IN INTERNATIONAL CRIMINAL LAW (2d rev. ed. 1999).

3. Geneva Convention for the Amelioration of the Condition of the Wounded and Sick in Armed Forces in the Field, Aug. 12, 1949, 6 U.S.T. 3114, 75 U.N.T.S. 31 [hereinafter Geneva Convention I]; Geneva Convention for the Amelioration of the Condition of Wounded, Sick and Shipwrecked Members

torture.[4] The goals of states engaged in such terrorism might include the subjugation of a foreign or domestic population or the continuation of a regime in the face of domestic opposition. Sometimes a regime like the Nazis in Germany, the U.S.S.R. under Lenin and Stalin, and the Khmer Rouge in Cambodia will engage in systematic terror-inspiring violence against a segment of the civilian population exclusively because of its race or political views. In these extreme cases, the ultimate goal of the terror-violence is the total elimination of that social or political group.

Non-state actors' terrorism can be distinguished on the basis of the number of the groups' adherents, their goals, and their capabilities. For purposes of this study, they are divided into two groups: insurgent and revolutionary groups, and ideologically motivated groups.

Insurgent and revolutionary groups are larger groups at war with a particular regime, and whose goal is the regime's demise.[5] Unlike the regimes they fight, insurgent and revolutionary groups do not have conventional military and police forces, but rather consist of volunteer fighters who do not have the military training and capabilities of their regime-force opponents. Anti-regime forces cannot therefore face the regime forces on the same military level, and must therefore resort to unlawful means of violence, including targeting civilians and public and private property in violation of international and humanitarian law and domestic criminal law.[6]

Ideologically motivated groups tend to have fewer members/adherents and do not have the capability of effectuating a regime change, but their terror-violence techniques are capable of destabilizing a regime and inflicting harm on members of its society to achieve politically related, often vengeful, goals. For instance, by revealing a regime's weaknesses, thereby causing terror in the society by exposing its vulnerability, such terrorist

---

of Armed Forces at Sea, Aug. 12, 1949, 6 U.S.T. 3217, 75 U.N.T.S. 85 [hereinafter Geneva Convention II]; Geneva Convention Relative to the Treatment of Prisoners of War, Aug. 12, 1949, 6 U.S.T. 3316, 75 U.N.T.S. 135 [hereinafter Geneva Convention III]; Geneva Convention Relative to the Protection of Civilian Persons in Time of War, Aug. 12, 1949, 6 U.S.T. 3516, 75 U.N.T.S. 287 [hereinafter Geneva Convention IV]; Convention Respecting the Laws and Customs of War on Land, Oct. 18, 1907, 36 Stat. 2277, 1 Bevans 631 [hereinafter 1907 Hague Convention IV]. *See also* Protocol Additional I to the Geneva Conventions of 12 August 1949, and Relating to the Protection of Victims of International Armed Conflicts, June 8, 1977, 1125 U.N.T.S. 3 [hereinafter Additional Protocol I]; Protocol Additional II to the Geneva Conventions of 12 August 1949, and Relating to the Protection of Victims of Non-International Armed Conflicts, June 8, 1977, 1125 U.N.T.S. 609 [hereinafter Additional Protocol II].

4. Convention Against Torture and Other Cruel, Inhuman or Degrading Treatment or Punishment, Dec. 10, 1984, S. Treaty Doc. No. 100-20, 1465 U.N.T.S. 85 [hereinafter Torture Convention].

5. Insurgent and revolutionary groups include those who participated in the 1917 revolution in czarist Russia, which resulted in the establishment of the U.S.S.R., and the VietCong in North Vietnam, who then spread into South Vietnam, resulting in the unification of the divided country. Most of the African and Asian countries under French colonization, such as Algeria, or British colonization, such as Kenya, had insurgent groups whose activities led to the removal of the colonial forces and the establishment of independent states.

6. Anti-regime forces include such groups as those in the 1960s and 1970s referred to as the Red Brigades in Italy, the Red Liberation Army in Japan, and the Bader-Meinhoff Group in Germany. The ETA in Spain continues its assassinations and bombings, as does the IRA in Northern Ireland and England.

groups place the regime in a situation where it is likely to overreact or commit unlawful acts, and thereby delegitimize itself. In turn, such terrorist groups gain a greater claim of legitimacy and engender more support among the domestic and foreign populations. Ideologically motivated groups engage in strategies of terror-violence to achieve a desired political result, propagandize a political message, punish the society with whom they deem themselves at odds or at war, obtain political concessions in exchange for either desisting from harm they can inflict (e.g., threat to bomb) or providing articles/persons they have taken from the regime (e.g., hostages).

In its common usage, the term "international terrorism" has come to exclude the activities of state actors and even insurgent and revolutionary groups. Instead it is applied to small, ideologically motivated groups, and whose strategies of terror-violence are designed to propagate a political message, destabilize a regime, inflict social harm as political vengeance, and elicit over-reactive state responses likely to create a political crisis.

Some of these groups are characterized by the international composition of their members, the transnational dimension to their operations, and their reliance on financial support from more than one state. Such groups necessarily rely on public sympathy and the support of others in several countries, which permit them to maximize their harmful capabilities. They also rely on easy access to the worldwide financial system for money-laundering purposes, and the lack of international cooperation in penal matters between states, including the lack of cooperation in law enforcement, intelligence, the extradition of suspects, and other prosecutorial/investigative activities.[7]

These ideologically motivated terrorist groups select particular targets with a view to enhance collective social fear and to demonstrate the government's vulnerability and inability to offer society adequate protection. Experience reveals that governments inevitably fall into the trap of responding to such acts in ways that increase social and political tensions. These reactions enhance levels of fear in society, which in turn place more pressure on governments to act. The result is usually the escalation of the violence, which is almost always what the terrorists want to accomplish.

Target selection is also based on the expectation of media attention, particularly from the sensationalistic elements of the media, which often both promote greater public visibility of such groups and contribute to collective social fear.[8] The media frequently develops a symbiotic relationship with the terrorist groups; by disseminating news about terrorist events, the media contributes further to terrorist goals. Extensive media coverage of these acts are almost always assured, and often lead to the government's over-reactive response. The extensive media coverage of the over-reactive state response

7. *See* M. Cherif Bassiouni, *The Face of Terror*, CHI. TRIB., Oct. 21, 2001, at 1; M. Cherif Bassiouni, *Cutting off the Easy Flow of Blood Money*, CHI. TRIB., Nov. 4, 2001, at 1.

8. *See* M. Cherif Bassiouni, *Terrorism, Law Enforcement and the Mass Media: Perspectives, Problems, Proposals*, 72 J. CRIM. L. & CRIMINOLOGY 1 (1981).

tends to undermine the legitimacy of the state's response and to give such groups more legitimacy in the eyes of their constituencies.

One example of such a state over-reaction is the U.S. war against Afghanistan on the basis of "credible," but unconfirmed, evidence that Osama bin Laden was involved in the September 11 attack, and that the Taliban government provide him support and was shielding him from extradition.[9] The United States, however, never formally sought bin Laden's extradition from Afghanistan, nor did it present to Afghanistan's government any evidence of his criminal involvement in the terrorist attacks on New York and Washington. The United States concluded that the Taliban regime was sponsoring international terrorism and should be removed from power by means of military force.[10] The war, however, has exacerbated Afghanistan's humanitarian and economic problems, creating an estimated two million new refugees and aggravating the situation for the country's existing millions of refugees,[11] many of whom may die as a result of starvation and the cold. U.S. bombings have also resulted in civilian casualties.[12] Without massive hmanitarian and economic aid, the level of harm suffered by the country's civilian population will delegitimize the U.S. action in the eyes of its populace, and provide legitimacy to the terrorist network called Al Qaeda. This can play into the hands of that terrorist group, providing it more general support and adherents from among the 1.3 billion Muslims in over 100 countries around the world. The criminal acts of September 11 were surely calculated to bring about that type of massive reaction. Even if bin Laden is killed, he becomes a martyr, and that will rally others to his movement or motivate them to engage in terrorist acts against the United States. But what else could the United States do? It was compelled by the circumstances to defend itself as best it could, and time will tell whether these measures were wise and effective in protecting it from such attacks in the future. This is precisely the type of conundrum that terrorist acts of that significance are intended to produce.

B. *The Impact of Globalization on Terrorism*

The advent of globalization has helped terrorist groups such as Al Qaeda. Globalization is characterized by the elimination of time and distance barri-

---

9. Various officials in the U.S. government have indicated that the Taliban government provided Osama bin Laden and Al Qaeda with a base of operation and support. *See, e.g.*, Interview by Peter Jennings with Secretary of State Colin L. Powell, Washington, D.C. (Sept. 20, 2001).

10. *See, e.g.*, President George W. Bush, Address to the Nation (Oct. 7, 2001), http://www.whitehouse.gov/news/releases/2001/10/20011007-8.html.

11. *See* Press Release, United Nations, Afghan Civilians to Face Increased Vulnerability after U.N. International Staffers are Evacuated to Pakistan (Sept. 14, 2001), http://www.unhchr.ch/huricane/huricane.nsf/view01/104CE9B697960E77C1256ACA0028CE35?opendocument.

12. *See* Press Release, Amnesty International, Afghanistan: Accountability for Civilian Deaths (Oct. 26, 2001), http://web.amnesty.org/ai.nsf/Index/ASA110222001?OpenDocument&of=COUNTRIES\AFGHANISTAN (noting that "U.S. officials have admitted that a number of civilian targets have been hit as a result of error," but lamenting the lack of public information on such attacks).

ers and the increased popular access to information, technology, and communications. These characteristics have been exploited by both legitimate and illegitimate enterprises. They have particularly benefited terrorist groups by allowing the groups' members and supporters to cross state borders, acquire and move equipment, obtain information, communicate with one another, and transfer funds transnationally with much greater ease, all the while relying on the worldwide media to broadcast both their message and the success of their operations. Globalization has also allowed terrorist groups to network with one another, permitting terrorist groups to develop strategic alliances with other groups engaged in transnational criminality in order to develop synergetic connections and to maximize respective capabilities and effectiveness. These networks have particularly developed between terrorist groups and organized crime; in Columbia, for example, the Revolutionary Armed Forces of Colombia (FARC) funds its rebellion by protecting the drug traffickers.[13] Terrorist groups also rely on techniques perfected by organized crime, particularly their methods of and sources for obtaining funding, arms, and military equipment on the illegal market. Because of economic globalization and the lack of international control of arms trafficking, terrorist groups seldom lack access to weapons and military equipment; the so-called "black market" is quite open and accessible to those with funds. For example, with arms purchased from funds obtained in the illegal diamond trade and laundered in European financial institutions, the Liberian and Sierra Leone rebels have terrorized their respective peoples for a decade, leaving an estimated 200,000 and 300,000 people dead, thousands of children mutilated, and thousands of women raped.[14] These rebels, particularly their leaders, have benefited from the loopholes in financial and criminal controls that have resulted from globalization.

III. The Weaknesses of Existing International Law in Addressing Terrorism

A. *Non-Specific Conventional and Customary International Law Applicable to Terrorism*

Given the advent of globalization and the development of international terrorism, the international community must establish effective means of punishing such international criminal acts. Currently, the conduct of state actors and insurgent or revolutionary groups is governed by the 1948 Genocide Convention,[15] customary international criminal law governing crimes against humanity (since there is no applicable international convention other than the 1998 Statute of the International Criminal Court which is not yet

13. M. Cherif Bassiouni & Eduardo Vetere, *Organized Crime and its Transnational Manifestations*, *in* 1 International Criminal Law 883 (M. Cherif Bassiouni ed., 2d ed. 1999).

14. *See* Human Rights Watch, Sierra Leone: A Call for Justice, http://www.hrw.org/campaigns/sleone.

15. Genocide Convention, *supra* note 1.

in effect), the 1984 Convention against Torture,[16] and the various norms against war crimes as reflected in the customary law of armed conflict, and the Four 1949 Geneva Conventions and their two 1977 Protocols.[17]

There is significant overlap between conventions and custom within the international criminal framework. The Convention against Torture, the Genocide Conventions, and the prohibitions on crimes against humanity apply in times of war and peace. However, the customary law of armed conflict and the Geneva Conventions apply only in times of war or armed conflict, either of an international or non-international character. These norms, applicable in the context of armed conflict, while sufficient, are seldom enforced against state actors and even less often enforced against non-state actors.[18] Furthermore, none of them makes distinctions in criminal responsibility between decision-makers and senior executors and lesser-rank personnel.[19]

In addition, these conventions lack an enforcement mechanism to truly deter and punish criminal behavior on an international scale. Certain international attempts have been made in the course of the last decade to provide effective enforcement. The Security Council established the International Criminal Tribunal for the Former Yugoslavia (ICTY) in 1993 and the International Criminal Tribunal for Rwanda (ICTR) in 1994 to prosecute persons charged with the first three of these crimes (genocide, crimes against humanity, and war crimes), committed in the context of these two conflicts. In no other conflict since World War II has such a post-conflict justice mechanism been established. Perhaps, when the ICC enters into effect after the sixtieth ratification (expected by the end of 2002), it will in time become a universal accountability mechanism for these three crimes. The extent to which the existence of such a system of international criminal justice can be an effective deterrent is, however, to be seen.

Further, universal jurisdiction of international conventions has spurred domestic attempts at enforcement of such laws against international crime.[20]

16. Torture Convention, *supra* note 4.

17. Geneva Convention I, *supra* note 3; Geneva Convention II, *supra* note 3; Geneva Convention III, *supra* note 3; Geneva Convention IV, *supra* note 3. Note that only Additional Protocol I applies to conflicts of an international character, while Additional Protocol II applies to conflicts of a non-international character. *See* Additional Protocol I, *supra* note 3; Additional Protocol II, *supra* note 3.

18. There is an absence of criminal prosecutions after conflicts occur, as evidenced by the fact that the Security Council had to establish the ICTY and ICTR in order to bring about the prosecution of crimes committed in, respectively, the former Yugoslavia and Rwanda. *See* M. Cherif Bassiouni, *Searching for Peace and Achieving Justice: The Need for Accountability*, 59 L. & CONTEMP. PROBS. 1, 9–28 (1996); STEVEN RATNER & JASON ABRAMS, ACCOUNTABILITY FOR HUMAN RIGHTS ATROCITIES IN INTERNATIONAL LAW: BEYOND THE NUREMBERG LEGACY (2d ed. 2001); Diane F. Orentlicher, *Settling Accounts: The Duty to Prosecute Human Rights Violations of a Prior Regime*, 100 YALE L.J. 2537 (1991).

19. *See* BASSIOUNI, *supra* note 2, at 369–446.

20. *See* INTERNATIONAL LAW ASSOCIATION, FINAL REPORT ON THE EXECUTION OF UNIVERSAL JURISDICTION IN RESPECT OF GROSS HUMAN RIGHTS OFFENCES 404 (2000); M. Cherif Bassiouni, *Universal Jurisdiction for International Crimes: Historical Perspectives and Contemporary Practice*, 42 VA. J. INT'L L. (2001) (forthcoming). *See also* PRINCETON UNIVERSITY PROGRAM IN LAW AND PUBLIC AFFAIRS, THE PRINCETON PRINCIPLES ON UNIVERSAL JURISDICTION (2001) (prescribing principles to govern the

Indeed, the Torture Convention may become more effectively enforced as the Pinochet experiment in the United Kingdom.[21] provides the precedent for increased state use of universal jurisdiction for national prosecutions. Universal jurisdiction can also be relied upon by national legal systems to prosecute genocide, crimes against humanity, war crimes, and torture. However, as crimes against humanity are not yet posited in conventional international criminal law other than in the two *ad hoc* tribunals of the ICTY and ICTR, and in the ICC Statute, it would be useful to have a specialized international convention on crimes against humanity, which, like Article 7 of the ICC Statute, would include non-state actors. In that way, crimes against humanity would encompass certain forms of terrorism committed by an "organization" which, on the basis of a "policy," engages in "widespread" or "systematic" attack upon "a civilian population," by means of killing and other specified acts.[22] An international convention prohibiting such crimes would likely allow for universal jurisdiction of the acts committed and thus increase national prosecution of terrorist acts.

The lack of coordinated international control of other dangerous and international criminal conduct also prevents effective enforcement. There is a significant legal gap, for example, in the control of weapons of mass destruction, such as nuclear, chemical, and biological weapons. For instance, there are no conventions on the prohibition of the use of nuclear weapons, whether by state or non-state actors. In addition, the 1993 Chemical Weapons Convention[23] lacks effective enforcement provisions applicable to unlawful terrorist use, and the 1972 Bacteriological Convention[24] does not criminalize the use of such agents for terrorist attacks. The Bacteriological Convention had been in the process of being amended for years, only to have a final draft opposed by the United States in 2001 as a result of pressures from the chemical and pharmaceutical industries. Thus, progress toward adopting a new convention with effective criminal provisions has been forestalled.

There is, in short, no normative fabric to international criminal law, just bits and pieces of overlapping norms with significant gaps as to their coverage. Even those norms that could be enforced, are subject to the recurring problem of a lack of effective enforcement by states. When states are permitted to rely on universal jurisdiction to enforce such norms, through their national legal systems, they fail to do so, even though such enforcement is

application of universal jurisdiction in light of its potential for abuse).

21. Regina v. Bow St. Metro. Stipendiary Magistrate, *ex parte* Pinochet Ugarte (No. 3), 1 A.C. 147 (2000); Christine M. Chinkin, *International Decision, Regina v. Bow Street Stipendiary Magistrate, Ex Parte Pinochet Ugarte (No. 3)*, 93 AM. J. INT'L L. 703, 704 (1999).

22. ICC Statute, *supra* note 1, art. 7. *See also* M. CHERIF BASSIOUNI, CRIMES AGAINST HUMANITY IN INTERNATIONAL CRIMINAL LAW (2d rev. ed. 1999).

23. Convention on the Prohibition of the Development, Production, Stockpiling and Use of Chemical Weapons and on their Destruction, Jan. 13, 1993, S. TREATY DOC. NO. 103-21, 1974 U.N.T.S. 3.

24. Convention on the Prohibition of the Development, Production and Stockpiling of Bacteriological (Biological) and Toxin Weapons and on their Destruction, Feb. 25, 1972, 26 U.S.T. 583, 1015 U.N.T.S. 163.

required by international humanitarian law and other norms. International criminal law, therefore, suffers from both substantive and enforcement deficiencies, leading to a substantial lack in deterrence.

B. Specific Treaty-Based International Law Applicable to Terrorism

Treaty-based international legal efforts to combat terrorism have suffered from similar problems in enforcement and deterrence, and are characterized in particular by the absence of a comprehensive convention governing the international dimensions of the fight against terrorism. Instead, the legislative international legal framework is comprised of thirteen international conventions,[25] adopted over a span of thirty-two years (1969–2001), that apply to different types of terrorist acts, including: airplane hijacking (4);[26] piracy on the high seas (2);[27] attacks or kidnappings of internationally protected persons, U.N. personnel, and diplomats (2);[28] attacks upon civilian maritime vessels;[29] attacks upon platforms on the high seas;[30] the taking of civilian hostages;[31] the use of bombings and explosives in terrorist acts;[32] the financing of terrorism;[33] and nuclear terrorism (pending).[34] Several regional intergovernmental organizations have established anti-terrorism conventions as well, including the Organization of American States (1971);[35] the Council of Europe (1977);[36] the South Asian Association for Regional Cooperation

25. *See* M. Cherif Bassiouni, International Terrorism: Multilateral Conventions 1937–2001 (2001).

26. Montreal Convention for the Suppression of Unlawful Acts Against the Safety of Civil Aviation, Sept. 23, 1971, 24 U.S.T. 564, 974 U.N.T.S. 177; Montreal Protocol for the Suppression of Unlawful Acts of Violence at Airports Serving Civil Aviation, Feb. 24, 1988, S. Treaty Doc. No. 100-19, 27 I.L.M. 627; Hague Convention for the Suppression of Unlawful Seizure of Aircrafts, Dec. 16, 1970, 22 U.S.T. 1641, 860 U.N.T.S. 105; Tokyo Convention on Offences and Certain Other Acts Committed on Board Aircraft, Sept. 14, 1963, 20 U.S.T. 2941, 704 U.N.T.S. 219.

27. Convention on the Law of the Sea, Dec. 10, 1982, 1833 U.N.T.S. 3; Convention on the High Seas, Apr. 29, 1958, 13 U.S.T. 2312, 450 U.N.T.S. 11.

28. Convention on the Safety of United Nations and Associated Personnel, Dec. 9, 1994, G.A. Res. 49/59, U.N. GAOR, 49th Sess., Supp. No. 49, at 299, U.N. Doc. A/49/49 (1994); Convention on the Prevention and Punishment of Crimes Against Internationally Protected Persons, including Diplomatic Agents, Dec. 14, 1973, 28 U.S.T. 1975, 1035 U.N.T.S. 167.

29. Convention for the Suppression of Unlawful Acts Against the Safety of Maritime Navigation, Mar. 10, 1988, S. Treaty Doc. No. 101-1, 27 I.L.M. 668.

30. Protocol for the Suppression of Unlawful Acts Against the Safety of Fixed Platforms Located on the Continental Shelf, Mar. 10, 1988, S. Treaty Doc. No. 101-1, 27 I.L.M. 685.

31. Convention Against the Taking of Hostages, Dec. 17, 1979, T.I.A.S. No. 11,081, 1316 U.N.T.S. 205.

32. International Convention for the Suppression of Terrorist Bombings, Jan. 9, 1998, S. Treaty Doc. No. 106-6, 37 I.L.M. 251.

33. International Convention for the Suppression of the Financing of Terrorism, G.A. Res. 109, U.N. GAOR, 54th Sess., Supp. No. 49, Agenda Item 160, at 408, U.N. Doc. A/54/109 (1999).

34. Draft Convention on the Suppression of Acts of Nuclear Terrorism, Jan. 28, 1997, U.N. Doc. A/AC.252/L.3.

35. Organization of American States: Convention to Prevent and Punish Acts of Terrorism Taking the Form of Crimes Against Persons and Related Extortion that are of International Significance, Feb. 2, 1971, 27 U.S.T. 3949, 1986 U.N.T.S. 195.

36. European Convention on the Suppression of Terrorism, Jan. 27, 1977, Europ.T.S. No. 90, 1979

(1987);[37] the League of Arab States (1998);[38] the Organization of African Unity (1999);[39] and the Organization of the Islamic Conference (2000).[40] Of these, only the European Convention on Terrorism has been invoked by its member-states.

As mentioned earlier, there is no comprehensive convention on terrorism that even modestly integrates, much less incorporates into a single text, these thirteen conventions so as to eliminate their weaknesses. The logic of such a comprehensive convention on terrorism is compelling, as is the logic against the current piecemeal approach taken by the separate conventions. Nevertheless, the United States has consistently opposed such a convention since 1972, ostensibly so that it can pick and choose from these disparate norms those that it wishes to rely upon. Above all, the United States does not want to have an effective multilateral scheme that would presumably restrict its unfettered political power to act unilaterally.

C. *International Institutions*

International legal crime-fighting institutions, in place to facilitate prevention of transnational crime, have also been ineffective. The United Nations has a Centre for International Crime Prevention in Vienna whose mandate includes fighting terrorism;[41] but the Centre has historically been underfunded, understaffed, and bereft of political influence within the U.N. system. Furthermore, in recent years it has suffered from disastrous leadership, further reducing its effectiveness.[42] Therefore, not only does it need new leadership, staff, and resources, but it needs a new mandate that better incorporates the fight against terrorism in this globalization-induced era of increased international and transnational criminal activity.

U.N.T.S. 94 [hereinafter European Terrorism Convention].

37. South Asian Association for Regional Cooperation Convention on Suppression of Terrorism, U.N. GAOR, 44th Sess., U.N. Doc. A/51/136 (1989).

38. The League of Arab States, The Council of Arab Interior and Justice Ministers: The Arab Convention on the Suppression of Terrorism, Apr. 22, 1998, http://www.leagueofarabstates.org/E_News_Antiterrorism.asp.

39. Organization of African Unity: Convention on the Prevention and Combating of Terrorism, July 14, 1999, http://untreaty.un.org/English/Terrorism.asp.

40. Organization of the Islamic Conference: Convention of the Organization of the Islamic Conference on Combating International Terrorism, Oct. 11, 2000, *reprinted in* U.N. Doc. A/54/637, Annex, http://www.oic-un.org/26icfm/c.html.

41. Operated within the United Nations' Office for Drug Control and Crime Prevention, the Center works closely with the United Nations' Terrorism Prevention Branch, also based in Vienna.

42. *See* Report of the Office of Internal Oversight Services, U.N. GAOR, 56th Sess., Agenda Item 130, U.N. Doc. A/56/381 (2001), http://www.un.org/Depts/oios/reports/a56_381.pdf. Report of the Office of Internal Oversight Services on the Inspection of Programme Management and Administrative Practices in the Office for Drug Control and Crime Prevention, U.N. GAOR, 56th Sess., Agenda Items 123, 124, 134, 143, U.N. Doc. A/56/83 (2001), http://www.un.org/Depts/oios/reports/a56_83.htm; Triennial Review of the Implementation of the Recommendations Made by the CPC at its Thirty-Eighth Session on the In-Depth Evaluation of the U.N. Crime Prevention and Criminal Justice, U.N. ESCOR, 41st Sess.

In October 2001, the Security Council established a committee to deal with terrorism, at the behest of the United States, following the adoption of Security Council Resolution 1373.[43] Because the Security Council deals only with international "peace and security" threats under its powers contained in Chapter VII of the U.N. Charter, the new committee's focus is necessarily confined to a limited set of terrorist acts (those that threaten international peace and security).[44] The *ad hoc* nature of this Committee also portends that it may not outlive its present usefulness.

The International Criminal Police Organization (INTERPOL) has been only marginally effective in combating terrorism because major powers, like the United States, do not fully trust it. Furthermore, INTERPOL is a police association and does not include intelligence agencies. It is self-evident that combating international terrorism cannot succeed while beholden to the same bureaucratic boundaries that exist between law enforcement and intelligence agencies in domestic contexts. In this sense, INTERPOL merely reflects a political and bureaucratic reality that exists in almost all countries of the world, and which inevitably reduces its effectiveness. In fact, until 1993, INTERPOL was effectively precluded from dealing with terrorism altogether because its Charter prohibited it from dealing with such "political" matters.[45] While INTERPOL has since changed, it remains ineffective for the reasons expressed above.

Certain regional intergovernmental organizations have bodies or committees that deal with transnational criminal activity, including terrorism;[46] but not one of these bodies has any intelligence or law enforcement function.[47] Instead, they essentially do research, develop policy recommendations, and prepare draft treaties—functions that only indirectly contribute to combating terrorism.

D. *Interstate Cooperation in Penal Matters*

There are presently 189 member-states of the United Nations, with significant variation among them in intelligence, law enforcement, prosecu-

43. S.C. Res. 1373, U.N. SCOR, 56th Sess., 4385th mtg., U.N. Doc. S/Res/1373 (2001).

44. *See id.* § 6.

45. *See* INTERPOL CONST., art. 3, http://www.interpol.int/Public/ICPO/LegalMaterials/constitution/constitutionGenReg/constitution.asp ("It is strictly forbidden for the organization to undertake any intervention or activities of a political, military, or religious or racial character."). However, the organization recognized the role it could play in combating international terrorism as early as 1985. *See* International Terrorism and Unlawful Interference with Civil Aviation, INTERPOL G.A. Res. No. AGN/54/RES/1 (1985), http://www.interpol.int/public/terrorism/default.asp. *See also* Mary Jo Grotenroth, *INTERPOL's Role in International Law Enforcement in* LEGAL RESPONSES TO INTERNATIONAL TERRORISM: U.S. PROCEDURAL ASPECTS 375, 381 (1988) (INTERPOL resolution on terrorism); J. Nepote, *The Role of the International Criminal Police (INTERPOL), in* I A TREATISE ON INTERNATIONAL CRIMINAL LAW: CRIMES AND PUNISHMENT 676 (M. Cherif Bassiouni & Ved P. Nanda eds., 1973).

46. These organizations include the Commonwealth Secretariat, the Council of Europe, the European Union, the League of Arab States, and the Organization of American States.

47. *See* M. Cherif Bassiouni, *Policy Considerations on Interstate Cooperation in Criminal Matters, in* II INTERNATIONAL CRIMINAL LAW, *supra* note 13, at 3.

torial, and judicial capabilities. Thus, it is easy for groups that engage in transnational criminality, including terrorism, to find countries where they can seek refuge, obtain support, or operate without much concern of detection.

Experience in combating transnational criminal activity, including terrorism, reveals that the first and most important stage in interdiction is intelligence and law enforcement cooperation. Such cooperation serves primarily as a means of prevention and deterrence, and only ultimately as a means of bringing perpetrators to justice. National systems, however, distribute these functions between competing bureaucratic agencies, thus reducing their individual and combined effectiveness. Furthermore, each separate national agency tends to develop *ad hoc* relationships with its counterparts in a select number of countries; so whatever information that is shared between corresponding agencies of different countries runs into the same intra-national bureaucratic impediments to information sharing and cooperation.

There is so far no international treaty that governs interstate law enforcement and intelligence cooperation. Thus, the international cooperation that does exist takes place outside international and national legal scrutiny. Therefore, there exists no protection of citizens against abuse of power and invasion of privacy, leading to a greater risk that those who are the victims of mistaken identity will have fewer means of protection at their disposal.

International criminal law has so far developed six modalities for international cooperation in penal matters. Agreements, in some form, exist covering extradition, legal assistance, transfer of criminal proceedings, recognition of foreign penal judgments, transfer of sentenced persons, and freezing and seizing of assets. These six modalities, however, are not contained in a single international convention that integrates them in a way that makes them more effective. Instead, they are scattered in the provisions of a number of multilateral regional conventions.[48] There are no U.N.-sponsored international conventions dealing with any of these areas.[49]

In dealing with cooperation in international criminal enforcement, states rely on a web of bilateral treaties, each dealing with a separate modality of interstate cooperation in penal matters. While multilateral conventions dealing with substantive international criminal law, such as the thirteen

48. *See, e.g.*, Inter-American Convention on Extradition, O.A.S. T.S. No. 60 (February 25, 1981), http://www.oas.org/juridico/english/sigs/b-47.html; Inter-American Convention on Mutual Assistance in Criminal Matters, O.A.S. T.S. No. 75 (May 23, 1992); European Convention on Extradition, Dec. 13, 1957, 359 U.N.T.S. 273. *See also* I–II Ekkehart Müller-Rappard & M. Cherif Bassiouni, European Inter-State Co-operation in Criminal Matters: The Council of Europe's Legal Instruments (2d ed. 1991) (for a discussion on the Council of Europe's conventions). The League of Arab States also has a convention on extradition and one on mutual legal assistance.

49. *See* U.N. Model Treaty on Extradition, G.A. Res. 116, U.N. GAOR, 45th Sess., Annex, at 211–15, U.N. Doc. A/RES/45/116 (1990); U.N. Model Treaty on Mutual Assistance in Criminal Matters, G.A. Res. 117, 45th Sess., Annex, at 215–19, U.N. Doc. A/RES/117 (1990).

aforementioned conventions dealing with terrorism,[50] do contain provisions on extradition and mutual legal assistance, these provisions are not consistent from convention to convention, and are usually limited to a few lines.[51] Instead, the United States, for example, has 137 bilateral extradition treaties applicable to 103 states, and 34 bilateral treaties on mutual legal assistance.[52] Worldwide, there are hundreds of bilateral treaties on extradition and mutual legal assistance. Other modalities, such as recognition of foreign penal judgments and transfer of criminal proceedings are seldom the subject of such bilateral agreements, while others still, such as the freezing and seizing of assets, are used only by a few states. Even the most significant for combating terrorism, the freezing and seizing of assets, until now has seldom been used except in connection with drug trafficking, due to the financial incentives that governments have in seizing assets derived from drug sales and then distributing them among their prosecutorial and law enforcement agencies.

States also rely on domestic legislation to enact these six modalities of interstate cooperation into law; as stated above, with the exception of Austria, Germany, Italy, and Switzerland, all other states deal with each of these modalities separately, thus precluding the integration of these modalities in order to make them more effective. For instance, the United States only has statutory provisions that deal with extradition and transfer of sentenced persons.[53] The extradition statute was drafted in 1825 with some recent modification.[54] At present, however, the provision is ridden with gaps that treaties and court decisions attempt to fill with considerable variation, rendering enforcement cumbersome, lengthy, and costly.[55]

The absence of both multilateral and domestic enforcement regimes that integrate the six modalities mentioned above has resulted in making interstate cooperation in penal matters cumbersome, lengthy, and, more often than not, ineffective. Developing countries, in particular, lack not only the legislative resources to engage in these modalities of interstate cooperation, but also the required expertise in their ministries of justice, interior, and foreign affairs to deal adequately with these processes. The United Nations' efforts to train experts in these areas, for instance, through its Crime Prevention Centre in Vienna, have been few and far between. Regional organiza-

---

50. *See supra* notes 26–34 and accompanying text.

51. *See* M. Cherif Bassiouni & Edward M. Wise, *Aut Dedere Aut Judicare*: The Duty to Prosecute or Extradite in International Law 7–19 (1995). *See also* M. Cherif Bassiouni, International Extradition in United States Law and Practice 295–382 (3d ed. 1996).

52. See 18 U.S.C. §§ 3181–3196 for a listing of these treaties.

53. *Id.* §§ 3181–3195.

54. Antiterrorism and Effective Death Penalty Act of 1996, Pub. L. No. 104-132, § 443(a), 110 Stat. 1280 (1996).

55. A 1984 proposal for comprehensive revision of the statute was rejected because it was deemed to contain too many individual guarantees. *See also* M. Cherif Bassiouni, *Extradition Reform Legislation in the United States: 1981–1983*, 17 Akron L. Rev. 495 (1984); *United States and United Kingdom Supplementary Extradition Treaty: Hearings Before the Subcomm. on Foreign Relations, United States Senate*, 99th Cong. (1985).

tions such as the Council of Europe, the Organization of American States and the Commonwealth Secretariat, have been better about undertaking such efforts. But these actions, too, have been limited.

In sum, the international community has not undertaken the effort of codifying international criminal law, either in its substantive or procedural aspects. Academic efforts in this direction have been sporadic,[56] and have not received significant governmental attention. As a result, there is a substantial weakness in the normative and procedural framework that is necessary to provide the bases for international cooperation in penal matters. Even reliance on national legal systems, for both the reasons stated above and those left unaddressed, has proved weak and inefficient.

IV. State Responsibility for the Sponsorship or Failure To Take Appropriate Preventive Measures of Terrorism

International law establishes a principle whereby states that breach their international obligations are held responsible for their breaches. That responsibility has historically been of a civil nature. The remedy for a state that is aggrieved by such a breach is to bring an action before the International Court of Justice, and to obtain damages or reparations. A breach based on omission occurs where a state's failure to take appropriate action to carry out its obligations, or to prevent harm from occurring to other states, can trigger liability.

Since the late 1970s, the International Law Commission, which had been working on the codification of the Principles of State Responsibility,[57] has also considered the concept of state criminal responsibility.[58] But the concept of state criminal responsibility has met with a great deal of opposition, as evidenced by the fact that the ICC Statute does not contain such international criminal responsibility. Nevertheless, in recent years the Security Council has imposed sanctions on both Libya[59] and Sudan[60] on the basis that these states have permitted terrorist organizations to operate from within their respective territories, but with the implication that these countries may have even been involved in more direct support for such organizations, both within and beyond their own territories. The imposition of sanctions, which have the effect of collective punishment on a given population, are certainly punitive. Consequently, even though state criminal responsibility has not been officially recognized, punitive consequences have been attached

56. *See* M. Cherif Bassiouni, A Draft International Criminal Code and a Draft Statute for an International Criminal Tribunal (1987).

57. The International Law Commission concluded its work in 2001. *See* International Law Commission, Report by the International Law Commission on the Work of its Fifty-Third Session, Apr. 23–June 1, July 2–Aug. 18, 2001, U.N. GAOR, 53d Sess., Supp. No. 10, U.N. Doc. A/56/10 (2001).

58. *See* M. Cherif Bassiouni, *The Sources and Content of International Criminal Law: A Theoretical Framework*, *in* 1 Int'l Crim. L. 3, *supra* note 13, at 27 (2d ed. 1999).

59. S.C. Res. 748, U.N. SCOR, 42d Sess., 3063d mtg., U.N. Doc. S/Res./748 (1992).

60. S.C. Res. 1054, U.N. SCOR, 46th Sess., 3660th mtg., U.N. Doc. S/Res/1054 (1996).

to states whenever the Security Council has determined that such state action constitutes a breach of peace under Chapter VII of the U.N. Charter.

International criminal law since the Nuremberg judgment has, however, recognized the concept of criminal responsibility for organizations such as the S.S. and S.A. of Nazi Germany.[61] The events of September 11 should raise the question of whether or not state responsibility should include the concept of state criminal responsibility, much in the same way as it includes breaches of other international obligations, including failure to act. Failure to act should encompass the failure to develop appropriate national legislation to prevent and suppress terrorism—and all other international crimes as well—and to enforce both international law and national legislation in connection with such crimes. The area of state criminal responsibility is an area of international law that has not so far been adequately developed, probably for the reason that international criminal law has not sufficiently evolved as a new discipline which bridges international and criminal law.

V. Old and New Concepts of Conflicts of a Non-International Character

Conflicts of a non-international character are regulated in conventional international humanitarian law by Common Article 3 of the four Geneva Conventions of August 12, 1949;[62] and further developed in Additional Protocol II of 1977.[63]

These norms were originally intended to give some protection to combatants and civilians in the context of wars of national liberation, which reached their height during the decolonization era of the 1950s to the 1970s. In turn, this period of national liberation insurgency was followed by a period of uprisings by revolutionary groups who fought their governments for regime-change. These insurgents and revolutionary groups[64] resorted to acts of terror-violence against colonizers/settlers and domestic regimes, acts which led to their being referred to as terrorists. While the term "terrorism" clashed with the legitimacy of such a right to engage in a war of national liberation or to topple dictatorial regimes, it properly described the means employed to those ends. This legitimacy-versus-means issue is still with us today.

---

61. *See* Bassiouni, *supra* note 58, at 24.

62. *See* Geneva Convention I, *supra* note 3, art. 3; Geneva Convention II, *supra* note 3, art. 3; Geneva Convention III, *supra* note 3, art. 3; Geneva Convention IV, *supra* note 3, art. 3. *See also* Documents on the Laws of War (Adam Roberts & Richard Guelf eds., 3d ed. 2000). With respect to the customary law of armed conflict, see International Committee for the Red Cross, International Law Concerning the Conduct of Hostilities (1996).

63. *See* Additional Protocol II, *supra* note 3.

64. The terms "insurgents" and "revolutionary groups" are just two of the terms used to describe groups of this type. *See* The International Law of Civil War (Richard Falk ed., 1971); Elizabeth Chadwick, Self-Determination, Terrorism, and the International Humanitarian Law of Armed Conflict (1996); 1 Restructuring the Global Military Sector: New Wars (Mary Kaldor & Basker Vaske eds., 1997).

The Geneva Conventions and Additional Protocols are based on the unarticulated premise that even legitimate ends do not justify certain means. Insurgents and revolutionaries, though not without right to resort to armed conflict, must nonetheless abide by the rules of armed conflict applicable to combatants and non-combatants in the context of non-international armed conflicts. The same applies to state forces fighting against such groups.[65] Violations by one side do not allow reprisals in kind by the other.[66] Thus, symmetry in legal obligations is established.

Insurgent and revolutionary groups, however, do not have the same military means and capabilities available to conventional state forces, and therefore feel that they cannot abide by the same rules if they are to succeed. They are reinforced in their disregard of these norms by the fact that state forces also seldom respect these rules. In addition, these groups are not professional combatants and have neither the command and control nor the training that regular and well-disciplined armed forces have. Additional Protocol II tried to take some of these factors into consideration by inducing compliance of insurgent and revolutionary groups with international humanitarian law through the relaxation of conditions for prisoner of war status under the 1949 Conventions.[67] This inducement – essentially one of status recognition – has naturally been met with considerable resistance on the part of states, who fear that this gives such groups misplaced legitimacy.

These problems were seldom resolved in the many conflicts of a non-international character that have occurred since World War II, where neither governments nor insurgent and revolutionary groups abided by either the terms of Common Article 3 or those of Additional Protocol II.[68] In fact, there has almost always been a premium for insurgent and revolutionary groups to increase their violence, including terror-violence, to levels that will garner them recognition and legitimacy, and eventually political settlements.[69] The result is that in conflicts of a non-international character the norms exist but are neither followed nor enforced.

This situation of lawlessness in the non-international context still exists. Governments do not want to give legitimacy to insurgent and revolutionary groups, while the latter are unwilling to abide by international humanitar-

---

65. *See, e.g.*, Howard S. Levie, Terrorism in War: The Law of War Crimes (1993). *See also* Hans-Peter Gasser, *Prohibition of Terrorist Attacks in International Humanitarian Law*, 1985 Int'l Rev. Red Cross 200, 203 (1985);

66. *See* Frits Kalshoven & Liesbeth Zegveld, Constraints on the Waging of War : an Introduction to International Humanitarian Law (3d ed. 2001).

67. *See* Additional Protocol II, *supra* note 3, art. 43. *See also* Commentary on the Protocols of 8 June 1977 to the Geneva Convention of 12 August 1949 (Yves Sandoz et al. eds., 1987).

68. The failure to resolve these problems has generated considerable harm in these conflicts. For a survey of such harm, see Jennifer Balint, *Conflict Victimization and Legal Redress*, 14 Nouvelles Etudes Penales 101 (1998).

69. This was the case with recent rebellions in Liberia and Sierra Leone, which resulted in approximately 200,000 and 300,000 victims, respectively, most of whom were innocent civilians, and many of whom had their limbs cut off or were raped.

ian law in view of the imbalance of power that exists between them and the states or regimes they are fighting against. They claim that legitimacy is on their side and that a double standard is used against them. Thus, they legitimize their terror-violence in their own perception.

With few exceptions, until September 11, conflicts of a non-international character occurred between an insurgent or revolutionary group and a state or regime. Probably the first conflict that at least began as one of a non-international character was the Vietnam conflict. The Viet Cong used Laos as a base and a travel route for operations in South Vietnam, which was deemed to be another country.[70] Another example is that of the U.S.-sponsored Nicaragua Contras whose base of operation was in Honduras. In the first case, the United States bombed Laos in violation of that state's sovereignty but the United States considered it an exercise of a legitimate right of self-defense. In the second case, the United States had no such legal justification.[71]

The operations of Al Qaeda against the interests of the United States, including both domestic[72] and foreign-based[73] actions, emanated from Afghanistan but with a support network in several countries. This raises novel questions in international humanitarian law. The first of these is whether a state can be at war with a group operating from another country (or from more than one country) with membership consisting of multiple nationalities, whose members comprise various nationalities . The second regards the legal implications of such an armed conflict.

The answer to the first question is in the negative, because only states can be at war. Clearly, however, a state can be engaged in an armed conflict with an insurgent or revolutionary group, irrespective of that group's legitimacy, and vice versa. This is reflected in Common Article 3 and Additional Protocol II.[74] The fact that, historically, such conflicts were confined to the territory of a given state does not alter the legal status of the participants in that conflict and the international humanitarian law applicable to them. The laws of armed conflict are not geographically bound. They relate to the conduct of combatants with clear limits and inderrogable prohibitions with respect to what these norms refer to as "protected targets." Thus, under no circumstances can, *inter alia*, non-combatant civilians, POWs, the sick, the wounded, and the injured at land, at sea, and in hospitals, be attacked. The rationale is simply a humanitarian one and the prohibition is absolute. The only available exonerating circumstance is a reasonable mistake of fact. But

---

70. North Vietnam and South Vietnam were legally deemed two different countries, but North Vietnam rejected that contention and argued that all of Vietnam was one country. *See* THE VIETNAM WAR AND INTERNATIONAL LAW (Richard Falk ed., 1976).

71. *See* Military and Paramilitary Activities in and Against Nicaragua (Nicar. v. U.S.), [1986] I.C.J. 14.

72. With respect to the September 11 attacks, both the hijacking and the subsequent destruction of the four airplanes occurred within the continental United States.

73. Foreign-based actions include attacks upon the U.S. Embassies in Kenya and Tanzania and against a U.S. naval vessel, the U.S.S. Cole, in Yemen.

74. *See* George Aldrich, *The Laws of War on Land*, 94 AM.J. INT'L L. 42 (2000).

no rule of military necessity exonerates those who commit such violations from criminal responsibility.[75]

International humanitarian law opted for a neutral rule that protects certain targets, but by implication it favors state forces over insurgent or revolutionary forces in light of the balance of power. Regardless, however, the law is binding on both state and insurgent or revolutionary forces.[76]

Al Qaeda's attacks against the United States on September 11 and earlier fall within this paradigm: they are subject to the strictures of international humanitarian law, regardless of the legitimacy of their perpetrators' cause. If Al Qaeda violates such norms (as it has), those who committed such acts may properly be considered war criminals. Furthermore, a country such as Afghanistan that has given such a group a base of operation is also responsible for the actions of that group, and the United States is entitled to use force based on its "inherent right of self-defense" under Article 51 of the U.N. Charter. If combatants from that group are seized in the field, that is, in Afghanistan, they can be tried by a Military Commission established by the Commander of U.S. forces in the field. This is permissible under the customary law of armed conflict, and there certainly is precedent. The United States did so in the Far East after World War II, and one case reached the United States Supreme Court, *In re Yamashita*.[77]

With respect to combatants from a foreign state with which the United States is formally at war and who are caught within the United States, the only precedent for a Military Commission was in 1942 when President Roosevelt established one to try eight German saboteurs. The validity of such a Commission was recognized by the Supreme Court in *ex parte Quirin*,[78] even if its jurisdiction in this case applied to U.S. citizens.[79] But these combatants were also nationals of a state with which the United States was at war in accordance with a proper declaration of a state of war by Congress in accordance with Article I of the Constitution.

There is therefore a valid legal basis for the Presidential Military Order of November 13, 2001, with respect to Military Commissions in the field that are outside the United States, and for Military Commissions in the United States for Violations of the Laws and Customs of War.[80] Not so for jurisdic-

75. *See, e.g.*, CHRISTOPHER GREENWOOD, A MANUAL OF INTERNATIONAL HUMANITARIAN LAW (1995); LESLIE .C. GREEN, ESSAYS ON THE MODERN LAW OF WAR (2d ed., 1999); THE LAW OF WAR CRIMES: NATIONAL AND INTERNATIONAL APPROACHES (Timothy L. H. McCormack & Gary J. Simpson eds., 1997) [hereinafter LAW OF WAR CRIMES].

76. *See* LAW OF WAR CRIMES, *supra* note 18.

77. 327 U.S. 1 (1946) (upholding the authority of Supreme Allied Command General Douglas MacArthur to establish such Commissions). *See also* In re Homma, 327 U.S. 759 (1946) ("The motion for leave to file petition for writ of habeas corpus and writ of prohibition is denied and the petition for writ of certiorari is also denied on authority of Application of Yamashita, and Yamashita v. Styer . . . ."); LAWRENCE TAYLOR, A TRIAL OF GENERALS: HOMMA, YAMASHITA, MACARTHUR (1981).

78. 317 U.S. 1 (1942).

79. *Id.* at 37.

80. Military Order, *Detention, Treatment and Trial of Certain Non-Citizens in the War Against Terrorism*, 66 Fed. Reg. 57, 833 (Nov. 13, 2001). *But see* Jordan Paust, *After MyLai: The Case for War Crimes Juris-*

tion over persons in the United States or outside the United States who do not fall within these categories. With respect to persons within the United States, other than those mentioned above, the Military Order violates the Constitutional doctrine of separation of powers, and in particular, Article 1, Section 8, Clause 4; Article III, Section 2; and the due process clauses of the Fourteenth and Fifth Amendments and the Fourth, Fifth, Sixth and Eighth Amendments. Regrettably, this type of legal analysis and resort to the norms of international humanitarian law have not been sufficiently aired in the post-September 11 context.

Finally, it should be noted that the attacks upon the United States of September 11 constitute "Crimes Against Humanity" as defined in Article 7 of the Statute of the International Criminal Court (ICC).[81] The provisions of the ICC Statute are not applicable to the United States, as the treaty establishing the ICC has not yet entered into effect and the United States has not ratified it. Further, the United States, unlike other countries, does not have a domestic statute on "Crimes Against Humanity," and the Uniform Code of Military Justice does not apply to acts committed by civilians in the United States.[82] This is an opportunity to pass appropriate legislation to include these crimes in Title 18 U.S.C. and make them subject to the jurisdiction of Federal Courts.[83]

VI. Conclusion

"Terrorism" is a value-laden term. Consequently, it means different things to different people, a characteristic that perhaps is best expressed in the saying, "What is terrorism to some is heroism to others," and has never been satisfactorily defined. Yet the phenomenon is as old as history, even as its manifestations have changed as a result of new technology. Both state and non-state actors have resorted to the same approaches in terrorizing civilian populations, while using different weapons and techniques. For both, the goals of terror-violence are political. However, where non-state actors are often ideologically motivated, state actors, soldiers and police personnel who are either conscripts or persons seeking a career or temporary job in these bodies, are usually not.

The need for a comprehensive convention on terrorism that is, as much as possible, value-neutral, encompassing all actors, and covering all modalities and techniques of terror-violence, is self-evident. Such a convention, though, has been politically elusive. Governments understandably seek to exclude state actors from the definition of terrorism, and reject the notion that a

---

diction over Civilians in Federal District Courts, 50 TEX. L. REV. 6 (1971).

81. *See* ICC Statute, *supra* note 1; BASSIOUNI, *supra* note 1; *International Criminal Court Ratification and National Implementing Legislation*, 71 REV. INT'L DE DROIT PENAL (2000).

82. *See* 10 U.S.C. §§ 801–946 (2000). *See also* JORDAN PAUST, M. CHERIF BASSIOUNI, ET AL., INTERNATIONAL CRIMINAL LAW: CASES AND MATERIALS (2d. rev. ed. 2000).

83. *See* Paust, *supra* note 80.

causal connection even exists between state-sponsored acts of terror-violence and terror-violence committed by non-state actors. Since governments inevitably prevail in the international arena, the definition of terrorism has been limited to encompass unlawful conduct by non-state actors. Even with respect to this confined definition, however, governments have avoided developing an international legal regime to prevent, control, and suppress terrorism, preferring instead the hodgepodge of thirteen treaties that currently address its particular manifestations. The absence of a coherent international legislative policy on terrorism is consistent with the *ad hoc* and discretionary approach that governments have taken toward the development of effective international legal responses to terrorism. Thus, international legal norms governing terrorism rest essentially on the identification of certain types of conduct or means employed. To date, there is no international initiative to systematize, update, integrate, or even harmonize these international norms.

Interstate cooperation in penal matters is also limited due to this lack of a coherent and cohesive international legal regime. National legal systems are therefore left with whatever jurisdictional and resource means they have at their disposal, making them ineffective in dealing with terrorism's international manifestations.

The exclusion of state actors' unlawful terror-violence acts from inclusion in the overall scheme of terrorism control highlights the double standard that non-state actors lament and use as a justification for their own transgressions. This disparity of treatment between state and non-state actors is plainly evident, and constitutes one of the reasons for the attraction of adherents to non-state terrorist groups.

Since the current renewed interest in the subject of terrorism is due to the tragic events of September 11, 2001, it may be useful to confront certain controversial questions. First, these attacks were not only criminal, but unconscionable as to their harmful consequences, both human and economic. Additionally, the incidents were a blow to the invulnerability of the world's only superpower. But in comparative terms, the estimated 3000 casualties of September 11 pale in contrast to some 15,000–23,000 people killed by other forms of violence, and the 15,000 people killed by drunk driving, in the United States every year.[84] The effect of the reaction on many throughout the Arab and Muslim world, which consists of 1.3 billion people worldwide is to ask why, applying the same legal and moral standards, is the U.S.-sponsored embargo on Iraq, which has caused the deaths of an estimated five hundred thousand innocent children, acceptable? Of course, there are several valid distinctions between the embargo and the attacks upon the United States, but not in comparative human terms. In the end, the United States bears an indirect responsibility for that outcome in Iraq. Similarly, a large

84. 23,040 cases in 1990, and 15,530 cases in 1999. See Federal Bureau of Investigation, Uniform Crime Reports: Crime in the United States—1999, Index of Crime, tbl.1, http://www.fbi.gov/ucr/99cius.htm.

segment of the world population asks why Israel's repression of the Palestinian people, which includes the commission of "grave breaches" of the Geneva Convention and what the customary law of armed conflict considers "war crimes," is deemed justified, while Palestinians' unlawful acts of targeting civilians are condemned? These are only some contemporary examples of the double standard that fuels terrorism. All these acts are unjustifiable, and one wrong does not make another right.

Terrorism springs out of despair and injustice; it is the weapon of the weak, not the coward; it is indiscriminate and a crime against its innocent victims. It must be addressed with effective and legitimate means by law enforcement and the national justice systems of all countries of the world. The control of its manifestations depends on international cooperation, but its prevention requires addressing its causes.

In 1961, President John F. Kennedy, addressing an Organization of American States heads of states meeting in Punta del Este, Uruguay, said "[t]hose who make peaceful evolution impossible, make violent revolution inevitable."[85] If we want to put an end to the forms of violence that we call terrorism, then we need an effective international legal regime with enforcement capabilities that can, as Aristotle once said, apply the same law in Athens as in Rome.[86] This is the only alternative to Mao Tse-tung's exhortation, to paraphrase, that truth comes out of the barrel of a gun.[87]

85. THE LAW OF DISSENT AND RIOTS 1 (M. Cherif Bassiouni ed., 1971).

86. *See* ARISTOTLE, THE NICOMACHEAN ETHICS (David Ross trans., Oxford Univ. Press, 1998).

87. QUOTATIONS FROM CHAIRMAN MAO TSE-TUNG 33 (Stuart Schram ed., 1967) ("Every communist must grasp the truth, 'Political power grows out of the barrel of a gun.'").

[6]

Terrorism as a Catalyst for the Emergence, Harmonization and Reform of Criminal Law

Kimmo Nuotio*

Abstract

Since incidents of terrorism have escalated around the world, the international community has become increasingly focused on ensuring that national criminal justice systems are well-equipped to deal with the issues raised. Despite the great willingness and growing consensus among states to reform and further develop the legal strategies of their respective criminal justice systems, this process has confronted many challenges. The author examines international and regional efforts to harmonize rules addressing terrorism at international, regional and national levels.

1. Introduction

Since the beginning of the new millennium, terrorism has been the number one issue in international politics, security and law. 'Terrorism' is a catch-word that captures our imagination immediately even though each person may understand its meaning differently.[1]

From the perspective of a criminal lawyer, I will examine some new developments that the recent terrorist phenomena have triggered internationally, regionally and domestically. Given the scope and variety of new developments in the law, it would be impossible to address them all here. Further, legal developments also vary from state to state, rendering it difficult to undertake a comparative up-to-date study examining the phenomenon across jurisdictions. For the purposes of this article, I will use the case of Finland to exemplify how some of the legal developments taking place on the national level relate to broader developments. The goal of this article is to illustrate that national jurisdictions remain the key bodies on the front lines of confronting terrorism.

* Professor of Law, University of Helsinki, Finland. [kimmo.nuotio@helsinki.fi]

1 On the problem of legally defining terrorism, see the contributions of G.P. Fletcher, T. Weigend, and A. Cassese in this issue.

Thus it is essential that national legal systems be efficient and just. But national legal systems may also be ill-equipped for the challenges posed by international terrorism, being either inefficient or too efficient. Being efficient in a wrong way may risk, in whole or in part, human rights protections guaranteed by the general penal doctrines. This article will examine current trends in the response to the threat or acts of terrorism.

In criminal law, terrorism is often grouped together with the phenomenon of conventional criminality. However, terrorism is multi-faceted and differs in many ways from ordinary forms of criminality. Terrorism is organized, it needs financial and other support and it requires access to weapons and explosives among other things. Terrorism may also be sustained with political support. Many of the difficulties involved in defining terrorism have revolved around such characteristic features.

Safeguarding a nation's security requires an adequate legal response to the risks that are inherent in terrorism. Since terrorism may be local, cross-border or international, so too should the legal response. Terrorism is a particularly difficult issue for democracies since some legal responses that would enable authorities to take action may quickly restrict the fundamental rights of citizens.[2] The quest for effective and adequate 'governance' in response to terrorism stretches to the limit the legal and political structures of the modern world. Conversely, the 'slow' legal approach that more firmly protects citizens' rights may, by definition, also pose many risks to society.

Terrorism presents a difficult issue for international organizations, such as the United Nations. This is so because powerful states, like the United States, which do not trust international organizations, may choose to take unilateral action against terrorism if they regard international legal arrangements as insufficient. Indeed, unilateral action has already taken place. Bardo Fassbender has pointed out that international institutions could play a more proactive role in preventing international terrorism rather than simply reacting to individual terrorist acts once they are known. Long-term preventive actions, rather than immediate responses, are better served under international institutions. Such a view, although pragmatic, poses a serious challenge to the means by which states can react under criminal law to the crimes committed.

Prevention of crime cannot be the sole function of criminal law. The United States has considered itself to be in a state of war against terror since 11 September 2001. This position involves an unwillingness to define the issue in terms of ordinary criminal justice or crime prevention only.[3] The doctrine of self-defence is being applied to the measures adopted. Within such a framework, a legalistic approach that stresses the necessity

2 P. Wilkinson, *Terrorism Versus Democracy: The Liberal State Response* (London: Frank Cass, 2001), Ch. 5.

3 See B. Fassbender, 'The UN Security Council and International Terrorism', in A. Bianchi (ed.), *Enforcing International Law Norms Against Terrorism* (Oxford: Hart Publishing, 2004) 83–102.

1000 *JICJ* 4 (2006), 998–1016

of acting within a criminal justice framework only does not have very good prospects for success.

Interestingly, terrorism does not fall within the core area of international criminal law.[4] However, terrorist action may, on occasion, be addressed as such if it has been committed in the context of a widespread and systematic attack on a civilian population. For this reason, terrorism will usually not be dealt with by international criminal courts but by domestic courts instead.[5] That said, the lack of a comprehensive legal definition of terrorism at the level of international law has slowed legal developments at all levels.

2. Terrorism and the Emergence of Domestic Criminal Law

Terrorism as a legal concept is a relatively recent phenomenon. To be sure, domestic criminal laws have, for centuries, contained provisions concerning highly dangerous activities, such as arson and political crimes. These crimes were not considered terrorist acts. Indeed, seldom have domestic provisions directly addressed issues that are today considered terrorism. Nevertheless, the criminal law that emerged from highly dangerous activities has provided the basis for national legislatures to examine these issues. Within this context, national features of terrorist offences have slowly taken shape. This emergence has been conditioned by historical developments that may have varied from one country to another. Today, most legal systems have devoted some considerations to the issues of terrorism.

In national legal systems, penal provisions for terrorist offences are usually not fully isolated from other legal norms. Terrorism is quite often characterized as a sort of qualified criminality, where terrorist motives are the primary feature.[6] If such a motive cannot be proven, often other penal provisions can be applied. For example, the provisions for terrorist crimes in the Finnish Penal Code Chapter 34a are not fully autonomous and independent. The legal-technical feature of the Finnish provisions is that terrorist intent renders as 'terrorist' certain actions that would have already been subject to penalization as ordinary crimes even without such intent. Another additional requirement for an act to qualify as 'terrorist' is that the act in question must be aimed at causing severe danger or harm to a state or to an international organization. The Finnish legal regime's response to terrorism, therefore, builds substantially upon provisions that define conventional criminal offences, such as aggravated assault, kidnapping, hostage taking, aggravated sabotage,

4 See also T. Weigend in this issue; *contra* A. Cassese in this issue.

5 For a detailed study, see R. Arnold, *The ICC as a New Instrument for Repressing Terrorism* (Ardsley: Transnational Publishers, 2004).

6 See also T. Weigend in this issue.

murder and aggravated endangerment of health. The legally protected interest of these underlying offences may range from private property, life, health, or freedom, or some combination thereof.

Given the notion, as exemplified by the example of Finland, that many domestic criminal justice systems tend to treat terrorist offences in a manner that conforms with their domestic criminal codes, any effort to 'harmonize' domestic definitions of terrorist offences across various states is likely to fail. Indeed, it would be nearly impossible to create a uniform legislation that would define internationally all of these underlying domestic criminal offences. Further, the harmonization of domestic criminal offences would contribute little to the challenge of solving the real problems that give rise to terrorism in the first place. Terrorist crimes when actually committed are already considered as severe crimes even if the specific elements characterizing terrorism are not satisfied. Rather, what may be most useful is for each state to revise its definitions of offences in such a way as to cover the areas of action that the internationally binding agreements have deemed worth including in a definition of terrorism.

Even with revised domestic definitions of criminal offences, a state will undoubtedly maintain a certain margin of discretion for implementation. As international law mainly restricts itself to determining the area of criminality, and seldom addresses other parts of penal liability — such as the general doctrines of liability or sentencing issues — these matters will normally be dealt with on a national basis alone. Typically, national legislatures find ways to incorporate these international criminal offences into their already-existing body of domestic criminal rules and principles.

In the Finnish context, for instance, current criminal legislation on terrorism has been closely connected to crimes of endangerment (*'yleisvaaralliset rikokset', 'gemeingefährliche Straftaten'*). The connection between these offences is a natural one, since the outward appearance of each of them is akin to the other. Finland, since its independence in 1917 and subsequent civil war, has been a country without strong separatist movements. Thus, the driving force behind the development of this part of the criminal legal framework has been the result of international legal cooperation. Domestic law amendments have kept close pace with international treaties. Hijackings of aeroplanes and maritime safety have also been addressed under domestic law since the 1970s, even though the actual experiences within Finland concerning such phenomena have been rather limited. Indeed, few acts that could be described as terrorist have ever been committed in Finland. As far as Finland is concerned, the development of domestic legislation has been contingent on the progress of the treatment of terrorist issues on the international scene. For this reason, the recent international activity on this topic has triggered rapid developments in law. In countries that have experienced terrorist problems domestically, this history looks quite different. In contrast to Finland, these countries have developed this branch of legislation, in part, for internally urgent reasons.

1002 JICJ 4 (2006), 998–1016

3. Terrorism and the International Legal Community

If legislating against terrorism domestically could be described as a gradual growth towards conceptualization, the same may be said for legislating against terrorism in international law. At present, there is no clear definition of terrorism in international law; only a 'rough consensus' has been reached. While the international legal community has produced a remarkable number of laws on this subject, a comprehensive legal apparatus is still lacking. The reasons are quite obvious: the political nature of terrorism renders it difficult to define. There are many ways to address the problem of terrorism: terrorism could be treated as a social problem, a political problem, a crime problem and a military problem. And different definitions suggest different solutions. Over time, the international legal community has shifted its conception of terrorism away from the amorphous paradigm of a social problem to that of a more narrowly construed problem of security and criminal justice.[7] Nevertheless, views still differ today as to how best to prevent terrorism. The strategy often adopted combines different methods.[8]

Terrorist phenomena are also problematic from the point of view of the boundaries between the realm of national law and that of international law. Terrorism as a national problem could be dealt with according to the paradigm of criminal law, that is, as an ordinary crime. International terrorism is more difficult to place within conventional paradigms. Despite the rhetoric, it is relatively clear that terrorist acts carried out by non-state actors are not acts of war in a proper sense.[9] Such terrorist acts are basically not considered violations of international law. For that reason, the international community has sought to handle terrorism as a crime problem.

A. The United Nations

The United Nations view of terrorism has developed gradually, proceeding through several stages. In the first stage, terrorism was considered a legally complex phenomenon but one that should be combated. For various reasons, terrorism was not regarded as being contrary to international law per se so long as no states were involved. Then, in a new stage, international terrorism was defined as presenting a threat to peace and security, resulting in a new

7 A more detailed discussion on this follows subsequently.

8 I do not wish to enter into a discussion as to whether a workable general definition of terrorism has already been reached by extrapolating it from various sources of international law. The gaps between existing definitions of terrorism have certainly narrowed. This topic will be dealt with in further detail in other articles in this volume. Cf. R. Kolb, 'The Exercise of Criminal Jurisdiction over International Terrorists', in Bianchi, *supra* note 3, 227–281; R. Young, 'Defining Terrorism: The Evolution of Terrorism as a Legal Concept in International Law and Its Influence on Definitions in Domestic Legislation', 29 *Boston College International and Comparative Law Review* (2006) at 23; see also the contributions of G.P. Fletcher, T. Weigend, and A. Cassese in this issue.

9 See also the contribution of M. Sassòli in this issue.

approach in international law. Today, the view is slowly emerging that acts of terrorism could be deemed illegal within international law per se. This latter approach is a recent development. If a comprehensive convention on international terrorism were to be adopted,[10] it would help clarifying how international law currently conceptualizes terrorism.

The role the UN has played in attempting to create a widely accepted definition of terrorism has been hampered by the fact that it is difficult for many states to agree on a definition. Terrorism has been condemned numerous times but the right to self-determination of people has also been acknowledged. Herein is the classic dilemma underlying the definition of terrorism: how can the definition of terrorism condemn acts of terrorism without simultaneously denying freedom-fighters the rights to self-determination and to oppose unlawful domination?

The first comprehensive international convention devoted to the Prevention and Punishment of Terrorism dates back to 1937 with the Terrorism Convention of the League of Nations.[11] In 1972, the General Assembly established an ad hoc committee on terrorism. This was followed by the General Assembly's Sixth Legal Committee. Since 1972, the General Assembly has passed several resolutions on terrorism. Several international treaties that addressed specific issues of terrorism have also been drafted by international organizations. The international community has chosen a piecemeal strategy in defining terrorism — dealing with one issue at a time — rather than choosing to address terrorism as a whole. From the outset, the UN itself was not very determined in its action. This piecemeal strategy at the international level caused national legislatures to also take a piecemeal approach to issues of terrorism.

The end of the Cold War marked a step forward for efforts to define terrorism because it became easier to condemn terrorism in all circumstances. This step also opened the way to a more comprehensive approach, allowing a larger role for UN bodies. For example, the Declaration on Measures to Eliminate International Terrorism adopted by the General Assembly in 1995[12] stated that certain criminal acts intended to or calculated to provoke a state of terror for political purposes committed for whatever reason were unjustifiable. Terrorism was thus defined as a crime problem. At the same time, the declaration stated that acts, methods and practices of terrorism could constitute a grave violation of the purposes and principles of the UN, and that terrorism could pose a threat to international peace and security as well.

In a 1996 resolution, the General Assembly established an Ad Hoc Committee to elaborate on an international convention for the suppression of terrorist bombings and, subsequently, an international convention for the

10 See in this context the contributions of T. Weigend and M. Hmoud in this issue.

11 Convention for the Prevention and Punishment of Terrorism, 16 November 1937, 19 *League of Nations Official Journal* (1938), at 23; the Convention did not enter into force.

12 GA Res. 49/60, 17 February 1995.

1004 JICJ 4 (2006), 998–1016

suppression of acts of nuclear terrorism, and to supplement related existing international instruments.[13] Thereafter, the Committee would address the means to further develop a comprehensive legal framework of conventions on international terrorism. The Committee's mandate has been renewed and revised on an annual basis by the General Assembly in its resolutions on the topic of measures to eliminate international terrorism. After the elaboration of two international conventions in the 1990s (the International Convention for the Suppression of Terrorist Bombings and the International Convention for the Suppression of the Financing of Terrorism),[14] the Committee's work has resulted in the International Convention for the Suppression of Acts of Nuclear Terrorism, which was adopted by the General Assembly in 2005.[15] The Convention on terrorism financing has been widely considered to be an important milestone because it contains a general definition of terrorism in its offence provision 1; this was the first such definition adopted at the level of an international agreement.[16]

Other UN bodies have also addressed terrorism issues from a broad perspective. Between 1990 and 2000, the Commission on Human Rights, a subsidiary body of the Economic and Social Council, passed 19 resolutions on human rights and terrorism.[17] The Commission has frequently called upon states to take all necessary measures to prevent, combat and eliminate terrorism. The Commission also repeatedly stressed that such measures should be taken in conformity with international standards of human rights.

In 2004, the UN Security Council adopted Resolution 1566 in which it, among other things, reaffirmed states' duties to prevent terrorist acts and to ensure that such acts are punished 'by penalties consistent with their grave nature'.[18] In paragraph 3 of the resolution, the Security Council formulated language that could be construed as a definition of terrorism. The wording was not, in a strict sense, regarded as a legal definition, but rather a working definition of terrorism. The language was considered an indirect definition as it refers to offences 'as defined in the international conventions and protocols relating to terrorism'. That same year, the General Assembly adopted a resolution on measures to eliminate international terrorism and in which it decided that the Ad Hoc Committee should continue to elaborate on the draft comprehensive convention on international terrorism.[19]

13 GA Res. 51/210, 17 December 1996.

14 International Convention for the Suppression of Terrorist Bombings, GA Res. 52/164, 15 December 1997, in force 23 May 2001, 37 *International Legal Materials* (1998) 249; International Convention for the Suppression of the Financing of Terrorism, GA Res. 54/109, 9 December 1999, in force 10 April 2002, 39 *International Legal Materials* (2000) 270.

15 GA Res. 59/290, 13 April 2005.

16 See also the contribution of M. Pieth in this issue.

17 M.C. Bassiouni, *International Terrorism: A Compilation of U.N. Documents*, vol. II (Ardsley: Transnational Publishers, 2002), 3 *et seq.*

18 SC Res. 1566 (2004).

19 GA Res. 59/46, 16 December 2004.

The UN Commission on Human Rights has appointed a Special Rapporteur for issues of human rights protection while combating terrorism. Further, a recent General Assembly resolution addresses the issue of protecting human rights and fundamental freedoms while countering terrorism.[20] Slowly, human rights law is becoming an important and growing consideration in the drafting of concrete international measures for combating terrorism. Additionally, the Security Council is increasingly bound by human rights concerns when framing its decisions. This heightened awareness of human rights and terrorism has cultivated a dialogue across the various bodies of the UN.

Prior to the attacks of 11 September 2001, work had begun on a draft comprehensive convention on international terrorism, but the road has been a long and winding one. A draft convention has been under discussion since 2000, but progress has been relatively slow.[21] The Ad Hoc Committee had a session also in 2006, and it is relatively close to reaching an agreement on the issue.

The events of 11 September 2001 transformed the debate on terrorism and compelled the Security Council to take charge. Through a series of resolutions, the Security Council defined terrorist acts as a threat to international peace and security, thereby triggering the Security Council's powers to act under Chapter VII of the UN Charter and to make decisions that are directly binding upon states. The first of these resolutions, Resolution 1368, adopted immediately after the attacks, merely contained vague obligations on states.[22] In contrast, however, the hitherto unprecedented Resolution 1373, adopted on 28 September 2001, contained detailed binding rules on the legislative measures to be adopted by states.[23] In Article 1 of the resolution, the Security Council required that all states criminalize terrorist financing, freeze certain funds and assets and prohibit certain further related actions. Article 2 contained further obligations, with Article 2(e) holding that states must

> [e]nsure that any person who participates in the financing, planning, preparation or perpetration of terrorist acts or in supporting terrorist acts is brought to justice and

20 GA Res. 60/158, 28 February 2006.

21 Draft Comprehensive Convention on International Terrorism, UN Doc. A/C.6/55/1 (28 August 2000). This convention was a revised version of the text that India had presented previously. For the original version, see UN Doc. A/C.6/51/6 (1996). For subsequent revised texts prepared by India, see e.g. UN Doc. A/C.6/55/WG.1/CRP.8 and 17 (2000), and UN Doc. A/C.6/55/WG.1/CRP.35 (2000). For an indication of subsequent developments concerning the negotiations of the Draft Comprehensive Convention, the following documents may be consulted: Report of the Ad Hoc Committee established by GA Res. 51/210, 17 December 1996, Sixth session (28 January–1 February 2002), UN GAOR, 57th Session, Suppl. No. 37, UN Doc. A/57/37, 11 February 2002; Letter dated 3 August 2005 from the Chairman of the Sixth Committee addressed to the President of the General Assembly, UN Doc. A/59/894, 12 August 2005; and Report of the Working Group on Measures to eliminate international terrorism, UN Doc. A/C.6/60/L.6, 14 October 2005.

22 SC Res. 1368 (2001).

23 SC Res. 1373 (2001).

1006 JICJ 4 (2006), 998–1016

ensure that, in addition to any other measures against them, such terrorist acts are established as serious criminal offences in domestic laws and regulations and that the punishment duly reflects the seriousness of such terrorist acts.

This sub-section entails a rather broad duty not only to criminalize terrorist acts as serious criminal offences domestically, but also to bring their perpetrators to justice. Very seldom did an instrument of international criminal law entail such a straightforward requirement concerning sentencing — that the punishment should duly reflect the seriousness of the terrorist act. It was clear from the outset that this principle was intended to be taken very seriously and that the Security Council would see to it that Member States make the necessary amendments in order to enforce this new regime. The third important element of this resolution called upon states to, among other things, become parties to the relevant international conventions and protocols relating to terrorism, including the International Convention for the Suppression of the Financing of Terrorism.[24] In contrast to Articles 1 and 2, this aspect of the resolution was not directly legally binding on states.

Resolution 1373 also called for the establishment of a separate body, a Committee of the Security Council, to monitor the implementation of the resolution. It also called upon all states to report to the committee on the steps each has taken to implement the resolution.[25] This reporting was to be an ongoing process followed according to a separate, fixed timetable. The Counter-Terrorism Committee (CTC) was promptly established. Since its inception 5 years ago, the CTC has actively monitored legal developments in practically every UN Member State. There can be no doubt that this activity has triggered law reform in various parts of the world. The constant pressure has likely also contributed to the actions being taken in a climate of haste and hurry.

Reports from various countries to the CTC present very detailed information on their respective legal developments. We must, however, bear in mind that this correspondence has been of diplomatic nature. The reports cannot be regarded as genuine legal sources. Most states have filed between two to four reports each of which represents detailed information about legislation, law reform plans and schedules. Many states have filed annual progress reports. Undoubtedly, the duty to report has motivated states to proceed as fast as possible to meet the required standards. Initial reports commonly contained detailed information on the status of a state's legislation at the time, whereas follow-up reports have tended to focus on the reforms states have carried out or are underway. The material available online[26] confirms that those states with previous experience with terrorism as well as those states that participate actively in international legislative cooperation are generally better equipped

24 The other conventions were not mentioned by name but, at the time the resolution was adopted, there were 12 applicable conventions.

25 See also the contribution of S. Betti in this issue.

26 See http://www.un.org/sc/ctc/(visited 19 May 2006).

than other states to deal with terrorism. The former have managed to conform their laws by implementing comparatively small-scale legal reforms, whereas the latter have had to address a great variety of qualitatively new legal issues in a very short period of time.

Finland serves as an example of a state that had a significant amount of homework to do. In Finland's first report, dated 21 December 2001, Finnish penal provisions on money laundering were evaluated as being relatively up-to-date and could, in limited cases, according to the view of Finland, be applied to the financing of terrorism. Finland was already a member of the Financial Actions Task Force (FATF), which was also geared towards addressing terrorism. The special and general recommendations of the FATF had provided the general framework for developing Finland's national legislation. The domestic legislation needed to be amended, however, so that Finland could ratify the International Convention for the Financing of Terrorism, which Finland had promised to do by the middle of 2002.

Finland had also promised to conduct a more comprehensive review of the penal provisions relating to terrorist offences by 2002 in connection with the national implementation of the Framework Decision on Terrorism of the European Union. From Finland's national point of view, the Framework Decision of the European Union on Terrorism, then in the process of being drafted, was crucial for the more general outline of the national legislation. In its letter dated 1 May 2002, the CTC asked particular questions that resulted in Finland's filing of its second report dated 11 July 2002. Finland's Parliament had just approved the Act on the Implementation of the Convention for the Suppression of the Financing of Terrorism.[27] The Penal Code was amended to establish the financing of terrorism as a criminal offence. As for the more comprehensive measures concerning terrorist offences, a Government Bill had been drafted on a new chapter concerning terrorist crimes and was submitted to experts for comments. The provision on the financing of terrorism would be transferred to the new chapter at the same time.

When Finland reported its plans and progress to the CTC, it did not directly refer to the Framework Decision mentioned above, which had been adopted just a few weeks earlier. On 25 November 2002, the CTC again requested certain information from Finland. In its third report dated 25 February 2003, Finland was finally in a position to inform the CTC that the amendment of the Penal Code concerning the financing of terrorism had entered into force in July 2002 and that the Government Bill for the enactment of the comprehensive reform of the provisions on terrorism had been passed after certain changes during the parliamentary proceedings. The amendments had been ratified, effective 1 February 2003. Several other questions posed by the CTC indicated that the CTC was not quite convinced that Finland had indeed complied with all the requirements.

27 Government Bill 43/2002 vp.

1008 *JICJ* **4** (2006), 998–1016

The CTC then sent a third letter to Finland dated 12 November 2003 which Finland answered with a fourth report dated 12 February 2004. Now the emphasis of the CTC letter was more on the effectiveness of the implementation of the obligations rather than the legal aspects of it. The CTC letter questioned the efficacy of Finland's legislation. The CTC also requested information concerning the legal definition of the words 'terrorist intention' in Section 34a of Finnish Penal Code. On 19 January 2005, the CTC sent its fourth letter to Finland with additional questions. Finland replied in its letter dated 20 April 2005. By this point, the CTC focused mainly on the details regarding the terrorist financing law, and it no longer seemed particularly concerned with Finland's more general provisions concerning terrorist crimes.

The CTC's monitoring appears to have been concrete and intensive. It ultimately had the effect of placing the reform of terrorist legislation very high on Finland's domestic agenda, at least for a period of time. Finland clearly wanted to fulfil the CTC's expectations, and the state fully supported the actions taken by the Committee. While as far as Finland was concerned, the CTC represented only one of the international bodies which exercised monitoring functions, it was nevertheless very influential.

B. European Union

The Council of the European Union adopted the Council Framework Decision on Combating Terrorism on 13 June 2002.[28] The Framework Decision contained a substantial definition of terrorist acts making it more helpful than other international instruments available at the time. In its preamble, the Framework Decision stated that the 'definition of terrorist offences should be approximated in all Member States, including those offences relating to terrorist groups. Furthermore, penalties and sanctions should be provided for natural and legal persons having committed or being liable for such offences, which reflect the seriousness of such offences'. Additionally, the need for a harmonization instrument for terrorist offences had been raised in several documents, including the Vienna Action Plan of 1998.[29]

Among its 13 articles, Article 1 of the Framework Decision defined terrorist offences generally. Articles 2 and 3 dealt with offences relating to a terrorist group and other offences linked to terrorist activities. Article 4 dealt with inciting, aiding or abetting and attempting terrorist acts. The Framework Decision also included provisions concerning the penalties and liabilities of legal persons. In its approach, the Framework Decision clearly went beyond what had been established in existing international conventions; it served as a kind of comprehensive legal instrument, albeit at a regional level only. The anti-terrorist regime of the European Union contained follow-up duties

28 *Official Journal* L 164 (22 June 2002), at 3.
29 *Official Journal* C 19 (23 January 1998), at 1–15.

as well. The European Union also monitors the effective implementation of its binding legal decisions.

Member States were required to take all necessary measures to comply with the Framework Decision by the end of 2002 — mere 6 months after it was adopted — an extremely short period of time. Only five of the 15 Member States succeeded in providing the European Commission with the necessary information by that date, and only two of them had included the texts of the actual provisions. By the middle of 2004, the Commission presented a report in which it assessed how Member States had complied with the requirements of the Framework Decision. Of 15 Member States, 12 had filed the requested information. Eight out of 12 Member States had specifically designated terrorist offences as a separate category of crime. Other Member States had tried to address the issue of terrorism by other means. The Commission further noted that most of the Member States had legislation in place that specifically addressed terrorist acts committed in relation to terrorist groups. The Commission also observed that most Member States had the greatest difficulty taking the necessary steps, pursuant to the requirements of Article 3 of the Framework Decision, to ensure terrorist-linked offences included particular acts enumerated therein; indeed, only four Member States had so complied.

A more detailed study of terrorist laws of Member States of the European Union was included in the Commission Staff Working Paper annexed to the report from the Commission in 2004.[30] The Commission Staff Working Paper observed that only two Member States — Spain and France — had not adopted specific legislation for implementing the Framework Decision, whereas the other Member States had done so or were in the process of doing so. Spain and France likely regarded the existing legal framework as sufficient.[31] Interestingly, both of these states have recently endured their own first-hand experiences with terrorism domestically.

It was difficult to assess Member States' compliance with the Framework Decision in large part because the Framework Decision allows for national discretion when being implemented. That said, Member States are required to choose the means of implementation in a manner that ensures that the directive functions effectively and that its aim is realized. With respect to many issues highlighted in the Framework Decision, Member States could achieve the required aim by following several kinds of legislative strategies. Nevertheless, this particular Framework Decision included relatively detailed provisions, which reduced the possible strategies available to Member States.

30 Commission Staff Working Paper, Brussels, COM (2004) 409 final, 8 June 2004. Three Member States failed to pass on the requested information.

31 In France, specific terrorist offences were enacted as late as in 1986; in Spain in 1984. See J. Borricand, 'France's responses to terrorism', in R. Higgins and M. Flory, *Terrorism and International Law* (London: Routledge, 1997), at 144.

1010 *JICJ* **4** (2006), 998–1016

The national implementation of this legal instrument brought about remarkable changes in the domestic legal systems. It was no longer regarded as sufficient that terrorist offences were considered simply common offences, but the terrorist nature of these offences was now required to be part of the definition. The new approach provided that a terrorist offence is a combination of objective and subjective elements; the former refers to a list of serious criminal conduct and the latter refers to the requirement of specific intent. Suffice it to say, the Framework Decision has played a crucial role in the emergence of terrorist offences in national legal systems as distinct offences — at least within the borders of the European Union. The Framework Decision is nearly a comprehensive legal instrument on terrorism because it includes both a substantive and general definition of terrorist offences.

C. *Council of Europe*

The Council of Europe, the guardian of human rights, democracy and rule of law in Europe, has long devoted its attention to terrorism issues. The Council of Europe used to be the forum for European states to develop common strategies for combating crime. Moreover, the Council of Europe is a regional organization in a broader sense, as it also has Member States outside European territory. Member States such as Russia and Turkey add an important aspect to this work. The Council of Europe concluded the Convention on the Suppression of Terrorism[32] in 1977. Soon after 11 September 2001, the Council of Europe once again addressed the issue of terrorism, which rapidly resulted in the drafting of a protocol that updated the previous convention. The review work was carried out by the Multidisciplinary Group on International Action against Terrorism (GMT), a governmental committee that brought together experts from the 45 Member States and a number of observer states and organizations. The protocol amending the Strasbourg Convention was adopted in 2003.[33]

A second group of experts (CODEXTER) drafted and finalized the Council of Europe Convention on the Prevention of Terrorism that was open for signature.[34] This convention is important mainly because it represents a somewhat more balanced and human rights-based approach in the fight against terrorism in contrast to the aforementioned Framework Decision of the European Union. But unlike the Framework Decision, this Convention does not contain a definition of terrorist offences, but refers instead to existing treaties. The work also resulted in the Council of Europe Convention on the Laundering, Search, Seizure and Confiscation of the Proceeds from Crime and on the Financing of Terrorism.[35] The Council of Europe is well equipped for tracking

32 Council of Europe Treaty Series (CETS) No. 90.

33 Protocol Amending the European Convention on the Suppression of Terrorism, CETS No. 190.

34 CETS No. 196.

35 CETS No. 198.

the legal developments within, as well as gathering materials from, its Member States. The country reports contain detailed information about domestic laws on terrorism.

Comparing the profiles of the Council of Europe with those of the European Union, we find some nuanced differences. Within the framework of the European Union, the anti-terror measures that deal with criminal justice and issues of definition are placed under the umbrella of building Europe as an area of freedom, security and justice. The approach of the European Union is security and criminal-justice based, seeking rapid solutions to problems. The European Union showed a remarkable ability to react to perceived threats, but this seems to have been at the cost of more fundamental considerations. The Treaty of the European Union listed the combating of terrorism under the joint efforts of the European Union.[36] One advantage was that in the structure of European Union law, measures aimed at the approximation of national criminal laws were closely connected with issues of European police cooperation as well as with prosecutorial cooperation. Europol's Counter Terrorism Unit represents a permanent structure that has developed operational projects for its purpose. 'Eurojust' was set up by a Council Decision on 28 February 2002 to improve judicial cooperation in matters involving serious crimes between Member States.[37]

Both the Council of Europe and the European Union showed great readiness to take action, but the European Union also had the opportunity to make use of tougher legal instruments as well as international treaties. The tougher law profile of the European Union does not mean that the process of harmonization of terrorist laws in the European Union has been especially easy. Indeed, it has been quite the contrary. From other points of view, such as protection of human rights, developments might look very different. As always, the real test will appear when concrete crimes are committed; only then will we see whether the perpetrators will be dealt with adequately and fairly in national courts.

4. Observations on the Logic of Legal Reform

A. *Problems of Pragmatism*

From the point of view of international criminal law, terrorism continues to be a hard case where definitional issues still hinder the progress. Some might see this as a sign of the impossible task of defining a phenomenon that itself is built on contradictions. The European Union approach has been more pragmatic, but it may face problems if at some point international efforts should lead to a definition of terrorism with a more nuanced approach. A one-sided criminal

36 Treaty of Amsterdam, Title VI, Art. 29.

37 European Council Decision, 2002/187/JHA (8 February 2002).

1012 JICJ 4 (2006), 998–1016

law approach might entail the risk of misuse of criminal justice for other purposes. It might produce terrorism laws that are too rigid and too broad. A broad national criminalization covering very loose forms of participation in terrorist organizations may lead to problematic restrictions of fundamental freedoms. Also many states may, when reforming their terrorist legislation, act so strongly out of external pressures that the quality of their domestic laws may suffer. In other words, 'legal irritants' could endanger the coherence of domestic criminal legislation. An apparent success in the short term might prove to be a failure in the long term. For many reasons, the real merits of harmonization of terrorist laws are, at present, very difficult to assess.

It seems clear that all strategies have some, albeit different, risks. The international system, particularly the UN, has exercised a very active policy control in this field, but as no comprehensive instrument was available at the time when political progress would have been easier, the best opportunities may have been missed. On the other hand, terrorist laws are likely better off if they are drafted slowly and carefully rather than created in an atmosphere of great insecurity and panic. This is certainly true at all levels of legislative work.

We should, thus, modulate our expectations of rapid progress in this field. Still, given how terrorism has been dealt with historically, the novel criminal justice approach does provide some hope for success. This approach is certainly more palatable than fighting terrorism with armed forces pursuant to a military approach. Terrorism laws can build on the growing grassroots consensus of what this phenomenon is all about. And, as is so often the case with other forms of criminality, 'hard' criminal law can often be combined with softer means that target the social and political roots of terrorism far more effectively than that accomplished by the warfare model.

B. Top-down or Bottom-up Approximation of Laws?

Despite great efforts internationally and domestically, the goal of harmonizing national laws is difficult to reach. We could say that there are always resistant forces at work. This resistance or, in some instances, opposition to harmonization emerges in part from the national civil service bureaucracy, which is charged with drafting the new provisions and which views the new rules with suspicion to the extent they depart from their own national legal traditions. Additionally, domestic resistance also comes from the need to preserve the coherence of domestic legal order and its principles and traditions of criminal justice. To better understand why things do not always work out smoothly, one must understand these underlying phenomena. I do not believe that any of the real forces of legal resistance have much connection with denying the severity of the threat posed by terrorism itself.

Legal regulations of international or regional origin containing ideologically or doctrinally 'abnormal' elements are likely to face problems when implemented nationally. In the context of the European Union, 'resistance' — a natural phenomenon in all reform efforts — has a two-fold role. First, Member States must agree on the legal instrument itself. This is the part that comes closest to original legislative work at a regional level. Second, the legal instrument must be nationally implemented. National parliaments may participate in the negotiations leading to the adoption of new instruments. In Finland, for example, Section 96 of the Constitution states that the Parliament is involved in the national preparation of legal matters of the European Union. The Parliament will be involved a second time when the national legislature implements the negotiated legal instruments.

A brief look at Finland's example may help shed light on some of the difficulties in legislating terrorism issues domestically. It is worth noting that the first stage of negotiating the Framework Decision meant an adaptation of the proposal first tabled by the European Commission on 19 September 2001. In October of that year, the proposal was twice renewed with some basic changes in Articles 1, 2 and 4 of the draft Framework Decision. The Framework Decision was finally accepted almost a year later on 13 July 2002. In Finland, Parliament addressed the matter in the autumn of 2001. After Parliament had been informed about the changes to the tabled proposal already accepted, the Constitutional Committee passed a statement in which it criticized various elements of the proposed Framework Decision. The Constitutional Committee mainly critiqued the vagueness of the definition of terrorism, holding that it contravened legal certainty and the principle of legality. In fact, most of the criticism stemmed from the Finnish Government's previous position.

With respect to the definition of terrorist offences relating to organized terrorist groups, the Constitutional Committee expressed worries about solutions that differed significantly from those resulting from traditional doctrines of participation in crime. Especially problematic was the position of the leader of such a terrorist organization. According to the Finnish view, leadership alone, without any connection to the activities themselves, would not suffice for penal liability. The Constitutional Committee also regarded the penal liability of participants to the activities of the group as too broad when measured against traditional principles of criminal law. The Constitutional Committee also raised doubts as to the prescribed penalty scales because they appeared to deviate excessively from the general approach under Finnish law.[38]

When the Law Committee of the Finnish Parliament dealt with the proposed Framework Decision, it noted, first of all, that owing to the recent changes, the Government's opinion on the last version of the proposal was no longer available. The Law Committee also noted that, as regarding the list of concrete terrorist offences, almost no justification was presented by the drafters of the law. The Law Committee further pointed out that its ability to assess the proposal was generally difficult given the number of recent changes to it,

38 Statement of the Constitutional Committee 41/2001, on file with the author.

but the Committee did not wish to provide further details. Instead, it stated only that the proposal was not satisfactory given the absence of precise definitions. The Committee suggested that one could strive for a definition that would be closer to the text of the UN Convention on the Financing of Terrorism. With respect to the criminalization of obligations pursuant to Article 2 of the Framework Decision, the Law Committee held that the current proposal was better than the earlier ones, but that problems still remained from the point of view of principles of Finnish penal legislation.[39]

The Finnish Parliamentary proceedings were initiated by the Government Bill 188/2001. In its statement on the Bill, the Constitutional Committee of the Parliament renewed some of its previous criticism, but the tone was more temperate. The remaining problems mostly concerned topics that were regarded as new issues under Finnish criminal law, including the participation in the activities of a terrorist organization.[40] One difficult problem that could now be resolved concerned how to implement the basic rule governing the maximum penalties for the leader of a terrorist group. The previous formulation had dropped from 20 to 15 years of imprisonment for someone convicted of being a leader of a terrorist group. Now, the 15 years of imprisonment could be reached legislatively without breaking with the traditional politics of penalty scales. A terrorist group leader could be regarded as having committed two or more crimes. In the case of multiple crimes, Finnish law allows a 15-years' maximum penalty. The Law Committee of the Parliament stated in its memorandum that the accepted framework decision had in many ways come closer to the views presented by the Committee at the earlier stage, but that the provisions of the Framework Decision still deviated in several respects from national principles of drafting law. The Committee was of the opinion, however, that the Member States could adjust the obligations arising from the Framework Decision to nationally adopted principles of drafting law.

The Law Committee took the remarks presented by the Constitutional Committee very seriously. In fact, the Law Committee scrutinized the whole proposed legislation carefully and, consequently, several of the provisions were rewritten. Indeed, only one of the eight provisions remained untouched.[41] In this way, the Law Committee accomplished the final checks to adapt to Finnish conditions the new provisions on terrorism.

From this history it is clear that the European model of how to define terrorism was not based on a 'dictate' from the Commission, but instead, was a result of intensive negotiations among different parties. The stakes were high, but still the governments and parliaments wanted to preserve values that were important from the point of view of domestic legal systems.

The reform of terrorist legislation has proved to be an important test case for transnational and regional law-drafting. My study has been very limited,

39 Statement of the Law Committee 20/2001, on file with the author.

40 Statement of the Constitutional Committee 48/2002, on file with the author.

41 Memorandum of the Law Committee 24/2002, on file with the author.

but similar examples of connections between regional law-drafting and national law-drafting could be found elsewhere. I believe that it is important to understand why national jurisdictions sometimes have a difficult time with the proposals tabled. The development of regional legislation is far from being a top-down project of imposing on domestic legal systems ready-made legal regulations. Counter-forces will have a profound impact on the rules that will eventually be adopted. This could, however, be seen rather as a merit than a defect. The main point, however, is that national authorities must share the same commitment to the problem of terrorism as shown by the original political actors.

As far as the Finnish case was concerned, the need to address the problems presented by terrorist crimes was never challenged by the institutional actors. It appears, however, that ultimately the balancing of freedom and security must be done at the national level. This is especially important when regional or international instruments operate on vague definitions that create uncertainties. These uncertainties may create risks to the protection of fundamental rights of persons, as the suspects will, in many ways, face actions by the police and other security bodies. The European Union Network of Independent Experts in Fundamental Rights has urged national parliamentary debates to develop the best possible text for this reason. The drafting of the national text should be accompanied as well by an independent assessment of compliance with the requirements of fundamental rights.[42]

The national margin of discretion may also lead to problems because the national differences may cause difficulties in international cooperation. As Reuven Young points out, '[a]n established minimum international law definition of terrorism that informs states' domestic criminal law is required to ensure a baseline of consistency and to facilitate international cooperation'.[43] It may be better to ensure that nationally adopted laws enjoy public support domestically and are not openly criticized for excesses. As the project of harmonizing legislation is always a long-term process, the experiences gathered may give impetus for new reforms in the future. If the work is done properly, future amendments are likely to be easier to accomplish.

C. *Contradictions Resolved?*

Finally, we should return to the question of whether the world needs a general definition of terrorism in the first place and whether the contradictions that have thus far hindered the international legal community from reaching consensus on such a definition still exist. It is very risky to make pronouncements on such questions at the moment. Most certainly, international

42 EU Network of Independent Experts in Fundamental Rights, *The Balance between Freedom and Security in the Response by the European Union and Its Members to the Terrorist Threat* (2003), at 11. See critical conclusions, at 51–52.

43 Young, *supra* note 8, at 26.

1016 JICJ 4 (2006), 998–1016

organizations will, in many cases, find themselves in the difficult position of determining whether the international system should classify a case as terrorist or whether some other formulation would suffice. Borderline cases will arise in the context of violent conflicts. The struggles around applications of definitions for terrorism will be more complicated the more open-ended the definitions. Therefore, precision is a virtue. New forms of terrorism, such as bio-terrorism and cyber-terrorism, might also call for attention from the domestic and international legislatures. International treaties are, almost inevitably, born after the fact.

Further, the ideological battles that have bogged down agreement on a definition of terrorism might appear as well in a domestic context. The exclusion of political justification for terrorist actions could lead to problems when such cases are handled by the courts. In the case of an armed conflict, state authorities are very likely to be involved in the event. If repressive actions attract terrorist responses, the state itself becomes involved. Labelling the 'enemy' as terrorist might be an easy way to justify control and repression, but problems may arise if domestic courts reinforce state authority in this respect.

The judiciary must remain impartial and independent. All major legal systems recognize doctrines of necessity and self-defence. As regards terrorist offences, motives of the perpetrators might sometimes be understandable. The legal system, if it 'normalizes' terrorist offences in ordinary legal life, must face all ordinary questions that arise in criminal trials. For that reason, such cases would be the ultimate test for the law on terrorism.

5. Conclusion

Terrorist laws are extreme examples of the modernization of criminal justice. Nevertheless, some cases will end up in ordinary courts. The legal framework of the criminal justice system must be equipped to identify terrorism as one crime among others, with all the necessary elements satisfied pursuant to penal law. But punishing terrorists ought to serve a rationale in terms of a punishment theory. Can terrorists be deterred? Do we rehabilitate terrorists? Do we believe in retribution? In addressing these questions, we should adhere to the traditional ways of addressing punishment, rather than inventing something new for these cases. The punishment should be a 'recognizing' one, and it should attribute certain acts to certain persons, as is done for ordinary criminal offences.[44] We should not let the 'militarism' of counter-terrorism militarize criminal justice by referring to enemy concepts.

44 Terrorism is surely a hard case, but no more difficult than criminal liability for large humanitarian disasters. Cf. the discussion and the critique of deterrence as a goal in M. Koskenniemi, 'Between Impunity and Show Trials', 6 *Max Planck Yearbook of United Nations Law* (2002) 1–36, and J. Klabbers, 'Just Revenge? The Deterrence Argument in International Criminal Law' 12 *Finnish Yearbook of International Law* (2001) 249–267.

[7]

Countering Nuclear Terrorism: A Conventional Response

Christopher C. Joyner*

Abstract

Nuclear terrorism poses a grave threat to national security, a fact dramatically demonstrated on 11 September 2001 by Al-Qaeda's attacks against the World Trade Center and the Pentagon. These strikes revealed the vulnerability of Western societies to foreign terrorist threats and underscored the real possibility that terrorist groups might use nuclear weapons against cities in the United States or Europe. This article analyses the nature of this threat and possible remedies within the context of a new multilateral instrument, the 2005 International Convention for the Suppression of Acts of Nuclear Terrorism. This Convention furnishes a legal basis for international cooperation to prevent terrorists from acquiring nuclear weapons. It criminalizes the possession of, use of, or threat to use radioactive devices by non-state actors, their accomplices, and organizers if intended to produce death, serious bodily injury or environmental or property damage. The agreement further encourages increased exchanges of information and greater collaboration between governments in the pursuit of terrorist suspects. But the effectiveness of this instrument depends on the degree to which state parties respect, abide by and enforce its provisions. Key in this regard is strengthening security of fissile materials stored in nuclear facilities. If governments fulfil their duties in this Convention, the agreement will work well and accomplish its purposes. To the degree that governments fall short of meeting their obligations, specific protections against nuclear terrorism in the Convention will be eroded, and the risk of nuclear terrorism will remain high.

Nuclear terrorism poses a grave threat to national security. While there was already awareness of this threat during the early 1990s, its stark importance was

* Professor of International Law, Department of Government and Edmund A. Walsh School of Foreign Service, Georgetown University; Director, Institute for International Law and Politics, Georgetown University; Ph.D. University of Virginia (Foreign Affairs, 1977); M.A. Florida State University (Government, 1973); M.A. Florida State University (International Relations, 1972); B.A. Florida State University (International Relations/History, 1970). The author would like to acknowledge the useful comments and suggestions made by the editor-in-chief and anonymous EJIL reviewers on an earlier version of this article. Email: joynerc@georgetown.edu.

226 *EJIL* 18 (2007), 225–251

dramatically demonstrated on 11 September 2001, when members of the Al-Qaeda terrorist organization hijacked four aircraft and flew three of them into the World Trade Center and the Pentagon.[1] These strikes revealed the vulnerability of Western societies to foreign terrorist threats. The 9/11 attacks also underscored the possibility that terrorist groups could use weapons of mass destruction against Western cities. The threat became clear that Al-Qaeda could similarly launch skyjacked aircraft strikes against nuclear power plants, with even more devastating impacts. More disturbing, it is well known that Al-Qaeda is seeking to acquire nuclear fissile materials – either plutonium or highly enriched uranium – and the necessary scientific expertise for making a nuclear weapon, presumably to detonate in a Western city.[2]

The possibility of future terrorist activities using nuclear devices is a concern that all governments must confront.[3] The puzzle confronting governments is what can be done to prevent such catastrophic nuclear attacks by terrorist groups. This study addresses one aspect of the solution to that puzzle, namely, the need to promote through international legal channels better intelligence-sharing and closer intergovernmental collaboration about terror groups and the storage and transfer of nuclear technologies.

On 15 April 2005, the UN General Assembly adopted and opened for signature the International Convention for the Suppression of Acts of Nuclear Terrorism (Convention on Nuclear Terrorism, or CNT).[4] The goal of this multilateral instrument is

1 On 11 Sept. 2001, hijacked aircraft were flown by 19 Al-Qaeda members into the two World Trade Center Towers in New York City and into the Pentagon Building in Virginia. Approximately 3,000 people were killed. A fourth hijacked aircraft crashed in the Pennsylvania countryside. See 'US Attacked: Hijacked Jets Destroy Twin Towers and Hit Pentagon in Day of Terror', *New York Times*, 12 Sept. 2001, at 1; 'Terrorists Hijack 4 Airliners, Destroy World Trade Center, Hit Pentagon; Hundreds Dead', *Washington Post*, 12 Sept. 2001, at 1. For an authoritative analysis of these events see T.H. Kean and L. Hamilton, *The 9/11 Report: The National Commission on Terrorist Attacks Upon the United States* (2004).

2 Rediff.com, 'Al Qaeda bought nuclear weapons', 22 Mar. 2004, available at: http://www.rediff.com/news/2004/mar/22mir.htm (accessed 18 Mar. 2006); 'Warning over al Qaeda nuclear weapons fear', *Daily Mail*, 24 May 2005, available at: http://www.dailymail.co.uk/pages/live/articles/news/news.html?in_article_id=349848&in_page_id=1770 (accessed 15 Mar. 2006). For an inventory of Al-Qaeda's efforts to secure nuclear weapons see Center for Nonproliferation Studies, 'Al-Qaeda's Nuclear Ambitions' (June 2005), available at: http://www.epsusa.org/publications/newsletter/june2005/alqaeda.htm (accessed 18 Mar. 2006).

3 See generally Rostow, 'Before and After: The Changed U.N. Response to Terrorism Since September 11th', 35 *Cornell Int'l LJ* (2002) 675.

4 International Convention for the Suppression of Acts of Nuclear Terrorism, UN Doc A/RES /59/290 (15 Apr. 2005), at Annex (hereinafter Convention on Nuclear Terrorism, or CNT), available at: http://www.un.int/usa/a-59-766.pdf (accessed 18 Mar. 2006). For initial reactions to the convention, see 'Statement by Ambassador Stuart Holliday, Alternate United States Representative to the UN for Special Political Affairs, on the Adoption of the International Convention for the Suppression of Acts of Nuclear Terrorism, in the General Assembly, April 13, 2005; United States Mission to the United Nations press release #68 (05), 13 Apr. 2005, available at: http://www.usunnewyork.usmission.gov/05_068.htm (accessed 18 Mar. 2006); 'New Convention Against Nuclear Terrorism Bolsters Global Framework', International Atomic Energy Agency staff report, 14 Apr. 2005, available at: http://www.iaea.org/NewsCenter/News/2005/conv_nuclterror.html (accessed 20 Mar. 2006); and 'Statement by Alexander Yakovenko, the Spokesman of Russia's Ministry of Foreign Affairs, Concerning the Adoption by UN General Assembly of an International Convention for the Suppression of Acts of Nuclear Terrorism', Russian Ministry of Foreign Affairs press statement, available at: http://www.russianembassy.org.za/statements/text/apr05/dyakovenko-terrorism140405.html (accessed 15 Mar. 2006).

to improve the existing legal framework against international terrorism 'for international cooperation in the investigation, prosecution, and extradition of those who commit terrorist acts involving radioactive materials or a nuclear device'.[5] But to what extent does the instrument actually make any real contributions toward countering acts of transnational nuclear terrorism? The study investigates three themes to address this central question. First, Section 1 examines the specific aims of the CNT, both regarding the reality of the threat of nuclear terrorism, as well as the policy provisions contained in its text. As a second theme, the study evaluates the ways and means proposed in the Convention to prevent nuclear terrorism and to deal with possible perpetrators. Section 2 sets out the background of the CNT, while the legal regime it creates is the subject of Section 3. This discussion sets out the strategies and procedures in the CNT for defining offences and improving multilateral efforts to suppress threats involving nuclear terrorism. The third theme is presented in Section 4 as the analysis assesses the realistic prospects for the CNT to coordinate successfully intergovernmental actions for deterring, preventing and punishing offenders accused of nuclear terrorism. The critical consideration here, as one might suppose, is likely to be found less in the content of the agreement's provisions or in its legal ambitions. Rather, ultimate success or failure of the CNT will rest on the degree to which its states parties are willing and able to make its provisions work.

1 Risks of Nuclear Terrorism

The risks posed by nuclear terrorism are threefold: (1) there is the need to protect nuclear reactors adequately; (2) there is the possibility that terror agents can construct or acquire nuclear weapons; and (3) there is the possibility that terror agents might build 'dirty bombs'.

A *Protection of Nuclear Reactors*

Most nuclear power reactors are openly vulnerable to attack from terrorist groups, as they are protected only by wire fences and local security personnel. The fear is that a terrorist attack against a nuclear plant could destroy redundant safety systems, thereby causing severe core damage, meltdown and catastrophic radioactive releases. Recent revelations that Al-Qaeda considered nuclear power plants as primary targets for sabotage escalated concern among experts that nuclear reactors worldwide, particularly in the United States, are not adequately protected.[6]

[5] Aita, Press Release, State Department Documents, 'U.N. General Assembly Adopts Nuclear Terrorism Treaty' (13 Apr. 2005), available at: http://www.globalsecurity.org/security/library/news/2005/04/sec-050413-usia02.htm (accessed 29 Dec. 2006).

[6] Starr, 'NRC memo warns of attacks on nuclear plants', CNN, 31 Jan. 2002, available at: http://archives.cnn.com/2002/US/01/31/ret.terror.threats/ (accessed 19 Mar. 2006); Grunwald and Behr, 'Are Nation's Nuclear Power Plants Secure?', *Washington Post*, 4 Nov. 2001.

B *Building Nuclear Weapons*

Closely related to plant security concerns are worries over whether a terrorist group could build a nuclear device. An emerging consensus suggests that such a scenario might be possible – that, if given scientific expertise and necessary fissile materials, a sophisticated terror group could construct an operational nuclear bomb, with a potential yield of around one kiloton. Documented attempts by Al-Qaeda to acquire nuclear materials and nuclear-weapon design information highlight the extreme gravity of this risk.[7] The key for this scenario to occur is the ability of a terror group to acquire fissile materials, either plutonium or highly enriched uranium, which is needed to make the bomb's core. These fissile materials might be purchased from foreign sources on the black market or stolen from a nuclear facility.[8]

The International Atomic Energy Agency (IAEA) sets safeguard standards and conducts inspections aimed at detecting whether there are substantial process losses of any fissile materials, or whether adequate protection is in place to ensure against the theft of materials in transit or in storage.[9] It remains problematic, however, that IAEA standards apply at present only to international shipments of fissile materials, not to the security of facilities where they are processed, used and stored. This invites genuine worry about whether fissile materials stored in these nuclear facilities are in fact secure, or have been misplaced, missing, or stolen.

C *Building 'Dirty Bombs'*

A third threat from nuclear terrorists is the possibility that they might detonate a 'dirty' bomb. A dirty bomb is a conventional explosive containing radioactive isotopes

7 Albright, 'Al-Qaeda's Quixotic Quest to Go Nuclear', *Asia Times*, 22 Nov. 2002, available at: http://www.atimes.com/atimes/Middle_East/DK22Ak01.html; Albright, 'Al Qaeda's Nuclear Program: Through the Window of Seized Documents', *Special Forum* 47 (The Nautilius Institute), 2 Nov. 2002, available at: http://www.nautilus.org/archives/fora/Special-Policy-Forum/47_Albright.html (accessed 9 May 2006). Significant evidence suggests that terrorist groups hostile to US interests have sought stolen nuclear weapons or weapons-usable nuclear materials, and have attempted to recruit nuclear-weapons expertise. See Bunn, 'The Threat: The Demand for Black Market Fissile Material' (Nuclear Treat Initiative, last updated 16 June 2005), available at: http://www.nti.org/e_research/cnwm/threat/demand.asp (accessed 19 May 2006). Evidence also suggests that most terror groups are not interested in destroying Western society with weapons of mass destruction: see Sands, 'The Nuclear Terrorists: Who, Why, and How Capable', in C.D. Ferguson and W.C. Potter (eds), *The Four Faces of Nuclear Terrorism* (2004); G. Allison, *Nuclear Terrorism: The Ultimate Preventable Catastrophe* (2004), at 19–42; and J. Stern, *The Ultimate Terrorists* (1999).

8 See generally Bunn, *supra* note 7; Testimony of Laura S.H. Holegate, Vice President for Russia/New Independent States Program, Nuclear Threats Initiative, 'Building a Nuclear Bomb: Identifying Early Indicators of Terrorist Activities' before the House Committee on Homeland Security Subcommittee on Prevention of Nuclear and Biological Attack, 26 May 2005. See Francis, 'Experts Warn Loose Russian Nuclear Materials Could Lead to WMD in Terrorist Hands', *NTI Global Security*, 27 May 2005, available at www.nti.org/d_newswire/issues/2005_5_27.html#3A7EDFED (accessed 5 Mar. 2007).

9 See IAEA, 'Nuclear Security Plan for 2006–2009', IAEA Doc GC(49)/17 and IAEA, 'Resolutions and Other Decisions of the General Conference, Forty-Ninth Regular Session, 26–30 September 2005' (GC(49)/RES/DEC(2005)).

in the form of powder or tiny pellets that, when exploded, will disperse the nuclear material and contaminate a wide area.[10] The main damage from a dirty nuclear bomb would come from the blast itself, while contamination from its radioactive material to people and the environment likely would be limited. The main intent of a dirty bomb is to incite panic and contaminate people and property with radioactive materials.[11]

These threats of nuclear terrorism are today real. That being the case, the overriding critical concern becomes: What can governments do to prevent such a nuclear incident from occurring? Fundamental to addressing this question is the need for genuine multilateral cooperation and collaboration to share intelligence information and coordinate individual national policies into unified international actions. Facilitating such cooperation are international law channels, especially through the promulgation of and mutual compliance with binding legal instruments. To this end, concerned governments worked for seven years under United Nations' auspices to negotiate a special multilateral agreement, the International Convention on the Suppression of Acts of Nuclear Terrorism.[12] This agreement represents the most authoritative international instrument to date for dealing with nuclear terrorism in terms of deterring such acts, defining them as criminal offences and for setting out means for bringing accused offenders to trial.

2 Background of the Convention

The international effort to criminalize nuclear terrorism is only a decade old. On 15 December 1997, the General Assembly recommended that the Ad Hoc Committee on Terrorism established by the General Assembly through its Resolution 51/210 of 17 December 1996 should convene to elaborate an international convention for the suppression of acts of nuclear terrorism.[13] To this end, in September 1998

[10] Nuclear Regulatory Commission, 'Fact Sheet on Dirty Nuclear Bombs', available at: http://www.nrc.gov/reading-rm/doc-collections/fact-sheets/dirty-bombs.html (revised Feb. 2004) (accessed 20 Mar. 2006); World Health Organization, 'Nuclear terrorism and dirty bombs' and WHO/RAD Information Sheet, 'Radiation Dispersion Devise (Dirty Bomb)', Feb. 2003, both available at: http://www.who.int/ionizing_radiation/a_e/terrorism/en/; and Karon, 'The "Dirty Bomb" Scenario', Time.com, 10 June 2002, available at: http://www.time.com/time/nation/article/0,8599,182637,00.html (accessed 18 Mar. 2006).

[11] See Ensor, 'Al Qaeda Interested in Dirty Bomb, U.S. says', CNN.com, 6 Dec. 2001, available at: http://archives.cnn.com/2001/US/12/04/ret.nuclear.report/; 'Analysis: Bin Laden's nuclear threat', BBC News, 26 Oct. 2001, available at: http://news.bbc.co.uk/1/hi/world/south_asia/1621819.stm (accessed 18 Mar. 2006).

[12] Convention on Nuclear Terrorism, *supra* note 4.

[13] 'Measures to eliminate international terrorism', GA Res 52/165, UN Doc A/RES/52/653 (15 Dec. 1997). See also GA Res 49/60, UN Doc A/RES/49/60 (9 Dec. 1994), by which the General Assembly adopted the Declaration on Measures to Eliminate International Terrorism; GA Res 51/210, P 9, UN Doc A/RES/51/210 (17 Dec. 1996); and GA Res 56/88, P 16, UN Doc A/RES/56/88 (24 Jan. 2002).

the Sixth Committee of the General Assembly established such a working group and elected Philippe Kirsch of Canada as its Chairman.[14] The Ad Hoc Committee on Terrorism convened in its second session from 17–27 February 1998 to peruse and revise a draft convention on nuclear terrorism that had been recently submitted by the Russian Federation.[15]

At the fifth meeting of the Ad Hoc Committee in 1998, the Russian delegation formally introduced its text for a draft convention on the suppression of acts of nuclear terrorism.[16] The drive behind Russia's initiative was its government's perception of the critical need to counter potential threats of terrorism involving the use of nuclear devices and the need to undertake effective international counteractions against those threats.[17] The Russians contended that current multilateral instruments were not sufficiently broad in reach or in means for responding to threats implicit in an act of nuclear terrorism. A new convention, they argued, would fill legal lacunae left by other relevant instruments, notably, the 1980 Convention on the Physical Protection of Nuclear Materials.[18] The Convention on Physical Protection only pertains to nuclear materials used for peaceful purposes; it does not extend to nuclear materials or facilities used for military purposes. The draft text submitted by the Russians aimed to cover more broadly possible targets and types of nuclear terrorism. Given that the Convention on Physical Protection fails to differentiate nuclear terrorism from other criminal acts involving nuclear materials, this new instrument would enable nuclear terrorism to be defined and distinguished more clearly as a terrorist act. The Russian draft convention also included provisions for countermeasures to combat nuclear terrorism, among them procedures to be taken after a crisis, such as the need to return to rightful owners any radioactive materials and devices involved in an offence. Importantly, also recognized during these discussions was that Russia's draft text mirrored

14 'Measures to Eliminate International Terrorism: Report of the Working Group', UN GA Doc A/C.6/53/L.4 53rd sess. (22 Oct. 1998), at 2.

15 UN Doc A/AC.252/L.3 (17 Dec. 1996).

16 See draft text of the convention on the suppression of acts of nuclear terrorism submitted by the Russian Federation, UN Doc A/AC.252/L.3 and Corr.1 and Corr. 2, in 'Report of the Ad Hoc Committee established by General Assembly Resolution 51/210 of 17 December 1996', UN GAOR 53rd sess. (Suppl No 37) (A/53/37) (23 July 1998), Annex I (hereinafter Russian draft text).

17 As privately reported, the impetus for Russia's initiative in introducing the draft was reports that about 100 of its portable nuclear weapons devices developed during Cold War years were unaccounted for and potentially vulnerable to theft by terror groups: see generally M. Bunn and A. Weir, *Securing the Bomb: An Agenda for Action* (2004); National Research Council (Committee on Indigenization of Programs to Prevent Leakage of Plutonium and Highly Enriched Uranium from Russian Facilities, Office for Central Europe and Eurasia), *Strengthening Long-Term Nuclear Security: Protecting Weapon-Usable Material in Russia: Development, Security, and Cooperation* (2005); National Research Council (Committee on International Security and Arms Control), *Monitoring Nuclear Weapons and Nuclear-Explosive Materials: An Assessment of Methods and Capabilities* (2005). The threat here concerns the possible use of 'suitcase atom bombs', which weigh as little as 65lb and could yield an explosion of between 0.5 and 2 kilotons: see N. Sokov, 'Suitcase Nukes: Permanently Lost Luggage', Paper for the Center for Nonproliferation Studies, Monterrey Institute of International Studies, 13 Feb. 2004, cited in Allison, *supra* note 7, at 49.

18 Convention on the Physical Protection of Nuclear Material, 3 Mar. 1980, TIAS No 11080, 1456 UNTS 101 (hereinafter Convention on Nuclear Materials).

criminal law provisions in other counter-terrorist conventions, which could be considerably reinforced by integrating relevant provisions from the recently concluded International Convention for the Suppression of Terrorist Bombings (CTB).[19] Implementation of this latter strategy, in fact, proved to be a viable approach as the convention text evolved over the next five years.

The committee conducted its work as a working group of the whole and proceeded in two phases. During the first phase, the Working Group concentrated on definitions and offences covered under the proposed convention, with a view to clarifying the need for such an instrument, along with its objectives and its substantive scope. To these ends, the group reviewed Article 1 of the Russian draft text, which contained definitions of select terms used in the text. During its second phase, the working group dealt with reviewing and assessing substantive provisions in the Russian text that differed from provisions in related UN counter-terrorism treaties.[20] From this process, 39 separate written amendments and proposals for rewording language in the draft text were submitted by at least 19 state delegations.[21] To follow up, the Working Group convened from 28 September to 19 October 1998, in 13 meetings to consider two documents. One was the draft text submitted by the Russian Federation; the second was a discussion paper prepared by 'the Friends of the Chairman'.[22] From these discussions, which included 38 additional written proposals and suggested amendments tabled before the Working Group, the Friends of the Chairman prepared a new discussion paper that was considered by the Working Group.[23] Based on comments made by delegations to this paper and proposals concerning provisions not included in the paper,[24] the Friends of the Chairman subsequently prepared a revised draft convention text. This revised text contains the entire final draft convention, save for draft Article 4. This provision delayed completion of the convention for four years. The main

19 International Convention for the Suppression of Terrorist Bombings, 15 Dec. 1997, S. Treaty Doc No. 106-6, 37 ILM 249 (hereinafter Convention on Terrorist Bombings).

20 Especially, the Convention on Plastic Explosives for the Purpose of Detection, 1 Mar. 1991, US Treaty Doc No. 103-8, 2122 UNTS 359 (hereinafter Convention on Plastic Explosives) and the Convention on Terrorist Bombings, *supra* note 21. Special attention in the draft negotiations focused mainly on draft Arts 2 (the nature of the offence), 4 (regarding the lawfulness of states using nuclear weapons), 5 (making offences domestic crimes), 6 (eliminating mitigating factors), 8 (protecting radioactive materials under IAEA standards), 10 (establishing conditions for investigating an alleged offence), 11 (making mandatory the duty to extradite or prosecute), 12 (ensuring fair treatment and human rights of the accused), 13 (setting conditions for extradition), and 14 (obligating parties to assist and cooperate).

21 See Annex II, 'Written amendments and proposal submitted by delegations', in 'Report of the Ad hoc Committee established by General Assembly resolution 51/210 of 17 December 1996', GAOR 53rd sess. Suppl No 37, UN Doc A/53/37 (23 July 1998), at 14–34, available at: www.un.org/documents/ga/docs/53/plenary/a53-37.htm (accessed 5 Mar. 2007).

22 The 'Friends' referred to a special group comprised of members of the Bureau of the Ad Hoc Committee that had been established by GA res. 51/210 of 17 Dec. 1996: see UN Doc A/C.6/53/WG.1/CRP.1.

23 UN Doc A/C.6/53/WG.1/CRP.1/Rev.1, noted in 'Measures to Eliminate International Terrorism: Report of the Working Group', UN Doc A/C.6/53/L.4, 53rd sess., at 2 (22 Oct. 1998).

24 Namely, Art. 2, para. 4 of Art. 4, Art. 10, and the preamble. See 'Measures to Eliminate International Terrorism: Report of the Working Group', UN Doc A/C.6/53/L.4, 53rd sess., at 2 (22 Oct. 1998), available at http://daccess-ods.un.org/access.nsf/Get?OpenAgent&DS=A/C:6/53/L.4&Lang=E (accessed 5 Mar. 2007).

concern centred on wording that attempted to determine the lawfulness or impermissibility of using nuclear weapons by states. In late 2001 a proposal submitted by Mexico amended this provision, which asserted that the convention 'does not address, nor can it be interpreted as addressing, in any way, the issue of the legality of the use or threat of use of nuclear weapons by States'.[25] Once this controversy was settled, the draft instrument was completed.[26]

The CNT represents a welcome and important contribution to the international legal framework for countering terrorism and ensuring nuclear security. Even so, it does not accomplish as much as some might have preferred. Some proposals were excluded from the CNT treaty's scope in order to facilitate its adoption by consensus. For example, considerable discussion occurred in the negotiating sessions over the merit of exempting military activities and personnel from prosecution for offences similar to those articulated in the CNT.[27] In the end, however, the exemptions remained. Other delegations suggested the insertion of specific provisions to protect against acts of terrorism involving nuclear weapons or materials that might be committed by state actors.[28] The final convention text, however, does not address the lawfulness of a state's use of nuclear weapons. Also significant is that delegations were unable to achieve consensus on a definition of terrorism, which contributed to prolonging the negotiations four years beyond completion of the draft text in 2001.[29] Producing a universally acceptable definition of 'terrorism' over the last four decades has proven to be a serious obstacle to the creation of a worldwide counter-terrorism regime, since, in the view of some governments, one man's terrorist remains another man's freedom fighter.[30] Not surprisingly, no definition of 'terrorism' appears in the final version of the CNT.

3 The CNT Regime

Treaty law serves as the chief source of modern international law. Treaties and conventions provide the principal legal frameworks within which modern international relations are conducted. A complex web of multilateral treaty-based rules, in fact, underpins contemporary international relations and strives to provide ways

25 Convention on Nuclear Terrorism, *supra* note 4, at Art. 4(4).

26 See Proposal submitted by Mexico, UN Doc A/C.6/56/WG.1/CRP.9, Art. 4(4), in UN Doc A/C.6/56/C.9 (29 Oct. 2001).

27 See the discussion in 'Measures to Eliminate International Terrorism: Report of the Working Group', UN Doc A/C.6/53/L.4 (22 Oct. 1998), at 50–52.

28 See Proposal by Mexico, UN Doc A/C.6/56/WG (2002).

29 See Center for Nonproliferation Studies, 'Draft International Convention for the Suppression of Acts of Nuclear Terrorism' (20 Sept. 2005).

30 A report by UN Secretary-General Kofi Annan, released for heads of governments in Sept. 2005, suggested a definition of terrorism that amounted to 'any action ... intended to cause death or serious bodily harm to civilians or non-combatants with the purpose of intimidating a population or compelling a government or an international organization to do or abstain from doing any act': see Annan, 'In Larger Freedom: Towards Security, Human Rights and Development for All; Report of the Secretary-General', UN Doc A/59/2005 (21 Mar. 2005), at 26.

and means to facilitate the ability of governments to deal with regional and global problems.

It is the same for the threat of nuclear terrorism. The Convention on Nuclear Terrorism, which embodies the first international counter-terrorism agreement since the 11 September 2001 attacks on the United States, was designed to strengthen the growing counter-terrorism regime that now includes 13 UN-sponsored multilateral agreements.[31] To this end, three fundamental presumptions anchor the CNT: (1) Nuclear terrorism could produce 'the gravest consequences' for humankind and therefore poses a threat to international peace and security; (2) the corpus of existing international law does not adequately cover attacks by terrorists on nuclear facilities or their use of nuclear weapons; and (3) international cooperation is urgently needed to devise and adopt 'effective and practical measures' to prevent nuclear acts of terrorism and to prosecute and punish their perpetrators.[32] To an impressive degree, the organizational structure and framework of the CNT, as well as the content of several of its provisions, are borrowed nearly verbatim from the Convention on Terrorist Bombings. This was done by the drafters in order to make the CNT legally compatible with its predecessors, as well as to minimize discontent over provisions dealing with jurisdiction, cooperation, exchange of information, extradition, the political offence exception, international transfer of accused persons, territorial sovereignty of a holding state, dispute settlement, and statements containing closing clauses for the Convention's entry into force.

A *Definition of the Crime*

The threat or use of nuclear weapons has been a paramount concern for governments for more than 60 years. The Cold War between the United States and the Soviet Union became framed by the strategy of nuclear deterrence, which dominated US–Soviet relations from the late 1940s until 1989, when the Soviet Union collapsed and the

31 In addition to the Convention on Nuclear Terrorism, other UN terrorism conventions include: International Convention for the Suppression of the Financing of Terrorism, 9 Dec. 1999, S. Treaty Doc No. 106-49, GA Res 54/109, UN GAOR, 54th Sess., Suppl No. 49, UN Doc A/54/49 (hereinafter Convention on Financing Terrorism); Convention on Terrorist Bombings, *supra* note 21; Convention on Plastic Explosives, *supra* note 22; Protocol for the Suppression of Unlawful Acts Against the Safety of Fixed Platforms Located on the Continental Shelf, 10 Mar. 1988, 27 ILM 685; Convention for the Suppression of Unlawful Acts Against the Safety of Maritime Navigation, 10 Mar. 1988, S. Treaty Doc No. 101-1, 27 ILM 668; Protocol for the Suppression of Unlawful Acts of Violence at Airports Serving International Civil Aviation (supplement to the Montreal Convention), 24 Feb. 1988, S. Treaty Doc No. 100-19, 1589 UNTS 474; Convention on the Physical Protection of Nuclear Material, 3 Mar. 1980, TIAS No. 11080, 1456 UNTS 101 (hereinafter Nuclear Materials Convention); International Convention Against the Taking of Hostages, 17 Dec. 1979, TIAS No. 11081, 1316 UNTS 205; Convention on the Prevention and Punishment of Crimes Against Internationally Protected Persons, Including Diplomatic Agents, 14 Dec. 1973, 28 UST 1975, 1035 UNTS 167; Convention for the Suppression of Unlawful Acts Against the Safety of Civil Aviation, 23 Sept. 1971, 24 UST 546565, 974 UNTS 178 (26 Jan. 1973); Convention for the Suppression of Unlawful Seizure of Aircraft, 16 Dec. 1970, 22 UST 1641, 860 UNTS 105 (hereinafter The Hague Convention); Convention on Offences and Certain Other Acts Committed on Board Aircraft, 14 Sept. 1963, 20 UST 2941, 704 UNTS 219 (hereinafter The Tokyo Convention).

32 Convention on Nuclear Terrorism, *supra* note 4, preamble.

Cold War ended.[33] Since then, the major threats to the West posed by nuclear weapons were thought to come from rogue states – North Korea and Iran in particular. The possible use of nuclear devices by terror groups was a concern, but was considered more a possible scenario than an actual likelihood. The 9/11 airliner attacks by Al-Qaeda against the World Trade Center and the Pentagon immediately transformed perceptions of this possible situation into a realistic probability. Such a development was viewed by governmental leaders as being so serious that it merited stipulation as a special criminal offence by individual persons in international law. The CNT was negotiated to meet that end.

A key achievement of the CNT is the definition of nuclear terrorism as a new crime under international law. As set out in Article 2 of the Convention, a person who 'unlawfully and intentionally' possesses radioactive materials or devices and intentionally aims to cause death or bodily injury or 'substantial damage to property or the environment' commits an international criminal offence.[34] An offence is also committed if a person threatens or damages a nuclear facility such that radioactive materials might be or are released with the intention of causing injury, death or extensive damage to property or the environment, or if that person threatens or attempts by use of force to 'demand unlawfully' any radioactive materials, a nuclear device or a nuclear facility.[35] A person who participates as an accomplice or 'organizes or directs others' to commit an offence is likewise construed to be an offender.[36] This provision lists actions done by individuals that amount to the commission of nuclear terrorism, a criminal act. Put succinctly, a person commits the unlawful act of nuclear terrorism if he or she acquires nuclear materials unlawfully, damages a nuclear facility, or participates in the planning or execution of such acts.[37]

B *Rights and Duties of Parties*

With regard to jurisdictional reach, the CNT defers to the principle of state sovereignty and territorial jurisdiction under specified circumstances. That is, the Convention does not apply in cases where an offence is committed within a state, presumably

[33] After the Soviet Union obtained atomic weapons in 1949, the US came to adopt a strategic doctrine through massive retaliation. This American strategy aimed to check Soviet use of nuclear weapons by threatening overwhelming retaliation with nuclear weapons on intercontinental ballistic missiles that would produce unacceptable damage on Soviet society. US strategic doctrine shifted in the 1960s to a strategy of mutually assured destruction (MAD), which sought to convince both sides that the costs of an exchange of nuclear-tipped ICBMs imposed unacceptability high costs on each other's homelands. Such a belief in MAD prompted each side to refrain from igniting a conflict that could lead to a direct nuclear attack against the other. The literature on this history of US–USSR strategic competition is voluminous: see, e.g., B. Brodie, *War and Politics* (1973); N. Brown, *Nuclear War: The Impending Strategic Deadlock* (1965); H. Kahn, *On Thermonuclear War* (1960); T.C. Schelling, *The Strategy of Conflict* (1960); and A. Wohlstetter, *The Delicate Balance of Terror* (1958).

[34] Convention on Nuclear Terrorism, *supra* note 4, art. 2.

[35] *Ibid.*, Art. 2 (1), (2), and (3).

[36] *Ibid.*, Art. 2 (4).

[37] The language of this provision is new since it pertains to a new crime in international law. Its format and wording, however, closely correspond to Art. 2 of the Convention on Terrorist Bombings, *supra* note 21.

by nationals of that state, who are apprehended within the territory of that state.[38] Authority over the apprehension, prosecution, and trial of such alleged offenders is left to the government of that particular state, to be executed under its domestic law.

It is from that explicit authority that certain rights and duties arise for other states parties. This Convention goes farther than many modern international agreements in this respect, as it clearly implies in Article 4 that states parties are bound to UN Charter law and international law in general. At the same time, the CNT demonstrates a reluctance to impinge on other rights, obligations or responsibilities of states and individuals under international law, including principles of humanitarian law.[39] It makes clear in that same provision that use of force during an armed conflict is to remain governed by the laws of armed conflict and the activities of a state's military forces remain under the jurisdiction of that state, not the Convention. Perpetration of the crime of nuclear terrorism lies outside the range of laws pertaining to the use of force during international armed conflict. In this way, the jurisdictional reach of the CNT avoids encroaching upon the international humanitarian law regime that governs activities of military forces during armed conflict. Likewise, this agreement does not attempt to tackle issues about the lawfulness of states using or threatening to use nuclear weapons in their relations with other states. Whether a state's use of nuclear weapons may be legal or impermissible is deliberately left unaddressed by this instrument.

38 Convention on Nuclear Terrorism, *supra* note 4, Art. 3. This provision is a nearly verbatim replica of Art. 3 of the CTB. Art. 3 embodies the principle of territorial jurisdiction in which jurisdiction is determined according to the location of an act. That is, a state is entitled to exercise its exclusive rights over acts done by a person within its territory. A variant of this, the theory of 'floating' territoriality, recognizes the jurisdiction of a state over criminal acts committed aboard its flag vessels and aircraft. This notion assumes that all flag-bearing air and sea vessels are detached pieces of a state's territory. Any harm to its vessels constitutes an offence against the state itself. Thus, criminal liability for terrorist acts committed against these vessels anywhere in the world attaches. Of the jurisdictional principles for extradition, the territorial principle remains the most widely accepted and most traditionally applied. See the text *supra* at notes 37–42. See also *Restatement (Third) of the Foreign Relations Law of the United States* (1987), sect. 402(1)(c). This theory is confirmed in the1963 Tokyo Convention by its reaffirmation of the 'law of the flag principle' that assigns the state of registration competence to exercise jurisdiction over offences and acts committed on board its aircraft: 1963 Tokyo Convention, *supra* note 31, Art. 3. See also Blakesley, 'United States Extradition Over Extraterritorial Crime', 29 *J Crim L & Criminology* (1982) 1109, at 1118–1119, 1123.

39 Convention on Nuclear Terrorism, *supra* note 4, Art. 4. Art. 4 of the Convention provides in full that:

'1. Nothing in this Convention shall affect other rights, obligations and responsibilities of States and individuals under international law, in particular the purposes and principles of the Charter of the United Nations and international humanitarian law.

2. The activities of armed forces during an armed conflict, as those terms are understood under international humanitarian law, which are governed by that law are not governed by this Convention, and the activities undertaken by military forces of a State in the exercise of their official duties, inasmuch as they are governed by other rules of international law, are not governed by this Convention.

3. The provisions of paragraph 2 of the present article shall not be interpreted as condoning or making lawful otherwise unlawful acts, or precluding prosecution under other laws.

4. This Convention does not address, nor can it be interpreted as addressing, in any way, the issue of the legality of the use or threat of use of nuclear weapons by States.'

Yet, the CNT does mandate that parties should adjust their national laws to criminalize offences set out in Article 2 of the Convention and, to that end, it also establishes penalties that reflect the gravity of these offences.[40] Another significant feature of the Convention is its directive that parties should adopt measures to ensure that 'criminal acts within the scope of this Convention, in particular where they are intended or calculated to provoke a state of terror in the general public or in a group of persons or particular persons, are under no circumstances justifiable by considerations of a political, philosophical, ideological, racial, ethnic, religious or other similar nature and are punished by penalties consistent with their grave nature'.[41] This provision aims to preclude any accused offender from being able to evade prosecution by invoking the criminal basis of an alleged crime being a 'political offence', which would therefore undercut prospects for extradition to a requesting state.[42]

If an international instrument is to accomplish its purposes, there must be broad, strong cooperation among all governments party to the agreement. Cooperation and collaboration are key to transforming an agreement from paper pledges to actual policy commitments. They are vital ingredients that any convention depends upon for any prospects of success.

A novel and notable strength of the CNT is the manner in which it spells out the ways and means that states parties should cooperate in devising and executing counter-terrorism strategies. The CNT mandates that governments should take 'all practicable measures' to thwart and deter terrorist preparations within their own territories that might be used to commit offences within or outside their state.[43] Such measures would include the prohibition of activities by persons, groups and organizations that 'encourage, instigate, organize, knowingly finance or knowingly provide technical assistance or information or engage in the perpetration of those offences'.[44]

The manner and efficacy in which the intelligence community serves the policies of states parties and their security interests remain critical to the operation of the Convention. Clearly, though, intelligence information about the members of terrorist groups, their planned attacks, what weapons they possess, and where they are located is vital for instigating preemptive or preventive action against possible acts of nuclear terrorism. Similarly, such information is necessary for parties to apprehend alleged offenders and perform extradition arrangements. As a consequence, the CNT calls for the exchange of 'accurate and verified' information, especially with other governments who seek jurisdiction over an alleged offender through extradition

[40] *Ibid.*, Art. 5. This provision corresponds verbatim to Art. 4 of the Convention on Terrorist Bombings, *supra* note 4.

[41] Convention on Nuclear Terrorism, *supra* note 4, Art. 6. This provision corresponds verbatim to Article 5 in the Convention on Terrorist Bombings, *supra* note 21.

[42] Article 15 of the CNT explicitly rejects the applicability of the exception to political offenses in cases of nuclear terrorism. See text at note 70 infra.

[43] *Ibid.*, Art. 7(1)(a).

[44] *Ibid.*

proceedings.[45] Information exchange between party governments also aims to detect, prevent, suppress and investigate offences, to lodge criminal proceedings against alleged offenders, and to notify international organizations about offences that might be committed.[46]

Securing classified information remains critical for national security. In the CNT, a confidentiality clause preserves the sovereignty of states parties, as it permits governments to protect in accordance with their national laws the confidentiality of information received from another state party or through participation in activities performed under the Convention.[47] The Convention does not compel governments to divulge information 'which they are not permitted to communicate pursuant to [their] national law or which would jeopardize the security of the State concerned or the physical protection of nuclear material'.[48] In the same vein, the Convention takes on a deterrent function. In striving to discourage offences from being committed, the CNT declares that parties must 'make every effort to ensure the protection of radioactive material, taking into account relevant recommendations and functions of the International Atomic Energy Agency'.[49]

Jurisdiction is critical as a legal ingredient for establishing the rights of states over an alleged offender. For action by a government to occur legally, a state must establish lawful jurisdiction over both a criminal offence and an accused offender. International law limits a state's jurisdiction to apply its statutes extraterritorially. Traditionally, a state may not prosecute a criminal seized beyond its borders unless it has lawful jurisdiction over the committed act. Similarly, for a government to exercise its rights and duties under international law, lawful jurisdiction must be secured by that state over action by another state or an individual offender. In effect, the jurisdiction to prescribe must exist before the jurisdiction to adjudicate, enforce and punish.[50]

Three jurisdictional principles specifically support the legal theory of extraterritorial jurisdiction needed to extradite nuclear-related terrorist offenders. In order of practical

45 *Ibid.*, Art. 7(1)(b).

46 *Ibid.*

47 *Ibid.*, Art. 7(2).

48 *Ibid.*, Art. 7(3). Art. 7 is unique to the Convention on Nuclear Terrorism, which underscores the gravity and concern that governments share about the need to gather and share intelligence to prevent and counter preparations for committing nuclear terrorism, as well as for punishing alleged offenders.

49 *Ibid.*, Art. 8. This provision is also unique to the NTC.

50 Obtaining extraterritorial jurisdiction for the exercise of a state's rights involves a two-step process. First, it must be determined whether a state's domestic law pertains to the act, i.e., whether there are grounds for exercising national jurisdiction. Secondly, it must be ascertained whether a sovereign state may proscribe such conduct extraterritorially under international legal rules. For this second criterion, governments can apply any of international law's 5 theoretical constructs for exercising prescriptive jurisdiction: (1) the territorial principle; (2) the nationality principle; (3) the protective principle; (4) the passive personality principle; and (5) the universality principle. To facilitate broader enforcement opportunities, these jurisdictional constructs are integrated, to a greater or lesser degree, into special provisions of the UN's anti-terrorism conventions, inclusive of the CNT.

legal priority, these are the universality principle,[51] the protective principle,[52] and the passive personality principle.[53] The principle of universal jurisdiction holds special standing, as it asserts that certain acts of terrorism are crimes against humanity and, as such, any state is permitted to arrest, prosecute or extradite accused offenders on behalf of the international community. The United Nations, by codifying such terrorist acts as international offences through prominent multilateral conventions, effectively renders these offences international crimes and activates the application of the universality principle for all states parties. An act of nuclear terrorism qualifies as such a crime.[54]

Viewed more in terms of national security, the protective principle justifies a state's right to punish offenders for crimes deemed harmful to the security or vital interests of the state. This notion provides jurisdiction on the basis of a perceived threat to national security, integrity or sovereignty by an extraterritorial offence.[55] Since an act of nuclear terrorism would be intended to impact the foreign policy of a state, vital interests of that state would be profoundly affected. Indeed, if a nuclear device were detonated in an urban area, tens of thousands of people would be killed and that state's civil society would never be the same. Extending protective jurisdiction, therefore,

51 The principle of universal jurisdiction recognizes that certain acts are so heinous and widely condemned that any states may prosecute an offender once custody is obtained. Such crimes are of universal interest to states and their perpetrators are considered to be the enemies of all humanity. That is, since acts of terrorism are universally recognized as international crimes, any government may extend jurisdiction over terrorists under the universal principle on the basis of *hoste humani generis:* Blakesley, 'Jurisdictional Issues and Conflicts of Jurisdiction', in M.C. Bassiouni (ed.), *Legal Responses to International Terrorism; US Procedural Aspects* (1988), at 142–153.

52 The protective principle concerns acts abroad that are considered prejudicial to the state's security interests. Under the protective principle, a state may exercise jurisdiction over certain acts that take place outside its territory, when such acts threaten the security, territorial integrity, or political independence of the state. Moreover, the protective principle permits governments to prosecute nationals of other states for their conduct outside the offended state: *Restatement (Third) of Foreign Relations Law of the United States, supra* note 38, sect. 402 cmt. f (hereinafter Third Restatement).

53 The passive personality principle gives a state extraterritorial jurisdiction over offences committed against its nationals, regardless of where the crime takes place. Jurisdiction is based on the nationality of the crime victim. The passive personality principle is not widely used, mainly because it is controversial and often conflicts with the territorial principle. Passive personality implies that people carry the protection of their state's law with them beyond the state's territorial jurisdiction. This assertion challenges the fundamental premise of a state's sovereign jurisdiction over its own territory, which would undercut the fundamental principle of territorial sovereignty: see *ibid.*, sect. 402 cmt g.

54 Under the principle of universal jurisdiction, a person accused of nuclear terrorism can be arrested and tried by any state without concern for the nationality of the accused or the location of the offence, and without establishing any link between the accused offender and the prosecuting state. All that is required is that the crime of nuclear terrorism qualifies as being universally condemned: *ibid.*, sect. 404. See also Donovan and Roberts, 'The Emerging Recognition of Universal Civil Jurisdiction', 100 *AJIL* (2006) 142; M.C. Bassiouni, 'Universal Jurisdiction for International Crimes: Historical Perspectives and Contemporary Practice', 42 *Virginia J Int'l L* (2001) 81 and Joyner, 'Arresting Impunity: The Case for Universal Jurisdiction in Bringing War Criminals to Accountability', 59 *Law & Contemporary Problems* (1996) 153, at 159–160.

55 *Third Restatement, supra* note 38, sect. 402 (3), cmt f.

would be lawful to establish jurisdiction over a would-be perpetrator of nuclear terrorism for purposes of extradition.

A third principle on which extradition of an alleged perpetrator of nuclear terrorism may be premised – passive personality – presents a more polemical basis on which to assign state jurisdiction. This view permits jurisdiction for extradition to be extended over persons who victimize citizens of the particular state seeking jurisdiction.[56] Though passive personality remains controversial, as a jurisdictional principle it applies to terrorism and other organized attacks against a state's nationals by reason of their nationality.[57] It seems reasonable that, if used in conjunction with other jurisdictional principles, application of the passive personality principle to bolster claims for extraterritorial jurisdiction could facilitate extradition in order to counter acts of nuclear terrorism.

It is not surprising that jurisdiction over offences emerges as a salient concern of the Convention. The CNT draws from earlier counter-terrorism instruments to establish territoriality as the principal form of jurisdiction over nuclear-terrorism offences committed within a state party or on board vessels flying the flag of that state.[58] In addition, the Convention allows for nationality to be asserted as a basis for jurisdiction

[56] *Ibid.*, sect. 402, cmt g.

[57] As the *Third Restatement* opines, the passive personality principle 'has not been ordinarily accepted or crimes, but it is increasingly accepted as applied to terrorists and other organized attacks on a state's nationals by reason of their nationality, or to assassination of a state's diplomatic representatives of other officials': *ibid.*, sect. 402 cmt g.

[58] Convention on Nuclear Terrorism, *supra* note 4, Art. 9(1). This provision reflects the principle of territorial jurisdiction. See *supra* note 37. In full, Art. 9 provides that:

'1. Each State Party shall take such measures as may be necessary to establish its jurisdiction over the offences set forth in article 2 when:

(a) The offence is committed in the territory of that State; or

(b) The offence is committed on board a vessel flying the flag of that State or an aircraft which is registered under the laws of that State at the time the offence is committed; or

(c) The offence is committed by a national of that State.

2. A State Party may also establish its jurisdiction over any such offence when:

(a) The offence is committed against a national of that State; or

(b) The offence is committed against a State or government facility of that State abroad, including an embassy or other diplomatic or consular premises of that State; or

(c) The offence is committed by a stateless person who has his or her habitual residence in the territory of that State; or

(d) The offence is committed in an attempt to compel that State to do or abstain from doing any act; or

(e) The offence is committed on board an aircraft which is operated by the Government of that State.

3. Upon ratifying, accepting, approving or acceding to this Convention each State Party shall notify the Secretary-General of the United Nations of the jurisdiction it has established under its national law in accordance with paragraph 2 of the present article. Should any change take place, the State Party concerned shall immediately notify the Secretary-General.

4. Each State Party shall likewise take such measures as may be necessary to establish its jurisdiction over the offences set forth in article 2 in cases where the alleged offender is present in its territory and it does not extradite that person to any of the States Parties which have established their jurisdiction in accordance with paragraph 1 or 2 of the present article.

5. This Convention does not exclude the exercise of any criminal jurisdiction established by a State Party in accordance with its national law.'

if an offence is committed by stateless persons within that state, or against nationals of that state, or against a government facility or diplomatic building of that state abroad, or on board an aircraft operated by that state.[59] A state party may also 'take such measures as may be necessary' to assert jurisdiction over an alleged offender apprehended in its territory, in the event that the government opts not to extradite the person to the state where the offence actually occurred.[60]

Counter-terrorism instruments are strengthened by provisions that facilitate apprehension, prosecution and punishment of offenders. If a government decides not to extradite an accused offender, one legal strategy that has proven practical is to mandate that government to prosecute him or her.[61] The legal principle here is *aut dedere aut judicare* – the duty to extradite or prosecute accused offenders.[62] This prescription requires the state party in which an alleged offender is discovered either to extradite that person to a state which is acknowledged to have jurisdiction over the offence, or alternatively if it opts not to extradite, 'to submit the case to its competent authorities for the purposes of prosecution'. It bears mentioning, however, that no UN counter-terrorism instrument directs that the state must prosecute an alleged offender through judicial proceedings, or proceed to punish him. All that is required is that a decision be taken by the competent authorities on whether to prosecute, given the factual circumstances of the situation. In essence, this language preserves the rights of due process, receiving a fair trial, and of being innocent until proven guilty. Presumably an investigation into the facts of the allegation against an accused offender would determine whether to proceed to the trial phase. If sufficient evidence is found, then prosecution through the courts may proceed.

59 *Ibid.* Art. 9(2). The nationality principle, which is generally accepted, allows a state to prescribe laws that bind its nationals, regardless of the location of either the national or where the offence occurs. The nationality principle extends a state's jurisdiction to actions taken by its citizens outside its territorial boundaries. The government is expected not only to protect its citizens when they are abroad, but it may also punish its citizens' criminal conduct, regardless of where it occurs: *Third Restatement*, *supra* note 38, sect. 402.

60 *Ibid.*, Art. 9(4).

61 The key provisions here are Arts 7 and 8 of the 1970 Hague Convention. Art. 7 of the Hague Convention provides that: 'The Contracting State in the territory of which the alleged offender is found shall, if it does not extradite him, be obliged, without exception whatsoever and whether or not the offence was committed in its territory, to submit the case to its competent authorities for the purposes of prosecution. Those authorities shall take their decision in the same manner as in the case of any ordinary offence of a serious nature under the laws of that State'. Hague Convention, *supra* note 31, Art. 7. Art. 8 of the Hague Convention sets out the conditions for extradition. Subsequent UN counter-terror agreements have replicated in great part the language of the Hague Convention's Arts 7 and 8 in the formulation of their extradite-or-prosecute obligations: see Montreal Convention, *supra* note 31, Arts 7 and 8; Internationally Protected Persons Convention, *supra* note 31, Arts 7 and 8; Hostage-taking Convention, *supra* note 31, Arts 9 and 10; IMO Convention, *supra* note 31, Art. 11; Convention on Physical Protection of Nuclear Materials, *supra* note 20, Arts 10 and 11; Terrorist Bombing Convention, *supra* note 31, Arts 8 and 9; and Convention on Financing Terrorism, *supra* note 31, Art. 10.

62 The duty to extradite or prosecute stems from the Roman notion of *aut dedere aut judicare*. The term *dedere* means to surrender or extradite, while *judicare* refers to the need to adjudicate or prosecute. For use of this expression see R. Jennings and A. Watts (eds), *Oppenheim's International Law* (9th edn, 1992), at 953, 971.

These arrangements are incorporated into the Convention on Nuclear Terrorism. Under this agreement, states are obliged to establish jurisdiction over and make punishable under their domestic laws the offences specified in the Convention. Governments are also required to extradite or to submit for prosecution persons accused of committing or aiding in the commission of the offences.[63] In these regards, extradition procedures provide a necessary conduit for bringing to justice individuals accused of international criminal offences, inclusive of terrorist activities involving nuclear devices or attacks on nuclear facilities. A criminal who succeeds in placing himself outside the territory of the state where he committed the crime also places himself beyond the reach of the law that he has violated. Through the formal process of extradition, one government transfers an accused person to the custody of another government. This process is usually done by treaty, reciprocity or comity. That vital role is highlighted by key provisions in contemporary legal efforts to suppress international terrorist activities, as extradition is used to facilitate the apprehension, prosecution, trial, and punishment of individuals who commit acts of terrorism.[64]

If vigorously exercised and enforced, extradition may serve as a viable deterrent to the commission of criminal terrorist acts. Moreover, parties often are obligated to assist each other with criminal proceedings under the Convention. To this end, Article 13 of the CNT stipulates that offences in the Convention are deemed to be extraditable offences between states parties under existing extradition treaties and under the Convention itself. Further, should states parties have no extradition treaty with one another, the CNT instrument may serve as the legal basis for extradition.[65]

[63] Art. 11 provides in full that:

'1. The State Party in the territory of which the alleged offender is present shall, in cases to which article 9 applies, if it does not extradite that person, be obliged, without exception whatsoever and whether or not the offence was committed in Its territory, to submit the case without undue delay to its competent authorities for the purpose of prosecution, through proceedings in accordance with the laws of that State. Those authorities shall take their decision in the same manner as in the case of any other offence of a grave nature under the law of that State.

2. Whenever a State Party is permitted under its domestic law to extradite or otherwise surrender one of its nationals only upon the condition that the person will be returned to that State to serve the sentence imposed as a result of the trial or proceeding for which the extradition or surrender of the person was sought, and this State and the State seeking the extradition of the person agree with this option and other terms they may deem appropriate, such a conditional extradition or surrender shall be sufficient to discharge the obligation set forth in paragraph 1 of the present article.'

Ibid., Art. 11. Compare the Convention against Terrorist Bombings, *supra* note 21, Art. 8.

[64] See generally Joyner, 'International Extradition and Global Terrorism: Bringing International Criminal to Justice', 25 *Loyola Los Angeles Int'l & Comp L Rev* (2003) 493.

[65] Convention on Nuclear Terrorism, *supra* note 4, Art. 13(2).

The Convention declares that universal jurisdiction may be used by parties as a lawful means for extradition as well,[66] and all parties are obliged to assist each other 'in the greatest measure' to advance investigatory, criminal, or extradition proceedings against an alleged offender.[67]

It is important to realize that, under contemporary international law, no universally accepted rule obligates governments to extradite, or even prosecute, alleged offenders who hide in their territory.[68] Indeed, the international extradition process today operates almost entirely through bilateral treaties, and certain conditions such as the nationality of the offender, concern over the fairness of a foreign trial, or the supposed political nature of the offence can obstruct the extradition process. The international extradition system, moreover, is neither comprehensive nor complete: no state has extradition treaties with every other state.[69]

Given defects in the extradition process, perhaps most problematic for extradition cases that might involve acts of nuclear terrorism is the political offence exception. Many modern extradition treaties specifically exempt political offences from extradition, since liberal and democratic governments developed a strong antipathy toward the idea of surrendering dissidents into the hands of a despotic government.[70] There

[66] In full, the Convention against Nuclear Terrorism makes extradition possible under the following circumstances:

'1. The offences set forth in article 2 shall be deemed to be included as extraditable offences in any extradition treaty existing between any of the States Parties before the entry into force of this Convention. States Parties undertake to include such offences as extraditable offences in every extradition treaty to be subsequently concluded between them.

2. When a State Party which makes extradition conditional on the existence of a treaty receives a request for extradition from another State Party with which it has no extradition treaty, the requested State Party may, at its option, consider this Convention as a legal basis for extradition in respect of the offences set forth in article 2. Extradition shall be subject to the other conditions provided by the law of the requested State.

3. States Parties which do not make extradition conditional on the existence of a treaty shall recognize the offences set forth in article 2 as extraditable offences between themselves, subject to the conditions provided by the law of the requested State.

4. If necessary, the offences set forth in article 2 shall be treated, for the purposes of extradition between States Parties, as if they had been committed not only in the place in which they occurred but also in the territory of the States that have established jurisdiction in accordance with article 6, paragraphs 1 and 2.

5. The provisions of all extradition treaties and arrangements between States Parties with regard to offences set forth in article 2 shall be deemed to be modified as between State Parties to the extent that they are incompatible with this Convention.'

Ibid., Art 13. Compare the language of Art. 8 of the Hague Convention, *supra* note 31; Art. 8 of the Montreal Convention, *supra* note 31; Art. 11 of the IMO SUA Convention, *supra* note 31; and Art. 9 of the Convention on Terrorist Bombings, *supra* note 21.

[67] Convention on Nuclear Terrorism, *supra* note 4, Art. 14(2).

[68] *Third Restatement*, *supra* note 38, at sect. 401 cmt B.

[69] The US, e.g., has extradition treaties with approximately 100 states, although today there are at least a total of 193 states in the international community. See US Dept. State, 'A List of Treaties and Other International Agreements of the United States in Force as of January 1, 2006', available at http://www.state.gov/s/l/treaty/treaties/2006/index.htm (accessed 18 May 2006), Sect.1 (Bilateral agreements), passim.

[70] For overviews of the political offence exceptions see M.C. Bassiouni, *International Extradition: United States Law and Practice* (2nd edn, 1996), at 502–583 and C.L. Blakesley, *Terrorism, Drugs, International Law, and the Protection of Human Liberty* (1992), at 264–270. The literature on the political offence exception is extensive: see, e.g., *ibid.*, at 264 n. 415.

are no recognized criteria, however, as to what constitutes a 'political offence', or any legal rule that prohibits the extradition of political offenders. As a result, the decision to extradite tends to rest on subjective criteria, as determined by the holding government. Given these conditions, the bilateral extradition system can provide only partial remedies for bringing international terrorists to justice. The consequence is that, while governments might agree that terrorist acts rise to being criminal offences against the international community, strict multilateral enforcement through extradition may still be lacking for prosecuting such acts.

In contrast to other UN counter-terrorism instruments, the CNT explicitly recognizes the problematic nature of the political offences exception, as it draws from the Terrorist Bombing Convention.[71] Accordingly, the CNT rejects the political offences exception bluntly as it avers in Article 15 that:

> None of the offences set forth in article 2 shall be regarded, for the purposes of extradition or mutual legal assistance, as a political offence or as an offence connected with a political offence or as an offence inspired by political motives. Accordingly, a request for extradition or for mutual legal assistance based on such an offence may not be refused on the sole ground that it concerns a political offence or an offence connected with a political offence or an offence inspired by political motives.[72]

This stipulation aims to contribute to legally differentiating terror violence from violent activities of national liberation movements. In the past, this conundrum generated not only considerable legal polemics to defining terrorism as a crime, but also formidable political encumbrances to exercising the extradition process between governments. To a certain degree, the provision succeeds in that ambition. But at the same time the Convention contains a caveat that governments could apply to refuse extradition of alleged offenders to another state. Like the 1979 Hostages Convention and the 1997 Terrorist Bombing Convention, the CNT asserts that no government is obligated to extradite if it has 'substantial grounds' to believe that an extradition request is being made 'for the purpose of prosecuting or punishing a person on account of that person's race, religion, nationality, ethnic origin or political opinion or that compliance with the request would cause prejudice to that person's position for any of these reasons'.[73] Such conditions normally are reserved for governments to consider in grants of political asylum to persons seeking refugee status. While this provision preserves that protection for refugees, it seems critical that governments must not abuse these conditions as loopholes or rationales to protect terrorist offenders. It remains unclear what impact the CNT presents for concerns over a government's possible effort to engage in the 'rendition' of detainees to other states for more 'aggressive' treatment. Under this Convention, a detainee would have to give his consent to be transferred unless there was a formal prosecution and extradition request. Even in the event that consent is given, the state to which a detainee is extradited is obligated to make appropriate notification of his detention, including reports of a conviction.[74]

71 See Convention on Terrorist Bombings, *supra* note 21, Art. 11.

72 Convention on Nuclear Terrorism, *supra* note 4, Art. 15.

73 *Ibid.*, Art. 16.

74 *Ibid.*, Art. 17.

A novel feature of the Convention on Nuclear Terrorism treats means and procedures for handling, controlling and returning radioactive materials, devices, or nuclear facilities seized from an offender. Nuclear materials and devices should be returned to the state of origin under safety standards approved by the IAEA. The object here is to ensure that radioactive materials, devices or nuclear facilities are put into the possession of a state that is lawfully empowered to possess and use them for peaceful purposes only.[75] Regarding prosecution of an alleged offender under a state

[75] As provided for in Art. 18:

'1. Upon seizing or otherwise taking control of radioactive material, devices or nuclear facilities, following the commission of an offence set forth in article 2, the State Party in possession of it shall:

(a) Take steps to render harmless the radioactive material, device or nuclear facility;

(b) Ensure that any nuclear material is held in accordance with applicable International Atomic Energy Agency safeguards; and

(c) Have regard to physical protection recommendations and health and safety standards published by the International Atomic Energy Agency.

2. Upon the completion of any proceedings connected with an offence set forth in article 2, or sooner if required by international law, any radioactive material, device or nuclear facility shall be returned, after consultations (in particular, regarding modalities of return and storage) with the States Parties concerned to the State Party to which it belongs, to the State Party of which the natural or legal person owning such radioactive material, device or facility is a national or resident, or to the State Party from whose territory it was stolen or otherwise unlawfully obtained.

3(1). Where a State Party is prohibited by national or international law from returning or accepting such radioactive material, device or nuclear facility or where the States Parties concerned so agree, subject to paragraph 3(2) of the present article, the State Party in possession of the radioactive material, devices or nuclear facilities shall continue to take the steps described in paragraph 1 of the present article; such radioactive material, devices or nuclear facilities shall be used only for peaceful purposes.

3(2). Where it is not lawful for the State Party in possession of the radioactive material, devices or nuclear facilities to possess them, that State shall ensure that they are as soon as possible placed in the possession of a State for which such possession is lawful and which, where appropriate, has provided assurances consistent with the requirements of paragraph 1 of the present article in consultation with that State, for the purpose of rendering it harmless; such radioactive material, devices or nuclear facilities shall be used only for peaceful purposes.

4. If the radioactive material, devices or nuclear facilities referred to in paragraphs 1 and 2 of the present article do not belong to any of the States Parties or to a national or resident of a State Party or was not stolen or otherwise unlawfully obtained from the territory of a State Party, or if no State is willing to receive such item pursuant to paragraph 3 of the present article, a separate decision concerning its disposition shall, subject to paragraph 3(2) of the present article, be taken after consultations between the States concerned and any relevant international organizations.

5. For the purposes of paragraphs 1, 2, 3 and 4 of the present article, the State Party in possession of the radioactive material, device or nuclear facility may request the assistance and cooperation of other States Parties, in particular the States Parties concerned, and any relevant international organizations, in particular the International Atomic Energy Agency. States Parties and the relevant international organizations are encouraged to provide assistance pursuant to this paragraph to the maximum extent possible.

6. The States Parties involved in the disposition or retention of the radioactive material, device or nuclear facility pursuant to the present article shall inform the Director General of the International Atomic Energy Agency of the manner in which such an item was disposed of or retained. The Director General of the International Atomic Energy Agency shall transmit the information to the other States Parties.

7. In the event of any dissemination in connection with an offence set forth in article 2, nothing in the present article shall affect in any way the rules of international law governing liability for nuclear damage, or other rules of international law.'

party's national law, that state is obliged to consult with and report the outcome of proceedings to the UN Secretary-General.[76] The Convention also reiterates the mandate that states parties should perform their obligations under the principles of sovereign equality, territorial integrity and non-intervention,[77] and provides that disputes between parties involving interpretation or application of the CNT be resolved through arbitration or the International Court of Justice, although parties may reserve exception to that procedure.[78] Finally, the CNT introduces a new opportunity into counter-terrorism law as it provides for the possibility of parties to make amendments to the Convention, which can be debated and approved at a later conference of states parties.[79]

4 Significance of the Convention

A *New Crime Defined*

The Convention on Nuclear Terrorism proscribes conduct and defines a new crime under international law. Prior to this Convention, nuclear terrorism was treated only as a criminal action by an individual under domestic law. The CNT raises an act of nuclear terrorism to the level of a crime against the law of nations, which involves commission by individuals of any of four acts: (1) the use of nuclear explosives against public targets with the intention to cause death, serious injury, or significant economic damage;[80] (2) the unlawful possession of radioactive material with the intention to cause death or serious injury; (3) the unlawful use of such material with the intention to cause death, serious bodily injury, substantial property or environmental damage; and (4) the threat or use of nuclear materials that cause or is likely to cause serious injury, death or property damage.[81] While 'terrorism' is not specifically used as a term in the text, the Convention's prohibitions aim to address acts that generally are viewed as terrorism. As international counter-terrorism law evolved, it became clear that interstate politics requires the ad hoc criminalization of specific actions perceived as terrorist in nature. It became apparent that some agreement on which actions should be proscribed was better than no progress or no agreement at all. The CNT sustains that rationale. Moreover, though similar to other counter-terrorism punitive conventions, the CNT refers to 'environmental damage', as well as that to persons and property.

76 *Ibid.*, Arts. 19 and 20.
77 *Ibid.*, Art. 21.
78 *Ibid.*, Art. 23.
79 *Ibid.*, Art. 26. Amendments need a two-thirds majority of all states parties to be adopted.
80 Cf. Convention on Terrorist Bombings, *supra* note 21, Art. 2(1).
81 Cf. Maritime Convention, *supra* note 27, Art. 3(1) (vessels); Fixed Platforms Convention, *supra* note 27, Art. 2(1).

B *Domestic Criminalization*

The CNT continues another trend in the development of multilateral counter-terrorism instruments – domestic criminalization. While the agreement requires that specific prohibitions be legislated into the domestic law of party states, it also leaves significant latitude to governments in implementing their own international obligations. The CNT generally follows the basic pattern set in previous counter-terrorism conventions. First, a category of terrorist activity that is explicitly of concern at the time is identified; second, governments are obliged to criminalize this conduct and impose penalties in their national laws proportional to the criminal act; and finally, governments are required to establish jurisdiction, usually based principally on territory, nationality and, if a vessel, state of registration.

A major purpose of the CNT is to prevent (or make less possible) perpetration of an offence by denying terrorists fissile materials, financial support or nuclear equipment. This purpose is contained in Article 7, which mandates that parties cooperate to 'prevent and counter preparations in their respective territories for the commission within or outside their territories of the offences . . . , including measures to prohibit in their territories illegal activities of persons, groups and organizations that encourage, instigate, organize, knowingly finance or knowingly provide technical assistance' to terrorist organizations or persons.[82] While making only a passing reference to financing, the CNT likewise prohibits in Article 7 raising funds for nuclear terrorism. This proscription draws upon the principles set out in the Convention on Financing Terrorism,[83] adopted by General Assembly Resolution in 1999,[84] that seeks to eliminate terrorism by cutting off funding streams, noting that the 'number and seriousness of acts of international terrorism depend on the financing that terrorists may obtain'.[85]

C *Civilian Victims Targeted*

The CNT also follows the pattern in counter-terrorism law that sets injuries or damage inflicted by an act as being standards for terrorist activity. The Convention on Nuclear Terrorism, like the Conventions on Financing Terrorism[86] and Terrorist Bombings,[87] explicitly proscribes acts that cause the death of or serious bodily injury to non-combatant civilians. This prohibition underscores the emerging standard for criminalizing nuclear terrorism as a crime in international counter-terrorism law, namely the

[82] Convention on Nuclear Terrorism, *supra* note 4, Art. 7. This obligation builds upon the 1980 Convention on Protection of Nuclear Material, *supra* note 18, and the 1991 Convention on Plastic Explosives, *supra* note 22, preamble. The Convention on Plastic Explosives also aims to restrict the availability of harmful radioactive materials to terrorists by requiring states to prohibit and prevent the manufacture of unmarked explosives: *ibid.*, Art. II.

[83] Convention on Financing Terrorism, *supra* note 27.

[84] GA Res 54/109, P 1, UN Doc A/RES/54/109 (25 Feb. 2000).

[85] Convention on Financing Terrorism, *supra* note 27, Art. 1.

[86] Convention on Financing Terrorism, *supra* note 31, Art. 2.

[87] Convention on Terrorist Bombings, *supra* note 21, Art. 2.

infliction of 'serious bodily injury' to human beings. Earlier counter-terrorism instruments prohibited 'injuries' or 'violence to persons'. In contrast, the CNT is expressly concerned with harm done to civilian persons. Any harm or injuries caused in the commission of an otherwise prohibited act rises to the level of an additional criminal offence.

The CNT requires that acts be independently 'unlawful' to contravene its provisions, which means that the unlawfulness of such acts is universal and not dependent upon the domestic law of a state. Nor is the CNT constrained by an attacker's motive. It does not require a religious, political or ideological motive to substantiate a person's status, nor does it necessarily separate terrorist groups from organized crime. The CNT requires that some form of *mens rea* be evident, namely, that the act of terrorism be a purposeful, intended act.

Mirroring its predecessors, the Convention on Nuclear Terrorism embodies international efforts to eliminate a specific form of terrorism in order to preserve peace, security and friendly relations among states. This instrument, like its 12 companion instruments, speaks to individual, not state-sponsored conduct. The CNT expressly provides that the activities of armed forces during an armed conflict are not within the legal purview of the Convention.[88] The reference to 'person' in the Convention[89] might be interpreted to bind government officials, and the CNT does not explicitly exclude within its text application to states. Yet, given that self-enforcement is not likely, it would seem probable that the Convention would have expressly obligated states if that was the original intent.

D *Treatment of Detainees*

In addition to defining the nature of offences, establishing appropriate means of jurisdiction, and affirming obligations of parties to investigate, prosecute or extradite alleged offenders, the Convention on Nuclear Terrorism focuses on the treatment of detainees. Unlike other counter-terrorism instruments, the CNT explicitly deals with the issue of offenders who are detained by a government. The Convention calls for 'fair treatment' of detainees and their full enjoyment of rights 'in conformity with' domestic law and 'applicable . . . international law, including international law of human rights'.[90] Even though 'fair treatment' and 'applicable . . . international law' are left undefined and unspecified, the CNT does stipulate that notifications should be made to a detainee's home country and to the UN Secretary-General. In addition, visits should be permitted by representatives of a detainee's home country and the International Committee for the Red Cross (ICRC), and protections should be invoked against unlawfully discriminatory extradition requests or non-extradition detainee transfers made without the detainee's consent.[91] These provisions would in effect curtail the practice of involuntary rendition of accused offenders. Finally, the CNT

88 Convention on Nuclear Terrorism, *supra* note 4, Art. 4(2).

89 Cf. Convention on Financing Terrorism, *supra* note 31, Art. 2(1).

90 Convention on Nuclear Terrorism, *supra* note 4, Art. 12.

91 *Ibid.*, Art. 10.

provides that a detainee shall enjoy rights and guarantees 'in conformity with' the law of the detaining power.[92]

No less problematic is the reference in the Convention to 'applicable provisions of international law', a phrase that begs the question concerning which provisions of international law, if any, should apply at all to a detainee situation.[93] It is similarly unclear whether adding the phrase 'including international law of human rights' should be interpreted as indicating that human rights law is, in fact, part of the international law. An argument can be made that the phrase 'applicable provisions of international law, including international law of human rights' is tantamount to meaning '. . . applicable international law, with human rights law included amongst the international law that is applicable'. Yet, others could contend that 'international law of human rights' is only meant to exemplify a subset of 'international law', with the word 'applicable' constraining both 'international law' in general and 'international law of human rights' in particular. Such reasoning suggests that the phrase 'applicable provisions of international law, including international law of human rights' means international law, including human rights law to the extent that it applies.

It seems plausible that the CNT could leave a detainee accused of nuclear terrorism in a status that straddles being a prisoner of war and an ordinary criminal. A prisoner of war would be entitled to visits from and registration with the ICRC, although no guarantees are made for visits by persons from their home state, especially understanding that in a traditional war, that state could be the enemy. On the other hand, a normal criminal would be entitled to contacts with his home government, but not necessarily with the ICRC. Yet, as previously noted, the CNT is not meant to function in a legal vacuum, as it aims to uphold respect for both international and national law given the conditions of any particular case.

By early 2007, the CNT had attracted 115 signatory states and 11 states parties.[94] The CNT will enter into force on the 30th day following the date of deposit of the 22nd instrument of ratification, acceptance, approval or accession. A number of non-party states, among them the United States and Russia, have expressed strong support for

[92] This provision revisits the argument concerning whether and how national law may be applied by a state's government, as in the case of the US and its Guantanamo Bay detentions. In that experience, some US government officials maintained that application of US law leads to the conclusion that rights of prisoners ordinarily enjoyed under US domestic law do not apply to detentions of foreign nationals held at Guantanamo Bay. Those persons are not members of regular armed forces, but instead are 'terrorists' who qualify as nothing more than 'unlawful, unprivileged combatants'. In other words, the argument made by the George W. Bush administration posits that application of US law effectively results in the non-application of US law, at least in the manner that it applies in other circumstances. Hence detainees are held in the Guantanamo detention facility indefinitely, without being formally charged with a crime, prosecuted for any offence, or given rights to legal counsel and a fair, speedy trial. Art. 12 of the CNT aims to preclude similar circumstances from arising in an event of nuclear terrorism.

[93] See Convention on Nuclear Terrorism, *supra* note 4, Art. 16. One might recall, e.g., that disparate views are held by the Bush administration and most other governments as to whether the 1949 Geneva Conventions on the Laws of War apply to the detention of foreign nationals who are incarcerated at Guantanamo Bay.

[94] States party to the CNT include Austria, the Czech Republic, El Salvador, India, Kenya, Latvia, Lebanon, Mexico, Mongolia, Seychelles, and Slovakia.

this instrument and it seems quite possible that it will enter into force in the near future.[95]

It warrants noting that the political credibility and legal reach of the CNT is bolstered by UN Security Council Resolution 1540, adopted in April 2004.[96] The resolution, which was done under Chapter VII of the UN Charter, carries the status of a mandatory legal obligation for the entire United Nations' membership. As the chief sponsor of this resolution, the United States sought to prompt the Security Council into authorizing practical measures to force governments to deal with the threat of non-state actors, principally terrorist groups, acquiring or trafficking in weapons of mass destruction. The impetus for this resolution was the revelation in 2003 of the nuclear proliferation network market organized by Pakistani scientist A. Q. Khan.[97]

While Resolution 1540 is not cited in the CNT's preambular paragraphs, its purposes are directly relevant to those of the Convention. The main obligation of the resolution is contained in operative paragraph 1, which prohibits states from providing 'any form of support to non-State actors that attempt to develop, acquire, manufacture, possess, transport, transfer or use nuclear, chemical or biological weapons and their means of delivery'. To prevent any non-state actor from engaging in these acts alone, without state support, operative paragraph 2 requires that states 'adopt and enforce appropriate effective laws' through national legislation that prohibit non-state actors from engaging in any of these activities. Operative paragraph 3 prescribes that states take and enforce effective measures to establish a comprehensive system of domestic controls to prevent the proliferation of weapons of mass destruction and related materials. To this end, the resolution also mandates that governments 'develop and maintain appropriate effective measures to account for and secure such items in production, use, storage or transport', strengthen border controls and law enforcement efforts to 'detect, deter, prevent and combat' unlawful trafficking and trade of these materials and develop and implement 'effective national export and trans-shipment controls' over such items.[98] Finally, operative paragraph 4 establishes a special committee, the '1540 Committee', which consists of all the Security Council members. The 1540 Committee is responsible for reviewing and assessing reports required of the member states that indicate what progress they have made in conforming to these obligations.[99]

95 CNT, *supra* note 4, Art. 25.

96 See UN Security Council Resolution 1540, UN Doc S/RES/1540 (2004) (28 Apr. 2004), available at: http://daccessdds.un.org/doc/UNDOC/GEN/N04/328/43/PDF/N0432843.pdf?OpenElement (accessed 3 Jan. 2007).

97 For discussion of A.Q. Khan's role in promoting nuclear proliferation for profit see Langewiesche, 'The Wrath of Khan', *Atlantic Monthly* (Nov. 2005) and Langewiesche, 'The Point of No Return', *Atlantic Monthly* (Jan./Feb. 2006).

98 Convention on Nuclear Terrorism, *supra* note 4, Art. 3(a)–(d)

99 See Olberg, 'Implementing Resolution 1540: What the National Reports Indicate', *Disarmament Diplomacy*, Issue 82 (Spring 2006), available at: http://www.acronym.org.uk/dd/dd82/82lo.htm (accessed 5 Jan. 2007).

These 1540 reports suggest that national governments bear the onus of enforcing the non-proliferation of nuclear weapons and maintaining security of nuclear materials in their state. Moreover, the reports should reveal the extent to which governments are complying with the obligations in SC Resolution 1540. For those states which fall short of meeting stipulations in the resolution, operative paragraph 7 suggests that other states should offer resources and advice on the legal and regulatory infrastructure needed for compliance. In this way, Resolution 1540 can be made more effective as a legally binding measure that fosters stronger compliance with provisions in the Convention on Nuclear Terrorism.

5 Conclusion

The Convention on Nuclear Terrorism expands the international legal framework for countering terrorist threats. In this regard, the instrument furnishes a legal basis for international cooperation aimed at preventing terrorists from acquiring weapons of mass destruction, the detonation of which could produce catastrophic consequences in a society. The CNT defines acts of nuclear terrorism in general terms and cites a broad range of possible targets, including nuclear power facilities and nuclear reactors. It criminalizes the possession of, use of, or threat to use radioactive devices by non-state actors, their accomplices and organizers if intended to produce death, serious bodily injury or environmental or property damage. States parties are obliged to adopt measures clearly stipulating that acts intended to provoke nuclear-related terror cannot be justified under any circumstances, particularly by political, philosophical, ideological, racial, ethnic, religious or other like considerations. Put another way, states are obligated to criminalize acts of nuclear terrorism as defined in the CNT and to adapt their domestic criminal codes in order to apprehend, prosecute and punish persons who violate its provisions. The agreement further encourages increased exchanges of information and greater cooperation between countries in the pursuit of terrorist suspects. While no specific forms of punishment are detailed in the Convention, punitive measures should correspond to the gravity of the breach.

The CNT encourages governments to cooperate in preventing terrorist attacks by sharing information and assisting each other in pursuing criminal investigations and extradition proceedings. The agreement also requires that any seized nuclear or radiological material be secured in accordance with IAEA safeguards and handled such that procedures conform to the IAEA's health, safety and physical protection standards. Similarly, peaceful uses of nuclear energy are preserved in this instrument. The Convention on Nuclear Terrorism recognizes the right of all states to develop and apply nuclear energy for peaceful purposes. This right, of course, is predicated upon ensuring that development of nuclear energy for peaceful purposes is not used as a guise for nuclear proliferation, as affirmed by Security Council Resolution 1540.

As contemporary events so vividly demonstrate, promulgation of multilateral conventions to counter acts of terrorism is not sufficient to prevent or deter their perpetration. An instrument's fundamental value lies in its being an integral component of a broader, more comprehensive coordinated strategy to combat terrorism. Yet, the fact remains that an international agreement alone cannot mitigate the threat of nuclear terrorism. If it is to be effective, the CNT must depend on the governments of states parties to respect, abide by, and enforce its provisions. Governments create the convention, they must implement it through their domestic law, they must comply with its requirements, and they must enforce its provisions. To the extent that governments fulfil these requisite duties, the agreement will work well and accomplish its purposes. To the degree that governments fall short of meeting their obligations, specific protections against nuclear terrorism in the Convention will be eroded.

In the end, while the Convention to Suppress Nuclear Terrorism emerges as a necessary component of the legal regime to counter terrorist activities, it is not sufficient. The Convention articulates new norms for international behaviour by individual persons, it establishes international legal rules to support those norms, and it imposes on states duties to execute those rules. Still, paper norms do not resolve real world threats. Governments must articulate and implement clear policy goals, especially regarding collaborative international efforts to secure and exchange intelligence information about the objectives, capabilities and operational plans of terrorist groups that intend to detonate nuclear devices. These policy goals, moreover, must be carried out by the resolute political willingness of governments of states, which includes their will to use armed force, if necessary, to attain those policy objectives. In the end, as an international instrument, the CNT establishes the legal framework for criminalizing acts of nuclear terrorism and for dealing with apprehended perpetrators. But it remains for governmental policy-makers to take whatever lawful means are necessary, including military force, to implement these legal mandates such that they protect and preserve their societies against such threats. To do otherwise is to squander the practical worth and utility of the CNT. Worse than that, however, it is also to put at risk the very societies that are threatened most by terrorists who seek to acquire nuclear arms. In an age where weapons of mass destruction held by one can threaten all, that is a price far too high for the international community to pay.

Part IV
War on Terror

[8]

THE LEGAL CASE AGAINST THE GLOBAL WAR ON TERROR*

Mary Ellen O'Connell†

I. Introduction

In the first confusing days after the September 11, 2001, attacks on the United States, President George W. Bush declared a war on terror. Many of us heard this declaration as stirring rhetoric to rally the nation. We understood it as a declaration that the President would direct a strong response against those responsible. We had heard this sort of rhetoric before when the nation faced powerful challenges—from illegal drugs and chronic poverty. Many of us understood President Bush's declaration of war to refer once again to the determined, persistent struggle to overcome a social blight—this time terrorism. We did not understand it as the kind of war Franklin Delano Roosevelt declared after the attack at Pearl Harbor. Indeed, how could we have understood it any other way? When President Bush made his declaration, he did not even know who had carried out the attacks.

Our government's actions in the first weeks after September 11 lent further support to this initial understanding. We did not engage our military against known terrorists just anywhere. We waited until facts were known and then we waged a war of self-defense against Afghanistan, beginning October 7, 2001. It was not until November 2001, as the Administration's legal policies regarding detainees started to emerge that we began to detect the rhetoric of war on terror might not be mere rhetoric. Apparently, some Administration lawyers took the President's declaration as the basis to allow the United States to claim certain wartime rights and privileges even outside the conflict in Afghanistan.

Academic international lawyers were perhaps slow to take this in, but by 2003, scholarly articles began to emerge countering the Administration's claims to privileges in the absence of actual hostilities. The International Court of Justice (ICJ) in its advisory opinion on the Legal Consequences of the Construction of a Wall in the Occupied Palestinian Territory has further undermined the possibility of declaring war against "terrorism" per se. By contrast, we find virtually no support from independent scholars or tribunals for the Bush Administration's case for global war.

---

* Presented at the War Crimes Research Symposium: "Terrorism on Trial" at Case Western Reserve University School of Law, sponsored by the Frederick K. Cox International Law Center, on Friday, Oct. 8, 2004.

† William B. Saxbe Designated Professor of Law, Moritz College of Law, and Fellow of the Mershon Center for the Study of International Security, The Ohio State University.

This essay reviews the Administration's case, contrasting the scholarship and jurisprudence against global war. The essay's contribution is to point out that three years after the declaration of global war, the Bush Administration's case has virtually no support in the wider international legal community—the community beyond the Administration's own people. The claim of global war is a radical departure from mainstream legal analysis. Moreover, claiming global war is turning out to have negative unintended consequences, such as enhancing the status of terrorists on the international plane and creating a dangerous legal precedent that other states are following.

A. The Bush Administration Case for Global War

President Bush declared global war on terrorism in his address to the nation following the attacks of September 11 and in his address to a joint session of Congress.[1] The President stated that the "war" "will not end until every terrorist group of global reach has been found, stopped and defeated."[2] The war attaches to individuals not to situations of armed hostilities. So wherever a suspected member of a terrorist organization is, there is an armed conflict. Former National Security Adviser, Condoleeza Rice has explained the global war on terror as a "new kind of war" to be fought on "different battlefields."[3]

In response to a question, "what is the legal basis for the global war on terror?" Deputy National Security Adviser Stephan Hadley in remarks at The Ohio State University explained that the legal basis was the attack on the United States on September 11. He said the American people could understand that the attacks were "an act of war."[4] Apparently as soon as the attacks occurred, the Bush Administration believed a war had begun and the law of war was triggered. In addition to the September 11 attacks,

---

[1] *See* President's Address to the Nation on the Terrorist Attacks, 37 WEEKLY COMP. PRES. DOC.1301, 1302 (Sept. 11, 2001); President's Address Before a Joint Session of the Congress on the United States Response to the Terrorist Attacks of September 11, *in* 37 WEEKLY COMP. PRES. DOC. 1347, 1347-49 (Sept. 20, 2001) [hereinafter Response to Terrorist Attacks]; President's Address to the Nation Announcing Strikes Against Al Qaida Training Camps and Taliban Military Installations in Afghanistan, *in* 37 WEEKLY COMP. PRES. DOC. 1432 (Oct. 7, 2001); President's Address Before a Joint Session of the Congress on the State of the Union, 39 WEEKLY COMP. PRES. DOC. 109, 112-13 (Jan. 28, 2003); http://www.whitehouse.gov.

[2] Response to Terrorist Attacks, *supra* note 1, at 1348.

[3] *Fox News Sunday* (Fox News television broadcast, Nov. 10, 2002), 2002 WL 7898884, at 9.

[4] Stephan Hadley, Remarks at the Moritz College of Law of the Ohio State University (Sept. 24, 2004).

Professor Ruth Wedgwood, who advises the Secretary of Defense, adds "Al Qaeda has declared jihad against the United States, and in *fatwa* after *fatwa*, Osama bin laden has announced that all Americans are valid targets."[5]

The U.S. Justice Department has also argued before US courts that the country is in a global war on terror.[6] It made this argument in three cases before the United States Supreme Court in the spring of 2004.[7] In December 2004, in a Federal district court case, the Administration took the position that where an elderly Swiss lady sends money to a charitable organization and the money ends up with Al-Qaeda, she could also qualify as a combatant.[8] Professor John Yoo, who was a member of the Justice Department and a chief architect of the "global war" argument, analyzed the Supreme Court's decisions, concluding "the Court agreed that the U.S. is at war against the al Qaeda terrorist network . . ."[9] And that it is allowed to "use all of the tools of war to fight a new kind of enemy . . ."[10]

Having characterized the world as at war after September 11, the Administration has claimed that three types of legal privilege flow from this: the right to declare individuals "enemy combatants" if they are suspected of terrorism; the right to target and kill individuals wherever they are if they are suspected terrorists; and the right to search ships and seize cargoes suspected of carrying weapons or materiel for terrorists.[11] Judge Alberto Gonzales, White House Counsel, explained to the ABA's Standing Committee on Law and National Security that the policy of declaring individuals "enemy combatants" is based on the view that "our conflict

---

[5] Ruth Wedgwood, *Combatants or Criminals? How Washington Should Handle Terrorists: Fighting a War Under its Rules*, 83 FOREIGN AFF., 126, 127 (2004), *available at* http://www.foreignaffairs.org/20040501faresponse83312/ruth-wedgwood-kenneth-roth/combatants-or-criminals-how-washington-should-handle-terrorists.html (last visited Feb. 26, 2005).

[6] *See, e.g.*, Brief for Respondents at 15, Hamdi v. Rumsfeld, 124 S. Ct. 2633 (2004) (No. 03-6696); Brief for Petitioner at 10, United States v. Alvarez-Machain, 124 S.Ct. 2739 (2004) (No. 03-485).

[7] *See* Rasul v. Bush, 124 S. Ct. 2686, 2710-11 (2004); Hamdi v. Rumsfeld, 124 S. Ct. 2633, 2636-37 (2004); Rumsfeld v. Padilla, 124 S. Ct. 2711, at 2712, 2716 (2004).

[8] Neil A. Lewis, *Searching for Limits on Power to Detain*, INT'L HERALD TRIB., Dec. 3, 2004, at 4, 2004 WL 90971627. The answer was given to a question by Judge Green during the oral arguments in In re Guantanamo Detainee Cases, No. 02-CV-0299CKK, 2005 WL 195356 (D.D.C. Jan 31, 2005).

[9] John Yoo, *The Supreme Court Goes to War*, WALL ST. J., June 30, 2004, at A8.

[10] *Id.*

[11] *See* Mary Ellen O'Connell, *Ad Hoc War, in* KRISENSICHERUNG UND HUMANITÄRER SCHUTZ [CRISIS MANAGEMENT AND HUMANITARIAN PROTECTION] 399 (Horst Fischer et al. eds., 2004).

with al Qaeda is clearly a war."[12] The Deputy General Counsel of the Department of Defense for International Affairs, Charles Allen, following the killing by the CIA of six men traveling in a vehicle in Yemen, justified the killing as lawful because the U.S. is at war with "Al Qaeda and other international terrorists around the world and those who support such terrorists."[13] In other words, the U.S. can kill *without warning*. To underscore his point that the "war" attaches to the individual, not the situation, Allen went on to suggest it would be lawful to kill an Al Qaeda suspect on the streets of a peaceful city like Hamburg, Germany.[14]

Interestingly, despite the legal controversy surrounding the assertion that war can exist based on the presence of an individual, rather than an armed conflict, we find virtually no scholarship arguing in favor of the Bush Administration's position. We certainly find very little from academics not connected with the Administration.

B. The Scholars Case Against Global War[15]

As I have written elsewhere:[16]

> Whether the U.S. was in fact in a war after September 11 depends on the definition of war in international law. Before the adoption of the UN Charter and its general prohibition on war, international law defined war with precision. A *de jure* war existed as soon as it was declared by a sovereign state. Real war, according to Oppenheim,

[12] Alberto R. Gonzales, Remarks Before the American Bar Association Standing Committee on Law and National Security (Feb. 24, 2004), http://www.abanet.org/natsecurity/judge_gonzales.pdf (last visited Feb. 26, 2005); Memorandum from William J. Haynes II, General Counsel of the Department of Defense, to Members of the ASIL-CFR Roundtable on Old Rules, New Threats, Enemy Combatants (Dec. 12, 2002), http://www.cfr.org/publication.php?id=5312 (last visited Feb. 26, 2005).

[13] Anthony Dworkin, *Law and the Campaign Against Terrorism: The View from the Pentagon* (Dec. 16, 2002), *at* http://www.crimesofwar.org/print/onnews/pentagon-print.html (last visited Feb. 26, 2005) (interview by Anthony Dworkin with Charles Allen, Deputy General Counsel for International Affairs at the Department of Defense).

[14] *Id.*

[15] In addition to the articles discussed more specifically herein, see O'Connell, *supra* note 6; Leila Nadya Sadat, *Terrorism and the Rule of Law*, 3 WASH. U. GLOBAL STUD. L. REV. 135 (2004); Gabor Rona, *Interesting Times for International Humanitarian Law: Challenges from the 'War on Terror,'* 27 FLETCHER F.WORLD AFF. 55, 57 (2003); Mary Ellen O'Connell, *Lawful Self-Defense to Terror*, 63 U. PITT. L. REV. 889 (2002); Mark Drumbl, *Victimhood in our Neighborhood: Terrorist Crime, Taliban Guilt and the Asymmetries of the International Legal Order*, 36 N.C. L. REV. 81 (2002).

[16] O'Connell, *supra* note 11 (some notes and parts of notes omitted).

was "a contention between two or more States through their armed forces, for the purpose of overpowering each other and imposing such conditions of peace as the victor pleases."[17] The term "war" fell out of use as a legal term of art with the adoption of the Charter in 1945. The Charter in Article 2(4) prohibits all uses of force, war and lesser actions, except in self-defense or as mandated by the Security Council. Following the adoption of the Charter, treaties relevant to war, such as the Geneva Conventions of 1949 substituted the term "armed conflict" for war. "War" ministries became "defense" ministries. States engaging in armed conflict rarely declared war. What mattered after 1945 was the actual fighting not the 19th century formalities that might mean a war was occurring legally even if no shot was ever fired. We still use the term "war" to refer to any serious armed conflict. Yugoslavia, Liberia, Sudan and Sri Lanka experienced civil war in the 1990s. We also had the Gulf War and the Ethiopia-Eritrea War in the 1990s. But indicative of the fact "war" is no longer the significant legal term it once was, the United States fought a war on poverty and a war on drugs. We would never say it was an armed conflict against poverty. The war on drugs does involve the military, but it is not an armed conflict against drugs.

Indeed, the division in the law depends today on the existence of actual armed conflict, not the rhetorical or even technical invocation or declaration of war. When President Bush first declared war on terrorism, many thought he was using the term war in the sense of the war on drugs. Presumably, the United States would use law enforcement methods and occasionally the military to pursue terrorists. And in fact that is largely what happened. But in the formation of [certain] policies ..., the Administration has acted as though the US is actually involved in armed conflict against terrorists everywhere. An armed conflict, however, has two important components. It consists of two or more armed groups engaged in armed hostilities. In *Prosecutor v. Tadić* before the International Criminal Tribunal for the Former Yugoslavia, the Tribunal defined "armed conflict" as existing "whenever there is a resort to armed force between States or protracted armed violence between governmental

[17] 2 L. OPPENHEIM, INTERNATIONAL LAW: A TREATISE 202 (Hersch Lauterpacht ed., 7th ed. 1952).

authorities and organized armed groups or between such groups within a state."[18] Thus, in distinction to the classic definition of war, armed conflict need not be between states or have domination of the other party as its goal. It occurs when organized groups use significant armed violence. The Geneva Conventions similarly incorporate a standard of intensity that must be reached to trigger the application of certain minimal rules in certain violent conflicts, namely those conflicts where all parties are not signatories to the Conventions.[19] Such conflicts must amount to "more than situations of internal disturbances and tensions such as riots and isolated and sporadic acts of violence."[20] We tend to refer to fighting below the threshold as "lawlessness" or criminality when it occurs within a state. Minimal-armed force between states is often referred to as an incident, as in "border incident" or "frontier incident."[21] Fighting serious enough to be above the threshold between two or more groups is an armed conflict. Once an armed conflict is triggered, whether internal or international, certain peacetime human rights protections will no longer apply. For example, most general human rights treaties protect the

[18] *Prosecutor v. Tadić*, Decision on the Defense Motion for Interlocutory Appeal on Jurisdiction, No. IT-94-1, para. 70 (Oct. 2, 1995), *available at*: http://www.un.org/icty/tadic/appeal/decision-e/51002.htm (last visited Feb. 26, 2005).

[19] *See* 3 JEAN DE PREUX, COMMENTARY TO THE 1949 GENEVA CONVENTION RELATIVE TO THE TREATMENT OF PRISONERS OF WAR 19-23 (Jean Pictet ed., 1960). Common Article 2 of the four Geneva Conventions provides that the Conventions "shall apply to all cases of declared war or of any other armed conflict which may arise between two or more of the High Contracting Parties, even if the state of war is not recognized by one of them." *Id.* at 19. The Commentary defines "armed conflict" as used in Article 2 as "any differences arising between two states and leading to the intervention of members of the armed forces." *Id.* at 23.

[20] 4 JEAN DE PREUX, COMMENTARY TO THE 1949 GENEVA CONVENTION RELATIVE TO THE PROTECTION OF CIVILIAN PERSONS IN TIME OF WAR 3-9 (Jean Pictet ed., 1958); *see also*, Alain Pellet, *No, This is Not War*, EUR. J. INT'L L., Oct. 3, 2001, http://www.ejil.org/forum_WTC/ny-pellet.html (last visited Feb. 26, 2005) ("[W]ar…presupposes an armed conflict between adversaries if not identified, at least identifiable, to which the 'laws and customs of war' can be applied….") In other words, Pellet believes that non-state actors cannot engage in armed conflict because of their limits as subjects of international law. This formalistic conclusion does not comport with the more contemporary tests of armed conflict based on the facts of fighting.

[21] Military and Paramilitary Activities In and Against Nicaragua (Nicaragua v. U.S.), 1986 I.C.J. 14, 102-03 (June 27) [hereinafter Nicaragua]; *see also* INTERNATIONAL INCIDENTS: THE LAW THAT COUNTS IN WORLD POLITICS (W. Michael Reisman & Andrew R. Willard eds. 1988).

> right to life, but the content of the right will differ depending on whether the right is invoked in war or peace.

Professor Christopher Greenwood shares this view with respect to the meaning of war:

> Terrorism is one of the greatest threats facing humanity today. It is therefore entirely understandable and justifiable that we mark the gravity of that danger and express a commitment to defeating it by using the language of a war on terrorism. That is, however, a far cry from using that language in a technical, legal sense. In the language of international law there is no basis for speaking of a war on Al-Qaeda or any other terrorist group, for such a group cannot be a belligerent, it is merely a band of criminals, and to treat it as anything else risks distorting the law while giving that group a status which to some implies a degree of legitimacy.[22]

And Professor Marco Sassoli shares my view with respect to the wartime privileges claimed by the Bush Administration:

> One of the dangerous effects of the U.S. characterization of the "war on terrorism" as a single global international armed conflict is that, if correct, such classification makes deliberate attacks upon members of the "enemy armed forces" lawful worldwide . . .. Thus, the United States justified an unmanned missile strike that hit and killed suspected members of Al-Qaeda in Yemen. Without this qualification under the laws of war, such targeted assassinations not preceded by an attempt to arrest the persons concerned would be classified as extra-judicial executions, which would seriously violate international human rights law. The latter accepts the deliberate killing of even the worst criminal only under the most extreme circumstances . . .. If fully applied, this theory would have justified, subject to the principle of proportionality, an ambush attack on Jose Padilla when he left his plane at a Chicago airport . . .. U.S. administration officials have indeed implied that the President's claimed authority to designate as an enemy combatant any individual, including

[22] Christopher Greenwood, *War, Terrorism, and International Law*, 56 CURRENT L. PROBS., 505, 529 (2004).

> a U.S. citizen within the United States, includes authority to carry out extra-judicial executions, within or outside the United States, of suspects so designated. Under the laws of war, if those persons were combatants, such claims would be correct. This absurd result, permitting targeted assassinations in the midst of peaceful cities, proves once more that all those suspected to be "terrorists" cannot be classified as combatants.[23]

Justice O'Connor, writing for the plurality in *Hamdi*, says the right to detain under "long-standing law-of-war principles...may last no longer than active hostilities."[24] She then describes those hostilities as existing in Afghanistan, where the United States has 13,500 troops engaged in active operations.[25] She talks about a real war, with real hostilities that will eventually end, but she does not address a so-called war on terror that will never end.[26] In the companion *Rasul* case, the majority allowed court review of Guantanamo Bay detentions. Concurring, Justice Kennedy gives guidance to reviewing courts when he refers to "a zone of hostilities,"[27] indicating that hostilities are occurring in specific locations and not everywhere in the world.

Finally, the International Court of Justice gave an advisory opinion to the UN General Assembly as to the legal consequences of Israel constructing a security barrier on occupied Palestinian territory. Israel cited Security Council resolutions acknowledging the right of a state to act in self-defense against terrorist attacks. Israel argued that if a state may use force in self-defense, then non-forcible measures are, a fortiori lawful. The ICJ replied to this argument that "Article 51 of the Charter . . . recognizes the existence of an inherent right of self-defence in the case of armed attack by one State against another State. However, Israel does not claim that the attacks against it are imputable to a foreign State."[28] In other words, the right to use armed force is connected with territory—facts of fighting on the ground, not the presence of an individual suspected of being a terrorist.

[23] Marco Sassòli, *Use and Abuse of the Laws of War in the "War on Terrorism"*, 22 LAW & INEQ. 195 (2004) (citations omitted).

[24] Hamdi v. Rumsfeld, 124 S.Ct. 2633, 2641 (2004).

[25] *Id.*

[26] *Id.*

[27] Rasul v. Bush, 124 S. Ct. 2686, 2700 (2005).

[28] *See generally* Legal Consequences of the Construction of a Wall in the Occupied Palestinian Territory, 2004 ICJ 131 (July 9), *available at*: http://www.icj-cij.org/icjwww (last visited Feb. 26, 2005) (decision is an advisory opinion).

Since Israel is in control of the Occupied Palestinian Territory it cannot claim self-defense—that would be self-defense against itself.

II. Conclusions

The decision to treat the struggle against terrorism as a global war, may well have had unintended consequences, including enhanced status for terrorists and setting dangerous precedent. I recently concluded:

> The puzzling decision of the Bush Administration to declare a global war on terror and to label terrorists "enemy combatants" has possibly had an unintended consequence for non-state actors. It has lifted certain individuals out of the status of *criminal* to that of *combatant*, the same category America's own troops have while engaging in armed hostilities. This move to label terrorists as combatants is contrary to strong historic trends. From earliest times, governments have struggled to prevent their enemies from approaching a status of equality. Even governments on the verge of collapse due to the pressure of a rebel advance have vehemently denied that the violence inflicted by their enemies was anything but criminal violence. Governments fear the psychological and legal advantages to opponents of calling them "combatants" and their struggle a "war." Yet, the Bush Administration, within days of the September 11 attacks in the United States, declared a "global war on terror" and designated terrorists "enemy combatants."[29]

And now we face the fact Russia has declared a global war on terror.[30] Now the Russians, in addition to Americans, believe they may target their enemies anywhere—including the streets of peaceful cities. These declarations of war are undermining the prohibition on the use of force, enhancing the status of terrorists and making the world a more dangerous place where human life is ever more de-valued.

It is time to call off the global war on terror.

---

[29] Mary Ellen O'Connell, *Enhancing the Status of Non-State Actors Through a Global War on Terror*, COLUM. J. TRANSNAT'L L. (forthcoming 2004).

[30] *See, e.g.*, *Putin's Chechnya War, Five Years and Still Counting*, AGENCE FR.-PRESSE, Oct. 1, 2004, *at* http://www.ivcc.edu/bigelow/Intro%20to%20Global/war%20on%20chechnya.htm (last visited Feb. 26, 2005).

[9]

Targeted Killing of Suspected Terrorists: Extra-Judicial Executions or Legitimate Means of Defence?

David Kretzmer*

Abstract

Whether a state that has been subject to attacks by a transnational terrorist group may target active members of that group who are not in its jurisdiction has caused controversy. Some refer to targeted killings of suspected terrorists as extra-judicial executions; others claim they are legitimate acts of war. The author examines the legality of such killings under norms of international human rights law and international humanitarian law. Under the former system, such killings can only be lawful when carried out to prevent an imminent attack that cannot be stopped by other means. Under the latter system, such killings may be lawful if the suspected terrorists are to be regarded as combatants. He argues that while in international armed conflicts suspected terrorists are generally not combatants, in non-international armed conflicts they may well be combatants. In such conflicts norms of international humanitarian law cannot stand on their own; the applicable system must be a mixed model, which incorporates features of international human rights law. In the final section the author discusses the Israeli policy of targeted killings and the US attack on suspected members of al-Qaeda in Yemen, and applies the mixed model to these cases.

1 Introduction

In November 2002 a car travelling in a remote part of Yemen was destroyed by a missile filed from an unmanned Predator drone. Six people in the car, all suspected members of al-Qaeda, were killed. While the US did not publicly acknowledge responsibility for the attack, officials let it be known that the CIA had carried it out.[1] One of

* Bruce W. Wayne Professor of International Law, Hebrew University of Jerusalem. Email: msmarcia@mscc.huji.ac.il. The writer wishes to thank Shiri Kribs and Nirit Lahav-Kanizo for their help in preparing this article. Ruth Gavison, Miri Gur Aryeh, and Daniel Reisner offered helpful comments. Obviously the responsibility for the final product lies with the author alone.

1 See Dworkin, 'The Yemen Strike: The War on Terrorism Goes Global', *Crimes of War Project*, 14 Nov. 2002, available at http://www.crimesofwar.org/onnews/news-yemen.html (last accessed 19 June 2004).

172 EJIL 16 (2005), 171–212

the men killed, Qaed Salim Sinan al Harethi, was said to be a former bin Laden security guard who was suspected of playing a major role in the October 2000 attack on the US destroyer Cole, in which 17 sailors were killed.[2]

The Yemen attack came two years after Israel adopted a policy of 'targeted killings' of Palestinians alleged to be active members of terrorist organizations involved in organizing, promoting or executing terrorist attacks in Israel and the Occupied Territories. This policy commenced with the attack on Hussein 'Abayat[3] and was followed by a series of attacks culminating recently in the attacks on the Hamas leaders Ahmed Yassin[4] and Abdel Aziz Rantisi.[5] In many of these attacks innocent bystanders were killed or wounded.[6] This policy has been officially acknowledged and is at the time of writing being defended by the government before the Supreme Court of Israel.[7]

2 See CNN report of 5 Nov. 2002, 'Sources: U.S. kills Cole suspect', available at http://www.cnn.com/2002/WORLD/meast/11/04/yemen.blast/index.html (last accessed 19 June 2004).

3 See B'Tselem The Israeli Information Centre for Human Rights in the Occupied Territories, *Israel's Assassination Policy: Extra-judicial Executions*, Position Paper, Jan. 2001, available at http://www.btselem.org/Download/Extrajudicial_Killings_Eng.doc (last accessed 19 June 2004). 'Abayat was killed in the West Bank village Beit Sahour by an IDF helicopter. Two bystanding women, Rahmeh Shahin and 'Aziza Muhammed Danun, were also killed in the attack.

4 See the official communiqué by the IDF spokesman issued by the Israel Ministry of Foreign Affairs, 'IDF strikes kills Hamas leader Ahmed Yassin', 22 Mar. 2004, available at http://www.mfa.gov.il/MFA/Terrorism-+Obstacle+to+Peace/Terrorism+and+Islamic+Fundamentalism-/Sheikh+Yassin+killed+in+IDF+attack+22-Mar-2004.htm (last accessed 1 June 2004). 4 people who were accompanying Yassin, including 2 of his sons, were killed in the attack.

5 See CNN International Report, 'Hamas leader killed in Israeli airstrike', 18 Apr. 2004, available at http://edition.cnn.com/2004/WORLD/meast/04/17/mideast.violence/ (last accessed 1 June 2004). In this attack 2 other people, 1 of whom was Rantisi's bodyguard, were killed and 10 people were wounded.

6 The most extreme case was the attack on Salah Shehadeh, leader of Hamas' military wing, Iz Adin al-Kassam, who was reportedly responsible for numerous attacks on Israeli soldiers and civilians. Besides Shehadeh, 16 people were killed, 15 of whom were civilians, including 9 children and Shehadeh's wife and child, and hundreds were wounded when an IDF plane dropped a 1-ton bomb on a house in a densely populated area of Gaza. See Meyerstein, 'Case Study: The Israeli Strike Against Hamas Leader Salah Shehadeh', *Crimes of War Project*, Sept. 2002, available at http://www.crimesofwar.org/onnews/news-shehadeh.html (last accessed 1 June 2004). As a result of the public outcry the IDF carried out an inquiry into this attack. According to the report of this inquiry published by the IDF spokesperson, there were 'shortcomings in the information available, and the evaluation of that information, concerning the presence of civilians near Shehadeh, who was in an operational hide-out'. See 'Findings of the inquiry into the death of Salah Shehadeh', 2 Aug. 2002, available at http://www.mfa.gov.il/mfa/government/communiques/2002/findings+of+the+inquiry+into+the+death+of+salah+sh.htm (last accessed 27 June 2004).

7 See H.C. petition 769/02, *Public Committee Against Torture in Israel* v. *Government of Israel*, pleadings on file with the author (hereinafter H.C. petition 769/02). This is not the first time the Court has been asked to rule on the legality of targeted killings. In a previous case the Court dismissed the petition in a few lines, merely stating that '[c]hoice of the means of fighting adopted by the respondents with the aim of frustrating murderous terrorist attacks in good time is not one of the matters in which this court will interfere. This is all the more so when the petition provides no concrete factual basis and asks for a wide remedy': H.C. 5872/2002, *M.K. Muhammed Barake v Prime Minister and Minister of Defence*, available at http://62.90.71.124/files/01/720/058/f04/01058720.f04.HTM (last accessed 25 Feb. 2004). The attitude of the Court in this case is criticized in Ben-Naftali and Michaeli, 'Justice-Ability: A Critique of the Alleged Non-Justiciability of Israel's Policy of Targeted Killings', 1 *J Int'l Criminal Justice* (2003) 368.

The Yemen attack by the US and the 'targeted killings' by Israeli forces have been castigated by human rights NGOs,[8] and some UN bodies[9] as 'extra-judicial executions'.[10] The states involved argue, on the other hand, that the killings were legitimate acts of war carried out as part of the state's inherent right to self-defence.[11] Some academic commentators have supported this view.[12] While few support the general Israeli policy, even some human rights experts have conceded that there are instances in which a targeted killing may be justified both legally and morally.[13]

8 See, e.g., Amnesty International, *Israel and the Occupied Territories: Israel Must End its Policy of Assassinations*, 4 July 2003 AI Index: MDE 15/056/2003; B'Tselem, *supra* note 3, at 2; Amnesty International Press Release, *Yemen/USA: government must not sanction extra-judicial executions*, 8 Nov. 2002, AI Index: AMR 51/168/2002; Amnesty International, *Yemen, The Rule of Law Sidelined in the Name of Security*, 24 Sept. 2003, AI Index MDE 31/006/2003.

9 See, e.g., Commission on Human Rights, *Question of the Violation of Human Rights in the Occupied Arab Territories, including Palestine, Report of the human rights inquiry commission*, (E/CN.4/2001/121), 16 Mar. 2001, at paras. 53–64 (hereinafter: *Report of the human rights inquiry commission*); *Report of the Special Rapporteur of the Commission on Human Rights on the situation of human rights in the Palestinian territories occupied by Israel since 1967*, 59th session, 17 Dec. 2002 (E/CN.4/2003/30); Statement of the UN Secretary General, New York, 10 June 2003 - Statement attributable to the Spokesman for the Secretary-General on the Middle East, available at http://www.un.org/apps/sg/sgstats.asp?nid=387 (last accessed 9 Feb. 2004). These attacks have also been castigated by governments of other countries: see US Department of State, *Country Reports on Human Rights, 2001, Israel and the Occupied Territories*, available at http://www.state.gov/g/drl/rls/hrrpt/2001/nea/8262.htm#ot (last accessed 20 Feb. 2004), strongly condemning the Israeli policy; statement of the Swedish foreign minister criticizing the US attack in Yemen, cited in Dworkin, *supra* note 1.

10 Many commentators and human rights groups have also referred to the Israeli killings as assassinations: see, e.g., reports of B'Tselem and Amnesty International, *supra* notes 3 and 8; Gross, 'Fighting by Other Means in the Mideast: a Critical Analysis of Israel's Assassination Policy', 51 *Pol Stud* (2003) 350. It seems to me that the term 'assassinations' should be reserved for deliberate killing of political figures, rather than killing of suspected terrorists. The Israeli authorities rarely, if ever, release evidence regarding the activities of the persons targeted, and it is quite possible that some of the cases indeed involved assassinations, in the above sense. And see Schmitt, 'State-Sponsored Assassination in International and Domestic Law', 17 *Yale J Int'l L* (1992) 609, who argues that in an armed conflict an assassination is killing of a specific person (whether a combatant or not) by treacherous means.

11 See, e.g., statement of National Security Advisor Condoleezza Rice, of 10 Nov. 2002, cited in Dworkin, *supra* note 1; Brief of Government of Israel, in H.C. petition 769/02, *supra* note 7.

12 See, e.g., Gross, 'Thwarting Terrorist Acts by Attacking the Perpetrators of their Commanders as an Act of Self-Defence: Human Rights Versus the State's Duty to Protect its Citizens', 15 *Temp Int'l & Comp LJ* (2001) 195; Rivkin, Jr., Casey, and Bartram, 'A Legal Analysis of the Attacks on Civilians and Infliction of "Collateral Damage" in the Middle East Conflict', *The Federalist Society for Law and Public Policy Studies*, available at http://www.fed-soc.org/Laws%20of%20war/collateral%20damage%20white%20paper%20cvr%20pg.pdf (last accessed 17 Feb. 2004).

13 According to a MERIP Report, Human Rights Watch Director Kenneth Roth stated in an interview with the press that his organization did not object to the Yemen attack as it saw it as an attack on an enemy combatant: Middle East Report Online, *Israel, the US and 'Targeted Killings'*, available at http://www.merip.org/mero/mero021703.html (last accessed 9 Feb. 2004). In a subsequent article, Roth states that if al-Harethi was indeed a top bin Laden operative, use of the rules of war against him might have been appropriate, especially seeing that arresting him might not have been a real option: Roth, 'The Law of War and the War on Terror', 83(1) *Foreign Affairs* 2, Jan./Feb. 2004. And see *Concluding Observations of the Human Rights Committee on Report of Israel*, 21/08/2003, CCPR/CO/78/ISR, discussed below, in the text accompanying note 38.

174 *EJIL* 16 (2005), 171–212

Granting licence to state authorities to kill suspected enemies of the state cannot appeal to anyone sensitive to human rights and suspicious of the uses and abuses of state power. On the other hand, one cannot simply dismiss out of hand the parallel drawn by the states involved between legitimate killing of enemy combatants during an armed conflict and the targeting of active members of terrorist organizations that have, for all intents and purposes, declared war on those states.[14]

The disparity in the attitudes taken towards 'targeted killings' reveals a fundamental disagreement not only regarding their morality or legality,[15] but also on the issue of the legal regime by which that legality should be judged. The states involved claim that such killings are legitimate means of fighting the 'war on terror', whose legality must be judged on the basis of the laws of armed conflict; those who label these killings 'extra-judicial executions' rely on a law-enforcement model of legality, which rests primarily, though not exclusively, on standards of international human rights law.[16]

Fundamental disagreement over the applicable legal regime is part of a wider controversy over the proper categorization of state measures to combat international or transnational terrorism. Are we talking about a 'war on terror' to be pursued according to the laws of armed conflict, or a struggle against a particularly pernicious form of criminal activity that should be managed according to a law-enforcement model?[17] Or perhaps we should be thinking of a new phenomenon, not adequately covered by either legal regime, so that a new, mixed legal regime should be devised.[18]

Human rights institutions, activists and NGOs generally reject the perception that existing norms of international law are inadequate to deal with domestic or transnational terror. With more than a measure of justification they still fear that the real threat in the present situation lies in over-reaction to terror by governments and adoption of measures that are incompatible both with human rights standards and rules of humanitarian law.[19] Their assumption is either that the constraints on state

14 See Statman, 'Targeted Killing', 5 *Theoretical Inquiries in Law* (2004) 179.

15 For an exchange on the moral and legal justification for Israeli targeted killings, see David, 'Israel's Policy of Targeted Killing', 17 *Ethics and International Affairs* (2003) 111; Stein, 'By Any Name Illegal and Immoral', *ibid.*, at 127; David, 'If Not Combatants, Certainly Not Civilians', *ibid.*, at 138. For arguments that the policy can be defended on moral grounds see Statman, *supra* note 14; Kasher and Yadlin, 'Fighting against Terror Morally', 2/3 *Bitachon Leumi* (2003) 5 (in Hebrew).

16 One of the most difficult questions in discussing the Israeli policy is whether the applicable norms are those which apply to an occupying power (fundamentally a law enforcement model based on international humanitarian law) or those which apply in a situation of active armed conflict. I will return to this question in part 5 B below.

17 For discussion of this question see: Slaughter and Burke-White, 'An International Constitutional Moment', 43 *Harv Int'l LJ.* (2002) 1; Fitzpatrick, 'Speaking Law to Power: The War Against Terrorism and Human Rights', 14 *EJIL* (2003) 241.

18 See Slaughter and Burke-White, *supra* note 17; Delbrück, 'The Fight Against Global Terrorism: Self-Defense or Collective Security as International Police Action?', 44 *German Yearbook on Int'l Law* (2001) 9; Watkin, 'Controlling the Use of Force: A Role for Human Rights Norms in Contemporary Armed Conflict', 98 *AJIL* (2004) 1.

19 See, e.g., statement of the UN High Commissioner on Human Rights, 'Terrorism and Human Rights', available at http://www.unhchr.ch/terrorism/index.html (last accessed 18 Feb. 2004); International Commission of Jurists, 'Declaration on Upholding Human Rights and the Rule of Law in Combating Terrorism', 6 Sept. 2004, available at http://icj.org/news.php3?id_article=3503?=en (last visited 28 Nov. 2004).

action against terror placed by existing standards do not hinder effective anti-terror measures, or that even if they do so, the dangers to human rights that result from relaxation of these standards is far greater than the danger presented to those rights from international terrorism itself. It has, however, recently been argued by the head of the American branch of a leading international human rights NGO that human rights NGOs have been somewhat selective in their concern for victims of human rights violations, showing little real concern for the victims of terror attacks.[20]

The issue of targeted killings has been analysed by a number of writers.[21] Their analyses reveal different ways of looking at the issue. My primary purpose in this paper is to examine the different perceptions and their difficulties. My conclusions are that neither the law-enforcement model, as reflected in standards of IHR, nor the armed conflict model, as reflected in standards of IHL, provides an adequate framework for the issue of transnational terror. I therefore conclude by suggesting a framework that combines elements of both models.

Before delving into the issue, some remarks about the terms I shall be using. It hardly bears repeating that the terms 'terror' and 'international terror' have proved notoriously difficult to define.[22] I do not intend to enter a debate on this question here. For the purposes of this discussion I will regard terrorism as the deliberate causing of death, or other serious injury, to civilians for political or ideological ends.[23] I will regard transnational terrorism as terrorism carried out across international lines or directed against the citizens or residents of a country that is not the country of the perpetrator.[24] An organization will be seen as a terrorist group, not only if terror is its sole aim or *modus operandi*, but also if it regularly employs terror as a means of achieving its aims. The legitimacy of those aims will be regarded as irrelevant.

[20] See Schulz, 'Security Is a Human Right Too', *NYTimes Magazine*, 18 Apr. 2004, available at http://www.amnestyusa.org/about/security.html (last accessed 19 June 2004). Mr. Schulz is the executive director of the American branch of Amnesty International.

[21] For recent analyses of this question, in the Israeli context, see Gross, *supra* note 10, at 350; Ben-Naftali and Michaeli, '"We Must Not Make a Scarecrow of the Law": A Legal Analysis of the Israeli Policy of Targeted Killings', 36 *Cornell Int'l LJ.* (2003) 233. Also see Rivkin, Casey, and Bartram, *supra* note 12; Kendall, 'Israeli Counter-Terrorism: "Targeted Killings" Under International Law', 80 *NCL Rev* (2002) 1069 and the exchange between David and Stein, *supra* note 15.

[22] For a discussion of the difficulties in finding an agreed definition see Teichman, 'How to Define Terrorism', 64 *Philosphy* (1989) 505; Primoratz, 'What is Terrorism?', 7 *J Applied Philosophy* (1990) 129. Also see Gearty, 'Introduction', in C. Gearty (ed.), *Terrorism* (1996), at p. xi (hereinafter: Gearty, *Terrorism*). For problems in reaching a legal definition of terrorism and international terrorism see UN Commission on Human Rights, *Specific Human Rights Issues: New Priorities, in Particular Terrorism, Additional Progress Report*, prepared by Ms. Kalliopi K. Koufa, Special Rapporteur on terrorism and human rights, E/CN.4/Sub.2/2003/WP.1, 8 Aug. 2003.

[23] Cf. Gearty, 'What is Terror?', *The Times Saturday Review*, 9 Mar. 1991; Cowdy, 'The Morality of Terrorism', 60 *Philosophy* (1985) 47; both articles are reprinted in Gearty , *Terrorism*, *supra* note 22, at 173 and 495 respectively. Like Gearty, I place the emphasis on the means employed, and not on the acceptability or non-acceptability of the aims. Furthermore, I too do not regard attacks on military targets as a form of terrorism. Finally, rather than using the notion of 'innocent persons' as the targets, I refer to attacks on civilians. This rests on the notion that even in situations in which killing and wounding is 'lawful', i.e., an armed conflict, it is never lawful to target civilians.

[24] Cf. Schachter, 'The Lawful Use of Force by a State Against Terrorists in Another Country', in H. H. Han (ed.), *Terrorism and Political Violence: Limits and Possibilities of Legal Control* (1993), at 243.

The typical case to be examined here is the targeting of a suspected terrorist who is not in the territory of the state which carries out the attack. While many of the same issues may arise in cases of internal terror, especially in a situation that has reached the scale of violence that justifies its categorization as a non-international armed conflict under Additional Protocol II to the Geneva Conventions, the present discussion shall not deal directly with this question.[25]

State A's civilians have been subject to terror attacks by a terrorist organization, which operates out of other countries. Is it ever legal for that state to target suspected members of that organization who are not at present in its borders? If so, in which situations would such targeting be legal?

2 Law Enforcement Model

Categorization of targeted killings as 'extra-judicial executions', rather than war crimes or grave breaches of international humanitarian law, implies that the relevant legal model is a law-enforcement model and that the applicable regime by which state action is to be assessed is the international human rights regime.[26] Under such a regime the intentional use of lethal force by state authorities can be justified only in strictly limited conditions. The state is obliged to respect and ensure the rights of every person to life and to due process of law. Any intentional use of lethal force by state authorities that is not justified under the provisions regarding the right to life, will, by definition, be regarded as an 'extra-judicial execution'.[27]

In examining application of international human rights standards to the issue of targeted killings of international terrorists, a number of questions have to be addressed:

A. Assuming that the regime of international human rights applies in such a situation, are there circumstances in which a targeted killing would *not* be regarded as a violation of the victim's right to life?

[25] There are differences between the non-international conflicts covered by Common Art. 3 of the Geneva Conventions and those covered by Additional Prot. II: see L. Moir, *The Law of International Armed Conflict* (2002). The main difference that interests me here is that under APII there must be some control over territory by the non-state party involved. It is this feature that could make a struggle with a terror group in the territory of a state similar to a case of trans-national terror.

[26] I stress that the emphasis is on state behaviour or responsibility, and not on individual criminal liability. Clearly, with the growing body of international criminal law and the establishment of the International Criminal Court, issues of individual liability of those who carry out the targeting on behalf of the state also needs to be addressed.

[27] In its report on the Israeli policy, *supra* note 8, Amnesty International defined an extrajudicial execution as follows: '[a]n extrajudicial execution is an unlawful and deliberate killing carried out by order of a government or with its acquiescence. Extrajudicial killings are killings which can reasonably be assumed to be the result of a policy at any level of government to eliminate specific individuals as an alternative to arresting them and bringing them to justice. These killings take place outside any judicial framework.'

B. Does the international human rights regime apply to the act of state A carried out on the territory of state B over which the state A does not exercise jurisdiction and has no control?
C. Does the international human rights regime apply in the 'warlike' situation of protracted violence between an international terror group and a given state?

A *Right to Life under the International Human Rights Regime*

All international conventions dealing with civil and political rights protect the 'inherent right to life'.[28] While all conventions classify this right as a non-derogable right, i.e., a right that may not be derogated from in times of emergency, none of them grants this right absolute protection. The International Covenant on Civil and Political Rights (ICCPR), the American Convention on Human Rights and the African Charter of Human and People's Rights prohibit *arbitrary* deprivation of life, leaving the question of when intentional deprivation of a person's life will violate that person's right to life to be determined by interpretation of the term 'arbitrary'.[29] The approach of the European Convention for the Protection of Human Rights and Fundamental Freedoms is somewhat different. Article 2(1) states that no one shall be deprived of his life intentionally. Under Article 2(2), however, deprivation of life shall not be regarded as a violation of the right to life when it results from the use of force which is no more than absolutely necessary in any of three cases, one of which is 'defence of any person from unlawful violence'.[30]

I shall in due course examine whether there may be cases of lethal force that do not amount to 'arbitrary' deprivation of a person's life, as this term is used in the ICCPR, American Convention or African Charter, even if they are not covered by the exceptions in Article 2(2) of the European Convention. For the moment, I shall concentrate on the European model, as it is widely accepted that this model provides a fair statement of cases in which such force may be regarded as non-arbitrary.[31] May targeting a person suspected of being a member of a terrorist organization that is waging a 'war of terror' against residents of the victim state be regarded as legitimate use of force under Article 2 of the European Convention?

The answer to this question depends on the meaning of the proportionality test adopted in Article 2(2) – that the use of lethal force is no more than absolutely necessary to defend persons whose lives are in danger. While the European Court of Human Rights

[28] See Art. 6 of the International Covenant on Civil and Political Rights, 1966. This is the only right referred to as an inherent right. It seems that reference to the right to life as 'inherent' is based on the notion that this right does not depend on the particular society or legal regime, but derives from the humanity of every individual, wherever he or she may be: see B.G. Ramcharan, *The Right to Life in International Law* (1985), at 51; M. Nowak, *U.N. Covenant on Civil and Political Rights, CCPR Commentary* (1993), at 105; W. Schabas, *The Abolition of the Death Penalty in International Law* (2nd edn., 1997), at 95.

[29] See Art. 6(1) of the ICCPR, Art. 4 of the American Convention on Human Rights, and Art. 4 of the African Charter.

[30] Art. 2(2) of the ECHR. The other cases are effecting a lawful arrest or to preventing the escape of a person lawfully detained and action lawfully taken for the purpose of quelling a riot or insurrection.

[31] See Nowak, *supra* note 28, at 111; N. Rodley, *The Treatment of Prisoners under International Law* (2nd edn., 1999), at 183.

178 *EJIL* 16 (2005), 171–212

has not had occasion to address the question of targeted killings, it has made it clear that the test to be employed in examining whether the use of lethal force is absolutely necessary is a strict one – the 'force used must be strictly proportionate to the achievement of the aims set out in sub-paragraphs 2(a), (b) and (c) of Article 2 (art. 2-2-a-b-c).'[32]

Establishing that the use of lethal force meets the absolute necessity tests involves examining two questions:

1. Is the use of *force* absolutely required, or could other measures be employed to protect the threatened persons?
2. Assuming that no other measures are available, is it absolutely necessary to use *lethal* force, or could some lesser degree of force be employed?

I shall concentrate on the first question, and shall assume that in cases regarding suspected terrorists, if force can be justified on the basis of Article 2(2), the seriousness of the threat and the need for effective frustration of that threat will generally lead to the conclusion that force may be lethal.[33]

The exceptions to the prohibition on intentionally depriving a person of his life must be interpreted in light of the fundamental assumption that international human rights law adopts a law-enforcement model based on principles of due process. All law-enforcement measures must be compatible with these principles, foremost amongst which are the following: 1. every individual benefits from the presumption of innocence; 2. persons suspected of perpetrating or planning serious criminal acts should be arrested, detained and interrogated with due process of law; and 3. if there is credible evidence that such persons were indeed involved in planning, promoting, aiding and abetting or carrying out terrorist acts they should be afforded a fair trial before a competent and independent court and, if convicted, sentenced by the court to a punishment provided by law. Under this model a state may not prevent criminal acts by eliminating the potential perpetrators. Prevention is to be achieved by apprehending those planning and preparing the violence and subjecting them to the criminal process. Deterrence is to be achieved by the threat of legal sanctions and enforcement of the criminal law against those convicted of breaking the law.[34]

[32] See *McCann v UK*, 21 EHRR (1996) 97, at para. 149.

[33] Support for this assumption may be drawn from the *McCann* case, *ibid.* This case involved the killing in Gibraltar by British special force soldiers of 3 IRA terrorists. The Court found that the soldiers involved honestly believed that the deceased would detonate a car bomb if they were given time to act after they realized that they were about to be apprehended. They therefore shot them several times, making quite sure that the force was lethal. The European Court of Human Rights found that this action by the soldiers did not amount to a violation of Art. 2 of the Convention. (The majority held, however, that in the planning of the action to apprehend the suspected terrorists, sufficient weight had not been given to alternative means that would not have involved lethal force, and that the UK was therefore liable for violation of Art. 2.)

[34] See F. Ni Aolain, *The Politics of Force: Conflict Management and State Violence in Northern Ireland* (2000), at 187. A state may derogate from certain rights during a state of emergency. Thus, for example, if the exigencies of the situation strictly demand it, a state may resort to administrative detention, which does not meet the principles of due process in criminal trials. However, the right curtailed in such cases is personal liberty. Unlike this right, the right to life is a non-derogable right. A state may not derogate from due process principles needed to protect this right: see Human Rights Committee, *General Comment No. 29 on Article 4 of ICCPR*, 31 Aug. 2001, CCPR/C/21/Rev.1/Add.11, at para. 15.

Under the law-enforcement model use of force can never be regarded as necessary (let alone absolutely necessary) unless it is clear that there was no feasible possibility of protecting the prospective victim by apprehending the suspected perpetrator. The paradigmatic case in which use of force would be justifiable is where serious violence against the person to be protected is so imminent that trying to arrest the perpetrator would allow him time to carry out his threat. It has been strongly argued that in no other case could we say that use of lethal force is absolutely necessary.[35] Borrowing US Secretary of State Daniel Webster's classic definition of a state's right to use force in self-defence in the exchange of notes following the *Caroline* incident, only where there is a concrete imminent threat can it be said that there is 'a necessity of self-defence, instant, overwhelming, leaving no choice of means, and no moment for deliberation'.[36]

The problem with the law-enforcement model in the context of transnational terror is that one of its fundamental premises is invalid: that the suspected perpetrator is within the jurisdiction of the law-enforcement authorities in the victim state, so that an arrest can be effected. What is the situation when, according to our premise, the terrorist is in the territory of another state? The victim state may not arrest or apprehend that person without the active assistance and support of that other state. But what if that state is either unwilling to arrest the suspected terrorist or incapable of doing so? Leaving aside issues of state sovereignty, and relying solely on the duty of the victim state under international human rights law to respect the right to life, could it not argue that it has no choice but to resort to force against the suspected terrorist? That force is absolutely necessary to protect its civilians against unlawful violence? Obviously it could not do so in every situation. Thus, it could not do so if its aim were to punish the suspected terrorist for past acts, or to deter potential terrorists from acting. But what if the state has strong evidence that the suspected terrorist is continuing to plan terrorist attacks against people in its territory? That if it does not either apprehend or target him, there is a very strong probability that he will carry out or organize further attacks? Would this also not be the kind of situation described

35 See Rodley, *supra* note 31, at 182–188; Nolte, 'Preventive Use of Force and Preventive Killings: Moves into a Different Legal Order', 5 *Theoretical Inquiries in Law* (2004) 111.

36 Note, *ibid.* According to this view, Art. 2(2) follows the model of self-defence in criminal law. In many legal systems this defence is available only when the threat to the life or body of the person against whom unlawful violence was to be used was imminent: see Bernsman, 'Private Self-Defence and Necessity in German Penal and in the Penal Law Proposal – Some Remarks', 30 *Israel L R* (1996) 171; B. Sanjero, *Self-Defence in Criminal Law* (2000), at 185–186 (in Hebrew). It should be noted that there is some limited authority for the view that the defence in Art. 2(2) may apply even when the danger is not imminent: see Rodley, *supra* note 31, at 188, who cites the decision of the European Commission of Human Rights in *Kelly v United Kingdom*, 74 D & R (1993) 139. In that case the authorities shot and killed a person who tried to avoid an army road block, as they thought he was a terrorist. The Commission found the complaint of violation of Art. 2 manifestly unfounded. Rodley remarks that 'the Commission's decision . . . seems to ignore any requirement of imminence of the anticipated threat as part of the necessity or proportionality tests'. The Commission's decision in this case has been strongly criticized: see Joseph, 'Denouement of the Deaths on the Rock: The Right to Life of Terrorists', 14 *Netherlands QHR* (1996) 5, at 9; Ni Aolain, *supra* note 34, at 196–198. Also see Smith, 'The Right to Life and the Right to Kill in Law', 144 *New L.J.* (1994) 354.

by Secretary of State Webster in his classic formulation of a state's right to self-defence? Could this not be regarded as a situation in which it was absolutely necessary to use lethal force? To put it another way: if the requirement of imminent danger rests on the availability of non-lethal, due process law-enforcement measures when the danger is not imminent, does the imminency requirement lose part of its force when such measures are unavailable?

As stated above, the ICCPR does not set out specific cases in which intentional use of lethal force does not involve violation of the right to life. The fear was that mentioning such cases might be regarded as an endorsement of killing.[37] Instead, Article 6 protects every person against arbitrary deprivation of his life. Where there is strong evidence that a suspected terrorist is preparing or planning a terrorist attack against residents of the victim state, will a pre-emptive attack be regarded as an arbitrary deprivation of his life, if there was no reasonable way of apprehending or arresting him? The Human Rights Committee addressed this question when considering the periodic report of Israel in July 2003. In its Concluding Observations the Committee stated:

> The Committee is concerned by what the State party calls 'targeted killings' of those identified by the State party as suspected terrorists in the Occupied Territories. *This practice would appear to be used at least in part as a deterrent or punishment, thus raising issues under article 6.* While noting the delegation's observations about respect for the principle of proportionality in any response to terrorist activities against civilians and its affirmation that only persons taking direct part in hostilities have been targeted, the Committee remains concerned about the nature and extent of the responses by the Israeli Defence Force (IDF) to Palestinian terrorist attacks.
>
> The State party should ensure that the utmost consideration is given to the principle of proportionality in all its responses to terrorist threats and activities. State policy in this respect should be spelled out clearly in guidelines to regional military commanders, and complaints about disproportionate use of force should be investigated promptly by an independent body. *Before resorting to the use of deadly force, all measures to arrest a person suspected of being in the process of committing acts of terror must be exhausted.* [38]

From the first part of this observation it would seem that the Human Rights Committee is of the opinion that targeted killings of suspected terrorists in the Occupied Territories only raise issues under Article 6, when they are used as a deterrent or punishment, and not, presumably, when they are used as a pre-emptive preventive measure. On the other hand, in its recommendation, the Committee refers to use of deadly force against a 'person suspected of being in the process of committing acts of terror'. This would seem to imply that the Committee adopts the approach that preventive force may only be used in the face of an imminent attack, which cannot be halted by arresting the perpetrator.

Ambiguity in interpretation of the term 'arbitrary' deprivation of life in the context of targeting terrorists is also apparent in the recent Inter-American Commission on Human Rights *Report on Terrorism and Human Rights*.[39] The Commission addresses

37 See Boyle, 'The Concept of the Arbitrary Deprivation of Life', in B.G. Ramcharan (ed.), *supra* note 28, at 221.

38 *Concluding Observations of the Human Rights Committee: Israel, supra* note 13 (emphasis added).

39 OEA/Ser.L/V/II.116, Doc. 5 rev. 1 corr, 22 Oct. 2002, available at http://www.cidh.oas.org/Terrorism/Eng/exe.htm (last accessed 15 Feb. 2004).

the use of lethal force by state agents. It mentions that 'in situations where a state's population is threatened by violence, the state has the right and obligation to protect the population against such threats and in so doing may use lethal force in certain situations'.[40] It goes on to give examples: the first, protection of persons from imminent threat of death or serious injury, and the second, 'to otherwise maintain law and order where strictly necessary and proportionate'.[41] The second example obviously refers to situations of violent riots or other disturbances and not to targeting a specific individual. However, in its attempt to pursue the issue further, the Commission creates some confusion.

The Commission states that in circumstances where force may be used:

> the state may resort to force only against individuals that threaten the security of all, and therefore the state may not use force against civilians who do not present such a threat. The state must distinguish between the civilians and those individuals who constitute the threat.[42]

This is a highly peculiar statement, which seems to confuse issues of international human rights law and international humanitarian law.[43] The status of a person as a civilian or combatant is only relevant in the latter system. In the former system, whether lethal force can be used against an individual is unconnected with that individual's status; it should depend entirely on the threat that the said individual poses, and the availability of alternative means of neutralizing that threat.

The confusion is compounded when the Commission continues with the following statement:

> Similarly, in their law enforcement initiatives, states must not use force against individuals who no longer present a threat as described above, such as individuals who have been apprehended by authorities, have surrendered, or who are wounded and abstain from hostile acts. The use of lethal force in such a manner would constitute extra-judicial killings in flagrant violation of Article 4 of the Convention . . .[44]

The examples given are impeccable. However, what about suspected terrorists who have not been apprehended or wounded and have not surrendered? If there is an assessment that they 'threaten the security threat of all' may lethal force be used against them?[45]

40 *Ibid.*, at para. 87.

41 *Ibid.*

42 *Ibid.*, at para. 90.

43 It must be stressed that this statement of the Commission is part of its discussion of protection of the right to life under international human rights law. In another part of its report the Commission addresses issues of IHL.

44 *Report on Terrorism and Human Rights, supra* note 39, at para. 91.

45 In another part of the report the Commission addresses '[t]he Right to Life and Terrorism'. In this part it compares norms of international human rights law and IHL. After mentioning the duty under IHL to distinguish between combatants and civilians, the Commission states: '[s]imilarly, in peacetime situations, state agents must distinguish between persons who, by their actions, constitute an imminent threat of death or serious injury, or *a threat of committing a particularly serious crime involving a grave threat to life*, and persons who do not present such a threat, and use force only against the former': *ibid.*, at para. 111 (emphasis added). From this section it seems that the Commission takes the clear stand that when there is a threat of a particularly serious crime involving a grave threat to life, use of force may be justified even if the threat is not imminent.

The Commission was apparently well aware that its analysis left matters unclear. In what reads as a somewhat feeble attempt to reduce the ambiguity, the Commission ends its analysis of the right to life issue with the following statement:

> It should be emphasized that, contrary to international humanitarian law governing situations of armed conflicts, relevant applicable norms of international human rights law require that state agents not use force to target individuals involved in a violent confrontation except in the above-mentioned circumstances.[46]

The problem is, of course, that 'the above-mentioned circumstances' are extremely vague. The question that interests us – targeting of suspected terrorists who are not within the state's jurisdiction – remains obscure.

Where does this all lead us? Clearly, the mere fact that a suspected terrorist is outside the territory of the victim state, and may therefore not be arrested by its authorities, does not mean that he has lost his right to life and that he may be targeted. It may be argued, however, that when there is strong evidence that the suspected terrorist is actually planning terrorist attacks against the victim state, and there is no feasible way of preventing those attacks by apprehending or arresting him, targeting him would not necessarily be regarded as an arbitrary deprivation of life. In such a case the unlawful violence might not be imminent, but the need to use lethal force in order to prevent that violence might be immediate, since if such force is not used now it may not be possible to prevent the violence later.[47] This may be what has been termed the last window of opportunity to frustrate further terrorist attacks.[48]

On the substantive level this argument may seem tempting. It should be noted, however, that the imminency requirement may be justified not only because of the lack of opportunity to use due process methods, but also on evidentiary grounds. When the violence is imminent we do not face the need to prove the intention to employ unlawful violence. The evidence is right there before us.[49] In the absence of such tangible evidence, can we rely on the law enforcement officials in the victim state to 'convict' persons of planning terrorist attacks? Should we not fear that this limited 'exception' may be exploited and abused by states eager to turn the struggle against terrorists into all-out war? Can we really create an exception that will be limited to the case of *absolute* necessity, in the sense mentioned above? The Israeli experience with the attempt to allow use of moderate physical force in the interrogation of suspected terrorists would seem to show that the answer is negative. While the original idea was that such force should only be used when all other methods of obtaining essential information for preventing terrorist attacks had failed, it would

46 *Ibid.*, at para. 92.

47 Under s.34J of the Israel Criminal Code, 1977, self-defence is a defence when violence was 'immediately required to ward off an unlawful attack which created a concrete danger of harm to life, body, liberty, property'. Under this provision the immediacy requirement does not relate to the danger to life, but to the need to use violence to frustrate that danger.

48 See Schmitt, 'Counter-Terrorism and the Use of Force in International Law', 32 *Israel Yrbk on HR* (2002) 53, at 110.

49 I am grateful to my colleague, Miri Gur-Aryeh, for raising this point.

seem that over time physical force and other unacceptable methods of interrogation became fairly standard methods of interrogation.[50]

When then may a state use lethal force against suspected terrorists? It seems that there are three possible approaches to this question:

a. Restricting the exceptions to the right to life (whether under Article 2(2) of the European Convention, or the 'arbitrary' deprivation escape clause in the ICCPR and American and African Conventions) to cases in which lethal force is used to thwart an imminent attack.[51] Absent imminency, pre-emptive targeting of a suspected terrorist will be regarded as not being absolutely necessary, or as an arbitrary deprivation of life, no matter how strong the evidence that he is planning further terrorist attacks and how high the probability that there may not be another opportunity to prevent such attacks.
b. Allowing the targeting in the very restricted circumstances in which apprehending or arresting the suspected terrorist is not feasible, provided there is extremely strong evidence that the suspected terrorist is involved in executing or planning a terrorist attack and there is a well-founded fear that other means of preventing that attack are likely to fail.[52] I have already described the difficulties of this approach. I shall return to it below.
c. Positing that the law-enforcement model, which lies at the basis of the treaty provisions on the right to life, does not provide an adequate answer to the issue of transnational terror. When the terror is intense, organized and protracted, the appropriate model should be the armed conflict model, which is not based on notions of imminent danger from the specific person targeted, but on notions of the danger posed by the group to which the person belongs.[53] I shall discuss this position below.

B *Jurisdictional Application of International Human Rights Norms*

Does the international human rights regime apply to actions of one state in the territory of another? Or to put it in another way, towards which individuals is a given

[50] I have addressed this question elsewhere: see D. Kretzmer, *The Occupation of Justice: The Supreme Court of Israel and the Occupied Territories* (2002), at 135 -143. Also see B'Tselem, *The Interrogation of Palestinians During the Intifada: Ill-treatment, 'Moderate Physical Pressure' or Torture?* (1991), available at http://www.btselem.org/Download/1991_Interrogation_Eng.doc (last accessed 19 June 2004); and *Routine Torture: Interrogation Methods of the General Security Service*, (1998), available at http://www.btselem.org/Download/eRTorture.rtf (last accessed 19 June 2004).

[51] This is the view of Nolte, *supra* note 35.

[52] This view would be consistent with the lenient approach adopted in *Kelly* v. *UK*, *supra* note 36, and could be consistent with *the Concluding Observations of the Human Rights Committee*, *supra* note 38, and the Inter-American Commission Report, *supra* note 39. And cf. Principle 4 of the *Basic Principles on the Use of Force and Firearms, adopted by the 8th UN Congress on Prevention of Crime and Treatment of Offenders, Havana, Cuba, 1990*:

> 'Law enforcement officials, in carrying out their duty, shall, as far as possible, apply non-violent means before resorting to the use of force and firearms. They may use force and firearms only if other means remain ineffective or without any promise of achieving the intended result'.

No mention is made of the imminency requirement, or the failure of an attempt to arrest the person.

[53] For this distinction see M. Walzer, *Just and Unjust Wars* (3rd edn., 2000), at 144–147.

state obligated under its international *human rights* obligations?[54] Under the ICCPR a state party is bound to respect and ensure the rights enshrined in the Covenant 'to all individuals in its territory and subject to its jurisdiction'; under both the European and American Conventions, the duty is to all persons subject to the state party's jurisdiction.

In the *Bankovic* case[55] the European Court of Human Rights took a narrow view of the concept of jurisdiction, when it held that a state party to the European Convention generally exercises its jurisdiction only in its own territory. The exceptions are cases where the state exercises all or some of the public powers of government in the territory of another state with that state's consent, invitation or acquiescence, or where it is occupying territory in which it exercises effective control.[56] Applying this approach, the Court held that when NATO forces bombed targets in Kosovo and Serbia from the air the persons in the bombed areas were not subject to the jurisdiction of the NATO states. Following this decision doubt has been expressed whether international human rights norms apply to actions of states against transnational terrorists outside their borders.[57] This doubt has been challenged.[58] In interpreting the ICCPR, the Human Rights Committee has adopted an approach similar to the cause and effect theory *rejected* by the European Court.[59] Under this approach anybody directly affected by a state party's actions will be regarded, for the purposes of the Covenant, as subject to that state party's jurisdiction.

Even if we are prepared to assume that neither the European Convention, nor the ICCPR, apply to persons who are not subject to the jurisdiction of a state party, within the meaning of this term adopted in the *Bankovic* decision, does this mean that a state has no obligations under *international human rights law* towards such persons? Answering this question in the affirmative would be incompatible with the very notion of the universality of human rights, which lies at the foundation of international human rights law. While a state party's *treaty* obligations are a function of the scope of application defined in the particular treaty, some of the substantive

54 I stress that for the moment I shall not refer to the state's general obligations under international law, such as the obligation to respect the sovereignty and territorial integrity of other states.

55 See *Bankovic v Belgium*, 11 BHRC (2000) 435. On application of human rights standards to armed conflict situations by the European Court of Human Rights see Heintze, 'The European Court of Human Rights and the Implementation of Human Rights Standards During Armed Conflict', 45 *German Ybk on Int'l L* (2002) 60.

56 See *Loizidou v Turkey*, 23 EHRR (1996) 513. In this case, the Court held that as an occupying power in northern Cyprus Turkey has jurisdiction over persons in that part of the island. Turkey could therefore be held liable for violations of an individual's rights under the European Convention.

57 See Neuman, 'Humanitarian Law and Counter-terrorist Force', 14 *EJIL* (2003) 283.

58 See Fitzpatrick, *supra* note 17, at 241. For a detailed criticism of the *Bankovic* decision see Ben-Naftali and Shani, 'Living in Denial: The Application of Human Rights in the Occupied Territories', 37 *Israel Law Review* (2004) 17.

59 See Communication No. 52/1979, *Lopez Burgos v Uruguay*, CCPR/C/OP/1 at 88 (1984); *General Comment No. 31: The Nature of the General Legal Obligation Imposed on States Parties to the Covenant*, 26 May 2004, CCPR/C/21/Rev.1/Add.13. The wide view has also been taken by the Inter-American Commission on Human Rights and by various learned writers: see Meron, 'Extraterritoriality of Human Rights Treaties', 89 *AJIL* (1995) 78; Fitzpatrick, *supra* note 17, at 241. But cf. Dennis, 'Application of Human Rights Treaties in Times of Armed Conflict: Fuzzy Thinking All Around?', forthcoming in 99 *AJIL* (2005).

norms in human rights treaties that have been ratified by the vast majority of states in the world, have now become peremptory norms of customary international law. The duty to respect the right to life is surely one of these norms.[60] A state's duty to respect the right to life (as opposed to its duty to ensure that right) follows its agents, wherever they operate. Any other approach would imply that in the absence of an armed conflict (to which IHL will apply) under international law a state may lawfully kill persons in the territory of another state.[61] Such a result is unconscionable and should be rejected.

C *International Human Rights Law in Armed Conflict*

The prevalent theory at one time was that the international human rights regime applies to the internal domestic situation of a state, both in times of peace and war. The authority given to a state to derogate from some of its obligations in times of emergency is directed towards its domestic front. On the battlefield, on the other hand, the applicable legal regime is the law of war, including international humanitarian law. In recent years this theory seems to have been abandoned. The prevailing theory is that even in the conduct of hostilities the international human rights regime applies, although in part it is superseded by the *lex specialis*, international humanitarian law.[62] This theory was adopted by the International Court of Justice (ICJ) in the *Nuclear Weapons* case.[63] In that case it was claimed that the use of nuclear weapons would inevitably involve violation of the right to life, protected under Article 6 of the ICCPR. In reply, it was argued that nuclear weapons would be used in war when international humanitarian law, and not the ICCPR, would apply.[64] Article 6 of the ICCPR was therefore not pertinent.

The ICJ rejected the argument that the ICCPR ceases to apply in times of war. It added:

> In principle, the right not arbitrarily to be deprived of one's life applies also in hostilities. The test of what is an arbitrary deprivation of life, however, then falls to be determined by the applicable *lex specialis*, namely, the law applicable in armed conflict, which is designed to regulate the conduct of hostilities. Thus whether a particular loss of life, through the use of

[60] See Dinstein, 'The Right to Life, Physical Integrity, and Liberty' in L. Henkin (ed.), *The International Bill of Rights – the Covenant on Civil and Political Rights* (1981), at 114, 115; Gormley, 'The Right to Life and the Rule of Non-derogability: Peremptory Norms of *Jus Cogens*', in Ramcharan (ed), *supra* note 28, at 120; Rodley, *supra* note 31, at 178–179.

[61] It may indeed be argued that by acting in the territory of another state, the targeting state would be violating that state's territorial integrity, protected under Art. 2(4) of the UN Charter. Even if this is the case, it cannot be the only reason why such an action should be regarded as unlawful under international law.

[62] See, e.g., Meron, 'The Humanization of Humanitarian Law', 94 *AJIL* (2000) 239; Doswald-Beck and Vité, 'International Humanitarian Law and Human Rights Law', 293 *IRRC* (1993) 94. Also see R. Provost, *International Human Rights and Humanitarian Law* (2002); Frowein, 'The Relationship between Human Rights Regimes and Regimes of Belligerent Occupation', 28 *Israel Yrbk on HR* (1998) 1; Watkin, *supra* note 18. But cf. Dennis, *supra* note 59.

[63] *Legality of the Threat or Use of Nuclear Weapons*, Advisory Opinion, 8 July 1996 [1996] ICJ Rep 226 (hereinafter: *Nuclear Weapons* case).

[64] *Ibid.*, at para. 24.

a certain weapon in warfare, is to be considered an arbitrary deprivation of life contrary to Article 6 of the Covenant can only be decided by reference to the law applicable in armed conflict and not deduced from the terms of the Covenant itself.[65]

The implications of this theory in the present context seem clear. If the targeted killings take place within the context of an armed conflict between the victim state and the terrorist group, or the states that harbour or host it, their legality will have to be decided on the basis of international humanitarian law. If such killings are permitted under IHL, they will not be regarded as arbitrary deprivations of life under Article 6 of the ICCPR.[66] I will argue below, however, that even if this is the situation in international armed conflicts, in non-international armed conflicts the connection between international human rights law and international humanitarian law is somewhat more complicated.[67] For reasons I shall explain below, in such conflicts one cannot divorce the question of 'lawful acts of war' from issues of due process under international human rights law. I shall try to show that the model for such conflicts must therefore be a mixed model, in which there is interplay of international human rights standards and international humanitarian law.

3 Armed Conflict Model

A *Terrorist Attacks and the Right to Self-Defence*

My main concern in this paper will be with *ius in bello*, i.e., international humanitarian law that applies to the parties involved in an armed conflict. It is important, however, to preface the discussion with a short review of issues of *ius in bellum* that have some relevance for the analysis.

In its recent Advisory Opinion on the *Legal Consequences of the Wall* the ICJ opined that only an attack by a state can constitute the type of armed attack contemplated by Article 51 of the UN Charter.[68] Three of the judges on the Court disassociated themselves from the Court's opinion on this issue,[69] which does not reflect the view of most experts.[70] Despite the ICJ Opinion, I shall assume that a transnational terrorist attack,

65 *Ibid.*, at para. 25. Also see *Report of the Human Rights Inquiry Commission, supra* note 9, at para. 62.

66 They may also be regarded as a legitimate derogation from the right to life, under Art. 15 of the ECHR, which states:

> 'No derogation from Article 2, *except in respect of deaths resulting from lawful acts of war*, or from Articles 3, 4 (paragraph 1) and 7 shall be made under this provision.' (emphasis added).

67 See Gasser, 'International Humanitarian Law and Human Rights Law in Non-international Armed Conflict: Joint Measure or Mutual Exclusion?', 45 *German Ybk Int'l L* (2002) 149.

68 ICJ, *Legal Consequences of the Construction of the Wall in the Occupied Palestinian Territory*, 43 ILM (2004) 1009, at para. 139 (hereinafter *Legal Consequences of the Wall*).

69 See *ibid.*, Separate Opinion of Judge Higgins, at paras. 33–34; Separate Opinion of Judge Kooijmans, at paras. 35–36; Declaration of Judge Buergenthal, at paras. 5–6.

70 See, e.g., Y. Dinstein, *War, Aggression and Self-Defence* (3rd edn., 2001), at 214; Franck, 'Editorial Comments: Terrorism and the Right of Self-Defence', 94 *AJIL* (2001) 839; Brown, 'Use of Force against Terrorism after September 11th: State Responsibility, Self-Defence and Other Responses', 11 *Cardozo J Int'l & Comp L* (2003) 1; Stahn, 'Terrorist Acts as "Armed Attack": The Right to Self-Defense, Article 51 (1/2) of the UN Charter, and International Terrorism', 27 *Fletcher Forum World Aff.* (2003) 35; Müllerson, '*Jus*

or a series of such attacks, of sufficient scale and effects, may constitute an armed attack that gives rise to the right of a state to use force in self-defence.[71] Even if one rejects this assumption, it is clear that if a state sponsors or controls a terrorist group, and possibly even if it takes no action to prevent use of its territory as a base for terrorist attacks against another state, such attacks may be imputed to the sponsor or host state. In such a case the attacks could certainly be the kind of armed attack contemplated by Article 51.[72]

The right of a state to use force in response to an armed attack by terrorists will depend on the degree of responsibility of the harbouring state for the attack, and possibly on its willingness or capability of acting to apprehend the terrorists and prevent them from carrying out further attacks.[73] Any use of force by the victim state must conform to requirements of necessity and proportionality.[74] Under the necessity principle, the victim state must not respond to the armed attack with force unless other means of defending itself are not available.[75] Furthermore, the aim of using

Ad Bellum and International Terrorism', 32 *Israel Yrbk on HR* (2002) 1; Schmitt, *supra* note 48. For the view that an attack by non-state actors cannot be an Art. 51 armed attack see Discussion Forum, *The Attack on the WTC: Legal Responses*, Pellet, 'No, This is Not war'; Gaga, 'In What Sense was there an "Armed Attack"?', Discussion forum of the European Journal of International Law, available at http://www.ejil.org/forum_WTC/index.html (last accessed 3 Feb. 2004). Also see Franck, *supra*, who mentions that this view was advanced at a conference of primarily German international lawyers.

71 On the scale required of a terrorist attack in order for it to meet the threshold of an armed attack see A. C. Arend and R. J. Beck, *International Law and the Use of Force* (1993), at 159–62. In the *Nicaragua* case, the ICJ stated that 'the prohibition of armed attacks may apply to sending by a state of armed bands to the territory of another State, if such operation because of its scale and effects, would have been classified as an armed attack rather than a mere frontier incident had it been carried out by regular armed force': *Case Concerning Military and Paramilitary Activities in and against Nicaragua (Nicaragua v United States)*, Merits [1986] ICJ Rep 14, at para. 195. And see Schachter, *supra* note 24, at 248. Schachter mentions that the attacks must be 'sufficiently grave to jeopardize the essential interest of the State in protecting its citizens and political order' and be 'part of a pattern of attacks accompanied by credible indications that future attacks are planned'. This also seems to be the view of Cassese, 'The International Community's "Legal" Response to Terrorism', 38 *ICLQ* (1989) 589. Cassese argues that not only must the attack be very serious, but it must form part of 'a consistent pattern of violent terrorist action rather than just being isolated or sporadic attacks': *ibid.*, at 596.

72 On the question of state responsibility for a terrorist attack see Travalio and Altenburg, 'State Responsibility for Sponsorship of Terrorist and Insurgent Groups: Terrorism, State Responsibility, and the Use of Military Force', 4 *Ch J Int'l L* (2003) 97; Jinks, 'State Responsibility for Sponsorship of Terrorist and Insurgent Groups: State Responsibility for the Acts of Private Armed Groups', *ibid.*, at 83; Brown, *supra* note 70; Frank and Rehman, 'Assessing the Legality of the Attacks by the International Coalition Against Al-Qaeda and the Taleban in Afghanistan: An Inquiry into the Self-Defense Argument Under Article 51 of the UN Charter', 67 *J Crim L* (2003) 415; Schmitt, *supra* note 48.

73 See Müllerson, *supra* note 70, and Schmitt, *supra* note 48, who both argue that even if the host state cannot be regarded as being responsible for the armed attack, if it is unwilling or unable to prevent the terrorist activities in its territory the victim state may use force against the terrorists.

74 See *Nicaragua* case, *supra* note 71, at para. 176; *Nuclear Weapons* case, *supra* note 63, at para. 41, and *Oil Platforms (Islamic Republic of Iran v USA)* 6 Nov. 2003, available at http://www.icj-cij.org/icjwww/idocket/iop/iopjudgment/iop_ijudgment_20031106.PDF (last accessed 19 June 2004), at paras. 73-77. Also see C. Gray, *International Law and the Use of Force* (2nd edn., 2004), at 120–126; Dinstein, *supra* note 70, at 207–213; Schmitt, *supra* note 48.

75 See Dinstein, *supra* note 70, at 198, who claims that 'reliance by the victim state on counter-force is contingent on its first seeking in vain a peaceful solution to the dispute'. Also see Cassese, *supra* note 71, at 597.

force must be future-oriented, i.e., halting or repelling an attack. This would seem to exclude attacks whose aim is punitive or retaliatory.[76] Under the proportionality principle the defensive measures should not exceed the degree of force needed to achieve the purpose of using counter-force, namely, defending the victim state against further terrorist attacks.[77]

Following the 9/11 attack on the US, there was a major debate whether this attack gave the US the right to use force against Afghanistan.[78] There did not, however, seem to be any disagreement over one issue: if the US was entitled to use force against Afghanistan in response to the attack, it was legitimate for it to target not only members of the armed forces of that country (presumably the Taliban), but members of al-Qaeda too. Intuitively, this seems self-evident. If a terrorist group mounts an armed attack against a state, that group obviously presents the threat against which the victim state is entitled to defend itself. The problem is that any act in self-defence must be compatible with norms of international humanitarian law.[79] And in order for an attack on members of a terrorist group to meet this requirement we have to adopt one of two theories:

1. The original armed attack, or the armed response of the victim state, has created an international armed conflict between the victim state and the host state, and within the context of this conflict the terrorists are legitimate targets; or
2. Whether or not an international armed conflict exists between the victim and host states, an armed conflict has been created between the victim state and the terrorist group, and within the context of this conflict the terrorists are legitimate targets.

I shall now examine the validity of these theories in international humanitarian law.

[76] See Gray, *supra* note 74, at 121; S.A. Alexandrov, *Self-Defence Against the Use of Force in International Law* (1996), at 184. Based on this requirement it has been argued that the legality of the US attack on Afghanistan following 11 Sept. was questionable, since it was not clear whether the US feared a further attack or was merely retaliating: Quigley, 'The Afghanistan War and Self-Defense', 37 *Valparaiso U LR* (2003) 541, at 561; Gray, *supra* note 74, at 167–172. But see Dinstein, *supra* note 70, at 199, who argues that what he terms 'defensive armed reprisals', whose object is future-oriented, and not purely punitive, may meet the necessity test. Also see Coll, 'The Legal and Moral Adequacy of Military Responses to Terrorism', 81 *Am Soc'y Int'l L Proc* (1987) 287, 297 and the remarks of Roberts, *ibid.*, at 318. And cf. the remarks of Boyle, *ibid.*, at 293–294; Rowles, 'Responses to Terrorism: Substantive and Procedural Constraints in International Law', *ibid.*, at 313.

[77] See Schmitt, *supra* note 48. But cf. Arend and Beck, *supra* note 71, at 165, who distinguish between three approaches to the proportionality requirement in this context: 'tit-for-tat' proportionality; 'cumulative' proportionality; and 'deterrent' proportionality.

[78] See, e.g., Murphy, 'Terrorism and the Concept of "Armed Attack" in Article 51 of the U.N. Charter', 43 *Harv Int'l LJ* (2002) 41; Bassiouni, 'Legal Control of International Terrorism: a Policy Oriented Assessment', 43 *Harv Int'l LJ* (2002) 83; Beard, 'Military Action against Terrorists under International Law: America's New War on Terror: The Case for Self-Defense under International Law', 25 *Harv J L & Pub Pol'y* (2002) 559; Byers, 'Terrorism, the Use of Force and International Law After 11 September', 51 *ICLQ* (2002) 401; Quigley, *supra* note 76; Gray, *supra* note 74, at 167–172.

[79] See Dinstein, *supra* note 70, at 195.

B *International Humanitarian Law*

When force is used against terrorists in a state regarded as responsible for an armed attack, an international armed conflict may be said to exist between the victim state and the host state.[80] But can an armed conflict exist between a victim state and an international terrorist group? And if so, what kind of conflict is this?

1 *International and Non-International Armed Conflicts*

The prevailing view seems to be that the very notion of an *international* armed conflict implies that the conflict is between states.[81] On the other hand, the typical non-international conflict contemplated in IHL instruments is a conflict between the authorities of a state and insurgents or rebels in its territory. Both Common Article 3 of the Geneva Conventions and Article 1(1) of Additional Protocol II to the Geneva Conventions relate to conflicts *occurring within the territory of a state party*.[82] This would seem to imply that the rules and principles regarding non-international conflicts are reserved for internal domestic armed conflicts, and do not apply to a conflict between a state and a terrorist group acting from outside its territory.

There is some debate in the literature whether a conflict between a state and a transnational terrorist group may constitute an armed conflict in international

[80] In its decision in the *Tädic* case, the Appeals Chamber of the ICTY held that an 'armed conflict exists whenever there is resort to armed force between States . . . ': *Prosecutor v Tädic* (Decision on the Defence Motion of Interlocutory Appeal on Jurisdiction), 2 Oct. 1995, App. Ch., IT-94-1-AR72, 35 ILM (1996) 32 (hereinafter: *Tädic , Jurisdiction Appeal*), at para. 70. Similarly the ICRC Commentaries on the Geneva Conventions state: '[a]ny difference arising between two States and leading to the intervention of armed forces is an armed conflict within the meaning of Article 2, even if one of the Parties denies the existence of a state of war. It makes no difference how long the conflict lasts, or how much slaughter takes place': ICRC, *Commentary on Convention (I) for the Amelioration of the Condition of the Wounded and Sick in Armed Forces in the Field. Geneva, 12 August 1949*, at 32.

[81] See Jinks, 'September 11 and the Law of War', 28 *Yale J Int'l L* (2003) 20. In the *Tädic* case, the Appeals Chamber of the ICTY stated:

> 'It is indisputable that an armed conflict is international if it takes place between two or more States. In addition, in case of an internal armed conflict breaking out on the territory of a State, it may become international (or, depending upon the circumstances, be international in character alongside an internal armed conflict) if (i) another State intervenes in that conflict through its troops, or alternatively if (ii) some of the participants in the internal armed conflict act on behalf of that other State. With the exception of Common Article 3, which shall be discussed below, the four Geneva Conventions of 1949 only apply to armed conflicts between states parties.'

Prosecutor v Tädic, Judgment, 15 July 1999, App. Ch., IT-94-1-A, at para. 84 (hereinafter: *Tädic, Merits Appeal*).

[82] Common Art. 3 of the Geneva Conventions refers to 'the case of armed conflict not of an international character occurring in the territory of one of the High Contracting Parties . . . '. Art. 1(1) of APII states that the Protocol applies only to non-international armed conflicts that 'take place in the territory of a High Contracting Party between its armed forces and dissident armed forces or other organised armed groups which, under responsible command, exercise such control over a part of its territory as to enable them to carry out sustained and concerted military operations and to implement [the] protocol'. The threshold for a non-international armed conflict under the API is much higher than that required under Common Art. 3. But this issue does not interest us here. The differences between Common Art. 3 and APII armed conflicts are discussed at length by Moir, *supra* note 25.

190 *EJIL* 16 (2005), 171–212

law.[83] Even though international instruments on IHL do not expressly address such conflicts, the implications of giving a negative answer to this question – that the parties are not subject to rules of IHL – should convince us that this answer should be rejected. Rather, we should choose between two possibilities: stretching the definition of an international armed conflict beyond an inter-state conflict, or widening the definition of a non-international conflict so as to include an armed conflict between a state and non-state actors, even if it is not in its own territory.

2 *Armed Conflicts with Terrorists as International Armed Conflicts*

Under the law of international armed conflicts the only legitimate aim of force is weakening the *military* potential of the enemy.[84] According to the fundamental principle of distinction, the parties must distinguish between combatants and civilians, and between military and non-military targets. In order to facilitate respect for this principle, combatants must distinguish themselves from other persons. Those who do not do so become 'unlawful' or 'non-privileged' combatants, who lose the privileges of combatants discussed below.[85] The distinction between combatants and civilians is clear: anyone who is not a combatant is, by definition, a civilian.[86] While combatants enjoy the privilege to fight, civilians are not permitted to do so and may be tried and punished if they do. Furthermore, civilians taking a direct part in hostilities lose their immunity from attack and become legitimate targets.[87]

Under this model whether an individual may be targeted and killed with impunity is generally dependent on his or her status rather than his or her actions.[88] If the

[83] See e.g., Goldman, 'Certain Legal Questions and Issues Raised by the September 11th Attacks', 9 *Hum Rts Brief* (2001) 2, arguing that the answer is positive; and cf. Discussion Forum, *The Attack on the WTC: Legal Responses*, Pellet, 'No, This is not war' and Gaga, 'In What Sense was there an "Armed Attack"?', both *supra* note 70, arguing the opposite. Also see Müllerson, *supra* note 70, at 36–44. The issue is addressed more fully below, in the text accompanying notes 107–121.

[84] This principle, originally adopted in the St. Petersburg Declaration Renouncing the Use, in Time of War, of Explosive Projectiles Under 400 Grammes Weight, 1868, is today reflected in the principle that the parties to an international conflict shall direct their operations only against military objectives: Art. 48 of API.

[85] The term 'unlawful combatant' dates back to *Ex Parte Quirin et al.*, 317 US (1942) 1, in which the US Supreme Court held that 4 German soldiers who were landed on the US coast during WWII, and proceeded in civilian dress to NYC, could be tried before a military commission for attempting to commit hostile acts against the US. The Court held that by passing US boundaries in order to destroy military targets 'without uniform or other emblem signifying their belligerent status, or by discarding that means of identification after entry, such enemies become unlawful belligerents subject to trial and punishment'. The question whether there is indeed a special category of 'unlawful combatants' and, if so, what this implies, has been the subject of great controversy. Nevertheless, the term 'unlawful' or 'unprivileged' combatant is widely used: see, e.g., *Report on Terrorism and Human Rights*, *supra* note 39, at para. 69; D. Fleck (ed.), *The Handbook of Humanitarian Law in Armed Conflicts* (1995), at para. 302; Dinstein, 'Unlawful Combatancy', 32 *Israel Yrbk on HR* (2002) 247; Dormann, 'The Legal Situation of "Unlawful/unprivileged Combatants"', 85 *IRRC* (849) (2003) 85; Col. K.W. Watkin, *Combatants, Unprivileged Belligerents and Conflicts in the 21st Century*, HPCR Policy Brief, Jan. 2003, available at http://www/hsph.harvard.edu/ hpcr (last accessed 25 Feb. 2004). It seems to me that the term now refers to persons who take an active part in hostilities although they do not meet the legal definition of combatants. I shall refer to such persons below, in the text accompanying notes 122–127.

[86] See Art. 50 of API.

[87] See Art. 51(3) of API.

[88] The exception is the case of a civilian who takes a direct part in hostilities. I shall discuss this in detail below, in the text accompanying notes 93–103.

individual is a combatant he or she becomes a legitimate target, whether or not he or she *personally* endangers the lives or interests of the other party to the conflict.[89] Furthermore, once an armed conflict exists, it is not incumbent on the army of the one party to inquire whether members of a military unit of the other party wish to surrender before attacking it. The onus is on the party that wishes to surrender and thereby prevent attack to make this wish clear.[90] The legality of an attack on a military unit is not dependent on the imminency of military action by that unit against the state of the attacking army.

Seemingly this is a closed model. One is either a combatant or a civilian. How do members of terrorist groups fit into this model? Assuming that there is an international armed conflict between two or more states, what is their status? They can be regarded as combatants only if they fall into one of two categories:

1. they are part of the armed forces of a state that is a party to the conflict; or
2. they are part of another armed group belonging to such a state which fulfils the four conditions laid out in Article 4(A)(2) of Geneva Convention III:
   a. being under responsible command;
   b. wearing a fixed distinctive sign;
   c. carrying arms openly; and
   d. conducting their operations in accordance with the laws and customs of war.[91]

International terrorists are generally not part of the armed forces of a given state, and even if they meet some of the conditions of Article 4(A)(2) of Geneva Convention III, the nature of their activities, i.e., the deliberate causing of death or serious injury to civilians, means that they never meet the condition in d. above.[92] They therefore do not meet the conditions to be regarded as combatants and must, by definition, be

89 See Walzer, *supra* note 53, at 144–145.

90 See Art. 41 of API, dealing with persons who are *hors de combat*. A person is *hors de combat* if, *inter alia*, 'he clearly expresses an intention to surrender'.

91 See Fleck, *supra* note 85, at para. 304. Under API, the application of the law relating to international armed conflicts was extended so as to apply to armed conflicts in which peoples are fighting against colonial domination, alien occupation, or racist regimes, and members of armed groups of such peoples are also regarded as combatants. For the present purposes I shall not discuss when terrorists could fit into this category, since the API extension of combatant status is not part of customary law, and the API has not been ratified by all states that are parties to the Geneva Conventions. It should be noted, however, that those states which refused to ratify API generally did so because they refused to acknowledge the combatant status of insurgents fighting against them. Most pertinently for the present discussion, API has not been ratified by either the US or Israel. For a discussion of the scope of combatants under API see Greenwood, 'Terrorism and Humanitarian Law – The Debate over Additional Protocol I', 19 *Israel Yrbk on HR* (1989) 187; Dinstein, *supra* note 85.

92 In most cases they would also not be a group belonging to a state involved in the conflict, and would therefore not qualify as combatants even if they met all the conditions: see *Military Prosecutor v Kassem and others*, decision of the Israeli Military Court sitting in Ramallah, 13 Apr. 1969, in M. Sassoli and A. A. Bouvier, *How Does Law Protect in War?* (1999), at 806. They would usually also not meet the conditions in subsections b. and c of Art. 4 A (2).

regarded as civilians.[93] As such, they shall not be the object of attack, 'unless and for such time as they take a direct part in hostilities'.[94] And indeed, in discussing the status of suspected terrorists in the territories occupied by Israel, Professor Cassese takes the view, based on the assumption that the conflict is an international armed conflict, that members of terrorist groups are to be regarded as civilians to whom this provision applies.[95]

If we adopt this view, the big question is when a terrorist may be regarded as taking a direct part in hostilities. In answering this question a few comments are called for:

1. Whether a particular civilian is taking a direct part in hostilities must be examined on an individual level. In other words, as opposed to targeting of combatants, which is based on their status, civilians may only be targeted because of their individual actions. The mere fact that a person belongs to a group, which promotes or carries out terrorist attacks, does not imply that he or she takes a *direct* part in hostilities. This would seem to imply that a state may never attack members of a terrorist group, as such, but would always have to concentrate on targeting specific terrorists.
2. What are 'hostilities'? According to the ICRC Commentary on Additional Protocol I (API), 'Hostile acts should be understood to be acts which by their nature and purpose are intended to cause actual harm to the personnel and equipment of the armed forces.'[96] This appears to be a somewhat narrow definition that would exclude terrorist acts, which, by definition, are intended to cause harm to civilians. Nevertheless, in his opinion to the Israel Supreme Court in the pending case on targeted killings, Professor Antonio Cassese does not contest that terrorist attacks on civilians are hostilities, within the meaning of Article 51(3) of API.
3. What activities will be regarded as a *direct* part in hostilities? Are planning a terrorist attack, manufacturing the explosives and supplying them included? And what about support of another nature? In a passage that adds little to the description of hostile acts, the ICRC Commentary on API merely states that '"direct" participation means acts of war which by their nature or purpose are likely to cause actual harm to the personnel and equipment of the enemy armed forces'.[97] On the other hand, in the commentary on the Joint Services Regulations of the *Bundeswehr*, the term is widened to include 'civilians who operate a weapons system, supervise such operation, or service such equipment' as well as 'preparation for a military operation and intention to take part therein', provided they are directly related to hostilities and 'represent a direct threat to the enemy'.[98]

93 See Brown, *supra* note 70, at 24–25, n. 112; Watkin, *supra* note 85, at 10. Also see Dinstein, *supra* note 70.

94 See Art. 51(3) of API. This provision is widely regarded as part of customary international law. But see *infra* note 99.

95 See *Cassese opinion* (on file with the author), at 16–18.

96 See ICRC, *Commentary on Protocol Additional to the Geneva Conventions of 12 August 1949, and relating to the Protection of Victims of International Armed Conflicts (Protocol I), 8 June 1977*, at para. 1942.

97 *Ibid.*, at para. 1944.

98 See Fleck, *supra* note 85, at 232.

4. Article 51(3) refers to such time as the civilians are taking a direct part in the hostilities. In the opinion mentioned above, Professor Cassese is adamant that this term must be given a narrow meaning. It is only while the persons are actually engaged in carrying out their hostile acts that they may be targeted. As soon as they have completed the hostile act, they once again enjoy the same protection as every other civilian. This view is supported by the ICRC Commentary on API.[99]

If we accept this narrow interpretation, terrorists enjoy the best of both worlds – they can remain civilians most of the time and only endanger their protection as civilians while actually in the process of carrying out a terrorist act. Is this theory, which has been termed the 'revolving door' theory,[100] tenable? The Inter-American Commission on Human Rights seemed to have its doubts.[101] So do some experts. It has been argued that the contemporary definition of civilians should rest on their inoffensive character and that civilians 'can lose their civilian status whenever they become "offensive" – that is, whenever they take action against military forces or their fellow citizens'.[102] Another argument is that a 'combatant-like' approach based on membership in the military wing of a group involved in hostilities, rather than on individual actions, should be adopted in deciding whether persons may be targeted.[103]

If we adopt the restricted theory, according to which international terrorists are civilians who may only be targeted while taking a direct part in hostilities, the right of self-defence under Article 51 of the UN Charter following an armed attack by a terrorist group may become meaningless. As any action carried out in self-defence must comply with *ius in bello*, targeting the terrorists regarded as responsible for the attack will not be lawful unless they are targeted while carrying out an attack. This does not seem to make much sense. As noted above, none of the experts who discussed the US response to the 9/11 attack contested that such force could be directed against al-Qaeda members in Afghanistan.

99 ICRC, *Commentary on Protocol Additional*, *supra* note 96, at para. 1944. And see Watkin, *supra* note 85, at 11–12; Behnsen, 'The Status of Mercenaries and Other Illegal Combatants Under International Humanitarian Law', 46 *German Ybk of Int'l L* (2003) 494, at 504. In its brief to the Supreme Court of Israel, the government argues, *inter alia*, that the wide definition of Art. 51(3), which speaks not only of taking a direct part in hostilities (language similar to that used in Common Art. 3 of the Geneva Conventions), but also 'for such time' as they participate, does not reflect customary international law. Support for this view may be found in Art. 8(2)(b)(i) of the Rome Statute on the ICC, which, in defining the crime involved in violence against civilians, omits reference to the words 'for such time'.

100 See Parks, 'Air War and the Laws of War', 32 *Air Force LR* (1990) 1, at 118–120; Watkin, *supra* note 85, at 12.

101 Report on *Terrorism and Human Rights*, *supra* note 39, at para. 69. In discussing Art. 51(3) of API the Commission stated that non-combatants who take a direct part in hostilities temporarily forfeit their immunity from direct individualized attack during such time as they assume the role of combatant. The Commission added: 'It is possible in this connection, however, that once a person qualifies as a combatant, whether regular or irregular, privileged or unprivileged, he or she cannot revert back to civilian status or otherwise alternate between combatant and civilian status'. And see Parks, *supra* note 100, who claims that under customary international law a civilian who crossed the line and committed combatant like acts could not revert to being a civilian and was a legitimate target.

102 Slaughter and Burke-White, *supra* note 17, at 13.

103 Watkin, *supra* note 18, at 16–17.

194 EJIL 16 (2005), 171–212

Aware of the inadequacies of a theory of self-defence which makes it unlawful to attack the very people who threaten the state, Michael N. Schmitt argues that '[s]tates should not be prevented from acting in self-defence by targeting individual terrorists simply because the mode of conflict exists on a different level'.[104] Schmitt argues that 'a state generally may target those reasonably believed to represent a violent threat to it'.[105] He suggests that four factors are relevant in determining the reasonableness of the belief that such a threat exists: the past practices of the terrorist group; whether the group has articulated goals which suggest a long-term conflict with the target state; whether contemporary events have exacerbated or relaxed tensions; and whether intelligence information shows that there are activities underway which suggest that an operation is being planned.[106]

That persons who do not belong to the armed forces of a party to the conflict, or do not have many of the characteristics of such forces, are to be regarded as civilians is understandable when the real armed conflict involved is between states. In such a situation a theory which posits that all persons who are not part of the fighting forces are to be regarded as civilians is not only credible; it is essential if we are to ensure respect for the principle of distinction. In this context, restricting the right to target civilians taking a direct part in hostilities to the actual time when they are so engaged can be explained not only because of the need to frustrate an imminent threat, but also on the evidentiary grounds mentioned above in the discussion of the imminency requirement in human rights law. When a person is actually taking part in hostilities, the evidence is before us, and we do not face difficult evidentiary issues, such as identification and credibility of intelligence sources.

When the armed conflict is essentially between a state and the terrorist group, the theory that the terrorists are civilians simply does not make sense. An armed conflict model of law (as opposed to a law-enforcement model) cannot be applicable if only one party to the conflict has combatants. If we concede, as many do, that protracted violence between an organized terrorist group and a state may constitute an armed conflict ruled by international humanitarian law, we have to find another, more feasible theory. Does that theory lie in regarding such a conflict as a non-international conflict?

3 *Armed Conflicts with Terrorists as Non-International Armed Conflicts*

Given the difficulties in regarding a conflict between a state and a trans-national terrorist group as an international armed conflict, it has been argued that such an armed conflict must be regarded as a non-international conflict.[107] This argument faces two difficulties.

As mentioned above, the definitions of a non-international armed conflict adopted in Common Article 3 of the Geneva Conventions and APII both refer to a conflict *within the territory of a state party*. Thus, even if we are to regard the conflict between

[104] Schmitt, *supra* note 10, at 648.

[105] *Ibid.*, at 649.

[106] *Ibid.* Also see Müllerson, *supra* note 70.

[107] See, e.g., Jinks, *supra* note 82, at 38.

a state and a transnational terrorist group as a non-international armed conflict, it is one to which the 'code on non-international conflicts' does not formally apply. This surely cannot mean, however, that a conflict between a state and a transnational terrorist group can never be an armed conflict, or that it may be an armed conflict to which IHL does not apply. It is difficult to believe that states agreed to the application of part of the norms of IHL to internal armed conflicts, but not to transnational armed conflicts that are not covered by the law regarding international armed conflicts.

There is no substantive reason why the norms that apply to an armed conflict between a state and an organized armed group within its territory should not also apply to an armed conflict with such a group that is not restricted to its territory. It therefore seems to me that to the extent that treaty provisions relating to non-international armed conflicts incorporate standards of customary international law, these standards should apply to all armed conflicts between a state and non-state actors. This means that, at the very least, Common Article 3 will apply to such conflicts.[108] The position in relation to APII is more complicated and we would have to be more discriminating, since not all its provisions have the status of customary law.[109]

While resort to force between states is always a situation in which the rules of international law in general, and international humanitarian law in particular, apply,[110] the general assumption is that violence involving non-state actors is primarily a matter for domestic law, relying on the law-enforcement model. States were reluctant to 'internationalize' internal conflicts, under the assumption that doing so might lend a degree of legitimacy to insurgents and might also unduly limit their own freedom of action in dealing with civil strife. Under APII 'situations of internal disturbances and tensions, such as riots, isolated and sporadic acts of violence and other acts of a similar nature', are expressly excluded from the definition of a non-international armed conflict.[111]

The scope and level of violence required in order for a conflict to be regarded as a non-international armed conflict has never been clearly defined. Acting on the assumption that classification of a conflict as an armed conflict would extend the legal protection offered to those affected, the ICRC has argued for a low threshold of application.[112] The ICTY has held that a non-international armed conflict exists when there is 'protracted armed violence between governmental authorities and organized

[108] In the *Nicaragua* case the ICJ stated that Common Art. 3 'defines certain rules to be applied in the armed conflicts of a non-international character. There is no doubt that, in the event of international armed conflicts, these rules also constitute a minimum yardstick, in addition to the more elaborate rules which are also apply to international conflicts; and they are rules which, in the Court's opinion, reflect what the Court in 1949 called "elementary considerations of humanity" (Corfu Channel, Merits . . .)'. *Nicaragua* case, *supra* note 71, at para. 218. Also see *Tädic, Jurisdiction Appeal*, *supra* note 81, at para. 98, in which the ICTY, citing the *Nicaragua* case, held that Common Art. 3 is part of customary law.

[109] See Moir, *supra* note 25, at 109.

[110] See *supra* note 81.

[111] Art.1(2) of APII. The ICRC, *Commentary on Protocol Additional to the Geneva Conventions*, *supra* note 96, at para. 4378, claims that the decision to exclude internal disturbances was based on the notion that 'these were considered to be covered by the instruments dealing with human rights'.

[112] See Moir, *supra* note 25, at 33.

196 *EJIL* 16 (2005), 171–212

armed groups'.[113] The ICTR added that this violence should also meet a fair level of intensity.[114]

Given the vagueness of the conditions for regarding violent confrontation between a state and non-state actors as an armed conflict, there will be room for disagreement whether a particular conflict between a state and transnational terrorists constitutes an armed conflict at all.[115] In the Israeli case, the authorities declared, soon after violence erupted in September 2000, that the level and scope of violence justified regarding the situation as one of 'armed conflict short of war'.[116] This classification is not shared by all.[117] The reason for the difference of opinion lies in the realization that classification of the confrontation between Israel and armed Palestinian groups as an armed conflict implies not only that protection of IHL is extended, but that the state will enjoy powers that it would not enjoy if the applicable regimes of international law were only the law of belligerent occupation and human rights law.[118]

Classifying an armed conflict with a transnational terrorist group as a non-international armed conflict does not imply that alongside this conflict there is not also an international conflict. The ICJ and the ICTY have held that there may be both international and non-international aspects in a particular conflict situation.[119] If another state is held responsible for an armed attack by a terrorist group, and the victim state responds by attacking the terrorists in that state's territory, an international armed conflict will certainly arise between the two states. Thus, when the US attacked Afghanistan in response to 9/11, claiming that the *de facto* Taliban government of Afghanistan was supporting al-Qaeda, an armed conflict was created between the US and Afghanistan. This surely does not mean that the conflict with al-Qaeda was swallowed up by the conflict with Afghanistan, and that the persons who had mounted the armed attack and presented the real threat to the United States were merely civilians taking a direct part in the hostilities between the states involved. Rather it means that the conflict became one that had both international and non-international aspects.

113 *Tädic case, Jurisdiction, supra* note 81, at para. 70. The ICRC Commentary places emphasis on the level of organization of the non-state actors rather than the level of violence involved: ICRC, *Commentary on the Protocol Additional, supra* note 111, at para. 4341.

114 See *The Prosecutor v Akayesu*, Case ICTR-94-4-T, 2 Sept.1998, at para. 625.

115 As we shall see below, this is one of the major bones of contention in the Israeli/Palestinian situation.

116 See *Sharm el Sheikk Fact-Finding Committee Report* (the *Mitchell Report*), citing from statements submitted by the Government of Israel, available at http://www.mideastweb.org/mitchell_report.htm; government brief submitted in H.C. 769/02 (on file with the author).

117 See, e.g., 'Legal Consequences of Israel's Construction of a Separation Barrier in the Occupied Territories', *International Law Opinion* by Oxford Public Interest Lawyers, Feb. 2004, (on file with author), at para. 115.

118 Thus, e.g., the authors of the *International Law Opinion* challenge the power of the Israeli authorities to seize and destroy property, permitted during hostilities if imperatively demanded by the necessities of war.

119 In the *Nicaragua* case, the ICJ held that that conflict between the contras and the Nicaraguan forces was an armed conflict not of an international character, whereas the conflict between the US and Nicaragua was an international armed conflict: Nicaragua case, *supra* note 71, at para. 219. In the *Tädic* case the ICTY held that an international conflict may exist alongside an internal conflict: *Tädic, Merits Appeal, supra* note 82, at para. 84.

Let us now assume that a conflict between a state and a transnational terrorist group has reached the necessary level and scope of violence so as to constitute a non-international armed conflict. Such a conflict is not a conflict between two collectives, some of whom are combatants, but most of whom are civilians, but between one such collective and an 'organized armed group'.[120] It is nevertheless perfectly clear that the fundamental principle of distinction, which applies in international armed conflicts, applies in such conflicts too. Thus, Article 13(2) of APII explicitly states that 'the civilian population as such, as well as individual civilians, shall not be the object of attack'. Article 13(3) adopts the principle laid out in Article 51(3) of API, namely that civilians shall be protected 'unless and for such time as they take a direct part in hostilities'. Article 8 of the Rome Statute, which defines war crimes in the jurisdiction of the ICC, includes among crimes that may be committed in armed conflicts not of an international character '[i]ntentionally directing attacks against the civilian population as such or against individual civilians not taking direct part in hostilities'.[121]

Use of the term 'civilians' in APII and the Rome Statute is based on the assumption that there must also be 'non-civilians' or combatants. But who is a combatant in a non-international armed conflict? International instruments do not even attempt to answer this question.[122]

The reasons for this lacuna are well known. States were, and still are, unwilling to grant the *status* of combatants to insurgents and other non-state actors who take part in non-international conflicts, as doing so would not only afford them an element of legitimacy, but would mean that they enjoy the two 'privileges' of combatants – immunity from criminal liability for fighting, and prisoner-of-war status when apprehended.[123] But does the lack of combatant *status* mean that there are in fact no combatants in such a conflict? Unless we give a negative answer to this question the protection extended to civilians becomes meaningless. If there are no combatants, all are civilians and there is no need for special provisions protecting them.

It therefore seems almost self-evident that in non-international armed conflicts there are indeed combatants, who, as opposed to civilians, may legitimately be targeted by the other side. Who are they? The answer lies in identifying the parties to the conflict. APII states that a non-international conflict is a conflict between the armed forces of a High Contracting Party 'and dissident armed forces or organized armed groups'.[124] While Common Article 3 of the Geneva Conventions does not state so

[120] Under Common Art. 3 it may also be a conflict between two or more groups of combatants.

[121] Art. 8(2)(e)(i) of the Rome Statute of the International Criminal Court. War crimes in non-international armed conflicts also include '[k]illing or wounding treacherously a *combatant* adversary' (Art. 8(2)(e)(ix), emphasis added).

[122] See Sassoli and Bouvier, *supra* note 92, at 208.

[123] See *Commentary on APII*, *supra* note 111, at para. 4441.

[124] APII, Art. 1. In order for APII to apply there are further conditions, namely that the armed groups are 'under responsible command, [and] exercise such control over part of [the State's] territory as to enable them to carry out sustained and concerted military operations and the implement this Protocol'.

198 *EJIL* 16 (2005), 171–212

expressly, it is agreed that in order for a non-international conflict covered by this article to exist, there must also be an organized group.[125]

The logical conclusion of the definition of a non-international armed conflict as one between the armed forces of a state and an organized armed group is that members of both the armed forces and the organized armed group are combatants. While these combatants do not enjoy the privileges of combatants in an international armed conflict, they may be attacked by the other party to the conflict. This is indeed the view adopted in the ICRC Commentary on APII, which states that '[t]hose who belong to armed forces *or armed groups* may be attacked at any time'.[126] According to this view, if an armed conflict exists between the United States and al-Qaeda, active members of al-Qaeda are combatants who may be targeted. Similarly, if an armed conflict exists between Israel and Hamas, Islamic Jihad and the Fatah/Tanzim in the West Bank and Gaza, active members of these groups are combatants who may legitimately be attacked.[127]

Regarding active members of organized armed groups as combatants who may be attacked raises a number of questions. In the first place, how are such combatants to be distinguished? As opposed to international armed conflicts, in which combatants are required to have 'a fixed distinctive sign recognizable at a distance',[128] absent a definition of 'combatants' in non-international armed conflicts, no similar demand exists. When the combatants are actually engaged in fighting, this may not create special difficulties. But can the opposing party to the conflict (in most cases, the state) be required to fight against combatants only when they are actually fighting? If we answer this in the affirmative there would seem to be no difference between combatants and civilians, as the latter may also be targeted when taking a direct part in hostilities.[129] As we have stressed above, fudging the differences between combatants and civilians would weaken the principles regarding protection of civilians, which form one of the foundations of international humanitarian law.[130]

One possible way out of this difficulty is to tie the definition of combatants to the provision in Common Article 3 of the Geneva Conventions, that persons who take no

125 In discussing non-international conflicts covered by Common Art. 3 of the Geneva Conventions, Pictet states that 'it must be recognized that the conflicts referred to in Article 3 are armed conflicts, with "armed forces" on either side engaged in "hostilities" – conflicts, in short, which are in many respects similar to an international war, but take place within the confines of a single country': ICRC, *Commentary on Geneva Convention (III) relative to the Treatment of Prisoners of War. Geneva, 12 August 1949*, at 37. Also see Moir, *supra* note 25, at 36; *Tădic, Jurisdiction Appeal*, *supra* note 81, at para. 70.

126 *Commentary on APII*, *supra* note 111, at para. 4789 (emphasis added).

127 This is indeed the view of Ben-Naftali and Michaeli, *supra* note 21, at 271. Also see Ni Aolain, *supra* note 34, at 241. In her discussion of the application of IHL in Northern Ireland the writer states: 'The corollary of this in Northern Ireland is that killing members of paramilitary organizations, if they are recognized as insurgents, is generally unproblematic if carried out in accordance with the laws of war. Additionally, the rules allow that a combatant need not be given a warning before being killed'.

128 Art. 4 A(2) of Geneva Convention III.

129 Common Art. 3 offers protection to 'persons taking no active part in the hostilities'. Art. 13 of APII forbids use of force against civilians, 'unless and for such time as they take a direct part in hostilities'.

130 Schmitt, 'The Principle of Discrimination in 21st Century Warfare', 2 *Yale HR & Dev LJ* (1999) 143, at 160-161; Dinstein, *supra* note 85, at 249.

active part in the hostilities shall be protected from violence to their life and body. Thus, combatants are only those persons who take an active part in hostilities.[131] Note, however, that this does not mean that such persons are combatants only for such time as they take part in the hostilities, but merely that their actual participation is what makes them combatants, and not their membership in a certain organization.[132] The conclusion would be that while the armed conflict continues members of the terrorist group who have taken an active part in hostilities are combatants who may be targeted.[133] Other persons are civilians who may only be targeted 'for such time as they take a direct part in hostilities'.[134]

It would seem that this was the approach taken by the UN Human Rights Inquiry Commission established by the Commission on Human Rights soon after the present *intifada* started. The inquiry commission adopted the view that *if* an armed conflict existed between Israel and Palestinian armed groups in the Occupied Territories (a question on which it found it difficult to make a final judgment), that conflict was a non-international conflict. It then stated that it found the Israeli argument that persons targeted were combatants 'unconvincing for two related reasons: they were not participating in the hostilities at the time they were killed; and no evidence was provided by Israel to back up its contention of a combat role despite their civilian appearance.'[135] The implication would appear to be that a person is a legitimate target while he or she is taking a direct part in hostilities (whether a combatant or a civilian) or *if there is other evidence of his or her combatant role.*

One of the obvious difficulties in this approach is the sort of evidence required to establish a combatant role.[136] In many cases such evidence will be based on intelligence information. But in other cases, leaders of a terrorist group may be involved who have made no bones about their role in the terrorist activities of the group.[137]

131 This seems to be the approach of Rodley, *supra* note 31, at 189. Also see Watkin, *supra* note 85, at 14.

132 The question which characteristics of combatant status are group characteristics and which are individual characteristics is discussed by Watkin, *ibid*, at 9–10.

133 See Ni Aolain, *supra* note 34, at 239, who claims that '[i]n a Common Article 3 armed conflict, the killing of an unarmed combatant, even if not immediately engaged in military activity, is legally unproblematic'.

134 APII, Art. 13(3).

135 *Report of the Human Rights Inquiry Commission*, *supra* note 9, at para. 62.

136 I shall not deal here with the question whether a state is obliged in advance to provide such evidence. A state may have to do so when called to account for its actions, but that does not mean that in the course of an armed conflict it has to provide evidence for all its acts: see Franck, *supra* note 70, at 842. In responding to the argument that the right of self-defence arises only upon proof that it is being directed against the actual attacker, Franck states that 'the right of a state to defend itself against attack is not subordinated in law to a *prior* requirement to demonstrate to the satisfaction of the Security Council that it is acting against the party guilty of the attack. The law does have an evidentiary requirement, but it arises after, not before, the right to self-defence is exercised.'

137 See, e.g., the interview with Salah Shehadeh, head of the 'Izz Al-Din Al-Qassam Brigades, the military wing of Hamas, who was killed by the IDF on 23 July 2002, published in Islam Online on 29 May 2002 and available at http://www.islam-online.net/arabic/politics/2002/05/article25.shtml (last accessed 19 June 2004). An English translation of the interview is available at http://www.bridgesforpeace.com/publications/dispatch/generaltopics/Article-2.html (last accessed 19 June 2004).

200 *EJIL* 16 (2005), 171–212

Defining combatants as members of terrorist groups who take an active part in hostilities forces us to distinguish between organized armed groups whose members are all actively involved in the hostilities, whether by planning, directing or executing attacks, and organizations that have both military and political branches. In the case of the latter, only members of the military branch may be regarded as combatants.[138] Targeting members of the political branch should be regarded as assassinations, which are outlawed even in the course of an armed conflict.[139]

Accepting that persons actively involved in the terrorist activities of an international terrorist group are combatants in a non-international armed conflict would seem to solve the problem involved in the tight definition of combatants in international armed conflicts. While the victim state does not have to accord such terrorists POW status if captured, nor are they immune from prosecution for fighting, they are legitimate targets. States would probably be very happy with this result, which allows *them* to enjoy the best of both worlds. But this is the very problem. Are we back to a licence to kill all persons suspected of being active members of the international terrorist group? How can we be sure that the targeted persons are indeed real terrorists? Doesn't this licence create an incentive for victim states to jump as soon as possible from the law-enforcement to the non-international armed conflict model, thus allowing them to ignore due process guarantees and to enjoy almost unrestricted discretion in targeting their suspected enemies? It would seem to me that these difficulties should lead us to the conclusion that the non-international armed conflict model cannot stand on its own. I shall return to the way in which it should be mitigated below.

4 *Proportionality*

Even if suspected terrorists are legitimate targets, every use of targeting must meet the demands of proportionality. Targeting a suspected terrorist will be regarded as an indiscriminate attack if it 'may be expected to cause incidental loss of civilian life, injury to civilians, damage to civilian objects, or a combination thereof, which would be excessive in relation to the concrete and direct military advantage anticipated'.[140] While this principle is as firmly entrenched in IHL as any, it is notoriously difficult to apply.[141] As the Committee Established to Review the NATO Bombing Campaign against the Federal Republic of Yugoslavia, stated in its report to the ICTY Prosecutor:

> The main problem with the principle of proportionality is not whether or not it exists but what it means and how it is to be applied. It is relatively simple to state that there must be an acceptable relation between the legitimate destructive effect and undesirable collateral effects. . . . It is much easier to formulate the principle of proportionality in general terms than it is to apply it to a particular set of circumstances because the comparison is often between unlike quantities

138 See Watkin, *supra* note 85, at 16.

139 David, *supra* note 15.

140 Art. 51(5)(b) of API. It is true that that provision refers to international armed conflicts but it clearly reflects a principle of customary international law that applies in all armed conflicts.

141 Gardam, 'Proportionality and Force in International Law', 87 *AJIL* (1993) 391; Ben-Naftali and Michaeli, *supra* note 21, at 278.

and values. One cannot easily assess the value of innocent human lives as opposed to capturing a particular military objective.[142]

How does one assess the concrete and direct military advantage gained by targeting a suspected terrorist? The state involved will probably claim that it has prevented terrorist attacks, which would have cost the lives of many civilians. Is such an assessment sufficient to show a concrete and direct military advantage? And assuming the answer is positive, how does one balance that advantage against the loss of life among innocent bystanders likely to be killed in the targeted killing? And are there cases, as the Israeli authorities argue, that even if it is totally certain that civilians (such as family members of the suspected terrorist) will be killed in the targeting, the targeting will still meet the proportionality test?

I shall not venture to provide a full answer to these questions. It seems to me that an extremely strong case has to be made to justify an attack on suspected terrorists when it is likely, not to mention inevitable, that the attack will cause the death of civilians. After all, unless the said terrorists are involved in a concrete terrorist attack that is about to take place and can only be thwarted by targeting them, the military advantages to be gained by targeting them are based largely on speculation. Can the assessment that an attack on civilians by the suspected terrorist might take place outweigh the high and concrete likelihood that the attack on the suspected terrorist will cause the death and wounding of other civilians?

Proportionality must be judged on the basis of the information available at the time of the attack, and not on the actual results. Nevertheless, when as a result of an attack innocent persons are killed or wounded, a heavy burden rests on the state to show either that this could not reasonably have been foreseen, or that even if it could have been foreseen, the necessity of the attack was great enough to justify the risk.

4 The Mixed Model

The analysis so far has been based on an either-or situation. Either we adopt the law-enforcement model or the armed conflict model. But neither of these models provides an adequate framework for dealing with transnational terror. The law-enforcement model is not suitable when the scale of violence has reached that of a non-international armed conflict and the terrorists operate from the territory of a state that is either unwilling or incapable of cooperating in law enforcement. The armed conflict model was not developed with the case of international terror in mind. Under the rules of international armed conflicts, terrorists are generally not combatants and may therefore only be attacked for such time as they take a direct part in hostilities, a legal conclusion that does not seem credible when the very conflict is between the victim state and the transnational terrorist group. On the other hand, if an armed

[142] *Final Report to the Prosecutor by the Committee Established to Review the NATO Bombing Campaign Against the Federal Republic of Yugoslavia*, available at http://www.un.org/icty/pressreal/nato061300.htm (last accessed 19 June 2004), at para 48. For a scathing criticism of the legal analysis in this report see Colangelo, 'Manipulating International Criminal Procedure: The Decision of the ICTY Office of the Independent Prosecutor not to Investigate NATO Bombing in the Former Yugoslavia', 97 *NW U LR* (2003) 1393.

conflict with a terrorist group is regarded as a non-international conflict, the state would seem to enjoy almost unlimited power to target persons it claims to be active members of that group, even when they pose no immediate danger and it might be feasible to apprehend them and place them on trial.

Extension of some of the rules of international law relating to armed conflicts to non-international armed conflicts was meant to extend the protection offered by IHL to cases in which it had not traditionally applied.[143] The assumption seems to have been that this was required not only so that these rules would apply to non-state actors, but also because if they were not extended the way such conflicts were handled was entirely within the domestic jurisdiction of the state involved.[144] This assumption may have been understandable at the time, as the first major step in international regulation of non-international armed conflicts, i.e. the adoption of Common Article 3 of the 1949 Geneva Conventions, was taken before the detailed development of international human rights law.

Following the dramatic development of international human rights law, it is no longer the case that if IHL is not applicable to non-international armed conflicts, states will have *carte blanche* to fight those conflicts as they see fit. On the contrary, in the type of non-international armed conflicts contemplated by Common Article 3 and APII, the state's freedom of action will be constrained by the standards of international human rights law. This means, *inter alia*, that the state will be prohibited from arbitrarily depriving individuals of their lives or personal liberty and that it will be bound to afford all persons accused of offences a fair trial before an independent and competent court. Any consideration of the legal regime applying in armed conflicts in general, and especially in non-international armed conflicts, must take these standards into account.[145]

An armed conflict between a state and a transnational terrorist group is not an international armed conflict. However, as it transcends the borders of the state involved it does not fully fit the model of a non-international armed conflict either. Applying human rights standards to such a conflict also faces a serious impediment. As the suspected terrorists are not within the jurisdiction of the victim state, one of the fundamental assumptions of the regimes contemplated in human rights treaties is lacking. While this impediment cannot simply be ignored, it should not lead to the conclusion that human rights standards may be abandoned. These standards must be maintained at all times. However, in their application the special features of a non-international conflict must be taken into account.

The only acceptable justification for targeting suspected terrorists is protection of potential victims of terrorist acts. Under ordinary human rights principles, based on a law-enforcement model with its guarantees of due process, use of lethal force to defend persons against unlawful violence is justified only when absolutely necessary.

143 For a history of the application of rules of international law to non-international armed conflicts, see Moir, *supra* note 25, at 1–16; *Commentary on Geneva Convention (III)*, *supra* note 125, at 28–35; *Commentary on Protocol II*, *supra* note 111, at paras. 4337–4418.

144 See UK Ministry of Defence, *The Manual of the Law of Armed Conflict* (2004), at para. 1.33.3.

145 See Ben-Naftali and Michaeli, *supra* note 21; Ben-Naftali and Shani, *supra* note 58; Watkin, *supra* note 18.

As seen above, the accepted view is that this test will be met only when force is used to stop an imminent attack. In other cases, law enforcement mechanisms must be employed. When the terrorists are not subject to the law enforcement jurisdiction of the victim state, and we are talking about violence of the scale and intensity required for the situation to be regarded as one of armed conflict, the parameters of absolute necessity have to be reconsidered.

When judging if use of force to defend potential victims of attacks by terrorists operating from outside the territory of the victim state is absolutely necessary, whether alternative law enforcement measures are available becomes a crucial question. As the object of such force must always be to prevent further attacks, rather than to punish, or even to seek general deterrence, I suggest that in deciding whether targeting suspected terrorists could be regarded as absolutely necessary we draw a parallel to a state's inherent right to self-defence under Article 51 of the UN Charter. In exercising this right, a state's actions are subject to the requirements of necessity and proportionality.[146] Under the principle of necessity, a state may not use force if there are other means of defending itself. In the present context the implication is that a state may not target suspected terrorists if there is a reasonable possibility of apprehending them and putting them on trial. Whether apprehension, arrest and trial are reasonable alternatives will depend on whether the victim state has effective control over the territory in which the terrorists are operating, and if it does not, on the degree of willingness or capability of the *de facto* force in control of that territory to arrest and try the terrorists, to extradite them, or, at the very least, to take effective steps to stop their activities.

As opposed to the general rule in armed conflicts, under which a party may target combatants of the other side even when they pose no immediate danger, under the necessity requirement the targeting of suspected terrorists must be restricted to cases in which there is credible evidence that the targeted persons are actively involved in planning or preparing further terrorist attacks against the victim state and no other operational means of stopping those attacks are available. As there is always a risk that the persons attacked are not in fact terrorists, even in such a case lethal force may be used against the suspected terrorists only when a high probability exists that if immediate action is not taken another opportunity will not be available to frustrate the planned terrorist attacks.[147]

Use of lethal force must always conform to the proportionality test. In this context this test should be based on balancing three factors: 1. the danger to life posed by the continued activities of the terrorists; 2. the chance of the danger to human life being realized if the activities of the suspected terrorist are not halted immediately; and 3. the danger that civilians will be killed or wounded in the attack on the suspected terrorist. As mentioned in the discussion above of the proportionality test, a heavy burden rests on the state to justify killing or wounding of civilians during an attack on

[146] See Schmitt, *supra* note 48.

[147] *Ibid.*, at 110.

suspected terrorists. The presumption should be that suspected terrorists may not be targeted when there is a real danger that civilians will be killed or wounded too.

There is no doubt that conceding the power of a state to target suspected terrorists, even in strictly limited circumstances, creates a real danger that states will adopt a liberal interpretation of those circumstances and will in fact use this exceptional measure as a general policy. Many will obviously argue that this danger is so great that we have to limit the right to use force to the case of an imminent threat to life. I do not deny that this danger indeed exists. I suggest, however, an institutional mechanism that may mitigate the danger, even if it does not eliminate it.

According to a series of decisions of the European Court of Human Rights, when state officials are involved in the use of lethal force, it is incumbent on the state to carry out an independent investigation in order to determine whether the action was compatible with the state's obligation to respect and ensure the right to life.[148] A state that fails to do so violates that obligation. Applying human rights standards in cases of an armed conflict with terrorist groups means that every case of targeted killings must be subjected to a thorough and credible legal investigation. If it transpires that the measure was used in circumstances that do not comply with international standards, legal action must be taken against those responsible.

5 The US and Israeli Cases

The above analysis reveals that one cannot give a clear and general answer to the question of whether targeting a suspected terrorist is an extra-judicial execution, a legitimate 'act of war' or a grave breach of international humanitarian law. The answer 'all depends' on a number of factors, among which is the legal regime that applies. I shall now return to the cases mentioned in the Introduction and apply the analysis suggested here to these cases.

A *The US Case*

In the absence of clear evidence about the identity of all those who were killed and the danger that they posed to the United States, it is extremely difficult to assess the legality of the US attack in Yemen. I shall therefore confine myself to a discussion of the parameters of the case.

In the first place, we have to ask whether there was an armed conflict involving the United States and al-Qaeda at the time of the attack. If the answer is negative, it is hard to escape the conclusion that the attack was unlawful. If the answer is positive, I have argued that the conflict should be regarded as one of a non-international nature. A strong case could be made for regarding al-Qaeda members who take an active part in hostilities as combatants, even if they were not directly involved in such hostilities when targeted.[149]

[148] See *McKerr v United Kingdom*; *Hugh Jordan v United Kingdom*; *Kelley and Others v United Kingdom*; *Shanaghan v United Kingdom*, Judgments of 4 May, 2001, available at http://www.echr.coe.int/Eng/Judgments.htm.

[149] According to reports the attack on al-Harethi was carried out by the CIA and not US armed forces. I shall not address the question whether use of non-combatants to carry out combatant activities is lawful.

According to the approach suggested here, the mere fact that persons are suspected combatants does not justify targeting them. The object of the attack has to be to prevent a concrete danger which could not reasonably be thwarted by other means and that was highly likely to be realized if immediate action was not taken. It is not at all clear that the Yemen attack was preventive, rather than retributive; neither is it clear whether al-Harethi presented a concrete danger that could not reasonably have been thwarted by other means.

Were all the persons killed combatants? This was not a case in which the suspected terrorist was targeted in a civilian area so that the other persons killed were innocent bystanders. It seems likely that the persons with al-Harethi in the desert were party to his activities, but there is no certainty about this. Thus, the issue of proportionality could be relevant. It would be hard to justify the inevitable killing of persons who did not take an active part in hostilities unless it could be shown that targeting of al-Harethi was absolutely necessary to save many lives.

It has been suggested that the US action was carried out with the consent of the Yemen Government whose forces had made several unsuccessful attempts to arrest al-Harethi in the course of which a number of Yemeni soldiers had been killed. The consent of the Yemen Government would mean that Article 2(4) of the UN Charter was not violated. But it would not mean that the targeting of al-Harethi and his companions was compatible with IHL. Had the Yemen authorities been able to arrest al-Harethi, the licence given to the US to act could not have made the targeting lawful. A state cannot avoid its obligations to respect and ensure the right to life, by allowing another state to deprive persons of that right.

B *The Israeli Case*

Assessing the legality of Israel's targeted killings of suspected members of Palestinian organizations that engage in terror attacks is more complicated than most, if not all, other cases. It would seem that the main bone of contention relates to whether, given Israel's status as an occupying power, terrorist attacks on civilians in Israel should be regarded as instances of *transnational* terror.[150] There is also little agreement on some fundamental legal questions that have an enormous bearing on the topic.

1 *Status of the West Bank and Gaza*

Most objective legal observers accept that at least until the Oslo and subsequent accords between Israel and the PLO, the status of the West Bank and Gaza was that of occupied territories to which the international law of belligerent occupation applied. While many government policies in these territories were incompatible with principles of this legal regime, when appearing before the Supreme Court of Israel to defend government actions there the framework of legal discourse adopted by government

[150] From its Advisory Opinion on the *Legal Consequences of the Wall*, *supra* note 68, at para. 139, one may deduce that the ICJ took the view that the answer to this question is negative. The ICJ opined that as the terrorist attacks originated in territory occupied by Israel it may not invoke its right to self-defence under Art. 51 of the Charter. But see Separate Opinion of Judge Higgins, *supra* note 69, at para. 34, in which this attitude of the Court is criticized.

lawyers has always been the law of belligerent occupation. There are numerous decisions and many dicta of the Court accepting this framework.[151] It is also the framework favoured by the whole international community.[152]

Had the situation remained as it was before the Oslo Accords and subsequent agreements, there could have been no doubt about the illegality of all targeted killings. All Palestinians in the West Bank and Gaza were protected persons under Geneva Convention IV, who were entitled, in all circumstances, to protection against all acts of violence.[153] The applicable legal model in occupied territories is the law-enforcement model, based in this case on the international law of belligerent occupation, complemented by international human rights law. Under this model force may only be used in the case of an imminent attack that cannot be halted by arresting the suspected terrorist.[154]

It is the considered view of many commentators that the Oslo Accords and subsequent agreements between Israel and the PLO effected a change in the status of some parts of the Occupied Territories.[155] Under these agreements, the West Bank was divided into three different zones: 'A' areas in which both civil and security matters were in the hands of the Palestinian Authority established under the agreements; 'B' areas, in which security control remained the responsibility of Israel, while civil matters were the responsibility of the Palestinian Authority; and 'C' areas in which Israel retained responsibility for security matters while responsibility for civil matters was divided between Israel and the Palestinian Authority. In Gaza there was a similar, although not identical, arrangement. While the status of 'C' areas, and probably 'B' areas too, remained unchanged, the status of 'A' areas became controversial.[156] On one hand, it was argued that having relinquished effective control over these areas, Israel could no longer be regarded as an occupying power; on the other hand, the claim was that since Israel still retained the ultimate power over all areas, including total control on who could enter or leave, it remained an occupying power in all parts of the West Bank and Gaza.[157]

151 I have discussed these decisions and dicta elsewhere: Kretzmer, *supra* note 50.

152 The ICJ recently confirmed that Israel's status on the West Bank was that of an occupying power: *Legal Consequences of the Wall, supra* note 68. The ICJ Advisory Opinion in this case did not relate to Gaza.

153 See Art. 27 of Geneva Convention IV.

154 It could also be used if it was the minimum force required in order to effect a lawful arrest or to quell a riot.

155 See Benvenisti, 'The Status of the Palestinian Authority', in E. Cotran and C. Mallat (eds.), *The Arab-Israeli Accords: Legal Perspectives* (1996), at 47.

156 The divergent views on this issue are presented in International Humanitarian Law Research Initiative, *IHL in Israel and Occupied Palestinian Areas, Briefing Note: Review of the Applicability of International Humanitarian law to the Occupied Palestinian Territory*, available at http://www.ihlreserach.or/opt/feature.ph?a=31 (last accessed 25 Feb. 2004).

157 The UN Commission of Inquiry found the argument that Israel is no longer an occupying power because it lacks effective control over 'A' areas untenable. It claimed that the test for application of the legal regime of occupation is not whether the occupying power fails to exercise effective control over the territory, but whether it has the ability to exercise such power. It added that the 'Oslo Accords leave Israel with the ultimate legal control over the OPT and the fact that for political reasons it has chosen not to exercise this control, when it undoubtedly has the military capacity to do so, cannot relieve Israel of its responsibilities as an occupying Power': *Report of the Human Rights Inquiry Commission, supra* note 9, at para. 41. I find this statement unconvincing. Under the Oslo Accords and subsequent agreements Israeli

If Israel retained its status as an occupying power in the 'A' areas it was bound to follow the law-enforcement model there. In the case of suspected terrorists acting in those areas, if the Palestinian Authority (under this theory a kind of sub-contractor of the Israeli authorities) refused to arrest or extradite the persons involved, the Israeli authorities were certainly entitled (and maybe even bound) to enter those areas in order to arrest them. On the other hand, if Israel ceased to be an occupying power in 'A' areas, and effective authority was in the hands of the Palestinian Authority, those areas took on many of the characteristics of a foreign state. Israel was not entitled to enter the area to arrest persons suspected of being active in organizing and executing terrorist attacks against its civilians, even if the Palestinian Authority refused to arrest or extradite them.[158] There was therefore some credence to the argument, similar to that raised by the US in the Afghanistan case, that the Palestinian Authority should be regarded as responsible for the attacks carried out from its territory, and that if it failed to act, Israel was entitled to do so. It would not seem reasonable to require a state to refrain from action against terrorists who plan, direct and execute attacks on its citizens from territory that is not under its effective control if the de facto government in that territory refuses to restrain them.[159]

After hostilities started in September 2000 between Israel and the Palestinians, and especially after the Israeli 'Defensive Shield' campaign of April 2002, the IDF took control of many of the 'A' areas. At the time of writing it has resumed effective control over all areas on the West Bank, while in Gaza most areas are still under control of the Palestinian Authority. Even if the 'A' areas ceased to be regarded as occupied territory after the Oslo Agreements, once the IDF resumed effective control they once again became occupied territory, with all that this implies.

2 Existence of an Armed Conflict

At the beginning of the present *intifada* the Israeli authorities redefined the legal situation pertaining in the West Bank and Gaza as 'armed conflict short of war.'[160] This view of the situation was based on the assessment that given the frequency and severity of the use of armed force against military and civilians, and the level of organization behind use of that force, there was now 'protracted armed violence between the IDF and organized Palestinian groups', the classic description of an

forces were not permitted to enter the 'A' areas, unless they were responding to an ongoing incident, and then only until they had handed the matter over to the Palestinian police. Thus, if Israeli forces refrained from entering 'A' areas, they were abiding by Israel's commitments under an international agreement, and not acting for political reasons.

158 Art. VIII(9)(b) to Annex I, Protocol Concerning Withdrawal of Israeli Military Forces and Security Arrangements, states that: '[w]ithin the territory under the jurisdiction of the Palestinian Authority, in places where Israeli authorities exercise their security functions in accordance with this Annex, and in their immediate vicinities, the Israeli authorities may carry out engagement steps in cases where an act or an incident requires such action', available at http://www.mfa.gov.il/MFA/Peace+Process/Guide+to+the+Peace+Process/Gaza-Jericho+Agremeent+Annex+I.htm (last accessed 19 June 2004). As can be seen, the right of Israeli authorities to carry out engagement steps is restricted to places where they exercise security functions. These places do not include 'A' areas.

159 See Schmitt, *supra* note 48; Müllerson, *supra* note 70.

160 See *supra* note 116.

armed conflict between a state and non-state actors.[161] This led to the next division of opinion: was there indeed an armed conflict going on?[162] The answer to this question has a decisive influence on whether targeted killings outside the context of an imminent attack could ever be legal.

It seems to me very difficult to support the view that the level of violence by organized armed groups against Israeli targets did not, at least at some stages of the *intifada*, reach the threshold required for the situation to be regarded as an armed conflict.[163] The situation could not be regarded as one of 'riots, isolated and sporadic acts of violence and other acts of a similar nature', which under APII do not constitute an armed conflict.[164] Many of the measures adopted by Israel in managing the conflict may well have exceeded requirements of necessity and proportionality.[165] However, this does not influence the conclusion that the protracted violence between Israel and the organized Palestinian armed groups amounted to an armed conflict.[166]

3 An International or Non-International Armed Conflict?

In his opinion to the Supreme Court of Israel, Professor Cassese works on the assumption that the applicable law 'is the body of international customary and treaty rules relating to international armed conflicts, in particular to *occupatio bellica* of foreign territory'. This assumption is highly problematical. Since Jordan has waived all claims to sovereignty over the West Bank, while Egypt never raised such claims over Gaza, the status of these territories as occupied territory does not imply that there is an ongoing conflict between two or more states.[167] It is for this very reason that

[161] See the government briefs in H.C. 769/02 (on file with the author).

[162] See the discussion on 'Arab-Israeli Conflict and the Laws of War', Interviews by Mark Dennis, *Crimes of War, How the Law Applies*, May 2001, available at http://www.crimesofwar.org/expert/arab-israel.html (last accessed 25 Feb. 2004).

[163] According to statistics published by the Israel Ministry of Defence, since Sept. 2000 there have been 21,657 attacks on Israeli military or civilians in the West Bank, Gaza, and Israel. In that period 672 civilians and 291 members of security forces were killed: The statistics are available at http://www1.idf.il/SIP_STORAGE/DOVER/files/7/21827.doc (last accessed 3 June 2004). In the *International Law Opinion, supra* note 117, the Oxford Public Interest Lawyers opine that '[t]he present level of violence in the Occupied Territories does not cross the threshold of gravity necessary for a state of hostilities to exist. Violence is low-level, isolated and sporadic and does not amount to widespread, organized, military resistance against the Israeli occupation'. This assessment does not seem to be compatible with the above statistics.

[164] As noted above, APII does not apply to the present situation for two reasons: it has not been ratified by Israel and it applies only to conflicts taking place in the territory of a High Contracting Party. However, as I stated above, whether an armed conflict exists depends on an analysis of the actual situation on the ground, and in evaluating such a situation the standards set out in APII provide useful guidelines, even if they do not formally apply. It should also be noted that the ICTY has held that many of the provisions in APII reflect standards of customary international law. It seems to me that the definition of the parameters of an armed conflict may be one of these provisions.

[165] See, e.g., *Report of the Human Rights Inquiry Commission, supra* note 9, at para. 45.

[166] I express no opinion on whether at the time of writing (Nov. 2004), given the reduction in the scale and level of terrorist attacks it is no longer possible to speak of an ongoing armed conflict in the area.

[167] It may very well be asked how these territories can be regarded as territories subject to the international law of belligerent occupation if no other states are involved. The Government of Israel has tried to argue that the lack of sovereignty of other states over the territories means that they are not to be regarded as occupied. This argument has been rejected by foreign governments, international bodies, many Israeli

Cassese's assumption was rejected by the UN Commission of Inquiry into Human Rights Violations in the Occupied Territories,[168] and by others.[169] Even if one assumes that at no time since 1967 did any parts of the West Bank and Gaza cease being territory to which the international law of belligerent occupation applied, this does not necessarily mean that any armed conflict which arises between armed groups in these areas and Israel itself is of an international nature. As we have seen above, both the ICJ and the ICTY have held that some situations involve armed conflicts that have both international and non-international aspects.

The conclusion to which Cassese's assumption leads him also reveals its weakness. Between whom exactly is the international armed conflict that Cassese speaks about? It is not between two states. Is it a conflict between a state and organized armed groups? It would seem so, but such a conflict is *not* regarded as an international armed conflict. Of course, one could say that the conflict is one between Israel and the Palestinian people. But a conflict between a state and a people under occupation is not regarded as an international armed conflict under customary international law,[170] and Israel has not ratified Additional Protocol I to the Geneva Conventions. Furthermore, if the conflict is to be regarded as an international armed conflict between Israel and the Palestinian people, at the very least members of the armed security forces of the Palestinian Authority would be regarded as combatants. But while there have been some incidents in which members of these security forces have been involved, the present conflict has not included hostilities between the IDF and units of the Palestinian security forces. It would therefore be totally unreasonable to argue that all members of these forces are combatants involved in an armed conflict with Israel.

The assumption that terrorists are merely civilians taking a direct part in hostilities might make sense if hostilities of an international nature were also taking place. But this is not the case. To the extent that an armed conflict does indeed exist, it is the very hostilities between Israel and the armed groups to which these terrorists belong that create this conflict. It is difficult to regard the fighting by one party to the armed conflict as 'direct participation of civilians in hostilities'.

Some commentators argue that since members of Palestinian armed groups are not recognized as combatants when captured, and as some captured members are prosecuted for killing Israeli soldiers or civilians, they cannot possibly be regarded as

---

academics, and, most recently, the ICJ. It seems to me that the territories became occupied since they were not Israeli territory when captured in the 1967 international armed conflict between Israel and two other states: Jordan and Egypt. The question then becomes whether they retained that status after these two states made peace treaties with Israel. Dinstein has argued that following these treaties the status of the territories changed from one of belligerent occupation to post-belligerent occupation: Dinstein, 'The International Status of the West Bank and the Gaza Strip – 1998', 28 *Israel Ybk on H R* (1998) 37. I do not intend to discuss this view here.

168 *Report of the Human Rights Inquiry Commission, supra* note 9, at para. 39.

169 See Ben-Naftali and Michaeli, *supra* note 21.

170 See Greenwood, 'Customary Law Status of the 1977 Geneva Protocols', in A. J.M. Delissen and G. J. Tanja (eds.), *Humanitarian Law in Armed Conflict – Challenges Ahead: Essays in Honour of Frits Kalshoven* (1991), at 93.

combatants who may be targeted.[171] It has even been argued that had Israel ratified API, the conflict would be regarded as an international conflict between Israel and a people fighting alien occupation. It would follow that members of the Palestinian armed groups would be entitled to combatant status, and would also be legitimate targets. However, since Israel has not ratified API, it may not target Palestinian terrorists.[172]

Had Israel ratified API the situation might have appeared to be a lot simpler. From a political point of view, Israel might have been able to justify targeting members of armed Palestinian groups more easily. Thus paradoxically, although Israel and some states in similar situations objected to the API and refused to ratify it,[173] ratifying API would not only have imposed certain obligations on them; it might also seem to have granted them some advantages. However, these advantages would have been purely political. From a legal point of view, even when API has not been ratified by a state, a conflict between that state and a people fighting against colonial domination or alien occupation, might constitute an armed conflict, albeit not an *international* one. One of the objects of API was to extend the protection offered to combatants in an international armed conflict to combatants involved in certain types of conflicts that are not inter-state conflicts. The innovation was in applying the law of *international* armed conflicts to such a conflict, not in recognizing it as an armed conflict. The question of whether a non-international armed conflict exists depends on an analysis of the factual situation – is there protracted armed violence between the state and organized armed groups (or between such groups within a given state)?

Absent ratification of API, Israel is not required to treat members of Palestinian armed groups as POWs. It may try members of such groups who have killed or wounded soldiers.[174] However, even if API had been ratified, Palestinians involved in terrorist activities (which by our definition involve deliberate killing and other severe violence against civilians) could have been tried for war crimes or crimes against humanity.[175]

It seems to me, following the line taken by the UN Commission of Inquiry, that the armed conflict between Israel and the Palestinian organizations which carry out terrorist attacks on civilians in Israel must be regarded as a non-international armed conflict.[176] In such a conflict active members of the organized armed groups are to be

[171] This argument is raised by the petitioner in H.C. 769/02, *supra* note 7.

[172] *Ibid.*

[173] On the objections of the US, Israel, and a few other states to the provisions of API see Greenwood, *supra* note 91.

[174] In non-international armed conflicts combatants may be prosecuted for fighting under the domestic law of the state involved. However, as opposed to terrorists, who commit a war crime under international law when they intentionally kill civilians in such a conflict, members of armed groups do not commit a crime under international law when they kill soldiers (unless they have laid down their arms or are *hors de combat*).

[175] On the notion that the deliberate organized attacks on Israeli civilians are to be regarded as crimes against humanity see Amnesty International, *Israel and the Occupied Territories and the Palestinian Authority: Without Distinction – Attacks on Civilians by Palestinian Armed Groups*, AI INDEX: MDE 02/003/2002, 11 July 2002; Human Rights Watch, *Erased In A Moment: Suicide Bombing Attack Against Israeli Civilians* (2002).

[176] This was also the view taken by Judge Kooijmans in his Separate Opinion in *Legal Consequences of the Wall*, *supra* note 68, at paras. 35–36.

regarded as combatants, even if they do not enjoy the privileges extended to combatants in an international armed conflict. If the law of armed conflict were to stand on its own, such combatants would be legitimate targets until such time as the armed conflict ended. However, as argued above, it does not stand on its own and must be considered together with international human rights law. I shall examine the way this system should work in the next section.

4 *Applying the Mixed Model*

In the present case we have a highly complicated legal situation which requires application of a model that incorporates elements of the laws of belligerent occupation, active armed conflict and international human rights. As Israel has reimposed its effective authority over all parts of the West Bank, it may not employ the armed conflict model in fighting suspected terrorists in this area. Force may be used only when absolutely necessary to halt an imminent attack on the military or on civilians or when an attempt to arrest suspected terrorists is resisted with force.

The issue is far more complicated when it comes to Gaza. Israeli forces have not reimposed military control over all sections of Gaza, and attempts to enter the areas under control of the Palestinian Authority in order to arrest suspected terrorists not only raise legal and political questions; they are invariably met with force that results in loss of life to Israeli soldiers and to Palestinian civilians. The situation there more closely resembles the case of transnational terrorists who are supported, or at least harboured, in another state.

This certainly does not mean that Israel is free to target all such suspected terrorists. As explained above, given the inherent uncertainty in identification, in order to justify targeting a suspected terrorist, not only must the authorities have clear and convincing evidence of that person's active involvement in terrorist activities. They must also have credible evidence that the person poses a real and concrete danger to the lives of others that cannot be thwarted without attacking him at the time he is attacked. Despite the difficulties, where apprehending the person involved is feasible, that avenue must be pursued. If it is not feasible, targeting the person may be lawful, but only if the object of the attack is preventive, and not punitive or deterrent.

But the issue does not end there. The question of proportionality looms large. As stated above, it is extremely difficult to assess the concrete and direct military advantage to be gained from targeting a suspected terrorist, and whether the expected loss to civilian life, injury to civilians, damage to civilian objects, or a combination thereof, are excessive in relation to that advantage. The presumption must be that if there is a danger that civilians may be killed or wounded in the attack, the attack will be unlawful. Lifting the burden imposed by that presumption depends on the information that decision-makers possessed, or should have possessed, when deciding on the attack. Nevertheless, I share the view of other commentators that even if the persons targeted by the IDF in some of the reported cases were legitimate targets, the results tend to show that the attacks did not meet the proportionality test.[177]

[177] See, e.g., Meyerstein, *supra* note 6; Ben-Naftali and Michaeli, *supra* note 21, at 280 (also analysing the attack on the commander of the military wing of Hamas, in which 16 people, including 9 children, were killed).

Finally, according to the demands of international human rights law, in every case of targeted killing a thorough legal investigation should be conducted. If it transpires that the conditions that justify use of the measure did not pertain, appropriate legal action should be taken. It is not clear whether this condition has been met in all cases of targeted killing.

6 Concluding Comments

The issue of transnational or international terror has generated a great deal of discussion, especially since the 9/11 attacks on the United States. Perceptions of the issues differ widely. Decision-makers in states that have been subjected to serious terrorist attacks often think that the 'war on terror' justifies actions that are totally inconsistent with standards of human rights and humanitarian law; human rights NGOs, some human rights institutions and politicians from states who have been free of terror see the great danger in over-reaction to terror, and sometimes offer what have been termed 'nice recipes . . . that have little practical relevance'.[178]

As intimated in the Introduction, I too believe that over-reaction of states acting outside accepted standards of human rights and international humanitarian law is a real danger. But this danger cannot be contained only by pious words and proposals for courses of action that 'seem to be blind to real life hard choices'.[179] International humanitarian law has always been based on recognition of the harsh reality of armed conflicts. It has not attempted to present idealistic standards of behaviour that cannot reasonably be demanded of parties faced with this reality. On the contrary it has made every attempt to lay down standards that recognize military necessity, but aim to spare those who do not participate in hostilities and to limit force to the amount necessary to weaken the fighting potential of the enemy.[180]

The assumption of this article has been that regarding suspected transnational terrorists as civilians who at times take part in hostilities is an unrealistic perception of the situation. On the other hand, regarding them as combatants who may be targeted at will opens the way to serious violations of the right to life in non-international armed conflicts. The middle road proposed here is an attempt to create a realistic alternative that allows states to defend their residents against terrorist attacks without abandoning commitment to standards of human rights and humanitarian law. It is based on the notion that unless realistic standards of conduct for states involved in armed conflicts with terrorist groups exist, they will act in an environment infected by the lawlessness that characterizes terrorism. The danger of this lawlessness is such that however imperfect these standards may be, they are preferable to no standards at all.

[178] Müllerson, *supra* note 70, at 18.

[179] *Ibid.*

[180] See Sassòli and Bouvier, *supra* note 92, at 67.

Part V
International Institutional Approaches

[10]

You are the Weakest Link and We will Help You! The Comprehensive Strategy of the United Nations to Fight Terrorism

Noëlle Quénivet*

Abstract

In 2004, the United Nations Secretary-General published the report of the high-level panel of experts on threats, challenges and change that projected a comprehensive strategy to fight various types of scourges that afflict humankind and notably terrorism. The report and the following world summit documents inscribe themselves in established trends set by the State community and the United Nations in the past decades. Since 11 September, five different wide-encompassing strategies have been offered to the State community to come to terms with terrorism. This article focuses on this proliferation of documents and their inconsistency in terms of content. Yet, it also pinpoints the common thread that runs through the documents, namely that the comprehensive strategy must address the root causes of terrorism, strengthen States and promote the rule of law and human rights, three targets that can be reached by the implementation of a strong policy of capacity-building. In all cases, the State community works on the premise that weak and rogue States will consent to be helped in building national and regional capacity to combat terrorism. Undoubtedly, convincing weak and rogue States to abide by international standards will require more than just capacity-building to deflect terrorism. Rather, the United Nations will need to conceptualise general measures to prevent and reverse state failure, which in turn means that the strategy must be indeed 'comprehensive'.

*Dr. Noëlle Quénivet is Senior Lecturer at Faculty of Law of University of the West of England (UK). E-mail: noelle.quenivet@uwe.ac.uk. I am thankful to Bernard Dougherty for his valuable comments.

1. Introduction

In 2004, the United Nations Secretary-General published the report of the high-level panel of experts on threats, challenges and change that projected a comprehensive strategy to fight various types of scourges that afflict humankind. Predictably, terrorism is one of the threats addressed at length by the panel because '[t]errorism attacks the values that lie at the heart of the Charter of the United Nations: respect for human rights, the rule of law; rules of war that protect civilians; tolerance among peoples and nations; and the peaceful resolution of conflict'.[1]

Although heralded as a new, if not revolutionary, policy proposal, the report and the following world summit documents inscribe themselves in established trends set by the State community and the United Nations (UN) in the past decades. In fact, these trends started already a long time ago and are the products of new actors and new actions or, in some cases, new perceptions activated by the sudden emergence of events. Indeed, since 1945, the fight against terrorism has mainly developed in three directions.

From a mere national issue to be combated at the domestic level by national legislation and law-enforcement agencies, terrorists reached the international plane. This demanded an international response. Furthermore, whereas in the past, terrorist activities were only viewed as falling within the purview of domestic criminal law and, therefore, predominantly fought by law-enforcement agencies rather than the armed forces, States as well as the United Nations decided from the 1980s onwards to go down the path of the use of force. The final trend is the growing combination between reactive (often punitive) and preventive (or pro-reactive) measures.

As a consequence, the comprehensive strategy elaborated in the high-level panel and other UN fora is nothing more than the outcome of these general trends. International co-operation and the issues of the use of force as well as pro-active and preventive measures are thoroughly discussed therein as most 'innovative' recommendations can be traced back to these universal tendencies. The novelty is that '[t]oday, more than ever before, threats are interrelated and a threat to one is a threat to all. The mutual vulnerability of weak and strong has never been clearer'.[2]

In reality, since September 11, five different wide-ranging strategies have been offered to the State community to come to terms with terrorism. Despite their differences, a thread runs through all of them, namely that the comprehensive strategy must address the root causes of terrorism, strengthen States and promote the rule of law and human rights, three targets that can be reached by the implementation of a strong policy of capacity building. With this aim, the international community is requested to assist States especially failed States to

1 UN High-level Panel on Threats, Challenges, and Change, *A More Secure World: Our Shared Responsibility*, UN doc. A/59/565, 2 December 2004, para. 145 [hereinafter *UN High-level Panel Report*].

2 *Ibid.*, para. 17.

develop legal and political devices to fight off terrorism and its roots. Yet, the question remains whether such States agree to benefit from such aid and, if not, whether the international community can oblige States to take such measures.

2. From the National to the International Level

One of the first general tendencies in the fight against terrorism is States' pooling and sharing of information and capacities. Indeed, in the past, counter-terrorist activities were undertaken by the State that had fallen prey to a terrorist act on the basis that '[t]he primary legal weapons against terrorism [were] national laws, and the task of applying them rest[ed] with the national criminal justice systems'.[3] Both the victims and the perpetrators were nationals of the same State, which did not pose any concerns regarding the application of national legislation and jurisprudence. As terrorism took an international dimension, so did counter-terrorism.

A. Changes in Reality and in Perception

First, whereas in the 1950s–1960s, one could safely regard terrorism as a national issue confined within the borders of a particular State,[4] such a viewpoint is absolutely untenable nowadays. Now, instead of carrying out activities only on the territory of the State, terrorist groups also attack the State's property and citizens wherever they are located, thereby also destroying the property of and killing or injuring the nationals of the State in which the attack occurs. Concomitantly, terrorists are not anymore always nationals of the State that they target but foreigners. The global reach of groups such as al-Qaeda is evidenced by its capacity to organise terrorist attacks in numerous States.[5] In addition, '[t]errorism in a single country can readily become a threat to regional peace and security owing to spill-over effects, such as cross-border violence and the creation of refugee populations'.[6]

Second, September 11 revealed that terrorist groups had organised themselves transnationally, because of which it was hard to trace them.[7] Whereas in

3 P. Wilkinson, *Terrorism Versus Democracy. The Liberal State Response* (2001) 118.

4 A closer look at the activities of terrorist groups such as the IRA, ETA and the Red Army Faction demonstrates that they had strong links with each other as well as with other groups such as the FARC in Colombia. Terrorist networks are consequently not new. Gus Martin, *Understanding Terrorism. Challenges, Perspectives, and Issues* (2003) 229.

5 Danish Institute for International Studies, *New Threats and the Use of Force* (2005) 22 [hereinafter *Danish Report*].

6 Report of the Policy Working Group on the United Nations and Terrorism, Annex to UN doc. A/57/273, UN doc. S/2002/875, 6 August 2002, para 12. [hereinafter Report of the Policy Working Group].

7 *Danish Report*, *op. cit.*, fn. 5, p. 23.

the past, terrorist groups could be readily categorised by reference to territory, the contemporary generation of terrorists does not have any territorial aspirations. Organised on a global scale, these loosely affiliated cells can operate simultaneously in various States by establishing a network. They are not unified by a single vertical command but rather linked in a horizontal fashion[8] by using modern communication and transportation technology. The integration of financial markets also facilitates their mobility and range of possible targets so as to allow them to exist without holding a particular territory or claiming one.[9] Although countless authors refer to the 'de-territorialisation' of terrorism as such groups and networks[10] can now operate without direct State participation,[11] one must bear in mind that terrorists need to keep training and fallback bases, which, inevitably, can only be located in a particular State,[12] often unable (weak State) or unwilling (rogue State) to counteract their activities.[13]

Terrorist groups benefit not only from the globalisation and the opening of borders but also from the existence of States that encounter difficulties in assuming full control over their territory. In this context, the jump from a national to an international movement is even easier for such groups. So, like terrorism, counter-terrorist activities moved from a purely national to an international plane. The response of the State community must accordingly be co-ordinated on the international level.

A third major change operated by terrorist groups in their activities is not only their increased means and methods of injuring the State and its nationals but also their will to employ such methods and weapons against larger groups of individuals,[14] as a consequence of which States realised that they had a shared interest in enhancing international co-operation to fight terrorism. No doubt, the September 11 attack was impressive in the damage it caused and this still with the use of more or less conventional means. Currently, the international community fears that such groups may be or will soon be in the possession of non-conventional weapons: biological, chemical and nuclear.[15]

8 C. Daase, 'Terrorismus und Krieg. Zukunftsszenarien politischer Gewalt nach dem 11. September 2001', in R. Voigt (ed.), *Krieg- Instrument der Politik? Bewaffnete Konflikte im Übergang vom 20. zum 21. Jahrhundert* (2002) 385.

9 Martin, *op. cit.*, fn. 4, p. 237. See also T. Müller, 'Der Kampf gegen den Terror', (2001) 12 *Internationale Politik* 47.

10 For an overview on how terrorist networks function, see L. Richardson, 'Terrorists as Transnational Actors', in M. Taylor and J. Horgan (eds.), *The Future of Terrorism* (2000) 216–218.

11 X. Raufer, 'New World Disorder, New Terrorisms: New Threats for Europe and the Western World', in Taylor and Horgan (eds.), *The Future of Terrorism* (2000) 30–31.

12 K. Hirschmann, *Terrorismus* (2003) 54.

13 G. Andréani, 'The "War on Terror": Good Cause, Wrong Concept', (2004) 46(4) *Survival* 38.

14 'Today, in contrast, it has become evident that many terrorist oganizations no longer seek to avoid mass casualties in their terror attacks'. B.N. Dunlap, 'State Failure and the Use of Force in the Age of Global Terror', (2004) 27 *Boston College International and Comparative Law Review* 463.

15 Terrorists already conducted several small-scale operations using such weapons. *Danish Report, op. cit.*, fn. 5, p. 24.

Especially in this field, it is necessary for the international community to work together as such a threat cannot be vanquished by single States.[16] Again in this context, the United Nations points the finger at certain States that are unable or unwilling to prevent or stop the traffic of such weapons. 'The ability of non-State actors to traffic in nuclear material and technology is aided by ineffective State control of borders and transit through weak States.'[17]

B. The International Community's Reaction to These Changes

For all these reasons, the international community must hold together and find common and/or co-ordinated solutions. Although September 11 undoubtedly showed the world that even a leading democracy in the world was not safe from terrorist attacks on its own territory, the event cannot in this particular aspect be regarded as the trigger of a new form of reaction. As in the past, co-operation with other States was inevitable. A key part of the 'old' response to terrorist threats consisted in adopting a series of diplomatic, economic and financial measures on the national level so as to recognise and fight terrorist structures.[18] To multiply the effect of such measures, States agreed to co-operate on the international level by using treaty law. So, about a dozen multilateral conventions were opened for signature, all covering specific aspects of anti- and counter-terrorism. Thus, all activities falling within the ambit of these conventions would be investigated and the perpetrators, according to the principle *aut judicare aut dedere*, either prosecuted or extradited.[19] In other words, no terrorist activity would go unpunished.[20] Moreover, internationally co-operative responses include intelligence gathering and tagging explosive materials as a way of facilitating law enforcement, regulating the sale of highly dangerous materials and tracing the money.

States have not given up on co-operation, rather they wish to reinforce it. The Club de Madrid stresses that '[g]overnments and civil society must reignite their efforts at promoting international engagement, co-operation and dialogue'.[21] Furthermore, September 11 triggered international co-operation

16 The Club de Madrid, *The Madrid Agenda: The Madrid Recommendations* (2005), vol. II, 49, reprinted in Club de Madrid, Addressing the Causes of Terrorism, The International Summit on Democracy, Terrorism and Security, 8–11 March 2005, Madrid [hereinafter *Madrid Agenda*].

17 *UN High-level Panel Report, op. cit.*, fn. 1, para. 20.

18 W. Schilling, 'Eine neue Dimension der Gewalt. Internationale Sicherheit nach dem 11. September', (2001) 12 *Internationale Politik* 34.

19 'Notwithstanding their diversity, these conventions, share the six modalities of international cooperation in penal matters, namely: extradition, mutual assistance, transfer of criminal proceedings, transfer of prisoners, seizure and forfeiture of assets and recognition of foreign penal judgments'. M.C. Bassiouni (ed.), 'International Terrorism', in *International Criminal Law*, vol. 1 (1999) 770.

20 C. Tomuschat, 'Der 11. September 2001 und seine rechtlichen Konsequenzen', (2002) 5 *Rechtspolitisches Forum* 6.

21 *Madrid Agenda, op. cit.*, fn. 16, p. 46.

by making it compulsory. Specifically to monitor States' obligations in the fight against terrorism, the Security Council established a Counter-Terrorism Committee to which States had to report on the implementation measures imposed by the Security Council in Resolution 1373. The difference in comparison to previous co-operation activities is the inclusion of the Security Council, trusted to be more effective than classical co-operation mechanisms enshrined in treaties. '[I]ts anti-terrorist measures applicable within all member states taken in response to September 11, 2001 look very much like global governance much more so than its previous sanctions regimes which were targeted at individual states'.[22]

Straight after September 11, the idea of a comprehensive convention on terrorism was revived. States should co-operate in fighting not only certain types of terrorist activities but also more generally terrorism. Renewed calls have been made to the State community to conclude a comprehensive convention on international terrorism.[23] Unfortunately, as of now, such a call has not been heeded due to political differences regarding the definition of 'terrorism'.

3. From the Criminal to the Use of Force

A second shift in counter-terrorist activities is that the State and the international community do not contemplate terrorist activities as falling solely within the purview of criminal law but also within the scope of the international use of force.[24]

Terrorists were initially only treated as criminals at the same level as murderers and rapists, their particular idiosyncrasy being that they are ideologically motivated, follow a political purpose and seek a certain power outcome.[25] Therefore, national penal laws and related enforcement institutions seemed to be an appropriate tool to deal with such activities.[26] With the growing use of force employed by terrorist organisations, States had recourse to the use of military force.

22 N.D. White, 'On the Brink of Lawlessness: The State of Collective Security Law', (2002) 13 *Indiana Intl CLR* 237.

23 Club de Madrid, Addressing the Causes of Terrorism, The International Summit on Democracy, Terrorism and Security, 8–11 March 2005, Madrid, vol. III, 8 [hereinafter Madrid III].

24 On a more general tone, the issue centres upon determining whether terrorism is 'war' or a 'crime'. Daase, *loc. cit.*, fn. 8, p. 373.

25 Bassiouni, *op. cit.*, fn. 19, p. 780.

26 'To keep terrorism as a police matter within the confines of civil society, it would be best if it could be considered as a form of criminality, which means that the most appropriate responses are found through the methods of law enforcement, involving domestic intelligence, the police and the judiciary. For this model to work, the terrorists must act as criminals.' Club de Madrid, Addressing the Causes of Terrorism, The International Summit on Democracy, Terrorism and Security, 8–11 March 2005, Madrid, vol. II, 21 [hereinafter Madrid II].

A. New Threats and Their Perceptions

Three reasons led particular States to take measures falling within the realm of the use of force. Not only did States realise that certain counter-terrorism activities were unfruitful but their perception of terrorist acts also changed.

First, the inability of States to combat national and/or international terrorism through an array of criminal laws and through traditional institutions such as the police and civil and criminal courts led some of them to look for short cuts and for a quick fix[27] especially when the terrorist attack was carried out abroad or seemed to have been planned from abroad.[28]

Second, States realised that terrorist groups should not be regarded as drug dealers and traffickers anymore but for what they are, that is good organised paramilitary groups which are highly motivated and able to carry out major attacks.[29] Moreover, as terrorists prefer to be viewed as warriors, States' reaction also falls more and more within the realm of 'war'.[30]

Third, as terrorists seek refugee or hide in another State sympathetic to their causes, international co-operation in the previously mentioned form fails to tackle the issue in an efficient manner, for weak States are unable to fulfil their international obligations.

B. The States' Powerful Responses

Hence, in addition to general crime prevention measures, a growing number of States opt for a military 'solution'. Inevitably, it is difficult for the reacting State to proceed against terrorists without violating several principles of international law, amongst them the prohibition of the use of force and the prohibition to intervene in a State's internal affairs. Furthermore, the use of force must be in conformity with international norms, that is it must be either a lawful act of self-defence or a measure adopted in the framework of the collective security mechanism embedded in the UN Charter,[31] whereby the right to self-defence is contemplated as subsidiary to the action of the Security Council.

27 Daase, *loc. cit.*, fn. 8, p. 375.

28 Armed forces are also used on national territory as the situations in Northern Ireland in the 1970s and in Algeria in the 1960s illustrate. States have recourse to armed forces when they realise that the police are not capable to face the threat created by the terrorists. In practice, the 'harmless' use of armed forces often ends up in a fully fledged military campaign. Andréani, *loc. cit.*, fn. 13, p. 37.

29 C. Carr, 'Terrorism as Warfare. The Lessons of Military History', (1996/1997) 13(4) *World Policy Journal* 5.

30 Another stance portends that drugs, crime and terrorism are recognised to be as dangerous and deadly as an armed conflict and so must States be as willing to fight these threats as wartime enemies. Andréani, *loc. cit.*, fn. 13, p. 31.

31 Madrid III, *op. cit.*, fn. 23, p. 14.

(i) The use of force through the collective security mechanism

The Security Council already determined a long time ago that acts of international terrorism were threats to international peace and security within the meaning of article 39 of the UN Charter.[32] Nevertheless, on no such occasions did the Security Council allow the use of military force. Resolution 1368 that followed the September 11 attack is a novelty in as much as the Security Council '[e]xpresses its readiness to take all necessary steps to respond to the terrorist attacks of 11 September 2001, and to combat all forms of terrorism, in accordance with its responsibilities under the Charter of the United Nations'.[33] However, as of now, the Security Council has not made use of its 'readiness'. More generally, Resolution 1377 declares that 'acts of international terrorism constitute one of the most serious threats to international peace and security in the twenty-first century'.[34]

The system of collective security could as well be initiated in cases where terrorist groups do not yet constitute an immediate threat that would allow States to have recourse to the right to self-defence. Preventive measures could hence be taken by the Security Council to avert terrorist attacks when these are incubating.[35]

(ii) The use of force according to the right to self-defence

Another way to bolster the claim that the use of force against terrorists is lawful is to demonstrate that it falls within the right to self-defence as encapsulated in article 51 of the UN Charter or as provided in customary international law. In the 1980s and 1990s, international terrorist activities were contemplated by only a few States as an armed attack, which entitled them to reply in self-defence. In reality, these were often punitive strikes[36] or unlawful reprisals[37] against States supportive of terrorist organisations that were severely criticised by the international community from a legal viewpoint.

32 For example, in 1988, the Security Council condemned the attack on the civilian aircraft at Lockerbie and urged Libya to respond immediately to international demands, i.e. the extradition or prosecution of those suspected to have committed the attack. Libya's failure to abide by the resolution led to another resolution imposing under chapter VII sanctions upon Libya. SC Res. 731 (1992), 21 January 1992; and SC Res. 748 (1992), 31 March 1992.

33 SC Res. 1368 (2001), 12 September 2001.

34 SC Res. 1377 (2001), 12 November 2001.

35 Madrid III, *op. cit.*, fn. 23, pp. 7–10.

36 A punitive attack can be defined as one 'launched as reprisals against terrorists for incidents that have already taken place. Successful punitive strikes require the attacker to symbolically and politically link the attacks to the terrorist incident.' Martin, *op. cit.*, fn. 4, p. 353. In view of the changes undergone by international terrorism in the last few years, it is argued that militarised responses do not serve any deterrent purpose, because they only attack certain cells but cannot target the entire terrorist organisation. Daase, *loc. cit.*, fn. 8, p. 385.

37 See the discussion in the *Danish Report*, *op. cit.*, fn. 5, p. 58.

While in the past such military actions were not perceived as lawful, the recent parallel drawn between terrorist activities and an armed attack implies the possibility for a State or a group thereof to respond by military means. The United States clearly took the stance that the events of September 11 constituted an armed attack by al-Qaeda on the United States. The fact that no State expressed its dissent as to the United States' right to self-defence led many legal scholars into thinking that either a new rule was instantaneously established[38] or that the rule that such acts amounted to armed attacks was this time legally confirmed. On the contrary, one may point at the ambiguities of Security Council Resolution 1373 that does not speak of an 'armed attack' but of a 'terrorist attack' in the main body and only refers to the right to self-defence, that can only be claimed if an armed attack occurred, in the preamble.[39]

The International Court of Justice confirmed in its advisory opinion on the legal consequences of the construction of a wall in the occupied Palestinian territory that (i) attacks that are not imputable to a foreign State and (ii) terrorist threats that originate within the territory of the same State as the one which suffered the injury do not give rise to the right to self-defence. It implies not only that the right to self-defence must be directed towards a State but also that individuals cannot violate the sovereignty of a State.[40] Therefore, although 'armed attacks' in the sense of the UN Charter may be carried out by non-State actors, the military reaction can only target a State to which the action is imputable according to the rules governing State responsibility.[41]

As the use of force can only be exercised against a State responsible for sending persons to carry out an attack, for adopting the acts of the terrorist group after the fact or for developing close ties with such a group, weak States that are merely unable to prevent and/or counteract terrorist activities may not be the subject of the right to self-defence.[42] Under the current circumstances, it is unlikely that a State can be held responsible on one of the first two grounds,[43]

38 B. Langille, 'It's "Instant Custom": How the Bush Doctrine Became Law after the Terrorist Attacks of September 11, 2001', (2003) 27 *Boston College International and Comparative Law Review* 145–156.

39 SC Res. 1373 (2001), 28 September 2001. Further resolutions referring to situations considered as terrorist, speak of 'bomb attack', 'terrorist bomb attack', 'attempted missile attack', 'heinous act of taking hostages', 'terrorist bombings' and 'terrorist attacks', the expression 'armed attack' being persistently ignored.

40 International Court of Justice, *Legal Consequences of the Construction of a Wall in the Occupied Palestinian Territory*, Advisory Opinion, General List No. 131, 9 July 2004, paras. 138–139.

41 'The acts of groups lacking these links to a state or territorial control are usually regarded as acts of criminal violence, not acts of war'. M.E. O'Connell, 'Enhancing the Status of Non-State Actors through a Global War on Terror?', (2005) 43 *Columbia Journal of Transnational Law* 445.

42 See Dunlap, *loc. cit.*, fn. 14, pp. 464–467. For an analysis of the US government opinion, see O'Connell, *loc. cit.*, fn. 41, p. 450.

43 As Dunlap explains '[a]rticle 51 offers dubious justification for counterterrorist operations in most cases and is practically useless in supporting the use of force against terrorists in failed states'. Dunlap, *loc. cit.*, fn. 14, p. 464.

because it is unlikely that a weak State would have such capacities. However, it is more likely that States' imputability may be demonstrated through cases, such as in Afghanistan under the Taliban regime, where the armed group involved in terrorist acts lives in symbiotic relationship with the government formally in charge of the State. Another case occurs where the State assists in the co-ordination and financing[44] of the operations as well as provides safe haven.[45]

On the contrary, 'there is an emerging consensus that it may be legitimate to take military action against terrorists in states that are either unwilling or unable to meet their legal obligations under UN Resolution 1373 to prevent terrorists from using their territory as launching pads for attacks on other countries'.[46] Nevertheless, most cases illustrating this position relate to focused military actions such as the drone manned attack in Yemen in 2002. As the report by the Danish Institute for International Studies explains 'limited preventive military actions against Al Qaida in weak states have generally been met with acceptance, if not outright support, from the international community'.[47]

As a consequence, post September 11, international law encounters a host of difficulties dealing with such a situation where the confines between State and armed/terrorist group are not clearly defined so as to distinguish the two protagonists.

(iii) Problems linked to the use of force against terrorists

An issue connected to the move from law enforcement to 'war' is the possible applicability of international humanitarian law. In case such *corpus juris* is pertinent, then the traditional definition of terrorists as criminals and not as combatants inevitably raises numerous problems concerning the way the armed forces can treat these individuals and their activities as well as act accordingly.[48] In any case, the use of military force against such persons increases their stature and provides them with a certain measure of legitimacy, if not legality.[49] Instead of a contest between the 'goodies' (the State) and the 'badies' (the terrorists) on the criminal level, the fight is levelled between two almost

44 See, for example, *United Nations, Terrorism Financing. Roots and Trends of Saudi Terrorism Financing*, Report Prepared for the President of the Security Council United Nations, 19 December 2002, JCB TF UN.

45 Often under these conditions, 'the barrier which usually separates the legitimate use of force by the state and illegitimate use of violence by private groups has broken down; the armed groups have at least partially substituted their own power to coerce those of the state'. R. Grote, 'Between Crime Prevention and the Laws of War: Are the Traditional Categories of International Law Adequate for Assessing the Use of Force Against International Terrorism?' in C. Walter, S. Vöneky, V. Röben and F. Schorkopf (eds.), *Terrorism as a Challenge for National and International Law: Security versus Liberation?* (2003) 954.

46 *Danish Report, op. cit.*, fn. 5, p. 46.

47 *Ibid.*, p. 48.

48 Daase, *loc. cit.*, fn. 8, p. 375.

49 Andréani, *loc. cit.*, fn. 13, p. 35; and Madrid III, *op. cit.*, fn. 23, p. 14.

equal groups, one of the criteria for this change of threshold being the requirements necessary for an armed conflict to take place according to the Geneva Conventions, their Additional Protocols and the jurisprudence of the international criminal courts.

Criticism is becoming ever louder against the disparate legal regimes of law enforcement and armed conflict that have merged and to some extent clashed.[50] Slowly, international lawyers argue for the dismissal of the distinction between the law of war and the law of peace in the fight against terrorism.[51] In particular, so they contend, this distinction is more and more difficult to apply in the light of the challenges posed more generally by non-State agents endowed with powers akin to States.

Until now, the Security Council has not favoured either the criminal or the use of force approach; it uses both to fight terrorism.[52] Yet, when it allows the use of force, it does so as a right to self-defence rather than in the framework of the collective security mechanism. In clear contrast, the Club de Madrid is reluctant towards the use of force against terrorists.[53] It is remarkable that in the long enumeration of activities in which the armed forces could be involved, the Club de Madrid does not mention the classical use of force to protect a country, the ultimate task entrusted to the armed forces. Additionally, the Secretary-General appears to refuse this move towards using force to solve the terrorist problem, a stance also taken by various States.

4. Combining Reactive and Preventive Measures

A third tendency is to combine reactive and preventive measures, the stress being put on the latter. In addition, a shift from short- to long-term thinking is noticeable both on the national and on the international scale, so that prevention covers not only hindrance of a single terrorist act or a set of terrorist activities but also terrorism in general.

A. The New Threats and Their Perceptions

Increasingly, States recognised that mere prevention and mere reaction did not work. Additionally, they began viewing certain changes in international relations as new threats.

50 W.K. Lietzau, 'Combating Terrorism: The Consequences of Moving from Law Enforcement to War', in D.H. Wippman and M. Evangelista (eds.), *New Wars, New Laws?* (2005) 32–33.

51 Bassiouni, *op. cit.*, fn. 19, p. 779.

52 'A military response to international terrorist acts is now widely considered lawful, alongside the law enforcement model previously relied upon for apprehending and punishing terrorists.' V.P. Nanda (ed.), 'Terrorism, International Law and International Oganizations', in *Law in the War on International Terrorism* (2005) 1.

53 Madrid II, *op. cit.*, fn. 26, p. 23.

One of the chief mistakes was simply that UN sanctions were not purely preventive but also contained punitive elements,[54] so that, in reality, most targeted States viewed themselves as punished, and their feeling of hatred towards the international community even increased. Factually, sanctions against States sponsoring or harbouring terrorist elements had failed in most cases, because some regimes were immune to international pressure and sanctions[55] and others, such as weak States, unable to eliminate the threat.[56]

Despite repeated efforts to suppress terrorism on the international level, States' co-operation is beset with considerable difficulties. One of them is linked to the fact that States 'continue to treat terrorism primarily, if not exclusively, as an internal responsibility'.[57] A second connected reason is the difference in criminal codes and procedures that often prevents co-operation with multiple actors. States tend to perceive their national systems for the prevention of terrorism as the best and most suitable for the type of terrorist threats they are facing.[58] In reality, only narrow bilateral co-operation seems to have worked in an efficient manner on such matters as intelligence-sharing, cross-border policing and the extradition of suspects.[59] Even in such cases, 'the exchange of data between national and international law enforcement agencies continues to be reactive rather than pro-active',[60] so that it is impossible to avert terrorist activities.

States' reaction to terrorism led to several problems. First, 'disproportionate reliance on military force to combat terrorism potentially feeds ongoing conflicts rather than repressing them'.[61] Second, in applying measures deemed to prevent terrorism, many States tend to obliterate human rights and the rule of law in the name of the fight against terrorism. For this reason, the United Nations feels obliged to remind States of their other international legal duties[62]

54 '[T]he distinction between enforcement to safeguard the peace and sanctions to punish violators is not so clear in practice, since enforcement action, especially non-military action, will often take the form of sanctions.' *Danish Report, op. cit.*, fn. 5, p. 92.

55 *Ibid.*, p. 113.

56 *Ibid.*, p. 114.

57 Wilkinson, *op. cit.*, fn. 3, p. 119.

58 The Club de Madrid also complains that '[n]arrow national mindsets are counterproductive'. *Madrid Agenda, op. cit.*, fn. 16, p. 46.

59 Against the odds, the system does not work very well on the European level. Müller, *loc. cit.*, fn. 9, p. 49.

60 Madrid II, *op. cit.*, fn. 26, p. 7.

61 J. Moore, 'Collective Security with a Human Face: An International Legal Framework for Coordinated Action to Alleviate Violence and Poverty', (2004) 13 *Denver Journal of International Law and Policy* 43.

62 'Development of better instruments for global counter-terrorism cooperation, all within a legal framework that is respectful of civil liberties and human rights, including in the area of law enforcement; intelligence-sharing, where possible, denial and interdiction, when required; and financial records.' *UN High-level Panel Report, op. cit.*, fn. 1, para. 148(c).

and to clearly spell out that 'the struggle against terrorism should be carried out in keeping with international human rights obligations'.[63]

Although there is nothing innovative in contemplating terrorism as a threat, the novelty lies in its combination with other kinds of threats. For example, until September 11, the problems of organised crime and terrorism were deemed as separate phenomena to be combated through separate means.[64] The report of the working group on terrorism recognises that 'international terrorism and transnational organized crime are often closely interrelated and connected'.[65] The experts of the high-level panel offer a similar viewpoint, for it is the combination of these 'new' threats, which renders the world less safe rather than their arithmetical sum.

A second perceived threat is that 'all these activities dramatically underscore the weakness of nation-states and of the international legal system'[66] to the level that States feel threatened even in their essence. Inevitably, as the 'central idea is that security is based on the survival of States',[67] the issue of weak States quickly rises to the fore. Specifically, September 11 triggered the recognition that weak States constituted an ever bigger threat when coupled with the presence of terrorist elements,[68] drug trafficking and private armies.[69] As Prins explains in her analysis of the high-level panel report, 'it is the very erosion of state capacity that is the principle catalyst energizing the interactions among the new security threats, thereby composing that new category of composite threat which is so particularly obscure to conventional analysis'.[70] Along these lines, the latest terrorist threat can only be understood in the general trend of the fall of the importance of the State in international relations and the growing significance of individuals and groups thereof on the international level.[71]

63 Report of the Policy Working Group, *op. cit.*, fn. 6, para. 27.

64 W. Bruggeman, *The ICC as an Important Partner in Enhancing Global Justice*, International Summit on Democracy, Terrorism and Security, 8–11 March 2005 in Madrid, 27 January 2005.

65 Report of the Policy Working Group, *op. cit.*, fn. 6, para. 25.

66 O. Schachter, 'The Decline of the Nation-States and its Implications for International Law', (1997) 36 *Columbia Journal of Transnational Law* 14–15.

67 M. Odello, 'Commentary on the United Nations' High Level Panel on Threats, Challenges and Change', (2005) 10 *JCSL* 234.

68 T.D. Grant, 'Partition of Failed States: Impediments and Impulses', (2004) 11 *Indiana Journal of Global Legal Studies* 51; and *Danish Report*, *op. cit.*, fn. 5, p. 25.

69 'In states plagued by what are now referred to as narco-terrorists, the corruption of officials may reach the very highest levels of government. States such as these prove particularly attractive to private armies, which require, in order to flourish and to pursue their special interests, space in which they are beyond the reach of governments.' W.M. Reisman, 'International Legal Responses to Terrorism', (1999) 22 *Houston Journal of International Law* 50.

70 G. Prins, 'Lord Castlereagh's Retun: The Significance of Kofi Annan's High Level Panel on Threats, Challenges and Change', (2005) 81(2) *International Affairs* 382.

71 F. Kohout, 'Krieg und Terrorismus. Zur Veränderung politischer Konflikte im 21. Jahrhundert', in R. Voigt (ed.), *Krieg- Instrument der Politik? Bewaffnete Konflikte im Übergang vom 20. zum 21. Jahrhundert* (2002) 343.

B. Prevention, Reaction and Comprehensive Prevention

The September 11 attack provided the impetus for a broader encompassing prevention policy to tackle the terrorist threat, the innovation lying in the range of prevention and co-operative measures adopted by the Security Council. In reality, the concept of 'prevention' should not be understood as the ability to hinder a terrorist attack but also as one aiming to impede further similar attacks after one was carried out. In this sense, prevention is a mixture of mere prevention and reaction. In contrast, reaction as such only includes a particular action or set of actions taken to punish or defend oneself.

The ever clearer links between the various scourges that affect today's world and States' fear from the unknown non-State actors allow the United Nations to promote a comprehensive strategy touching upon various threats and embracing broad prevention activities. Again, this idea is not a novelty as an *ad hoc* committee established by the General Assembly already recommended in 1977 the investigation of the underlying causes of terrorism.[72] Several States also supported this approach inasmuch as they believed that to effectively address the daunting challenge of terrorism, its causes must be understood and appreciated. The international community has realised that '[t]errorism flourishes in environments of despair, humiliation, poverty, political oppression, extremism and human rights abuse; it also flourishes in contexts of regional conflict and foreign occupation',[73] and the link among transnational crime, corruption and terrorism is becoming stronger day by day. In other words, the United Nations recognises and admits that to hinder terrorism, one must also tackle its societal and economic roots, an idea also shared by the Club de Madrid.[74]

5. The Comprehensive Strategy

Because the threats are interconnected, a comprehensive strategy covering them all must be envisaged. This broad vision of collective security, adopted in all United Nations documents dealing with terrorism, is already envisaged in the UN Charter and, thus, is not as new as some claim.

Unsurprisingly, this strategy is part of a general trend set by the United Nations in establishing prevention programmes in various fields of activity. So, prevention is also the lead word of the reports of the Policy Working Group and the high-level panel[75] and subsequent reports on collective security including terrorism.

72 Cited in Nanda, *op. cit.*, fn. 52, p. 7.

73 *UN High-level Panel Report, op. cit.*, fn. 1, para. 145.

74 'In the fight against terrorism, forceful measures are necessary. Military action, when needed, must always be co-ordinated with law enforcement and judicial measures, as well as political, diplomatic, economic and social responses.' Madrid Agenda, *op. cit.*, fn. 16, p. 45.

75 'Preventive actions are addressed for all the six main threats, including inter- and intrastate conflicts.' Odello, *loc. cit.*, fn. 67, p. 237.

Accordingly, this pro-active counter-terrorism policy must be conceived in terms of an offensive *intervention* policy led under the heading of collective security.[76]

A. *Terrorism and Human Security*

The general opinion holds that 'collective security can both promote the peaceful settlement of situations that endanger peace (chapter VI processes) and take action with respect to threats to the peace, breaches of the peace or acts of aggression (chapter VII action)'.[77] Two organs are responsible for ensuring peace and security on the international plane, the Security Council, which in pursuance of article 24(1) of the UN Charter is entrusted with the primary responsibility to keep the peace, and the General Assembly.

If the United Nations wishes to develop a truly comprehensive strategy to fight terrorism, it must involve both organs because, due to the difference of powers and composition, these two bodies have different visions of what 'peace' and 'collective security'[78] are as well as how terrorism should be combated. Slowly, the United Nations admits that '[w]hat is required is a comprehensive strategy that incorporates but is broader than coercive measures'[79] and moves from a security peace to an effort to install a structural peace based on improved economic, social and political conditions as it realises the failure of military interventions to address structural and societal problems in an effective fashion.[80] In particular, the Security Council adopts a more open-minded definition of the concept of threats to peace and security. Here again, the preventive approach is at the heart of the United Nations' work.[81]

In this context, the concept of 'human security'[82] was taken over to describe the combination of measures aimed to secure peace and security in strategic and humanistic terms. The notion places the individual and his/her community instead of the State in the centre of attention and defines security according to threats posed to humankind. Inevitably, 'human security highlights the interconnection between different dimensions of security and puts into evidence the global nature of security challenges'.[83]

76 Daase, *loc. cit.*, fn. 8, pp. 386–387.
77 White, *loc. cit.*, fn. 22, p. 237.
78 Until the end of the Cold War, the Security Council adopted a conception of peace that identified the lack of war with peace. Hence, it predominantly acted in cases where armed conflicts had already emerged and only reluctantly engaged itself in other conflicts and crises that were likely to turn into full armed conflicts. In contrast, the General Assembly offered a conception of peace that encompassed broader issues such as economic, social, cultural and human rights issues.
79 *UN High-level Panel Report*, *op. cit.*, fn. 1, para. 148.
80 R. Dupuy, 'The United Nations Facing the Crisis of the Nation State', in N. Jasentuliyana (ed.), *Perspectives on International Law* (1995) 207.
81 V. Matthies, *Krisenprävention: Vorbeugen ist besser als Heilen* (2000) 30.
82 It is thought that the concept originated in the 1994 Human Development Report.
83 Bruggeman, *loc. cit.*, fn. 64.

Although the concept may sound new, it is well enshrined in the UN Charter and other documents of the United Nations. For example, article 1 of the UN Charter, which articulates the mandate of the organisation, integrates the maintenance of peace and security with the promotion of human rights and the resolution of global economic and social problems. Article 55 of the UN Charter also closely links economic, social, cultural and human rights issues to peace. Furthermore, articles 2(3) and 2(4) 'suggest that socio-economic justice is linked to the maintenance of peace and security'.[84] Moreover, not only does the Universal Declaration of Human Rights[85] link civil and socioeconomic rights in a single instrument, but it also declares in its preamble that human rights are a precondition of 'freedom, justice and peace', thereby strengthening the attestation to the interdependence of military/strategic and human security. A similar enunciation is enshrined in the preambles of the International Covenant on Civil and Political Rights[86] and the International Covenant on Economic, Social and Cultural Rights.[87]

As the human security approach is well entrenched in the *raison d'être* of the UN work, it should also be employed by this organisation when tackling terrorism.

B. Various Comprehensive Strategies

All three aforementioned tendencies have put the United Nations in the centre of all strategies to the level that '[t]he UN thus emerged as the principal international forum for establishing norms and co-operation to counter the new threats'.[88] Subsequently, the United Nations felt obliged to suggest various comprehensive strategies.

(i) Brief description of the comprehensive strategies

A so-called pre-comprehensive strategy can be seen in Resolution 1373 that imposes a wide-encompassing regime of measures to prevent and suppress the preparation and financing of terrorist acts.

The first 'comprehensive strategy' was put forward by the Policy Working Group in 2002.[89] It recommends a three-tiered approach:

84 J. Moore, *loc. cit.*, fn. 61, p. 64.

85 GA Res. 217 A (III): Universal Declaration of Human Rights, 10 December 1948.

86 GA Res. 2200 A (XXI): International Covenant on Civil and Political Rights, 16 December 1966.

87 GA Res. 2200 A (XXI): International Covenant on Economic, Social and Cultural Rights, 16 December 1966.

88 *Danish Report, op. cit.*, fn. 5, p. 26.

89 Report of the Policy Working Group, *loc. cit.*, fn. 6,.

(1) to dissuade disaffected groups from embracing terrorism;

(2) to deny groups or individuals the means to carry out acts of terrorism and

(3) to sustain broad-based international co-operation in the struggle against terrorism.

The second strategy is suggested in the 2004 high-level panel report. Accordingly, the comprehensive strategy includes five components that can be summarised under the following headings:[90]

(1) to dissuade individuals from using terrorism by tackling the roots and facilitators of terrorism;

(2) to act against extremism and intolerance;

(3) to develop better instruments of global co-operation;

(4) to build State capacity and

(5) to control dangerous materials and public health defence.

Later on, the Secretary-General adopts a different approach towards the comprehensive strategy by focusing on the '5 ds':

(1) to dissuade disaffected groups from choosing terrorism as a tactic to achieve their goals;

(2) to deny terrorists the means to carry out their attacks;

(3) to deter States from supporting terrorists;

(4) to develop State capacity to prevent terrorism and

(5) to defend human rights in the struggle against terrorism.[91]

Although a five-tiered approach had already been adopted by the high-level panel, the one that stems from the Madrid Summit does not reproduce it. On the contrary, it adds new elements and regroups some others.

A couple of days later, the Secretary-General presents his report entitled 'In Larger Freedom',[92] which again contains references to terrorism, albeit only to 'catastrophic terrorism', thereby brushing aside other forms of terrorist activities.

90 *UN High-level Panel Report*, *op. cit.*, fn. 1, para. 148(a).

91 United Nations, *Secretary-General Offers Global Strategy for Fighting Terrorism*, in Address to Madrid Summit, Press Release SG/SM/9757, 10 March 2005.

92 United Nations, *In Larger Freedom. Towards Development, Security and Human Rights for All*, UN doc. A/59/2005, 21 March 2005.

After shortly restating the five pillars of the Madrid Summit,[93] the Secretary-General concentrates his attention on

(1) a comprehensive convention on terrorism (which is in fact a means to achieve one of the goals of the strategy);

(2) nuclear terrorism;

(3) the need to gather as many resources as possible to carry out the comprehensive strategy and

(4) the establishment of a special rapporteur on terrorism and human rights law.

(ii) The main issues raised in the comprehensive strategies

The existence of an entire series of comprehensive strategies (see annex 1) is rather worrying. Although it may be linked to the fact that the aforementioned reports were designed by various actors, two of them by experts (Policy Working Group amd High-Level Panel Report), two others by States (Madrid Summit and World Summit) and one by the Secretary-General himself (In Larger Freedom), this lack of overall consistency is particularly deplorable. Generally, Mack and Furlong remark that '[o]utsiders trying to follow a paper trail of the emerging consensus on prevention within the UN have often been surprised by the inconsistency of various reports and extraordinary confusion of terms used to describe the organization's prevention policies'.[94] Hence, this inconsistency is not solely linked to the issue of terrorism but rather to the general manner in which United Nations reports are designed. The general aim of documents produced by the United Nations is to examine the current political and legal situation in terms of security and peace as well as to recommend States to adopt pertinent measures, so that they can appropriately direct the work of the United Nations.[95] Consequently, if the United Nations seriously wishes to agree on a comprehensive strategy, it ought to propose a common and single approach sanctioned and blessed by the Secretary-General. On the contrary, it is true that, inevitably, many issues broached in the reports can be put under the headings of other official documents, but the general impression remains that there is no united front in terms of solution.

93 *Ibid.*, para. 88.

94 A. Mack and K. Furlong, 'When Aspiration Exceeds Capability: The UN and Conflict Prevention', in R.M. Price and M.W. Zacher (eds.), *The United Nations and Global Security* (2004) 68.

95 S. Weinlich, *Prävention und Intervention: Konzeptionelle Entwicklungen in den Vereinten Nationen von der Agenda für den Frieden bis zum Bericht des High-Level Panel on Threats, Challenges and Changes* (2005) 26, TranState Working Paper No. 23, University of Bremen.

Generally, it transpires from the reports that the United Nations believes the world community to be ready to approve such a broad-encompassing strategy in the fight against terrorism. However, a first look at the 2005 World Summit report is disappointing as it seems that the States are unable to suggest efficient and comprehensive means to counteract terrorism. Instead, it takes ten paragraphs to enumerate activities that must be undertaken to come to terms with terrorism. A second look at the report nevertheless reveals that, in fact, all these activities can be put under the categories mentioned in previous reports and that, thus, the State community pays attention to the United Nations' viewpoints and expectations. Unfortunately, it does so in a less categorised and consistent manner than one may wish.

Despite all the criticism that can be raised against the latest documents of the United Nations in the fight against terrorism, '[a] thread that runs through all such concerns is the imperative to develop a global strategy of fighting terrorism that addresses root causes and strengthens responsible States and the rule of law and fundamental human rights'.[96] The focus lies therefore in combating the root causes through empowering States in the fight against terrorism still ensuring that both the rule of law and human rights are preserved in this battle. To some degree, it implies that States are not able to cope with the terrorist threat alone and, hence, must be assisted by the State community for the sake not only of the individual life of the State but also of the international community.

It also takes into consideration that weak States may become harbourers of current and future terrorists. What is more, the radicalisation and isolation of these States inevitably contribute to their being pushed even further aside from the international community. So, one of the goals of the comprehensive strategy is to assist weak States that are for various reasons unable to cope with the terrorist threat and even less with the primary causes that stimulate terrorist violence.

6. Capacity Building

The issue of capacity building deserves more attention not only because it is mentioned in most UN documents but also because it is a vector of other policies such as co-operation, dissuasion, deterrence and control.[97] Moreover, capacity building is probably one of the most comprehensive and long-term approaches towards the fight against terrorism, especially in weak States.

The three aforementioned trends, the move of terrorist and counter-terrorist activities from the national to the international level, the combination of criminal

96 *UN High-level Panel Report*, *op. cit.*, fn. 1, para. 148.

97 As the report devotes two sub-sections on (c: to develop better instruments of global co-operation) and (d: to build State capacity), there is no doubt that the United Nations' aim for the next few years is to develop State capacity as well as enhance international co-operation in the fight against terrorism. *UN High-level Panel Report*, *op. cit.*, fn. 1.

and use of force measures to fight off terrorism and the adoption of a more pro-active and preventive stance towards terrorism, in the fight against terrorism are again present in this partial strategy. First, States are required to 'help themselves' either alone or in collaboration with other States (international co-operation). Second, as a subsidiary means, the United Nations is asked to assist such States. In this context, the United Nations may employ measures linked to both prevention and intervention (pro-active measures) to the level that the use of force may be allowed (from criminalisation to the use of force).

A. States' Responsibility in the Fight Against Terrorism

The 2005 World Summit resolution puts the stress on States' international obligations because States are the front line responders to today's threats. Instead of entrusting the implementation of the comprehensive strategy, which is nominally mentioned in the section on terrorism, to UN organs, the General Assembly requests States to deal with the matter. In this regard, the General Assembly reminds States to comply with their obligations and encourages them to acknowledge the importance of the issue and, thus, the necessity to request co-operation. Much is left to States in the implementation of the comprehensive strategy, so that territorial integrity is put at the forefront. Many deplore that States are left alone steering the wheel although they are bad drivers.

Yet, the definition of territorial integrity is not as narrow as suggested by some legal documents and scholars. Already in 1928, international law recognised that States were not only sovereign but also responsible for the acts that took place within the confines of their territory.[98] Unfortunately, a series of the so-called weak States are unable to abide by their responsibility to protect, because they are no longer able to impose law and order and project sufficient authority within their own borders. As a result, they 'pose dangers not only to themselves and their neighbors, but also to people around the globe'[99] and need the world institutions' assistance.

B. The United Nations' Responsibility in Capacity Building in the Elimination of Terrorism

The United Nations is therefore strongly asked to develop the capacities of those States that cannot help themselves. Yet, the idea of capacity building is not fresh

98 'Territorial sovereignty [. . .] involves the exclusive right to display the activities of a State. This right has as corollary a duty: the obligation to protect within the territory the rights of other States, in particular their right to integrity and inviolability in peace and in war, together with the rights which each State may claim for its nationals in foreign territory.' Island of Palmas Case (*US v The Netherlands*), 2 R.I.A.A. 829, 839 (1928).

99 Dunlap, *loc. cit.*, fn. 14, p. 454.

either. Already in Resolution 1373, the Security Council pinpointed the expediency to upgrade States' capacities in terms of legislation and executive machinery to fight terrorism. The Policy Working Group also believes that preventive action in the form of capacity building is urgently required to dissuade individuals from embracing terrorism.[100] What may be a novelty is the will to apply and implement this approach. Indeed, some years later, in 2004, the Committee on Counter-Terrorism came forward with a clear identification of steps needed to deter terrorism. In stage A, States should put in place adequate legislation; in stage B, executive machinery must be established; and before, in stage C, terrorism is fought through international co-operation based on appropriate international legislation.[101]

This capacity building task could be either undertaken by the United Nations or delegated to regional international organisations. Should the latter alternative be chosen, there is no doubt that '[t]he potential role of the UN in working with regional multilateral efforts fits within the Organization's roles of norm setting, coordination, cooperation and capacity-building'.[102] In addition, it must be noted that already '[v]arious multilateral groups provide technical assistance to States to help them to develop or enhance a variety of legal, financial and other actions to counter terrorism'.[103] The Club de Madrid suggests that '[p]olice services across the world need to engage in capacity building. Distinguished units should be invited to assist smaller countries, for example in the standardisation of travel and transport documents, or the creation of joint investigation teams.'[104] On a more practical side, the United Nations may help in building indigenous law enforcement and intelligence infrastructure as well as capabilities to secure porous borders.

As of now, all measures cited in various reports of the United Nations are built upon the premise that weak States consent to being assisted. Indeed, the UN vision is based, as said earlier, on *prevention* rather than *intervention*.[105] Similarly, the Club de Madrid expects 'States in need of assistance in the process of ratifying and implementing conventions against terrorism [to] declare their preparedness to accept such assistance'.[106]

To some degree, it shows that the United Nations believes weak States to be the unwilling objects of terrorist groups, thereby refusing to consider the fact that some weak States are *per se* non-compliant. Even if it is true that '[w]eak States are helpless but not inherently evil',[107] the possibility that they turn into

100 Report of the Policy Working Group, *op. cit.*, fn. 6, para. 41.
101 Note by the President of the Security Council, UN doc. S/2004/70, Annex, 26 January 2004.
102 Report of the Policy Working Group, *op. cit.*, fn. 6, para. 47.
103 *Ibid.*, para. 46.
104 Madrid II, *op. cit.*, fn. 26, p. 11.
105 For a distinction between these two concepts, see Weinlich, *op. cit.*, fn. 95, pp. 3–4.
106 Madrid III, *op. cit.*, fn. 23, p. 15.
107 I. Österdahl, '... But some Are more Equal than Others – On Weak and Rogue States in the National Security Strategy of the United Nations', (2004) 73 *Nordic Journal of International Law* 248.

non-compliant States because they do not have the means to abide by international law must not be overlooked. The only trace of the United Nations' understanding of the harsh reality on the ground is found in the high-level panel report that recognises that '[t]he crucial need, in relation to the States in the region from which terrorists originate, is to address not only their capacity but their will to fight terrorism'.[108] The Club de Madrid repeats that 'the global threat from terrorism requires international solidarity, mutual trust and the willingness for cooperative support'.[109] In such States a collective will cannot be ascertained as often the government represents a minority. Unfortunately, UN documents do not offer any solution to this tremendous and extremely practical problem as terrorist groups are often based in non-compliant States. In this case, it is unclear which measures can be undertaken to constrain a State to adopt anti-terrorist measures. Some authors contend that the difficulty in solving this issue lies in the fact that 'rogue states and global terrorist networks remain distinct categories of threats, which do not call for the same strategic response'.[110] Yet, here again, scholars as well as the United Nations only see a part of the problem in the sense that in their opinion non-compliance automatically means 'rogue'. In reality, a rogue State is one that is willingly engaged in an adverse behaviour. This dichotomy between weak and rogue States must be revised to understand the difficulty in undertaking capacity-building activities.

The issue as to whether it is lawful for the United Nations to intervene in weak States without their consent is currently the centre of a heated debate.

On the contrary, every type of activity undertaken by the United Nations without the express consent of the State may be considered as intervention in its internal affairs unless permitted by the Security Council under chapter VII. So, strictly speaking, one must perceive each activity linked to conflict prevention as unlawful *per se*.[111] In 1992, the Agenda for Peace stressed States' fundamental and territorial sovereignty on which each United Nations activity should be based,[112] thereby espousing an old and conventional understanding of sovereignty, at least on the rhetorical level. Some States claim that prevention measures, especially relating to human rights and humanitarian issues, are illegitimate intervention. In their opinion, prevention amounts to 'anticipatory intervention'.[113] If one toes this line, it is impossible for the United Nations to engage in capacity-building measures to counteract terrorist activities without the express consent of the State. As a result, weak States continue to offer terrorist groups the cover of State sovereignty,

108 *UN High-level Panel Report*, *op. cit.*, fn. 1, para. 147.
109 Madrid II, *op. cit.*, fn. 26, p. 10.
110 Andréani, *loc. cit.*, fn. 13, p. 44.
111 Weinlich, *op. cit.*, fn. 95, p. 8.
112 UN Secretary-General, Agenda for Peace, UN doc. A/47/277–S/24111, 17 June 1992, para. 17.
113 M. Griffin, 'Retrenchment, Reform and Regionalization: Trends in UN Peace Support Operations', (1999) 6(1) *International Peacekeeping* 486.

and little can be done either peacefully or forcefully on behest of the right to self-defence.[114] Only collective measures adopted under chapter VII would be possible to remove the threat.

At the heart of the controversy lies the definition of the latest version of 'sovereignty' in terms of 'responsibility' as well as the argument that such States lose their statehood if they do not fulfil certain requirements.[115] On the one hand, it is argued that '[a] state that allows its citizens "to suffer in a vacuum of responsibility" temporarily forfeits its moral claim to be treated as legitimate. Therefore its sovereignty and its right to non-intervention are suspended'.[116] In a sovereign-centric vision of international law, the loss of sovereignty of a weak State produces an entity that can no longer be deemed a subject of international law and thereby loses certain rights and obligations associated with statehood.[117] The right to non-interference in internal affairs is thus contingent on the fulfilment of the State's responsibilities towards its population and the international community. Accordingly, States as well as international institutions are free to intervene in the affairs of weak States and do not need their consent.

Combined with the subsidiary responsibility of the United Nations to prevent, protect and rebuild,[118] it means that the United Nations would be put in a position, if not obligation, to rebuild the State and provide it with the capacity to deter terrorism. First, the United Nations 'recognizes the problem of failed states and considers itself the vital instrument in managing state failure and stemming its consequences'.[119] Second, '[t]he responsibility of the international community to prevent and punish serious violations of human rights comes into play [. . .] in the case of "weak" or "failed" states, unable to prevent serious violations from being committed on its territory by private parties'.[120] As terrorism is perceived as a threat to the State community[121] as well as a violation of

114 'So the ineffective or failed state is an ideal incubator; it is itself unable to restrain the private army that uses terrorism, yet its state status insulates the private army from other states upon whom the private army may prey'. Reisman, *loc. cit.*, fn. 69, p. 50.

115 S. Mohamed, 'From Keeping Peace to Building Peace: A Proposal for a Revitalized United Nations Trusteeship Council', (2005) 105 *Columbia Law Review* 816.

116 S. Wills, 'Military Interventions on behalf of Vulnerable Populations: The Legal Responsibilities of States and International Organisations Engaged in Peace Support Operations', (2004) 9(3) *JCSL* 392.

117 R. Gordon, 'Saving Failed States: Sometimes a Neocolonialist Notion', (1997) 12 *American University Journal of International Law and Policy* 967. See also the discussion in Österdahl, *loc. cit.*, fn. 107, pp. 247–263.

118 See the International Commission on Intervention and State Sovereignty, *The Responsibility to Protect*, December 2001.

119 Mohamed, *loc. cit.*, fn. 115, p. 817.

120 Wills, *loc. cit.*, fn. 116, p. 391.

121 A plethora of UN Security Council resolutions describes terrorism as a threat to peace and security. The Declaration on the Issue of Combating Terrorism reiterates that 'terrorism in all its forms and manifestation constitutes one of the most serious threats to peace and security'. SC Res. 1456 (2003), 20 January 2003.

international law,[122] the United Nations is entitled to intervene without the consent of the State. It is nevertheless unlikely that the United Nations would intervene in a particular country without its consent and furthermore without the express authorisation of the Security Council.

A third possibility would be for the Security Council to declare that a particular situation amounts to a threat to international peace and security according to article 39 of the UN Charter and, thereby, allow the use of forceful measures. For example, the Club de Madrid suggests the possibility for the Security Council to launch on-site investigations where it is believed that terrorist groups are hiding in a particular State that is actively sheltering or assisting them.[123] Unfortunately, although the Club de Madrid mentions that the Security Council disposes of the full range of measures under chapter VII, it restricts its enumeration of possible measures to sanctions such as those adopted against Libya, Sudan and Afghanistan before September 11. To build up capacities to fight terrorism, the Security Council must allow for more than just on-site investigations; it must also adopt positive measures, such as capacity-building, once it has established that the State is complicit in terrorist activities. Under chapter VII, the Security Council could indeed lawfully force a State to engage in capacity-building measures by imposing a UN presence on the ground.

The necessity to have recourse to the Security Council raises two major issues. The first problem focuses on the political selectivity of the Security Council decisions, as the trigger mechanism for the United Nations being engaged in capacity-building activities entirely lies in its hands and upon its determination of a situation as a threat to international peace and security. Moreover, the vagueness and political characterisation made by the Security Council inevitably poses a problem.[124] As White underlines, '[e]ven relatively clear terms such as "breach of the peace", while retaining their core certainty, have been applied selectively, while other terms, such as "threat to the peace", have an inherent ambiguity, deliberately chosen so as to allow a significant amount of discretion'.[125] As a result, it is difficult to gauge when the Security Council is ready to engage in capacity-building operations.

Second, the practicability of imposed capacity-building measures comes to the fore. How can such a system be enforced once the United Nations arrives in a State whose government refuses to co-operate and, maybe, does everything

122 'Terrorism is a violation of human rights.' Report of the Policy Working Group, *op. cit.*, fn. 6, para. 26; 'Terrorism is a serious crime of concern to the international community as a whole.' Madrid III, *op. cit.*, fn. 23, p. 14.

123 Madrid III, *op. cit.*, fn. 23, p. 9.

124 However, the Appeals Chamber in Tadic noted that 'threat to the peace is more of a political concept. But [that] the determination that there exists such a threat is not a totally unfettered discretion, as it has to remain, at the very least, within the Purposes and Principles of the Charter'. ICTY, *Prosecutor v Tadic*, Decision on the Tadic Jurisdictional Motion, Case No. IT-94-1-AR72, 2 October 1995, para. 27.

125 White, *loc. cit.*, fn. 22, p. 237. See also *Danish Report, op. cit.*, fn. 5, p. 91.

possible to prevent the United Nations from working properly? In this case, one can surmise that the United Nations would have to act against the State and maybe remove and replace its government for a certain period of time. In other words, this comprehensive strategy would empower the United Nations to take over a State and proceed with its capacity-building tasks. To some extent, the Kosovo or the East-Timor 'model' could be adopted and adapted to the situation on the ground but then, the United Nations could not limit itself to capacity-building measures related to terrorism.

7. Conclusion: The Future of Such a Strategy

Last but not least, a crucial question is whether this comprehensive strategy would reduce or suppress the terrorist threat. There is no expediency to develop another strategy that is neither feasible nor efficient. What the international community needs is a strategy that has some chance of success.

In fact, it is feared that the implementation of the comprehensive strategy will overburden the UN institutions. In addition, the positive effect of such activities may only be felt in the long term, so that the United Nations may be committed in these countries for decades. Meaningful results could only be gauged in several decades provided enough financial support is secured for such long-term activities. In the immediate future, no positive outcome will be seen and, hence, support may be quickly reduced if not suppressed.

Furthermore, capacity building limited to punctual aid in specific fields may not be sufficient to counteract terrorism in weak States, because the State may not have the ability to fulfil the most basic functions of a State. Indeed, the State may not be able to prevent their officials from being bribed and their institutions from being infiltrated to the level that terrorists obtain official documents, weapons and information.[126] In other words, '[terrorism] profits from weak State capacity to maintain law and order'.[127] Therefore, '[t]he surest method for denying havens for terrorists in failed states is to prevent and reverse state failure itself',[128] a statement based on the idea that the best guarantor of peace is an efficient State.[129] This task encompasses, amongst others, rebuilding physical infrastructures and establishing internal security and peace that are indispensable to avert the terrorist threat as well as its emergence.[130] The financial and political efforts undertaken by the United Nations in State building may be even more drastic than those deployed for sustaining capacity-building measures.

126 *Danish Report, op. cit.*, fn. 5, p. 25.
127 *UN High-level Panel Report, op. cit.*, fn. 1, para. 145.
128 Dunlap, *loc. cit.*, fn. 14, p. 455.
129 S. Sur, 'Sur quelques tribulations de l'Etat dans la société internationale', (1993) 4 *Revue Générale de Droit International Public* 892.
130 W. von Erffa, 'Internationale des Terrors. Panislamische Netzwerke im Nahen Osten', (2003) 10 *Internationale Politik* 30–31.

On the one hand, '[t]he financial burdens and political risks associated with interventions of the scope and duration necessary to effectuate the remaking of a state pose a powerful deterrent to governments'.[131] Consequently, intervention in weak States does not fail on the basis of a lack of proper international norms but on the political will of States potentially able to intervene.[132] On the other hand, repairing failed States has also become part of the national security agenda against terrorism and, hence, some governments may be more willing to participate in the gigantic task of reconstructing the State. Yet again, selectivity of the decisions, and hence the priorities, of the Security Council must be taken into consideration. In other words, we fall back into the old scheme of collective security that is in the hands of the permanent five.

131 Grant, *loc. cit.*, fn. 68, p. 72.

132 S. Mair, 'Intervention und 'state failure': Sind shwache Staaten noch zu retten?', (2004) 3 *Internationale Politik und Gesellschaft* 89.

ANNEX 1

Working Policy Group (2002)	High-Level Panel (2004)	Madrid (2005)	In Larger Freedom (2005)	World Summit (2005)
To dissuade disaffected groups from embracing terrorism	To dissuade individuals from using terrorism by tackling the roots and facilitators of terrorism	To dissuade disaffected groups from choosing terrorism as a tactic to achieve their goals		
	To act against extremism and intolerance			To promote dialogue, tolerance and understanding among civilisations
To deny groups or individuals the means to carry out acts of terrorism		To deny terrorists the means to carry out their attacks		
	To control dangerous materials and public health defence		To agree on an international convention from the suppression of acts of nuclear terrorism	States must become parties to the convention for the suppression of acts of nuclear terrorism
To sustain broad-based international cooperation in the struggle against terrorism	To develop better instruments of global cooperation			The Security Council must monitor and enforce States' obligations in the fight against terrorism
				States must become parties to the anti-terrorism conventions
	To build State capacity	To develop State capacity to prevent terrorism		The UN should assist States in building national and regional capacity to combat terrorism
		To deter States from supporting terrorists		States must refrain from supporting terrorist activities and must take measures to ensure that their territories are not used for such activities
		To defend human rights in the struggle against terrorism	To create a special rapporteur on the compatibility of counter-terrorism measures with international human rights law	States must ensure that any measures taken to combat terrorism comply with their obligations under international law

[11]

THE LEGISLATIVE ROLE OF THE SECURITY COUNCIL IN ITS FIGHT AGAINST TERRORISM: LEGAL, POLITICAL AND PRACTICAL LIMITS

LUIS MIGUEL HINOJOSA MARTÍNEZ*

Abstract This article studies the normative activity developed by the Security Council (SC) in recent years, particularly in the fight against terrorism. This legislative activity has aroused a great deal of controversy both among scholars and the States. Is the SC acting ultra vires? Has it revealed a new form of creating of international norms, which overrides definitively States' consent as the only material source of international law? This contribution tries to answer these questions by investigating the scope of the SC powers in the Charter, their historical background and the reaction of UN Member States towards its Resolutions. After this analysis, it is submitted that the SC does have a legislative capacity, but with important legal, political and practical limits.

I. INTRODUCTION

Since the beginning of the 1990s, the revitalization of the Security Council (SC) has resulted in an extraordinary increase in its activity and in the imagination with which its powers have been implemented. In recent years, the SC has taken decisions on general issues, not necessarily linked to a particular conflict, and has established rules of general scope that oblige Member States of the United Nations (UN) to adopt legislation and administrative acts in their internal legal systems. This has particularly been the case in the fight against terrorism, where it has been said that the SC has begun to behave as a global legislator.

This legislative activity of the SC has aroused a great deal of controversy both among scholars and the States. Is the SC acting ultra vires? Has the SC revealed a new form of creating international norms, which definitively overrides State consent as the only material source of international law? This article tries to answer these questions by investigating the scope of the SC powers in the Charter within the context of its recent normative activity. After this analysis, it is submitted that the SC does have this legislative capacity, but with important legal, political and practical limits.

* PhD: LLM (LSE, London); Licence spécial en droit européen (ULB, Brussels); Professor of International Law, Department of Public International Law, University of Granada <hinojosa@ugr.es>.

II. CHAPTER VII OF THE CHARTER AS THE LEGAL BASIS FOR LEGISLATIVE ACTIVITY

As is usual in the practice of the SC, the two Resolutions most clearly identified as 'legislative', Resolution 1373 (2001) and Resolution 1540 (2004), were adopted 'acting under Chapter VII of the Charter'. The use of this Chapter as a generic legal base is questionable, but not novel.[1] In any event, it seems clear that when the SC describes 'any act of international terrorism' as 'a threat to international peace and security' it is acting under the provisions of Article 39 of the Charter, and when it decides that all States shall necessarily apply specific measures that do not imply the use of force to fight against that terrorism, it does so under the powers granted by Article 41 of that text.[2] Resolution 1373 itself seems to seek elements of justification in its Preamble when it makes reference to the need to work together 'urgently' to prevent and suppress acts of terrorism. Similar arguments were used in relation to Resolution 1540.[3]

Examining the practice of the SC from the beginning of the 1990s, it can be seen that Article 41 has been used with enormous creativity, going far beyond the merely indicative list of examples that the provision contains. The progressive extension of the concept of threat to peace[4] has led the Council to widen the range of applicable measures in an attempt to adapt its intervention to the needs of each specific case. Thus, the SC has instituted a Claims Commission to determine the indemnities that Iraq had to pay after its invasion of Kuwait,[5] has established as 'final' the border demarcation between these two States made by a body that it itself had created,[6] has set up

[1] Although in Resolution 232 (16 Dec 1966), the SC explicitly mentioned Articles 39 and 41 of the Charter as the legal ground of its decision, since Resolution 253 (29 May 1968), it has referred to 'Chapter VII of the Charter' as the generic legal basis for its actions in situations where it estimates that there is a threat to international peace and security, apart from very specific exceptions (see, eg, Resolution 1718 (14 Oct 2006), in which it clarifies that the SC adopted measures in accordance with Article 41 of the Charter).

[2] Colombia's representative, a member of the SC when Resolution 1373 was adopted, expressly cited Article 41 of the Charter as the legal basis of that Resolution (Doc S/PV.4394 (Resumption 1) (25 Oct 2001) 7).

[3] SC Res 1540 (2004) was also justified by the urgency of the circumstances. In a press conference prior to the commencement of the debates on this Resolution (2 April 2004), the President of the SC pointed out, 'there was a gap in international law pertaining to non-State actors. So, either new international law should be created, either waiting for customary international law to develop, or by negotiating a treaty or convention. Both took a long time, and everyone felt that there was an "imminent threat", which had to be addressed and which could not wait for the usual way', (available at <http://www.un.org/News/briefings/docs/2004/pleugerpc.DOC.htm>).

[4] The SC not only considers inter-State conflicts as threats to peace, but also clearly has extended that concept to include internal conflicts (Sierra Leona, Somalia, Sudan, etc). In the same way, it has incorporated into that notion other forms of violence distinct from armed conflicts, such as a coup d'état against a democratically chosen President that generates a humanitarian crisis (Resolution 841 (16 June 1993)), ethnic cleansing (Resolution 808 (22 Feb 1993)), or terrorism (Resolution 1269 (19 Oct 1999)).

[5] SC Res 687 (3 April 1991) para 18.

[6] SC Res 833 (27 May 1993) para 4.

international criminal courts and has approved their Statutes,[7] has established sanctions against particular physical and legal persons,[8] and even decreed that all States adopt the necessary measures to return artefacts removed from a national museum.[9]

Regardless of the opinions that can be expressed about these and other initiatives, it is not surprising that with these antecedents, the International Criminal Tribunal for the Former Yugoslavia (ICTY) has suggested in its jurisprudence that the SC possesses a normative capacity in the development of its functions. In the UN there is no clear division between the legislative and executive powers that attributes each of them to a specific organ. Article 41 of the Charter contains a 'negative definition' of the SC's powers, since it only lays down what the measures 'cannot be' (armed force cannot be used); however, 'it does not say or suggest what they have to be'.[10] In such circumstances, as nothing in the Charter contradicts it, the SC would enjoy the normative power necessary for the efficient accomplishment of its mission to safeguard international peace and security.[11]

Moreover, it can be argued that Article 31 (3)(b) of the Vienna Convention on the Law of Treaties establishes that 'any subsequent practice in the application of a treaty which establishes the agreement of the parties' can be used as the appropriate criterion for the interpretation of its provisions.[12] In this sense, the unanimity with which Resolutions 1373 (2001) and 1540 (2004) were adopted in the SC, together with the support for them shown by the General Assembly (GA), may account for the general acceptance of the SC's interpretation made in the said Resolutions on the powers derived from Article 41 of the Charter.[13] The statement of the ICJ in its Opinion in *Certain Expenses of the United Nations* case would also favour this interpretation when it said that in the absence of any specific procedure to clarify the validity

[7] Eg, the ICTY in SC Res 808 (22 Feb 1993) and 827 (25 May 1993), or the Special Tribunal for Lebanon in Resolution 1757 (30 May 2007).

[8] See the sanctions against a list of persons connected to Al Qaeda and the Taliban, based on SC Res 1267 (15 Oct 1999), 1333 (19 Dec 2000) and 1390 (28 Jan 2002).

[9] SC Res 1483 (22 May 2003).

[10] See *Tadić (Jurisdiction)* ICTY-94-1 (2 October 1995) para 35.

[11] ibid paras 43–44. The preparatory work of the Charter sheds no light in this respect, since it only discusses (and rules out) the possibility of expressly granting the GA legislative competence (P De Visscher, 'Valeur et autorité des actes des organisations internationales' in RJ Dupuy (ed), *Manuel sur les organisations internationals* (Académie de Droit International de la Haye/Nihoff, The Hague, 1988) 324). However, the fact that this question was not even discussed in relation to the SC allows various interpretations, from completely rejecting this possibility to not wanting to limit the SC's discretion by imposing conditions on its action.

[12] In the *Namibia* case ([1971] ICJ Rep 22), the ICJ alludes to the practice of SC members, generally accepted by the members of UN, as a criterion of interpretation of Article 27 (3) of the Charter, in order to *assert* that the abstention of one of the States with a permanent seat in the SC cannot prevent the adoption of decisions.

[13] For a defence of this evolving interpretation of Article 41 of the Charter, see R Lavalle, 'A Novel, if Awkward, Exercise in International Law-Making: Security Council Resolution 1540 (2004)' (2004) 51 Netherlands Intl L Rev 419–23 (NILR).

of the acts of this organization's institutions, each of them must determine its own jurisdiction.[14] Thus there are well-founded arguments that support in general terms the Council's normative capacity in the development of its mission to maintain international peace and security when some circumstances put them at risk.

I do not share the opinion of a sector of the doctrine that considers that the SC enjoys a general legislative competence on the basis of Article 25 of the Charter, which does not depend on other more specific powers granted by the Charter itself.[15] Although it is true that in the negotiations on the text of Article 25 the drafters did not want to introduce particular allusions to any Chapter of the Charter so as not to limit the role granted to the SC within the UN,[16] any of its actions must be grounded on a legal basis. Of course, the ICJ introduced a certain confusion by indicating, in the *Namibia* case (in which South Africa questioned the validity of a SC Resolution because it lacked a legal basis), that a general Resolution may be based on Article 24 (1) of the Charter, without needing to be remitted to the Chapters mentioned in paragraph 2 of the Article. Later, the Court added that Article 25 is applicable to all the decisions of the SC, and not only to those adopted under Chapter VII.[17] Nevertheless, in my opinion the interpretation referred to previously would empty Article 24 of all meaning and make it superfluous. In reality, since Article 25 makes no mention whatever of any material sphere, it would convert the SC into a type of universal legislator without limits *ratione materiae*, which, without doubt, would go beyond the intentions of the Charter's drafters.

III. THE SHARING OUT OF THE NORMATIVE COMPETENCES BETWEEN THE GENERAL ASSEMBLY AND THE SECURITY COUNCIL

The United Nations Charter provides certain criteria to delimit the functions between the GA and the SC in the context of the fight against terrorism. Articles 11 and 12 of the Charter give wide competences to the GA for the maintenance of international peace and security. More concretely, Article 11 (1) establishes that the GA 'may consider the *general principles* of co-operation in the maintenance of international peace and security' (emphasis added). From a more general perspective, Article 13 (1)(a) confers on the GA a limited normative function (something very different

[14] [1962] ICJ Rep 168.

[15] C Tomuschat, 'L'adaptation institutionnelle des Nations Unies au nouvel ordre mondial' in R Ben Achour and S Laghmani, *Les nouveaux aspects du droit international* (Pedone, Paris, 1994) 163.

[16] B Simma (ed), *The Charter of the United Nations. A Commentary* (Oxford University Press, Oxford, 2002) vol I, 454.

[17] *Legal Consequences for States of the Continued Presence of South Africa in Namibia (South West Africa) notwithstanding Security Council Resolution 276 (1970)* [1971] ICJ Rep, paras 110 and 113.

from legislative competence), by indicating that it can promote studies and make recommendations for 'encouraging the progressive development of international law and its codification'.

In practice, these competences have been translated into the drafting of resolutions in which the GA identified the international law in force,[18] in a declarative function,[19] although it could not draw up additional or complementary norms that imposed new obligations on the States.[20] For the latter, and on the basis of Article 13 (1) of the Charter, the GA created its Sixth Committee and the International Law Commission (ILC).[21] The States' debates in the Sixth Committee, and in other subsidiary bodies created ad hoc for the negotiation of certain international conventions, enable treaties to be drawn up that are subsequently approved by the GA, but which lack binding force until they have been ratified by a sufficient number of States. In short, what makes these conventions obligatory is the States' expression of consent, since the GA possesses competence to 'encourage' the progressive development of international law, but it cannot take the place of the indispensable consent of the States in that process.

All this explains why the adoption of general measures against terrorism was in the past considered a function of the GA. Several of its Resolutions identified the obligations that both the Charter and international law imposed on the States in the fight against terrorism.[22] From a normative perspective, it

[18] See, eg, the well-known GA Res 2625 (XXV) (24 Oct 1970), or 3314 (XXIX) (14 Dec 1974).

[19] The ICJ has referred on numerous occasions to GA Resolutions to clarify the concrete content of the norms of customary international law. See, eg, the Advisory Opinion on the *Legal Consequences of the Construction of a Wall in the Occupied Palestinian Territory* [2004] ICJ Rep 136, which remits to Resolution 2625 (XXV) to set out the specific content of the principle of the prohibition of the use of force (para 87), or of the principle of free determination of peoples (para 88). However, the fact that a Resolution of the GA indicates that a given action is contrary to the Charter or international law does not signify that this is necessarily so. In the Advisory Opinion on the *Legality of the Use by a State of Nuclear Weapons in Armed Conflicts* [1996] ICJ Rep, paras 70–71, after pointing out that 'General Assembly resolutions, even if they are not binding, may sometimes have normative value. They can, in certain circumstances, provide evidence important for establishing the existence of a rule or the emergence of an *opinio juris*', the ICJ indicated, 'several of the resolutions under consideration in the present case have been adopted with substantial numbers of negative votes and abstentions'. In consequence, the Court considered that, in spite of their forceful asseverations, those GA resolutions did not prove the existence of an *opinio iuris* that enabled the existence of a customary norm to be proved.

[20] As is well known, GA Resolutions are not binding on States, since it can only make 'recommendations' (Article 10 of the Charter).

[21] Although Article 16 of the ILC Statute reserves to the GA the 'progressive development' of international law, the ILC does not distinguish in practice its work of 'codification' from that of 'progressive development', carrying out both tasks together (Doc A/51/10, paras 157–58) On the other hand, over recent years the GA has habitually created ad hoc subsidiary bodies, outside the ILC, to draw up particular conventions. On these questions, see Y Daudet, 'Actualités de la codification du droit international' (2003) 303 Recueil des Cours de l'Académie de la Haye 9 (RCADI).

[22] See, in particular, GA Res 49/60 (17 Feb 1995) and 51/210 (16 Jan 1997), which preceded Resolution 60/288 (20 Sept 2006).

has also been the GA that has sponsored several international agreements against terrorism, fundamentally through the work of its Sixth Committee and the Special Committee created by its Resolution 51/210.[23]

On the other hand, the Charter seems to outline essentially executive competences for the SC. It can only make use of the powers granted by Chapter VII of the Charter after a declaration of the existence of a threat to the peace, a breach of the peace, or an act of aggression. In such circumstances, the examples set out in Article 41 on the measures that the SC can take, show the Charter's drafters were thinking of executive functions.[24]

This has led a substantial sector of the doctrine to point out that the SC only has competences to confront particular cases that threaten international peace and security,[25] and that it lacks legislative competence,[26] understood as the capacity to issue binding norms of general scope on abstract questions.[27] Other authors recognize, at most, an exceptional normative competence to resolve those concrete cases,[28] or even an 'administrative regulatory' competence.[29]

At the other extreme of the doctrinal spectrum are those authors who defend the SC's legislative capacity,[30] basing their argument on the fact that no provision of the Charter rules out that possibility, nor establishes limits on its discretion other than respect for the purposes and principles for the UN (Article 24 (2) of the Charter) when deciding what measures to adopt under

[23] On the base of this Special Committee's work the GA has drafted and approved three 'new generation' treaties that have notably completed international conventional law against terrorism: the International Convention for the Suppression of Terrorist Bombings (1997), the International Convention for the Suppression of the Financing of Terrorism (1999), and the International Convention for the Suppression of Acts of Nuclear Terrorism (2005). At present, and since the year 2000, the Special Committee established by Resolution 51/210 is working on drawing up a draft General Convention for the Suppression of International Terrorism.

[24] Article 41 of the Charter speaks of the interruption of economic relations and of rail, sea, air, postal, telegraphic, radio, and other means of communication, and the severance of diplomatic relations.

[25] M Happold, 'Security Council Resolution 1373 and the Constitution of the United Nations' (2003) 16 Leiden Journal of International Law 600; G Arangio-Ruiz, 'On the Security Council's "Law Making"' (2000) 83 Rivista di Diritto Internazionale 692–700; V Gowlland Debbas, 'The Limits of Unilateral Enforcement of Community Objectives in the Framework of UN Peace Maintenance' (2000) 11 Eur J Intl L 377 (EJIL).

[26] E Lagrange, 'Le Conseil de sécurité des Nations Unies peut-il violer le droit international?' (2004) 37 Revue belge de droit international 577 (RBDI).

[27] M Koskenniemi, 'The Police in the Temple. Order, Justice and the UN: A Dialectical View' (1995) 6 EJIL 345; A Pellet, 'Peut-on et doit-on contrôler les actions du Conseil de sécurité?' in M Boutros Ghali et al, *Le Chapitre VII de la Charte des Nations Unies* (Pedone, Paris, 1995) 236.

[28] S Sur, 'Conclusions' in Boutros Ghali et al (n 27) 311.

[29] Corten considers that SC Resolutions 1373 (2001) and 1540 (2004) 'se présentent comme des décisions de type réglementaire et non comme l'expression de règles générales' (O Corten, 'La participation du Conseil de Sécurité à l'élaboration, à la cristallisation ou à la consolidation de règles coutumières' (2004) 37 RBDI 562).

[30] JE Álvarez, 'Hegemonic International Law Revisited' (2003) 97 AJIL 874; PA Szasz, 'The Security Council Starts Legislating' (2002) 96 AJIL 904–5; C Tomuschat, 'Obligations Arising for States Without or Against their Will' (1993) 241 RCADI 344–46.

Chapter VII. It would be simply a question of making a teleological interpretation of a text drawn up in 1945,[31] to enable the SC to tackle the threats to international peace and security, such as terrorism, which nowadays have a worldwide dimension.[32]

It has already been indicated that, from my point of view, the Charter can be interpreted in such a way that the SC is not prevented from adopting the normative measures necessary to confront the direct and concrete threats to international peace and security. In spite of that, it has to be admitted that in the normative field the Charter imposes a first limit on the SC derived from the balance of power between the two main organs of the United Nations: the SC lacks competence for the codification and the progressive development of international law because that function is explicitly assigned to the GA by the Charter (Article 13 (1)(a)).[33]

In fact, it is not even the GA itself, through the subsidiary organs it has created to that end, that progressively develops international law but rather, in the last instance, the States, which by expressing consent to be bound by its conventions, or by behaving in a constant and uniform manner, and by being aware of the legal obligation to do so, create new norms of international law. In short, the Charter is built on the cornerstone that serves as the basis for the international legal system: State consent is the only origin of the obligations imposed by that system.[34] In such circumstances, if the SC assumes a general

[31] The ICJ has recognized in its jurisprudence the convenience of making a teleological interpretation of the Charter in such a way that the United Nations can carry out effectively the missions that are assigned to it (*Reparation for Injuries Suffered in the Service of the United Nations* [1949] ICJ Rep 182). There are even some authors who point out that it is only now that the SC is 'functioning as was originally intended under the United Nations Charter' (P Wallensteen and P Johansson, 'Security Council Decisions in Perspective' in DM Malone (ed), *The UN Security Council from the Cold War to the 21st Century* (Lynne Rienner Publishers, Boulder, 2004) 17). For an examination of the changes that the SC has undergone since its creation, while requiring scarcely any reforms in the Charter, see FL Kirgis, 'The Security Council's First Fifty Years' (1995) 89 AJIL 506.

[32] 'If the Council thought that the lack or weakness of existing counter-terrorism . . . legislation . . . in a particular country posed a specific threat to peace and security, few would question its authority under Chapter VII to adopt a resolution requiring that State to take certain steps to enhance its capacity. It is also difficult to dispute the fact that existing terrorist . . . threats are global in nature, and thus, . . . it would be logical for the Council to claim the authority under Chapter VII to impose the same requirements on all States' (E Rosand, 'The Security Council as a "Global Legislator": *Ultra Vires* or Ultra Innovative?' (2005) 28 Fordham Intl L J 559–60 (FILJ)).

[33] There are objective data that show the SC's progressive invasion of the GA's competences. The expansion of SC competences has increased the average length of its Resolutions, so that they now extend to considerations that previously were only seen in those of the GA (see, eg, the reflections in SC Res 1624 (14 Sept 2005), on the need to promote dialogue among civilizations, paying special attention to the problems of development as an element that contributes to strengthening the fight against terrorism). But even more, the SC has permitted itself to identify what rules set out in a Convention must be considered norms of customary international law (SC Res 1067 (26 July 1996) para 6).

[34] It can be argued here that the States 'consent' when they ratify the UN Charter, thus accepting the obligatory nature of the SC's decisions; but this would only be so in the case that the Charter itself effectively granted the SC competence for the progressive development of

legislative function of progressive development of international law, not only would it be overlapping the GA's modest competences, but rather it would be subverting the structural bases of the international legal order itself, by acting as if State consent were no longer necessary for the creation of new international norms.[35]

Of course, in legal terms it would be tremendously complicated to identify the moment in which such a step has been taken, and even more so bearing in mind the SC's discretionality both to determine the existence of threats to peace and security and to decide on the measures to oppose them, including creating norms. However, that discretion is clearly overstepped if the SC uses it to impose abstract norms of general scope that meet significant opposition in the GA.

IV. THE LEGISLATIVE NATURE OF SOME SC RESOLUTIONS

As a first step to the analysis of the scope of the SC's normative competence, it is necessary to decide whether Resolutions 1373 and 1540 effectively constitute legislative acts, and whether they are truly new, even revolutionary, in the SC's practice.

Of all the precedents in the SC's activity, the creation of international criminal courts has probably been the most clearly legislative.[36] The approval of the Statutes of those courts, in which the crimes to be judged and the procedural norms are laid down, can only be described as a normative act, and in the *Tadić* case, the ICTY recognized the SC's competence to carry out such acts.[37] These assertions do not contradict the fact that in its report on the creation of ICTY, the Secretary-General stated that by punishing serious

international law. As Judge Sir Gerald Fitzmaurice pointed out in his separate opinion in the *Namibia* case ([1971] ICJ Rep 294, para 115), 'It was to keep the peace, not to change the world order, that the Security Council was set up'.

[35] In the debate that took place in the SC prior to the adoption of Resolution 1540 (2004), some States indicated that its legislative initiatives might break the balance of power between the GA and the SC (see, eg, the intervention of the Indian representative in Doc S/PV.4950, 22 April 2004, 25), while other States explicitly pointed out that the SC's legislative role was supplanting State competences (see, eg, the intervention of the Indonesian representative in Doc S/PV.4950, 34); nevertheless, a majority of States accepted the Council's legislative capacity in exceptional circumstances and in response to an urgent need (for example, see the Swiss representative's intervention in Doc S/PV.4950, 31).

[36] Other precedents can also be mentioned, such as SC Res 687 (3 April 1991), which for its scope and thoroughness can be considered as the equivalent of a peace treaty between Iraq and Kuwait; SC Res 1031 (15 December 1995), which established in detail the criteria of the application of the General Framework Peace Agreement in Bosnia and Herzegovina; or the approval of a criminal code for Somalia by the UN Secretary-General's Representative on the basis of a mandate conferred by the SC under Chapter VII of the Charter (see the reference in D Sarooshi, *The United Nations and the Development of Collective Security* (Clarendon Press, Oxford, 1999) 62–63).

[37] In paras 33–36 of *Tadić (Jurisdiction)* ICTY-94-1 (2 Oct 1995), the argument was put forward as to why the SC could create international criminal courts and, in paras 43–44, it was asserted that no clear division between legislative and executive power existed in the UN's

violations of international humanitarian law, 'the SC would not be creating or purporting to "legislate" that law'.[38] These considerations were directed at refuting the violation of the principle *nullum crimen, nulla poena sine lege*.[39]

In any case, the procedural norms set out in the Statutes,[40] or their provisions relating to their competence *ratione personae*, are enough to describe their content as legislative. Moreover, the fact that two members of the SC showed, when Resolution 827 (1993)[41] was adopted (under which the ICTY was created), that they would have preferred this institution to have been set up through an international treaty, demonstrates the legislative nature of such a Resolution.[42]

With this background, it has to be recognized that many of the obligations imposed by the SC in Resolution 1373 had already been included in earlier resolutions of the GA as derived from customary international law,[43] and that other obligations established in the same Resolution had been set out in the International Convention for the Suppression of the Financing of Terrorism.[44]

On the other hand, it must be remembered that prior to 11 September 2001, the SC had already condemned terrorism in general terms and without referring to any specific attack in Resolution 1269 (1999).[45] Nevertheless, it had done so without inferring from that condemnation the imposition of any

institutional framework, suggesting a justification of the SC's legislative capacity on the basis of Chapter VII of the Charter.

[38] Doc S/25704 (20 May 1993) para 29. [39] ibid para 34.

[40] Eg, Article 10 of the ICTY Statute establishes that no State could judge persons tried before the ICTY in its own courts for the same crimes, while Article 19 of the same text imposes exacting obligations of judicial cooperation on all States.

[41] SC Res 827 (25 May 1993).

[42] The words of the Chinese representative, as a permanent member of the SC are particularly clarifying: 'the Statute of the International Court that has just been approved is a legal instrument that enjoys the attributes of an international treaty that involves complex legal and financial questions. It should only come into force after having been negotiated and concluded by sovereign States and having been ratified by their national legislative organs in accordance with their national laws' (Doc S/PV.3217 (25 April 1993) 32). In spite of these words, China voted in favour of Resolution 827 (1993). However, to show its growing dissatisfaction at this formula for creating international criminal courts, it abstained in the vote on Resolution 955 (8 Nov 1994), which set up the International Criminal Tribunal for Rwanda (ICTR).

[43] The second paragraph of Resolution 1373 (2001) incorporated no new obligations on the States that the GA had not already accepted as arising from general international law in its previously mentioned Resolutions 49/60 and 51/210, with the exception of those relating to the financing of terrorism. Eg, the fifth paragraph of the Declaration annexed to Resolution 49/60 considers as arising from international law the obligations to refrain from 'tolerating terrorist activities and to take appropriate practical measures to ensure that their respective territories are not used . . . for the preparation or organization of terrorist acts intended to be committed against other States', 'to ensure the apprehension and prosecution or extradition of perpetrators of terrorist acts', or 'to take appropriate measures . . . for the purpose of ensuring that the refugee status is not used' for the preparation of terrorist acts.

[44] Eg, Resolution 1373, in para 1(b), requires the financing of terrorism to be classified as a crime, so extending to all States the obligation imposed by Article 4 of the 1999 Convention.

[45] SC Res 1269 (19 Oct 1999).

specific obligation on Member States, beyond the explicit backing mentioned in that Resolution to the Declaration annexed to Resolution 49/60 of the GA.

All these antecedents enable us to understand the evolution that led to the drafting of Resolution 1373, but cannot hide its revolutionary nature. With this Resolution, for the first time the SC acted by establishing general, permanent[46] obligations, unconnected to any given controversy. They are new obligations—or at least some of them are[47]—created by the SC, so the argument that this institution is limited to codifying pre-existing law cannot be defended. The Resolution imposes on all States, independently of their relation to the terrorist phenomenon, the adoption of a series of penal, administrative and procedural measures that require legislative reforms in national law. Therefore, the legislative (and not the administrative regulatory[48]) nature of Resolution 1373 is clear. Besides, most of the doctrine understands it that way.[49]

The normative nature of the Resolution is well demonstrated if its effects are compared with the conclusion of a multilateral convention in which all the

[46] It seems evident that the measures envisaged in Resolution 1373 will only give results in the medium and long term, and that terrorism will not be eradicated, if at all, for many years.

[47] Eg, in para 1 (c) of Resolution 1373, the SC imposes on all States the duty of freezing the funds and resources, not only of all persons related to the commission of terrorist acts, but also of businesses they own, under their direct or indirect control, which act under their orders, and even of other '*associated* persons and entities' (emphasis added); for its part, the 1999 Convention limits itself to requiring the confiscation or seizure of funds 'used or allocated' to commit terrorist crimes (Article 8 of the Convention), and referring to legal persons, it only demands that their liability is established 'when a person responsible for the management or control of that legal entity has, in that capacity, committed an offence' of terrorism (Article 5 (1) of the Convention). It can also be mentioned that para (1)(d) of Resolution 1373 lays down that States shall 'prohibit their nationals or any persons and entities within their territories from making any funds, financial assets . . . or financial or other related services available' to persons or entities related with terrorism. This obligation does not seem to be contained in the 1999 Convention, which is limited to regulating the intentional crime of terrorism financing. The only obligations that the latter text imposes on legal persons that are not directly implicated in these crimes are those of identifying their clients, and informing the authorities of all suspicious transactions (Article 18 (1)(b) of the Convention). Therefore, Resolution 1373 again shows itself to be more rigorous than the Convention and fills a gap it has left.

[48] In that line, see Corten (n 29) 562. However, to be able to classify a norm as administrative, it has to be based on a general law that it details or applies to the particular case. In the case of Resolution 1373, the SC creates new norms, such as requiring the provision of funds to terrorists to be categorized as a crime, which do not appear in the Charter, nor could be considered as derived from customary international law.

[49] JE Álvarez, *International Organizations as Law-Makers* (Oxford University Press, Oxford, 2005) 196–98; S Talmon, 'The Security Council as a World Legislature' (2005) 99 AJIL 176–77; J Delbrück, 'Transnational Federalism: Problems and Prospects of Allocating Public Authority Beyond the State' (2004) 11 Indiana Journal of Global Legal Studies 37; S Szurek, 'La lutte internationale contre le terrorisme sous l'empire du chapitre VII: un laboratoire normatif' (2005) 109 Revue Générale de Droit international public 15–16 (RGDIP); A Pellet and V Tzankov, 'L'État victime d'un acte terroriste peut-il recourir à la force armée ?' in Société Française pour le Droit International, *Les nouvelles menaces contre la paix et la sécurité internationales* (Pedone, Paris, 2004) 98; N Angelet, 'Vers un renforcement de la prévention et la répression du terrorisme par de moyens financiers et économiques?' in K Bannelier et al (eds), *Le droit international face au terrorisme après le 11 septembre* (Pedone, Paris, 2002) 219–20.

members of the United Nations appeared as parties. An instrument of that nature would have brought about the same consequences, but with the advantage that Resolution 1373 produces immediate effects without having to wait for the slow process of ratification, and furthermore guarantees that all countries are bound by it.[50] Another legal difference with the option of the Resolution is that the latter is not ruled by the 1969 Vienna Convention on the Law of Treaties for its modification, interpretation or the control of its compliance. It is the SC itself that carries out all those functions. In short, we find a formidable accumulation of power because of the concentration of normative and executive powers in a single organ.

Also related to the terrorist phenomenon, Resolution 1540 (2004) of the SC,[51] dealing with the non-proliferation of weapons of mass destruction, reproduces various of the essential characteristics of Resolution 1373: it establishes general obligations on all States, relating to an international problem on which the GA had pronounced with consensus,[52] and sets up a Committee to evaluate the reports that the members of the organization have to present on the application of the Resolution.[53]

Again this is a basically normative Resolution of the SC that sought to fill a gap in the international law then in force:[54] it aims to prevent terrorist groups from having access to nuclear, biological or chemical weapons. In the face of that possibility, qualified on repeated occasions by the SC as a 'threat to international peace and security', this body has not hesitated to approve (unanimously) another legislative Resolution of universal scope, which obliges all States to adopt specific normative provisions in their domestic law, including the application of penal or civil sanctions for certain acts.[55]

In the same line, the SC has consolidated its role as a general watchdog over specific international problems, adopting decisions with suitable sanctions for

[50] I Thomas, 'La mise en œuvre en droit européen des dispositions internationales de lutte contre le terrorisme' (2004) 108 RGDIP 464; L Condorelli, 'Les attentats du 11 septembre et leurs suites: où va le droit international?' (2001) 105 RGDIP 834.

[51] SC Res 1540 (5 Nov 2004).

[52] See GA Res 57/83 (9 Jan 2003) and 58/48 (8 Jan 2004).

[53] For comments on the content of SC Res 1540 (2004), see S Sur, 'La résolution 1540 du Conseil de sécurité (28 avril 2004): entre la prolifération des armes de destruction massive, le terrorisme et les acteurs non étatiques' (2004) 108 RGDIP 855; Lavalle (n 13) 411.

[54] In the exchange of opinions that took place in the SC, numerous delegations started from the basis that none of the international Conventions on this issue (1968 Treaty on the Non-Proliferation of Nuclear Weapons, the 1972 Convention on the Prohibition of the Development, Production and Stockpiling of Bacteriological (Biological) and Toxin Weapons and on Their Destruction, the 1993 Convention on the Prohibition of the Development, Production, Stockpiling and Use of Chemical Weapons and on Their Destruction) adequately treated the question of the measures to adopt in order to prevent non-State actors, in particular terrorists, from having access to these types of weapons. See those debates in Doc S/PV.4950 (22 April 2004).

[55] See, eg, para 2 and 3(d) of Resolution 1540 (2004), in which the obligation is imposed on the States to adopt 'appropriate effective laws which prohibit any non-State actor to manufacture, acquire, posses, develop, transport, transfer or use nuclear, chemical or biological weapons', or pass 'appropriate laws and regulations to control export, transit, trans-shipment and re-export' of these arms and related materials.

those subjects of international law who contravene its instructions. Thus, for example, in its Resolution 1612 (2005) it has created a working group to examine the reports presented by the parties to a conflict, previously identified in a report of the Secretary-General, with a view even to adopting sanctions against those who do not respect the rights of children in armed conflicts.[56] In this way, the obligation contained in Article 38 of the 1989 UN Convention on the Rights of the Child is extended to all States, and provided with a surveillance and sanction mechanism not envisaged by the Convention.

In short, SC normative Resolutions in the fight against terrorism are no isolated act, an accident justified by the pressures of a given moment in history, but are rather the starting point for a new dimension in its functions. In the absence of other more efficient international mechanisms, the SC has decided to tackle some of the challenges of international security by redefining its role and its functions, although it does so by using the same legal grounds as it did in the past: Chapter VII of the Charter. Thus it puts in place the basis to enable it to go beyond the traditional instruments for the creation of international norms in the field of security in the international legal system.

V. THE LIMITS OF THE NORMATIVE COMPETENCE OF THE SC

A. Legal Limits

In the first place, it should be remembered that the SC is an organ of an international organization. In consequence, the constituent treaty of the organization is the foundation and, at the same time, the limit, of its competences. In that context, the reading of Articles 24–26 of the Charter indicates that the mission of the SC is the maintenance of international peace and security, and that it has been given a series of powers to fulfil that role that 'are laid down in Chapters VI, VII, VIII and XII' (Article 24 (2) of the Charter). Therefore, the SC's powers are regulated.

Thus, for example, Article 26 of the Charter imposes an explicit limit on the SC's normative powers when it envisages that in matters of disarmament and regulation of armaments, this institution can formulate 'plans to be submitted to the Members of the United Nations' that enable the resources dedicated by States to that activity to be reduced. This means that, although the SC can impose obligations to disarm on a given State when it considers that its arsenals constitute a threat to international peace and security (Chapter VII of the Charter),[57] this institution has no capacity to establish a universal system of regulation of armaments, since this would only be possible through a multilateral agreement that enjoyed the consent of the States. This demonstrates the importance given by the Charter to State consent as the source of

[56] See points 2, 8 and 9 of SC Res 1612 (26 July 2005).

[57] See eg, para C of SC Res 687 (3 April 1991), which imposed many very specific disarmament obligations on Iraq.

international obligations, and the exceptional character that any normative activity by the SC should have.[58]

Similarly, the Charter makes express reference to certain general limits that the SC must respect in the development of its functions. The second paragraph of Article 24 indicates that 'the Security Council shall act in accordance with the Purposes and Principles of the United Nations'. These purposes and principles are those set out in Articles 1 and 2 of the Charter,[59] and have been developed by GA Resolution 2625 (XXV), which nowadays is universally accepted as a central element of the model of legitimacy articulated around the United Nations. From these truly elemental considerations, the first limits to the SC's normative capacity must be deduced: it has to confine itself to questions directly tied to the maintenance of international peace and security, and must scrupulously respect both the purposes and principles of the Charter and the specific provisions that regulate the SC's functions and powers.[60]

A second limit to the SC's legislative capacity is imposed by the need to respect general international law. To ground this requirement, it is enough to recall that the SC is a body of an international organization, and that it has to be presumed that all international organizations, as subjects of the international legal system, are bound by the norms of general international law.[61]

[58] Article 26 of the Charter has been interpreted in many different ways. While for Happold, Article 26 shows that 'even in an area where the Security Council has been given a specific mandate to act, it is not permitted to impose general obligations on the UN membership', thus demonstrating the Council's lack of legislative competence (Happold (n 25) 605–7), for Kelsen, the SC can change the plans drawn up on the basis of Article 26 into obligations, by deciding that non-compliance entails a threat to international peace and security (H Kelsen, *The Law of the United Nations: A Critical Analysis of its Fundamental Problems* (London Institute of World Affairs, Stevens & Sons, London, 1951) 106; in the same line, see Tomuschat (n 30) 344–46). From my point of view, both postures are partly right, but both strain the meaning of Article 26. I agree with Happold when he points out that this provision 'submits' clearly the final decision on the general system of regulation of armaments to the Member States, so that the SC lacks competence to establish it on its own and with a binding character. However, it seems equally clear that this Article is limited to speaking of the 'regulation of armaments', and a general and absolute limitation on the SC's normative capacity cannot be deduced from it (a contrary reading could even lead some to deduce a regulatory competence in the other security spheres). I also agree with Kelsen when he indicates that the SC can declare that the behaviour in armament matters of a State or group of States which ignore its plans constitutes a direct threat to peace and security, giving rise to the adoption of measures on the basis of Chapter VII of the Charter. Nevertheless, I understand that that such a declaration cannot be used as a short cut to impose general disarmament plans drawn up by the SC on States that are not in accord with them. To do so would violate the principle of sovereignty, as seems to be defended in Article 26 of the Charter.

[59] In spite of the very general wording of these provisions, their legal content cannot be underestimated as a limit on the SC's activities. Eg, the text of the principle of non-intervention in the domestic affairs of Member States (Article 2 (7) of the Charter), expressly envisages an exception for cases in which the SC acts in 'application of enforcement measures under Chapter VII'. This indicates that the SC cannot intervene in questions of State competence on the basis of the powers that the other Chapters of the Charter confer.

[60] Talmon (n 49) 182–83.

[61] *Interpretation of the Agreement of 25 March 1951 between the WHO and Egypt* [1980] ICJ Rep 89–90, para 37.

That said, in the particular law of an international organization, nothing prevents it from authorizing a body to act without regard for the *ius dispositivum* of general international law in its relations with Member States. As no normative hierarchy exists between distinct international norms, the principle *lex posterior derogat priori* governs, and the Charter can enable the SC to act outside international law,[62] in given circumstances, and always provided that it respects the *ius cogens*.[63]

The preparatory work of Article 1 (1) of the Charter provides sound arguments to maintain that the SC, when it 'adopts efficient collective measures to prevent and eliminate threats to peace' in crisis situations, can disregard the *ius dispositivum* of international law without questioning the validity or binding nature of its decisions.[64] In particular, the purpose was to enable this institution to put an end to hostilities in armed conflicts, without having to decide on the rights of the parties in conflict in accordance with the international legal order. However, apart from exceptional circumstances such as these, no provision of the Charter authorizes the SC to violate international law.[65]

Hence, when the SC establishes general rules whose validity is not subject to a time limit, and is not dealing with a specific crisis, but seeking to give an answer in the medium to long term to a permanent threat to international peace and security, it is bound by general international law, and lacks authority to derogate these norms, which result from inter-State consensus. In this context, it is revealing that the SC has taken care to reiterate on numerous occasions that it acts in accord with international law, in a clear effort to reinforce the

[62] Lagrange (n 26) 571–72.

[63] It seems to me impossible to admit that the intention of the drafters of the Charter was to create an organ with the capacity to dispose of the very structural elements of the legal order on which its power and competences are founded. As the ad hoc Judge E Lauterpacht indicated in a separate Opinion on the Order of 13 Sept 1993, relating to Further Requests for the Indication of Provisional Measures, in the *Application of the Convention on the Prevention and Punishment of the Crime of Genocide* case ([1993] ICJ Rep 440, para 100), 'the relief which Article 103 of the Charter may give to the Security Council in case of conflict between one of its decisions and an operative treaty obligation cannot—as a matter of simple hierarchy of norms—extend to a conflict between a Security Council resolution and *ius cogens*. Indeed, one only has to state the opposite proposition thus—that a Security Council resolution may even *require* participation in genocide—for its unacceptability to be apparent'. See, in this line, E Papastavridis, 'Interpretation of Security Council Resolutions under Chapter VII in the Aftermath of the Iraqi Crisis' (2007) 56 ICLQ 107–10.

[64] During the deliberations in the Conference of San Francisco, some States proposed that the limitation that measures be adopted 'in conformity with the principles of justice and international law' should also apply to the first phrase of the first paragraph of Article 1 (collective measures against threats to the peace) and not only to the second (dispute settlement). From these debates it is deduced that the proposal was rejected to prevent the binding nature of SC decisions from being questioned in a crisis situation, alleging that some norm of international law was being breached (Simma (n 16) 43; B Martenczuk, 'The Security Council, the International Court and Judicial Review: What Lessons from Lockerbie?' (1999) 10 EJIL 545).

[65] For Lagrange, 'la Charte attribue au Conseil de sécurité le pouvoir de déroger aux règles du droit international lorsqu'il agit sur le fondement du chapitre VII, non par de règles, mais par des décisions' (Lagrange (n 26) 574–82).

legitimacy of its actions.[66] In the same way, the members of the SC usually refer to the consistency between the Resolutions and the norms of international law as justification of the positive nature of their vote.[67] Additionally, international jurisprudence provides arguments from which the SC's general obligation to respect international law seems to be deduced.[68]

The question of determining whether the SC can modify or annul the effects of international treaties in force is more controversial. In the debates that took place while approving SC Resolutions 1422 (2002) and 1487 (2003), numerous States stated that such Resolutions entailed a modification of the Statute of the International Criminal Court, and that the SC lacked power to act in that manner.[69]

Unlike the situation with customary international law, the Charter does provide a literal argument for those who defend the pre-eminence of SC Resolutions over the provisions of any international convention. Its Article 103 establishes that, 'in the event of a conflict between the obligations of the Member States ... under the present Charter and their obligations under any other international agreement, their obligations under the present Charter shall prevail'. In fact, interpreting this provision in the *Lockerbie* case, the ICJ considered that, prima facie, the Court could not protect the rights of the Libyans under the 1971 Montreal Convention for the adoption of cautionary

[66] In its Resolution 1377 (12 Nov 2001), the SC, meeting at ministerial level shortly after adopting Resolution 1373, to give greater significance to the Declaration on its new role in the fight against terrorism, stated that to combat the scourge of international terrorism what is essential is 'a sustained and comprehensive approach ... in accordance with the Charter of the United Nations and international law'. In the same way, the SC has made an effort to remind Member States on many occasions that, 'they must ensure that any measures taken to combat terrorism comply with all their obligations under international law' (SC Res 1787 (10 Dec 2007); 1566 (8 Oct 2004), both in the Preamble).

[67] See, eg, the intervention of President of the Council, although speaking in the name of Pakistan, when explaining his vote in favour of Resolution 1483 (22 May 2003), relating to the finalization of the sanctions against Iraq and the recognition of the role of the Authority created by the occupying forces for the political transition in that country (Doc S/PV.4761 (22 May 2003) 11–12).

[68] *Namibia* [1971] ICJ Rep 51–52, especially paras 111–12. See also *Tadić (Jurisdiction)* ICTY-94-1 (2 October 1995) paras 28 and 42, which, on examining whether the SC enjoyed powers to create an international criminal court, laid down that in order for that to be possible, 'such a court ought to be rooted in the rule of law and offer all guarantees embodied in the relevant international instruments'.

[69] Resolutions 1422 (12 July 2002) and 1487 (12 June 2003). In these Resolutions, the SC used the prerogative set out in Article 16 of the Statute of the International Criminal Court to prevent persons who participated in peace-keeping operations, and who came from States that were not parties to the Statute, from being tried before that Court. Numerous States, and even the UN Secretary-General, expressed the view that in Article 16 that type of exemption was not permitted, and some countries even stated that the incorrect use of this norm by the SC was equivalent to its modification (see Docs A/57/PV.22 (4 Oct 2002) 6, in which the Liechtenstein representative firmly asserted that, 'the functions and powers of the SC do not encompass the competence to alter or interpret international treaties'; and S/PV.4772 (12 June 2003), in particular the interventions of Greece, in the name of the European Union (8–9), Iran (10) or Brazil (13)).

measures, to the extent that these seemed incompatible with the provisions of SC Resolution 748 (1992).[70]

In any case, Article 103 of the Charter must be interpreted in a manner compatible with the principle of sovereignty (set out in Article 2 (1) of that same text), which is the cornerstone of international law, a consensual legal order. This leads one to think that, although the SC can make the 'obligations' that it imposes in a particular matter prevail over those foreseen in any international treaty apart from the Charter, it lacks the competence to modify or interpret those international conventions, since this would be only in the hands of the States who were party to them. For the same reasons, no State can be obliged to ratify a given international convention.[71]

However, Article 103 seems a sufficient legal basis to permit the SC, in an extreme case, to declare that a particular provision of an international treaty constitutes a threat to international peace and security, demanding the States Parties not to comply with it. In this line, although it is a controversial question, I think that the same argument would seem strong enough to justify the pre-eminence of the SC's legislative Resolutions over the norms of conventional law,[72] since it must be presumed that its demands are justified by the need to safeguard international peace and security, on the basis of Articles 25 and 103 of the Charter.

Nevertheless, three limits can be identified that qualify this formidable power of the SC: first, it has to be competent to adopt the Resolution;[73] secondly, it has to respect the norms of general international law, since, in principle, as indicated above, these also bind the SC; thirdly, respect for the principle of sovereignty compels this organ to make an effort of self-restraint, limiting itself to adopting the measures which are indispensable to the maintenance of international peace and security. In short, the SC would be acting ultra vires, if it used the powers that Chapter VII of the Charter confers on it to modify the rights and obligations of States party to a treaty, if it is not indispensable for safeguarding international security.[74]

[70] *Questions of Interpretation and Application of the 1971 Montreal Convention arising from the Aerial Incident at Lockerbie*, Order of 14 April 1992 [1992] ICJ Rep paras 39–40. See, also in this matter, the Joint Declaration by Judges Evensen, Tarassov, Guillaume and Aguilar, of 9 April 1992, on the change that the Resolution brought about in relation to the rights of the parties to the controversy, as reflected in the 1971 Montreal Convention.

[71] Both in Resolution 1373 (see its para 3 (d)), as in the other Resolutions that complement and develop it, the SC limits itself to 'calling' upon States to adhere 'as soon as possible' to the international conventions and protocols to prevent and suppress terrorist attacks, without ever formulating this petition as an obligation.

[72] Condorelli (n 50) 835.

[73] In this sense, Talmon considers that the SC could not impose universal rules on the control of armaments that would modify the States' rights and obligations under the Non-Proliferation Treaty, since it lacks competences to impose general obligations on Member States in the field of arms regulation (Article 26 of the Charter) (Talmon (n 49) 185).

[74] With an optimistic vision, Rosand considers that this self-restraint is very likely because of the care that the governments of Member States of the SC must take not to establish norms that could offend or upset their national Parliaments (Rosand (n 32) 578–79). In effect, the rules established by the SC are imposed on the States, and national Parliaments have no capacity to

These last reflections lead us to examine another legal limit to the SC's discretionality: respect for the principle of proportionality. In various provisions of the Charter reference is made to enabling the SC to adopt the measures 'necessary' for the maintenance of international peace and security.[75] From this it can be inferred that the SC cannot go beyond what is indispensable when using the exceptional powers conferred by Chapter VII of the Charter.[76] The fact that Article 2 (7) of that same text states as a general principle that the United Nations shall not intervene in the internal affairs of States, and puts forward as an exception the application of 'enforcement measures' laid down in Chapter VII, would also lead to a restrictive interpretation of the SC's capacity to intervene in that context.[77]

Nevertheless, it has to be said that in practice this principle has played a very modest role as a limit on the SC's discretion. It is the SC itself that decides on the necessity for its actions, and on their scope,[78] without any direct mechanism of legal review of its decisions. On many occasions, an evaluation of respect for the principle of proportionality depends on a rule of reason that will be mediated by political considerations, over which no legal control in the strict sense can be exercised. All this gives the SC an enormous margin of appreciation. In consequence, respect for this principle constitutes a rather theoretical limit that until now has not had any relevant function in demarcating the SC's powers.

B. Political Limits

The vitality the SC has acquired since the beginning of the 1990s has enabled it to become progressively aware of its potential. In that process, it has ceased to respond exclusively to concrete incidents, paying attention to some problems from an ever more general perspective, developing medium- and short-term policies in various fields related to international peace and security.[79]

In any case, it is undeniable that Resolution 1373 (2001) entailed a widening of the powers traditionally assigned to the SC. Although sound arguments can be put forward to defend the 'constitutionality' of its normative competence (as well as the contrary opinion), almost nobody postulated this possibility openly before 1990. There is no doubt that Resolution 1373 of the

influence the terms or alter the wording of any of their provisions. However, in some circumstances, this could make the SC's 'legislative option' even more tempting for governments.

[75] Articles 24 (3), 40, 42, 43 (1) and 51 of the Charter.

[76] Talmon (n 49) 184–85; E De Wet and A Nollkaemper, 'Review of Security Council Decisions by National Courts' (2002) 42 German Ybk Intl L 179–81.

[77] G Nolte, 'Article 2 (7)' in Simma (n 16) 171, para 75.

[78] In principle, it is the SC itself that determines the scope of its competence and, in that sense, the legality of its intervention (*Namibia* [1971] ICJ Rep 21–22, para 20).

[79] See SC Res 1170 (28 May 1998), on UN activities on the African continent; 1261 (30 Aug 1999), on the situation of children in armed conflicts; or 1325 (31 Oct 2000), on the role of women in the resolution of conflicts and humanitarian aid programmes.

SC was approved in an emotionally charged atmosphere. The closeness of the 11 September attacks clearly influenced the drafting of a text that introduced substantial innovations in the conception that the SC itself had of its mission and its powers on the basis of Chapter VII of the Charter. However, in spite of the pressure of the moment, the Member States of the United Nations were fully conscious of the historic step they were taking.[80]

Although it would have been better to take this type of decision after a pause for reflection, which would have permitted an express and generalized consensus of the international community on the reinterpretation of Chapter VII of the Charter,[81] it is no less true that a process of that nature could have dragged on forever, and that at times history precipitates innovations, when the circumstances move in that direction. Nevertheless, the legitimacy of Resolution 1373 does not depend so much on the situation in which it was adopted as on its acceptance by the generality of States.

Here, it should be indicated that in the debates on the measures to eliminate international terrorism that took place in the GA in the days immediately after the adoption of Resolution 1373, the States' representatives systematically supported it, while at the same time they encouraged the prompt ratification of the 1999 Convention for the Suppression of the Financing of Terrorism by those States who still had not done so.[82] Subsequently, in successive Resolutions, the GA has expressly backed Resolution 1373, reminding States of its binding nature and encouraging them to adopt the measures necessary to ensure its full compliance.[83]

Despite this, in the discussions leading up to the adoption of Resolution 1540 (2004),[84] an ever-greater number of States criticized the Council's growing legislative work, questioning its capacity to act as a universal legislator, when imposing obligations that could only be assumed under the

[80] As an illustration, the words of the French representative in his address to the GA on 1 Oct 2001, 'On the evening of Friday, 28 September, the Security Council unanimously adopted resolution 1373 (2001), a resolution that will stand out in history. By virtue of its global and binding nature, this resolution traces the new and ambitious path to which the Council has resolutely committed itself in order to contribute to eradicating acts that constitute a threat to international peace and security' (Doc A/56/PV.13 (1 Oct 2001) 24–25).

[81] Resolution 1373 was approved in record time. The USA presented the proposal to the other permanent members on 26 Sept 2001 (Doc S/2001/921 (28 Sept 2001)), and it was informally discussed the following day with the rest of the SC members. On 28 Sept 2001 the Resolution was unanimously approved in a five-minute session, at which only members of the Council attended (the other countries were neither invited nor consulted) (Doc S/PV.4385 (28 Sept 2001)).

[82] A reading of the Minutes of the GA's plenary sessions that took place between 1 and 5 Oct 2001, and that they were devoted solely to measures against international terrorism, is enough to verify the overwhelming support of the speakers on SC Resolution 1373 (see Docs A/56/PV.12–A/56/PV.22). Even States that, like Mexico, had argued that the SC lacked competences to create international criminal tribunals (Doc A/55/PV.95 (14 March 2001) 3) supported Resolution 1373 (Doc S/PV.4453 (Resumption 1) (18 Jan 2002) 26–27).

[83] See, eg, GA Res 62/71 (8 Jan 2008) para 9; 60/43 (6 Jan 2006) para 7; 60/1 (24 Oct 2005) para 90; 59/46 (16 Dec 2004) para 7; or 58/81 (8 Jan 2004) para 7.

[84] SC Res 1540 (5 Nov 2004).

expression of consent in an international treaty.[85] In any case, it must be made clear that these criticisms were directed at the formula chosen for the establishment of norms (SC Resolution), and not at their content, on which there was a broad consensus. These types of arguments have been repeated in the debates on subsequent Resolutions.[86]

Therefore, until now, the States have accepted the SC's legislative initiatives,[87] but have shown that this way of proceeding has its legal and political limits.[88] The use of this fast track for creating obligations has been justified to the international community by its effectiveness[89] in the generalization of obligations that enjoy wide international consensus. As against the exasperating slowness with which the GA's normative projects progress,[90]

[85] See the various speeches that took place in the SC on 22 April 2004, Doc S/PV.4950, especially the words of the Indian representative at 23–24: 'The issue goes beyond a mere legal consideration of the Council's allocated powers under the Charter. The credibility and even respect that the Security Council can garner depend on its actions being the product of internal cohesion and universal acceptability'. Although in different tones, countries as distinct as Cuba, Namibia, Nepal, Mexico or Indonesia showed their concern, or opposition, in regard to the fact that the SC assumed the role of universal legislator. Other countries, such as Switzerland or the Philippines, accepted this initiative as exceptional due to its 'urgent need'. See a comment on the different interventions in the SC in Lavalle (n 13) 425–28. For a systematic exposition of the arguments against the SC's legislative capacity, consult J Tercinet, 'Le pouvoir normatif du Conseil de Sécurité: le Conseil de Sécurité peut-t-il légiférer?' (2004) 37 RBDI 53–42; B Elberling, 'The Ultra Vires Character of Legislative Action by the Security Council' (2005) 2 International Organizations Law Review 337–360.

[86] In the explanatory session on the vote after the approval of Resolution 1566 (8 Oct 2004), which contained a definition of terrorism, Brazil's representative regretted (despite having voted in favour of the Resolution) the excessive recourse to Chapter VII of the Charter, pointing out that such a tendency was 'unnecessary and counterproductive', and that during the negotiations 'this point was raised by several other delegations'. In particular, the Brazilian representative insisted that 'no constraints should be imposed on States' freedom to negotiate the terms of international conventions' (Doc S/PV.5053 (8 Oct 2004) 7).

[87] Very explicitly, in the Plan of Action of the 'United Nations Global Counter-Terrorism Strategy', approved under GA Res 60/288 (20 Sept 2006) Annexe, para (2)(c), it was established that Member States of the UN resolve 'to implement all Security Council resolutions related to international terrorism and to cooperate fully with the counter-terrorism subsidiary bodies of the Security Council in the fulfilment of their tasks'.

[88] On the need to make these legal and political limits on the SC's legislative capacity more explicit through the reform of the Charter, see the report *The United Nations and the New Threats: Rethinking Security* (2004) 13–14 (available online at <http://www.un-globalsecurity.org>), which summarizes the results of the Conference on 'Threats, Challenges and Change', held in Rome in May 2004, and organized by the United Nations Foundation.

[89] 'The perils of an "imperial" Security Council are as real as is the promise that it will take effective action. An effective Council may well be an imperial one' (Álvarez (n 49) 201). Also see A Bianchi, 'Assessing the Effectiveness of the UN Security Council Anti-terrorism Measures: The Quest for Legitimacy and Cohesion' (2006) 17 EJIL 888–89.

[90] It is enough to remember that the negotiations for drafting a general Convention against terrorism have been blocked for several years due to the lack of agreement on the definition of terrorism in the Committee created by GA Res 51/210. In fact, the 1999 Convention for the Suppression of the Financing of Terrorism had not entered into force when SC Res 1373 (2001) was approved, and the rhythm of ratifications promised several years of waiting before that would occur (the adoption of Resolution 1373 spectacularly speeded up ratifications).

which afterwards require various years to come into force[91] (due to the delays typical of all ratification processes of conventions that seek universality), it offers an expeditious formula,[92] which gives worldwide cover, 'in order to ensure prompt and effective action by the United Nations (Article 24 (1) of the Charter).

However, this new formula can only be effective if it is perceived as legitimate by the vast majority of States, that is if the SC continues establishing in its Resolutions obligations on which there is a high degree of international consensus.[93] If a significant group of States considers that the line that delimits the essential elements of their sovereign capacity of decision has been overstepped, and they deliberately cease to cooperate with the SC, its Resolutions will stop being efficient, and a crack will have been opened up that will be difficult to repair in the already deteriorated building that houses the collective security system of the United Nations.

To achieve broad international consensus in the SC, it is not enough to obtain nine votes in favour of a Resolution, including the five permanent members[94] (Article 27 (3) of the Charter). Although this in itself is a first political filter,[95] the SC does not have a large enough membership to assume that capacity of representation.

The participation of all States that desire to do so in the preparatory work seems to be a necessary political condition in drawing up this type of

[91] A typical example related to terrorism is the International Convention against the Recruitment, Use, Financing and Training of Mercenaries, which took ten years to be negotiated, and after finally being approved through GA Res 44/34 (4 Dec 1989), did not come into force until 20 Oct 2001. This Convention still only has 30 States as parties.

[92] Nevertheless, the SC's efficiency should not be mythified. One only has to read the reports of the Counter-Terrorism Committee (CTC) to appreciate the enormous difficulties this organ faces in numerous countries. See, eg, its considerations on the fight against money-laundering, or the absence of legal mechanisms in national legal systems to freeze and seize funds in procedures of mutual international judicial assistance (Doc S/2004/70 (26 Jan 2004) 4–5), which demonstrate that total compliance with the provisions of Resolution 1373 can only be a medium or long-term objective in some States. Besides, the CTC Executive Directorate was not declared operative until 15 Dec 2005, and its first mission was the elimination of the backlog accumulated in the review of the reports presented by the States on the basis of Resolution 1373 (Doc S/PV.5375 (21 Feb 2006) 2–3). This organ did not expect to conclude its preliminary implementation assessments of Resolution 1373 until the end of 2007 (Doc S/2007/254 (4 May 2007) 5; see also the Briefing to the SC by the CTC Chairman of 14 Nov 2007).

[93] When there is no international consensus on a rule, the SC cannot substitute, and even less impose, its will over that of the sovereign will of the States if it does not want to be ignored. In the work carried out in the Special Committee established by the GA to negotiate a general Convention against terrorism, the definition of terrorism given by the SC in its Resolution 1566 (8 Oct 2004), has been considered simply irrelevant, and the States continue discussing this point, which is the main obstacle to achieving an agreement on that general Convention (Doc A/63/67 (11 March 2008) Annex II).

[94] It must be remembered that both of the normative Resolutions (1373 and 1540) adopted by the SC in the framework of the fight against terrorism have been unanimous.

[95] In spite of this, Anghie considers that the SC Resolutions against terrorism of recent years are a clear manifestation of US hegemony in international law (A Anghie, *Imperialism, Sovereignty and the Making of International Law* (Cambridge University Press, Cambridge, 2005) 298–303).

Resolution.[96] This involvement would enable us to asses whether its content effectively meets with international consensus. Fortunately, this is the direction in which the SC practice appears to be heading, because in the drafting of Resolution 1540 (2004) all States that requested it were permitted to intervene.[97] Although Article 31 of the Charter gives the SC itself the power to decide whether States that are not members of this institution can participate (with voice but without vote) in its deliberations,[98] the usual practice is for the Council to invite all States that request it to its meetings.[99] Any future normative Resolution should follow this precedent, rather than that of Resolution 1373, approved in scarcely 48 hours and without an explanatory session for the vote.[100]

C. Practical Limits

The normative resolutions of the SC must be implemented by the Member States in accordance with their respective constitutional procedures and their technical, economic and human possibilities.[101] Logically, that reality determines the content of SC Resolutions, since they can only impose rules that can be universally applied within a reasonable time, if such Resolutions are not to be mere statements of intent, or even worthless paper.

Thus, for example, although the States have for the most part complied with the obligation to present the reports required under Resolution 1373 (2001), that does not mean that all the measures included in it have been put into practice.[102] In particular, the work of the CTC has shown the enormous

[96] Lavalle (n 13) 436; Talmon (n 49) 186–88.

[97] See Doc S/PV.4950 (22 April 2004) 1, in which it is stated that 36 countries not members of the SC applied to attend, and the majority of them participated, in the debate on the adoption of what would subsequently be SC Res 1540, that being accepted by SC members by assent.

[98] By virtue of Article 31 of the Charter, the SC can authorize the participation in its deliberations of a State that is not a member of that organ whenever it 'considers that the interests of that Member are specially affected'. Obviously, it would be difficult to argue this for normative resolutions of general scope. However, from the political point of view, the most elemental requirements of legitimacy demand that all States that wish to do so are permitted to participate in SC deliberations on this type of Resolutions.

[99] For this to be possible, it is indispensable that the SC makes its initiatives public beforehand. Taking into account that it is usual for Council members not to inform the rest of UN members of their proposals, and that these are discussed in informal and private meetings, the adoption of normative Resolutions would require a significant change in this practice. It is revealing that Rule 48 of the SC Provisional Rules of Procedure lays down that SC meetings should be public, unless this body decides to the contrary (something which has never happened), with the intention of distancing the Council from the practice of secret diplomacy, which aroused so much prejudice against the League of Nations. Paradoxically, the fact that all the meetings are public has resulted in the decisions taken by the SC being previously 'cooked up' in informal and often secret meetings of Council members.

[100] Doc S/PV.4385 (28 Sept 2001).

[101] Bianchi (n 89) 892–903.

[102] Talmon (n 49) 190–92. Often the reports are used to show the political opinion of the government of the State in question, without contributing really relevant information (K Von Hippel, 'Improving the International Response to the Transnational Terrorist Threat' in J Boulden and TG Weiss (eds), *Terrorism and the UN* (Indiana University Press, Bloomington, 2004) 112–13).

amount of technical assistance that will be needed for many countries really to be able to apply the Resolution.[103] Compliance with the obligation to present reports under Resolution 1540 (2004) has been rather less, and some of the States that have cooperated made it clear that they did not consider it necessary to promulgate special laws to control the use, sale or transport of weapons of mass destruction or connected materials that are not found on their territory.[104] In this sense, the more complex the SC Resolutions, the less stringently must their content be considered, so that the only thing that can be demanded of numerous States is that they should not adopt an attitude manifestly opposed to their compliance.

VI. SC LEGISLATIVE RESOLUTIONS AND PROCEDURES FOR THE FORMATION OF INTERNATIONAL LAW

State consent is found in the origin of the creation of all international obligations. The nexus between State consent and the formation of international norms is more evident in the case of international treaties and customary international law; however, that nexus is more indirect in the case of the acts of international organizations, since in that case it is the consent of the State to be bound by the constituent treaty of the organization that compels the State to comply with the organization's binding decisions.

That greater distance between State consent and the genesis of international obligations in the acts of international organizations has generated some doctrinal debate. Tomuschat has come to describe as 'fictitious' the argument that the obligatory force of an act adopted by the majority in an international organization, against the will of a State, has its origin in that State's consent. He bases that on the evolutionary interpretation of the provisions of constituent treaties that, at times, leads international organizations to exercise competences that were not foreseen at the time they were created.[105]

Although this theory appears attractive, I cannot share that view of the relativization of the role of State consent, which, in the end, would lead to

[103] The reports of the CTC and its Executive Directorate show that at present its main task is supplying technical assistance to members that request it, with the aim of creating conditions necessary for the effective application of Resolution 1373 (See, eg, Docs S/2006/107 (16 Feb 2006) 6–8; S/2006/607 (4 Aug 2006) 3–4). In fact, the reports serve essentially to identify those shortages that can only be solved through external aid (See, eg, the fourth report of Kyrgyzstan, in which that country asked for three computers with external modem, three printers, and one fax machine so that its Parliament could tackle the legislative work necessary to comply with Resolution 1373 (Doc S/2006/350 Add.1 (23 Aug 2006) 4)).

[104] Doc S/2006/257 (25 April 2006) 2–4. By 20 April 2006, 62 Member States still had not presented any report on their compliance with SC Res 1540 (2004).

[105] 'Even if the requirements for the exercise of a regulatory power are relatively well defined, any grant of such a power opens up a dynamic process whose ultimate outcome can hardly be forecast with any degree of reliability. . . . In any event, the more the act of ratification as an actual political decision disappears in the shadows of the past, the less convincing it becomes to trace back the binding force of a resolution adopted against the declared will of the State concerned to the remote act of ratification' (Tomuschat (n 30) 326–29).

announcing the overcoming of the principle of State sovereignty. In the first place, the obligations directly derived from the constituent treaty must be clearly distinguished from those imposed by the institutional law of the organization. Evidently these must be different obligations, since otherwise, that institutional law would not be necessary. What is indispensable is that the organ that adopts a binding decision has competence to do so, because there is a legal basis in the constituent treaty that gives it such a capacity. Therefore, when a State agrees to participate in an organization in which there are bodies with specific normative functions, the State consents to be bound by the obligatory decisions of those bodies, always provided that they are acting within the framework of their competences.[106]

Those principles are not lessened by the passing of time or by the creativity of the organ in the exercise of its normative functions. Moreover, by consenting to be bound by the treaty, the State not only assumes obligations, but also rights. In particular, the Member State can use all the mechanisms that the constituent treaty offers to defend its sovereign competences and, in any case, is not obliged to comply with institutional decisions of the organization if it is acting ultra vires.[107] These guarantees, conferred when the constituent treaty is ratified, but which remain in force throughout its existence (however long that may be), mark the limits of State consent to be bound, and hence the limits of the international organization's normative capacity.

This is the framework within which one has to evaluate the statements of a broad sector of the doctrine who consider that SC Resolutions 1373 and 1540 deviate from the traditional method of creating multilateral obligations,[108] or that they have substituted the conventional procedure for drawing up norms at the international level.[109] In my opinion, the legislative initiatives of the SC must continue to be situated within the general theory of international organizations' acts, both for their adequate understanding and for the

[106] It is true that in the UN each institution interprets the provisions of the Charter on the scope of its powers and functions. However, this does not mean that such a reading cannot be questioned. The preparatory work for the Charter demonstrates that it was not intended to attribute an express competence to make an authentic interpretation of the Charter to any organ of the UN. In a Report of the Special Subcommittee of Committee IV/2 on the Interpretation of the Charter, 13 UNCIO (1945) 831–32, it is explained that 'it is inevitable that each organ will interpret such parts of the Charter as are applicable to its particular functions. ... Accordingly, it is not necessary to include in the Charter a provision either authorizing or approving the normal operation of this principle. ... It is to be understood, of course, that if an interpretation made by any organ of the Organization ... is not generally acceptable *it will be without binding force*' (emphasis added).

[107] For a study of the theory of ultra vires acts in the context of international organizations, see CF Amerasinghe, *Principles of the Institutional Law of International Organizations* (Cambridge University Press, Cambridge, 2005) 193–216; R Bernhardt, '*Ultra Vires* Activities of International Organisations' in J Makarczyk (ed), *Theory of International Law at the Threshold of the 21st Century. Essays in Honour of K. Skubiszewski* (The Hague, Kluwer, 1996) 599.

[108] Rosand (n 32) 548.

[109] N Krisch, 'The Rise and Fall of Collective Security: Terrorism, US Hegemony, and the Plight of the Security Council' in C Walter et al (eds), *Terrorism as a Challenge for National and International Law: Security versus Liberty?* (Springer, Berlin, 2004) 884.

determination of their limits. I do not think, therefore, that we find ourselves before a new means of creating international obligations.[110]

Comment has already been made on the reasons why it seems possible to deduce from a flexible and evolutionary interpretation of the Charter[111] the SC's capacity to lay down rules of general scope and indefinite legal effect, with the aim to confront direct threats to international peace and security that pose urgent challenges. Nevertheless, at the same time, there are significant limits on this normative power so that we cannot speak of a general legislative competence or of a universal legislator. This is so, first, because the SC can only lay down rules in relation to the safeguarding of international peace and security. Secondly, it must be done respecting the text of the Charter, which imposes fundamental procedural and material obligations. Furthermore, as previously pointed out, the SC must respect general international law when approving legislative initiatives.

To all these legal limits we must add the political limits faced by this type of decision and, in particular, the impossibility of acting with a minimum of efficiency in fields where no broad international consensus is found. In this sense, the enormous differences that exist between one State and another oblige the SC to formulate very general norms, in which the distinct countries have leeway both for the interpretation of the rules and in the choice of the mechanisms used to apply them. In such circumstances, it is most likely that recourse to normative Resolutions will not be common in the SC. The practice subsequent to Resolution 1373, and the debates following Resolution 1540, seem to indicate as much.[112]

In any case, it is not possible to predict the future and once one sets out on a journey, one often does not know where it will end. The widening of the notion of threat to peace from the beginning of the 1990s could lead the Council to adopt normative Resolutions in many spheres more or less related to international peace and security, which would end by transforming it into a true universal legislator.[113] Nevertheless, the limits that have just been outlined should prevent that drift.

In these circumstances, it does not seem that the SC normative Resolutions can substitute, or even overshadow, the task of codification and progressive development of international law which is driven by the GA and its subsidiary organs. First, because of the SC's unique subject-matter: international peace

[110] For the opposite position, see Lavalle (n 13) 436.

[111] For a defence of an evolutionary interpretation of the Charter, giving various convincing examples showing the creativity with which this treaty has been applied to adapt it to historic necessities, see Rosand (n 32) 569–73.

[112] See above notes 83 and 84.

[113] Bearing in mind that the SC's discretion to qualify a situation as a threat to peace, it cannot be ruled out that in the future massive displacements of immigrant populations, generalized famine or specific genetic research programmes will be considered as such. If the SC ends by laying down norms in a range of issues of that variety, evidently it will have become a universal legislator.

and security. Secondly, even in that sphere, the development of more plural negotiations will be necessary to reach universal consensus in many matters, and this only seems possible in the more heterogeneous framework of the GA.[114] To some extent, there could be greater collaboration between both organs. For example, the adoption of SC Resolution 1540 (2004), not only did not prejudice the deliberations developed in the GA for the adoption of an International Convention for the Suppression of Acts of Nuclear Terrorism, but rather its measures are perfectly complementary with the agreement finally reached.[115]

Moreover, in its normative Resolutions, the SC is obliged to respect general international law and, therefore, the codification conventions, to the extent that they codify customary international law.[116] As has been submitted in this article, the SC can only act outside that general international law in exceptional circumstances and for specific cases. Moreover, it is subject to the norms of *ius cogens* in any case.[117]

Until now, however, the role of the SC has been very modest in the consolidation or generation of customary international law.[118] Due to its restricted composition, it does not seem to be the most appropriate institution to show the existence of a universal *opinio iuris*,[119] and for its traditional task in dealing with specific cases, it was not thought that its actions, at times erratic and incoherent, were evidence of a uniform and constant practice.[120] This

[114] In this sense, the declarations of various countries after the GA's approval of the Convention for the Suppression of Acts of Nuclear Terrorism were enlightening; in these they praised the fact that the forum for the negotiation of the Convention had been that created by the GA (See, eg, the intervention of the Indonesian representative in Doc A/59/PV.91 (13 April 2005) 9–10).

[115] The Convention was finally approved by GA Res 59/290 (15 April 2005).

[116] But instead, as indicated previously, the obligations imposed by SC Resolutions would have priority over those derived from particular conventional law, in virtue of what is provided in Article 103 of the Charter.

[117] The European Court of First Instance has declared its 'indirect' competence to control the legality of SC Resolutions in relation to the norms de *ius cogens*, when considering that in the case (which it considers 'improbable') that the latter were breached by a Resolution, that Resolution 'would bind neither the member States of the UN, nor, in consequence, the Community' (Cases T–315/01 *Kadi* [2005] ECR II-0000, paras 226–31 and T–253/02 *Ayadi* [2006] ECR II-0000, para 116).

[118] Corten (n 29) 562–66.

[119] This does not mean that SC work has not been used to identify the *opinio iuris* in order to prove the existence of a customary norm. Eg, in *Tadić (Jurisdiction)* ICTY-94-1 (2 October 1995) para 133, it was held that the customary norms of international humanitarian law were applicable to internal armed conflicts, and that their breach generated the liability of the individuals who violate them. To prove the *opinio iuris* in this sense, the Court referred, among other arguments, to the SC Resolutions dealing with the armed conflict in Somalia.

[120] In any case, it is necessary to recall that international jurisprudence has alluded on some occasions to the SC's practice to prove the existence of a customary norm, although always as one further element among other evidence. See, eg, in *Legal Consequences of the Construction of a Wall in the Occupied Palestinian Territory* [2004] ICJ Rep, paras 89–101, the references to the practice of the States that demonstrated that the IV Geneva Convention of 1949, on the Protection of Civilian Persons in Time of War, was applicable to the Palestinian territories occupied by Israel, among which various SC Resolutions were cited (para 99 of the Advisory Opinion).

situation could change in relation to the normative Resolutions, that for the most part do not include customary international law, but rather create new obligations. As these are grouped together in a universally binding decision of the SC, it could have the effect of generating an international custom, above all if its future Resolutions continue to lay down (as has occurred until now) rules that enjoy broad international backing.

VII. CONCLUSIONS

Obviously, the panorama described shows a far from satisfactory situation. Not even the most ardent supporters of the SC's normative capacity would dispute that it was not created to legislate. As a consequence of that, the adoption of normative Resolutions generates various dysfunctions in the UN system and attracts no few criticisms. However, since this type of initiative can be repeated in the future, it is worth considering the realistic possibilities of improving this system of creating international obligations.

The work of the Counter Terrorism Committee (CTC) shows the main lines along which this form of activity must be conducted. This Committee works from a promotional perspective, focusing on aiding Member States to achieve the construction of a legislative and executive framework that permits them to pursue terrorists and their activities with greater efficiency. From that standpoint, each country is given a wide margin of discretion, as the economic circumstances, human resources and social reality vary enormously. The examination of the reports presented by the States and the visits to the different countries, at least until now, are more concerned with the technical assistance than with control over compliance with the Resolution. This has facilitated the generalized acceptance of Resolution 1373, and has stimulated cooperation with the CTC.[121]

Of course, the SC must limit itself to responding to urgent questions that can admit no delay in their regulation and on which there is broad international consensus. This should not prevent the parallel negotiation of more detailed international conventions on the same subjects in the GA context, but should rather stimulate it. The setting up of the International Criminal Court, created to put an end to the proliferation of ad hoc criminal tribunals, is a good example of the right dynamic.[122]

[121] For a detailed analysis of the CTC's role, see Szurek (n 49) 22–42; E Rosand, 'Security Council Resolution 1373 and the Counter-Terrorism Committee: the Cornerstone of the United Nations Contribution to the Fight against Terrorism' in C Fijnaut, J Wouters and F Naert (eds), *Legal Instruments in the Fight against International Terrorism. A Transatlantic Dialogue* (Nijhoff, Leiden, 2004) 608–31.

[122] 'Unless the Council soon stipulates that these are emergency regulations to contain an imminent threat to peace and security, perhaps of time-limited duration till more legally founded instruments of law can be negotiated and come into force, the Council's authority and legitimacy will almost certainly come under intensifying attack' (*The United Nations and the New Threats: Rethinking Security* (n 88) 13–14).

Nevertheless, any attempt to increase substantially the legitimacy of the procedure for the adoption of legislative Resolutions by the SC requires the institutional reform of the United Nations. On one hand, the SC has to be reformed, adding to the number of its members to make it more representative,[123] or demanding unanimity for this type of Resolutions. On the other, clearer and more explicit legal limits to that normative capacity should be established, so that the GA's competences in that process would be reinforced. In this sense, a limit could be set to the time these Resolutions remain in force, or their validation/derogation by the GA could be stipulated. Finally, the jurisdiction of the ICJ should be amended to institute a direct mechanism to facilitate the exercise of a legal control.[124] The great discretion that the Charter confers on the SC protects it from ill-founded proceedings, and the prima facie validity of its Resolutions prevents their effectiveness and application from being questioned in the short and medium term. It could even be argued such a judicial review would contribute to legitimating the Council's 'new' powers, by consolidating in the UN system one of the main factors limiting arbitrariness in the rule of law.

In the absence of those reforms, the dangers hidden behind the SC's normative activity are many and serious. It cannot be ruled out that, at a given moment, a SC under pressure from the circumstances would opt to impose general obligations, with the aim to break the tough opposition of a significant group of States to accept certain compromises. However, the international legal order is based on State consent, as a corollary of an international society made up of independent sovereign States. If the foundations are attacked, the whole edifice can collapse.

[123] In the debate that took place in the GA in 2004 on the 'Question of equitable representation on and increase in the membership of the Security Council and related matters', the German representative used the argument of this institution's new legislative function to justify the need for its enlargement (Doc A/59/PV.26 (12 Oct 2004) 18). In the never-ending discussion on the need to reform the SC, see Doc A/61/47 (14 Sept 2007). The consultations held in the GA from 12 to 14 November 2007 showed that we are still very far from consensus on this issue.

[124] During the San Francisco Conference, Belgium presented a proposal that would have enabled a direct claim to the ICJ to be lodged in the event of a State considering that a decision of the SC breached its essential rights (3 UNCIO (1945) 336). However, the great powers opposed this initiative because they considered it could entail an excessive reduction in the SC's effectiveness (12 UNCIO (1945) 49–66). Therefore, although the ICJ is the main judicial organ of the United Nations (Article 92 of the Charter), the Member States of the Organization cannot initiate proceedings directly to challenge the legality of the SC's acts. However, this does not mean that this Court cannot pronounce on the legality or on the effects of the acts of other UN organs. Despite lacking 'powers of judicial review or appeal' in respect of the decisions taken by UN organs, it can be argued that the ICJ has recognized its capacity to review the validity of such organs' Resolutions indirectly, to the extent that it is necessary to resolve legal questions that have been validly put to it, both in its advisory opinions (*Namibia* [1971] ICJ Rep 45), and in contentious cases (*Lockerbie* [1998] ICJ Rep paras 41–42 and 50). For a submission that the ICJ assume its full responsibility in solving today's international legal problems, see HE Judge P Kooijmans, 'The ICJ in the 21st century: Judicial Restraint, Judicial Activism, or proactive Judicial Policy' (2007) 56 ICLQ 741.

[12]

The UN Anti-terror Sanctions Regime under Pressure

Helen Keller* and Andreas Fischer**

1. Introduction

The plague of international terrorism has not only resulted in a ripple effect on national legislative activity, particularly in the wake of the 11 September 2001 attacks, but it has also led to wide consensus within the international community to adopt a prompt and effective response to counter the financing of terrorism. In its fight against terrorism, the United Nations Security Council (SC) has resorted to the same strategy inaugurated in 1997 (and supplemented in 1998) with the introduction of travel and financial restrictions against members of the UNITA[1].

Targeting individuals, rather than a specific State, marked a qualitative change in the SC's sanctions policy. These so-called 'targeted sanctions', also known as 'smart sanctions', have been introduced in a number of SC resolutions directed against individuals and entities allegedly associated with the Taliban and Al-Qaida. By means of Resolution 1267,[2] the SC, *inter alia*, required States to freeze funds and financial assets controlled directly or indirectly by the Taliban; likewise, Resolution 1333[3] ordered as much with regard to Osama bin Laden and his associates. To these resolutions, blacklists were attached for listing the targeted individuals and corporate entities. Resolution 1390[4] renewed the Taliban/Al-Qaida blacklists and expanded the reach of the sanctions to any person associated with the Taliban, Osama bin Laden or

*Professor of Public International Law, University of Zurich; Member of the Human Rights Committee (helen.keller@rwi.uzh.ch).
**PhD student at the Law Faculty of the University of Zurich (andreas.fischer@rwi.uzh.ch).

1 Portuguese acronym for União Nacional para a Independência Total de Angola (National Union for the Total Independence of Angola).
2 SC Res. 1267, 15 October 1999, S/RES/1267 (1999).
3 SC Res. 1333, 19 December 2000, S/RES/1333 (2000).
4 SC Res. 1390, 16 January 2002, S/RES/1390 (2002).

Al-Qaida, imposing on the latter a travel ban and arms embargo. It was the first resolution which dispensed with any link to a specific territory or State.[5] The Resolutions setting out the targeted sanctions regime are binding on all United Nations (UN) Member States because they were adopted under Chapter VII of the UN Charter.

Under the three Resolutions, a Sanctions Committee was established with a mandate to maintain a list of individuals and corporate entities that are to be subjected to the sanctions as well as monitoring the implementation of the sanctions by the States. Listings are done upon a corresponding request by a State. Targeted individuals and entities may submit a request for de-listing through the State of their residence or citizenship or through a 'focal point' in the UN Secretariat. The Sanctions Committee operates on the basis of consensus.

In view of the grave consequences of these sanctions for the targeted individuals, from a rule of law perspective, it is imperative that legal avenues are available for individuals to claim some form of review of the measures imposed on them. However, the lack of legal safeguards countervailing a possible arbitrary exercise of political power of the SC (through its Sanctions Committee) has been a major problem with the SC targeted sanctions.

While initially, under Resolution 1267, sanctions were imposed without any specific procedural standards, the procedural flaws have been addressed in subsequent resolutions setting up listing criteria[6] and providing for a 'statement of case' to be submitted by the nominating State and obligatory notification of inclusion on the list to the relevant individuals and entities.[7] Furthermore, the establishment of a 'focal point' within the UN Secretariat[8] to which individuals can directly lodge their de-listing requests is certainly an improvement, as the individual is no longer dependent on his State of nationality or residence to initiate a de-listing procedure on his behalf. A further welcome development has been the adoption of SC Resolution 1822, which provides that the Sanctions Committee shall conduct a review of all names on the UN sanctions list at the date of adoption of that resolution by 30 June 2010 and thenceforth to undertake 'an annual review of all names on the Consolidated List that have not been reviewed in three or more years . . ..'[9]

5 See Cameron, 'UN Targeted Sanctions, Legal Safeguards and the European Convention on Human Rights', (2003) 72 *Nordic Journal of International Law* 159 at 164.

6 SC Res. 1526, 30 January 2004, S/RES/1526 (2004) called upon States to include in their listing requests identifying and background information 'to the greatest extent possible' and SC Res. 1617, 29 July 2005, S/RES/1617 (2005) clarified the meaning of the term 'associated with'.

7 SC Res. 1617 mandated that proposing States submit a 'statement of case describing the basis of the proposal'. SC Res. 1735, 22 December 2006, S/RES/1735 (2006) specified the content of the statement of case and provided for the obligatory notification of listed individuals and entities, though this does not necessarily include the reasons for listing.

8 SC Res. 1730, 19 December 2006, S/RES/1730 (2006).

9 SC Res. 1822, 30 June 2008, S/RES/1822 (2008) at paras 25 and 26.

Yet, these improvements are clearly insufficient. With respect to the listing procedure, individuals have no right to be heard, let alone in the context of judicial proceedings where a decision is rendered by an impartial judicial or quasi-judicial body. Fair trial standards as enshrined in the relevant human rights instruments are only engaged if the sanctions are considered to be 'criminal' in nature, and not merely of a preventative, administrative nature as characterised by the UN organs.[10] Whilst views by scholars and (quasi-)judicial bodies[11] diverge on whether targeted sanctions are to be regarded as civil, criminal, or administrative in character,[12] the fact remains that the sanctions which give rise to severe consequences for the targeted individuals are imposed on them without there being any international legal mechanism for reviewing the accuracy of the information forming the basis of a State's listing request or the proportionality of the measures adopted.[13] Thus, '[t]here is still the prospect that individuals might be listed based on mistaken identity.'[14] To quote Council of Europe Parliamentary Assembly investigator Dick Marty (Switzerland): 'A country proposes that a person be added, often without giving any detailed reasons, even to the other members of the Sanctions Committee, and the Committee agrees without hearing or even notifying the person concerned.'[15] Furthermore, the consensus nature of the Sanctions

10 The targeted sanctions are characterised by SC Res. 1735, supra n. 7, as being 'preventative in nature and not reliant upon criminal standards set out under national law'. See also the Guidelines of the Committee for the Conduct of its Work, adopted on 7 November 2002 and last amended on 9 December 2008, at para. 6: 'A criminal charge or conviction is not necessary for inclusion on the Consolidated List as the sanctions are intended to be preventive in nature.' The revised Guidelines are available at: http://www.un.org/sc/committees/1267.Guidelines.pdf [last accessed 18 May 2009].

11 While not expressly pronouncing itself on the legal nature of the sanctions, the European Court of Justice (ECJ) in Joined Cases C-402P and C-415/05P, *Yassin Abdullah Kadi and Al Barakaal International Foundation v Council of the European Union and Commission of the European Communities* [2008] ECR I-(nyr) held the fair trial guarantees and the right to an effective remedy applicable. See Ziegler, 'Strengthening the Rule of Law, but Fragmenting International Law: The *Kadi* Decision of the ECJ from the Perspective of Human Rights', (2009) 9 *Human Rights Law Review* 288–305. In contrast, the Sanctions Committee in the present case concluded that the sanctions were in effect administrative, see below.

12 For a discussion on the proper characterisation see, for example, Bianchi, 'Assessing the Effectiveness of the UN Security Council's Anti-terrorism Measures: The Quest for Legitimacy and Cohesion', (2006) 17 *European Journal of International Law* 881 at 905; and van den Herik, 'The Security Council's Targeted Sanctions Regimes: In Need of Better Protection of the Individual', (2007) 20 *Leiden Journal of International Law* 797 at 806.

13 Cameron, supra n. 5 at 159. See also van den Herik, ibid at 798: '[S]till there is no possibility whatsoever of some independent substantive review at UN level. Here again it becomes clear that, more than anything else, the real stumbling block is the substantive review of intelligence information by an independent and impartial organ.'

14 Marty, 'United Nations Security Council and European Union blacklists', Report of the Committee on Legal Affairs and Human Rights, Parliamentary Assembly, 16 November 2007, Doc. 11454 at Point C. II. ii. A., available at: http://www.assembly.coe.int/Mainf.asp?link=/Documents/WorkingDocs/Doc07/eDOC11454.htm [last accessed 12 April 2009].

15 Marty, 'UN Security Council black lists: Introductory memorandum', Committee on Legal Affairs and Human Rights, Parliamentary Assembly, AS/Jur 9 (2007) 14, 19 March 2007, ajdoc14 2007, available at: http://assembly.coe.int/CommitteeDocs/2007/20070319.ajdoc14.pdf [last accessed 12 April 2009].

260 *HRLR* **9** (2009), 257–266

Committee's decision-making means that, once a name is on a list, any SC Member can block its removal, even in the face of a national court decision affirming the innocence of a listed individual, and despite the fact that the State which originally submitted an individual's name for listing itself requests the removal of that individual from the sanctions list. The procedure at the 'focal point' is also political and based on consensus, lacking any proper legal safeguards.

Over the past years, targeted sanctions have been the focus of criticism by scholars, reports commissioned by international organisations[16] and governments,[17] and were not least challenged in legal proceedings. The most recent case exposing the problems of wrong listings and the glaring deficiency of the de-listing procedure concerns a Belgium couple—Nabil Sayadi, who is of Lebanese descent, and his wife Patricia Vinck. Sayadi and Vinck were, respectively, the director and secretary of *Fondation Secours Mondial* (FSM), the Belgium office of the Global Relief Foundation (GRF), an Islamic charitable organisation based in the United States. The United States suspected the GRF of having provided financial and other assistance to, and receiving funding from, individuals associated with Al-Qaida. On the basis of a request from the United States, the GRF was placed on the Sanctions Committee list in October 2002. Subsequently, upon a proposal for listing by Belgium, the names of Sayadi and his wife were added to the UN sanctions list on 22 January 2003, which was subsequently appended to a European Community regulation[18] and a ministerial order issued in the State party.[19]

The consequences for the Sayadi couple and their four children were harsh. As a result of their listing, all of the couple's financial assets were frozen and, because of the travel ban, they could no longer travel within or leave Belgium, and Mr Sayadi was unable to take up an offer of employment in another country. Mr Sayadi and his wife have neither been prosecuted nor convicted, and they boast a clean criminal record.

Sayadi and Vinck submitted several requests in 2003 to the Belgian Government, European Union (EU) Commission and to diverse organs of

16 See Cameron, *The European Convention on Human Rights, Due Process and United Nations Security Council Counter-terrorism Sanctions* (commissioned by Council of Europe, 2006), available at: http://www.coe.int/T/E/Legal_Affairs/Legal-co-operation/Public_international_law [last accessed 10 April 2009]; and Fassbender, *Targeted Sanctions and Due Process* (commissioned by the UN Office of Legal Affairs, 2006), available at: http://www.un.org/law/counsel/Fassbender_study.pdf [last accessed 10 April 2009]..

17 See White Paper prepared by the Watson Institute, *Strengthening Targeted Sanctions through Fair and Clear Procedures*, A/60/887–/2006/331 (2006), available at: http://www.watson institute.org/pub/Strengthening_Targeted_Sanctions.pdf [last accessed 12 April 2009].

18 Commission Regulation (EC) No. 145/2003 of 27 January 2003 amending Regulation (EC) No. 881/2002 for the ninth time.

19 Ministerial order of 31 January 2003 amending ministerial order of 15 June 2000 implementing the Royal Decree of 17 February 2000 concerning the restrictive measures directed against the Taliban in Afghanistan.

the UN in an attempt to have their names struck off the sanctions list. On 11 February 2005, after two and half years of investigation without an indictment, the Brussels Court of First Instance ordered the Belgian State to file a de-listing request with the Sanctions Committee. The Judge's Chambers of the Brussels Court of First Instance exonerated the plaintiffs of any suspected criminal activities, dismissing the case on 25 February 2005. Although Belgium promptly complied with the Court of First Instance's ruling, and repeated its de-listing request a year later, the de-listing procedures were blocked each time by members of the Sanctions Committee. Thus, despite these clear judicial decisions in favour of the plaintiffs, Sayadi and Vinck continue to be subjected to the sanctions.

2. Disputed Competence

Whilst roaming the institutional landscape, Sayadi and Vinck also filed an individual complaint with the Human Rights Committee (HRC). Belgium disputed the HRC's competence to consider the complaint on the basis of Article 1 of the Optional Protocol to the International Covenant on Civil and Political Rights 1966 (the Covenant)[20] which stipulates that for a complaint to be admissible, the individual in question must be subject to the jurisdiction of a State party.[21] Since its measures taken to implement the UN anti-terror sanctions were dictated by its international obligations to comply with SC decisions adopted under Chapter VII, Belgium alleged that the actions against Sayadi and his wife fell beyond the scope of its domestic jurisdiction. Thus, Sayadi and Vinck were not subject to Belgium's jurisdiction within the meaning of Article 1 of the Optional Protocol, and could not challenge Belgium's measures taken to implement its UN Charter obligations.[22] In the same vein, in her dissenting opinion, Ruth Wedgwood held that the complaint was 'inadmissible because it [pleaded] no cognizable violation by the State party'.[23] In conclusion, she stated that '[t]he only actions taken by Belgium were in accordance with the binding mandate of the Security Council.'[24]

Belgium's argument weighed heavily. Indeed, pursuant to Article 25 of the UN Charter, States must accept and carry out the decisions of the SC, and Article 103 of the UN Charter sets out the primacy of the States' Charter obligations *vis-à-vis* their other international obligations. It is generally argued that because of the pre-eminent role of the SC and the importance of the interests

20 99 UNTS 171.
21 *Sayadi and Vinck v Belgium* (1472/2006), CCPR/C/94/D/1472/2006 (2008); 16 IHRR 427 (2009) at para. 6.1.
22 Ibid.
23 Ibid. at Dissenting Opinion of Ruth Wedgwood.
24 Ibid.

at stake, the SC enjoys a wide measure of discretion under Chapter VII both to determine the existence of one of the situations that could trigger its powers and in respect of the choice of measures contemplated under the Charter to be employed. By signing the UN Charter, UN Member States have implicitly accepted the supremacy of the SC, which is not checked by any body with explicit powers to monitor and control it.[25] Article 24 of the UN Charter provides that the SC shall act in accordance with the purposes and principles of the Charter, including the maintenance of international peace and security in accordance with the principles of justice and international law, and the protection and promotion of human rights. However, in the absence of a judicial body at the UN level which could check the actions of the SC, the latter, it is claimed, has the *kompetenz-kompetenz* in deciding to what extent it is bound by human rights.[26] However, to accept such an argument would be to accept the irrelevance of international law to international politics. The debate about the limits to the SC's exercise of its powers has been a well-rehearsed topic. Here, it should suffice to state that the view of the SC being unfettered by law is untenable. [27]

Conceptually distinct from the previous issue is the question of whether States are bound by the rule of law when implementing SC Resolutions. This issue was addressed in SC Resolution 1456, according to which 'States must ensure that any measure taken to combat terrorism comply with all their obligations under international law, in particular human rights, refugee and humanitarian law . . . '.[28] Hence, regardless of whether the SC sanctions are consistent *per se* with international law, States are obliged to ensure that their implementation does not violate international law.

25 Cameron, supra n. 5 at 174. Compare Belgium's contentions in *Sayadi*, supra n. 21 at para. 6.3: 'In ratifying the Charter, the State party transferred powers to the Security Council, and it has subsequently ratified the Covenant. At the time when the State party ratified the Covenant, the powers it had transferred to the Security Council were no longer within its competence, and so the State party cannot be held responsible under the Covenant for how those powers are exercised.'

26 Ibid. at 173.

27 Angelet, 'International Law Limits to the Security Council', in Gowlland-Debbas (ed.), *United Nations Sanctions and International Law* (The Hague: Kluwer Law International, 2001) 71; De Wet, *The Chapter VII Powers of the United Nations Security Council* (Oxford: Hart, 2004) at 133–216; Dugard, 'Judicial Review of Sanctions', in Gowlland-Debbas, ibid. at 83; Gill, 'Legal and Some Political Limitations on the Power of the UN Security Council to Exercise its Enforcement Powers under Chapter VII of the Charter', (1995) 26 *Netherlands Yearbook of International Law* 33; Lamb, 'Legal Limits to United Nations Security Council Powers', in Goodwin-Gill and Talmon (eds), *The Reality of International Law: Essays in Honour of Ian Brownlie* (Oxford: Clarendon Press, 1999) 361; Nolte, 'The Limits of the Security Council's Powers and its Functions in the International Legal System: Some Reflections', in Byers (ed.), *The Role of Law in International Politics* (Oxford: Oxford University Press, 2000) 315; and Schweigman, *The Authority of the Security Council under Chapter VII of the UN Charter: Legal Limits and the Role of the International Court of Justice* (The Hague: Kluwer Law International, 2001).

28 SC Res. 1456, 20 January 2003, S/Res/1456 (2003) at para. 6.

The consistency of State conduct in the context of implementing SC sanctions with legally binding rules is thus susceptible to judicial or quasi-judicial review. As for the latter, the HRC concluded that while it could not pass judgment on the legality of SC measures taken under the UN Charter, it was competent to consider whether 'a State party had violated rights set forth in the Covenant, regardless of the source of the obligations implemented by the State party'.[29]

3. Dilemma in International Law

As a matter of fact, the Belgian State found itself in a dilemma: if it chose to lift the financial ban, it would breach its obligations under the UN sanctions regime. If it left the sanctions in place against Sayadi and Vinck, without any incriminating evidence found against them, it would violate their human rights.

Concerning the merits, the Belgian Government maintained that, because of the primacy accorded to UN Charter obligations by Article 103 of the Charter, it had no option but to comply with the SC Resolutions.[30] If Belgium was held to be in violation of the Covenant, taken in isolation, Articles 25 and 103 of the UN Charter would nonetheless absolve the Belgian State of responsibility for failure to fulfil its lower ranking obligations under the Covenant.[31] Furthermore, the Belgian Government asserted that it had taken all appropriate measures within its powers to have the authors' names de-listed.[32]

The HRC accepted Belgium's argument that the SC sanctions, though involving serious consequences for the complainants, are of a preventive rather than a punitive nature and thus cannot be characterised as 'criminal' for the purposes of Article 14(1) of the Covenant.[33] Consequently, fair trial guarantees (Article 14) and the principle of legality of penalties (Article 15) were not engaged. Nonetheless, the HRC held Belgium in breach of its obligations under the Covenant. Concerning the liberty of movement as protected under Article 12 of the Covenant, the HRC observed that because of the travel restrictions imposed on Sayadi and Vinck, the latter were unable to travel freely within Belgium or to leave it. Measuring these restrictions against the yardstick of Article 12(3), it found that in view of the dismissal of the criminal investigation against Sayadi and his wife in 2005 and Belgium's requests for the removal of their names from the UN sanctions list, these restrictions were 'not necessary to protect national security or public order' and thus amounted

29 *Sayadi*, supra n. 21 at para. 7.2.
30 Ibid. at paras 4.12, 6.3 and 8.1–8.2.
31 Ibid. at para. 8.1.
32 Ibid. at para. 8.3.
33 Ibid. at para. 10.11.

to a violation of Article 12.[34] Furthermore, the HRC considered that the stigmatisation involved in the inclusion of the complainants' names together with their full contact details on the SC anti-terror list, and in view of the many press articles tarnishing their reputation, amounted to an unlawful attack on the honour and reputation of Sayadi and Vinck (Article 17).[35] In its reasoning, the HRC refuted Belgium's argument that it was obliged to transmit the names of Sayadi and his wife to the Sanctions Committee, in view of the fact that Belgium was the only State to have transmitted names associated with GRF to the Sanctions Committee, and because it did so without awaiting the outcome of the national criminal investigation.[36] Thus, the HRC found that 'even though the State party is not competent to remove the author's names from the United Nations and European lists, it is responsible for the presence of the . . . names [of Sayadi and his wife] on those lists.'[37] With respect to Belgium's obligation to provide the complainants with an effective remedy (Article 2), the HRC held that Belgium had to undertake all that was in its power to have the complainant's names removed from the list as soon as possible and to prevent similar violations from occurring in the future.[38]

In its reasoning, the HRC performed a balancing act. On the one hand, well aware of the legitimacy problems involved in any pronouncement on the compatibility of the SC sanctions regime with the UN Charter, the HRC steered around this delicate issue. On the other hand, it made it unambiguously clear that State measures taken to give effect to SC resolutions must respect human rights. Regardless of whether or not SC resolutions *per se* are consistent with human rights, in implementing them the Member States do not have a *carte blanche*; they are constrained by the rule of law. While the HRC's decision is merely directed against the Belgian State, it ultimately sends an indirect signal to the UN, namely the SC.

4. Urgent Need for Reform

The HRC's criticism is the most recent of a range of authoritative judicial and quasi-judicial comments on the inadequacy of the extant system of SC anti-terror sanctions. The procedural flaws involved in the process of adopting and implementing SC targeted sanctions have been exposed in various judgments by the judiciary of the EU, such as in the *Mojahedin*[39] and the

34 Ibid. at para. 10.8.
35 Ibid. at para. 10.13.
36 Ibid. at paras 10.7 and 10.13.
37 Ibid. at para. 10.13.
38 Ibid. at para. 12.
39 Court of First Instance, Case T-228/02, *Organisation de Modjahedines du people d'Iran v Council of the European Union*, Judgment, 12 December 2006 (insufficient statement of reasons,

Sison[40] cases. In contrast to the *Sayadi* case, the listing in the *Mojahedin* and *Sison* cases was not done on the basis of Resolution 1267, but pursuant to Resolution 1373.[41] Whereas under the former, listing was undertaken by the Sanctions Committee, the latter Resolution left the listing task up to each State. In the context of the EU, the lists were established and maintained by the Council of the EU. In the *Mojahedin* and *Sison* cases, the European Court of First Instance annulled the decision to place the complainants on the EU anti-terror blacklist on the grounds that the Council of Europe had not provided sufficient reasons for listing the organisation and because the listing procedure did not respect the right to a fair hearing. As for listings under SC Resolution 1267, a landmark ruling was issued by the ECJ in September 2008. In *Kadi and Al Barakaat v Council of the EU and Commission of the EC*,[42] the ECJ was the first among regional and international tribunals to hold that the sanctions imposed by the SC anti-terror resolutions infringed certain fundamental rights under European Community (Community) law, namely the right to be heard, the right to an effective legal remedy and the right to property. It also marked the first time that a court confirmed its jurisdiction to review the lawfulness of a measure giving effect to a SC resolution. Despite ruling that the implementing measure—Council Regulation (EC) 881/2002 of 27 May 2002—violated fundamental rights under Community law, the ECJ, like the HRC, was anxious to stress that its judicial review did not extend to the SC resolution as such. It held that 'any judgement by the Community judicature deciding that a Community measure intended to give effect to . . . a [UN SC] resolution is contrary to a higher rule of law in the Community legal order would not entail any challenge to the primacy of that resolution in international law.'[43] An application against Switzerland concerning the implementation of SC sanctions measures has also been lodged with the European Court of Human Rights.[44]

While improvements have been made with regard to the listing and de-listing procedures, these still fall short of full respect for the rule of law principle. Importantly, the *modus operandi* of the listing process in the

violation of the applicant's right to a fair hearing); Case T-256/07, *People's Mojahedin Organization of Iran v Council of the European Union*, Judgment, 23 October 2008 (insufficient statement of reasons); and Case T-284/08, *People's Mojahedin Organization of Iran v Council of the European Union*, Judgment, 4 December 2008 (violation of the applicant's rights of defence and right to effective judicial protection).

40 Court of First Instance, Case T-47/03, *Jose Maria Sison v Council of the European Union*, Judgment, 11 July 2007.

41 SC Res. 1373, 28 September 2001, S/RES/1373 (2001).

42 Supra n. 11. See also Ziegler, supra n. 11.

43 Ibid. at para. 288.

44 Identical letters dated 23 June 2008 from the Permanent Representative of Switzerland to the United Nations addressed to the President of the General Assembly and the President of the Security Council, Enclosure: 'Improving the implementation of sanctions regimes through "fair and clear procedures",' A/62/891-S/2008/428, at 4, available at: http://www.security councilreport.org [last accessed 12 April 2009].

Sanctions Committee and at 'focal point' are political. In this regard, a group of countries[45] have advanced the idea of establishing an independent, impartial expert panel to assist the Sanctions Committee in the consideration of de-listing requests. This would be a step in striking 'a careful balance between the competence and authority of the Security Council and its Sanctions Committee(s) in the area of international peace and security on the one hand, and the substantive requirements of "fair and clear procedures" on the other'.[46]

It is to be hoped that the increasing criticism on the part of various international (non-governmental) organisations will garner the necessary political support to buttress the efforts to bring the anti-terror fight under the banner of justice and the rule of law. Otherwise, the chances are that the UN counter-terrorism efforts may backfire. States may become increasingly reluctant[47] to comply with the SC sanctions regime and submit new names for listing, or may begin to lift the freezing of bank accounts and travel bans on their own account. Such undercutting of the UN sanctions system would herald its end. To be sure, fair listing and de-listing procedures, in enhancing the States' perceived legitimacy of the SC targeted sanctions, would improve the sanctions' 'compliance pull'[48] and thus also their overall effectiveness. One should be mindful of the words of former Secretary-General Kofi Annan: '[The Security] Council has a very heavy responsibility to promote justice and the rule of law in its efforts to maintain international peace and security.'[49]

45 The States concerned include: Denmark, Germany, Liechtenstein, the Netherlands, Sweden and Switzerland.

46 'Improving the implementation of sanctions regimes through "fair and clear procedures"', supra n. 44 at 4.

47 Compare ibid.: 'These deficiencies have caused countries to hesitate with the submission of names for listing. They also underline existing concerns about the integrity and legitimacy of targeted sanctions in general.'

48 See Franck, *The Power of Legitimacy Among Nations* (New York: Oxford University Press, 1990) at 24; and Hurd, 'Legitimacy and Authority in International Politics' (1999) 53 *International Organization* 379 at 387ff.

49 Former UN Secretary-General Kofi Annan at the Security Council's meeting on justice and the rule of law, 24 September 2003.

Part VI
State Responses

[13]

SECURITY DETENTION, TERRORISM AND THE PREVENTION IMPERATIVE*

John P. McLoughlin,† *Gregory P. Noone*‡ *& Diana C. Noone*§

[T]he Government's regulatory interest in community safety can, in appropriate circumstances, outweigh an individual's liberty interest. For example, in times of war or insurrection, when society's interest is at its peak, the Government may detain individuals whom the Government believes to be dangerous. Even outside the exigencies of war, we have found that sufficiently compelling governmental interests can justify detention of dangerous persons.

—*United States v. Salerno*,
481 U.S. 739, 748 (1987)

The events of September 11 transformed the mission of the Department of Justice . . . . Indeed, the protection of our national security and the prevention of terrorist acts are our number one goal. On every level, we are now committed to a new strategy of prevention.

—*U.S. Department of Justice*
Counterterrorism White Paper

* The authors would like to thank Laura Fridley for her outstanding research for this article, and Brianne Draffin, Lara Nochomovitz, Gwen Gillespie, and Philip Hadji for their outstanding editing. The positions and opinions stated in this article are those of the authors and do not represent the views of the United States Government, the Department of Defense, the United States Navy, the Defense Institute of International Legal Studies, or any other governmental or nongovernmental entity. All information obtained for this article was gathered through open sources.

† John P. McLoughlin (A.B. Georgetown University, J.D. University of Virginia) is an international attorney at the Defense Institute of International Legal Studies, where he serves as Regional Program Director for Africa.

‡ Gregory P. Noone (B.A. Villanova University, J.D. Suffolk University Law School, M.A. The Catholic University of America, Ph.D. West Virginia University) is the Director of the National Security and Intelligence Program and an Assistant Professor of Political Science and Law at Fairmont State University.

§ Diana C. Noone (B.A. Virginia Polytechnic Institute and State University, J.D. Widener University School of Law, M.S.W. The Catholic University of America, Ph.D. University of Maryland) is the Chair of Social Sciences and an Assistant Professor of Criminal Justice at Fairmont State University.

INTRODUCTION

Since the events of September 11, 2001, the United States and many of its allies in the global campaign against terrorism have adopted a new dominant security imperative: prevention of terrorist attacks against their homelands and national interests. In succinct terms, the prevention imperative posits that the U.S. will engage all elements of national power (legal, economic, diplomatic, financial, military, intelligence, and information) to neutralize the threat posed by al Qaeda and other non-state actors. Detention of suspected terrorists has become a main facet of this prevention strategy, and several legal mechanisms have been employed in this regard in the U.S.

The primary purpose of this article is neither to assess the rectitude or efficacy of the current multi-prong approach to detention of suspect individuals, nor to assess the imperative placed on prevention as a strategy. Rather, this article will review the recent calls for a new system of preventive detention and the legal landscape of preventive detention in the U.S., and will survey several preventive detention systems used by the U.S.'s allies. The goal of the article is to outline the likely characteristics of, and fundamental questions associated with, any new security detention process the U.S. might consider adopting.

At the outset, this article is written with certain premises in mind. First, terrorism experts agree that the U.S. homeland likely will be the target of future attacks. Second, it is also likely that at some future point those attacks will be perpetrated by homegrown individuals, including U.S. citizens.[1] Third, the design of any system of preventive detention should be consistent with the U.S.'s obligations under both the U.S. Constitution and international law. Finally, it is better to discuss the controversial issue of preventive detention in a calm and deliberate manner rather than in the wake of another terrorist attack, when fear, anger, and calculations of political advantage may rule the day.

I. THE CURRENT APPROACH TO DETENTION OF TERRORIST SUSPECTS

The United States currently uses a multi-prong approach to detain suspected terrorists. As former Attorney General Alberto Gonzalez acknowledged, to many outsiders the U.S. government's decision-making process about how to deal with a particular individual "is a black box that raises the specter of arbitrary action," despite what he described as "a

---

1 Timothy McVeigh's 1995 bombing of the Alfred P. Murrah Federal Building in Oklahoma City has already demonstrated this reality.

thoughtful, deliberate and thorough analysis of the relevant facts and law at many levels of the Executive branch."[2]

One of the legal mechanisms that the U.S. has employed to detain suspects is traditional criminal law enforcement, which the U.S. has relied on to investigate and prosecute both terrorism-specific and other crimes. This reliance on criminal law enforcement procedures principally has involved the "material support" statutes found at 18 USC §§ 2339A and 2339B. More ordinary offenses such as conspiracy, document fraud, obstruction of justice, perjury, and the like also have played a critical role.[3] This criminal law enforcement element of the prevention strategy has been used with respect to both U.S. citizens and aliens, and persons apprehended both in the U.S. and in foreign nations. The U.S. has employed other tools from the law enforcement paradigm more aggressively to neutralize perceived terrorist threats. Perhaps the most notable example is the use of the power to detain persons that qualify as material witnesses for ongoing criminal investigations and prosecutions.[4] Moreover, the U.S. and other nations have undertaken numerous measures, both in domestic and international law, to enhance the criminal law enforcement powers available to combat terrorism.

In addition to the criminal law enforcement paradigm, the U.S. has expanded and employed its framework of immigration laws as an alternate detention mechanism. As in the arena of criminal law enforcement, the years since 9/11 have witnessed enhanced government powers and in-

---

[2] Alberto R. Gonzalez, Counsel to the President, Remarks before the American Bar Association Standing Committee on Law and National Security (Feb. 24, 2004), *available at* http://fas.org/irp/news/2004/02/gonzales.pdf.

[3] *See generally* U.S. Department of Justice, *Counterterrorism White Paper* (June 22, 2006), *available at* http://trac.syr.edu/tracreports/terrorism/169/include/terrorism.whitepaper.pdf.

[4] The primary provision regarding material witnesses can be found at 18 U.S.C. § 3144 (2006). For example, both Jose Padilla, a U.S. citizen, and Ali Saleh Kahlah al Marri, an alien resident in the U.S., were initially detained in 2001 as material witnesses for the investigation into the 9/11 attacks. *See* Al-Marri v. Wright, 487 F.3d 160, 164 (4th Cir. 2007); Steve Fainaru & Margot Williams, *Material Witness Law Has Many in Limbo; Nearly Half Held in War on Terror Haven't Testified*, WASH. POST, Nov. 24, 2002, at A1. Both were ultimately transferred to military custody and further detained as enemy combatants. 487 F.3d at 165; Kirk Semple, *Padilla Sentenced to 17 Years in Prison*, N.Y. TIMES, Jan. 23, 2008. The U.S. government eventually transferred Padilla back to the ordinary civilian criminal justice system, where he was tried and convicted for terrorism-related crimes that were unrelated to the original basis for his detention. Peter Whoriskey & Dan Eggen, *Judge Sentences Padilla to 17 Years, Cites His Detention*, WASH. POST, Jan. 23, 2008, at A3. According to the Washington Post, between September 2001 and November 2002, at least forty-four persons were detained as material witnesses in connection with terrorism investigations. Steve Fainaru & Margot Williams, *Material Witness Law Has Many in Limbo; Nearly Half Held in War on Terror Haven't Testified*, WASH. POST, Nov. 24, 2002, at A1. Of those forty-four, twenty were never brought before a grand jury. *Id.*

creased enforcement operations with respect to foreign nationals.[5] Although immigration laws and processes generally do not apply to citizens, immigration laws do apply to foreign nationals who legally have entered and resided in the U.S. for extended periods, not just illegal immigrants or those foreign nationals who are stopped at the border.

A third—and in some quarters more controversial—legal mechanism used to effectuate the prevention imperative is the law of armed conflict (LOAC). Framing the conflict with al Qaeda and its network of affiliates as a "global war on terror" and relying on the 2001 Authorization for the Use of Military Force (AUMF) adopted by Congress,[6] the U.S. has cited the long-established customary and conventional power of nations to detain enemy combatants as the legal basis for holding many suspected terrorist operatives in military custody. This power, which permits a nation to hold enemy combatants for the duration of a conflict to prevent them from returning to the battle, also has been asserted by the U.S. government to detain both U.S. citizens and foreign nationals, and with respect to both persons detained in the U.S. and persons detained in foreign nations.

Despite the availability and use of these multiple legal mechanisms, a growing number of prominent U.S. legal scholars and practitioners have suggested that the U.S. should enact a new system of security detention (also termed "preventive detention" or "administrative detention"). These scholars and practitioners suggest that the challenges facing the government under the current multi-prong approach, and the questions of fundamental fairness to some detainees under that approach, necessitate such a new system. Moreover, these commentators have expressed concern that the current strategy is accomplished only by distorting these legal paradigms in ways that will ultimately spill over into government efforts to combat threats other than terrorism.

---

[5] *See* OFFICE OF THE INSPECTOR GEN., U.S. DEP'T OF JUSTICE, THE SEPTEMBER 11 DETAINEES: A REVIEW OF THE TREATMENT OF ALIENS HELD ON IMMIGRATION CHARGES IN CONNECTION WITH THE INVESTIGATION OF THE SEPTEMBER 11 ATTACKS, 2, 15, 47 (2003), http://www.usdoj.gov/oig/special/0306/full.pdf. (stating that approximately 762 aliens were detained in the U.S. in connection with the 9/11 investigation). By far, most of those aliens were detained under immigration provisions related to illegal entry or expired visas, and the overwhelming number of those charges were found to be invalid. The vast majority of the detained aliens were never connected to terrorism, and prior to 9/11 many of them would not have been detained for those violations. *Id.*

[6] Authorization for Use of Military Force, Pub. L. No., 115 Stat. 224 (2001) (codified at 50 U.S.C. § 1541).

A. *The Challenges of the Current Approach*

1. Shortcomings of old and new paradigms to combat terror threats

Before 9/11, the United States and many other nations viewed terrorism primarily as an issue of criminal law enforcement. Efforts to combat terrorism too often focused on *post hoc* criminal investigations that were designed to develop criminal cases for prosecution. Generally, *post hoc* criminal investigations often involve interdicting terrorist activity close to the point of attack, or, too frequently, after an attack has occurred, when evidence of offensive conduct and intent naturally is more unequivocal. This strategy largely permits shielding sensitive intelligence information—including evidence from intelligence investigations—from disclosure during judicial proceedings.

This approach might be understandable in response to a brand of terrorism that: (1) involves sporadic attacks; (2) limits civilian casualties (through advance warnings and the like) to insulate political agendas (e.g. the Marxist and nationalist terror groups of the 1970s); (3) primarily targets property interests (for example, modern eco-terrorists); (4) is secularly inspired; and (5) is almost exclusively domestic. However, this historical brand of terrorism has been joined, and to some extent eclipsed, by a fundamentally different terrorist threat, namely one perpetrated by religiously inspired radical extremist groups such as al Qaeda and its associated organizations around the world. These modern terrorist groups employ a wide web of support for recruitment, procurement, logistics, and operational planning. They present a global terrorist threat interested in carrying out repetitive attacks involving indiscriminate mass casualties and severe damage to economic and social infrastructure (including critical systems such as energy, communications, and food and water supplies). These groups have a genuine interest in the use of chemical, biological, radiological, and nuclear weapons, and a willingness, if not a desire, to die (through suicide or otherwise) to achieve their mission.

Just as the nature of the modern terrorist threat has evolved, so have the challenges of investigating and prosecuting that threat. Terrorist investigations are increasingly multi-jurisdictional. Differences in capabilities, timeframes of action, judicial systems (accusatorial versus inquisitorial, common law versus civil law, and the like), willingness to cooperate, availability of resources, and enforcement authority create serious investigative obstacles. These obstacles make it far more difficult for government agencies to obtain relevant, useful evidence while simultaneously increasing the time and cost of trying to do so. In addition, the global nature of modern terrorism means that evidence may often be obtained under extraordinary circumstances or in extraordinary places.[7]

The forensic requirements of modern terrorism investigations are also far more complex and time consuming than in the past, particularly given the possibility of WMD hazards. The methodology of simultaneous attacks extends and complicates forensic examination and analysis, especially when the forensic sites are located in major metropolitan areas and infrastructure systems. Modern forensic investigations also require deployment of specialized teams, the number of which are limited and the functions of which are often sequential in nature, meaning that parallel efforts are difficult, if not impossible.[8]

As a result of the changed threat environment and these investigative challenges, suspected terrorist activities must be disrupted earlier in the planning and preparation cycle. Terrorism investigations now are more of-

---

[7] Operation Springbourne, an investigation by the British Metropolitan Police of a terrorism plot using ricin, provides a demonstration of obstacles to terrorism investigations. Conducted between 2002 and 2005, Operation Springbourne spanned twenty-seven jurisdictions. HOME AFFAIRS COMMITTEE, TERRORISM DETENTION POWERS, 2005–06, H.C. 910-I, at 56, *available at* http://www.publications.parliament.uk/pa/cm200506/cmselect/cmhaff/910/910i.pdf. Because U.K. law required charging decisions within a short timeframe and evidence was not able to be developed from the many jurisdictions within that timeframe, the authorities were unable to prosecute the suspects for terrorism charges. *Id.* Instead, the suspects were prosecuted for ordinary crimes such as fraud or forgery arising from some peripheral document and credit card fraud schemes. *Id.* A suspect later determined to be a prime conspirator fled the country while on bail awaiting trial on the lesser charges. *Id.*

[8] For example, the July 2005 London bombings created the largest crime scene in the United Kingdom's history—and it took place in the heart of London's critical transport infrastructure. *See Minutes of Evidence Before the British H. of Commons Home Affairs Comm.*, Session 06 (2005) (testimony of British Metropolitan Police Commissioner Ian Blair and Assistant Commissioner Andy Hayman to the British House of Commons Home Affairs Committee) [hereinafter *Minutes of Evidence*], *available at* http://www.publications.parliament.uk/pa/cm200506/cmselect/cmhaff/462/5091305.htm. As of September 2005, law enforcement authorities had collected over 38,000 evidentiary exhibits. *See id.* The evidence to be preserved, collected, and analyzed included thousands of hours of closed circuit television (CCTV) videos and over 1,400 fingerprints. *See id.* As the investigations expanded, over 160 sites became potential crime scenes. *See id.* According to the British Metropolitan Police, one such site involved a so-called "bomb factory" discovered in the Yorkshire area. *See* HOME AFFAIRS COMMITTEE, *supra* note 7, at 19. Investigators required over two weeks to secure safe access to the site, and examination required another six weeks. *See id.* Definitive forensic analysis of the explosive devices could not be completed before charging decisions were required under U.K. law, and thus a much more limited assessment of the device had to be used to interrogate the suspects prior to charge. *See id.* at 56–57. New technology also increases the time required for terrorism investigations. These investigations often involve seizure of large numbers (i.e., into the hundreds) of computer hard drives that store vast amounts of data. *See id.*at 18–19. That data must be secured, often decrypted, examined, and ultimately assessed prior to being incorporated into investigative interviews or other steps. *Id.* Many of these steps cannot be done simultaneously, and thus the time involved is necessarily increased. *See id.*

ten viewed as intelligence cases, and prosecution of terrorist crimes is only one tool available to neutralize terrorist threats. However, the realities of intelligence pose serious problems. The key limit on intelligence is its incompleteness; rarely does intelligence tell the whole story, and terrorists take proactive steps to secure and obscure information. Intelligence is sporadic, fragmentary, often inferential at best, and difficult to interpret. It requires validation, prioritization, sifting, assessment and judgment. Intelligence is also fragile. It comes from human sources who risk their lives to obtain it, and from sensitive technologies that can be countered by skilled and informed opponents. Highly dependable intelligence information may have been provided by a foreign government on the condition that the information, or the government's cooperation, is not publicly disclosed.[9]

Statutes such as the Classified Information Procedures Act (CIPA)[10] provide limited relief for these concerns. To be sure, CIPA provides a valuable procedural mechanism for making determinations about the disclosure of national security information in criminal proceedings and to help "prevent[] unnecessary or inadvertent disclosures of classified information."[11] CIPA accomplishes this goal through: pre-trial conferences; notice requirements; judicial protective orders; *ex parte* and *in camera* submissions; court authorized deletions, summaries and stipulations; pre-trial evidentiary hearings; and interlocutory appeals. But CIPA "neither adds to nor detracts from the substantive rights of the defendant or the discoery [sic] obligations of the government."[12] Instead, it merely permits the government "to know in advance of a potential threat from a criminal prosecution to its national security . . . and advis[es] the government of the national security 'cost' of going forward."[13] Indeed, where a court rejects protective measures pro-

---

[9] *See* Dame Eliza Mannignham-Buller, Dir. Gen., British Security Services, Address at the Dutch General Intelligence and Security Service (AIVD) (Sept. 1, 2005), *available at* http://www.mi5.gov.uk/print/Page387.html [hereinafter Mannigham Speech].

[10] 18 U.S.C. App. 3 §§ 1–16 (1980).

[11] U.S ATTY. CRIM. RESOURCE MANUAL, SYNOPSIS OF CLASSIFIED INFORMATION PROCEDURES ACT, HTTP://WWW.USDOJ.GOV/USAO/EOUSA/FOIA_READING_ROOM/USAM/TITLE 9/CRM02054.HTM [hereinafter U.S. ATTORNEY MANUAL].

[12] *Id.*

[13] *Id.* The ABA has concluded that CIPA

> provides procedures for notice to the government and judicial screening when the defendant wishes to reveal classified information. It is designed to limit the defense's ability to leverage its possession of classified information in plea negotiations. CIPA provides no protection for information that the prosecution might need to introduce or for information that the defense is permitted to introduce.

ABA TASK FORCE ON TERRORISM AND THE LAW, REPORT AND RECOMMENDATIONS ON MILITARY COMMISSIONS, Jan. 4, 2002, at 14, n.33. Thus, although "mechanisms exist to protect evidence of a classified nature from public exposure, these may not suffice to protect the information from the defendants and, through them, others who may use such information to the harm of the U.S. and its citizens." *Id.* at 14.

posed under CIPA, the government "ha[s] two options: (1) order the case to be dismissed; or (2) file an affidavit effectively prohibiting the use of the contested classified information. At that point, the court may impose sanctions against the government, which may include striking all or part of a witness's testimony, resolving an issue of fact against the United States, or dismissing part or all of the indictment."[14]

Perhaps the most important aspect of this new paradigm is the critical dilemma it poses to both governments and societies alike. Specifically, how does a government protect its citizens within the rule of law when intelligence that is considered reliable does not meet the high evidentiary thresholds developed by society in the context of ordinary criminal prosecutions, and still protect the sources and methods essential to acquiring that critical information? For example, authorities could correctly believe that a terrorist attack is being planned, but the authorities must release any individuals arrested in connection with the suspected threat because the plan is too embryonic and vague to obtain criminal charges and convictions, or because the intelligence underlying the authorities' belief is too sensitive to reveal the sources, methods, or technological capabilities that gave rise to the information.[15] Accordingly, it may be in the best interest of society to

---

[14] Jim McAdams, The Classified Information Procedures Act: An Introduction and Practical Guide for Criminal Investigators (Nov. 13, 2007), http://www.fletc.gov/training/programs/legal-division/downloads-articles-and-faqs/articles/the-classified-information-procedures-act.html; *see also*, U.S. ATTORNEY MANUAL, *supra* note 11 (citing a specific example of where this issue might arise: the testimony of covert intelligence operatives). According to § 2054 of the U.S. Attorney's Criminal Resource Manual, the success of the intelligence community

> turns in significant part upon the ability of its intelligence officers covertly to obtain information from human sources. In carrying out that task, the intelligence officers must, when necessary, be able to operate anonymously, that is, without their connection to an intelligence agency of the United States being known to the persons with whom they come in contact. For that reason, an intelligence agency is authorized under Executive Order 12958 to classify the true name of an intelligence officer. During the pre-trial progression of an indicted case, as the court enters its CIPA rulings …, it may become apparent to the prosecutor that testimony may be required from an intelligence officer or other agency representative engaged in covert activity, either because the Court has ruled under CIPA that certain evidence is relevant and admissible in the defense case, or because such testimony is necessary in the government's rebuttal. Just as the substance of that testimony, to the extent it is classified and is being offered by the defense, must be the subject of CIPA determinations by the court, the prosecutor must also ensure that the same considerations are afforded to the true names of covert intelligence community personnel, if those true names are classified information.

Id.

[15] *See* Manningham Speech, *supra* note 9. *But see Minutes of Evidence, supra* note 8 (testimony of British Home Secretary Charles Clarke), *available at* http://www.publications.parliament.uk/pa/cm200506/cmselect/cmhaff/462/5091302.htm (observing that, in the weeks before the bombings, the U.K.'s Joint Terrorism Analysis Center concluded that there was no

intervene in the absence of substantial admissible evidence in order to prevent or disrupt a terrorist plot, even if the effect is to compromise a related criminal investigation and jeopardize follow-up prosecutions.

Although the U.S. has prosecuted a number of terrorism cases in the ordinary criminal courts, many of the "successful" cases have involved highly unusual circumstances.[16] Others cases only have succeeded in obtaining convictions of significantly lesser charges,[17] failed altogether,[18] or involved novel (some would say troubling) applications of the law. Moreover, despite U.S. efforts to prosecute some terrorist suspects before military commissions as unlawful combatants under the law of armed conflict, as of

single terrorist group "with both the current intent and the capability to attack the UK," and the threat level under which the authorities operated was reduced accordingly). Home Secretary Charles Clarke testified,"[I]ntelligence is not knowledge." *Id.* Rather, intelligence is an effort to understand threats to a nation using a variety of techniques and sources, and then assessing the information gathered to come to a view. *See id.*

[16] For example, Richard Reid, the so-called "shoe bomber," was prosecuted for attempting to detonate an explosive device on a trans-Atlantic commercial flight in December 2001. *See* Indictment, United States v. Reid, 206 F.Supp.2d 132 (D. Mass 2002). The explosives were hidden in the soles of his shoes. *Id.* Had he succeeded in lighting one of the several matches he struck, Reid would have killed more than 180 innocent passengers and crew members. *Id.* Reid ultimately pled guilty to virtually all charges, likening himself a soldier at war against the U.S., and was sentenced to life imprisonment. Richard Reid's Response To Government's Motion To Vacate Or Modify Appointment Of Counsel For Defendant, United States v. Reid, 206 F.Supp.2d 132 (D. Mass 2002). Similarly, Zacarias Moussaoui also pled guilty to terrorism offenses related to the 9/11 plot. *See* Motion to Withdraw Guilty Plea, United States v. Moussaoui, 282 F.Supp.2d 480 (E.D. Va. 2003). Like Reid, Moussaoui used his trial to cast himself as a warrior against the U.S., and was ultimately sentenced to life imprisonment. *Id.*

[17] *See, e.g.*, Dan Eggen, *Justice Dept. Statistics on Terrorism Faulted*, WASH. POST, Feb. 21, 2007, at A08 (explaining that Department of Justice Inspector General report shows that many terrorism-related cases result in charges on minor crimes or immigration violations unrelated to terrorism); Dan Eggen & Julie Tate, *U.S. Campaign Produces Few Convictions on Terrorism Charges*, WASH. POST, June 12, 2005, at A01 (reporting that out of 200 terrorism-suspect convictions reviewed, only 39 convictions were for terrorism or other national security charges; most were for more ordinary crimes such as making false statements or immigration violations). For an overview of U.S. terrorism-related prosecutions between 2001 and 2006, *see generally* U.S. Department of Justice, *supra* note 3.

[18] *See, e.g.*, Adam Liptak & Leslie Eaton, *Financing Mistrial Adds to U.S. Missteps in Terror Prosecution*, N.Y. TIMES, Oct. 24, 2007, at A16 (noting a larger percentage of terrorism prosecutions brought since 9/11 have been lost compared to pre-9/11 terrorism prosecutions, in part because pre-9/11 terrorism convictions "were for completed acts of violence . . . or for conspiracies that were relatively close to fruition," whereas post-9/11 prosecutions tend to be for less definitive activities, "reflective of a conscious change in Washington's law enforcement strategy, to prevention from punishment"); Leslie Eaton, *U.S. Prosecution of Muslim Group Ends in Mistrial*, N.Y. TIMES, Oct. 23, 2007, at A1 (detailing lack of a single conviction in the trial of the Holy Land Foundation, one of the largest terrorist financing prosecutions in U.S. history); Eric Lichtblau, *Setback for U.S. in Terror Trial*, N.Y. TIMES, Dec. 7, 2005, at A1 (detailing failure of seventeen counts against former professor Sami al-Arian for providing support and resources for the Palestinian Islamic Jihad).

November 2008, only two such commissions have been completed. A series of challenges (many of them successful) to the legal basis and structure of the commissions are largely responsible for the failure of these efforts.[19]

2. Scholarly criticism of the current approach

Concern for the difficulties facing investigators and prosecutors has led a growing number of commentators to conclude that the U.S. should consider adopting a new system of preventive detention, or perhaps some form of modified criminal process, for terrorism and other national security cases. Additionally, some commentators have suggested that the current seemingly *ad hoc* approach to detention of terrorism suspects poses more risk to civil liberty than the adoption of a formal system of preventive detention would pose.

For example, Professors Jack Goldsmith (former head of the Office of Legal Counsel at the U.S. Department of Justice) and Eric Posner have argued that the U.S. should abandon trials of terrorist suspects before military commissions in favor of preventive military detention subject to more rigorous standards and enhanced oversight.[20] Professor Goldsmith later concluded, together with Professor Neal Katyal (counsel for the detainees in the case of *Hamdan v. Rumsfeld* [21]), that Congress should explicitly establish and sanction "a comprehensive system of preventive detention . . . that would . . . supplement the criminal process . . . [and] . . . would have greater legitimacy than our current patchwork system."[22]

Similarly, prior to his current post as U.S. Attorney General, Michael Mukasey (a former Federal district court judge who handled several of the most prominent U.S. terrorism cases) wrote that Congress should deliberate "how to fix a strained and mismatched legal system, before another cataclysm calls forth from the people demands for hastier and harsher results."[23] Mukasey urged Congress to consider proposals to create national security courts or to develop measures akin to civil commitment to "incapa-

---

[19] *See, e.g.*, William Glaberson, *U.S. Seeks Execution for 6 in Sept. 11 Case*, N.Y. TIMES, Feb. 11, 2008, at A1 (discussing military tribunal's failure to begin any trials as of early 2008).The only military commissions completed as of November 2008 were the guilty plea of the Australian David Hicks and the conviction of Salim Hamdan (a.k.a. "bin Laden's driver") for providing material support.

[20] *See* Jack Goldsmith & Eric A. Posner, Editorial, *A Better Way on Detainees*, WASH. POST, Aug. 4, 2006, at A17.

[21] 548 U.S. 557 (2006).

[22] Jack L. Goldsmith & Neal Katyal, Op-Ed, *The Terrorists' Court*, N.Y. TIMES, July 11, 2007, at A19.

[23] Michael B. Mukasey, Op-Ed, *Jose Padilla Makes Bad Law*, WALL ST. J., Aug. 22, 2007, at A15.

citate dangerous people" suspected of involvement in terrorism.[24] He reached this conclusion not simply as a result of the prosecutorial, financial and intelligence challenges faced by the government, but also because "if conventional legal rules are adapted to deal with a terrorist threat, whether by relaxed standards for conviction, searches, the admissibility of evidence or otherwise, those adaptations will infect and change the standards in ordinary cases with ordinary defendants in ordinary courts of law."[25]

Most recently, Professor John Farmer, a former Attorney General of the State of New Jersey and former senior counsel to the 9/11 Commission, reviewed the terrorism-related prosecutions of Jose Padilla and others since 9/11 for crimes such as material support and conspiracy, and determined that "[t]hey cry out for the creation of a form of preventive detention adapted to terrorism, and outside the criminal justice system."[26] Professor Farmer concluded that "the continued reliance on our criminal justice system as the main domestic weapon in the struggle against terrorism fails on two counts: it threatens not only to leave our nation unprotected but also to corrupt the foundations of the criminal law itself."[27] According to Farmer, "[i]n order to make the criminal justice system an effective weapon [against terrorism], we have already started extending the reach of criminal statutes to conduct that has never before been punishable as a crime,"[28] and

> [t]he urgency involved in terrorism cases has also led courts to accept conduct by the government that might well have been disapproved in other contexts . . . .
>
> . . . .
>
> . . . When terrorism cases are treated as ordinary criminal prosecutions, the principles of law that they come to embody will guide law-enforcement conduct and be cited by the government not just in terrorism cases but in other criminal contexts.
>
> Over time, we may well transform the law of conspiracy to the point where an agreement alone is a crime. This would render thoughts punishable, reward government overreaching and erode our civil liberties. All because the criminal law is being used not primarily to punish crimes but for purposes of detaining people we are worried about.[29]

---

[24] *Id.*

[25] *Id.*

[26] John Farmer, Op-Ed., *A Terror Threat in the Courts*, N.Y. TIMES, Jan. 13, 2008, ¶ 4, at 14.

[27] *Id.*

[28] *Id.*

[29] *Id.*

3. Judicial responses to the current approach

Apprehension about stretching the bounds of established legal doctrines to fit difficult terrorism matters has surfaced in a number of recent cases both in the U.S. and abroad. The increasingly broad scope of the material support and conspiracy doctrines used in cases such as *Padilla*, which gave rise to Mr. Mukasey's and Mr. Farmer's commentaries, is just one example. Indeed, the federal court that handled the criminal prosecution of Jose Padilla ultimately imposed a significantly shorter term of imprisonment than that requested by U.S. prosecutors, at least in part because, in the court's view, the evidence did not link Padilla to any specific act of terrorism.[30]

A related concern centers on the growing tendency to criminalize conduct that is ever more remote from the actual commission of a terrorist attack or conduct that is not supported by sufficient proof of terrorist intent. Earlier this year a court of appeal in the United Kingdom reversed the convictions of five young Muslim students prosecuted for "possess[ing] an article in circumstances which give rise to a reasonable suspicion that [it was possessed] for a purpose connected with the commission, preparation or instigation of an act of terrorism,"[31] contrary to Article 57 of the U.K.'s Terrorism Act 2000.[32] The articles included documents, compact discs and computer hard drives that contained extremist religious and political propaganda (described by the prosecution as al Qaeda recruiting material) and communications that allegedly revealed a plan by the men to travel to Pakistan and receive terrorist training.[33] Among the articles was a martyrdom song, a letter from one of the men saying he had left to take part in warfare, a military manual, and communications with a contact in Pakistan about how to travel without raising suspicion.[34] The British court ruled that, despite the potentially broad scope of the statutory language:

> It was necessary for the prosecution to prove first the purpose for which each appellant held the [articles at issue] . . . and then to prove that this purpose was "connected with the commission, preparation or instigation" of the prospective acts of terrorism relied on by the prosecution . . . .
>
> . . . .

30 *See* Kirk Semple, *Padilla Gets 17-Year Term For Role in Conspiracy*, N.Y. TIMES, Jan. 23, 2008, at A14. ("In explaining her decision, [the judge] . . . questioned the effects of the conspiracy, saying that there was no evidence linking Mr. Padilla and two co-defendants to specific terrorism acts anywhere.").

31 *E.g.*, Zafar v. Regina [2008] EWCA (Crim) 184, [15] (Eng.).

32 *Id.* at [49].

33 *Id.* at [1], [40], [44].

34 *Id.* at [1], [8].

> We have concluded that, if section 57 is to have the certainty of meaning that the law requires, it must be interpreted in a way that requires a direct connection between the object possessed and the act of terrorism. . . .
>
> . . . .
>
> . . . [T]he prosecution's case [suggested] that a much looser connection between the material possessed by the appellants and the terrorist act ... would suffice to establish the appellants' guilt.[35]

Another example of judicial pushback occurred in the June 2007 case of *al-Marri v. Wright*.[36] The United States Court of Appeals for the Fourth Circuit examined whether military detention of terrorist suspects designated as enemy combatants could be extended to a foreign national who legally entered and resided in the U.S. prior to his detention[37]—a doctrine that the Supreme Court affirmed in the case of *Hamdi v. Rumsfeld* in 2004.[38] Al-Marri was originally arrested and charged with several crimes in the civilian criminal justice system,[39] but before his case went to trial, al-Marri was transferred to military custody pursuant to a Presidential Order determining that, among other things, al-Marri was an enemy combatant in possession of intelligence that would aid U.S. efforts to prevent attacks by al Qaeda.[40]

---

[35] *Id.* at [24], [29], [34]; *See also Five Students Win Terror Appeal*, BBC NEWS, Feb. 13, 2008 (discussing Appellate Court decision).

[36] Al-Marri v. Wright, 487 F.3d 160 (4th Cir. 2007).

[37] *See id.* at 164.

[38] Hamdi v. Rumsfeld, 542 U.S. 517, 519 (2004).

[39] *See Al-Marri,* 487 F.3d at 164. Al-Marri, a citizen of Qatar, entered the U.S. on September 10, 2001, and resided legally in the State of Illinois. *Id.* He was originally arrested by civilian authorities in the U.S. as a material witness to the 9/11 investigation and eventually indicted for several domestic crimes. *Id.* None of the charges against al-Marri were terrorism-specific crimes; instead, he was charged with more general crimes that often arise in terrorism investigations, such as "possession of unauthorized or counterfeit credit card numbers with intent to defraud . . . making false statements to the FBI [and] . . . on a banking application, and . . . using another person's identification for the purpose of influencing the action of a federally insured financial institution." *Id.* "Al-Marri pleaded not guilty to these charges." *Id.*

[40] *See id.* at 164–66 ("The declaration of Jeffery N. Rapp, Director of the Joint Intelligence Task Force for Combatting Terrorism . . . asserts that al-Marri: (1) is 'closely associated with al Qaeda, an international terrorist organization with which the United States is at war"; (2) trained at an al Qaeda terrorist training camp . . . ; (3) in the summer of 2001, was introduced to Osama Bin Laden by Khalid Shaykh Muhammed; (4) . . . volunteered for a ''martyr mission''on behalf of al Qaeda; (5) . . . enter[ed] the United States sometime before September 11, 2001, to serve as a ''sleeper agent'' to facilitate terrorist activities and explore disrupting this country's financial system through computer hacking; (6) . . . met with [and received funds from] terrorist financier; (7) gathered technical information about poisonous chemicals . . . (8) undertook efforts to obtain false [and stolen] identification, credit cards, and banking information . . . ; (9) communicated with known terrorists including, Khalid Shaykh Mu-

The court's answer was an emphatic "No." According to the court, even assuming all of the allegations about al-Marri's conduct were true, the government had no authority to treat al-Marri as an enemy combatant or as anything other than a civilian.[41]

> If the government accurately describe[d] al-Marri's conduct, . . . [he could] be returned to civilian prosecutors, tried on criminal charges, and, if convicted, punished severely. But the government cannot subject al-Marri to indefinite military detention. For in the United States, the military cannot seize and imprison civilians—let alone imprison them indefinitely.[42]

Given the level of concern of courts, legal scholars and practitioners alike, perhaps it is time to re-examine the issue of preventive detention in the U.S. in the context of terrorism.

B. The Legal Landscape of Preventive Detention in the United States

Preventive detention refers to the detention or confinement of a person believed to pose a threat to national security or to public safety and order, or a person whose presence at a public proceeding is required but cannot be guaranteed.[43] The purpose of the detention is avoidance of the potential danger or absence rather than the punishment of a criminal offense. Although many, if not most, people held under some form of preventive detention are in fact criminal defendants, others may not have been accused of crimes.[44]

Some might suggest that preventive detention necessarily infringes fundamental principles of both U.S. Constitutional law and international

---

hammed and Al-Hawsawi, by phone and e-mail; and (10) saved [jihadist] information . . . on his laptop computer . . . Rapp [did not allege] that al-Marri [was] a citizen, or affiliate of the armed forces, of any nation at war with the United States . . . [or] directly participated in any hostilities against United States or allied armed forces.").

41 *See id* at 164. The Fourth Circuit later vacated the panel decision and reviewed al-Marri's case *en banc*. The *en banc* court held: (1) assuming the government's allegations about al-Marri's conduct were true, Congress had authorized his detention as an enemy combatant; but (2) al-Marri had not been afforded sufficient process to challenge his designation as an enemy combatant. Al-Marri v. Pucciarelli, 534 F.3d 213 (4th Cir. 2008) (per curiam) (reversing the district court and remanding for further proceedings). The U.S. Supreme Court has recently agreed to review the *al-Marri* case during the 2008 term. *See* Robert Barnes, *Supreme Court to Hear Case of Accused Al-Qaeda Member*, WASH. POST, Dec. 6, 2008, at A2.

42 *Id.*

43 *See, e.g.*, Zadvydas v. Davis, 533 U.S. 678, 690 (2001) (discussing rationale behind preventive detention).

44 *See, e.g.*, Hamdi v. Rumsfeld, 542 U.S. 517, 518–19 (2004).

law.[45] Others might contend that preventive detention is a widely accepted practice that is thoroughly consonant with the concept of ordered liberty.[46] The truth lies somewhere in the middle. Multiple sources of legal authority govern the standards and conditions of detention, including domestic law, international human rights law, and, in certain circumstances, the law of armed conflict (also called international humanitarian law).[47] Preventive detention by its very nature therefore has one foot in the international legal world and one in the world of domestic law.

The basic instruments of international human rights law neither explicitly permit nor prohibit preventive detention, although they do establish certain basic substantive and procedural standards relevant to the issue. Most important is the freedom from arbitrary arrest or detention, and the requirement that arrest, detention and other deprivations of liberty must be for lawful grounds and according to established legal procedures.[48] Further, anyone arrested or detained has a right to: (1) information about the grounds underlying the deprivation; (2) independent proceedings to determine the lawfulness of the detention; and (3) freedom from torture or any other form of cruel, inhuman or degrading treatment or punishment.[49] The law of armed conflict provides for many similar detainee rights.[50]

---

45 *See, e.g.*, Al-Marri, 487 F.3d at 163–64 (stating the court's view that al-Marri's detention violated constitutional principles).

46 *See id.* (discussing the Government's perspective that it had the authority to detain al-Marri).

47 *See, e.g.*, Universal Declaration of Human Rights, G.A. Res. 216 (III), U.N. GAOR, 3d Sess., 1st plen. mtg., U.N. Doc. A/810 (Dec. 10, 1948); International Covenant on Civil and Political Rights, Dec. 19, 1966, 999 U.N.T.S. 171, 6 I.L.M. 368 [hereinafter ICCPR]; Geneva Convention Relative to the Treatment of Prisoners of War, Aug. 12, 1949, 972 U.N.T.S. 1950, 4 Bevans 852 [hereinafter POW Convention].

48 *See, e.g.*, Universal Declaration of Human Rights, *supra* note 47.

49 *See* Universal Declaration of Human Rights, G.A. Res. 217A, arts. 5, 8, 9, U.N. GAOR, 3d Sess. 1st plen. mtg., U.N. Doc. A/810 (Dec. 21, 1948); ICCPR, *supra* note 47, at arts. 7, 9(1), 9(2), 9(4); Body of Principles for the Protection of all Persons under any Form of Detention or Imprisonment, G.A. Res. 43/173, principles 2, 4, 6, 11, U.N. Doc. A/RES/43/173 (Dec. 9, 1988); United Nations Convention Against Torture, G.A. Res. 39/46, arts. 2(1), 16(1), U.N. Doc. A/RES/39/46 (Dec. 10, 1984) [hereinafter CAT]. Note that, except for the prohibition on torture and cruel, inhuman or degrading treatment, each of the freedoms and rights mentioned may be subject to derogation if necessary during times of officially proclaimed public emergency. *See* ICCPR, *supra* note 47, at art. 4.

50 The Geneva Conventions permit internment of prisoners of war in international armed conflicts until the cessation of hostilities. *See* POW Convention, *supra* note 47, arts. 4, 21, 118. The Geneva Conventions also provide for review by a "competent tribunal" of the basis for prisoner of war status "[s]hould any doubt arise." *Id.* at art. 5. The Geneva Conventions permit the internment of certain civilians when necessary for security, and provide for reconsideration or appeal of such decisions (and further periodic review) by an appropriate judicial or administrative body. *See* Geneva Convention Relative to the Protection of Civilian Persons in Time of War, arts. 42, 43, 78, Aug. 12, 1949, 6 U.S.T. 3516, 75 U.N.T.S. 287 [herei-

More importantly, the U.S. Supreme Court has clearly stated that "[f]reedom from imprisonment—from government custody, detention, or other forms of physical restraint—lies at the heart of the liberty that [the Due Process] Clause protects."[51] As a result,

> government detention violates [the Due Process] Clause unless the detention is ordered in a criminal proceeding with adequate procedural protections, or in certain special and narrow non-punitive circumstances where a *special justification*, such as harm-threatening mental illness, outweighs

nafter Civilian Persons Convention]. The law of armed conflict also prohibits torture and other inhumane treatment of combatants and civilians both in international and non-international armed conflict. *See* POW Convention, *supra* note 47, arts. 3(1), 13, 17; Civilian Persons Convention, *supra*, arts. 27, 31, 32, 37. Further, whereas the provisions of both international human rights treaties and law of armed conflict treaties may be limited in their application based on the terms of the treaty (for example, many provisions of human rights treaties do not strictly apply to State activities outside the territory of the State at issue), customary international law outlines certain fundamental human rights guarantees that bind all states, in all circumstances. *See, e.g.*, Press Release, United Nations Information Service, Prohibition of Torture "Absolute" U.N. Doc. SG/SM/9373, OBV/428 (June 18, 2004) *available at* http://www.unis.unvienna.org/unis/pressrels/2004/sgsm9373.html. These rights generally are understood to include freedom from "prolonged arbitrary detention" and "torture or other cruel, inhuman or degrading treatment." THE JUDGE ADVOCATE GENERAL'S SCHOOL, UNITED STATES ARMY, OPERATIONAL LAW HANDBOOK 6-1, 6-2 (2000); THE JUDGE ADVOCATE GENERAL'S DEPARTMENT, UNITED STATES AIR FORCE, AIR FORCE OPERATIONS & LAW 127–28 (2002). As a statutory matter, U.S. law explicitly forbids any cruel, inhuman or degrading treatment (including torture) of detainees in U.S. custody regardless of their geographical location, and prohibits the U.S. Department of Defense from interrogating detainees in any manner not authorized by the U.S. Army Field Manual on Military Interrogations. *See* Detainee Treatment Act of 2005, Pub. L. No. 109-148, Tit. X, 119 Stat. 2739 (2005). In September 2006, the U.S. Army replaced the Field Manual on Military Interrogations with a new Field Manual on Human Intelligence Collection Operations, which prohibits torture and other cruel, inhuman, or degrading treatment. U.S. DEPT. OF THE ARMY, HUMAN INTELLIGENCE COLLECTOR OPERATIONS, FM 2-22.3 viii (2006). It also contains a list of interrogation techniques that are specifically forbidden, including sexually humiliating acts, hooding, infliction of physical pain, "water-boarding," and the use of military working dogs to instill fear. *Id.* at 5–21. Nevertheless, the issue of detainee treatment persists, in part because the U.S. government asserts the right of agencies other than the Department of Defense (e.g., the Central Intelligence Agency) to use unspecified enhanced interrogation techniques beyond those in the Field Manual, provided they do not constitute torture or mistreatment as defined by the U.S. government. *See, e.g.*, Pamela Hess, *House Fails to Override Torture Veto*, THE ASSOCIATED PRESS, Mar. 11, 2008; Dan Eggen, *Bush Announces Veto of Waterboarding Ban*, WASH. POST, Mar. 8, 2008, at A02; George W. Bush, President of the U.S., Text of the President's Weekly Radio Address (Mar. 8, 2008), *available at* http://www.whitehouse.gov/news/releases/2008/03/20080308.html.

[51] Zadvydas v. Davis, 533 U.S. 678, 690 (2001) (citing Foucha v. Louisiana, 504 U.S. 71, 80 (1992)).

the individual's constitutionally protected interest in avoiding physical restraint.[52]

A statutory bias against emergency detention of citizens also has existed in the U.S. since 1971 when Congress enacted the Non-Detention Act as part of legislation that repealed the earlier Emergency Detention Act.[53] The Non-Detention Act plainly states that "[n]o citizen shall be imprisoned or otherwise detained by the United States except pursuant to an Act of Congress."[54]

As the Supreme Court indicated, the U.S. has recognized several exceptions to the general rule against detention of individuals absent the ordinary protections afforded a criminal defendant. The fundamental nature of the liberty interest involved compels that such exceptions be fairly limited. As such, preventive detention in the U.S. is a more recent, circumscribed power (both substantively and procedurally)[55] than many would prefer to accept, particularly in cases that do not involve post-charge, pretrial detention of a criminal defendant.

1. Pre-trial detention

For most of the 20th Century, preventive detention was largely limited to criminal defendants awaiting trial for murder, criminal defendants who posed a flight risk, insane persons and other dangerous incompetents, and those with infectious diseases.[56] Other serious criminal defendants considered dangerous to the community may have been placed under *de facto* preventive detention through the imposition of high bail amounts, but the general practice in criminal proceedings was to set bail and provide conditional release pending trial. In the 1970s, state and local governments increasingly instituted preventive detention for criminal defendants accused of

---

[52] *Zadvydas*, 533 U.S. at 690–92 (emphasis added) (internal quotations and citations omitted) (original emphasis omitted). This fundamental right to due process finds its origin in both the Fifth Amendment guarantee against deprivations of liberty without due process of law and the Fourth Amendment guarantee against unreasonable seizures. U.S. CONST. amends. V, IV.

[53] LOUIS FISHER, DETENTION OF U.S. CITIZENS, 1 (2005). The Emergency Detention Act, which provided procedures for emergency executive detention of individuals deemed likely to engage in espionage or sabotage, was adopted in 1950 during another period of intense national security concerns. *Id.*

[54] 18 U.S.C. § 4001(a) (1948).

[55] "[T]he Due Process Clause contains a substantive component that bars certain arbitrary, wrongful government actions regardless of the fairness of the procedures used to implement them." *Foucha*, 504 U.S. at 80 (internal quotation omitted).

[56] One example of preventive detention that does not fit this mold is the Japanese internment cases from World War II. Although these cases have been largely discredited, they have not been formally overruled.

dangerous or violent crimes, and in 1984 Congress passed the Federal Bail Reform Act,[57] which authorized pre-trial preventive detention for defendants accused of a much broader range of violent crimes and other demonstrably dangerous defendants.

The U.S. Supreme Court upheld the preventive detention provisions of the Act in *United States v. Salerno*,[58] in which the defendants were charged with numerous violent racketeering and organized crime offenses. Reversing the Second Circuit Court of Appeals, the Supreme Court found that the Bail Reform Act satisfied both substantive and procedural due process concerns.[59] Pre-trial detention imposed under the Act was regulatory (administrative) in nature rather than punitive; it served not to punish the defendant but to prevent danger to the community—a legitimate and compelling regulatory goal.[60] Though seemingly indefinite, detention under the act was limited to a pre-trial period, which was not excessive relative to the purpose of the detention.[61] The Act also provided for a prompt judicial hearing—at which the detainee had the right to request counsel, testify, present evidence, confront witnesses, and from which he could appeal—to determine the propriety of detention.[62] Moreover, the Act, which required holding a defendant apart from the ordinary prison population to the extent possible, reserved detention for "individuals who have been arrested for a specific category of extremely serious offenses" and whose danger had been proved by clear and convincing evidence.[63]

In the wake of *Salerno*, the U.S. now regularly permits pre-trial preventive detention of a wide range of dangerous criminal defendants, and

57 Federal Bail Reform Act, 18 U.S.C. §§ 3141–3150 (1984).

58 *See* United States v. Salerno, 481 U.S. 739, 755 (1987).

59 *See id.* at 752–55.

60 *Id.* at 747.

61 *See id.* at 747. The Speedy Trial Act limits the length of the pre-trial detention. *Id.*

62 *Id.* at 739.

63 *Id.* at 747–752. Of course, in the U.S. pre-trial detention differs in one critical way from the other bases for preventive detention discussed in this article, as all pre-trial defendants have at least been charged with a criminal offense on the finding of probable cause to believe that the defendant committed the crime. 18 U.S.C. § 1342(a) (2006). The U.S. is not the only system to permit extended pre-trial detention of dangerous criminal defendants; for example, in the terrorism context both France and Spain permit pre-trial detention of up to four years. *See* HOME OFFICE, TERRORIST INVESTIGATIONS AND THE FRENCH EXAMINING MAGISTRATES SYSTEM 7 (2007) ("In France, the period of pre-trial detention can last up to 4 years."); HUMAN RIGHTS WATCH, COUNTER-TERRORISM MEASURES IN SPAIN: PROLONGED PRE-TRIAL DETENTION (2005), *available at* http://www.hrw.org/reports/2005/spain0105/9.htm (explaining that persons accused of serious crimes "may be held in pre-trial detention for up to 4 years").

pre-trial preventive detention is routinely available for federal criminal defendants charged with terrorism-related offenses.[64]

2. The mentally ill and recidivist sex offenders

Due Process also permits preventive detention for certain classes of persons in the U.S. other than pre-trial criminal defendants, notably those who are mentally impaired and, more recently and more controversially, recidivist sex offenders.[65] A review of the seminal case law surrounding

[64] The Bail Reform Act now includes a rebuttable presumption in favor of pre-trial detention of any person accused of a "federal crime of terrorism" (as defined in 18 U.S.C. §2332b(g)(5)(B)) for which a prison term of ten years or more is applicable. *See* 18 U.S.C. § 3142(e) (2006). The Supreme Court has also upheld pre-trial preventive detention of juvenile criminal suspects considered to present a danger to the community. *See* Schall v. Martin, 467 U.S. 253 (1984). An issue related to, but distinct from, pre-trial detention is pre-charge detention. In the past several years, the United Kingdom has extended the pre-charge period during which terrorist suspects may be detained in connection with criminal investigations. Recent legislation in the United Kingdom allows terrorist suspects to be detained for up to twenty-eight days before charges must be filed or the detainee released. *See* Terrorism Act, 2006, c. 11 (Eng.), § 23.

[65] The U.S. is not the only country to have enacted legislation permitting the civil detention of the mentally ill, sexual offenders and other criminals who continue to pose a danger after their criminal sentences are completed. For example, in 2003 the parliament of Queensland, Australia enacted the Dangerous Prisoners (Sexual Offenders) Act 2003, which authorizes a court to order post-sentence imprisonment of serious sexual offenders where the court has found reasonable grounds to believe the prisoner will commit a serious sexual offense if released. *See Patrick Keyser & Sam Blay, Double Punishment? Preventive Detention Schemes Under Australian Legislation and Their Consistency with International Law: The Fardon Communication*, 7 MELBOURNE J. OF INT'L L. (2006). In early 2008 France adopted a new law permitting the continued detention of certain dangerous criminals even after they served their full sentence. *See French Pass Bill on Lifelong Internment for Deranged Convicts*, DEUTSCHE PRESSE-AGENTUR, Jan. 10, 2008, *available at* http://www.monstersandcritics.com/news/europe/news/article_1385786.php/French_pass_bill_on_lifelong_internment_for_deranged_convicts. Inspired by a 2007 kidnapping and rape of a 5-year-old boy by a 61-year-old sexual predator, the law originated as a measure to be applied only to persons convicted of serious crimes against children. *Id.* However, the final law passed applied to anyone convicted of a broader range of serious crimes and subject to imprisonment for 15 years or more. *Id.* The law establishes a multi-disciplinary commission including medical and legal professionals to make the detention determination. *Id.* Detention is renewable each year without limit. *Id.*; *see also* Press Release, Amnesty International, France: Amnesty International's Concerns on 'Preventive Detention' Bill (Feb. 8, 2008), http://www.amnestyusa.org/document.php?lang=e&id=ENGEUR210022008 (discussing human rights concerns related to France's preventive detention bill). Similarly, in 2004 Germany enacted legislation permitting post-sentence detention of those convicted of a crime against life, bodily integrity, personal freedom, or sexual self-determination when facts "indicate a considerable danger from the prisoner for the general public." Andrew A. Hammel, *Preventive Detention in Comparative Perspective*, *in* ANNUAL OF GERMAN & EUROPEAN LAW VOLUME II & III, at 89–115 (R. Miller & P. Zumbanse, eds., Berghahn Books 2006) (discussing and quoting §66b of the German Penal Code), *available at* http://works.bepress.com/andrew_hammel/1. Such detention can be ordered by a court "if a complete evaluation of the prisoner, his crimes, and

these doctrines, however, indicates that the circumstances justifying preventive detention are quite limited.

In *Addington v. Texas* the Supreme Court upheld the preventive detention of a mentally incapacitated person upon a showing by clear and convincing evidence that the person posed a danger to himself or to others, and where the person was entitled to a periodic release hearing.[66] Detention could continue provided the person remained mentally ill and continued to pose a danger to society.[67]

Foucha v. Louisiana[68] highlighted the limits of the *Addington* doctrine by holding that due process prohibits the continued detention of a person who ceases to suffer from mental illness, even if he continues to pose a danger to the community. According to the Court, the continued detention of Foucha bore no "reasonable relation to the purpose for which the individual was committed,"[69] namely mental disease or illness, regardless of his dangerousness. Moreover, the statute at issue failed to provide substantive and procedural safeguards of the kind identified in *Salerno*.[70]

Another area where the Supreme Court has permitted preventive detention involves violent sex offenders, particularly those convicted of crimes involving children. Starting mainly in the 1990s, many U.S. states adopted new civil commitment laws for sexual predators who continued to pose a danger after completing their criminal sentences. In *Kansas v. Hendricks*, the Court considered one such statute and found it satisfied the Constitution's due process requirement, both substantively and procedurally.[71] The statute required a "special justification" beyond mere dangerousness and so applied only to "a small segment of potentially dangerous individuals," and it also provided "strict procedural safeguards."[72] Although the statute did not require the finding of a mental illness to justify civil commitment, the Court held that the statute required some form of mental abnormality or anti-social personality disorder, thus limiting detention to individuals with "volitional impairment[s] rendering them dangerous beyond their control."[73] Further, it provided stringent procedural safeguards including:

. . . his development during prison confinement reveal, that with a high probability he will commit serious crimes, through which the victims will be seriously psychologically or bodily injured." *Id.* at 97.

66 Addington v. Texas, 441 U.S. 418 (1979).

67 *Id.* at 426.

68 Foucha v. Louisiana, 504 U.S. 71 (1992).

69 *Id.* at 78.

70 *See id.* at 71–72. The Supreme Court has also permitted detention of dangerous defendants who become mentally incompetent before trial. *See Id.*

71 Kansas v. Hendricks, 521 U.S. 346, 371 (1997).

72 *Id.* at 368.

73 *Id.* at 358–59.

(1) an initial finding of probable cause to believe that person is a dangerous sexual predator; (2) an independent professional evaluation of the individual; and (3) a full trial on the merits of the question.[74] The individual possessed the right to counsel (funded if necessary) and the right to a jury.[75]

3. Aliens

One area where preventive detention has received more deference from the courts is under immigration laws. Despite the lack of an explicit Constitutional power to control immigration, the U.S. Supreme Court has found that the power to exclude or deport aliens is inherent in the concept of a sovereign nation.[76] The Court has also consistently held that potentially dangerous aliens may be detained pending removal proceedings,[77] much as dangerous criminals may be held pending trial pursuant to *Salerno*.

The Court has not reached these conclusions because aliens are wholly without Constitutional rights. Although the Constitution ordinarily does not protect aliens in foreign territory,[78] it does provide some rights to aliens who have entered and developed substantial connections with U.S.

---

[74] *Id.* at 352–53. The statute required proof beyond a reasonable doubt at the trial. *Id.*

[75] *Id.* at 352–59; Kansas Inpatient SVP Act, Kan. Stat. Ann. §§ 59–29a01. In a subsequent case, the Court had occasion to clarify the special factor that permitted detention of sexual predators. According to the Court, the Constitution does not "permit[] commitment of the type of dangerous sexual offender considered in *Hendricks* without any lack-of-control determination. *Hendricks* underscored the constitutional importance of distinguishing a dangerous sexual offender subject to civil commitment 'from other dangerous persons who are perhaps more properly dealt with exclusively through criminal proceedings' . . . The presence of what the 'psychiatric profession itself classifies[] . . . as a serious mental disorder' helped to make that distinction in *Hendricks*. And a critical distinguishing feature of [the serious mental disorder in *Hendricks*] consisted of a special and serious lack of ability to control behavior. . . . [W]e recognize that in cases where lack of control is at issue, 'inability to control behavior' will not be demonstrable with mathematical precision. It is enough to say that there must be proof of serious difficult in controlling behavior. And this . . . must be sufficient to distinguish the dangerous sexual offender whose mental illness, abnormality, or disorder subjects him to civil commitment from the dangerous but typical recidivist convicted in an ordinary criminal case." Kansas v. Crane, 534 U.S. 407, 412-13 (2002) (internal citations omitted).

[76] *See* Chae Chan Ping v. United States (*The Chinese Exclusion Case*), 130 U.S. 581, 603–06 (1889) ("[The power of the government to] exclude aliens from its territory is a proposition which we do not think open to controversy. Jurisdiction over its own territory to that extent is an incident of every independent nation. It is part of its independence."); Fong Yue v. United States, 149 U.S. 698, 707 (1893) (holding that the right to deport foreign aliens already in the country "rests upon the same grounds, and is as absolute and unqualified as the right to prohibit and prevent their entrance into the country").

[77] *See, e.g.*, Demore v. Kim, 538 U.S. 510, 524–26 (2003).

[78] *See, e.g.*, United States v. Curtiss-Wright Export Corp., 299 U.S. 304, 318 (1936) (U.S. Constitution has no force "in foreign territory unless in respect of our citizens").

territory.[79] Most provisions of the Bill of Rights, the Fourteenth Amendment, and other individual rights in the Constitution, including the Due Process Clauses, apply to "persons" rather than "citizens." [80] Accordingly, these rights generally protect aliens present in the U.S. as well as citizens.

However, due process guarantees in immigration proceedings are not equivalent to those applicable in criminal proceedings. Immigration proceedings "are civil, not criminal, and . . . are nonpunitive in purpose and effect"[81] and do not require the same procedural safeguards as criminal proceedings. The courts also have drawn distinctions between the process that is due to aliens excludable prior to admission into the U.S. and the process due to aliens subject to deportation after entry.[82] Because the regulation of aliens is related to issues of national security and foreign relations, U.S. courts have shown deference to the judgment of Congress and the President in these matters.[83]

---

[79] *See, e.g.*, United States v. Verdugo-Urquidez, 494 U.S. 259, 271 (1990); Wong Wing v. United States, 163 U.S. 228, 238 (1896); Yick Wo v. Hopkins, 118 U.S. 356, 369 (1886).

[80] *See* U.S. CONST. amend V; *but see* U.S. CONST. amend. XIV, § 1 (defining "citizenship"). Aliens are not afforded the rights that are limited to citizens such as those in the Privileges and Immunities Clauses. *Cf. id.* (explicitly prohibiting abridging the rights of citizens only).

[81] Zadvydas v. Davis, 533 U.S. 678, 690 (2001).

[82] *See, e.g.*, *id.* at 678, 679, 719–21 (distinguishing Shaughnessy v. United States ex rel. Mezei, 345 U.S. 206 (1953), and concluding that "[t]he distinction between an alien who has effected an entry into the United States and one who has never entered runs throughout immigration law" and "once an alien enters the country, the legal circumstance changes, for the Due Process Clause applies to all 'persons' within the United States, including aliens, whether their presence here is lawful, unlawful, temporary or permanent"). The question of whether the Due Process Clause provides protection to aliens held outside the U.S. but on territory over which the U.S. exercises exclusive authority and control was recently before the Supreme Court. *See* Brief for Petitioner at i, Boumediene v. Bush, 128 S.Ct. 2229 (2007) (No. 06-1195). Although the Court did not explicitly hold that the protections of the Due Process Clause apply to aliens held in such circumstances, it did hold that the protections of the Suspension Clause apply, and that the limited process established by the Detainee Treatment Act to review Combatant Status Review Tribunal (CSRT) determinations was a constitutionally inadequate substitute for the habeas review to which the petitioners were entitled. *See* Boumediene v. Bush, 128 S.Ct. 2229, 2244–2262 (2008). *See infra* note 110 for a discussion of CSRTs.

[83] *See, e.g.*, Knauff v. Shaughnessy, 338 U.S. 537 (1950) ("Whatever the procedure authorized by Congress is, it is due process as far as alien denied entry is concerned"); Restatement (Third) of the Foreign Relations Law of the United States, §§ 721 and 722 (and comments and notes thereto) (the U.S. may deport permanent resident aliens even if the person peacefully resided in the U.S. for many years if sufficient procedural safeguards are followed; such aliens can be deported even for activities that Congress could not define and punish as a crime, such as political activities otherwise protected by the first amendment). The Court also has broadly continued to affirm the broad powers of the political branches with regard to immigration controls, including upholding the more controversial ideological provisions found in the national security grounds for removal, and even in cases involving

Still, when it comes to preventive detention of removable (that is, excludable or deportable) aliens, the Supreme Court has taken a more rigorous approach in recent years in recognition of due process concerns. Under U.S. immigration law, aliens ordered removed from the U.S. are detained for up to 90-days during a statutory "removal period" after the removal order has been issued.[84] The immigration law also authorizes further detention of certain removable aliens whose removal is not accomplished during the removal period.[85] Prior to 2001, the U.S. immigration authorities maintained a practice pursuant to this statute of indefinitely detaining these categories of removable aliens if not removed during the statutory 90-day "removal period."[86]

In June 2001, the Court limited this practice in *Zadvydas v. Davis*, a case involving two resident aliens ordered removed due to convictions for aggravated crimes.[87] To avoid a constitutional due process problem, the Court read the statute to "limit[] an alien's post-removal-period detention to a period reasonably necessary to bring about that that alien's removal from the United States. [The statute] does not permit indefinite detention."[88] The Court also imposed a 180-day period during which post-removal detention is presumptively valid, but after which the government generally must show evidence of a significant likelihood of removal in the foreseeable future in order to continue the detention.[89]

The Court compelled these requirements even though eventual removal of the alien remained possible, good faith efforts at removal continued, and the detention underwent periodic administrative review.[90] The Court held that these considerations were outweighed by the fact that "the civil confinement at issue is not limited, but potentially permanent,"[91] and

---

longtime lawful resident aliens. *See, e.g.*, Kleindienst v. Mandel, 408 U.S. 753 (1972); Harisiades v. Shaughnessy, 342 U.S. 580 (1952).

[84] 8 U.S.C. § 1232 (2006).

[85] *See* 8 U.S.C. § 1231(a)(6)(2006); *see also* DEPARTMENT OF HOMELAND SECURITY, OFFICE OF INSPECTOR GENERAL, REPORT OIG-07-28, ICE'S COMPLIANCE WITH DETENTION LIMITS FOR ALIENS WITH A FINAL ORDER OF REMOVAL FROM THE UNITED STATES 3–4 (Feb. 2007) [hereinafter DHS OIG Report]. The provision of the statute allowing for extended post-removal period detention applies to aliens who are: (1) inadmissible; (2) removable as a result of violations of entry conditions, violations of criminal law, or reasons of national security or foreign policy; or (3) represent a threat to the community or a flight risk if released. *See* 8 U.S.C. § 1231(a)(6).

[86] *See* DHS OIG Report, *supra* note 85, at 3.

[87] *Zadvydas*, 533 U.S. 678, 690 (2001).

[88] *Id.* at 689.

[89] *See id.* at 701. In some cases, the government is not required to release an alien who was not removed after 180 days. *Id.*

[90] *See id.* at 685, 696.

[91] *Id.* at 691.

"[t]he provision authorizing detention does not apply narrowly to 'a small segment of particularly dangerous individuals,' *say suspected terrorists*, but broadly to aliens ordered removed for many and various reasons, including tourist visa violations."[92] Further, "the sole procedural protections available to the alien are found in administrative proceedings, where the alien bears the burden of proving he is not dangerous, without . . . significant later judicial review. . . . [T]he Constitution may well preclude granting an administrative body the unreviewable authority to make determinations implicating fundamental rights."[93] Once again considerations about whether the detention power was narrowly tailored to a specially dangerous class of persons, and subject to adequate procedural safeguards, guided the Court's decision. Yet, despite these due process concerns, the Court indicated that the restrictions imposed would not necessarily apply in a case that involves a suspected terrorist alien or a case that raises other national security concerns.

Indeed, the *Zadvydas* Court stressed that it was not considering "terrorism or other special circumstances where special arguments might be made for forms of preventive detention and for heightened deference to the judgments of the political branches with respect to matters of national security."[94] And when the Court extended the *Zadvydas* rule to inadmissible aliens in *Clark v. Martinez*, it took pains to point out that "sustained detention of alien terrorists is a 'special arrangement' authorized by a different statutory provision."[95] Moreover, the Court held that the capacity of Congress to "secur[e] our borders" against non-removable aliens

> is demonstrated by [the fact that] [l]ess than four months after the release of our opinion [in *Zadvydas*], Congress enacted a statute which expressly authorized continued detention, for a period of six months beyond the removal period (and renewable indefinitely), of any alien (1) whose removal is not reasonably foreseeable and (2) who presents a national security threat or has been involved in terrorist activities.[96]

The U.S. government also adopted this approach in immigration regulations issued after the *Zadvydas* case. The regulations established three categories of aliens who may be detained beyond the presumptive 180-day

---

[92] *Id.* (quoting Kansas v. Hendricks, 521 U.S. 346, 368 (1997) (emphasis added)).

[93] *Id.* at 692 (internal quotations and citations omitted). *Cf.* Rasul v. Bush, 452 U.S. 466 (2004) (holding that U.S. district courts can hear habeas corpus petitions from aliens captured on a battlefield and detained at a location over which the U.S. exercises plenary jurisdiction, albeit on statutory rather than constitutional grounds).

[94] *Zadvydas*, 533 U.S. at 696. The Supreme Court, interpreting the Attorney General's authority to detain aliens, noted that "if Congress had meant to authorize long-term detention of unremovable aliens, it certainly could have spoken in clearer terms." *Id.* at 697.

[95] Clark v. Martinez, 543 U.S. 371, 379, n.4 (2005).

[96] *Id.* at 386, n.8 (citing USA PATRIOT Act § 412(a), 8 U.S.C. § 1226a(a)(6)(2001)).

period even if not likely to be removed in the reasonably foreseeable future, including aliens: (1) who have highly contagious diseases; (2) whose release may cause serious adverse foreign policy consequences; and (3) who are being detained for national security or terrorism concerns.[97]

4. Enemy combatants

Enemy combatants also are subject to preventive detention absent conviction in a criminal proceeding.[98] The Supreme Court has repeatedly upheld the preventive detention of enemy combatants under the customary law of armed conflict, which helps to explain the robust efforts of the U.S. government to apply this legal paradigm to the problem of international terrorism in the wake of 9/11. The application of this customary power to certain international terrorist suspects (U.S. citizens and non-citizens alike) was squarely addressed by the Supreme Court in *Hamdi v. Rumsfeld*.[99] The Court, in a plurality opinion, held that the Authorization for Use of Military Force (AUMF) provided "explicit congressional authorization for the detention" of "individuals who fought against the United States in Afghanistan as part of the Taliban, an organization known to have supported the al Qaeda terrorist network responsible for those attacks,"[100] and that "the AUMF satisfied [the Non-Detention Act's] requirement that a detention be 'pursuant to an Act of Congress' (assuming, without deciding, that [the Non-Detention Act] applies to military detentions)."[101] According to the Court, "[t]he capture and detention of lawful combatants and the capture, detention, and trial of unlawful combatants, by universal agreement and practice, are important incidents of war. The purpose of detention is to prevent cap-

---

97 8 C.F.R. § 241.14(a)–(d) (2001); DHS OIG REPORT, *supra* note 85, at 4–5. Certification that an alien meets one or more of these criteria requires substantial factual support and approval by senior government officials. *See* 8 C.F.R. § 241.14. The statute also allows for detention of aliens determined to be "specially dangerous" beyond the 180-day presumptive period; however, during 2008 two Federal courts held that this provision of the statute was unconstitutional. *See* Tran v. Mukasey, 515 F.3d 478 (5th Cir. 2008); Hernandez-Carrera v. Carlson, 546 F. Supp. 2d 1185 (D. Kan. 2008).

98 During times of war Congress may also authorize the detention of "alien enemies," meaning "[s]ubjects of a foreign state at war with the United States." Johnson v. Eisentrager, 339 U.S. 763, 769, n.2 (1950) (internal quotation marks omitted) (quoting Techt v. Hughes, 128 N.E. 185, 186 (1920)); see also Ludecke v. Watkins, 335 U.S. 160 (1948) (approving executive power to detain enemy aliens in times of war).

99 Hamdi v. Rumsfeld, 542 U.S. 507 (2004) (plurality opinion).

100 *Id.* at 518. Congress adopted the AUMF in September 2001. *Id.* The AUMF empowered the President to "use all necessary and appropriate force" against "nations, organizations, or persons" that he determines "planned, authorized, committed, or aided" in the September 11, 2001 terrorist attacks. *Id.* (citing Authorization for Use of Military Force, Pub. L. No. 107-40, 115 Stat. 224 (2001)).

101 *Hamdi*, 542 U.S. at 517.

tured individuals from returning to the field of battle and taking up arms once again."[102] Moreover, "there is no bar to this Nation's holding one of its own citizens as an enemy combatant . . . . A citizen, no less than an alien, can be 'part of or supporting forces hostile to the United States or coalition partners' and 'engaged in an armed conflict against the United States"; "such a citizen, if released, would pose the same threat of returning to the front during the ongoing conflict."[103]

But just as we have seen under the other categories of preventive detention, the Court limited this power in three important substantive or procedural regards. First, the Court acknowledged Hamdi's concern for the "substantial prospect of indefinite detention" given that "the national security underpinnings of the 'war on terror,' although crucially important, [were] broad and malleable" and reflective of the unconventional nature of the conflict at issue.[104] Much like in the *Salerno* case, the Court resolved this issue by differentiating between indefinite detention and detention with an uncertain end. Hamdi's detention could only last as long as "the record establishes that United States troops are still involved in active combat in Afghanistan."[105] While this period had no fixed end date, the period's end date could be determined with relative certainty, and thus was not an "indefinite" period in the Court's view. Nonetheless, the Court emphasized that it affirmed the detention power "based on long-standing law of war principles" and "[i]f the practical circumstances of a given conflict [were] entirely unlike those of the conflicts that informed the development of the law of war, that understanding [would] unravel."[106] Second, the Court specifically stated that "indefinite detention for the purpose of interrogation is not authorized."[107] Third, the Court concluded that a citizen such as Hamdi, who disputed the enemy combatant designation underlying his detention, was entitled to notice of the factual basis for his detention and a meaningful opportunity to challenge his detention before a neutral decision maker.[108] While recognizing these procedural safeguards, the Court acknowledged that under some circumstances such proceedings could be tailored to the situation; evidentiary rules, burdens of proof and other aspects of such a hearing might be

---

102 *Id.* at 515 (internal quotation marks and citations omitted). Note that the *Hamdi* case involved a U.S. citizen captured on foreign soil. The same power of detention, however, applies to foreign nationals who satisfy the Court's descriptive category.

103 *Id.* at 519.

104 *Id.* at 520.

105 *Id.* at 521.

106 *Id.* (noting that Afghanistan *was* similar to conflicts that contributed to the development of the law of war because "[a]ctive combat operations" continued in Afghanistan).

107 *Id.*

108 *Id.* at 533.

significantly altered from those applicable in criminal proceedings.[109] The Court noted, however, that Hamdi's right to an attorney in such proceedings was "unquestionabl[e]."[110]

In *Padilla v. Hanft*, the United States Court of Appeals for the Fourth Circuit closely followed the *Hamdi* decision, permitting enemy combatant detention of a U.S. citizen who took up arms against the United States in Afghanistan on behalf of the Taliban.[111] Padilla left the battlefield in Afghanistan for the alleged purpose of carrying out terrorist attacks on U.S. soil, and was initially arrested by civilian law enforcement authorities upon his arrival in the U.S.[112] However, as discussed above, the Fourth Circuit later initially refused to extend this power to sanction enemy combatant detention of the resident alien in the *al-Marri* case, reasoning that *Hamdi* and *Padilla* stand for the proposition that "who fits within the 'legal category' of enemy combatant . . . rest[s] . . . on affiliation with the military arm of an enemy nation."[113] According to the court, al-Marri did not qualify for the enemy combatant "exception to the usual criminal process" because, unlike Hamdi and Padilla, al-Marri was not alleged to have taken up arms against the U.S. in Afghanistan on behalf of the Taliban or "to have engaged in combat with United States forces anywhere in the world."[114] Indeed, the court explicitly rejected the government's argument that "al-Marri's seizure and indefinite military detention . . . are justified because he engaged in, and continues to pose a very real threat of carrying out, . . . acts of international

---

109 *Id.* at 533–34.

110 *Id.* at 539. The U.S. government responded to the *Hamdi* decision and to the decision of the Court in *Rasul v. Bush*, 542 U.S. 466 (2004), by instituting Combatant Status Review Tribunals (CSRTs) for enemy combatants held in the war on terror. COMBATANT STATUS REVIEW TRIBUNALS, Sept. 28, 2006, http://www.defenselink.mil/news/Jul2007/CSRT%20 %Fact%Sheet.pdf. Among other things, the CSRTs provide for the right to: (1) review the unclassified basis for the detainees detention; (2) have hearing in front of a tribunal of neutral military officers; (3) testify or introduce documentary evidence; (4) call (if reasonably available) and question witnesses before the tribunal; (5) attend all proceedings except when matters that would compromise national security are involved; (6) receive assistance of an appointed personal representative; and (7) submit the tribunal decision to automatic review by a higher authority. *See, e.g.*, Memorandum from Gordon England, U.S. Deputy Secretary of Defense, to Secretary of the Military Departments Joint Chief of Staff Under Secretary of Defense for Policy, Implementation of Combatant Status Review Tribunal Procedures for Enemy Combatants Detained at U.S. Naval Base Guantanamo Bay, Cuba (July 14, 2006), *available at* http://www.defenselink.mil/news/ Aug2006/d20060809CSRTProcedures.pdf.

111 *See* Padilla v. Hanft, 423 F.3d 386 (4th Cir. 2005).

112 *Id.*

113 Al-Marri v. Wright, 487 F.3d 160, 182 (4th Cir. 2007).

114 *Id.* at 183.

terrorism" on behalf of al Qaeda.[115] Thus, the Fourth Circuit panel would not extend the "special justification" of enemy combatant status to a person alleged only to be an operative of a non-state international terrorist organization such as al Qaeda.[116]

In sum, preventive detention in the U.S. generally requires not just a finding of dangerousness, but a finding of dangerousness combined with: (1) adequate procedural safeguards; and (2) some "special justification" such as mental illness, incompetence, abnormality, lack of control, communicable disease, or special status as an alien or enemy.[117] Potentially indefinite detention is particularly suspicious.

In light of these cases, the question becomes whether ties to terrorism suffice as an appropriate "special justification" and, if so, what procedural safeguards should apply?

C. *Does Terrorism Pose the "Special Danger" Required by the U.S. Supreme Court?*

In the *Zadvydas* and *Clark* cases, the Supreme Court suggested that terrorism indeed may justify an exception to the general rule against indefinite preventive detention, particularly where aliens are involved. On the other hand, the Fourth Circuit panel in the *al-Marri* case explicitly held that

---

115 *Al-Marri*, 487 F.3d at 183–84 (internal quotation and alteration omitted) ("[T]he government is mistaken in its representation that *Hamdi* and *Padilla* recognized [t]he President's authority to detain 'enemy combatants' during the current conflict with al Qaeda. No precedent recognizes any such authority.") (internal quotations omitted).

116 Again, the original *al-Marri* decision, which was issued by a split panel, was vacated and reheard *en banc*. Al-Marri v. Pucciarelli, 534 F.3d 213 (4th Cir. 2008). Unlike the original panel, the *en banc* court held that al-Marri could be held as an enemy combatant, assuming the government's allegations about his conduct were true. *Id.* at 216–17. In fact, Judge Traxler, the sole member of the court concurring in all aspects of the *en banc* judgment, vehemently disagreed with the original panel's premise that "because al Qaeda is not technically in control of an enemy nation or its government, it cannot be considered as anything other than a criminal organization whose members are entitled to all the protections and procedures granted by our constitution. . . . [A]l Qaeda is much more and much worse than a criminal organization. And while it may be an unconventional enemy force in a historical context, it is an enemy force nonetheless." *Id.* at 160 (Traxler, J., concurring). The *al-Marri* case is subject to further proceedings on remand, *see supra* note 41, and the tension about the proper application of LOAC doctrines to a conflict as unconventional as the global campaign against international terrorism is not likely to go away soon. In fact, the U.S. Supreme Court has recently agreed to review the *al-Marri* case during the 2008 term. *See* Robert Barnes, *Justices to Decide Legality of Indefinite Detention*, WASH. POST, Dec. 6, 2008, at A2.

117 *See* Zadvydas v. Davis, 533 U.S. 678, 690–91 (2001) ("[W]e have upheld preventive detention based on dangerousness only when limited to specially dangerous individuals and subject to strong procedural protections . . . . In cases in which preventive detention is of potentially *indefinite* duration, we have also demanded that the dangerousness rationale be accompanied by some other special circumstance, such as mental illness, that helps to create the danger.") (internal citations and quotations omitted).

alleged involvement with international terrorism is insufficient to warrant extension of the enemy combatant exception, even to an alien, and a similar argument was raised by the petitioners in *Boumediene v. Bush.*[118] Can terrorism qualify as a sufficient special danger justifying preventive detention?

Concerns about both security and liberty strongly suggest the answer is "Yes." As recounted earlier, international terrorism poses significant investigative and prosecutorial challenges that the ordinary criminal justice system is not equipped to handle. And, as former U.S. Attorney Mary Jo White has indicated, the ordinary criminal justice system is not capable of deterring large numbers of committed extremists who are "willing, indeed anxious, to die in service of their cause."[119] Furthermore, the nature and magnitude of the injury that modern international terrorist organizations seek to inflict is categorically different from the harms that the ordinary criminal justice system was designed to remedy. It seems clear that (the Fourth Circuit's initial *al-Marri* panel notwithstanding) individual operatives of sub-state terrorist organizations can pose the kind of special danger the Supreme Court has identified. For example, suppose that the U.S. government—using sensitive, credible, but ultimately inadmissible intelligence information—succeeded in disrupting an al Qaeda plot to simultaneously fly multiple airliners into iconic buildings in various U.S. cities, and the operatives involved were U.S. citizens and/or aliens who never fought against the U.S. forces in Afghanistan or elsewhere.

---

[118] The *Boumediene* petitioners argued, among other things, that their detention as enemy combatants was illegal. They contended that aliens allegedly connected to al Qaeda, but arrested by civilian police in a friendly country and not alleged to have participated directly in armed combat against the U.S., do not satisfy the enemy combatant exception pursuant to the AUMF and *Hamdi*. Further, they argued that the CSRT process established in the wake of *Hamdi* did not provide meaningful notice of the basis of detention, an opportunity to be heard, representation by counsel, or a neutral decision maker, which they claimed are required by Fifth Amendment due process. The government strongly disagreed, arguing that petitioners were aliens detained outside the U.S. and as such were not entitled to constitutional due process guarantees, and that in any event the CSRT process provided even more due process than *Hamdi* required for U.S. citizens held as enemy combatants or than is provided under the process in place to comply with Article 5 of the Geneva Convention Relative to the Treatment of Prisoners of War. *See* Briefs for Petitioner and Respondent, Boumediene v. Bush, 128 S.Ct. 2229 (2008) (No. 06-1195). In its decision, the Court declined to address whether the President had authority to detain the petitioners. Boumediene v. Bush, 128 S.Ct. 2229, 2240 (2008). Moreover, the Court rendered no judgment as to whether the CSRTs satisfy due process standards. *Id.* at 2270. The Court did hold, however, that the petitioners were entitled to constitutional habeas review and to protection of the Suspension Clause, and that the limited process established by the Detainee Treatment Act to review CSRT determinations was a constitutionally inadequate substitute for such habeas review. *Id.* at 2244–2262.

[119] Mary Jo White, *Prosecuting Terrorism in the Criminal Justice System*, XV(1) ARMS CONTROL, DISARMAMENT, AND INT'L SECURITY 3, 8 (2003).

The *al-Marri* case seems to direct that, absent criminal prosecution, those involved must be released or, if aliens, deported. Preventive detention would be impossible. This outcome seems inappropriate and unnecessary.[120] Moreover, the liberty concerns underlying *al-Marri* and other cases also favor a preventive detention system (with strong substantive and procedural safeguards built in) to handle terrorism cases that do not easily fit within the traditional categories of detention, lest the pressures on the traditional law enforcement and enemy combatant models permanently warp the principles that underlie them.

II. A "SECURITY DETENTION ACT" FOR THE U.S.?

If terrorism does represent the special danger that justifies preventive detention, then one must ask what such a security detention system for terrorist suspects would look like? The foregoing analysis of U.S. and international law, and a review of several preventive detention programs proposed or adopted by other countries,[121] identifies eight fundamental issues that must be addressed in any legislation of this type.

A. *Nature of the System*

Legislation must address the nature of the system. To this point, this article has discussed exclusively actual physical detention of terrorist suspects. Israel's Administrative Detention Act employs this approach. However, several systems adopted in recent years provide control options that represent a less drastic intrusion of the liberty interest at stake. For example, both the United Kingdom and Australia have enacted legislation permitting authorities to impose "control orders" on terrorist suspects without subject-

---

[120] As Justice John Paul Stevens acknowledged when the *Padilla* case initially reached the Supreme Court in 2004, "[e]xecutive detention of subversive citizens, like detention of enemy soldiers to keep them off the battlefield, may sometimes be justified to prevent persons from launching or becoming missiles of destruction." Rumsfeld v. Padilla, 542 U.S. 426, 465 (2004) (Stevens, J., dissenting).

[121] The preventive detention schemes reviewed for this article include the system of derogating and non-derogating control orders established by the United Kingdom's Prevention of Terrorism Act 2005, c. 2 (Eng.); the system of control orders and preventive detention orders established by Australia's Anti-Terrorism Act (No. 2), 2005, c. 144 (Austl.); Israel's Emergency Powers (Detention) Law 1979, 33 L.S.I. 89 (1978-99), *reprinted in* Emanual Gross, *Human Rights, Terrorism and the Problem of Administrative Detention in Israel: Does a Democracy Have the Right to Hold Terrorists as Bargaining Chips?*, 18 ARIZ. J. INT'L & COMP. L. 721 (2001); and the system of investigative hearings and recognizance orders contemplated by Canada's Bill S-3, *see* LAURA BARNETT, AN ACT TO AMEND THE CRIMINAL CODE, (INVESTIGATIVE HEARING AND RECOGNIZANCE WITH CONDITIONS), LS-574E, at 3–6 (2008), *available at* http://www2.parl.gc.ca/HousePublications/Publication.aspx?Docid=3334060&file=4, as adopted by the Canadian Senate on March 6, 2008 and on first reading in the Canadian House of Commons.

ing them to arrest or detention.[122] The Parliament of Canada is presently considering[123] a system of "recognizance" orders that are very similar.

Control order schemes allow imposition of a broad range of restrictions and prohibitions,[124] and generally provide an option that is subject to fewer procedural safeguards than actual physical detention. However, the British, Australian, and Canadian control order systems also authorize more drastic measures under certain circumstances. Under the U.K. legislation, the government may at times seek a control order that derogates from the U.K.'s arrest and detention obligations under Article 5 of the European Convention on Human Rights.[125] Similarly, the Australian and the Canadian

---

122 The United Kingdom's Anti-terrorism, Crime and Security Act permitted the U.K. to deport aliens who were suspected international terrorists, or to detain such aliens indefinitely where deportation could not be accomplished. Anti-terrorism, Crime and Security Act, 2001, c. 24 §§ 22–23 (Eng.). If either an international legal obligation or a practical consideration (for example, human rights concerns in the receiving country, documentation issues, etc.) prevented removal pursuant to such an order, the U.K. authorities were authorized to detain the suspected terrorist indefinitely. *Id.* In December 2004, the U.K. House of Lords invalidated the alien detention provisions of the ATCSA. A v. Secretary of State [2004] UKHL 56. The Lords ruled that the detention provisions, in particular the indefinite detention provisions, violated the European Convention on Human Rights in that their effect on foreign nationals was a disproportionate, irrational, and discriminatory deprivation of liberty compared to the threat posed by foreign nationals. *Id.* In response to the House of Lords judgment, the British Parliament enacted the Prevention of Terrorism Act 2005 (PTA), which explicitly repealed the detention provisions of the ATCSA and instituted the current system of derogating and non-derogating control orders. Prevention of Terrorism Act 2005, c. 2 (Eng.).

123 The Canadian legislation is largely identical to the system enacted by Canada's Anti-Terrorism Act of 2001, which expired after five years and was not immediately re-authorized. *Compare* Anti-terrorism Act, 2001 S.C., c. 41 (Can.), *with* BARNETT, *supra* note 121.

124 Examples include restrictions on movement, premises, communications, associations, activities, use or possession of articles or substances, and the wearing of electronic tracking devices. *See, e.g.*, Prevention of Terrorism Act 2005, c. 2 (Eng.).

125 Prevention of Terrorism Act 2005, c.2, § 1 (Eng.). Article 5 of the European Convention on Human Rights stipulates that "[n]o one shall be deprived of his liberty save in the following cases," which include: (1) detention upon criminal conviction; (2) detention for non-compliance with a lawful court order; (3) criminal pre-trial detention; (4) detention of a minor for educational supervision; (5) detention of the mentally ill, controlled substance abusers, and those with infectious diseases; and (6) detention with a view toward deportation or extradition. Convention for the Protection of Human Rights and Fundamental Freedoms as Amended by Protocol No. 11 art. 5(1), Nov. 1, 1998, 213 U.N.T.S. 222. A control order that impinges these rights is called a "derogating" order under the U.K. system, and must be imposed by a court. Prevention of Terrorism Act 2005, c.2, § 4 (Eng.). An order that imposes restrictions but that does not violate the person's rights relating to physical arrest and detention is called a "non-derogating" order, and may be imposed by the Secretary of State for the Home Department. *Id.* § 2. However, it seems at least one U.K. court has held that certain orders imposed by the government, though styled as non-derogating orders, impose restrictions that in fact amount to deprivation of liberty prohibited by the arrest and detention

legislation each permit physical detention in exigent circumstances.[126] Control order systems also provide that failure to observe the conditions imposed by the order, or obstruction of those exercising the control order powers, may be grounds for arrest, detention, and potential imprisonment.[127]

The dual approach of control order systems is appealing in light of the U.S. case law outlined above. The ability to impose lesser intrusions on all but the most dangerous suspects works to limit the class of potential detainees in the manner required by the Supreme Court. Moreover, less intrusive restrictions generally require less burdensome procedural guarantees.

B. Definitional Threshold

Any new security detention system should not broadly authorize detention for *anyone* who poses a threat to national security. Rather, preventive detention should be available only for those individuals who represent the central threat of modern terrorism and who cannot be handled without straining ordinary criminal justice processes or law of armed conflict doctrines. One of the principal concerns with the U.S.'s current multi-prong approach to the detention of terror suspects is that it has ensnared individuals and conduct that are increasingly remote from the primary terrorist actors and activities. Similarly, the Supreme Court has expressed concern with preventive detention schemes that define the pool of potential detainees too broadly.[128] If suspected involvement with international terrorism is to justify preventive detention outside one of the existing categories, the definitional threshold must be strict.

A comparison of other systems is instructive. Israel, for example, permits administrative detention of anyone when reasonable cause exists to believe that reasons of State security or public security require detention.[129] While this is an exceptionally broad threshold, it is subject to some limitations. For example, administrative detention can only occur during a state of emergency (which has existed continuously in Israel since 1948), and may be imposed only if it is the sole means available to detain the person,[130] meaning that criminal prosecution must not be a practical option.

provisions of Article 5, not merely a restriction of liberty. *See* JJ and Others v. Sec'y of State for the Home Dep't, [2006] EWHC 1623.

126 Anti-Terrorism Bill (No. 2), 2005, § 105.4, sched. 4 (Austl.); Anti-terrorism Act, 2001 S.C., c. 41, § 4 (Can.).

127 *E.g.*, Anti-Terrorism Bill (No. 2), 2005, § 104.27, sched. 4 (Austl.); Anti-terrorism, Crime and Security Act, 2001, c. 2 § 9 (Eng.).

128 *See, e.g.*, *supra* text accompanying notes 51–52, 58-63, 66–74, 87–93.

129 Israel's Emergency Powers (Detention) Law 1979, 33 L.S.I. 89 (1978–99), *reprinted in* Gross, *supra* note 121, at 725.

130 *Id.*

The threshold for imposition of a control order in Britain depends on the nature of the order and reflects the different restrictions of liberty at stake. Derogating orders may be confirmed by the court only if: (1) it is more probable than not that the person is or has been "involved in terrorism-related activity"; (2) the obligations imposed are necessary to protect members of the public from a risk of terrorism; (3) the risk at issue is associated with a public emergency for which the government has issued a formal notice of derogation from all or part of Article 5 of the ECHR; and (4) the obligations imposed by the order are among those listed in the government's derogation notice.[131] Non-derogating control orders, however, have a lesser threshold. The Secretary of State may issue a non-derogating control order if he: (1) has reasonable grounds to suspect that the person is or has been "involved in terrorism-related activity"; and (2) considers the imposition of the order and the obligations it imposes necessary to protect the public from a risk of terrorism.[132] But, much like Israel, where the "involvement with terrorist-related activity" that gives rise to a control order suggests the commission of a criminal offense, the Secretary of State must consult with police and prosecution officials before making or applying for the order to determine if evidence exists that could realistically be used to prosecute the subject of the order for an offense related to terrorism.[133] If the order is issued, the police officials must continue to investigate to determine if prosecution becomes possible during the duration of the order.[134]

The Australian system seems to have the highest threshold to obtain a control order. A federal police officer may apply for a preventive detention order with respect to a person for either of two reasons: (1) if he reasonably suspects that the person "will engage in a terrorist act, possesses a thing connected with the preparation for, or engagement … in, a terrorist

---

131 Prevention of Terrorism Act 2005, c.2, § 4 (Eng.).

132 *Id.* The terms "involvement in terrorism-related activity" and "terrorism" are defined very broadly. "Involvement in terrorism-related activity" means: (a) the commission, preparation or instigation of terrorism; (b) facilitating, encouraging, or intending to facilitate or encourage the same; or (c) giving support or assistance to those known or believed to be involved in terrorism-related activity. It does not matter if the foregoing conduct relates to a specific act of terrorism, or to terrorism in general. *See* Prevention of Terrorism Act 2005, c.2, § 1.9 (Eng.). "Terrorism" has the same meaning as in the Terrorism Act 2000, which defines the term as the use or threat of action that (a) involves serious violence against a person, involves serious damage to property, endangers a person's life, creates a serious risk to the health or safety of the public or a section of the public, or is designed seriously to interfere with or seriously to disrupt an electronic system; (b) is designed to influence the government or to intimidate the public or a section of the public; and (c) is made for the purpose of advancing a political, religious or ideological cause. Terrorism Act, 2000, c. 11, § 1(Eng.).

133 *See* Prevention of Terrorism Act 2005, c.2, § 8 (Eng.).

134 *See id.*

act," or has taken an action in preparation for a terrorist act; or (2) if a terrorist act has occurred within the past 28 days and detention of the person for the period imposed is reasonably necessary to preserve evidence relating to the act.[135] A future terrorist act must be imminent, meaning at the most it is expected to occur within the following 14 days.[136]

C. *Duration of Detention*

Any new legislation on preventive detention must address the duration of detention. As discussed, the U.S. Supreme Court has demonstrated a decided bias against indefinite detention, particularly absent the existence of some special factor that both narrowly limits the class of people to which the detention potentially applies and confirms the heightened danger that class poses, as well as the existence of strict procedural safeguards. Thus, potentially lengthy detention periods require a stricter definitional threshold and more robust procedural safeguards.

The foreign detention schemes reviewed for this article vary broadly in potential duration. For example, preventive detention orders in Australia may not exceed 48 hours and are subject to restrictions on the imposition of multiple detention orders.[137] In contrast, detention orders under Israel's Administrative Detention Act may be imposed for up to six months and are renewable indefinitely for successive six-month periods.[138] In Britain, duration depends on the nature of the control order, again reflecting the degree of infringement of the person's liberty. Non-derogating control orders in Britain last for up to 12 months and are renewable for successive 12-month periods, while derogating control orders may be issued for six-month periods, subject to renewal by the court.[139] Further, the legislation provides that persons may be arrested and detained for up to 96 hours during the pendency of an application for a derogating control order.[140]

D. *Appropriate Decision-maker*

Preventative detention legislation must authorize an official to impose the detention. Most foreign preventive detention systems involve an initial determination made by order of a competent and independent judicial

---

135 Anti-Terrorism Bill (No. 2), 2005, § 105.4, sched. 4 (Austl.).

136 *Id.*

137 Anti-Terrorism Bill (No. 2), 2005, § 105.1, sched. 4 (Austl.). ("[T]he object of this [Act] is to allow a person to be taken into custody and detained *for a short period of time . . . .*") (emphasis added).

138 Israel's Emergency Powers (Detention) Law 1979, 33 L.S.I. 89 (1978-99), *reprinted in* Gross, *supra* note 121, at 725.

139 *See* Prevention of Terrorism Act 2005, c.2, §§ 2, 4 (Eng.).

140 *See Id.* § 5.

official upon application of an executive official at a sufficiently high level to provide subsequent accountability. In urgent circumstances, however, provisions are usually made for an initial detention decision by an appropriately high-ranking executive official, with subsequent confirmation by a judicial authority.[141]

E. *Nature of Process, Including Standard of Proof, Evidentiary Rules, and Detainee Rights*

A security detention system also should specify any detainee rights and the procedural safeguards associated with the protection and exercise of detainee rights. As outlined earlier, notice of the basis for detention and the ability to seek independent review are basic standards.[142] Other important issues include a detainee's right to counsel, standards and burdens of proof, evidentiary rules on admissibility and reliability, rules for the use and protection of classified information, rules regarding the interrogation of detainees, presence of counsel during interrogation, and the permitted uses of information obtained from such interrogation. Israel, Australia, and the U.K. each provide different procedural safeguards and assurances of a detainee's rights.

In Israel, an administrative detainee must be brought before a district court judge within 48 hours or be released.[143] While the detainee has the right to know the basis for his detention, to have access to counsel, and to be present and have counsel present at the judicial confirmation hearing, the detention court may rely on hearsay and other evidence, if such evidence is deemed reliable, even if that evidence would ordinarily be inadmissible in criminal proceedings.[144] The court also may order sensitive evidence with-

141 For example, in Israel's administrative detention may occur upon an order issued by the Minister of Defense, subject to judicial confirmation. *See* Israel's Emergency Powers (Detention) Law 1979, 33 L.S.I. 89 (1978–99), *reprinted in* Gross, *supra* note 121, at 725. In Australia, a federal police officer may apply to a senior police official for a preventive detention order lasting up to 24 hours. Anti-Terrorism Bill (No. 2), 2005, § 105.8, sched. 4 (Austl.). A judge or federal magistrate may extend a preventive detention order for up to a total of 48 hours. *Id.* § 105.12. In Britain, under normal circumstances, the Secretary of State for the Home Department may apply to a court for imposition of a non-derogating control order. Prevention of Terrorism Act 2005, c.2, § 2 (Eng.). The Secretary of State may issue a non-derogating control order in urgent circumstances, subject to subsequent confirmation by the court. *Id.* Control orders that derogate from Article 5 of the ECHR may only be issued, regardless of circumstances, by a court. *Id.* § 1(2).

142 *See, e.g., supra* text accompanying notes 48–52, 58–63, 66–74, 87–93, 104–09.

143 Israel's Emergency Powers (Detention) Law 1979, 33 L.S.I. 89 (1978–99), *reprinted in* Gross, *supra* note 121, at 756.

144 Israel's Emergency Powers (Detention) Law 1979, 33 L.S.I. 89 (1978–99), *reprinted in* Gross, *supra* note 121, at 773.

held from a detainee if disclosure would threaten national security.[145] Commentators suggest that the applicable evidentiary standard is generally accepted to be a "clear and convincing" standard and that more evidence is thought to be required as a practical matter the longer detention continues (a proportionality rule of sorts).[146]

Australian detainees and their lawyers must be given a copy of the detention order and a summary of the grounds for detention.[147] Detainees have the right to contact lawyers, family members, and employers for limited purposes, and to contact the police Ombudsman.[148] However, the government may seek an order restricting the person's ability to contact virtually any person, including particular family members and particular attorneys, and the content of a detainee's communications may be monitored.[149] The Australian Act specifically requires that a person detained under the Act must be treated humanely and may not be subjected to any cruel, inhuman, or degrading treatment.[150] The government may not question a detainee during detention, for law enforcement or intelligence purposes,[151]

145 *Id.*

146 *See id.* at 773–74.

147 Anti-Terrorism Bill (No. 2), 2005, § 105.32, sched. 4 (Austl.).

148 *Id.* §§ 105.35–105.37.

149 *Id.* §§ 105.34–38.The content of such communications with a lawyer may not, however, be admitted in any criminal proceedings. *Id.* Family members, lawyers and others may be subject to up to five years imprisonment for improperly disclosing information pertaining to a detention order. *Id.* § 105.41.

150 *Id.* § 105.33.

151 Considering that the justification for preventive detention is the potential dangerousness of the detainee and not his intelligence value, some systems impose strict limits on intelligence interrogations of detainees. *See, e.g.*, *id.* a § 105.42. But the issue of interrogation of detainees, particularly for intelligence purposes, is important and must be resolved. Many of the procedural and substantive rights associated with preventive detention programs may prove problematic for intelligence gathering, which is a critical element of the new prevention imperative. For example, most experienced interrogators maintain that isolation can be among the most useful interrogation techniques, and interruption of the interrogation process (for example, to meet with legal counsel) can negatively impact information gathering. *See, e.g.*, Paul Rosenzweig & James Jay Carafano, *Preventive Detention and Actionable Intelligence*, 13 LEGAL MEMORANDUM 1 (The Heritage Found., Washington, D.C.), Sept. 16, 2004, at 3, *available at* http://www.heritage.org/Research/HomelandSecurity/lm13.cfm. Professors Goldsmith and Katyal have suggested a system of delayed access to counsel to permit limited interrogation as a possible solution. Jack L. Goldsmith & Neal Katyal, Op-Ed, *The Terrorists' Court*, N.Y. TIMES, July 11, 2007, at A19. One potential solution might involve a process modeled on that used in Spain, where terrorism suspects may be held in police custody for up to five days before a decision to commence criminal proceedings is made. Maria Alvanou, *Terrorism Legislation Issues in Spain: Terrorism Offenses and 'Incommunicado' Procedures*, RESEARCH INSTITUTE FOR EUROPEAN AND AMERICAN STUDIES, 2007, http:/rieas.gr/index.php?option=com_content&task=view&id=405&Itemid=41. The person may be held incommunicado during that period pursuant to court authorization. *Id.* Moreover, the incommunicado period may be extended for an additional eight days if the decision

except to confirm identity and safety, and any questioning must be video-taped.

Once again, the rights and procedures applicable under Britain's control order system vary with the nature of the order. The subject of any control order must be informed of the imposition of a control order.[152] For non-derogating control orders, the court may conduct an *ex parte* hearing of the government's basis for issuing the order.[153] If convinced that the government's decision is not "obviously flawed," the court must conduct a full hearing to determine the appropriateness of the order and the obligations imposed.[154] At the full hearing, the court must determine whether the government's decision was flawed in respect of any of the following issues: (1) the existence of reasonable grounds to suspect that the person was "involved in terrorism-related activity"; (2) that a control order was necessary to protect members of the public from the risk of terrorism; or (3) the necessity of the particular obligations imposed.[155] The court may order the government to revoke or modify the order as appropriate. Non-derogating control orders issued by the government in exigent circumstances must be referred to the court immediately, and the court must commence consideration of the order no more than seven days after the order took effect.[156] In the case of derogating control orders, upon application by the British government, the court will hold an immediate preliminary hearing (which, again, may be *ex parte*) to determine if a *prima facie* case exists for the imposition of an order.[157] If such a case exists, the court will impose the order subject to a subsequent full hearing.[158] At that hearing, the court will confirm the control order only if it is convinced that the threshold standard has been met and if it has not been met, the court may quash or modify the obligations originally imposed.[159]

---

is made to commence criminal proceedings. *Id.* During an incommunicado period, a suspect's relatives may not be informed of the detention and legal services are provided by a duty solicitor, not an attorney chosen by the suspect. *Id.* A suspect held incommunicado may be questioned in the presence of the duty solicitor, who may advise the suspect on matters of procedure but may not consult privately with the suspect. *Id.* Note, however, that a forensic physician is assigned to examine the suspect during the period and ensure the suspect is not abused, and must make a report to the supervising judicial authority. *Id.* The suspect may not see a lawyer of his choosing or notify anyone of his detention until the end of the incommunicado period, which may last a total of thirteen days. *Id.*

152 *See* Prevention of Terrorism Act 2005, c.2, § 7 (Eng.).

153 *Id.* § 3.

154 *Id.* § 4.

155 *See id.*

156 *Id.* § 3.

157 *See id.* § 4.

158 *Id.*

159 *Id.*

The British system also addresses a number of evidentiary and related procedural concerns. For example, the Prevention of Terrorism Act imposes an obligation on the government to disclose all evidence relevant to the control order proceedings.[160] However, the Act directs the courts to establish rules allowing the government to withhold sensitive information from anyone other than the court or certain qualified lawyers designated as "special advocates," and to exclude the controlled person and his legal counsel from proceedings when considering such evidence.[161] In those circumstances, the special advocates shall represent the interests of the controlled person, but shall not be responsible to him or his legal counsel. [162] The British Act does not, however, address the extent to which those subject to control orders may be interrogated, or any restrictions on potential uses of the information that may be obtained from interrogation.

U.S. law provides a relevant example of how these issues have been handled in a non-criminal context involving terrorism and preventive detention. In 1996, as part of the Anti-Terrorism and Effective Death Penalty Act (AEDPA), the U.S. created a new removal process for aliens called the Alien Terrorist Removal Court (ATRC), which is comprised of five federal district court judges appointed by the Chief Justice of the Supreme Court.[163] ATRC proceedings are available to the government in any case where, on application by the Attorney General, the Court finds probable cause to believe that: (1) the alien is a terrorist; (2) the alien is present in the U.S.; and (3) ordinary removal proceedings would pose a risk to national security due to disclosure of classified information.[164]

More specifically, the ATRC legislation allows the government to use classified information to establish grounds for removal without disclosure to the alien if a risk to national security would result. In place of the

---

[160] *Id.* § 4, sched. Control order proceedings, etc.

[161] *Id.* §§ 4, 7. When the court opts to withhold evidence, the courts may also provide for summaries of the sensitive evidence. *Id.* § 4.

[162] *Id.* § 7.

[163] 8 U.S.C. § 1532(a)(2000). Recall that removable aliens are detainable pending the removal determination and pending actual removal, particularly in cases involving terrorism. *See supra* text accompanying notes 76–83. Note also that the Alien Terrorist Removal Court provisions rarely, if ever, have been used since their adoption in 1996, primarily because the provisions' intricate procedures are considered unworkable, but also in part because of due process concerns. Steven R. Valentine, *Flaws Undermine Use of Alien Terrorist Removal Court*, 17(12) WASH. LEGAL FOUNDATION 1, 2 (2002). One other potential example of how current U.S. law and practice address these issues is the CSRT. COMBATANT STATUS REVIEW TRIBUNALS, Sept. 28, 2006, http://www.defenselink.mil/news/Jul2007/CSRT%20%Fact% Sheet.pdf. However, as previously mentioned, the CSRT system continues to face significant constitutional challenge. The *Boumediene* case recently decided by the Supreme Court is just one example. Boumediene v. Bush, 128 S.Ct. 2229 (2008).

[164] 8 U.S.C. § 1533(a) (1996).

classified information, unclassified summaries approved by the court can be provided to the alien and his attorney. Where unclassified summaries are not possible, and the alien is a legal permanent resident, special pre-cleared attorneys who can review the classified material are available.[165] The removal hearing may continue without disclosure or summaries if the court determines that serious and irreparable harm to national security might otherwise result.

The AEDPA also spells out the rights of the aliens in ATRC proceedings, including (1) notice of the nature of charges; (2) a public hearing and the right to be present at the hearing (except when considering sensitive information); (3) a compensated right to counsel; and (4) a reasonable opportunity to call and confront witnesses and to offer evidence.[166] The government bears the burden of proof in ATRC proceedings under a preponderance of the evidence standard, but the ordinary rules of evidence do not apply, meaning that the government may use virtually any and all relevant evidence, including evidence alleged to have been obtained unlawfully.[167]

F. Appeals and Periodic Review

Most preventive detention systems provide for rights of appeal and periodic automatic review of detention. For example, under the British Prevention of Terrorism Act, all persons subject to control orders have a right of appeal on matters of law.[168] Under the ATRC provisions in U.S. law, removable aliens may appeal the removal determination to the U.S. Court of Appeals, and in cases involving permanent legal residents the appeal is automatic.[169] The standard of review is the same as in criminal proceedings—*de novo* review for matters of law, and a clearly erroneous standard for factual matters.[170]

Automatic periodic review typically involves the same standard used to impose detention in the first instance, and usually occurs no less than once each year depending on the intrusiveness of the liberty restriction. In Israel, administrative detention orders must be reviewed by the court

165 Other options that might be considered in place of such special counsel are a permanent staff of skilled defense lawyers similar to the Federal Public Defender system, as proposed by Professors Goldsmith and Katyal, Jack L. Goldsmith & Neal Katyal, Op-Ed, *The Terrorists' Court*, N.Y. TIMES, July 11, 2007, at A19, or a system of pre-clearance for lawyers who are not associated with the government but who are experienced human rights practitioners.

166 8 U.S.C. § 1534 (2001).

167 *Id.*

168 *See* Prevention of Terrorism Act 2005, § 11 (Eng.).

169 8 U.S.C. § 1535 (1996).

170 *Id.*

every three months.[171] In Britain, there is no automatic periodic review during the course of the order, but the order must be affirmatively renewed at the end of each period for it to continue in effect.[172] Persons subject to control orders may seek revocation or modification of the order either from the government (non-derogating orders) or the court (derogating orders).[173] Moreover, the government may revoke or relax a non-derogating control order at any time, and the court is obligated to revoke a derogating control order if the derogating restrictions are no longer required.[174]

G. *Reporting and Oversight*

Preventive detention systems also tend to impose oversight and reporting obligations on an appropriate independent authority, such as an Inspector General.[175] These provisions usually require periodic evaluation of the use of the preventive detention powers, the outcome of the detention proceedings, the nature and conditions of the detention imposed, and any other material matters associated with the preventive detention program.[176] Reports normally must be submitted to a responsible executive agent (such as a Minister of Justice or State) and to a designated legislative committee.[177]

For example, in Australia the Attorney General must make an annual report to the Parliament regarding the functioning of the Act, including the number of orders issued and people detained, the nature of complaints made by those detained, and the number of detention orders found invalid by a court, among other issues.[178] The British scheme has several periodic reporting and oversight provisions. For example, the Secretary of State must provide a report to Parliament on a quarterly basis detailing his use of the control order powers and appoint an independent reviewer to report on the operation of the Act and other related matters.[179]

171 Israel's Emergency Powers (Detention) Law 1979, 33 L.S.I. 89 (1978–99), *reprinted in* Gross, *supra* note 121, at 775.

172 *See* Prevention of Terrorism Act 2005, c.2, § 4 (Eng.).

173 *See id.* § 7.

174 *Id.*

175 *See, e.g.*, *id.* § 14.

176 *See, e.g.*, Anti-Terrorism Bill (No. 2), 2005, § 105.47, sched. 4 (Austl.).

177 *E.g.* Prevention of Terrorism Act 2005, c.2, § 14 (Eng.).

178 Anti-Terrorism Bill (No. 2), 2005, § 105.47, sched. 4 (Austl.).

179 Prevention of Terrorism Act 2005, c.2, § 14 (Eng.).

H. *Sunset Provisions*

Preventive detention systems may be subject to a legislative sunset provision that requires the systems to cease operation unless reauthorized.[180] The sunset provisions, however, vary significantly. For example, the control order provisions of the British Prevention of Terrorism Act 2005 must be reauthorized annually, subject to approval by the British Parliament.[181] By contrast, the Australian law has a 10-year sunset clause.[182]

CONCLUSION

The U.S.'s current multi-prong approach to detention of terrorist suspects has a number of strengths. Its central strength is that it takes advantage of every legal tool available and attempts to use those tools that best fit the particular situation. It is, in short, fact driven and adaptive. Moreover, the U.S. approach relies on doctrines and powers that have lengthy pedigrees in U.S. jurisprudence. The detention of material witnesses, for example, dates from Sixteenth Century England and has been permitted under U.S. law since the first Judiciary Act of 1789.[183] The prosecution of well-established lesser offenses such as obstruction of justice and document fraud proved a valuable law enforcement tool in other contexts, such as the fight against organized crime. Similarly, the right of a nation to detain aliens that pose serious threats to national security is largely uncontroversial. And invocation of the right to detain enemy combatants for the duration of hostilities under LOAC is, as the Supreme Court acknowledged in *Hamdi*, "by universal agreement and practice [an] important incident[] of war."[184]

Nevertheless, the current approach also has many weaknesses. There is growing concern that these law enforcement, immigration and LOAC doctrines are being stressed beyond their limit.[185] Indeed, Attorney

---

180 *See, e.g.*, *id.* § 13; Anti-Terrorism Bill (No. 2), 2005, § 105.53, sched. 4 (Austl.).

181 Prevention of Terrorism Act 2005, c.2, § 13 (Eng.).

182 Anti-Terrorism Bill (No. 2), 2005, § 105.53, sched. 4 (Austl.).

183 Stacey M. Studnicki, *Material Witness Detention: Justice Served or Denied?*, 40 WAYNE L. REV. 1533, 1534–36 (1994) (explaining that the concept of material witnesses began in England in the 1500s); Judiciary Act of 1789, ch. 20, sec. 33, 1 Stat. 73, 91 (1789) ("Recognizances of the witnesses for their appearance to testify . . . may [be] require[d] on pain of punishment.").

184 Hamdi v. Rumsfeld, 542 U.S. 517, 518 (2004) (citing Ex parte Quirin, 317 U.S. 1, 30 (1942)).

185 For instance, detention of material witnesses was conceived to compel individuals with relevant testimony to appear as witnesses; detention of material witnesses was not intended to be a proxy for preventive detention of those considered dangerous to society. *See* Studnicki, *supra* note 183, at 1539–37. Because these warrants were conceived for short-term detention of witnesses, there are few procedural safeguards such as meaningful judicial review or a robust ability to challenge the basis for detention. *See id.* at 1536–39.

General Mukasey and the other commentators previously cited seem to have reached just that conclusion, as did the Fourth Circuit panel in *al-Marri.*[186] The pressure on traditional doctrines to accommodate the challenges of modern international terrorism tends to skew those doctrines in disturbing ways. There also is genuine concern in the legal community that the current approach damages our fundamental rights, and harms our international relationships—the very partnerships the United States must strengthen to effectively defeat al Qaeda and its allies, as well as presently unknown or future terrorist organizations.

These concerns warrant a call for the U.S. Congress to explore a new system of security detention for terrorism suspects. It is not entirely clear that a system of security detention for terrorist suspects would pass constitutional muster. Whether a sufficient nexus with terrorism would qualify as a constitutionally permissible "special justification" is largely an open question, and the adequacy of any procedural safeguards will depend on the totality of the specific provisions adopted. Further, for such a system to be of value, it must avoid becoming just one more tool used in the current *ad hoc* system. Instead, it must clearly define when it applies and direct the executive and judicial branches to apply the system in cases that push the bounds of existing detention categories. This goal is not obviously achievable.[187]

Moreover, there are countless possible variations on the preventive detention model that have not been discussed. For instance, a security detention system might concentrate preventive detention decisions, terrorism-related criminal prosecutions, and other national security matters into specialized national security courts, as several commentators have previously suggested—a concept with its own set of concerns. However, this approach might serve to free ordinary criminal courts from the challenges of handling terrorism matters, and stimulate development of a cadre of investigators, prosecutors and judges experienced in terrorism and national security matters—similar to the system used in France and Spain, where terrorism cases are handled by centralized courts. Another variation could involve the adoption of investigative hearing measures similar to those currently under contemplation in Canada, which permit a court to compel the examination of

---

186 *See supra* text accompanying notes 24, 37–43.

187 For example, the U.S. government has asserted on several occasions that the President has inherent constitutional power to detain enemy combatants even in the absence of a congressional authorization to use force such as the AUMF. *Cf.*, *e.g.*, *Hamdi*, 542 U.S. at 513–15 (2003) (discussing both the Government's argument that the President's war powers authorize detention of enemy combatants and skepticism that the Government requires a Congressional authorization to detain enemy combatants). The courts have not yet fully resolved that question.

any person reasonably believed to have information related to a terrorism matter.

Let us be clear. We do not urge the consideration of such a system because we believe that the government officials who designed or operate under the current multi-prong approach are ill-motivated or purposely distorting the legal authorities under which they operate. To the contrary, we believe the vast majority have acted in good faith and have done the best they can with, in the words of Attorney General Mukasey, "a strained and mismatched legal system."[188] If structured properly, a new security detention system might relieve the pressures currently distorting the existing detention mechanisms and provide a more definite, regular, and widely accepted standard of detention in difficult terrorism cases.

[188] Michael B. Mukasey, Op-Ed, *Jose Padilla Makes Bad Law*, WALL ST. J., Aug. 22, 2007, at A15.

[14]

GUANTANAMO BAY: THE LEGAL BLACK HOLE[1]

JOHAN STEYN*

The most powerful democracy is detaining hundreds of suspected foot soldiers of the Taliban in a legal black hole at the United States naval base at Guantanamo Bay, where they await trial on capital charges by military tribunals. This episode must be put in context. Democracies must defend themselves. Democracies are entitled to try officers and soldiers of enemy forces for war crimes. But it is a recurring theme in history that in times of war, armed conflict, or perceived national danger, even liberal democracies adopt measures infringing human rights in ways that are wholly disproportionate to the crisis. One tool at hand is detention without charge or trial, that is, executive detention. Ill-conceived rushed legislation is passed granting excessive powers to executive governments which compromise the rights and liberties of individuals beyond the exigencies of the situation. Often the loss of liberty is permanent. Executive branches of government, faced with a perceived emergency, often resort to excessive measures. The litany of grave abuses of power by liberal democratic governments is too long to recount, but in order to understand and to hold governments to account, we do well to take into account the circles of history.

Judicial branches of government, although charged with the duty of standing between the government and individuals, are often too deferential to the executive in time of peace. How then would the same judges act in a time of crisis? The role of the courts in time of crisis is less than glorious. On this side of the Atlantic *Liversidge v Anderson* (1942)[2] is revealing. The question before the House of Lords was a matter of the interpretation of Defence Regulation 18B which provided that the Home Secretary may order a person to be detained 'if he has reasonable cause to believe' the person to be of hostile origin or associations. A majority of four held that if the Home Secretary thinks he has good cause that is good enough. Lord Atkin chose the objective interpretation: the statute required the Home Secretary *to have* reasonable grounds for detention. Lord Atkin said: 'amid the clash of arms the laws are not silent' and warned against judges who 'when face to face with claims involving the liberty of the subject show themselves more executive minded

* A Lord of Appeal in Ordinary.

[1] This is the text of the Twenty-Seventh FA Mann Lecture, organized by the British Institute of International and Comparative Law and Herbert Smith and held in Lincoln's Inn Old Hall, 25 November 2003 with Sir Lawrence Collins in the chair.

[2] [1942] AC 206.

than the executive'. At the time the terms of Lord Atkin's dissent caused grave offence to his colleagues. But Lord Atkin's view on the interpretation of provisions such as Regulation 18B has prevailed: the Secretary of State's power to detain must be exercised on objectively reasonable grounds. To that extent *Liversidge v Anderson* no longer haunts the law.[3] I have referred to a case sketched on the memory of every lawyer because, despite its beguiling framework of a mere point of statutory interpretation, it is emblematic of the recurring clash of fundamentally different views about the role of courts in times of crisis. How far contemporary decisions match Lord Atkin's broader philosophy is far from clear. The theory that courts must always defer to elected representatives on matters of security is seductive. But there is a different view, namely that while courts must take into account the relative constitutional competence of branches of government to decide particular issues, they must never, on constitutional grounds, surrender the constitutional duties placed on them.[4]

Even in modern times terrible injustices have been perpetrated in the name of security on thousands who had no effective recourse to law. Too often courts of law have denied the writ of the rule of law with only the most perfunctory examination. In the context of a war on terrorism without any end in prospect this is a sombre scene for human rights. But there is the caution that unchecked abuse of power begets ever-greater abuse of power. And judges do have the duty, even in times of crisis, to guard against an unprincipled and exorbitant executive response.

Not every one will agree with the picture I have put before you. Let me therefore explain, with reference to Second World War experience, on both sides of the Atlantic, why I feel justified in what I have said. During the Second World War the United States placed more than 120,000 American citizens of Japanese descent in detention camps. There was no evidence to cast doubt on the loyalty of these people to the United States. The military authorities took the view, as a general put it, that 'a Jap is a Jap'. In due course it was recognized by the United States that a grave injustice was done. In 1988 Congress enacted legislation acknowledging that the 'actions were taken without adequate security reasons' and that they were largely motivated by 'racial prejudice, wartime hysteria and a failure of political leadership'.[5] Restitution was made to individuals who were interned. This is to the great credit of the United States. On the other hand, it must be remembered that an earlier opportunity arose in 1944 in *Korematsu v United States*[6] for the Supreme Court to redress the injustice. Korematsu was a Californian of Japanese ancestry. After

[3] *Nakkuda Ali v Jayaratne* [1951] AC 66.

[4] J Jowell, QC, 'Judicial Deference: Servility, Civility or Institutional Capacity?' [2003] PL 592. I deal with this point in my recent lecture *Dynamic Interpretation Amidst an Orgy of Statues*, The Brian Dickson Memorial Lecture, Ottawa, 2 Oct 2003.

[5] The Civil Liberties Act 1988.

[6] 332 US 214.

the bombing of Pearl Harbor he volunteered for the army but was rejected on health grounds. He obtained a defence industry job. In June 1942 he was arrested for violation of the internment orders. He challenged the constitutionality of the orders. The issue was whether military necessity was established. The court was divided. Delivering the opinion of the majority of the Court, Justice Black stated: 'To cast this case into outlines of racial prejudice, without reference to the real military dangers which were presented, merely confuses the issue.' Demonstrating significant deference to the executive, he concluded:

> the military authorities considered that the need for action was great, and time was short. We cannot—by availing ourselves of the calm perspective of hindsight—now say that at that time these actions were not justified.

Not many in the United States, in the moderate spectrum of views, would now defend this outcome, even viewed from the perspective of 1942. In any event, in 1984 a federal district court overturned Korematsu's conviction on the ground that the government had 'knowingly withheld information from the courts when they were considering the critical question of military necessity.'[7] In giving judgment Judge Patel observed that the case 'stands as a caution that in times of distress the shield of military necessity and natural security must not be used to protect governmental institutions from close scrutiny and accountability'.[8]

The second decision of the United States Supreme Court which I must mention is *Ex parte Quirin* (1942), the so-called 'Saboteurs case'.[9] It is a case of a very different kind and in many ways more understandable than *Korematsu*. It is cited by United States government spokesmen as authority for the detentions at Guantanamo Bay. In June 1942, when the United States was at war with Germany, eight Nazi agents, including one American citizen, arrived by submarine in the United States. They intended to commit acts of sabotage. Two among them revealed the plot. On 2 July 1942 President Roosevelt ordered the men to be tried by military commission for offences against the law of war and the Articles of War. The Proclamation also provided that they were to be denied access to the courts. On 8 July 1942 the trial commenced and proceeded in secret. Three weeks later the Supreme Court convened a special Summer session to consider petitions for habeas corpus made on behalf of the saboteurs. The saboteurs argued that they had a constitutional right of due process and that they were entitled to be tried before an ordinary civilian court. On 31 July 1942 the Supreme Court made a unanimous order that the military commission was legally constituted and the petitioners were lawfully detained. By 8 August 1942 all the saboteurs had been found guilty and six of the eight had been executed. The turncoats had their sentences commuted. Almost three months after the saboteurs were executed,

[7] *Korematsu v United States*, 584 F Supp (1984), at 1406 (ND Cal 1984).
[8] At 1420.
[9] 317 US 1.

the Supreme Court made public a unanimous decision holding that Congress had validly authorised military commissions to try violations of the laws of war. The court did, however, hold that the exclusion of judicial review did not apply to habeas corpus. Secret trials without the usual guarantees of fair trial were, however, constitutionally acceptable. In the context of the detentions at Guantanamo Bay it will be necessary to return to this case.

Between 1939 and 1945 almost 27,000 persons were detained in Britain without charge or trial and 7,000 were deported. The danger facing Britain was, of course, immeasurably greater than that of the United States. In the circumstances the total figure does not seem excessive. But most detentions were probably not justified. Not all cases of detention ended as happily as that of the German born Michael Kerr who was detained in 1940 for 6 months, released to fly for the RAF during the rest of the war, and rose to become a Lord Justice of Appeal.[10] In his book *In the Highest Degree Odious*[11] Professor AW Brian Simpson concluded that the courts washed their hands enthusiastically of responsibility for the legality of detentions. He said:

> the courts did virtually nothing for the detainees, either to secure their liberty, to preserve what rights they did possess under the regulation, to scrutinize the legality of Home Office action, or to provide compensation when matters went wrong. The legal profession too, as a profession, did nothing; I am told that it was not easy to persuade lawyers to act for detainees at all. . . . So far as the government lawyers were concerned, the Treasury Solicitor's Department comes across as unattractive; its ethos was ruthless determination to win cases at the least possible cost. One cannot but be struck by the absence in the papers of any hint of sympathy to those who litigated, or any generosity of spirit to individuals none of whom had been charged or convicted of any crime. Of the Law Officers Somervell seems to have sailed very close to the wind, and both he and Jowitt changed their tune over the relationship between the courts and the regulation. I cannot but suspect that other examples of dubious conduct have been concealed by the accidental loss of Treasury Solicitor's files . . . (418–19).

The 'hands off' approach continued after the war. In *R v Secretary of State, Ex p Hosenball* from 1977, a deportation case, Lord Denning said:[12]

> There is a conflict between the interests of national security on the one hand and the freedom of the individual on the other. The balance between these two is not for a court of law. It is for the Home Secretary. He is the person entrusted by Parliament with the task.

Exhibiting great deference to the executive Lord Denning added:

> In some parts of the world national security has on occasions been used as an excuse for all sorts of infringements of individual liberty. But not in England. Both during the wars and after them, successive ministers have discharged their duties to the complete satisfaction of the people at large.

[10] M Kerr *As Far As I Remember* (Oxford Hart 2002).
[11] Oxford Clarendon Press 1994. [12] [1977] 1 WLR 766, at 783.

Possibly we would now say that such instinctive trust in public servants, executive or judicial, has been replaced by a culture requiring in principle openness and accountability from all entrusted with public power.

During the Second World War a new idea took root. Previously there had been an assumption that however outrageously a government treated individuals, it was not properly the concern of other governments. The Third Reich and the Holocaust changed that perception. Out of the ashes of the war came the creation in 1945 of the United Nations, committed by its charter to uphold 'the dignity and worth of the human person'. The adoption on 10 December 1948 in Paris of the Universal Declaration of Human Rights—the legacy of Mrs Roosevelt—was a momentous event. It gave birth to the human rights movement and the rights revolution. Eighteen years later it became known together with the International Covenant on Social and Cultural Rights (1966) and the International Covenant on Civil and Political Rights (1966) as the International Bill of Rights. Central to these instruments is the dignity of the human person and the maintenance of the rule of law to protect that most fundamental of rights. A large number of treaties, regional and specific, the descendants of the Universal Declaration, enshrine the same principle. For present purposes the Convention Relative to the Treatment of Prisoners of War of 12 August 1947 (the Third Geneva Convention III) is relevant. It contained detailed provisions protecting prisoners of war. I am content to assume that the Taliban soldiers detained at Guantanamo Bay are on a literal interpretation not covered by the Third Geneva Convention because they did not wear uniforms on the battlefield. But Article 75 of the First Protocol Additional to the Geneva Conventions of 12 August 1949, dated 8 June 1977, contains more far-reaching provisions to protect prisoners captured during armed conflicts. Whatever their status, such prisoners are entitled to humane treatment. It is true that the United States has not ratified this Protocol. But it is generally accepted that Article 75 reflects customary international law.[13] Indeed when the United States government decided not to ratify the Protocol, it had before it expert advice that many Articles of the Protocol accurately reflect customary international law. Specifically it was advised that Article 75 was an Article which was already part of customary international law and therefore binding on the United States.[14] Many of the provisions of Article 75 are relevant. The use of torture and inhuman or degrading treatment is prohibited. The authorities are entitled to question a prisoner but there is no obligation on the prisoner to answer the questions put. Coercing a prisoner to confess is unlawful. Article 75(4) is particularly significant. It provides:

[13] C Greenwood, 'International Law and the "War Against Terrorism"', International Affairs 78, 2 (2002) 307, at 315.

[14] T Meron, *Human Rights and Humanitarian Norms of Customary Law* (Oxford Clarendon Press 1989), at 62–9.

> No sentence may be passed and no penalty may be executed on a person found guilty of a penal offence relating to the armed conflict except pursuant to a conviction pronounced by an impartial and regularly constituted court respecting the generally recognized principles of regular judicial procedure . . .

In the 1990s there were important developments. On 16 October 1998 Augusto Pinochet, the former President of Chile, was arrested in London in response to an arrest warrant issued by a Spanish court. Henry Kissinger has described him as 'a fashionably reviled man of the right'. Given what we now know the verdict of history may be a little more severe. In any event, the warrant alleged crimes of murder, torture and 'disappearances'. The final decision of the House of Lords was to the effect that crimes under international law, such as torture, could not be acts within the official capacity of a Head of State and that extradition proceedings could continue. Despite the fact that due to his mental state Pinochet could eventually not be tried, the decision of the House of Lords was an important breakthrough on immunities and universal jurisdiction.[15] Equally important was the creation of ad hoc international criminal tribunals in the case of Rwanda, Yugoslavia, and Milosevic to try defendants on war crimes.[16] Despite the negative role of the United States, the International Criminal Court was set up. To date 91 countries have ratified or acceded to the Treaty. The court is fully operational. Recently Madam Justice Arbour of the Canadian Supreme Court has eloquently summed up what this means. She said:

> We have witnessed a maturation process from the declaratory era of some 50 years ago, through a monitoring and denunciatory phase, and now into the modern era of efficient enforcement through personal criminal responsibility. This culture carries with it the expectations of millions of human rights holders who until very recently did not perceive themselves as such. But globalization of the culture of rights, combined with the spread of democracy, has irreversibly changed their sense of entitlement . . . [17]

There was great progress on the humanitarian front between 1948 and 2001.

Then came the horror of 11 September 2001. Using civilian aircraft as missiles, Al-Qaeda terrorists attacked and attempted to attack the great symbols of the United States government and nation. A military response was inevitable. Three days later President Bush declared a national emergency.[18] Congress rushed through the Patriot Act[19] which gave to the executive vast

[15] *R v Bow Street Stipendiary Magistrate, Ex P Pinochet (No 3)* [2000] 1 AC 147.

[16] The International Criminal Tribunal for Rwanda was created by Security Council resolution 955 of 8 Nov 1994; The International Criminal Tribunal for the former Yugoslavia ('ICTY') was established by resolution 827 of 25 May 1993 and the case of Milosevic was transferred to the ICTY on 29 June 2001.

[17] *'Is The Growth of International Criminal Law A Threat to State Sovereignty?'* Irving R. Segal Lecture, University of Pennsylvania, Philadelphia, PA, 24 Sept 2003.

[18] Proc 7463 '*Declaration of National Emergency by Reason of Certain Terrorist Attacks*'.

[19] USA PATRIOT Act 2001.

powers to override civil liberties. Congress promptly authorised the President to use all necessary force against, inter alia, those responsible for the terrorist attacks of 11 September to prevent further attacks.[20] On 7 October 2001 the air campaign against Afghanistan began. In military terms the action was successful. But now the region is left with a ravaged country which under its warlords has enormously increased its production of opium grown for the world market. Afghanistan was followed by the deeply controversial Iraqi war of 'shock and awe' which fractured the international legal order so carefully crafted in the crucible of Lake Success in 1945. It is easier to destroy than to develop international institutions. But tonight I must concentrate on Guantanamo Bay.

On 13 November 2001 the President issued an order providing for the trial by military commissions of persons accused of violations of the laws of war.[21] That order has been repeatedly amended.[22] Beginning in January 2002 some 660 prisoners have been transferred at first to Camp X-Ray and then Camp Delta at Guantanamo Bay. The number included children between the ages of 13 and 16 as well as the very elderly.[23] Virtually all the prisoners are foot soldiers of the Taliban. It has been reported that there are no 'big fish' among the prisoners.[24] Contemporaneous reports stated that the prisoners, who are Muslims, were compelled contrary to the tenets of their religion to shave off their beards.

By a blanket presidential decree all prisoners have been denied prisoners of war status. Before the armed conflict started, the Taliban government had been in effective control of Afghanistan. The vast majority of the prisoners were soldiers of the Taliban forces. Let me assume that at Guantanamo Bay there are also some prisoners who are Al-Qaeda terrorists. But if there are such prisoners, criminal outlaws as they may be, they are also in law entitled to the protection of humanitarian law.[25]

How prisoners at Guantanamo Bay have been treated we do not know. But what we do know is not reassuring. At Camp Delta the minute cells measure 1.8 m by 2.4 m. Detainees are held in these cells for up to 24 hours a day. Photographs of prisoners being returned to their cells on stretchers after interrogation have been published. The Red Cross described the camp as principally

[20] 'Authorization for Use of Military Force' Public Law 107–40, 115 Stat 224 18 Sept 2001.

[21] Military Order of 13 Nov 2001, 'Detention, Treatment and Trial of Certain Non-Citizens in the War Against Terrorism' 66 FR 57833 (16 Nov 2001) 'The Presidential Order'.

[22] *Trials Under Military Order: A Guide to the Final Rules for Military Commissions*, Lawyers Committee for Human Rights Briefing Paper, July 2003.

[23] United States of America, *The Threat of a Bad Example: Undermining international standards as 'war on terror' continues*, Amnesty International, 19 Aug 2003, at 21.

[24] *Call for release of 'low-level' Guantanamo inmates,* J Borger, The Guardian, 20 Aug 2002.

[25] George H Aldrich, *The Taliban, Al-Qaeda, and The Determination of Illegal Combatants*, 96 AJIL 891.

a centre of interrogation rather than detention.[26] The *Washington Post* suggested there has been a sweeping change in United States policy on torture since 11 September, despite public pronouncements against its use. It quotes Cofer Black, the former director of the CIA's counter-terrorist branch, as telling a congressional intelligence committee: 'All you need to know: there was a before 9/11, and there was an after 9/11 . . . After 9/11 the gloves came off'.[27] The United States website records thirty-two attempted suicides committed by twenty-seven prisoners.[28] A report of 16 March 2003 reported officials as saying that the techniques of interrogation are 'not quite torture, but as close as you can get'.[29] It appears likely that 'stress and duress' tactics of disrupting sleep and forcing prisoners to stand for extended periods, which have been used by United States interrogators in Afghanistan, are also employed at Guantanamo Bay.[30] The purpose of holding the prisoners at Guantanamo Bay was and is to put them beyond the rule of law, beyond the protection of any courts, and at the mercy of the victors. The procedural rules do not prohibit the use of force to coerce prisoners to confess. On the contrary, the rules expressly provide that statements made by a prisoner under physical and mental duress are admissible 'if the evidence would have value to a reasonable person', ie, military officers trying enemy soldiers.[31] At present we are not meant to know what is happening at Guantanamo Bay. But history will not be neutered. What takes place there today in the name of the United States will assuredly, in due course, be judged at the bar of informed international opinion.

Having invoked a historical perspective, I must acknowledge that, despite the Magna Carta, in harsher times England resorted to the expedient of sending prisoners beyond the reach of the rule of law. One of the charges made against Edward Hyde, the First Earl of Clarendon, in his impeachment in 1667 was that he had attempted to preclude habeas corpus by sending persons to 'remote islands, garrisons, and other places, thereby to prevent them from the benefit of the law', that is by sending persons to places where the writ of habeas corpus would not be available. In 1679 this loophole was blocked by section 11 of the Habeas Corpus Amendment Act 1679.[32] For more than three centuries such stratagems to evade habeas corpus have been unlawful in England.

[26] C Girod quoted in *La Vigilance inquiète de la Croix-Rouge à Guantanamo*, P Jarreau, Le Monde, 18 Oct 2003.

[27] *'Stress and Duress' Tactics Used on Terrorism Suspects Held in Secret Overseas Facilities*. D Priest and B Gellman, Washington Post, 26 Dec 2002.

[28] *Suicide Attempts at Guantanamo Reach 32*, Associated Press, 26 Aug 2003.

[29] *Interrogation or torture: Blurred line?*, D Van Natta Jr, New York Times, 8 Mar 2003.

[30] The Amnesty report cited above, at 23.

[31] Presidential Order s 4(3).

[32] I am indebted to Lord Bingham of Cornhill for this reference. See his Romanes Lecture given on 15 Oct 2002 in Oxford, 52 ICLQ 2003, at 841–58.

The regime applicable at Guantanamo Bay was created by a succession of presidential orders. It can be summarised quite briefly. The prisoners at Guantanamo Bay, as matters stand at present, will be tried by military tribunals. The prisoners have no access to the writ of habeas corpus to determine whether their detention is even arguably justified. The military will act as interrogators, prosecutors, defence counsel, judges, and when death sentences are imposed, as executioners. The trials will be held in secret. None of the basic guarantees for a fair trial need be observed. The jurisdiction of the United States courts is excluded. The military control everything. It is, however, in all respects subject to decisions of the President as Commander-in-Chief even in respect of guilt and innocence in individual cases as well as appropriate sentences. It is an awesome responsibility. The President has made public in advance his personal view of the prisoners as a group: he has described them all as 'killers'.

At Guantanamo Bay arrangements for the trials are proceeding with great efficiency. A courtroom with an execution chamber nearby has apparently been constructed. But the British prisoners will not be liable to be executed. The Attorney General has negotiated a separate agreement with the Pentagon on the treatment of British prisoners. He has apparently received a promise that the British prisoners of war will not face the death penalty. This gives a new dimension to the concept of 'most favoured nation' treatment in international law. How could it be morally defensible to discriminate in this way between individual prisoners? It lifts the curtain a little on the arbitrariness of what is happening at Guantanamo Bay and in the corridors of power on both sides of the Atlantic.

The United States government seeks to justify its action by relying on the *Quirin* case. It is a case rooted in the circumstances of the Second World War. Humanitarian law was not yet developed. It is worth recalling that at Yalta, Churchill, a humane man, argued that the Nazi leaders should be shot after the war as soon as they were caught. Stalin, who knew a thing or two about trials, said that they should be tried before they were shot.[33] Roosevelt had no trouble with a trial as long as it was, in his words, 'not too judicial'. That was a long time ago. In any event, the circumstances of the Nazi saboteurs were very different from the position at Guantanamo Bay. Now there has been no declared war. Congress has not authorised the military commissions. The Guantanamo Bay prisoners are subject to military prosecution for violations never before considered war crimes. They are deprived of the right of confidential communications with their lawyers, access to all relevant evidence, and judicial review—all of which were afforded to the German saboteurs. Most importantly, the status of the German saboteurs as enemy aliens was beyond dispute, whereas the 660 prisoners at Guantanamo Bay are not enemy aliens, ie, citizens of a State at war with the United States, and in any event,

[33] M Gilbert, *Winston S. Churchill*, Vol VII, *Road to Victory, 1941–1945*, at 1201–2.

are not a homogeneous group since some were captured on the battlefield in Afghanistan and some elsewhere. They are deprived of any right to test the legality of their detention. The *Quirin* case does not therefore support the action taken at Guantanamo Bay. In any event, today it is widely regarded as a sordid episode in United States history. Legal scholars are agreed, as Professor Bellknapp put it, 'that the court had fallen into step with the drums of war'.[34] Professor Danelski described *Quirin* as 'an embarrassing tale of . . . a prosecution designed to obtain the death penalty . . . a rush to judgment and agonising effort to justify a fait accompli.' He ended by saying that if there is a lesson to be learned, 'it is that the court should be wary of departing from its established rules and practices, even in times of national crisis, for at such times the court is especially susceptible to co-optation by the executive.'[35] The reliance of the United States Administration on this discredited precedent ignores more than half a century of progress of humanitarian law, notably in response to prisoners captured during armed conflict.

The Court of Appeals for the District of Columbia Circuit has recently in consolidated cases ruled that, despite the fact that the United States has had exclusive control over Guantanamo Bay since 1903, the courts have no jurisdiction to examine the legality of the detention of the prisoners. The Court of Appeals decided that it has no jurisdiction to consider the claims by nationals of Kuwait, Australia and Britain, captured by United States military forces in Afghanistan or Pakistan.[36] The applicants were not enemy aliens. Each of the applicants denied that he had engaged in hostilities against America, sought an explanation for the indefinite detention and complained of the refusal of access to legal counsel. Judge A Raymond Randolph (for the three-judge panel) concluded that the American courts had no jurisdiction because the claimants were aliens, were captured during military operations abroad, were now detained outside the United States, and had never been present in the United States. Even evidence of torture by the military authorities, however compelling, may not be examined. In other words, the court ruled that the United States government might legally evade the jurisdiction of the United States courts in the case of foreign nationals by its choice of a place of imprisonment beyond American soil. But on 10 November 2003 the United States Supreme Court granted *certiorari* for the case to proceed to a substantive hearing on the question whether the lower courts were right to conclude that they had no jurisdiction to entertain habeas corpus applications. This will be the only issue on which the Supreme Court will rule.[37] That hearing will take

34 'The Supreme Court Goes to War: The Meaning and Implications of the Nazi Saboteur case' Military Law Review, vol 89, 59, at 95.

35 *The Saboteurs' case,* Journal of Supreme Court History, vol 1, 61–82.

36 *Al Odah v US* 321 F 3d 1124 (2003).

37 The order reads as follows: 'The petitions for writs of certiorari are granted limited to the following Question: Whether United States courts lack jurisdiction to consider challenges to the legality of the detention of foreign nationals captured abroad in connection with hostilities and incarcerated at the Guantanamo Bay Naval Base, Cuba.' A powerful amicus curiae brief signed,

place in the Spring next year. When the matter is considered by the United States Supreme Court, it will have before it the considered view of our Court of Appeal. When an action was brought in British courts on behalf of a British citizen detained at Guantanamo, the Master of the Rolls, Lord Phillips of Worth Matravers, said:

> We find surprising the proposition that the writ of the United States courts does not run in respect of individuals held by the United States government on territory that the United States holds . . . under a long-term treaty.

He called it 'objectionable' that a prisoner had no opportunity to challenge the legitimacy of his detention before a court or tribunal.[38]

It is now necessary to bring some of the threads together. In doing so a distinction must be drawn between two principal features. First, on the basis of the decision of the Court of Appeals for the District of Columbia Circuit, the prisoners have no right of recourse to any courts to determine on an individual basis their status or to rule on the lawfulness of their treatment. Secondly, there is the failure of the procedures and rules governing trials before military tribunals at Guantanamo Bay to measure up to minimum international standards. I turn to the first aspect.

The United States has a long and honourable commitment to the Magna Carta and allegiance to the rule of law. In recent times extraordinary deference of the United States courts to the executive has undermined those values and principles. As matters stand at present the United States courts would refuse to hear a prisoner at Guantanamo Bay who produces credible medical evidence that he has been and is being tortured. They would refuse to hear prisoners who assert that they were not combatants at all. They would refuse to hear prisoners who assert that they were simply soldiers in the Taliban army and knew nothing about Al-Qaeda. They would refuse to examine any complaints of any individuals. The blanket presidential order deprives them all of any rights whatever. As a lawyer brought up to admire the ideals of American democracy and justice, I would have to say that I regard this as a monstrous failure of justice.

In English law the writ of habeas corpus protects citizens and aliens alike. That is how it should be because foreign nationals must obey our laws and therefore deserve the protection of our laws. The writ is available whenever the detained person enters territory under the control of the Crown. That is consistent with human rights law. In *Cyprus v Turkey* (1982), the European Court of Human Rights held that States are: 'bound to secure the said rights and freedoms of all persons under their actual authority and responsibility, whether that authority is exercised within their own territory or abroad'.[39] Let

inter alia, by Sir Sydney Kentridge QC, Colin Nicholls QC, and Timothy Otty on the law of habeas corpus has been placed before the United States Supreme Court.

[38] *R (Abbasi) v The Secretary of State for Foreign Affairs* [2002] EWCA Civ 1598.

[39] 1982 4 EHRR 482, at 586, para 8.

me illustrate the point. Reports have been published in the media and by human rights groups of the detention of suspected Al-Qaeda suspects at the United States military facility at Diego Garcia.[40] The British government has denied this allegation. One must accept this categorical assurance. But if the allegation had been true, the writ of habeas corpus would have been available in respect of prisoners at the United States military facility because this small island is part of British Indian Ocean Territory and is leased to the United States. It would have been sufficient that the British government controls the territory. Until 11 September the understanding of the law of habeas corpus would have been the same in the United States. Deference to the executive has so far eroded the cardinal principles of habeas corpus. By denying the prisoners the right to raise challenges in a court about their alleged status and treatment, the United States government is in breach of the minimum standards of customary international law. The importance of this right is underlined by the experience of the Gulf war when the military held about 1,200 hearings to assess the status of captured prisoners, and about two-thirds were found not to be combatants.[41] It is surely likely that in the chaos of the Afghanistan war and its aftermath the United States military forces picked up a great many who were not even combatants.

While my focus is on the prisoners at Guantanamo Bay, denial of justice to foreigners was bound to erode the civil liberties of citizens in the United States. It was said that the Patriot Act is largely targeted at foreign nationals. The background is that 20 million non-citizens living in the United States cannot vote. In a book published in May this year David Cole, Professor at Georgetown University Law Centre, has shown how oppressive treatment of foreign nationals paves the way for similar measures against American citizens.[42] In recent times the United States government has imposed military custody on two United States citizens. In *Hamdi* the prisoner had been arrested on the battlefield in Afghanistan. In January 2002 he was transported to Guantanamo Bay. In April 2002 he was moved to military detention at a military base in Norfolk, Virginia. The Court of Appeals for the Fourth Circuit upheld the indefinite military detention of the prisoner as an unlawful combatant.[43] Padilla is an American citizen arrested on American soil. In June 2002 he was transferred to a military brig in South Carolina. He challenged the lawfulness of his detention. A District judge held that 'the commission of a judge . . . does not run to deciding de novo whether Padilla is associated with

[40] *Questioning Terror Suspects in a Surreal World*, D Van Natta Jr, New York Times, 16 Mar 2003. *Wake-Up call to UK government on torture*, Amnesty International, 7 Mar 2003.

[41] D Cole, *Enemy Aliens: Double Standards and Constitutional Freedoms in the War on Terrorism*. 2003, at 42.

[42] (As n 37).

[43] *Hamdi v Rumsfeld* (ED Va 11 June 2002) (No 02 CV 439); (4th Cir 12 July 2002) (No 02-6895); (ED Va 16 Aug 2002) (No 2: 02 CV 439); (4th Cir 8 Jan 2003) (No 02-7338); (4th Cir 9 July 2003) (No 02-7228).

Al Qaeda and whether he should therefore be detained as an enemy combatant'.[44] Previously, there had been very little protest about the United States government's actions at Guantanamo Bay. But the action against United States citizens has caused a chorus of disapproval. Objectively these protests are justified but inherent in them are double standards which are deeply troubling. In a review of David Cole's book in the New York Review of Books Anthony Lewis commented:[45] 'We must respect the humanity of aliens lest we devalue our own. And because it is the right thing to do.' That observation is one that we, in the United Kingdom, ought also to heed.

Let me now turn to the second matter. The question is whether the quality of justice envisaged for the prisoners at Guantanamo Bay complies with minimum international standards for the conduct of fair trials. The answer can be given quite shortly: it is a resounding 'No'. The military commissions contemplated by the United States government have been described by Professor Ronald Dworkin as the type of trials one associates with utterly lawless totalitarian regimes.[46] David Pannick QC invoked Joseph Kafka's *The Trial* in which the great novelist describes how Kafka's advocate warns him of the difficulties of presenting a defence when 'the proceedings were not only kept secret from the general public, but from the accused as well.' But as David Pannick observed, Kafka could see his lawyer, however incompetent, and there was a court, however imperfect, making the decision.[47] The military commissions are not independent courts or tribunals. The term 'kangaroo court' springs to mind. It derives from the jumps of the kangaroo, and conveys the idea of a pre-ordained arbitrary rush to judgment by an irregular tribunal which makes a mockery of justice. Internationally military commissions at Guantanamo Bay will be so regarded. Trials of the type contemplated by the United States government would be a stain on United States justice. The only thing that could be worse is simply to leave the prisoners in their black hole indefinitely.

Does the United States Administration care about international opinion? In his dissenting opinion in *Atkins v Virgina*,[48] which was concurred in by the Chief Justice and Justice Thomas, Justice Scalia observed in a death penalty case: 'Equally irrelevant are the practices of the world "community", whose notions of justice are (thankfully) not always those of our people.' This isolationist approach may also be the response of the United States government to criticism about Guantanamo Bay. On the other hand, there may possibly be winds of change. On 26 June 2003 the Supreme Court by a majority decision in *Lawrence et al v Texas* overruled an earlier Supreme Court decision in

44 *Padilla v Bush* (SDNY 4 Dec 2002) (No 01 Civ 4445 (MBM)).

45 *Un-American Activities,* Anthony Lewis, New York Review of Books, Vol L, No 16, 23 Oct 2003, at 19.

46 *The Threat to Patriotism,* New York Review of Books, 28 Nov 2002, 44.

47 The Times, 25 Mar 2003, Law 4.

48 20 June 2002, 122 Supreme Ct 2242 (2002).

Bowers v Hardwick,[49] which had upheld Georgia's sodomy law as constitutional. For the first time in its history the court (as opposed to individual justices) relied on international human rights law and practice. Justice Kennedy observed:

> When homosexual conduct is made criminal by the law of the State, that declaration in and of itself is an invitation to subject homosexual persons to discrimination both in the public and private spheres. The central holding of *Bowers* has been brought into question by this case, and it should be addressed. Its continuance as precedent demeans the lives of homosexual persons.

Justice Scalia, with whom Chief Justice Rehnquist and Justice Thomas agreed, said that the majority had signed up to what he called the homosexual agenda. He observed:

> The court's discussion of these foreign views (ignoring, of course, the many countries that have retained criminal prohibitions on sodomy) is . . . meaningless dicta. Dangerous dicta, however, since this court . . . should not impose foreign moods, fads, or fashions on Americans.

The relevance of this ongoing debate about the place of United States law in a global world is, of course, that it may in time become possible in the United States to look at Guantanamo Bay in the context of human rights law and humanitarian law regarding the rights of captured prisoners. It is also just possible that the Supreme Court could be persuaded to rule that United States courts have jurisdiction to entertain habeas corpus applications from prisoners at Guantanamo Bay. That would be an important vindication of the rule of law, but it would leave the prisoners at Guantanamo Bay with a long struggle to attain (a) justice on the merits of their habeas corpus applications, and (b) fair trials before regular courts.

So far I have considered what is happening at Guantanamo Bay in largely legal terms. There is, however, a wider view. Looking at the hard realities of the situation, one wonders what effect it may have on the treatment of United States soldiers captured in future armed conflicts. It would have been prudent, for the sake of American soldiers, to respect humanitarian law. Secondly, what must authoritarian regimes, or countries with dubious human rights records, make of the example set by the most powerful of all democracies? In his recent John Galway Foster lecture, Professor Koh of Yale University has shown how many foreign governments, who want to free themselves of the restraints of human rights, have already directly invoked the United States policy in regard to the Guantanamo Bay prisoners as justification for their actions.[50] Thirdly, the type of justice meted out at Guantanamo Bay is likely to make martyrs of the prisoners in the moderate Muslim world with whom the West must work to ensure world peace and stability.

[49] 478 US 186 (1986).
[50] *The United States and Human Rights*, Oct 2003, London.

What other route could the United States have taken? The International Criminal Court could not be used to try the Guantanamo Bay prisoners because the Rome Treaty applies prospectively only, and the prisoners were captured before the Treaty came into force in July 2002. The United States courts could have assumed universal jurisdiction for war crimes. The prisoners would have received fair trials before ordinary United States courts. It would have been an acceptable solution. On the other hand, the Muslim world would probably not have accepted this as impartial justice. The best course would have been to set up through the Security Council an ad hoc international tribunal. That would have ensured that justice is done and seen to be done.

There is, of course, a dilemma facing democracies. Aharon Barak, President of the Supreme Court of Israel, presided in a case in which the court held that the violent interrogation of a suspected terrorist is not lawful even if doing so may save human life by preventing impending terrorist acts. He confronted the problem created for democracies by terrorism. He said: [51]

> We are aware that this decision does not make it easier to deal with the reality. This is the fate of democracy, as not all means are acceptable to it, and not all methods employed by its enemies are open to it. Sometimes, a democracy must fight with one hand tied behind its back. Nonetheless, it has the upper hand. Preserving the rule of law and recognition of individual liberties constitute an important component of its understanding of security. At the end of the day, they strengthen its spirit and strength and allow it to overcome its difficulties.

Such restraint is at the very core of democratic values.

It may be appropriate to pose a question: ought our government to make plain publicly and unambiguously our condemnation of the utter lawlessness at Guantanamo Bay?[52] John Donne, who preached in the Chapel of Lincoln's Inn, gave the context of the question more than four centuries ago:

> No man is an Island, entire of it self; every man is a piece of the Continent, a part of the main; . . . any man's death diminishes me, because I am involved in Mankind; And therefore never send to know for whom the bell tolls; it tolls for thee.

[51] The citation relies on the magisterial essay of President Aharon Barak, 'A Judge on Judging: The Role of a Supreme Court in a Democracy', Harvard LR vol 116, no 1 Nov 2002, at 148.

[52] I have been greatly helped in preparing this lecture by my wife, Susan, by Laura Johnson, my judicial assistant, and by Alex Glassbrook, my son-in-law.

[15]

Terrorism and the Non-derogability of Non-refoulement

RENE BRUIN* AND KEES WOUTERS**

Abstract

After the terrorist attacks on 11 September 2001, is it permitted to strike a balance between the national security of a State and the obligation to provide protection against *refoulement*? In the war on terrorism, this option seems to be open for discussion. Although no uniform or single definition of terrorism in international law exists, it is clear that the *opinio communis* wants the perpetrators, planners or facilitators to be prosecuted. If they flee prosecution, no safe haven should be granted. Membership of a terrorist organization cannot in itself be qualified as a terrorist act. Nevertheless, the danger exists that mere membership will suffice to be excluded from refugee status or from protection against *refoulement*. The European Commission has stated in a Working Document that the European Court of Human Rights should reconsider the decisions in which the absolute character of Article 3 ECHR was laid down. In the *Suresh* case, the Canadian Supreme Court deemed a decision to expel to be possible even if there is a chance the alien will become a victim of a human rights violation as proscribed in Article 3 Convention Against Torture. If there are reasonable grounds for regarding a refugee a danger to the national security or the community of the country of refuge, he is not protected against *refoulement* under Article 33 (1) Refugee Convention. This rule needs to be interpreted restrictively and applied with particular caution. The assessment of the danger needs to be individual and *ex futuro*. Article 33 (2) Refugee Convention allows *refoulement* if a provable danger to the national security or community of the country of refuge exists, unless *refoulement* entails a risk of the individual being subjected to torture or inhuman or degrading treatment or punishment. In such cases *refoulement* is prohibited. The obligation of *non-refoulement* under Article 3 of the European Convention on Human Rights, Article 7 International Covenant on Civil and Political Rights and Article 3 Convention Against Torture is absolute. No exceptions and no derogations are permitted, not even if an alleged terrorist constitutes a

* Rene Bruin is a lawyer and senior staff member of the refugee department of the Dutch section of Amnesty International.

** Kees Wouters is a legal researcher and lecturer at the Institute of Immigration Law of the Universiteit Leiden, the Netherlands and the E.M. Meijers Institute of Legal Studies, Leiden University, where he is conducting a PhD research on the different obligations of *non-refoulement* in international law. He is also a lecturer at and staff member of the Office of Human Rights at Mahidol University, Thailand.

danger to the national security of a country. In search of a way to derogate from the obligations of *non-refoulement*, States may look for safety guarantees to allow expulsion. In cases involving the imposition or the carrying out of legal sentences, for example the death penalty, the issue of guarantees is clear. However, cases involving extra-judicial acts like torture are much more complicated. There is a real risk that a balancing act can be avoided and will be 'found' in the assessment of the risk of being subjected to prohibited treatment by trying to expel an alien after guarantees have been obtained. We believe exclusion is no solution and prosecution of alleged terrorists may be a better solution than co-operating with further violations of human rights by refraining to give protection. The possibility of prosecuting perpetrators of serious human rights violations is quickly gaining ground. The legal tension between absolute protection against *refoulement* and the States' responsibility for national security can be reduced, now that States can hold those who have perpetrated serious violations of human rights and humanitarian law criminally accountable. We strongly urge States to uphold the non-derogability of *non-refoulement* and to take those steps necessary to prosecute perpetrators of serious human rights violations.

1. Introduction

The attack on the World Trade Center and the Pentagon on 11 September 2001 has led to serious world-wide discussions. Many changes have been suggested, especially in the field of migration and asylum. The fear of new attacks has led to new case law and a number of proposals in which the issue of national security is gaining momentum. The attacks on the United States could mean a turning point in applying obligations of *non-refoulement*.

This article addresses the balance between issues of national security and the protection against *refoulement*. We will discuss several developments that have a direct influence on obligations of *non-refoulement*. These include both global as well as European developments. Within the United Nations several resolutions have been adopted, both by the General Assembly as well as the Security Council.[1] Security Council resolution 1373 (28 September 2001) is of major importance regarding asylum law.

Within Europe, the European Commission of the European Communities has adopted a Working Document entitled: 'The Relationship between safeguarding internal security and complying with international protection obligations and instruments'. In this document a 'balancing act' between the protection needs of the individual, set off against the security interests of a State, is mentioned. Of further interest is the proposal for a Council Directive on minimum standards for the qualifications and status of third country nationals and stateless persons as refugees or as persons who otherwise need international

[1] UNGA res. 56/1, 18 Sept. 2001; SC res. 1368, 12 Sept. 2001; SC res. 1373, 28 Sept. 2001; SC res. 1377, 12 Nov. 2001.

protection. We will focus on the negotiations and redrafting of articles 14, 17 and 19 of this proposal, dealing with the exclusion from a protection status and the principle of *non-refoulement.*

Furthermore, to illustrate the political debate concerning terrorism, the judgment of the Canadian Supreme Court in the Suresh case will also be discussed. With explicit reference to the events of 11 September 2001 the Court considered a fair balance not in violation of the obligation of *non-refoulement.* The focus of this article will be on the non-derogability of some of the most important obligations of *non-refoulement.* Finally, we will describe the possibility of expulsion after having received assurances regarding the safety of the person to be deported and the possibility of prosecution to eliminate the dangers of terrorist activities.

2. The war on terrorism: global and European developments

2.1 UN Security Council Resolution 1373

In Security Council resolution 1373, States are called upon to:

> (f) take appropriate measures in conformity with the relevant provisions of national and international law, including international standards of human rights, before granting refugee status, for the purpose of ensuring that the asylum-seeker has not planned, facilitated or participated in the commission of terrorist acts;
> (g) ensure, in conformity with international law, that refugee status is not abused by the perpetrators, organizers or facilitators of terrorist acts, and that claims of political motivation are not recognized as grounds for refusing requests for the extradition of alleged terrorists.[2]

The text indicates that Member States are called upon to exclude terrorists from refugee status under Article 1F of the 1951 Refugee Convention even though their actions may be politically motivated. In this resolution terrorism is conceptualized as acts that can be defined as terrorism. Excludable are those persons that have committed, planned or one way or the other contributed to these acts. However, no uniform international definition of terrorism exists. It remains the prerogative of States to decide who is excludable from refugee status as a terrorist. Based on this resolution, could it be that a member of an alleged terrorist organization solely because of his membership be excluded from refugee status? One can argue, only if being a member

[2] SC res. 1373 28 Sept. 2001. Contrary to UNGA res. 51/210, 17 Dec. 1996 with Annex 'the Declaration to Supplement the 1994 Declaration on Measures to Eliminate International Protection', SC res. 1373 has no explicit reference to the obligation of *non-refoulement* as laid down in the 1951 Refugee Convention.

in itself is a terrorist act. However, that rule is nowhere to be found. The relevant question is whether or not membership of and/or sympathizing with an alleged terrorist organization is a legitimate ground for excluding a person from refugee status. In the U.N. Draft Comprehensive Convention on International Terrorism, currently under preparation, membership of a terrorist organization in itself is not listed as an offence within the meaning of this Convention.[3] Even though exclusion does not seem to be in accordance with this draft convention or resolution 1373, there is a genuine danger that the listing of an organization as a terrorist organization will have a significant impact on exclusion cases. Yet, the international community has no uniform idea which organization should be characterized as a terrorist organization. For example, Canada and the United States have both listed the Tamil opposition group in Sri Lanka, the LTTE, as a terrorist organization. However, the LTTE is not mentioned on a list prepared by the European Union.[4] It is obvious that characterizing an organization as terrorists is to a large extent based on a political motivation and can have profound political impact.

2.2 The European Commission Working Document

On 20 September 2001 the European Council on Justice and Home Affairs adopted several conclusions (SN 3926/6/01). In these conclusions, the Council requests the competent authorities of Member States: to strengthen controls at external borders (conclusion 24); request Member States to apply procedures for the issue of visas with maximum rigour (conclusion 26); invites those States participating in the Schengen Information System (SIS) to provide more systematic input into the system of alerts under Articles 95, 96 and 99 of the Schengen Convention (conclusion 27); and invites the Commission to examine urgently the relationship between safeguarding internal security and complying with international protection obligations and instruments (conclusion 29). According to the European Commission, consideration is being given on how existing EU legislation can be made 'terrorism proof' (Report from the Commission, 17 October 2001 (COM (2001) 611).

Furthermore, the European Commission has presented a proposal for a Council Framework Decision on the European arrest warrant and the surrender procedures between the Member States (COM (2001) 522) and a proposal for a Council Framework Decision on combating terrorism (COM (2001) 521).

[3] Article 2 Draft Comprehensive Convention on International Terrorism, UN doc. A/C.6/56/L.9, 29 Oct. 2001.

[4] European Council Common Position, 17 June 2002, Official Journal of the European Communities, L 160/32.

On 5 December 2001 the European Commission finalized a Working Document entitled: 'The relationship between safeguarding internal security and complying with international protection obligations and instruments' (COM (2001) 743 final).

A Common Position of the Council of the European Union on the application of specific measures to combat terrorism was adopted on 27 December 2001 (Official Journal of the European Communities, 28 December 2001, L 344/70). The adopted measures include the freezing of funds and other financial assets or economic resources of persons, groups and entities listed in the Annex. The Annex contains a list of persons, groups and entities that are involved in terrorist acts (29 individuals and 13 groups). Updated lists have been published on 2 May 2002 (Official Journal of the European Communities, 3 May 2002, L116/75), 17 June 2002 (Official Journal of the European Communities, 18 June 2002, L 160/32) and 28 October 2002 (Official Journal of the European Communities, 30 October 2002, L 295/1). The list now comprises 35 individuals and 32 groups.

The Working Document of 5 December 2001 clearly indicates that the European Commission wants to nullify the non-derogability of Article 3 of the European Convention on Human Rights (ECHR). This stems from the following text: (paragraph 2.3.1, p. 16):

> The European Court of Human Rights has repeatedly affirmed that the European Convention on Human Rights, even in the most difficult circumstances, such as the fight against terrorism and organised crime, prohibits, in absolute terms, torture and inhuman or degrading treatment or punishment. The European Court of Human Rights has emphasised that, unlike most of the substantive clauses of that particular Convention, Article 3 makes no provision for exceptions and no derogation from it is permissible even in the event of a public emergency threatening the life of the nation. Following the 11th September events, the European Court of Human Rights may in the future again have to rule on questions relating to the interpretation of Article 3, in particular on the question in how far there can be a "*balancing act*" [emphasis added, authors] between the protection needs of the individual, set off against the security interests of a state. "And in paragraph 2.4 (p. 17)" In addition to their possible criminal prosecution it may also be necessary to harmonise the basic rights granted to this category of excludable but non-removable persons, and to assess the different means for dealing with these persons if they pose a security risk.

It is clear that the Commission wants to initiate an investigation to examine possible measures other than prosecution that can be adopted against terrorists and other serious criminals. In paragraph 2.3.2 of the document the Commission writes:

> Extradition must be considered legal when it is possible to obtain legal guarantees from the State that is going to try the person, addressing the

concerns connected to the potential violations of the European Convention of Human Rights. Such 'guarantees' by third States could for instance relate to the non-application of capital punishment in that particular case, though the law of that State allows for such punishment.

Surprisingly, there is no mention of guarantees regarding the risk of being subjected to torture, inhuman or degrading treatment or punishment.

Several important legal questions arise from reading the Working Document. First, how will the European Court of Human Rights deal with the political pressure in adopting a 'balancing act' between the protection needs of the individual and the security interests of a State? Second, a more fundamental question is whether or not Article 3 ECHR leaves any room for adopting a 'balancing act'. In the *Ahmed*[5] and *Chahal*[6] cases, the European Court considered that the respective applicants could not be expelled under Article 3 ECHR even though Article 33 (2) of the Refugee Convention was applicable and the applicants could not claim protection under the obligation of *refoulement* laid down in Article 33 (1) Refugee Convention. A final question concerns the influence of legal (safety) guarantees regarding the obligation of *refoulement.*

Articles 14 and 17 of the proposal for a Council Directive on minimum standards for the qualifications and status of third country nationals and stateless persons as refugees or as persons who otherwise need international protection (COM (2001) 510 final, d.d.12 September 2001) have been changed drastically.[7] Both articles deal with the exclusion of persons in need of protection. Articles 14 and 17 oblige Member States not to grant refugee status or subsidiary protection to applicants if undeserving. In previous drafts, paragraph 4 of both Articles stated that not granting international protection to those undeserving of it, 'is without prejudice to Member States' obligations under international law, in particular under the European Convention on Human Rights'. Both paragraphs are of the utmost importance in the context of this article. The Commission upheld the absolute character of Article 3 ECHR. However, since then the Commission has changed its attitude. We have noticed above the text of the Working Document of December 2001. In the last version of the proposal for a Council Directive on minimum standards for the qualifications and status of third country nationals and stateless persons as

[5] *Ahmed v. Austria*, (17 Dec. 1996), European Court of Human Rights, Appl.no. 25964/94.

[6] *Chahal v. United Kingdom*, (15 Nov. 1996), European Court on Human Rights, Appl.no. 22414/93.

[7] See Council of Europe, Asylum Working Party , Document ASILE 45, Brussels 25 September 2002.

refugees or as persons who otherwise need international protection, dated 25 September 2002, paragraph 4 has been deleted for both Articles. In addition, the first paragraph of Article 19 stipulates that Member States shall respect the principle of *non-refoulement* in accordance with their international obligations. In spite of that, paragraph 2 reads as follows:

> Without prejudice to paragraph 1, a Member State may refoule a refugee or a person eligible for subsidiary protection when there are reasonable grounds for considering:
>
> (a) him or her as a danger to the security of the country in which he or she is; or
> (b) having been convicted by a final judgement of a particular serious crime, he or she constitutes a danger to the community of that country.

It is obvious that the absolute character of Article 3 ECHR, Article 3 Convention against Torture and Article 7 of the International Covenant on Civil and Political Rights is not reflected in this proposal.

2.3 The *Suresh* case

In the *Suresh* case,[8] the Supreme Court of Canada considered whether expulsion or deportation of an alien is prohibited if there is a substantial risk of torture except if the alien constitutes a serious danger to the national security of Canada. An alien involved in terrorist activities could not claim protection.

Suresh is a Sri Lankan citizen of Tamil descent. In 1990 he entered Canada and was recognized as a Convention refugee in April 1991. In the summer of 1991, Suresh applied for landed immigrant status in Canada. His application was not finalized and in late 1995 Canada started proceedings to deport Suresh to Sri Lanka on security grounds.

Since his youth, Suresh was a member of the LTTE and is now a member of the LTTE executive. He is well-known within the LTTE and is mainly involved in fundraising for the LTTE. The Canadian authorities acknowledged the fact that Suresh has not personally committed any acts of violence either in Canada or Sri Lanka. His activities on Canadian soil were non-violent in nature. However, they concluded that membership of the LTTE, an organization listed as a terrorist organization by Canada, was a sufficient ground for deportation. The Canadian authorities recognized that Suresh would be at risk on returning to Sri Lanka, but that this risk was difficult to assess and that it might be tempered by his high profile. They

[8] *Suresh v. Canada*, (11 Jan. 2002), Supreme Court of Canada, 2002 SCC 1, File no. 27790, published on www/lexum.umontreal.ca/csc-scc/en/rec.

concluded that expulsion or deportation of Suresh was legitimate. Both the judicial review as well as the appeal were dismissed. Eventually Suresh appealed to the Supreme Court of Canada.

The main legal issue in the *Suresh* case was whether Canadian Law precluded deportation to a country where Suresh ran a risk of being tortured. Related questions were concerned with when there is a danger to the national security of Canada (regarding combating terrorism) and whether mere membership of an alleged terrorist organization sufficed.

The main legal issue indicated a balancing act between the protection needs of Suresh (that is, the risk of being tortured upon return) and the security interests of Canada. According to the Canadian Supreme Court, a balancing act is permitted but needs to be in accordance with the principles of fundamental justice. These principles are defined by Canadian municipal law and applicable international law.

From the Canadian domestic perspective, the Supreme Court concluded that:

> The outcome [of the balancing act] will depend not only on considerations inherent in the general context but also on considerations related to the circumstances and condition of the particular person whom the government seeks to expel. (. . .) Canadian jurisprudence suggests that this balance will usually come down against expelling a person to face torture elsewhere (paragraph 58).

After careful consideration, the Supreme Court seems to conclude that only a small or theoretical possibility exists for deporting a recognized refugee to face torture. The Supreme Court went on:

> We have examined the argument that from the perspective of Canadian law to deport a Convention refugee to torture violates the principles of fundamental justice (paragraph 59)

and in paragraph 75:

> We conclude that the better view is that international law rejects deportation to torture, even where national security interests are at stake. This is the norm which best informs the content of the principles of fundamental justice under s. 7 of the Charter.

Here, the Supreme Court referred to the Convention Against Torture and Other Cruel, Inhuman or Degrading Treatment and Punishment (CAT) and the International Covenant on Civil and Political Rights (ICCPR).

In spite of this small, and in our opinion, rather theoretical possibility to apply a balancing test the Supreme Court leaves the door open that 'in an exceptional case such deportation might be justified (. . .) in the balancing approach (. . .)' (paragraph 129).

In this regard the Canadian Supreme Court raises the question how terms like 'danger to the security of Canada' and 'terrorism' need to be defined. According to the Supreme Court, the security of Canada is in danger if there is a real and serious possibility of adverse effect to Canada. However, the threat need not be direct; rather it may be grounded in distant events that indirectly have a real possibility of harming Canadian security (paragraph 88). The term terrorism has no single internationally accepted definition. The Supreme Court referred to the recently adopted International Convention for the Suppression of the Financing of Terrorism.[9] This Convention defines terrorism in two ways. First, it employs a functional definition in Article 2 (a) by defining terrorism as 'any act which constitutes an offence within the scope of and as defined in one of the treaties listed in the annex' (consisting of nine treaties that are commonly viewed as relating to terrorist acts) and second, this offence-based definition is supplemented by a stipulative definition in Article 2 (1) (b):

> any act intended to cause death or serious bodily injury to a civilian, or to any other person not taking an active part in the hostilities in a situation of armed conflict, when the purpose of such act, by its nature or context, is to intimidate a population, or to compel a government or an international organization to do or to abstain from doing any act.

The Supreme Court concluded that both the terms 'danger to the security of Canada' and 'terrorism' are not defined as unconstitutionally vague. It was concluded that deportation of Suresh was *prima facie* permitted provided the Minister certified him to be a substantial danger to Canada and provided he was found to be engaged in terrorism or a member of a terrorist organization (paragraph 99).

In the end, the Supreme Court concluded that Suresh made a *prima facie* case that he might be tortured on return if expelled to Sri Lanka and that accordingly he should have been provided with the necessary procedural safeguards. Because these safeguards were not provided for, the case was remanded to the Minister for reconsideration (paragraph 130).

With regard to the standard that should be adopted with respect to the Minister's decision that a refugee constituted a danger to the security of Canada, the Supreme Court considered that the reviewing court:

> should adopt a deferential approach to this question and should set aside the Minister's discretionary decision if it is patently unreasonable in the sense that it was made arbitrarily or in bad faith, it cannot be supported on the evidence, or the Minister failed to consider the appropriate factors. The Court should not reweigh the factors or interfere merely because it would have come to a different conclusion (paragraph 29).

[9] UNGA res. 54/109, 9 Dec. 1999, entry into force 10 April 2002.

Clearly, according to the Supreme Court, the Minister has a discretionary power and the courts should adopt a test of reasonableness. The Supreme Court emphasized this in the following quote (paragraph 33):

> (. . .) the recent events in New York and Washington. They are a reminder that in matters of national security, the cost of failure can be high. *This seems to me to underline the need for the judicial arm of government to respect the decisions of ministers of the Crown on the question of whether support for terrorist activities in a foreign country constitutes a threat to national security*. It is not only that the executive has access to special information and expertise in these matters. It is also that such decisions, with serious potential results for the community, require a legitimacy which can be conferred only by entrusting them to persons responsible to the community through the democratic process. If the people are to accept the consequences of such decisions, they must be made by persons whom the people have elected and whom they can remove. [Emphasis added.]

Like the European Court of Human Rights, we do not see any reason for judicial restraint in assessing a possible danger to national security.

Finally, we note that the Canadian Supreme Court considers deportation of a refugee to face torture should only be permitted in exceptional cases. However, it did not, in our opinion, make clear why the *Suresh* case was exceptional.

3. Terrorism in international law

There is no uniform or single definition of terrorism in international law. Since 1963 a number of global and regional treaties have been drafted and adopted in which specific crimes have been defined that are commonly viewed as terrorist acts.[10] Among these offences are hijacking, kidnapping and bombing. It stems from these treaties that terrorism is a collective term for a number of serious offences for which

[10] Global Conventions: 1963 Convention on Offences and Certain Other Acts Committed on Board Aircraft, 1970 Convention for the Suppression of Unlawful Seizure of Aircraft, 1971 Convention for the Suppression of Unlawful Acts against the Safety of Civil Aviation, 1973 Convention on the Prevention and Punishment of Crimes against Internationally Protected Persons, 1979 International Convention against the Taking of Hostages, 1980 Convention on the Physical Protection of Nuclear Material, 1988 Protocol on the Suppression of Unlawful Acts of Violence at Airports Serving International Aviation, 1988 Convention for the Suppression of Unlawful Acts against the Safety of Maritime Navigation, 1988 Protocol for the Suppression of Unlawful Acts against the Safety of Fixed Platforms Located on the Continental Shelf, 1991 Convention on the Marking of Plastic Explosives for the Purpose of Detection, 1997 International Convention for the Suppression of Terrorist Bombings and the 1999 International Convention for the Suppression on the Financing of Terrorism. Regional Conventions: 1971 OAS Convention to Prevent and Punish Acts of Terrorism Taking the Form of Crimes against Persons and Related Extortion that are of International Significance, 1977 European Convention on the Suppression of Terrorism, 1987 SAARC Regional Convention on Suppression of Terrorism, 1998 Arab Convention on the Suppression of Terrorism, 1999 Convention of the Islamic Conference on Combating International Terrorism, 1999 OAU Convention on the Prevention and Combating of Terrorism and the 1999 Treaty on Co-operation among States Members of the Commonwealth of Independent States Combating Terrorism.

persons should be prosecuted. By focusing on the act rather than the actor, an objective legal concept is created by which the difficult issue of terrorism versus freedom fighting can be resolved.

This legal concept does not seem to correspond with the current political train of thought. For example, the European Union, Canada and the United States have all drafted lists of terrorist groups. The mere fact that a person is a member of a listed organization suffices to characterize this person as a terrorist. It will not be necessary to determine whether or not this person is responsible for any act described in the above mentioned treaties. At most one can argue that members of the listed groups have committed terrorist acts in the past. Therefore, the suspicion might exist that this person was one way or the other involved in these acts. Nevertheless, an individual assessment needs to be made whether or not this person can be held criminally responsible for a certain terrorist act. In this respect the presumption of innocence is very important.[11]

The thin line between fighting for freedom or self-determination and terrorism became clear during the negotiations on drafting a Statute for the International Criminal Court (ICC). Talks were held to include terrorism as one of the crimes for which the ICC should have jurisdiction. However, no agreement was reached on a definition of terrorism. A number of States suggested defining terrorism as a crime against humanity.[12] This proposal was rejected, among others, by the United States, for the following reasons: (a) the offence (terrorism) was not clearly defined; (b) the inclusion of terrorism as a crime would politicize the ICC; (c) some terrorist acts would not be sufficiently serious to warrant prosecution by an international court; (d) prosecution and punishment by national courts was considered more efficient and (e) the ICC Statute does not make any difference between terrorism and the struggle for self-determination.[13]

We share the criticism of the United States: Terrorism is a political term and not a legal term.

4. The obligations of *non-refoulement* and national security interests of states

4.1 Articles 1F and 33 (2) of the 1951 Refugee Convention

There are several ways by which States can refuse entry to individuals who constitute a danger to the security of the State. Within Europe, for

[11] See Article 14 (2) ICCPR, Article 6 (2) ECRM, Article 7 (1) African Charter on Human and Peoples' Rights and Article 8 (2) American Convention on Human Rights.

[12] UN doc. A/CONF.183/C.1/L 27.

[13] Antonio Cassese, 'Terrorism is also disrupting some crucial legal categories of international law', (2001) *European Journal of International Law* website (www.ejil.org), World Trade Center Forum.

example, States parties to the Schengen Agreement can issue an alert in the joint Schengen Information System for the purpose of refusing entry (Article 96 Schengen Agreement). In practice, States can also simply stop an alien from entering the country or refrain from giving access to asylum procedures, for example, by strictly applying the concept of safe third countries. In its Working Document of 5 December 2001 the European Commission proposed the immediate suspension or *freezing* of the actual examination of the asylum request in two situations (paragraph 1.4.2.1): first, 'in cases in which an international criminal tribunal has indicted the individual who has claimed asylum', and secondly, 'where an extradition request from a country other than the country of origin of the asylum seeker, relating to serious crimes, is pending'.

These measures could all be taken by States when confronted with an asylum seeker who might fall under Article 1F Refugee Convention, by which asylum seekers are excluded from refugee status because there are serious reasons for considering that they have committed particularly serious crimes. However, it is also possible for States to apply Article 33 (2) of the Refugee Convention. Contrary to Article 1F, this Article applies to persons who are recognized as refugees.

The relationship between Article 1F and Article 33 (2) of the Refugee Convention is complex, both in terms of offences that fall within the scope of the Articles as well as the applicable standard of proof. We believe that Article 1F applies to those persons who have committed certain offences outside the country of refuge and before they have applied for asylum. On the other hand, Article 33 (2) Refugee Convention in principle applies to those persons who have committed offences or are planning to commit offences within the country of refuge. However, offences committed outside the country of refuge do not necessarily fall outside the scope of Article 33 (2) if the perpetrator constitutes a danger to the security of the country of refuge. The objective of Article 33 (2) is the protection of the country of refuge, whereas the objective of Article 1F is to define who should be excluded from refugee status. Excludable persons cannot claim protection against *refoulement* under Article 33 (1) of the Refugee Convention.

According to Article 33 (2) of the Refugee Convention, a refugee is not protected against *refoulement* if there are *reasonable grounds* for regarding the refugee as a danger to the security of the country in which he or she is, or who, having been convicted by a final judgment of a particular serious crime, constitutes a danger to the community in that country. The threshold for applying Article 33 (2) is high. The standard of proof is higher than when applying Article 1F. Hathaway and Harvey write: 'In particular, the evidentiary standard for denying protection under Article 33(2), "reasonable grounds", is higher than that for exclusion under Article 1F(b), "serious reasons for considering" '.[14] Contrary to excludable persons under Article 1F, Article 33 (2) applies to refugees who in principle have a right to be protected. Therefore, the exception needs to be applied restrictively. In the 1997 Note on the Principle of *Non-refoulement*, UNHCR wrote that: '14. In view of the serious consequences to a refugee of being returned to a country where he is in danger of persecution, the exception provided for in Article 33(2) should be applied with the greatest caution. It is necessary to take fully into account all the circumstances of the case (. . .)'.[15] Furthermore, Lauterpacht and Bethlehem write: 'given the humanitarian character of *non-refoulement* and the serious consequences to a refugee or asylum seeker of being returned to a country where he or she is in danger, the exceptions to *non-refoulement* must be interpreted restrictively and applied with particular caution'.[16]

4.1.1 Danger to the security of the country

When does a refugee constitute a danger to the national security of a country? The text of Article 33 (2) Refugee Convention indicates that there needs to be a danger to the country of refuge. Therefore, danger to other States or to the international community falls outside the scope of this Article. Lauterpacht and Bethlehem write:

> It does not address circumstances in which there is a possibility of danger to the security of other countries or to the international community more generally. While there is nothing in the 1951 Refugee Convention which limits a State from taking measures to control activity within its territory or persons subject to its jurisdiction that may pose a danger to the security of other States or of the international community, they cannot do so, in the case of refugees or asylum seekers, by way of *refoulement*.[17]

In the *Suresh* case, the Canadian Supreme Court indicates it knows the history of Article 33 (2) Refugee Convention by considering that there needs to be a danger to Canada (paragraph 90). However, the Supreme Court believes this approach is no longer valid. According to the Supreme Court, the security of one State depends on the security of other States. The Supreme Court further considers: 'It may once have made sense to suggest that terrorism in one country did not necessarily implicate other countries. But after the year 2001, that approach is no longer valid' (paragraph 87).

[14] James C. Hathaway and Colin Harvey, 'Framing Refugee Protection in the New World Disorder,' (2001) 43:2 *Cornell International Law Journal*, 288; see also Sir Elihu Lauterpacht and Daniel Bethlehem, 'The Scope and Content of the Principle of *Non-refoulement*' (2001), *Opinion for UNHCR's Global Consultations*, 147.

[15] UNHCR 'Note on the Principle of *Non-refoulement*,' UN doc. EC/SCP/2, August 1997.

[16] Cf. Sir Elihu Lauterpacht and Daniel Bethlehem, above, n. 14, at 52.

[17] Ibid. at 54.

The Supreme Court of Canada concludes that since the terrorist attacks of 11 September 2001 'courts may now conclude that the support of terrorism abroad raises a possibility of adverse repercussions on Canada's security' (paragraph 87). Nevertheless, the text of Article 33 (2) Refugee Convention still indicates that even in these situations a provable danger to the security of Canada needs to exist. The mere 'possibility of adverse repercussions' will be insufficient. The threshold indicated by the text of Article 33 (2) needs to be applied. Therefore, there needs to be a danger to the security of the country of refuge or its international relations. The danger needs to be proven and cannot be based on assumptions. Hathaway and Harvey write in a comment on previous decisions in the *Suresh* case: 'In line with the general evidentiary standard of Article 33(2), the connection between an impact on the integrity of Canada's international relations and Canada's essential welfare should have been proved, not simply assumed.'[18] We conclude that 'possible adverse repercussions' are insufficient.

Although Article 33 (2) Refugee Convention does not specify the facts and circumstances that constitute a danger to the national security and leaves a margin of appreciation for States, the Article does demand a level of risk substantiated by proof. The threshold is high. It applies to persons who try to overthrow the government by force or other illegal means, who are endangering the constitution, the territorial integrity, the independence or the peace of the country of refuge.[19]

4.1.2 Danger to the community of the country

The second part of Article 33 (2) Refugee Convention applies to refugees who have been convicted in the country of refuge. According to the text and history of Article 33 (2) a provable danger to the community of the country of refuge needs to exist and the Article needs to be applied with great caution. The mere fact that a refugee has been convicted will not be sufficient to apply Article 33 (2) Refugee Convention. First, the text makes clear it only applies in cases of particularly serious crimes. Second, the assessment of the danger needs to be *ex future*, namely it concerns a future risk. Once again we quote Hathaway and Harvey (p. 292):

> Third and finally, the nature of the conviction and other circumstances must justify the conclusion that the refugee constitutes a danger to the community from which he or she seeks protection. Because the danger flows from the

[18] Cf. James C. Hathaway and Colin Harvey, above, n. 14 , at 290.

[19] A. Grahl-Madsen, *The Status of Refugees in International Law* (Sijthoff, 1966), 235–236; W. Kalin, *Das Prinzip des non-refoulement* (Peter Lang, 1982), 131; Thomas Spijkerboer and Ben Vermeulen, *Vluchtelingenrecht* (NCB, 1997), 302; cf. Sir Elihu Lauterpacht and Daniel Bethlehem, above, note 14, 56.

refugee's criminal character, it does not matter whether the crime was committed in the state of origin, an intermediate state or the asylum state.

We believe a refugee who has been convicted, punished and served his time should not beforehand be excluded from protection under Article 33 (1) Refugee Convention. If in this situation deportation of the refugee is still in violation of the obligation of *non-refoulement*, and the refugee constitutes no danger to the community of the country then granting the refugee a residence permit will contribute to the safety of the individual and of the community. Not granting him any form of legal status within the country will be an extra punishment.

4.1.3 Assessing the Suresh *case*

According to the Canadian Supreme Court in the *Suresh* case, Suresh constitutes a danger to the national security of Canada because of the mere fact that he is a member and fundraiser of the LTTE, listed by Canada as a terrorist organization. According to the judgment, Suresh is a well-known LTTE member and part of the LTTE executive. No further details are given. For example, it does not become clear how much money Suresh contributes to the LTTE. On the other hand, it does become clear that Suresh himself has never been directly involved in any terrorist or otherwise violent act in Sri Lanka or Canada (paragraphs 13, 14 and 16).

The fact that Suresh did financially contribute to the LTTE could mean that the International Convention for the Suppression of the Financing of Terrorism is applicable, if it was known to Suresh that his contributions were allocated to acts prohibited under the Convention (Article 2). Because of the high profile of Suresh within the LTTE organization it is not unlikely that he knew what his contributions were used for. The question then is whether the destination of the money is in violation of the Convention. If so the LTTE can be characterized as a terrorist organization according to the International Convention for the Suppression of the Financing of Terrorism. However, with regard to the question whether Suresh has a right to be protected against *refoulement*, it still needs to be assessed if Suresh constitutes a provable danger to the security of Canada. From the facts and circumstances of the case, this is far from clear.

Does the LTTE constitute a danger to the security of Canada? It is well known that the LTTE limits its actions largely to Sri Lanka. It certainly has not committed any violent actions in Canada. Furthermore, it needs to be seen whether the LTTE constitutes a future danger. Recently the first round of peace negotiations between the LTTE and the Sri Lankan authorities has taken place in Thailand in which a cease-fire has been agreed upon. We believe no real or provable danger to the national security of Canada exists.

4.1.4 The possibility of a balancing act?

Does Article 33 (2) Refugee Convention leave any room for a balancing act between the national security of a State and the protection needs of the individual? Hathaway and Harvey believe that no room is available. They write: 'If compelling evidence exists that the refugee is a danger to asylum-state security or safety of the community of that country, there is no additional proportionality requirement to satisfy.' However, they continue: 'Refoulement is instead authorized only where genuinely necessary to protect the asylum-state community from an unacceptably high risk of harm.'[20] Hathaway and Harvey believe that a balancing act may lead to an interpretation of Article 33 (2) Refugee Convention in which disputable dangers to the national security might be weighed more heavily than the protection needs of a refugee.

Lauterpacht and Bethlehem approach Article 33 (2) Refugee Convention in the context of developments regarding *non-refoulement* that have occurred after the adoption of the Refugee Convention. They, for example, refer to Human Rights Committee General Comment 20 regarding ICCPR. Lauterpacht and Bethlehem do not seem to exclude a balancing act. In cases where danger to the national security exists, the obligation of *non-refoulement* is only applicable if there is a risk of torture or other cruel, inhuman or degrading treatment or punishment: '(. . .) the State proposing to remove a refugee or asylum-seeker to his or her country of origin must give specific consideration to the nature of the risk faced by the individual concerned'. This is because exposure to some forms of risk will preclude *refoulement* absolutely and without exception. This applies notably to circumstances in which there is a danger to torture, cruel, inhuman or degrading treatment or punishment.[21] In such cases, the obligation of *non-refoulement* is non-derogable or absolute. If there is a risk of other forms of persecution a balancing act is possible.

Combining Hathaway/Harvey and Lauterpacht/Bethlehem it can be concluded that Article 33 (2) Refugee Convention allows deportation if a provable danger to the national security of the country of refuge exists or if the refugee is convicted for a particularly serious crime and constitutes a provable danger to the community of the country of refuge, irrespective of the persecution the refugee might be subjected to, unless the persecution can be qualified as torture or inhuman or

20 James C. Hathaway and Colin Harvey, above n. 14, 294.
21 Sir Elihu Lauterpacht and Daniel Bethlehem, above n. 14, 57.

degrading treatment or punishment. In those cases, deportation is not permitted.

4.2 Article 3 European Convention on Human Rights (ECHR)

According to Article 3 ECHR no one shall be returned to a country where he or she runs a real risk of being subjected to torture or inhuman or degrading treatment or punishment. In its Working Document of 5 December 2001 the Commission of the European Union has stated that the European Court of Human Rights on several occasions has confirmed the non-derogability and the absolute and fundamental character of Article 3 ECHR. Under no circumstances are exceptions or derogations under Article 3 ECHR allowed. That includes dangers to the national and public security. Even in cases of a 'public emergency' (Article 15 ECHR) no derogation is permitted. Regarding alleged terrorists, the European Court has also confirmed the non-derogability of Article 3 ECHR. In *Chahal v. United Kingdom*,[22] the applicant, an Indian national belonging to the Sikh population, was suspected of having committed terrorist acts. He had asked for asylum in the United Kingdom. Although the British authorities considered a balancing act between the national security of the United Kingdom and the protection needs of Chahal to be necessary, the European Court ruled that the absolute character of Article 3 does not permit deportation to India if there is a real risk of being subjected to torture or inhuman or degrading treatment or punishment, irrespective of the conduct of the applicant or a possible danger to the national security of the United Kingdom. The Court concluded that if returned to India, Chahal would run a real risk of being subjected to torture or inhuman or degrading treatment or punishment. Therefore, deportation would lead to a violation of Article 3 ECHR. We conclude that Article 3 ECHR does not allow any balancing act between the security interests of State parties and the protection needs of individuals.[23]

Contrary to the Supreme Court of Canada in the *Suresh* case, the European Court concluded in the *Chahal* case that a test of reasonableness should not be applied. In paragraph 131 the Court:

> recognizes that the use of confidential material may be unavoidable where national security is at stake. This does not mean, however, that the national authorities can be free from effective control by the domestic courts whenever they choose to assert that national security and terrorism are involved. With reference to Canada, the European Court considers a more effective form of

[22] *Chahal v. United Kingdom*, (15 Nov. 1996), European Court of Human Rights, Appl.no. 22414/93; See also *Ahmed v. Austria*, (17 Dec. 1996), Appl.no. 25964/94.

[23] The Dutch Minister of Justice has stated that he wants to know to what extent deportations are possible in cases in which this may violate Article 3 ECHR; see the Official Parliamentary Publication 'TK 2001–2002, 27 925, nr. 58, p. 6'.

judicial control has to be adopted 'which both accommodate legitimate security concerns about the nature and sources of intelligence information and yet accord the individual a substantial measure of procedural justice' (paragraph 131).

The Court reiterated this opinion in the case of *Al-Nashif v. Bulgaria*.[24] In paragraphs 123 and 124 the Court stated:

> Even where national security is at stake, the concepts of lawfulness and the rule of law in a democratic society require that measures affecting fundamental human rights must be subject to some form of adversarial proceedings before an independent body competent to review the reasons for the decision and relevant evidence, if need be with appropriate procedural limitations on the use of classified information (see the judgements cited in paragraph 119 above). The individual must be able to challenge the executive's assertion that national security is at stake (. . .).

4.3 The International Covenant on Civil and Political Rights (ICCPR) and the Convention against Torture and Other Cruel, Inhuman or Degrading Treatment or Punishment (CAT)

Like the ECHR, the Convention against Torture includes an absolute or non-derogable obligation of *non-refoulement*, in Article 3. Under this Article no exception or derogation is allowed. In the case of *Paez v. Sweden*, the Committee Against Torture has explicitly stated that the activities of Paez as a member of the alleged terrorist organization *Sendero Luminoso* in Peru, cannot be a material consideration in determining his right to be protected under Article 3 of the Convention against Torture. The Committee considered:

> the text of article 3 of the Convention is absolute. Whenever substantial grounds exist for believing that an individual would be in danger of being subjected to torture upon expulsion to another State, the State party is under obligation not to return the person concerned to that State. The nature of the activities in which the person concerned engaged cannot be a material consideration when making a determination under article 3 of the Convention.[25]

The relationship between the non-derogable character of Article 3 and the fight against terrorism became clear in the case of *Arana v. France*. The applicant, a member of the Basque separatist movement ETA, was about to be extradited to Spain.[26] The Committee Against Torture adopted its view on 5 June 2000, long before the attacks on New York and Washington. It is an important view as the Committee confirms

[24] *Al-Nashif v. Bulgaria*, (20 June 2002), European Court of Human Rights, Appl. no. 50963/99.
[25] *Paez v. Sweden*, (28 April 1997), Committee Against Torture, no. 39/1996, at 14.5.
[26] *Arana v. France*, (5 June 2000), Committee Against Torture, no. 63/1997 at 11.5.

the importance of procedural safeguards:

> The Committee recognizes the need for close co-operation between States in the fight against crime and for effective measures to be agreed upon for that purpose. It believes, however, that such measures must fully respect the rights and fundamental freedoms of the individuals concerned.

No exceptions or derogation as to the obligation of *non-refoulement* are permitted under Article 7 of the International Covenant on Civil and Political Rights (ICCPR). Similar to Article 3 ECHR, Article 7 ICCPR prohibits torture and other forms of cruel, inhuman or degrading treatment or punishment. This prohibition contains an implicit obligation of *non-refoulement*, according to the Human Rights Committee in its General Comment number 20 (1992).[27] In this General Comment the Human Rights Committee confirms the non-derogability or absolute character of Article 7 ICCPR.[28]

4.4 The African Charter on Human and Peoples' Rights and the American Convention on Human Rights

An obligation of *non-refoulement* can also be found in Article 5 of the African Charter on Human and Peoples' Rights and in Articles 5 (2) and 22 (8) of the American Convention on Human Rights.

According to Article 5 of the African Charter: 'Every individual shall have the right to the respect of the dignity inherent in human beings and to the recognition of his legal status. All forms of exploitation and degradation of a man particularly slavery, slave trade, torture, cruel, inhuman or degrading punishment and treatment shall be prohibited.' This provision is absolute and contains an implicit obligation of *non-refoulement*.[29] Likewise, Article 5 (2) of the American Convention reads: 'No one shall be subjected to torture or to cruel, inhuman or degrading punishment or treatment (. . .)'.

An explicit obligation of *non-refoulement* can be found in Article 22 (8) of the American Convention on Human Rights: 'In no case may an alien be deported or returned to a country, regardless of whether or not it is his country of origin, if in that country his right to life or personal

[27] General Comments number 20, (1992), Human Rights Committee, at 9; see also *Kindler v. Canada*, (18 November 1993), Human Rights Committee, no. 470/1991 at 13.2: 'If a State extradites a person within its jurisdiction in circumstances such that as a result there is a real risk that his or her rights under the Covenant will be violated in another jurisdiction, the State party itself may be in violation of the Covenant,' and *C v. Australia*, (13 November 2002), Human Rights Committee, no. 900/1999 at 8.5.

[28] General Comment number 20, (1992), Human Rights Committee, at 3 and General Comment number 29, (2001), Human Rights Committee, at 7.

[29] Joan Fitzpatrick (ed.), *Human Rights Protection for Refugees, Asylum-seekers and Internally Displaced Persons, A Guide to International Mechanisms and Procedures* (Transnational Publishers Inc., New York, 2002), 264–265.

freedom is in danger of being violated because of his race, nationality, religion, social status, or political opinions.' However, this obligation is not absolute. In times of 'public emergency' a State party may derogate (Article 27 American Convention).

Finally, the OAU Convention governing specific aspects of refugee problems in Africa (1969) also includes an obligation of *non-refoulement* in Article II (3).

4.5 Charter of Fundamental Rights of the European Union

It is important to note that within the European Union, the Charter of Fundamental Rights of the European Union — a non-binding document — contains an explicit and absolute obligation of *non-refoulement*. According to Article 19 (2) 'no one may be removed, expelled or extradited to a State where there is a serious risk that he or she would be subjected to the death penalty, torture or other inhuman or degrading treatment or punishment.'

4.6 The *jus cogens* nature of *non-refoulement*

Protection against *refoulement* based on several treaty obligations cannot be seen separately. There is mutual influence of the different obligations of *non-refoulement*. A treaty shall be interpreted in good faith in accordance with the ordinary meaning to be given to the terms of the treaty in their context and in the light of its object and purpose (Article 31 Vienna Convention on the Law of Treaties).Treaties need to be interpreted in light of their current juridical context and in the juridical context of subsequent agreements by State parties, including human rights treaties and related case law.[30] Article 33 (2) Refugee Convention needs to be interpreted in light of the other *non-refoulement* obligations.[31] In the case of *Paez v. Sweden*, for example, the Committee Against Torture considered that if an alien is excludable under Article 1F Refugee Convention from refugee status, he still can have a right to be protected against *refoulement* under Article 3 of the Convention Against Torture.[32]

A step further is the question if the obligation of *non-refoulement* can be qualified as a peremptory norm of general international law, or '*jus cogens*' (Articles 53 and 64 Vienna Convention on the Law of Treaties).

The object and purpose of asylum law is the protection of individuals against violations of fundamental human rights. This objective is not

[30] Tom Clark and François Crépeau, 'Mainstreaming Refugee Rights: The 1951 Refugee Convention and International Human Rights Law' (1999) 17:4 *Netherlands Quarterly on Human Rights*, 389–390.

[31] EXCOM Conclusion number 79, (1996); Tom Clark and François Crépeau, above note 30, p. 390.

[32] *Paez v. Sweden*, (28 April 1997), Committee Against Torture, no. 39/1996.

subject to discussion, at least not until the attacks of 11 September 2001. After this date the objective seems to be no longer that clear. To characterize the obligation of *non-refoulement* as *jus cogens* might therefore be a powerful weapon to guarantee protection of individuals and their human rights. Therefore, it is important to see if the obligation of *non-refoulement* is accepted and recognized as a peremptory norm of international law. If so, every treaty, every treaty obligation and every unilateral, bilateral or multilateral act by a State or international organization that is in conflict or violation with this norm, is void.

According to Article 53 of the Vienna Convention on the Law of Treaties, a norm can be characterized as *jus cogens* if it is 'accepted and recognized by the international community of States as a whole as a norm from which no derogation is permitted and which can be modified only by a subsequent norm of general international law having the same character.' Although we have already concluded that the obligations of *non-refoulement* stemming from Article 3 ECHR, Article 3 CAT and Article 7 ICCPR are non-derogable, it is still useful to examine if *non-refoulement* can be characterized as *jus cogens*, irrespective of treaty obligations. The relevant questions is: is the obligation of *non-refoulement* a non-derogable norm and as such accepted and recognized by the international community of States as a whole? In other words, is the obligation of *non-refoulement* part of international customary law? Goodwin-Gill and Allain believe *non-refoulement* is part of international customary law.[33] According to Goodwin-Gill, it is especially important to note that international organizations like the United Nations General Assembly and UNHCR have regularly confirmed *non-refoulement* as a rule of international customary law, without any objection of States. Furthermore, Allain[34] considers that mainly because of different EXCOM Conclusions (Conclusions of the Executive Committee of UNHCR),[35] and because of the State practice which has emerged in Latin America on the basis of the 1984 Cartagena Declaration on Refugees, the obligation of *non-refoulement* can be characterized as *jus cogens*.[36] It is not relevant that in practice States do not always act according to the obligation.[37] Allain concludes that 'as long as there is an insistence on the non-derogable nature of *non-refoulement*, its status is secure'.[38]

33 Guy S. Goodwin-Gill, *The Refugee in International Law* (OUP 1996), 167; Jean Allain, 'The *Jus cogens* Nature of *Non-refoulement*,' 13 *IJRL* 538 (2001).

34 Jean Allain, above note 33.

35 EXCOM Conclusions on International Protection No. 25 (1982), No. 55 (1989), No. 79 (1996).

36 See also e.g. Sir Elihu Lauterpacht and Daniel Bethlehem, above n. 14, 62.

37 Military and Paramilitary Activities in and against Nicaragua, ICJ Rep. 1986.

38 Allain, above n. 33.

Besides the obligation of *non-refoulement*, the prohibition on torture can also be characterized as a peremptory norm of general international law.[39] In General Comment 24 (1994) the Human Rights Committee has recognized the prohibition on torture and other cruel, inhuman or degrading treatment or punishment also as a peremptory norm of general international law.[40]

Recognizing and accepting the obligation of *non-refoulement* as a peremptory norm of general international law (*jus cogens*) means that States and international organizations such as the United Nations and the European Union cannot just derogate from the norm. This is only possible by a subsequent norm of general international law having the same character (Article 53 Vienna Convention on the Law of Treaties).

The major practical problem remains the burden of proof to be able to actually characterize the obligation of *non-refoulement* as a peremptory norm of general international law and to claim this in a court of law.

5. The future of the non-derogable nature of *non-refoulement*

5.1 Safety guarantees

It is not unthinkable that the European Commission will come up with a proposal for a Directive in which the Commission will interpret Article 3 ECHR in such a manner that expulsion will be possible after having obtained safety guarantees. If there is a request for extradition this certainly will be a possibility.[41] If no extradition request has been received, the State willing to send back the alleged terrorist can, until now, not obtain any guarantee because it is forbidden to contact the authorities of the country of origin.[42]

In the Canadian *Suresh* case, the Sri Lankan authorities gave assurances that on return Suresh would not be subjected to torture. The Supreme Court of Canada considered these assurances to be insufficient. They considered it difficult to rely:

> too heavily on assurances by a State that it will refrain from torture in the future when it has engaged in illegal torture or allowed others to do so on its

[39] Sir Elihu Lauterpacht and Daniel Bethlehem, above n. 14, 73.

[40] General Comment number 24, (1994), Human Rights Committee, at 8: 'Accordingly, provisions in the Covenant that represent customary international law (and a fortiori when they have the character of peremptory norms) may not be the subject of reservations. Accordingly, a State may not reserve the right to engage in slavery, to torture, to subject persons to cruel, inhuman or degrading treatment or punishment (. . .).'

[41] See 'Guidelines of the Committee of Ministers of the Council of Europe on human rights and the fight against terrorism', 15 July 2002, para. XIII.

[42] See, for example, Art. 22 of the proposal for a Council directive on minimum standards on procedures in Member States for granting and withdrawing refugee status (COM (2002) 326 final), 3 July 2002: 'Member States shall not disclose the information regarding individual applications for asylum to the authorities of the country of origin of the applicant for asylum.'

territory in the past [(paragraph 124).They further considered:] 125. In evaluating assurances by a foreign government, the Minister may also wish to take into account the human rights record of the government giving the assurances, the government's record in complying with its assurances, and the capacity of the government to fulfil the assurances, particularly where there is doubt about the government's ability to control its security forces.

Safety assurances or guarantees given by the country of origin to which an alien is to be returned can be of influence in the risk assessment. In the case of *Soering v. United Kingdom* before the European Court of Human Rights,[43] the question arose whether extradition of the applicant to the United States would lead to a violation of Article 3 ECHR because capital punishment might be imposed and hence the applicant might be subjected to the death row phenomenon. The final decision was influenced by the certainty of guarantees given by US authorities. The US Public Prosecutor for example officially declared that: '(. . .) should Soering be convicted of the offence of capital murder as charged (. . .) a representation will be made in the name of the United Kingdom Government that the death penalty should not be imposed or carried out.' According to the European Court guarantees 'must at the very least significantly reduce the risk of a capital sentence either being imposed or carried out' (paragraph 93). The British authorities admitted that the guarantees given did not significantly reduce the risk. The decision to impose the death penalty and to take into account the wishes of the United Kingdom lay, in this case, with the judge and the governor of the State, not with the federal authorities and they did not give any guarantees.

In the *Soering* case, the issue of guarantees is clear: if significant guarantees would have been given that the death penalty would not be imposed or carried out, then the risk of subjection to the death row phenomenon would have been nullified and a real risk of a violation of Article 3 ECHR would not have arisen. It is much more complicated in cases not involving the imposition or the carrying out of legal sentences, but subjection to extra-judicial torture or inhuman or degrading treatment or punishment. By expelling an alien after guarantees are given, a balancing act can be avoided and will be found in the assessment of the risk of being subjected to prohibited treatment.[44]

[43] *Soering v. the United Kingdom*, (7 July 1989), European Court of Human Rights, Appl.no. 14038/88.

[44] In *G.T. v. Australia*, (4 Dec. 1997), Human Rights Committee, no. 706/1996 at 8.4, the Human Rights Committee considered with respect to a drugs smuggler no significant guarantees are necessary: 'Although the Committee considers that the "assurances" given by the Malaysian Government do not *as such* preclude the possibility of T.'s prosecution for exporting or possessing drugs, (. . .).'

5.2 Applying criminal law in cases involving Articles 1F and 33 (2) of the 1951 Refugee Convention

The documents the European Union has adopted since 11 September 2001 propose deportation and extradition of persons suspected of serious crimes who at the same time may claim their right to be protected against violations of fundamental human rights. It is feared that the European Commission and the EU Member States are trying to balance the interest of the individual in search and need of protection, on the one hand, and the interest of the State and its community on the other hand, by trying to get guarantees from the countries of origin or by expelling the alien to a third country outside the European Union that is willing to admit the alien.

However, would prosecution of alleged terrorists not be a better solution than by refraining to give protection and thereby co-operating with further violations of human rights? The fundraising activities of Suresh might fall within the scope of the International Convention for the Suppression of the Financing of Terrorism. According to Article 4 of this Convention, all State parties are obliged to take all necessary measures: '(a) To establish as criminal offences under its domestic law the offences set forth in article 2; (b) To make those offences punishable by appropriate penalties which take into account the grave nature of the offences.' Hereby an obligation is created for State parties to prosecute alleged terrorists, as defined by this treaty. This is similar to the 1996 UN General Assembly Declaration to Supplement the 1994 Declaration on Measures to Eliminate International Protection:[45] 'The States Members of the United Nations reaffirm the importance of ensuring effective cooperation between Member States so that those who participated in terrorist acts (. . .) are brought to justice'. Recent developments in international criminal law, such as the creation of an International Criminal Court, have shown that the prosecution of perpetrators of serious human rights violations is quickly gaining ground (in spite of objections by the United States). The legal tension between absolute protection against human rights violations and responsibility mechanisms can be reduced now that the possibility of holding terrorists, war criminals and other perpetrators of serious human rights violations criminally accountable has significantly increased.

The legal procedures to assess cases involving Article 1F Refugee Convention lack the legal guarantees of criminal proceedings. If, like in the Netherlands, the assessment of exclusion under Article 1F Refugee Convention precludes the assessment of inclusion under Article 1A (2)

[45] UNGA res. 51/210, 17 Dec. 1996, with Annex 'Declaration to Supplement the 1994 Declaration on Measures to Eliminate International Protection'.

Refugee Convention, early co-operation between the Immigration Service that is responsible for status determination of asylum seekers and the Public Prosecutor is of vital importance.

The protection of individuals against *refoulement* should never lead to impunity. Asylum law is not meant to be an escape route to avoid prosecution. Not only should States take responsibility whenever an individual is in need of protection, but they also should hold individuals criminally accountable for their acts. The current measures proposed by States neglect both international responsibilities.

6. Conclusion

On 14 December 1967, the United Nations General Assembly adopted a Declaration on Territorial Asylum. It stated: 'Recognizing that the grant of asylum by a state to persons entitled to invoke article 14 of the Universal Declaration of Human Rights is a peaceful and humanitarian act that as such cannot be regarded as unfriendly by any other State.' Thirty-five years later it becomes clear this objective has not been reached. Over the years, asylum law has been politicized. Since the 1990s States have adopted lists of so-called safe countries of origin and safe third countries. Not being mentioned on such a list can be highly politically significant. The attacks on New York and Washington have led to new lists. This time, lists of wanted persons and forbidden organizations. Not being mentioned on these lists is also highly politically significant. Being mentioned can have far-reaching consequences for members and sympathizers of forbidden organizations and groups. They will probably not be able to claim international protection. Thereby, absolute and fundamental norms such as the prohibition on torture and other cruel, inhuman or degrading treatment or punishment will be balanced.

In sum, the war on terrorism is harmful for human rights. In the *Suresh* case, the Supreme Court of Canada considered the prohibition of torture to be 'less' than absolute. They made clear that States have the power to declare a person to be a terrorist without effective control by the judiciary. The European Commission adopted proposals and asked the European Court of Human Rights to find ways to allow States to refuse a person entry if he constitute a danger to national security. We would strongly urge States to uphold the absolute or non-derogable character of *non-refoulement* and to take those steps necessary, both legal as well as practical, to prosecute suspected terrorists.

[16]

Extraordinary Rendition and the Law of War

Ingrid Detter Frankopan[†]

I. Introduction

There is, when discussing the now fashionable topic of extraordinary rendition, a certain conceptual confusion: when we consider semantic arguments, even the verb *rendere*, in Latin, would normally signify to "give something back," normally to someone who has the right to ask for such restitution. The term rendition, as a derivation of the Latin term *rendere* thus means to "hand back," a meaning which is often lost in the current debate about rendition.

Rendition, in legal terms, implies the transfer of a person from

---

[†] Ingrid Detter de Lupis Frankopan, D.Phil., Oxon; J.D., Stockholm; *Lic. en Droit*, Paris; Dipl. European Law, Turin; Emeritus Lindhagen Professor of International Law, Stockholm; former Fellow of Lady Margaret Hall and of St. Antony's College, Oxford.

one jurisdiction to another. In the case of what is usually called "ordinary rendition," the procedure has kept its original meaning of handing over (or back) a person to another jurisdiction with better rights to instigate a trial.[1]

II. Ordinary Rendition

Ordinary rendition in the United States has its historical roots in the need to recapture fugitive slaves.[2] Nowadays rendition often takes place between the various States of the United States when trial is more appropriate in another State.[3] Rendition procedure is authorized by article 4(2) of the U.S. Constitution.[4] Such rendition is internal to the United States in character and clearly does not involve any other countries.[5] Such ordinary rendition continues to be used in intra-U.S. situations.

---

1 BLACK'S LAW DICTIONARY 1298-99 (7th ed. 1999).

2 U.S. CONST. art. IV, § 2, cl. 3 ("No Person held to Service or Labour in one State, under the Laws thereof, escaping into another, shall, in Consequence of any Law or Regulation therein, be discharged from such Service or Labour, but shall be delivered up on Claim of the Party to whom such Service or Labour may be due."), *repealed by* U.S. CONST. amend. XIII.

3 *See* U.S. CONST. art. IV, § 2, cl. 2; 18 U.S.C. § 3182 (2000). This procedure is also called interstate rendition. BLACK'S LAW DICTIONARY 1298-99 (7th ed. 1999).

4 U.S. CONST. art. IV, § 2, cl. 2.

5 On federal interests in interstate renditions, see Puerto Rico v. Branstad, 483 U.S. 219, 221 (1987) (holding that Puerto Rico had authority under the Extradition Act to invoke power of federal courts by mandamus action to demand extradition of fugitive from asylum state); Innes v. Tobin, 240 U.S. 127, 134-135 (1916) (stating that a state is free to surrender a fugitive to the state from which he has fled); Roberts v. Reilly, 116 U.S. 80, 94 (1885) (holding that extradition procedure is governed by U.S. Congressional legislation and that individual states do not have the discretion to deviate from its uniformity); *cf.* Taylor v. Taintor, 83 U.S. (16 Wall.) 366, 371 (1872) (holding that the Constitutional provision requiring the surrender of a person charged in any state with treason, felony, or other crimes is obligatory upon every state and a part of the law of every state); Com. of Kentucky v. Dennison, 65 U.S. (24 How.) 66, 83-84 (1861) (holding that it is the duty of the state, upon proper demand by another state, to surrender a fugitive); Prigg v. Com. of Pennsylvania, 41 U.S. (16 Pet.) 539, 616, 618–619 (1842) (holding that, because the extradition of fugitive slaves is exclusively regulated by U.S. Congressional legislation permitting slave owners to retrieve their slaves from where they have fled, a state may not punish such an act of retrieval as unlawful). In 1934, it was made unlawful for "any person to flee from one State to another for the purpose of avoiding prosecution . . . in certain cases." Act of May 18, 1934, Pub. L. No. 73-233, 48 Stat. 782 (1934) (current version at 18 U.S.C. § 1073 (2000)).

III. Deportation, Extradition and Extraordinary Rendition

Deportation and extradition are forms of rendition, although rarely referred to as such, and involve the sending of a person to be tried or otherwise dealt with by another jurisdiction.[6] Deportation implies the expulsion of an alien whose presence in the territory of a State is deemed undesirable.[7] Deportation often takes place after an alien has served a prison sentence or otherwise been convicted by a court in one country;[8] the court issues a judgment or a decision that the convicted person shall, possibly after having served a prison sentence, be sent out of the country, normally to his original home State.[9]

There are safeguards in international law that a person lawfully residing in a country will not be deported without the judgment of a court or another State authority.[10] Extradition, on the other hand,

---

6 BLACK'S LAW DICTIONARY 450, 605 (7th ed. 1999). In fact, the definitions of "extradition" and "rendition" each reference the other as an analogous term. BLACK'S LAW DICTIONARY 605, 1298-99 (7th ed. 1999).

7 BLACK'S LAW DICTIONARY 450 (7th ed. 1999).

8 *See* 8 U.S.C. § 1251 (1996) (listing the circumstances upon which an alien shall be deported).

9 "If an alien defendant is subject to deportation, the court may provide, as a condition of supervised release, that he be deported and remain outside the United States, and may order that he be delivered to a duly authorized immigration official for such deportation." 18 U.S.C.A. § 3583(d) (2006).

10 Protocol No. 7 to the Convention for the Protection of Human Rights and Fundamental Freedoms, art. 1, Nov. 22, 1984, Eur. T.S. No. 117. Article 1, titled "Procedural safeguards relating to expulsion of aliens," provides that:

1. An alien lawfully resident in the territory of a State shall not be expelled therefrom except in pursuance of a decision reached in accordance with law and shall be allowed: *a.* to submit reasons against his expulsion, *b.* to have his case reviewed, and *c.* to be represented for these purposes before the competent authority or a person or persons designated by that authority. 2. An alien may be expelled before the exercise of his rights under paragraph 1.*a*, *b* and *c* of this Article, when such expulsion is necessary in the interests of public order or is grounded on reasons of national security.

Id. Furthermore, Article 13 of the International Covenant on Civil and Political Rights provides that:

An alien lawfully in the territory of a State Party to the present Covenant may be expelled therefrom only in pursuance of a decision reached in accordance with law and shall, except where compelling reasons of national security otherwise require, be allowed to submit the reasons against his expulsion and to have his case reviewed by, and be represented for the purpose before, the competent authority or a person or persons especially designated by the competent authority.

is performed under international agreements,[11] transferring normally a person of a specific nationality to his home country or, alternatively, transferring a person to a place where he is alleged to have committed a crime.[12]

Straightforward extradition implies the handing over of a person to another State, normally in order for that other State to try the person in its own courts. Extradition is usually carried out under specific treaties and numerous countries have ratified such agreements to facilitate trial in another country of persons indicted in criminal proceedings. Such procedure is sometimes called for if a person is a citizen of another State and that State claims to be better suited to try the person. There is rarely a case for claiming that extradition would violate a person's human rights.[13] In other cases, a person may be extradited to a State whose interests he is said to have violated or whose citizens have had their rights infringed. In other cases, again, a person is extradited to another State as he is alleged to have committed a crime in that other State which would, in a trial, apply the *lex loci delicti*, that is to say the law in the State where the crime took place.[14]

Under extradition treaties there is usually a clause that exempts "political" crimes from the list for which extradition may take place.[15] Nor is a person normally extradited to a country where he

---

International Covenant on Civil and Political Rights art. 13, *opened for signature* Dec. 16, 1966, 999 U.N.T.S. 171 [hereinafter ICCPR].

11 *See, e.g.*, Extradition Treaty Between the Government of the United States of America and the Government of the United Kingdom of Great Britain and Northern Ireland, U.S.-U.K., Mar. 31, 2003, S. Treaty Doc. No. 108-23 [hereinafter U.S.-U.K. Extradition Treaty].

12 BLACK'S LAW DICTIONARY 605 (7th ed. 1999).

13 Ocalan v. Turkey, 41 Eur. Ct. H.R. 45 (2005).

14 The *lex loci delicti* is the law of the place where the crime took place. BLACK'S LAW DICTIONARY 923 (7th ed. 1999).

15 "The first provision to protect political offenders appeared in a Belgian extradition act in 1833 and has since been incorporated into most Western extradition treaties." Antje C. Petersen, *Extradition and the Political Offense Exception in the Suppression of Terrorism*, 67 IND. L.J. 767, 774 (1992); *see also id.* & n.23 (citing an extradition treaty with such a clause between the U.S. and Germany). The extradition treaty between the United States and the United Kingdom also contains a clause pertaining to political offenses. U.S.-U.K. Extradition Treaty, *supra* note 11, art. 4. For a detailed analysis of extradition, see generally IVAN ANTHONY SHEARER, EXTRADITION IN INTERNATIONAL LAW (1971).

may be subjected to harsh interrogation or torture, or to a country which applies the death penalty if the sending State would not impose such sanctions for the suspected crime.[16] On the other hand, the European Convention on the Suppression of Terrorism of 1977,[17] was adopted to avoid that specific acts, like acts of terrorists, would be classified as "political" and lead to denial of extradition. There is now a dilemma: a suspected terrorist may not be exempt from extradition as his acts are not, under the said Convention, to be considered as "political"; but, on the other hand, he must not be extradited to a country which might subject him to torture or harsh treatment, even if there are diplomatic assurances to the contrary.[18] At times, however, it may be that diplomatic pledges are effective and prevent the real risk of torture and an extraditing State is enabled to proceed with the extradition.[19]

Many problems concerning deportation and extradition, in particular in so far as possible torture may ensue in the destination country, also arise in the field of extraordinary rendition. Extraordinary rendition, however, involves different methods and practices than either deportation or extradition.

IV. Essential Features of Extraordinary Rendition

In the discussions on extraordinary rendition there are a host of misunderstandings and conflicting definitions. It may be possible to reach at least provisional common ground by a stringent analysis of what specific terms actually mean. Extraordinary rendition is quite different from ordinary rendition and extradition

---

16 *See, e.g.*, Soering v. United Kingdom, 161 Eur. Ct. H.R. (ser. A) at 8 (1989); Chahal v. United Kingdom (No. 22), 1996-V Eur. Ct. H.R. 1831, 1855 para. 80; Nivette v. France, 2001-VII Eur. Ct. H.R. 493, 501 (emphasizing that extradition to a State imposing the death sentence violates Article 3 of the Convention for the Protection of Human Rights and Fundamental Freedoms).

17 European Convention on the Suppression of Terrorism, Jan. 27, 1977, Europ. T.S. No. 90.

18 Ahmed Hussein Mustafa Kamil Agiza v. Sweden, Comm. No. 233/2003, U.N. GAOR Comm. Against Torture., 34th Sess., para. 13.4, U.N. Doc. CAT/C/34/D/233/2003 (May 20, 2005) (stating that the fact that diplomatic assurances had been issued was not sufficient where the extraditing country, Sweden, should have known that Egypt resorts to widespread torture of prisoners).

19 *See* Mamatkulov and Askerov v. Turkey, 41 Eur. H.R. Rep. 494, 495-97 (2005); *see also* Cruz Varas v. Sweden, 14 Eur. H.R. Rep. 1, 35 para. 75 (1991); Vilvarajah & Others v. United Kingdom, 14 Eur. H.R. Rep. 248, 288 para. 107 (1991).

described above.

Extraordinary rendition signifies the handing over of a person to be questioned in another jurisdiction. The significance of extraordinary rendition changed substantially when the practice was introduced by the United States in the 1980s to transfer foreign delinquents to be tried or, more often, interrogated in other countries outside such extradition treaties,[20] and such countries were chosen where one might suspect that a different level of treatment of detainees was afforded than what might be expected in the Western world.[21]

The difference to ordinary rendition and to deportation or extradition is essentially that, in the case of extraordinary rendition, there is no link between the person "rendered" and the country to which he is sent. In the case of extraordinary rendition, a person is transferred to a country where he is not (normally) a citizen. Nor is that country the scene of any alleged crimes committed by the person in question.

Extraordinary rendition or irregular rendition is thus a term used to describe the transfer of a person from one State to another State, normally for the purposes of being subjected to some form of interrogation. During the last few years this practice has been criticized as some States to which such rendition has been effectuated are countries with a questionable human rights record.[22] It has, at times, appeared that such States might use harsh interrogation techniques or torture to extract information

20 For an explanation of rendition taking place outside the framework of extradition treaties and its implications on human rights, see Edmund S. McAllister, *The Hydraulic Pressure of Vengeance*: United States v. Alvarez-Machain *and the Case for a Justifiable Abduction*, 43 DEPAUL L. REV. 449, 474-76 (2004); Jimmy Gurule, *Terrorism, Territorial Sovereignty, and the Forcible Apprehension of International Criminals Abroad*, 17 HASTINGS INT'L & COMP. L. REV. 457, 490-93 (1994).

21 *See* Leila Nadya Sadat, *Ghost Prisoners and Black Sites: Extraordinary Rendition Under International Law*, 37 CASE W. RES. J. INT'L L. 309, 320 (2006) (stating that Egypt, Syria, Saudi Arabia, Pakistan, and Uzbekistan are nations known to take part in extraordinary rendition and are identified by the U.S. State Department as countries that practice torture).

22 *See* A. John Radsan, *A More Regular Process For Irregular Rendition*, 37 SETON HALL L. REV. 1, 62 (2006) (identifying Uzbekistan, Egypt and Syria as nations being used for extraordinary rendition even though these nations have questionable human rights records).

from the person whom has been rendered.[23]

On the other hand, during the more or less emotional debates on extraordinary rendition, commentators have often deviated to discuss prison conditions and treatment in general of suspected terrorists.[24] The subject of extraordinary rendition is sufficiently vast for laudable attempts to keep an analysis of the subject to narrow latitudes, corresponding to the definition set out above.

According to a Report of the Parliament of European Union (often cited but usually attributed to the Parliament of the Council of Europe, a totally different organization), extraordinary rendition could be defined as "an extra-judicial practice which contravenes established international human rights standards and whereby an individual suspected of involvement in terrorism is illegally abducted, arrested and/or transferred into the custody of US officials and/or transported to another country for interrogation which, in the majority of cases, involves *incommunicado* detention and torture."[25] This is not an acceptable definition. Numerous conditions of this attempted definition are uncertain or vague: should "illegal" be understood to mean illegal under the law of the sending and/or receiving State or under international law? Is the prohibition of being held "incommunicado" on the same level as the prohibition of torture? Does the *caveat* of "in majority of cases" mean that there can be legal and acceptable forms of extraordinary rendition?

It is essential to underline that extraordinary rendition is not *per se* illegal. It is only if torture ensues that such rendition violates legal rules. There is, in effect, an acceptable practice whereby States resort to extraordinary rendition under various Mutual Assistance Treaties to send an arrested person to be interrogated in another country.[26] This can be done outside

---

23 *See id.* at 3 (citing Dana Priest & Barton Gellman, *U.S. Decries Abuse but Defends Interrogations*, WASH. POST, Dec. 26, 2002, at A1).

24 *See* Leila Nadya Sadat, *Extraordinary Rendition, Torture, and Other Nightmares from the War on Terror*, 75 GEO. WASH. L. REV. 1200, 1211-15 (2007); Sadat, *supra* note 21, at 313.

25 Report on the Alleged Use of European Countries by the CIA for the Transportation and Illegal Detention of Prisoners, para. 36, EUR. PARL. DOC. A6-0020/2007 (2007).

26 *See, e.g.*, Treaty on Extradition and Mutual Assistance in Criminal Matters, U.S.-Turk., June 7, 1979, 32 U.S.T. 3111; Treaty on Mutual Assistance in Criminal Matters,

extradition treaties in cases where it is more appropriate to interrogate a person elsewhere, for example under Interpol or Europol mechanisms or in procedures involving the European Arrest Warrant.[27] Such procedures resemble in every detail extraordinary rendition as the term is usually understood without any indication of harsh treatment or torture.

Extraordinary rendition may not be a good term for practices where torture is actual or presumed: it would be more appropriate to speak of "outsourcing" of practices which a State would rather not perform itself. "Torture by proxy" could also be used to describe transfers of suspected terrorists to countries for harsh interrogation techniques or torture.

There is also a serious problem of proof of actual torture and it is clearly essential to establish to what extent reports are correct that suspected terrorists have been flown from the United States or from elsewhere and have subsequently been subjected to torture in a third State. It is important to clarify to what extent evidence that torture has been inflicted is reliable and, furthermore, to establish what actually constitutes torture.

Lawyers have not devoted much attention to the practices of extraordinary rendition.[28] There are some factual, but often sensationalist, accounts[29] written by journalists, politicians, human right movements and pressure groups on this practice. When one

May 25, 1973, U.S.-Switz., 27 U.S.T. 2019. For a list of Mutual Legal Assistance Treaties to which the U.S. is a party, see U.S. Dept. of State, Mutual Legal Assistance (MLAT) and Other Agreements, http://travel.state.gov/law/info/judicial/judicial_690.html (last visited Mar. 6, 2008).

27 *See* Council Framework Decision 2002/584/JHA, 2002 O.J. (L 190) 1, 1-2 (explaining the replacement of extradition procedures between E.U. Member States with the European arrest warrant). The European arrest warrant is designed to replace formal extradition by requiring each national judicial authority to "*ipso facto* recognize requests for the surrender of a person made by the judicial authority of another Member State with a minimum of formalities." *Commission Proposal for a Council Framework Decision on the European Arrest Warrant and the Surrender Procedures Between the Member* States, at 2, COM (2001) 522 final (Sept. 25, 2001).

28 For examples of analysis by lawyers of extraordinary rendition, see Sadat, *supra* note 24; Margaret L. Satterthwaite, *Rendered Meaningless: Extraordinary Rendition and the Rule of Law*, 75 GEO. WASH. L. REV. 1333 (2007).

29 *See, e.g.*, STEPHEN GREY, GHOST PLANE: THE TRUE STORY OF THE CIA TORTURE PROGRAM (St. Martin's Press 2006); TREVOR PAGLEN & A. C. THOMPSON, TORTURE TAXI: ON THE TRAIL OF THE CIA'S RENDITION FLIGHTS (Melville House Publishing 2006).

examines the material on this topic, however, much consists of newspaper articles and more or less tendentious articles. Even international organizations, like the UN Human Rights Commission, the European Union and the Council of Europe, mostly cite newspaper reports when they make their own assessment as to what extraordinary rendition involves.[30]

Much is also written on this subject, in the United States and elsewhere, to criticize the present Republican administration in the United States for its policies in Iraq and for ensuing policies on the "War on Terror."[31] Before one continues to analyze the legal position with regard to extraordinary rendition, it may be useful to underline that it was indeed a Democratic administration that initially allowed such questionable methods of interrogation of detainees. The CIA was granted permission to use rendition in a presidential directive signed by President Bill Clinton in 1995.[32] Nor is there any sign that the Democrats, if they come into power after the next election, would cease the practice of extraordinary rendition.

It is, however, correct that the practice of extraordinary rendition has grown sharply under the Bush administration since the 9/11 attacks.[33] There has been an enhanced need to deal with suspected terrorists by forceful interrogation tactics, clearly to preempt further attacks on the civilian population. It is important to establish where the limit goes for the permissible techniques of interrogation as balanced against the interest to safeguard citizens of the State. It is now alleged that some detainees are sent to receiving States such as Egypt, Jordan, Syria, Morocco, and Uzbekistan[34] where, reportedly, some interrogation practices are

---

30 *See, e.g.*, Report on the Alleged Use of European Countries by the CIA for the Transportation and Illegal Detention of Prisoners, *supra* note 25, paras. 17, 148–149.

31 *See, e.g.*, Satterthwaite, *supra* note 28, at 1333-34; Sadat, *supra* note 24, at 1200-06.

32 U.S. Policy on Counterterrorism, Presidential Decision Directive/NSC-39 (June 21, 1995), *available at* http://www.fas.org/irp/offdocs/pdd39.htm.

33 *See* Robert M. Chesney, *State Secrets and the Limits of National Security Litigation*, 75 GEO. WASH. L. REV. 1249, 1255 (2007); Craig Whitlock, *Europeans Investigate CIA Role in Abductions*, WASH. POST, Mar. 13, 2005, at A1.

34 *Extraordinary Rendition, Extraterritorial Detention and Treatment of Detainees: Restoring Our Moral Credibility and Strengthening Our Moral Standing: Hearing Before the S. Comm. on Foreign Relations* 10, 36 (2007) (statements of Tom Malinowski, Washington Advocacy Director, Human Rights Watch, and Dr. Daniel

used which might violate basic human rights.[35]

It is, on the other hand, quite obscure as to what the *quid pro quo* might be when a State sends a person to be interrogated in another State. What does the receiving State get in return for its interrogating services? This is a question rarely raised and not ever clearly addressed.

V. Extraordinary Rendition and *Réfoulement*

Réfoulement means the expulsion of persons who have the right to be recognized as refugees. The principle of non-réfoulement was first codified in 1954 in the UN Convention relating to the Status of Refugees which, in Article 33(1), provides that: "No Contracting State shall expel or return ("réfouler") a refugee in any manner whatsoever to the frontiers of territories where his life or freedom would be threatened on account of his race, religion, nationality, membership of a particular social group or political opinion."[36] The principle of non-réfoulement does not only forbid the expulsion of refugees to their country of origin but to any other country where they might risk being persecuted. Only if the person to be expelled constitutes a danger to national security may transfer be possible under the UN Convention.[37]

Problems still arise due to the fact that some States have not ratified the Refugee Convention. Some States might even lack formal procedures for determining refugee status.[38] It is suggested

---

Byman, Director, Center for Peace and Security Studies, Edmund A. Walsh School of Foreign Service, Georgetown University); *Extraordinary Rendition in U.S. Counterterrorism Policy: The Impact on Transatlantic Relations: Joint Hearing Before the Subcomm. on International Organizations, Human Rights, and Oversight and the Subcomm. on Europe of the H. Comm. on Foreign Affairs*, 110th Cong. 4 (2007) (statement of Amnesty International USA).

35 *Extraordinary Rendition in U.S. Counterterrorism Policy*, *supra* note 34, at 4.

36 Convention Relating to the Status of Refugees art. 33(1), *adopted* July 28, 1951, 19 U.S.T. 6259, 189 U.N.T.S. 137 [hereinafter Refugee Convention].

37 *Id.* art. 33(2). For a discussion of réfoulement in general, see Sir Elihu Lauterpacht & Daniel Bethlehem, *The Scope and Content of the Principle Non-Réfoulement: Opinion*, *in* REFUGEE PROTECTION IN INTERNATIONAL LAW: UNCHR'S GLOBAL CONSULTATIONS ON INTERNATIONAL PROTECTION, 87, 87-179 (Erika Feller, Volker Türk & Frances Nicholson eds., 2003).

38 *See* Stephen H. Legomsky, *Secondary Refugee Movements and the Return of Asylum Seekers to Third Countries: The Meaning of Effective Protection*, 15 INT'L J. REFUGEE L. 567, 593-94 (2003) (naming Jordan, Syria, Pakistan, Indonesia, and

that the same principle applies to extraordinary rendition, that a person must thus not be rendered to a country where his life or freedom would be threatened or to a country where he can be expected to be tortured.[39] Any State through which transit takes place would appear to assume an obligation to prevent, and preempt, that this occurs.[40]

VI. Relevance of Legal Prohibitions of Torture

For some time there have been efforts to forbid or condemn torture by express provisions in international law. The Universal Declaration of Human Rights of 1949, in Article 5, states that "[n]o one may be subjected to torture or to cruel, inhuman or degrading treatment or punishment."[41] The Declaration adopted by the General Assembly on 9 December 1975[42] also concerns the Protection of All Persons from Being Subjected to Torture and Other Cruel, Inhuman or Degrading Treatment or Punishment.

These Declarations have predominantly only declaratory force, but it could also be argued that they re-state a rule that already exists in international law.[43] This pre-existing rule that the Declarations confirm is probably an expression of a form of minimum standards[44] rather than any customary rule; any argument on "custom," "usage" or "practice" relies on the absurd notion of "negative custom."[45]

Thailand as having no domestic refugee law as well as not being parties to the Refugee Convention).

39 *See* COMM. ON INT'L HUMAN RIGHTS OF THE ASSOC. OF THE BAR OF THE CITY OF N.Y. & CTR. FOR HUMAN RIGHTS AND GLOBAL JUSTICE, N.Y. SCHOOL OF LAW, TORTURE BY PROXY: NATIONAL AND DOMESTIC LAW APPLICABLE TO "EXTRAORDINARY RENDITIONS" 31-83 (2004), *available at* http://www.chrgj.org/docs/TortureByProxy.pdf; David Weissbrodt & Amy Bergquist, *Extraordinary Rendition: A Human Rights Analysis*, 19 HARV. HUM. RTS. J. 123, 139-41 (2006).

40 *See* Council Directive 2003/110/EC, art. 8, 2003 O.J. (L 321) 26, 26, 29.

41 Universal Declaration of Human Rights, G.A. Res. 217A, at 71, 73, U.N. GAOR, 3d Sess., 1st plen. mtg., U.N. Doc. A/810 (Dec. 12, 1948).

42 G.A. Res. 3452 (XXX), at 91, U.N. Doc. A/10034 (Dec. 9, 1975).

43 INGRID DETTER, INTERNATIONAL LEGAL ORDER 294 (1994).

44 For further discussion on the concept of minimum standards, see *infra* Part IX.

45 Ingrid Detter, *The Law of War and Illegal Combatants*, 75 GEO. WASH. L. REV. 1049, 1054 (2007). It is not logical to claim that a State, or combatants in the field, air, or sea, having *refrained* from certain cruel practices would, on account of this passivity, be bound in the future not to commit such acts. *Id.* In other words, it is not by the force

The prohibition against torture is more emphatically confirmed in straightforward treaty stipulations, on a regional scale in Europe by the European Convention on Human Rights[46] and by the specific European Torture Convention of 1987[47] and in North and South America by the American Convention on Human Rights of 1969[48] and by the Inter-American Convention of Torture of 1985.[49] There is also a much neglected African Charter on Human and People's Rights of 1981.[50]

On the universal and global scene, torture is forbidden by the International Covenant on Civil and Political Rights[51] and, above all, by the United Nations Convention Against Torture (UNCAT) of 1984, a treaty entirely dedicated to the prohibition of torture.[52]

It is to be noted that the United States has incorporated provisions prohibiting torture in internal law in the U.S. War Crimes Act (WCA), as amended by the Military Commissions Act

of "negative custom" that a prohibition becomes effective but because of an imperative diktat of conscience and of normal human attitudes, as reflected in a minimum standards of civilized behavior. *Id.* at 1054, 1086-87.

46 Council of Europe, Convention for the Protection of Human Rights and Fundamental Freedoms, art. 3, *opened for signature* Nov. 4, 1950, Europ. T.S. No. 5, 213 U.N.T.S. 222.

47 European Convention for the Prevention of Torture and Inhuman or Degrading Treatment or Punishment, Nov. 26, 1987, Europ. T.S. No. 126, 27 I.L.M. 1152 (1988) (securing the prohibition against torture and inhuman or degrading treatment found in Article 3 of the European Convention on Human Rights by authorizing visits to sites where persons are being denied their liberty by a governmental authority).

48 Organization of American States, American Convention on Human Rights art. 5, *opened for signature* Nov. 22, 1969, O.A.S.T.S. No. 36, 1144 U.N.T.S. 123.

49 Organization of American States, Inter-American Convention to Prevent and Punish Torture, *opened for signature* Dec. 9, 1985, O.A.S.T.S. No. 67, 25 I.L.M. 519 (1986).

50 Organization of African Unity, African [Banjul] Charter on Human and Peoples' Rights art. 5, *adopted* June 27, 1981, 1520 U.N.T.S. 217, 21 I.L.M. 58 (1982).

51 ICCPR, *supra* note 10, art. 7.

52 Convention Against Torture and Other Cruel, Inhuman or Degrading Treatment or Punishment, *adopted* Dec. 10, 1984, S. Treaty Doc. No. 100-20, 1465 U.N.T.S. 85 [hereinafter Convention Against Torture]. On 18 December 2002, an Optional Protocol to the Torture Convention was adopted with the intent to establish a preventive system of regular visits to places of detention by a special Subcommittee and by independent international and national bodies. Optional Protocol to the Convention Against Torture and Other Cruel, Inhuman or Degrading Treatment or Punishment, G.A. Res. 57/199, U.N. Doc. A/RES/57/199 (Dec. 18, 2002).

of 2006 (MCA).[53] The Torture Convention Implementation Act of 1994 also incorporate international prohibitions into domestic law of the United States[54] and the Detainee Treatment Act of 2005 also prohibits torturous, or as it is often called "enhanced" interrogation practices.[55]

Less attention has been devoted by commentators to the fact that "inhuman treatment" is also prohibited by the Torture Convention[56] and under other international instruments.[57] The difference between inhuman treatment and torture is that inhuman treatment need not be "intended" to cause suffering.[58] But latitudes may change: the European Court of Human Rights held in the *Ireland* case that the so called "five techniques" amounted to inhuman treatment but not to torture.[59] The five techniques are: wall-standing; hooding; subjection to noise; deprivation of sleep; and deprivation of food and drink.[60] A later case, however, clarified that the same practices today might well be considered to amount, not only to inhuman treatment, but to torture as the high standard demanded today in the field of human rights demands more "firmness."[61]

On the other hand it is important to note that, for example, deprivation of sleep, which by commentators is often regarded as outright torture, may not unquestionably be classified as torture when seeking to extract information from a suspected terrorist if such information might save the lives of other innocent citizens.

The United States admits that it has schemes allowing for extraordinary rendition, but the United States Administration has

---

53 War Crimes Act of 1996, 18 U.S.C.A. § 2441 (West 1998 & Supp. 2007); Military Commissions Act of 2006, Pub. L. No. 109-366, § 6, 120 Stat. 2600, 2632-35 (to be codified at 18 U.S.C. § 2441).

54 18 U.S.C. §§ 2340–2340B (2000).

55 42 U.S.C.A. §§ 2000dd–2000dd1 (West 2003 & Supp. 2007).

56 Convention Against Torture, *supra* note 52, art. 1.

57 Council of Europe, *supra* note 46, art. 3.

58 Convention Against Torture, *supra* note 52, arts. 1, 16. The same absence of subjective criterion is applied to degrading treatment. *See* Tyrer Case, 26 Eur. Ct. H.R. (ser. A) at 15 (1978).

59 Ireland v. United Kingdom, 25 Eur. Ct. H.R. (ser. A) at 67 (1978).

60 *Id.* at 41.

61 Selmouni v. France, 1999-V Eur. Ct. H.R. 151, 183.

formally denied that such practices entail torture. On July 20, 2007 President Bush clarified in an Executive Order the treatment that must afforded to detainees and repeated that the United States does not condone torture of captives by intelligence officials.[62] The President insisted that Common Article 3 of the Geneva Conventions would apply: this article provides some minimum guarantees to soldiers and shipwrecked as well as to the civilian population.[63]

The President was possibly wrongly advised by referring to the requirements of Common Article 3 of the Geneva Conventions as this article is not applicable in situations of suspected terrorists.[64] The article only protects "real" combatants and "real" civilians and not those who do not wear a uniform but clandestinely take up arms to commit terrorist acts.[65] Instead, the Order could have referred to international minimum human rights standards.[66]

As has been suggested above and which will be shown later in this text, the very question of legality or illegality turns on actual proof and reliable evidence as to whether extraordinary rendition as practiced nowadays by the United States and several other consenting States actually involves an accepted definition of prohibited torture.

Some claim that extraordinary rendition violates Article 3(2)

62 Exec. Order No. 13440, 72 Fed. Reg. 40,707 (July 20, 2007).

63 Geneva Convention for the Amelioration of the Condition of the Wounded and Sick in Armed Forces in the Field art. 3, *opened for signature* Aug. 12, 1949, 6 U.S.T. 3114, 75 U.N.T.S. 31; Geneva Convention for the Amelioration of the Condition of Wounded, Sick and Shipwrecked Members of Armed Forces at Sea art. 3, *opened for signature* Aug. 12, 1949, 6 U.S.T. 3217, 75 U.N.T.S. 85; Geneva Convention Relative to the Treatment of Prisoners of War art. 3, *opened for signature* Aug. 12, 1949, 6 U.S.T. 3316, 75 U.N.T.S. 135; Geneva Convention Relative to the Protection of Civilian Persons in Time of War art. 3, *opened for signature* Aug. 12, 1949, 6 U.S.T. 3516, 75 U.N.T.S. 287. Common Article 3 provides some minimum guarantees to soldiers and shipwrecked as well as to the civilian population. Detter, *Illegal Combatants*, *supra* note 45, at 1057. Article 3 of the above Geneva Conventions is referred to as "Common Article 3" because it appears in the same form in all four Conventions. *Id.* at 1079 n.191.

64 *See* Detter, *Illegal Combatants*, *supra* note 45, *passim* (discussing reasons why Common Article 3 may not apply to terrorists).

65 *Id.* at 1058-60.

66 *Id.* at 1086-92.

of the Torture Convention which the United States has ratified.[67] The article provides that:

> 1. No State Party shall expel, return ("refouler") or extradite a person to another State where there are substantial grounds for believing that he would be in danger of being subjected to torture.
>
> 2. For the purpose of determining whether there are such grounds, the competent authorities shall take into account all relevant considerations including, where applicable, the existence in the State concerned of a consistent pattern of gross, flagrant or mass violations of human rights.[68]

The prohibition derives its phrasing from the prohibition of *réfoulement* in refugee law,[69] in the rules concerning extradition, and other rules in the field of conflict of laws.[70]

But Article 3(2) of the Torture Convention does not really cover extraordinary rendition involving torture: the United States is not "expelling" or "returning" persons under this scheme.[71] Suspected terrorists are dispatched for interrogation elsewhere and, furthermore, at no stage does the United States relinquish control of the fate of the detainees sent for such questioning.[72]

Even if the Torture Convention were applicable, the question arises as to whether a State might be relieved from certain obligations in the case of national emergency. This question thus concerns the right of derogation. A most important question concerns whether a situation of national emergency dispenses with obligations assumed under the Torture Convention and under other international engagements. It is to be noted that the Convention

67 Satterthwaite, *supra* note 28, at 1367-69; *see also* David Weissbrodt & Amy Bergquist, *Extraordinary Rendition and the Torture Convention*, 46 VA. J. INT'L L. 585, 599 (2006).

68 Convention Against Torture, *supra* note 52, art. 3.

69 Refugee Convention, *supra* note 36, art. 33.

70 For a treaty-specific overview of conflict of laws principles in the field of extradition, see Yaffa Zilbershats, *Extraditing Israeli Citizens to the United States—Extradition and Citizenship Dilemmas*, 21 MICH. J. INT'L L. 297, 301-10 (2000).

71 *See* Convention Against Torture, *supra* note 52, art. 3.

72 *See* Beth Henderson, *From Justice to Torture: The Dramatic Evolution of U.S.-Sponsored Renditions*, 20 TEMP. INT'L & COMP. L.J. 189, 197 (2006) ("U.S. participation in a rendition will not serve to insulate the rendered individual from trial in the United States.").

for the Protection of Human Rights and Fundamental Freedoms ("European Convention on Human Rights") allows a contracting State to derogate from certain obligations "[i]n time of war or other public emergency threatening the life of the nation" to the extent that this is strictly required "by the emergencies of the situation" and on the condition that such derogations "are not inconsistent with other obligations under international law."[73] A State bound by the Convention may thus derogate from the obligation under Article 5 of not depriving a person of his liberty and under Article 6 to give a fair trial within a certain time period.[74] However, derogations from Article 3, which deals with the prohibition of torture, inhuman or degrading treatment, are not permitted.[75]

The International Covenant on Civil and Political Rights also provides for the possibility of derogations in time of national emergencies.[76] The Torture Convention, however, excludes all such possibility of derogation, even in the case of serious national emergency.[77]

There is no doubt that the United States did find itself in a situation of national emergency after 9/11 but, as shown above, relevant conventions do not allow for derogation even in such situations. On the other hand, national courts have not found any

---

73 Council of Europe, *supra* note 46, art. 15.

74 *Id.* arts. 5, 6.

75 *Id.* art. 3.

76 ICCPR, *supra* note 10, art. 4(1); *cf.* U.N. Econ. & Soc. Council [ECOSOC], Sub-Comm. on Prevention of Discrimination and Prot. of Minorities, Comm'n on Human Rights, *Note Verbale Dated 24 August 1984 from the Permanent Representative of the Netherlands to the United Nations Office at Geneva Addressed to the Secretary-General*, Annex, U.N. Doc. E/CN.4/1985/4 (Sept. 28, 1984) (setting forth the Siracusa Principles on the Limitation and Derogation Provisions in the International Covenant on Civil and Political Rights). A State may derogate from its article 4 obligations under the International Covenant on Civil and Political Rights "only when faced with a situation of exceptional and actual or imminent danger which threatens the life of the nation." *Id.* para. 39. A "threat to the life of the nation" is defined as a threat that:

(a) Affects the whole of the population and either the whole or part of the territory of the State, and (b) Threatens the physical integrity of the population, the political independence of the territorial integrity of the State or the existence or basic functioning of institutions indispensable to ensure and protect the rights recognized in the Covenant.

Id.

77 Convention Against Torture, *supra* note 52, art. 2.

need for relaxation of stringent rules forbidding enhanced interrogation methods.[78]

It is futile to rely on the Torture Convention or other formal treaties to prove the illegality of extraordinary renditions involving torture. Numerous States have not ratified these agreements and it is essentially to these non-party States to which suspected terrorists have been sent under the extraordinary rendition schemes.[79]

There may, however, be other rules of international law more on point than the Torture Convention and other formal treaties to

---

78 *See, e.g.*, Bundesverfassungsgericht [BVerfG] [Federal Constitutional Court] Feb. 15, 2006, docket number 1 BvR 357/05, at juris online/Rechtsprechung, *available at* http://www.bverfg.de/entscheidungen/rs20060215_1bvr035705.html (declaring the Aviation Security Act, which authorized the shooting down of aircraft controlled by those seeking to use it as a weapon, void as an impermissible derogation from the Basic Law); HCJ 3239/02 Marab v. Commander of IDF Forces in the West Bank [2002] IsrSC 57(2) 349, paras. 26-34, *available at* http://elyon1.court.gov.il/eng/verdict/search_eng/verdict_by_misc.html (search "Search by Case no." for "case no. 3239" and "year 2002," then follow "PDF" hyperlink) (discussing how judicial intervention for detainees is a necessary right that should not be delayed); HCJ 3278/02 Ctr. for the Def. of the Individual v. Commander of IDF Forces in the West Bank [2003] IsrSC 57(1) 385, para. 24, *available at* http://elyon1.court.gov.il/eng/verdict/search_eng/verdict_by_misc.html (search "Search by Case no." for "case no. 3278" and "year 2002," then follow "PDF" hyperlink) ("Even [prisoners] suspected of terrorist activity of the worst kind are entitled to conditions of detention which satisfy minimal standards of humane treatment and ensure basic human necessities."); HCJ 5100/94 Pub. Comm. Against Torture in Isr. v. Israel et al. [1999] IsrSC 53(4) 1, para. 40, *available at* http://elyon1.court.gov.il/files_eng/94/000/051/a09/94051000.a09.pdf (holding that the General Security Service does not have the authority to use the "necessity defense" as a tool for utilizing inhumane interrogation tactics); A (FC) & Others (FC) v. Sec'y of State for the Home Dep't [2005] UKHL 71, paras. 33, 45, 52, 53, [2006] 2 A.C. 221, 261, 268, 270-72 (appeal taken from Eng.) (discussing the potentially broadening scope of what constitutes torture and the admissibility of evidence procured by torture). For a Press Release explaining the German case regarding the Aviation Security Act cited above, see Press Release No. 11/2006, Bundesverfassungsgericht [Federal Constitutional Court], Authorization to Shoot Down Aircraft in the Aviation Security Act Void (Feb. 15, 2006), http://www.bundesverfassungsgericht.de/en/press/bvg06-011en.html.

79 For a list of countries to which suspected terrorists have been rendered, see sources cited *supra* notes 21–22; *see also supra* note 34 and accompanying text. For an updated list of countries who have ratified (or failed to ratify) the Torture Convention, see United Nations, Office of the United Nations High Commissioner for Human Rights, 9. Convention Against Torture and Other Cruel, Inhuman or Degrading Treatment or Punishment, New York, 10 December 1984, http://www2.ohchr.org/english/bodies/ratification/9.htm (last visited Mar. 7, 2008).

clarify the prohibition of extraordinary rendition involving torture. For example, the question as to whether extraordinary rendition would have been compatible with international law before the adoption of the Torture Convention in 1984 is usually avoided in subsequent discussions. Yet, extraordinary rendition cases involving torture have been reported before this date but, still, the question of ancillary prohibitive rules is rarely, if ever, raised in discussions on extraordinary rendition.[80] Yet, it is fairly certain that practices involving subjecting detainees to torture were prohibited even before 1984, as perhaps most strikingly shown by evidence given in the Nuremberg and Tokyo Trials.[81]

VII.Torture Flights, Ghost Detainees and Black Sites

A whole new language has evolved around the relatively new practice of extraordinary rendition. Many now speak of "torture flights" to signify the chartered planes that have taken some detainees to be interrogated in specific countries known to practice harsh interrogation methods and torture. Most of these countries have not ratified the Torture Convention.

A number of airlines, for example, Jeppesen, a subsidiary of Boeing and Tepper Airlines, are said to be involved in such torture flights.[82] It is clear that actual precise evidence is not available: most consist of reports in newspapers which may or may not be reliable.[83] It is, however, highly likely that a least some of these

---

80 For further discussion on fundamental or intrinsic human rights, see DETTER, INTERNATIONAL LEGAL ORDER, *supra* note 43, at 288-305; INGRID DETTER, CONCEPT OF INTERNATIONAL LAW 46-51, 119 (2d ed. 1995).

81 *See* 20 INTERNATIONAL MILITARY TRIBUNAL FOR THE FAR EAST, THE TOKYO WAR CRIMES TRIAL 49,663-49,761 (R. John Pritchard & Sonia Magbanua Zaide eds., 1981); United States v. von Weizsaecker (The Ministries Case), *in* XII TRIALS OF WAR CRIMINALS BEFORE THE NUERNBERG MILITARY TRIBUNALS UNDER CONTROL COUNCIL LAW NO. 10, at 35-38 (1949); XII TRIAL OF THE MAJOR WAR CRIMINALS BEFORE THE INTERNATIONAL MILITARY TRIBUNAL, NUREMBERG, 14 NOVEMBER 1945 – 1 OCTOBER 1946, at 257 (1947).

82 *See* Complaint, Mohamed v. Jeppesen Dataplan, Inc., No. C 07-2798 (N.D. Cal. May 30, 2007) (asserting that Jeppensen aided the CIA in its extraordinary rendition practices). *See also* Bob Egelko, *Judge Dismisses Renditions Lawsuit in San Jose*, SAN FRANCISCO CHRONICLE, Feb. 13, 2008, at B2(reporting that Judge Ware in a San Francisco Court blocked the hearing of a case brought by the American Civil Liberties Union against Jeppesen Data Plan, alleging that the airway company ran "torture flights." The Judge held that such matters were a "state secret.").

83 *See, e.g.*, Dan Bilefsky, *European Inquiry Says C.I.A. Flew 1,000 Flights in*

flights have taken place, and that detainees have been taken from one jurisdiction to another, usually to one of these countries where torture is likely to be used.[84]

The CIA is also said to hold certain "ghost detainees," that is to say detention of prisoners who are not officially registered. Such "ghost detainees" are kept outside of judicial oversight, sometimes without ever entering US territory.[85]

Some detainees are, according to reports, taken through secret detention centres: so called "black sites" are normally used by the CIA in cooperation with other governments.[86] States that cooperate in such schemes may have their international responsibility engaged under various international agreements if such detention precludes the defence rights of a detainee,[87] especially if detention is prolonged in time.[88]

It is this cooperation by other states that has provoked a series of investigations and reports in various international organizations.

Secret, N.Y. TIMES, Apr. 27, 2006, at A12; Nat Hentoff, *Have a Nice Flight*, The Village Voice, Feb. 7, 2007, at 14; Daniel McGrory, *U.S. Torture 'were Refuelled in Britain*, TIMES (U.K.), Dec. 16, 2005, at 16; Marie Woolf, *Torture Flights Landed in U.K., Admit Air Controllers*, INDEPENDENT (U.K.), Feb. 19, 2006, at 23.

84 AMNESTY INT'L, U.S.A: BELOW THE RADAR: SECRET FLIGHTS TO TORTURE AND 'DISAPPEARANCE' 24-32 (2006) [hereinafter Amnesty Int'l Report].

85 *See, e.g.*, INTELLIGENCE AND SECURITY COMMITTEE, RENDITION, 2007, Cm. 7171.

86 *Id.*

87 *See, e.g.*, Kurt v. Turkey (No. 74), 1998-III Eur. Ct. H.R. at 1185, para. 124, where the European Court of Human Rights stated that "arbitrary deprivation of . . . liberty" and "the unacknowledged detention of an individual is a complete negation" of the rights guaranteed by Article 5 of the European Convention for the Protection of Human Rights. Council of Europe, Convention for the Protection of Human Rights and Fundamental Freedoms, art. 5, *opened for signature* Nov. 4, 1950, Europ. T.S. No. 5, 213 U.N.T.S. 222.

88 *See, e.g.*, Ocalan v. Turkey, 2005-IV Eur. Ct. H.R. 131 (imposition of death penalty following an unfair trial and prolonged detention violated Articles 3, 5, and 6 of European Convention); Suárez-Rosero Case, 1997 Inter-Am. Ct. H.R. (ser. C) No. 35, paras. 90-91 (Nov. 12, 1997) (prolonged detention and poor treatment of detainee violated Article 5(2) of the American Convention on Human Rights); Velásquez Rodríguez Case, 1998 Inter-Am. Ct. H.R. (ser. C) No. 4, para. 187 (July 29, 1988) (prolonged detention and poor treatment of detainee violated Articles 5(1) and 5(2) of the American Convention on Human Rights); Polay Campos v. Peru, Comm. No. 577/1994, U.N. GAOR Hum. Rts. Comm., 61st Sess., paras. 8.4, 8.6-.7, U.N. Doc. CCPR/C/61/D/577/1994 (Jan. 9, 1998) (prolonged detention and poor treatment of detainee violated Articles 7 and 10(1) of the International Covenant on Civil and Political Rights).

A number of states, such as France, Spain, Sweden, Denmark, Norway, Germany, Portugal, Austria, Italy, Poland, Romania, United Kingdom and Ireland have all been accused of facilitating extraordinary rendition by allowing transit of such flights.[89] In most countries investigations have been launched only to result in statements that no evidence has been found to support the claim of such cooperation.[90]

These sites have been claimed to exist in Afghanistan at the Bagram Air Base[91] and in Iraq[92] at Camp Cropper.[93] It has also been claimed that the Abu Ghraib prison worked as a black site, but there is less evidence of this assertion.[94] In addition Jordan[95] and Pakistan have been claimed to be black site hosts.[96] Black sites are also alleged to exist in Egypt,[97] and Morocco, for example at the al-Tamara interrogation centre near Rabat.[98] In Thailand, the Voice of America relay station in Udon Thani has been said to host a black site.[99] Claims have also been made that black sites have existed in several European countries, especially in the post-communist states, such as Poland,[100] at Mihail Kogălniceanu near Constanta, in Romania,[101] Armenia,[102] Georgia,[103] Latvia,

89 *See* European Parliament Report, *supra* note 30.

90 *See* Intelligence and Security Committee, *supra* note 85.

91 European Parliament Report, *supra* note 25, at para. 160.

92 Josh White, *Army, CIA Agreed on 'Ghost' Prisoners*, WASH. POST, Mar. 11, 2005, at A16.

93 Jamie McIntyre, *Pentagon: Iraqi Held Secretly at CIA Request*, CNN, Jun. 16, 2004, http://www.cnn.com/2004/US/06/16/ghost.prisoner/index.html.

94 White, *supra* note 92.

95 European Parliament Report, *supra* note 30, at para. 105.

96 Amnesty Report, *supra* note 84, at 8

97 European Parliament Report, *supra* note 25, at para. 107.

98 European Parliament Report, *supra* note 25, at para. 89; Jason Burke, *Secret World of U.S. Jails*, THE OBSERVER (U.K.), Jun. 13, 1994, http://www.guardian.co.uk/world/2004/jun/13/usa.terrorism.

99 EUR. PARL. ASS. Report, *Secret Detentions and Illegal Transfers of Detainees Involving Council of Europe Member States: Second Report*, Doc. 11302 (June 11, 2007) at n. 27; *see also* Dana Priest, *CIA Holds Terror Suspects in Secret Prisons*, WASH. POST, Nov. 2, 2005, at A1.

100 Amnesty Report, *supra* note 84, at 15; European Parliament Report, *supra* note 25, at 174 (mentioning Szymany Airport as involved in rendition flights).

101 See The Associated Press, *Romanian President Says CIA Flights May Have*

Bulgaria[104] and Slovakia.[105] Not only ex-communist states have been implicated, but many Western states have been accused of tolerating activities by the CIA including, Austria, Belgium, Cyprus, Denmark, Germany, Greece, Ireland, Italy, Poland, Portugal, Romania, Spain, Sweden and the United Kingdom.[106]

As for documentary proof of such sites, it is sadly lacking. It is obviously in the nature of things that first hand sources will not be readily available. However, one would have expected some form of effort on behalf of organizations of human rights to seek some form of primary sources, at least as far as pronouncements, and denials, of by United States government are concerned. Even parliamentary reports like those of the EU Parliamentary Assembly[107] and of the Parliament of the Council of Europe[108] (two bodies often confused), as well as the UN High Commission for Human Rights,[109] generally refer only to newspaper articles, and refrain from citing any first hand documentary sources. This practice of resorting to secondary and even tertiary sources is even used for references to statements of the United States government, such as denials or for the Executive Orders prohibiting torture for which official documents are readily available.[110]

Landed in Country, Feb. 8, 2006, *available* at, http://www.tkb.org/NewsStory.jsp?storyID=105414; *see also* European Parliament Report, *supra* note 25, at 149.

102 Amnesty Report, *supra* note 84, at 16.

103 *Id.*

104 *Id.*

105 *Id.*

106 European Parliament Report, *supra* note 25.

107 *See e.g.*, European Parliament Report, *supra* note 25.

108 *See, e.g.*, EUR. PARL. ASS., *Report from the Comm. on Legal Affairs & Human Rights: Lawfulness of Detentions by the United States in Guantánamo Bay*, Doc. No. 10497, § III (2005), http://assembly.coe.int/Main.asp?link=http://assembly.coe.int/Documents/WorkingDocs/Doc05/EDOC10497.htm (citing The Washington Post, The New York Times, The Guardian, The Observer, and Vanity Fair).

109 *See* Office of the United Nations High Commissioner for Human Rights, Comm. against Torture, *Conclusions and Recommendations of the Committee against Torture*, U.N. Doc. CAT/C/USA/CO/2, at 5 (July 25, 2006).

110 *See, e.g.*, Exec. Order No. 13, 440, 3 Fed. Reg. 40, 707 (July 20, 2007). This document is rarely cited and often replaced by a secondary newspaper reference.

VIII. Legality or Illegality of Extraordinary Rendition

Some international bodies have criticized the system of extraordinary rendition. On May 19, 2006, the United Nations Committee Against Torture, the U.N. body that monitors compliance with the United Nations Convention Against Torture, recommended that the United States cease holding detainees in alleged secret detention facilities and stop the practice of rendering prisoners to countries where they are likely to be tortured.[111]

The Parliamentary Assembly of the Council of Europe on January 23, 2008 backed a report saying the use of arbitrary terrorist black-lists by the UN and the EU violate fundamental rights.[112]

Such attitudes, however, may fail to take into consideration that a state's most important duty is to its own citizens and in the present volatile world a state is certainly expected to do its utmost to protect its citizens from terrorist attacks.

It is possible that this duty cannot be discharged unless certain suspected terrorists are allowed to be subjected to fierce and effective interrogation. If there is no mistaken identity and the arrested person actually is a genuine risk to the citizens in a state, officials must be entitled to question him using some form of pressure, where the limits of such pressure are a matter of common sense. It cannot not be right – or even efficient – to subject a person to torture. Nor can it be right to be so lenient that the arrested person feels no pressure to part with vital information, for example with regard to a planned terrorist attack.

IX. Compatibility of Extraordinary Rendition with International Law

There are three main questions that should be raised when assessing the legality or illegality of extraordinary rendition.

One question is whether suspected terrorists that have been subjected to extraordinary rendition are "protected persons" under

---

111 Office of the United Nations High Commissioner for Human Rights, Committee Against Torture, *Conclusions and recommendations of the Committee against Torture*, 36th Session, CAT/C/USA/CO/2 (May 1-19, 2006).

112 *See* EUR. PARL. ASS., *United Nations and European Union blacklists: Resolution 1597*, 5th Sitting (Jan. 23, 2008), http://assembly.coe.int/Main.asp?link=/Documents/AdoptedText/ta08/ERES1597.htm.

the Geneva Conventions, specifically whether they form part of the group of persons who, cannot be forcibly moved under Article 49 of the Geneva Convention Relative to the Protection of Civilian Persons in Time of War ("Geneva Convention IV").[113]

A second question concerns whether the Torture Convention or any other rules in international law prohibits torture to interrogate suspected terrorists, and whether or not they qualify as protected persons. An additional question under this heading concerns whether torture is only prohibited in the territory of states bound by the Torture Convention or are signatories bound outside of their territory.

A third question relates to the view that there are binding rules on minimum standards of behavior with regard to the treatment of individuals, rules which form part of international peremptory norms or *jus cogens*.

It is important to keep these three questions distinguished.

A. The Protected Persons Argument

The first question must probably be answered in the negative as the Geneva Convention IV is designed to protect "real" civilians,[114] and those who take up arms and engage in hostilities, which at least some suspected terrorists certainly do, fall outside all protection under the Convention.[115] However, this does not necessarily mean that there are not other rules under international law which protect persons from torture or other harsh forms of interrogation, as will be explored later in this text.

In 2004 United States Assistant Attorney General Jack Goldsmith stated that "protected persons" apprehended in Iraq could be subjected to so called extraordinary rendition and sent to

---

113 Geneva Convention Relative to the Protection of Civilian Persons in Time of War, *supra* note 63, art. 49.

114 *Id.* art. 3. "Civilians" are "persons taking no active part in the hostilities, including members of armed forces who have laid down their arms and those placed hors de combat by sickness, wounds, detention, or any other cause, shall in all circumstances be treated humanely, without any adverse distinction founded on race, colour, religion or faith, sex, birth or wealth, or any other similar criteria ..." and under Article 4 are "persons protected by the Convention are those who, at a given moment and in any manner whatsoever, find themselves, in case of a conflict or ocçupation, in the hands of a Party to the conflict or Occupying Power of which they are not nationals." *Id.* arts. 3-4.

115 *See* Detter, *Illegal Combatants, supra* note 45, at 1060.

be "interrogated" in another state.[116]

"Protected persons" are those who form part of the civilian population in an occupied area. Under the Geneva Convention IV on Civilians such people must not be moved. Article 49 of IV Geneva Convention of 1949 concerning Civilians states that:

"Individual or mass forcible transfers, as well as deportation of protected persons from occupied territory to the territory of the Occupying Power or to that of any other country, occupied or not, are prohibited, regardless of their motive"[117]

However the captured persons to whom the Assistant Attorney General referred are not any such civilians: they are unlawful or illegal combatants and do not enjoy any protection under the Law of War. It was indeed unfortunate that the Attorney General referred to "protected persons." There is no question that if real "protected persons" had been at issue it would certainly be illegal under international law to remove such civilians from the territory in question.[118] However, the whole point is that at least some of the persons removed were not such civilians and thus not "protected persons." If a person takes up arms and engages in hostilities, as some of the transferred person are alleged to have done, they have lost their status of "civilians" and are no longer "protected persons."[119] It was also unfortunate that the Memorandum specifically refers to Article 49, claiming that transfers would be compatible with this provision in the case of "illegal aliens." The Memo states that:

"The United States may, consistent with Article 49:

(1) remove "protected persons" who are illegal aliens from Iraq

---

116 Draft Memorandum from Jack Goldsmith, III, Assistant U.S. Attorney General, to Alberto R. Gonzales, U.S. Attorney General, regarding the Permissibility of Relocating "Protected Persons" from Occupied Iraq (Mar. 19, 2004), *in* THE TORTURE PAPERS: THE ROAD TO ABU GHRAIB 366-80 (K.J. Greenberg & J.L. Dratel eds., 2005) [hereinafter *March Draft Memo*].

117 Geneva Convention Relative to the Protection of Civilian Persons in Time of War, *supra* note 63, art. 49.

118 *Id.*

119 *See* Detter, *Illegal Combatants*, *supra* note 45, at 1060; *see also* INGRID DETTER, THE LAW OF WAR 136-37, 148 (2d ed. 2000) (explaining that because civilians who take up arms and engage in hostilities are not protected as soldiers, they are not regarded as POWs under Geneva Convention II and, unless they wear uniforms and fulfill other criteria of a soldier, they are "illegal" or "unlawful" combatants).

> pursuant to local immigration law; and
>
> (2) relocated "protected persons" (whether illegal aliens or not) from Iraq to another country to facilitate interrogation, for a brief but not indefinite period, as long as adjudicative proceedings have not been initiated against them"[120]

Geneva Convention IV provides that violations, *inter alia*, of Article 49 concerning forced transfers constitutes a "grave breach" of the accord, and thus a "war crime" under U.S. federal law, according to a footnote in the Justice Department draft.[121] "For these reasons," the footnote reads, "we recommend that any contemplated relocations of "protected persons" from Iraq to facilitate interrogation be carefully evaluated for compliance with Article 49 on a case by case basis."[122] It says that even persons removed from Iraq retain the treaty's protections, which includes the right to humane treatment and to contact with international monitors.[123]

It is of considerable importance, however, that the often cited Memorandum of March 19, 2004 is marked as a "Draft." It is not compatible with correct legal assessment to treat this document as if it were an official and final document authorizing extraordinary rendition.

According to unconfirmed claims that surrounds the process of extraordinary rendition, the CIA is said to have "used" the March draft memo as legal support for secretly transporting detainees out of Iraq to be interrogated elsewhere for a "brief but not indefinite period" and has permanently removed persons deemed to be "illegal aliens" under "local immigration law." Another OLC draft memorandum from August 1, 2002 is said to exist that again authorizes the removal of suspected terrorists from Iraq and from other locations.[124]

A point may be made initially about the importance of

120 March Draft Memo, *supra* note 116, at 367-68.

121 *Id.* at 379.

122 *Id.*

123 *Id.* at 379-80.

124 *See, e.g.*, Memorandum Jay S. Baybee, Assistant U.S. Attorney General, to Alberto R. Gonzales, Counsel to the President, regarding Standards of Conduct for Interrogations under 18 U.S.C. §§ 2340-2340A (Aug. 1, 2002), *in* THE TORTURE PAPERS: THE ROAD TO ABU GHRAIB 172-217 (K.J. Greenberg & J.L. Dratel eds., 2005).

establishing the true identity of a suspected terrorist. There have been some scandals involving cases when innocent persons have been held and treated as possible terrorists. In some cases persons have certainly been subjected to erroneous rendition, usually as a result of mistaken identity. In December 2005 the CIA's Inspector General admitted that the CIA was investigating what the Agency called "erroneous renditions."[125] Khalid El-Masri is one such case.[126] Another incident concerned the radical Islamist cleric Hassan Mustafa Osama Nasr, also known as Abu Omar, who was kidnapped in Milan on February 17, 2003, and sent to Egypt, where he was held until February 11, 2007, when an Egyptian court ruled his imprisonment was "unfounded."[127]

It is important to retain the qualification of "combatants" to ensure that the Law of War protects those that most deserve to be protected, that is to say real soldiers and real civilians. To enjoy full protection under the Law of War a combatant must wear a distinctive sign or uniform showing that he is a soldier, be under military command, carry arms openly and follow himself the rules of the Law of War.[128]

B. *The Torture Argument*

The second question concerns precisely what limits international law poses to prevent suspected terrorists form being tortured or subjected to other forms of harsh treatment.

In this context it must first be analyzed what actually constitutes "torture." It is clear that to some extent some forms of treatment may be experienced differently by different people.

---

125 Dana Priest, *Wrongful Imprisonment: Anatomy of a CIA Mistake*, WASH. POST, Dec. 4, 2005, at A1.

126 *Id.*

127 The Associated Press, *Abducted Egyptian Cleric Released*, WASH. POST, Feb. 12, 2007.

128 *See* Detter, The Law of War, *supra* note 119, at 136-148; Detter, *Illegal Combatants*, *supra* note 45, at 1058-59. For a questionable decision regarding the requirement that lawful combatants wear distinctive insignia, see Military Prosecutor v. Omar Mahmud Kassem and Others, 42 I.L.R. 470 (Israeli Military Ct. at Ramallah, 1969) (holding that "dark green dress and mottled peaked caps" do fulfill the requirement because "civilians resident in the area where the encounter with the Israeli forces took place do not usually wear green clothes or mottled caps."); *see also* Dinstein, *Conduct of Hostilities Under the Law of International Armed Conflict* 48 (2004).

Some, with a low threshold of pain, may consider even light pressure as unbearable and would consider this as torture. Other more courageous persons may find, when subjected to fierce interrogation, that they do not place this on the level of torture.

The inevitable subjective element, that is to say how different persons experience specific interrogation methods, is also reminiscent of the discrepancy between the English and French versions of the Geneva Conventions. The English version speaks of "unnecessary suffering" which certainly involves a subjective evaluation.[129] The French version, on the other hand, speaks of *maux superflus*, ("excessive wounds"), which, of course, has a far more objective meaning.[130]

Nevertheless there is normally a vague agreement that any considerable physical harm inflicted on a person does constitute torture. What is more difficult to ascertain is whether psychological pressure, which can be far more effective in terms of interrogation, amounts to torture. There is also an ancillary question as to whether threats to harm other members of a person's family amounts to torture; such threats can cause immense suffering to a person held for questioning.

It is also relevant that the United States has made some significant reservations to the Torture Convention. The term "cruel, inhuman or degrading treatment" will be interpreted according to United States rules.[131] This evokes the famous reservation that the United States appended to its accession to the Statute of the International Court of Justice, stating that the United States itself would decide what question concerns national security for which the ICJ is not competent.[132]

---

129 Protocol Additional to the Geneva Conventions of 12 August 1949, and Relating to the Protection of Victims of International Armed Conflicts (Protocol I) art. 47, June 8, 1977, 1125 U.N.T.S. 3 (English language); *see also* Detter, The Law of War, *supra* note 119, at 165.

130 Geneva Conventions *supra*, note 129 (French language).

131 Namely, "cruel, unusual and inhumane treatment" or punishment is interpreted through the law of the Fifth, Eighth, and/or Fourteenth Amendments to the Constitution of the United States. *See* 136 Cong. Rec. 17,486 (1990) (resolution of ratification of the Convention Against Torture and Other Cruel, Inhuman or Degrading Treatment or Punishment).

132 *See* Reservation to the Optional Clause of the ICJ by the United States, 61 Stat. 1218, 1946 WL 25470 (US Treaty).

The Torture Convention is slightly unhelpful with regard to the definition of torture. Article 1 provides that:

"For the purposes of this Convention, torture means any act by which severe pain or suffering, whether physical or mental, is intentionally inflicted on a person for such purposes as obtaining from him or a third person information or a confession, punishing him for an act he or a third person has committed or is suspected of having committed, or intimidating or coercing him or a third person, or for any reason based on discrimination of any kind, when such pain or suffering is inflicted by or at the instigation of or with the consent or acquiescence of a public official or other person acting in an official capacity. It does not include pain or suffering arising only from, inherent in or incidental to lawful sanctions."[133]

It is vital to note the very last sentence, which removes all sense to the prohibition as any state involved in extraordinary rendition programs would argue that the interrogation methods are, indeed, part of lawful sanctions in the case of suspected terrorists. Furthermore, the condition that pain and suffering must have been inflicted by an "official," or by someone with "official" sanction, also removes certain scenarios from the ambit of the Convention.

In any event, the states to which extraordinary rendition flights are said to have been sent are virtually all non-signatories of the Torture Convention.

The question as to what sort of pressure can be allowed in order to extract information from suspected terrorists must also be addressed. Some forms of interrogations have clearly produced important results. It is clear that some interrogations have yielded valuable results in the sense that projected terrorist attacks have been foiled. According to White House, interrogation by CIA has often preempted serious terrorist attempts.[134] For example, the interrogation of Abu Zubaydah and Ramzi Binalshibh helped to break up a cell of Southeast Asian terrorist operatives preparing

133 Convention Against Torture and Other Cruel, Inhuman or Degrading Treatment or Punishment, Dec. 10, 1984, S. Treaty Doc. No. 100-20, 1465 U.N.T.S. 112.

134 President George W. Bush, President Bush Discusses Global War on Terror at Wardman Park Marriott Hotel, Wash., D.C. (Sept. 29, 2006), *available at* http://www.whitehouse.gov/news/releases/2006/09/20060929-3.html.

attacks in the United States, foil an al Qaeda operation to develop anthrax, expose planned strikes on a U.S. Marine camp in Djibouti, as well as on the U.S. Consulate in Karachi, and finally thwart plots to hijack passenger planes and to fly them into installations and buildings at Heathrow Airport and in London's Canary Wharf.[135]

Further, on December 26, 2005, it was reported that the capture of al Qaeda leaders Ramzi Binalshibh in Pakistan, Omar al-Faruq in Indonesia, Abd al-Rahim al-Nashiri in Kuwait and Muhammad al Darbi in Yemen were all partly the result of information gained during interrogations.[136]

The core of the question is actually a matter of the territorial reach of prohibitions of torture. Some assume that states which have not adhered to the Torture Convention (or other binding treaty on the matter) are free to practice torture. Others appear to think, as some in the US Administration do, that, although a ratifying state is not free to practice torture in its own territory, it is free to do so elsewhere or that it is free to delegate the process of applying such pressure in interrogations.[137] Hence the expression "torture by proxy."[138]

But this is a fallacy. To apply some historical perspective to the question, the German government during World War II had not signed any treaties or conventions on genocide; the Genocide Convention had not even come into existence. Nor had wartime Germany adhered to any binding agreements forbidding torture (or

---

135 Dan Eggan and Dafna Lizner, *Secret World of Detainees Grows More Public*, WASH. POST, Sept. 7, 2006, at A18.

136 *Id.*

137 *See* Craig Forcese, *A New Geography of Abuse? The Contested Scope of U.S. Cruel, Inhumane and Degrading Treatment Obligations*, 24 BERKELEY J. INT'L L. 908, 908-09 (2006) (illuminating Attorney General Alberto Gonzalez's account of the United States' position regarding the applicability of the Torture Convention to treatment of aliens beyond the nation's borders).

138 On the prohibition of torture in areas outside the territory of the State see R. (on the application of Al-Skeini) v. Sec'y of State for Def., 2004 WL 2810920 (Q.B.D. Admin. Ct. Dec. 14 2004) (holding that the fundamental scope of jurisdiction under Article 1 is territorial). *But see*, Loizidou v. Turkey, App. No. 15318/89, 310 Eur. Ct. H.R. (ser. A) 513, 515 (1995) (preliminary objections) ("the responsibility of Contracting Parties *can* be involved because of acts of their authorities, whether performed within or outside national boundaries, which produce effects outside their own territory") (emphasis added).

other gruesome practices) outside its own territory, for example in Auschwitz in Poland. Yet the War Crime Tribunal in Nuremberg came to the conclusion that Germany had severely violated international law for which even individual responsibility could be incurred.[139]

The question concerning the territorial reach of the prohibition of torture is linked to the next problem discussed here, that concerning minimum standards in international law.

C. The Minimum Standards Argument

There is room for suggesting that even though certain countries have not ratified the Torture Convention, and even though the harsh interrogations takes place outside the territory of the United States, *all states* have an obligation under international law to behave in a civilized way and refrain from torture or other inhumane treatment of individuals.[140]

One question concerns whether the application of the Law of War has territorial limitations. The theatre of the War on Terror may be global, and the rules which are part of the Law of War, for example those concerning the prohibition of torture, may *appear* to apply. Some then insist that it is by virtue of the rules of the Law of War that the torture of suspected terrorists is prohibited, while others would contend that this is so on the basis of the Torture Convention.[141] On closer analysis, neither of these assumptions may be correct: there might be a prohibitive rule because of *another basis of obligation*, for example a prohibition under peremptory rules of international law.

These are the other rules of international, outside formal treaties, which cannot be ignored when assessing the legality or illegality of torture.

The International Court of Justice has repeatedly insisted that *all* states are bound to respect *fundamental human rights*.[142] Some

---

139 *See, e.g.* Christian Tomuschat, *The Legacy of Nuremberg*, 4 J. INT'L CRIM. JUST. 830, 839-40 (2006).

140 *See* Detter, *Illegal Combatants*, *supra* note 45, at 1089.

141 *See* International Committee of the Red Cross, International Humanitarian Law and the Challenges of Contemporary Armed Conflicts 9 (2003), *available at* http://www.icrc.org/Web/eng/siteeng0.nsf/htmlall/5XRDCC/$File/IHLcontemp_armedconflicts_FINAL_ANG.pdf.

142 *See, e.g.*, Legal Consequences for States of the Continued Presence of South

twenty-eight years ago the Court confirmed this view in the *Hostage Case* and stated:

"Wrongfully deprive human beings of their freedom and subject them to physical hardship is in itself manifestly incompatible with the principles of the Charter of the United Nations, as well as with the Universal Declaration of Human Rights."[143]

Here the Court did not even mention torture but only "hardship" which clearly sets a lower level for what is acceptable as treatment of others. The Court, however, inserts the proviso of "*wrongfully*" which just might exclude certain forms of interrogation of suspected terrorists.

Courts in many countries have also claimed that torture is forbidden under general international law.[144] In other words, states may be held responsible for acts they have procured or allowed in areas under their control or occupation, or, indeed, for acts committed in territories to which they have deliberately dispatched a person for interrogation.[145] States, companies and individuals that connive in such transport where torture might be the

Africa in Namibia (South West Africa), Notwithstanding Security Council Resolution 276 (1970), Advisory Opinion, 1971 I.C.J. 16, 57 (June 21); *see also* Detter, International Legal Order, *supra* note 43, at 290.

143 (1980) ICJ *Reports* 1980, 42.

144 *See* Detter, INTERNATIONAL LEGAL ORDER, *supra* note 43, at 290. General international law is clearly a wider concept than "customary international law," even though many in the United States use the terms interchangeably. But general international law obviously also includes treaties and agreement, as well as rules on ethics and on *jus cogens*. None of which are necessarily tied to "customary" law; *see also* Detter, *Illegal Combatants*, *supra* 45, at 1054 (noting the absurdity of a "negative custom").

145 *See* Issa v. Turkey, no. 31821/96, ¶¶ 71-74 (Eur. Ct. H.R. Nov. 16, 2004), http://cmiskp.echr.coe.int/tkp197/view.asp?item=1&portal=hbkm&action=html&highlight=issa%20%7C%20turkey&sessionid=6048954&skin=hudoc-en; Legal Consequences of the Construction of a Wall in the Occupied Palestinian Territory (2004) I.C.J. 136, 179 (July 9); López Burgos v. Uruguay, No. 52/1979, Views of the H.R.C., ¶ 12.3, U.N. Doc. CCPR/C/13/D/52/1979 (July 29, 1981); Casariego v. Uruguay, No. 56/1979, Views of the H.R.C., ¶10.3, U.N. Doc. CCPR/C/13/D/56/1979 (July 29, 1981); Coard et al. v. United States, Case 10.951, Inter-Am. C.H.R., Report No. 109/99, OEA/Ser.L/V/II.106, doc. 6 rev. ¶ 37 (1999), *available at* http://www.cidh.org/annualrep/99eng/Merits/UnitedStates10.951.htm; Alejandre et al. v. Cuba, Case 11.589, Inter-Am. C.H.R., Report No. 86/99, OEA/Ser.L/V/II.106, doc. 6 rev. ¶ 23 (1999), *available at* http://www.cidh.org/annualrep/99eng/Merits/Cuba11.589.htm.

foreseeable result may also have their responsibility engaged as they, too, have the duty to prevent torture.[146]

It is essential to establish that the minimum standards evoked in this context are not necessarily those found in treaties and international conventions. It may be that the rules laid down in Articles 27-78 of the Fourth Geneva Convention and the provisions of Article 75 of the Second Protocol of 1977 to the Geneva Conventions *correspond*, roughly, to the minimum standards. But it is most important to underline that terrorists are not protected by the Law of War as they do not wear uniforms and do not qualify as soldiers, nor as civilians.[147]

When the Red Cross attempted to suggest that "no one must be left unprotected" by the Law of War, that organization did not service to the soldier in the field, nor to the real civilian: both would suffer by this dissipation of the rules of protection under the Law of War.[148] If we dilute the contents of protection to protect those who do not deserve to be protected we will alter the whole essence of the Law of War and make such rules worthless, and the soldier and the civilian will be exposed to much danger.

This is not to say that states may treat suspected terrorists as they please. Although, it must be insisted, the suspected terrorist does not have the right to be protected as a prisoner of war nor as a civilian, there are some minimum standards that apply. It is clear he must not be subjected to torture. But one comes back to the question of definition: water-boarding and outright physical harm is certainly prohibited under general international law (not under

146 *See* Z and Others v. U.K. No. *29392/95*, 10 Eur. Ct. H.R. 384 (2001), *available at* http:// www.echr.coe.int/eng, *see also* A v. U.K. No. 100/1997/884/1096, 5 Eur. Ct. H.R. 137 at para. 22 (1998), *available at* http:// www.echr.coe.int/eng, *see also* Ilascu and Others v. Mold. and Russ. *9*, (2004) Eur. Ct. H.R. 48787/ at para. 318, *available at* http:// www.echr.coe.int/eng.

147 *See* Geneva Convention Relative to the Treatment of Prisoners of War art. 4, Aug. 12, 1949, 6 U.S.T. 3316, 75 U.N.T.S. 135 (explaining the criteria that establish whether a combatant will be protected by the Geneva Conventions, including the requirement that a soldier wear a uniform or other distinctive dress). The point about uniforms is clearly the question of *distinction* that you show to your enemy that you are a member of the armed forces. Although the Law of War allows ruses and surreptitious practices, it does not allow soldiers to be disguised as civilians; *see also* Detter, The Law of War, *supra* note 119 , at 135.

148 *See* ICRC 2003 Report, *supra* note 141; *see also* Detter, *Illegal Combatants*, *supra* note 45, at 1058-59.

customary law, as some pretend as "negative custom" is an absurd notion).[149] But some pressure must be allowed, such as sleep deprivation, in cases such as when a suspected terrorist has information as to where there is a bomb which might kill a great number of people. It is not that the suffering of one is worth that of thousands, but a matter of common sense, that interrogation must be allowed to use some form of minor force.[150]

X. Conclusions.

No state can escape responsibility for inflicting harm on individuals during interrogations. It should also be underlined that the state cannot claim that its security services have exceeded their power as the state has a duty to supervise and closely monitor such activities.[151]

On the other hand, it is clear that some pressure is allowed to extract information from suspected terrorists but there is also a certain level beyond which questioning should not proceed.

The whole system of extraordinary rendition has overemphasized the territoriality aspect. If captives cannot be subjected to techniques of interrogation legally in the United States, some find it acceptable that they are sent abroad to states where such methods are not illegal. But all this ignores the fact that the procedure might be illegal under *international law* and it may be futile to use domestic law arguments to evade obligations under the international legal system.[152] In *Filartiga v Pena-Irala* a United States court held that the torturer has become "like the pirate and the slave trader before him – *hostis humani generis*, an enemy of all mankind."[153] Recently it has been possible to claim that it is the terrorist who has become such an outlaw and enemy of mankind.[154] But by resorting to torturer the torturer thus places

---

149 *See* Detter, *Illegal Combatants*, *supra* note 45, at 1054.

150 *See* The Ireland Case, *supra* note 59; *see also* the text accompanying Refugee Convention, *supra* note 36.

151 *See* Klass and Others v. F.R.G No. 5029/71, 2 Eur. H.R. Rep. 214 at para. 71 and 75 (1980), *available at* http:// www.echr.coe.int/eng. *See also* Leander v. Swed., No. *9248/81*,9 Eur. H.R. Rep. 433 at para. 84 (1987), *available at* http:// www.echr.coe.int/eng.

152 *See* Detter, International Legal Order, *supra* note 43, at 168-170.

153 D. Filartiga and J. Filartiga, v. Pean-Irala, 630 F.2d 876, 890 (2d Cir. 1980).

154 *See* Detter, *Illegal Combatants*, *supra* note 45, at 1096.

himself on the same unacceptable level as the terrorist.

A state may not use its own legislation to escape obligations under international law.[155] The *Alabama Arbitration* illustrates that a state is *under a duty to make sure that its internal laws comply with international law* and, if they do not, the state may incur responsibility for consequences of the discrepancy between international law and municipal law.[156] The Permanent Court of International Justice also held in *Polish Nationals in Danzig*[157] that a state cannot invoke its own constitution or other internal rules to escape obligations under international law. In the same way, then, the United States cannot justify moving detainees to other locations only on the ground that the interrogations techniques to be used are illegal under US law. Such methods are also illegal under international law and the state's responsibility is engaged when seeking to evade obligations under internal law which, ironically, also apply world wide under the minimum standard rules of the international legal system.

Furthermore, the International Court of Justice has also spoken to a state's responsibility for of extraterritorial acts in *Legal consequences of the Construction of a Wall in the Occupied Palestinian Territory.*[158]

Just as much as those responsible for Germany's practices during the Second World War could not escape responsibility for war crimes by claiming that acts committed were legal (and even commended) by the internal legal system, so a state cannot now claim that because something is illegal in its own state, it would be legal to arrange to have such acts carried out elsewhere.

---

155 *Id.*

156 For a discussion of the Alabama Claims and their outcome resulting in the Treaty of Washington see CALEB CUSHING, THE TREATY OF WASHINGTON: ITS NEGOTIATION, EXECUTION, AND THE DISCUSSIONS RELATING THERETO (Harper & Bros. 1873). For the Case presented by the U.S. stating their claims in the Alabama Claims *see The Case of the United States, to be Laid Before the Tribunal of Arbitration: to be Convened at Geneva under the Provisions of the Treaty Between the United States of America and Her Majesty the Queen of Great Britain, concluded at Washington, May 8, 1871* (Richard Bently & Sons, 1872).

157 Treatment of Polish Nationals and Other Persons of Polish Origin or Speech in the Danzig Territory, Advisory Opinion, 1933 P.C.I.J. (ser A/B) no. 44 (Feb. 4).

158 Legal Consequences of the Construction of a Wall in the Occupied Palestinian Territory, Advisory Opinion, 2004 I. C. J. 136 (July 9).

The argument that a state is not liable for what it allows or organizes in the territory of other states, indeed, in territories outside its sovereignty like Guantanamo Bay, is a fallacy. The arguments is based on the faulty premise that territoriality is all and that actions beyond a state's territory can somehow be distanced from government action. This is not correct and there is still a question of liability for such action which in due course might mature.

The United States would probably gain far more sympathy even for fierce or enhanced interrogation practices of suspected terrorists if such questioning took place in the United States. But what is not acceptable in international law is to seek to escape liability by organizing interrogations clandestinely, involving torture flights (at what cost?) and black sites.

It is also beyond doubt that information obtained through torture is notoriously unreliable and it is therefore perhaps not wise to engage the state's responsibility (and probably damage its good name) by arranging torture flight abroad.

The European Court of Human Rights has also confirmed that the prohibition of torture extends to areas under effective control of the state.[159] The same attitude has been taken by English courts.[160] Occupied territories over which a state has established authority thus come within the ambit of the human rights obligations of the state.[161]

Delegation of interrogation procedures to another state can thus not rid a state of its responsibility for torture if it arranges flights to areas outside its own territory. On the other hand, at the root of the problem, it is not quite established what sort of practices and in how many cases interrogations practices have exceeded what is permissible under international law. Newspaper reports and evidence given by released detainees, possibly

---

159 *See* Loizidou v. Turkey, App. No. 15318/89, 310 Eur. Ct. H.R. (ser. A) 513, 515 (1995) (preliminary objections) ("The responsibility of a Contracting State can also arise when as a consequence of military action—whether lawful or unlawful—it exercises effective control of an area outside its national territory.")

160 *See* R. (on the application of Al-Skeini) v. Sec'y of State for Def., 2004 WL 2810920 (Q.B.D. Admin. Ct. Dec. 14, 2004).

161 *See, e.g.*, EXTRATERRITORIAL APPLICATION OF HUMAN RIGHTS TREATIES (Fons Coomans & Menno T. Kamminga, eds. 2004) for a comprehensive publication devoted to this subject.

delivered during a post-traumatic state of mind, must be largely discarded and only clear evidence as to excessive interrogation methods must be accepted.[162] The truth about such practices is not easy to establish. Nor is the truth of what is revealed under torture easy to ascertain.

On the other hand, it is clear that the prohibition of torture is one of the basic tenets of *jus cogens*, the peremptory rules from which no derogation is permitted.[163] Along with genocide, slavery and genocide, it must be noted that torture is also forbidden by these fundamental and intrinsic rules of international law.[164]

In a landmark case in the House of Lords in England it was decided that evidence obtained through torture is not allowed in English courts.[165] The main reason for this attitude is clearly that such evidence is not sufficiently reliable to form the basis for ensuing convictions. The same attitude should prevail in the international field and it should be accepted that torture is rarely the appropriate method to arrive at the truth.

---

162 *See, e.g.*, Richard Bonner, *Detainee Says he was Tortured while in US Custody*, N.Y. TIMES, Feb. 13, 2005, at A1.

163 Vienna Convention on the Law of Treaties art. 53, May 23, 1969, 1155 U.N.T.S. 331.

164 *See, e.g.*, The Tokyo and Nuremberg Trials, *supra* note 81; *see also* Prosecutor v Furundzija, 38 ILM 317, 349 (1999).

165 *A(FC) and Others v Secretary of the Home Department, 2005 U.K.H.L. 71 (2005)*. The unanimous judgment confirmed that, under English law, "torture and its fruits" could not be used in evidence in court. *See id.* at para 51. But the information obtained could be used by the police as "it would be ludicrous for them to disregard information [about a ticking bomb] if it had been procured by torture." *Id.* at para 68. The Law Lords thus dismissed, to some extent, concerns about the accuracy of information obtained under torture.

Part VII
Judicial Responses

[17]

DECISIONS OF INTERNATIONAL COURTS AND TRIBUNALS

PAUL JAMES CARDWELL, DUNCAN FRENCH AND NIGEL WHITE

Edited by J Craig Barker

I. European Court of Justice, *Yassin Abdullah Kadi and Al Barakaat International Foundation v Council and Commission* (Joined Cases C-402/05 P And C-415/05 P) Judgment of 3 September 2008
II. International Tribunal for the Law of The Sea, *Hoshinmaru (Japan v Russian Federation)* and *Tomimaru (Japan v Russian Federation)* Prompt Release Judgments of 6 August 2007

I. EUROPEAN COURT OF JUSTICE, *Yassin Abdullah Kadi and Al Barakaat International Foundation v Council and Commission* (JOINED CASES C-402/05 P AND C-415/05 P) JUDGMENT OF 3 SEPTEMBER 2008

A. Summary of Facts and Judgment

UN Security Council (UNSC) Resolution 1267 (1999) was one in a series of resolutions which attempted to prevent the planning and carrying out of terrorist attacks by Usama bin Laden and the Al-Qaeda network. The freezing of funds of the Taliban, who the Security Council saw as providing both a safe haven for bin Laden and a base for developing international terrorist activities, as well as the funds of those suspected of being associated with bin Laden, is one of the principal means by which the aims of the Resolutions are to be achieved. Paragraph 6 of the Resolution established a Sanctions Committee, which is responsible, amongst other tasks, for creating a list of individuals and entities designated as associates of bin Laden. States are responsible for freezing the funds and assets of those individuals and entities on the list.

The European Union (EU) adopted Common Position 1999/727/CFSP pursuant to the provisions on the Common Foreign and Security Policy (CFSP) which prescribed the freezing of funds according to the terms of Resolution 1267. The common position was swiftly followed in February 2000 by Council Regulation 337/2000 concerning a flight ban and the necessary freezing of funds. Further UNSC Resolutions were passed, followed by CFSP Common Positions and EC Regulations, which strengthened the restrictive measures. Regulation 467/2001 defined the nature of 'funds' and 'freezing of funds' and listed, in Annex I, the individuals and entities designated by the Sanctions Committee as affected by the freezing of funds.

Kadi, a national of Saudi Arabia, and the Al Barakaat International Foundation, established in Sweden, were placed on the Sanctions Committee's renewed lists on 17 October and 9 November 2001 respectively. They were subsequently added to Annex I of Regulation 467/2001.[1] The contested Regulation (881/2002) was adopted

[1] Namely regulations 2062/2001 of 19 October 2001 (Kadi) and 2199/2001 of 12 November 2001 (Al Barakaat).

on 27 May 2002 following a further UNSC Resolution and CFSP common position, all which continued and widened the measures directed at the Taliban, bin Laden and Al-Qaeda. The regulation repealed the previous Regulation 467/2001 but the definitions of funds and freezing of funds were identical. Both Kadi and Al Barakaat remained on the list in Annex I. Regulation 561/2003 introduced an amendment whereby a Member State may allow for exceptions to the freezing of funds as permitted by the UNSC: the Member State must inform the Sanctions Committee (and the other Member States), who must not object to the exception being granted.

Kadi, as a 'non-privileged applicant' for the purposes of judicial review at the EU level, brought an action before the Court of First Instance (CFI) seeking annulment of the Regulation in so far as it related to him. His arguments were based on four grounds: one on lack of EC competence and three on breaches of his fundamental rights (right to a fair hearing; the right to respect for property and the principle of proportionality; and the right to effective judicial review).

The CFI rejected all of the arguments.[2] On the competence issue, the CFI found that although articles 60 and 301 EC only expressly mention sanctions which can be imposed on third countries (and not, therefore, individuals), recourse to the 'residual powers' of article 308 EC[3] was justified. However, the Court refused to endorse the Commission's argument that the fight against international terrorism fell within the residual competence of article 308 in order to achieve a Community objective. This, in the view of the CFI, would 'deprive many provisions of the Treaty on European Union of their ambit and would be inconsistent with the introduction of instruments specific to the CFSP'.[4] Nevertheless, when the effects of articles 60, 301 and 308 were combined, this justified their use in the present case and did not constitute a widening of 'the scope of Community powers beyond the general framework created by the provisions of the Treaty'.[5]

On the fundamental rights arguments, the CFI was unwilling to find that it had the power to review UNSC resolutions to assess their conformity with the fundamental rights at stake. The CFI concluded that since UNSC resolutions are binding on Member States and, as a matter of customary international law, a state 'may not invoke the provisions of its internal law as justification for its failure to perform a treaty',[6] such resolutions fall outside the ambit of the Court's judicial review, the Court cannot therefore 'call in question, even indirectly, their lawfulness in the light of Community law'.[7] The CFI noted, however, one limit on the binding nature of UNSC resolutions, namely that they must observe peremptory norms of general international law, or *jus cogens*. If the resolution did not do so, then the Court would be empowered to carry out indirect judicial review; as the CFI noted 'in connection with an action for annulment of a Community act adopted, where no discretion whatsoever may be exercised, with a view to putting into effect a resolution of the Security Council may therefore, highly exceptionally, extend to determining whether the superior rules of international law

[2] Judgments of 21 September 2005 in Case T-306/01 *Yusuf and Al Barakaat International Foundation v Council* and Case T-315/01 *Kadi v Council and Commission*.

[3] 'If action by the Community should prove necessary to attain, in the course of the operation of the common market, one of the objectives of the Community, and this Treaty has not provided the necessary powers, the Council shall, acting unanimously on a proposal from the Commission and after consulting the European Parliament, take the appropriate measures'.

[4] Above (n 2) para 156.

[5] ibid, paras 132–3.

[6] ibid, para 182.

[7] ibid, para 225.

falling within the ambit of *jus cogens* have been observed, in particular, the mandatory provisions concerning the universal protection of human rights'.[8] On this basis, the CFI considered the claims based on fundamental human rights and found that none could succeed.

Both applicants lodged appeals with the European Court of Justice (ECJ) on the same grounds. Advocate General Maduro's opinion on the *Kadi* case[9] proposed that the Court should set aside the CFI's decision and annul the Regulations in so far as they concern the applicant. On the issue of competence, the Advocate General found that the CFI's interpretation of articles 60 and 301 was too narrow in restricting the imposition of sanctions on the governing regimes of third countries only. The mentioning of 'third countries' in these articles includes, according to the Advocate General, the economic relations with individuals and entities *within* third countries since 'the sanctions necessarily affect the overall state of economic relations between the Community and that country'.[10] There was no need, in his view, to bring in article 308 and to do otherwise would be to deprive article 301 of much of its use.

The Advocate General's opinion placed great emphasis on the right of the Community courts to review whether the regulation complies with the respect for the individual's fundamental rights as protected *within* the EU legal order. In a strongly worded assertion, the Advocate General found that 'it would be wrong to conclude that, once the Community is bound by a rule of international law, the Community Courts must bow to that rule with complete acquiescence and apply it unconditionally in the Community legal order'.[11] As such, the Community institutions 'cannot dispense with proper judicial review proceedings when implementing the Security Council resolutions in question within the Community legal order'[12] and cannot depart from their usual interpretation of fundamental rights as invoked by the applicant. Given the proposed availability of review of these measures by the ECJ, the Advocate General found that the closely connected rights invoked form part of the general principles of Community law as laid down by the ECJ in a series of cases.[13] Though the Court cannot necessarily know or second-guess whether or not the sanctions are disproportionate or misdirected, since there is no 'genuine and effective mechanism'[14] for allowing a right to be heard at the UN level, but merely an intergovernmental process to petition the Sanctions Committee, it must fall to the powers for judicial review within the Community legal order to ensure that a right to be heard is allowed.

The Grand Chamber of the ECJ gave its judgment on 3 September 2008.[15] It rejected the argument, put forward by the Commission and accepted by the Advocate General, that articles 60 and 301 are sufficient alone in allowing for the competence to

[8] ibid, para 231.

[9] Opinion of Poiares Maduro Advocate General, delivered on 16 January 2008. Similar wording is found in the Opinion delivered on the Al Barakaat International Foundation case on 23 January 2008.

[10] Above (n 9) paras 12–13.

[11] ibid, para 24.

[12] ibid, para 54.

[13] See Case C-32/95 P *Lisresal* [1996] ECR I-5373, Case C-50/00 P *Unión de Pequeños Agricultores v Council* [2002] ECR I-6677.

[14] Above (n 9) para 54.

[15] Judgment of the Court (Grand Chamber) of 3 September 2008—*Yassin Abdullah Kadi, Al Barakaat International Foundation v Council of the European Union and Commission of the European Communities* (Joined Cases C-402/05 P and C-415/05 P).

adopt the contested regulation.[16] However, it accepted that article 308 could be used jointly with articles 60 and 301 'if such powers appear none the less to be necessary to enable the Community to carry out its functions with a view to attaining on the objectives laid down by the Treaty'.[17] Such an objective in the present case was met, and the ECJ dismissed the appeal on this point.

As regards the substantive issues on the fundamental rights claims, the ECJ's approach is strikingly different from the CFI's judgment. In his appeal, Kadi claimed that the CFI erred in law in accepting the nature of UNSC resolutions as automatically part of European law and stating that the Community Courts have no power to review the lawfulness of UNSC resolutions except in relation to *jus cogens*. Kadi referred to the judgment of the European Court of Human Rights in *Bosphorus*[18] as evidence of the requirement of judicial review to be available at Community level when rights are at stake, even if the measure is ultimately derived from international law.

The ECJ confirmed that fundamental rights, in particular those found in the European Convention on Human Rights (ECHR), are an integral part of the general principles of law[19] and that the lawfulness of Community acts depends on their respect for human rights,[20] despite the general obligation on the Community to respect international law.[21] A review, such as the one in the present case, is of the Community act, and not the international agreement.[22] The ECJ utilized various EC Treaty provisions in support of its view that derogations from the principles of human rights are not possible and that these constitute a 'constitutional guarantee stemming from the EC Treaty as an autonomous legal system which is not to be prejudiced by an international agreement'.[23] The existence of the procedure whereby states may petition the Sanctions Committee on behalf of an individual did not constitute a generalised immunity from jurisdiction within the EC legal order.[24] The ECJ was therefore unimpressed with arguments that it should show full deference to the UN's legal order since the guarantees for judicial protection were not in place at the UN level. Since the ECJ found that the CFI was wrong to find that it had no jurisdiction to consider the claims based on fundamental rights, the ECJ felt no need to consider the aspects of the appeal dealing with *jus cogens*.

The ECJ did, however, consider the nature of the fundamental rights at stake. The Court felt that neither the regulation nor the CFSP Common Position afforded Kadi the right to be heard. Though this would not be expected before the act comes into effect—the 'element of surprise' being an essential component of the freezing of funds—as there was no means by which they could make their point of view or exercise rights of defence,[25] they were therefore deprived of this right. On the right to property, whilst a relationship of proportionality between the aim and means of the restrictive measure 'might, in principle, be justified',[26] the current application of the regulation to Kadi infringed his fundamental right to respect for property. The ECJ's reasoning on this point was closely linked to the lack of opportunity for him to put his case to the

[16] ibid, paras 174–6.

[17] ibid, para 211.

[18] *Bosphorus Hava Yollari Turizm ve Ticaret Anonim Sirketi v. Ireland* (2005) (Application no. 45036/98).

[19] Above n 15, para 283.

[20] ibid, para 284. See also *Opinion 2/94* [1996] ECR I-1759, para 34 and Case C-112/00 *Schmidberger* [2003] ECR I-5659 para 73.

[21] ibid, para 291.

[22] ibid, para 286.

[23] ibid, para 316.

[24] ibid, paras 318–21.

[25] ibid, para 348.

[26] ibid, para 366.

authorities.[27] However, since the ECJ was unaware of the evidence which had led to Kadi being placed on the Sanctions Committee list in 2001, it also stated that 'on the merits of the case, the imposition of those measures on the appellants may for all that prove to be justified'.[28] The result was that notwithstanding the upholding of the appeals, the effects of the regulation would be maintained (pursuant to article 231 EC) for a period of three months until the Council could remedy the infringements, which it since has done.

B. Commentary

The judgment of the ECJ in *Kadi* is a significant—though perhaps not a ground-breaking—decision in understanding the relationship between EU law and public international law, specifically the UN Charter and, more especially, the exercise of Chapter VII powers by the Security Council. The approach of the ECJ is ultimately premised upon three key understandings, namely the autonomy of the EU legal system, the constitutionality of the EU legal system and the centrality of fundamental rights to the operation of that legal system. Thus, the reason that the *Kadi* judgment should not be characterised as radical is because it reflects the long-standing view of the Court that the EU legal system is an autonomous legal framework independent of, and not reliant upon, public international law. Moreover, the ECJ in seeing and speaking of itself as a court protecting constitutional guarantees is also not a novel innovation.[29] In both respects, the Court has simply applied its settled jurisprudence in a way that is consistent with past practice.

The judgment nevertheless raises a range of issues on both EU and international law; this note limits itself to two. First, the place of the UN Charter and UNSC resolutions in EU law, and second, whether the current understanding of article 103 UN Charter in marginalising human rights arguments in favour of security measures can be supported in the light of a less atomistic interpretation of the UN Charter.

1. EU law and UN Security Council resolutions

The upholding, by the Court, of fundamental rights by the way of 'the guarantee of judicial protection'[30] has unquestionably powerful symbolic rhetoric, especially when placed against the revised, yet still limited, political review mechanism of the Sanctions Committee. The Court can barely hide its criticism of the 'diplomatic and intergovernmental' procedure, which it states 'cannot give rise to generalised immunity from jurisdiction within the internal legal order of the Community'.[31] In developing this line of argument, the Court adopts the general view that 'the Community judicature must . . . ensure the review, in principle the full review, of the lawfulness of all Community acts in the light of the fundamental rights forming an integral part of the general principles of Community law'.[32] In the abstract, this would appear both reasonable and sound; it is when it is placed against the normative framework of

[27] ibid, para 372–3. [28] ibid, para 374.
[29] See, inter alia, *Internationale Handelsgesellschaft* [1970] ECR 1125.
[30] Above (n 15) para 322. [31] ibid, para 321. [32] ibid, para 326.

binding resolutions of the UN Security Council however that it becomes contentious in its application.

Nevertheless, in many ways, the Court's judgment is clearly to be favoured over that of the decision of the Court of First Instance (CFI). Although some welcomed the CFI's step in acknowledging the primacy of the UN legal system over the Community legal order,[33] the argument that the EU was denied the right to judicially review one of its own measures simply because it was adopted to implement a UN resolution, particularly one that potentially infringed the fundamental rights inherent within the Union's legal framework, seemed incompatible with the whole tenor of the ECJ's jurisprudence on fundamental rights. At the same time, the CFI's certainty at being able to review the compatibility of the regulation against norms of *jus cogens*, seemed inconsistent with the continuing doctrinal debate surrounding judicial review at the global level.[34] It is perhaps wise, therefore, that the ECJ declined to confront this issue directly.

The ECJ emphasised in its judgment that 'an international agreement cannot affect the ... autonomy of the Community legal system'[35] and the constitutional guarantee 'stemming from the EC Treaty as an autonomous legal system which is not to be prejudiced by an international agreement'.[36] It is not stated by the ECJ whether the UN Charter is considered to be an international agreement for these purposes, which is problematic given the requirement, also recognised by the Court, for EC law to 'respect international law in the exercise of its powers' and that 'a measure adopted by virtue of those powers must be interpreted, and its scope limited, in the light of the relevant rules of international law'.[37] Reading the latter in the light of the former suggests that the ECJ itself was not following its own dicta.

On this point, the wording of paragraph 286 is instructive: '[T]he review of lawfulness thus to be ensured by the Community judicature applies to the Community act intended to give effect to the international agreement at issue, and not to the latter *as such*'.[38] While the inclusion of the words 'as such' may be incidental and insignificant, on the other hand it leaves open the possibility—doctrinal if not actual—of the ECJ undertaking a de facto review of the underlying UN resolution.

More specifically, was the ECJ right to equate the UN Charter with international agreements adopted under article 300(7) EC Treaty[39] and thus not hierarchically superior to the primary law of the EU, including fundamental rights?[40] One argument is that the ECJ was clearly wrong on this point as the UN Charter does not fall under article 300(7) EC Treaty[41] but article 307 EC Treaty?[42] On this issue, does the Court adopt a purposive (rather than a textual) approach when it notes that while article 307

[33] For example, C Tomuschat, 'Note on Kadi v Council and Commission (CFI)' (2006) 43 Common Market Law Review 537–551.

[34] See generally R Wessel, 'The UN, the EU and *Jus Cogens*' (2006) 3 International Organizations Law Review 1–6.

[35] Above (n 15) para 282.

[36] ibid, para 316.

[37] ibid, para 291.

[38] Emphasis added.

[39] Above (n 15) para 307.

[40] ibid, para 308.

[41] Article 300(7) EC Treaty: 'Agreements concluded under the conditions set out in this Article shall be binding on the institutions of the Community and on Member States'.

[42] Article 307 EC Treaty: 'The rights and obligations arising from agreements concluded before 1 January 1958 or, for acceding States, before the date of their accession, between one or more Member States on the one hand, and one or more third countries on the other, shall not be affected by the provisions of this Treaty'.

may allow derogations from the primary law in certain instances, '[t]hose provisions cannot, however, be understood to authorise any derogation from the principles of liberty, democracy and respect for human rights and fundamental freedoms enshrined in article 6(1) EU as a foundation of the Union'.[43] These are grand words, but they also contribute to a perceivable tension between the Court's insistence on respect for international law and the 'special importance' attached to the role of the UNSC under Chapter VII of the Charter[44] on the one hand, and its own right to review measures in terms of fundamental rights, on the other.

1. An alternative approach: revisiting the scope of article 103 UN Charter

There is a growing tendency, albeit a reluctant one, to accept the Security Council as increasingly omnipotent, especially when dealing with global threats such as Al-Qaeda, so that a combination of articles 25[45] and 103[46] of the UN Charter will even override human rights.[47] In effect, supposedly constitutional provisions (especially article 103)[48] are being used to override constitutional rights. This seemed, until the European Court of Justice's judgment in *Kadi* in 2008, to be the orthodoxy emerging in a number of judgments from various regional and domestic courts (the English House of Lords in *Al-Jedda*,[49] the European Court of Human Rights in *Behrami*,[50] and the European Court of First Instance in *Kadi*—notwithstanding the token *jus cogens* point). This note seeks to argue that such a doctrinal position is not clearly established in international law, either by the International Court or is indeed what the Security Council itself intends.

The Security Council is a political body whose decisions have legal consequences, but the political compromise behind each resolution does not anticipate with any precision what those consequences might be. Admittedly resolution 1267 (1999), which is the decision that initiated the listing of suspected terrorists and terrorist organizations, calls upon 'all States to act strictly in accordance with the provisions of this resolution, notwithstanding the existence of rights and obligations conferred or imposed by any international agreement or any contract entered into or any licence or permit granted prior to the date of coming into force of the' measure. Though this could be said to rely on article 103, it is interesting that it uses the invocation 'calls upon' instead of 'decides' and is therefore a weak assertion of primacy, and further its references to

[43] Above (n 15) para 303.
[44] ibid, para 294.
[45] Article 25 UN Charter: 'The Members of the United Nations agree to accept and carry out the decisions of the Security Council in accordance with the present Charter'.
[46] Article 103 UN Charter: 'In the event of a conflict between the obligations of the Members of the United Nations under the present Charter and their obligations under any other international agreement, their obligations under the present Charter shall prevail'.
[47] See, for example, JE Alvarez, *International Organizations as Lawmakers* (Oxford University Press, Oxford, 2005) 207.
[48] See R Bernhardt, 'Article 103' in B Simma (ed), *The Charter of the United Nations: A Commentary* (2nd edn, Oxford University Press, Oxford, 2004) 1299.
[49] *R (on the application of Al-Jedda) v Secretary of State for Defence* [2007] UKHL 58.
[50] *Behrami and Saramati v France, Germany and Norway* (2007) (Admissibility of Application No 71412/01, and Application No 78166/01). Though the case was decided on the basis that the acts and omissions in question were attributable to the UN and not a state party to the ECHR, the Court did seem to accept the supremacy of Security Council decisions at paras 147–8.

contracts and licences in the latter part of the paragraph suggests that the type of international agreement referred to might only be a bilateral one governing trade or assets, rather than a multilateral one, particularly one governing human rights. In other words the intent may be simply to push aside inconsistent contractual treaty obligations, not inconsistent constitutional ones.

Furthermore, such an approach is not out of line with the original purpose of article 103, which was to remove directly conflicting obligations—so that an arms embargo imposed by the Security Council would absolve member states from any treaty commitments they had made with the target state to supply it with arms.[51] Of course, it is possible for a provision such as article 103 to be widened by practice but that practice has to be accompanied by clear institutional intent, which is not present here.

In its Declaration on Combating Terrorism (2003) the Security Council, meeting at the level of Foreign Ministers, declared that states 'must ensure that any measure taken to combat terrorism comply with all their obligations under international law, and should adopt measures in accordance with international law, in particular international human rights, refugee, and humanitarian law'.[52] This is hardly institutional *opinio juris* to the effect that its resolutions enable states to by-pass their human rights obligations because they are subject to a binding resolution of the Council requiring them to freeze the assets of named individuals. Rather, such assets must be frozen in accordance with the human rights obligations of the member states, including those arising under a regional treaty. On this basis a Member State would be in compliance with Resolution 1267 if it froze the assets of a named individual, but that person had the opportunity to challenge it before a court. The lack of human rights mechanisms at the Security Council level does not mean that they are also rendered inapplicable at the domestic or indeed regional levels by means of a Security Council resolution.

At the outset of the *Kadi* judgment the ECJ does cite relevant provisions of the UN Charter (including articles 25 and 103), but also significantly mentions article 24,[53] paragraph 2 of which states that the Council in carrying out its duties to maintain international peace and security 'shall act in accordance with the Purposes and Principles of the United Nations'. The purposes and principles contained in articles 1 and 2 of the Charter are broad but they include the achievement of international co-operation 'in promoting and encouraging respect for human rights and for fundamental freedoms for all without distinction as to race, language, or religion'. It is in fulfilment of this purpose that instruments such as the 1948 Universal Declaration of Human Rights were adopted by the General Assembly, embedding human rights in the UN system, and being the source of customary law and the inspiration for treaties both international and regional. Thus when article 103 speaks in terms of 'a conflict of obligations . . . under the present Charter and . . . obligations under any other international agreement', the matter is not a simple application of articles 25 and 103, as stated—if only prima facie—at the provisional measures stage of the 1992 *Lockerbie* cases[54] and, it seems, more conclusively in the recent spate of cases mentioned above.

[51] N Bentwich and A Martin, *A Commentary on the Charter of the United Nations* (Routledge & Kegan Paul, London, 1950) 179–80; J Frowein and N Krisch, 'Article 41' in Simma (n 48) 745.

[52] SC Res. 1456 of 20 January 2003.

[53] Above (n 15) para 4. Article 24 of the UN Charter is also mentioned at para 294.

[54] *Questions of Interpretation and Application of the 1971 Montreal Convention Arising from the Aerial Incident at Lockerbie* [1992] ICJ Rep 114, 126.

Article 103 applies to both primary and secondary obligations arising under the Charter,[55] but only, it is argued, to Security Council resolutions adopted in accordance with the Purposes and Principles of the UN. Thus the targeted sanctions against Kadi created overriding obligations for member states only to the extent that they were consistent with 'promoting and encouraging respect for human rights'. Member states are obliged to apply them within their legal orders as far as they are consistent with respect for human rights. The Court of First Instance made a mistake in restricting the applicability of human rights limitations on the freezing order to *jus cogens* norms. Although the Security Council is bound by *jus cogens* norms, it is also limited in its competence by the Purposes and Principles of the Charter, and therefore arguably it also cannot adopt measures which oblige member states to disregard the broader array of human rights.[56]

Given that the Charter does not itself contain a list of human rights the question is always raised as to which human rights must be respected. At this point we must avoid falling back just on *jus cogens*, and instead look to the basic international instruments promoting and respecting human rights, which are binding upon states, either in terms of customary (some or all of the Universal Declaration) or treaty law (under international or regional treaties on human rights). By adopting this approach the European Court of Justice could have expressly reconciled its judgment with the UN Charter. Indeed, this type of reasoning seems to underlie its judgment, but the Court failed to be clear on this issue, possibly out of deference to the fact that that would amount to review of Council decisions, a power that should be exercised by the International Court alone. The ECJ refused to review Security Council resolutions, even for their incompatibility with *jus cogens*.[57] But as the Advocate General argued in his opinion in the absence of any effective mechanism of review at the UN level, regional courts may be faced with no choice on the matter.[58]

The Court's reasoning is not incompatible with the above approach to Security Council resolutions, though it was limited to the issue of the implementation of regulations within the EU legal order. The Court was very clear though on the fundamentals of the EU legal order which is based on the rule of law, and a legal order which contains a 'complete system of legal remedies and procedures designed to enable the Court of Justice to review the legality of acts of the institutions'.[59] Unlike in the Advocate General's opinion[60] there is no critique of the UN system, but there is clearly a less developed legal order within the UN, to the extent that we can say that though lawmaking and judicial elements are present it is not governed by the strict application of the rule of law, exemplified in the workings of the Security Council where judicial, legislative and executive powers are intertwined and almost completely subject to political judgment. To give a political body power to override human rights, even in the name of peace and security, would be to allow it to subvert the rule of law in domestic and regional systems.

[55] LM Goodrich, E Hambro and P Simons, *Charter of the United Nations* (3rd edn, Columbia University Press, New York, 1969) 616.

[56] R Liivoja, 'The Scope of the Supremacy Clause of the United Nations Charter' (2008) 57 ICLQ 586.

[57] Above (n 15) para 287.

[58] Above (n 9) para 54.

[59] Above (n 15) para 281.

[60] Above (n 9) para 54.

Unlike under the European legal order, decisions of the Security Council do not have direct effect so that States decide on how to implement these decisions within their domestic legal orders,[61] and while accepting their obligations to implement these decisions governments must also uphold other obligations that may qualify but do not prevent the implementation of the decision. While human rights obligations may mean that freezing orders cannot remain unchallenged in the domestic order, they do not directly conflict with the freezing order unlike, say, an obligation to trade would conflict with a trade embargo. Thus there is a choice as to the breadth and depth of the effects of article 103 within any legal order—we can disregard all potential hurdles to the most efficient implementation of the decisions, or we can disregard only those treaty obligations that are directly in the path of the obligations created by the resolution. In the context of *Kadi*, while an asset freeze might directly infringe an individual's right to property, at least temporarily, it does not conflict with a right to a fair hearing. In the context of *Al-Jedda*, the power to detain granted by Security Council Resolution 1546 (2004) clearly conflicts with the right to liberty, but again only temporarily since it does not directly conflict with due process rights. However, the House of Lords appeared to interpret the effect of the overriding obligations deriving from Resolution 1546 more broadly than necessary to uphold the detention of the appellant without charge or trial, though Lord Bingham did say that the UK 'must ensure that the detainee's rights under article 5 [of the ECHR] are not infringed to any greater extent than is inherent in such detention'.[62]

It is strongly argued that the effect of executive orders within any legal order based on the rule of law must be interpreted narrowly. It must not simply be assumed that they override human rights. As has been stated in a different security context, the term 'necessary measures' used by the Security Council to authorize a use of force is not intended to signify that the use of force can be exercised with disregard to inconsistent humanitarian norms, such as the prohibition on targeting civilians.[63] It would be inconceivable to read a Security Council resolution such as Resolution 678 (1990) authorizing the use of force against Iraq as allowing violations of humanitarian law, so why should targeted sanctions be interpreted to permit a violation of human rights norms?

The European Court of Justice in *Kadi* puts fundamental rights at the heart of the EU legal order drawing 'inspiration' from the domestic legal order of member states and from international instruments, especially the ECHR. Thus 'respect for human rights is a condition of the lawfulness of Community acts',[64] with the result that implementation of obligations imposed under the UN Charter within the EU legal order cannot undermine human rights.[65] As has been stated, this approach could be applied, at least

[61] Above (n 15) para 298.

[62] Above (n 49) para 39. In her opinion in *Al-Jedda*, Baroness Hale said that the right to liberty 'is qualified but not displaced . . . the right is qualified only to the extent required or authorised by the resolution' (para 126). Lord Carswell went further and identified a number of safeguards that would minimise the infringement of the detainee's rights: '[T]he compilation of intelligence about such persons which is accurate and reliable as possible, the regular review of the continuing need to detain each person and a system whereby that need and the underlying evidence can be checked and challenged by representatives on behalf of the detained persons, so far as is practicable and consistent with the needs of national security and the safety of other persons' (para 130).

[63] Liivoja (n 56) 589.

[64] Above (n 15) paras 283–4.

[65] ibid, para 285.

in principle, to the Security Council itself on the basis of article 24(2) of the UN Charter, so that any Security Council resolution cannot be used to undermine the human rights obligations of member states. The Court however stopped short of reviewing Security Council resolutions in this light stating that it was simply reviewing the Community acts that implemented Security Council resolutions. Nevertheless, the Court's statement that its judgment did 'not entail any challenge to the primacy of that resolution in international law',[66] is only truly reconcilable with Security Council resolutions if the above interpretation—that is founded upon respect for human rights within the UN as well as European legal order—is adopted.

By allowing the Council of Ministers a brief period of time to fix the regulations 'to remedy the infringements found, but which also takes account of the considerable impact of the restrictive measures concerned on the appellant's rights and duties',[67] the European Court of Justice is in effect recognising that targeted sanctions are lawful if they are imposed in such a way as to be human rights compliant. The essence of the above argument is this reasoning is not incompatible with the UN order, indeed it reflects the approach that should be taken to the Security Council resolutions themselves. Maybe the ECJ is not the right judicial forum to make this statement, but in failing to do so it leaves itself open to the argument that its reasoning is undermining the international legal order. It could and should have based its arguments more clearly on the international legal order, which has a central place for human rights, though not always the mechanisms to protect them.[68] The Court did state that 'the European Community must respect international law in the exercise of its powers' and that 'a measure adopted by virtue of these powers must be interpreted, and its scope limited, in the light of the relevant rules of international law',[69] but it failed to clarify the limitations imposed by international law. While welcoming its protection of human rights, which are after all fundamental elements of the international, as well as regional, legal orders, the Court's failure to put the Security Council's decisions themselves within that international legal order was disappointing though not unexpected.

C. Conclusion

Ultimately, regardless of the technicalities of the legal issues in question, the European Court justifies its decision on meta-political grounds; upon the autonomy of the EU legal order and that this constitutional framework would be undermined if it was 'prejudiced by an international agreement',[70] seemingly regardless of the international agreement at issue. This is a narrow, but not unsurprising, view from Luxembourg. However, as the European Court of Human Rights has shown, it is both possible for a regional convention to be self-standing while also situating itself within general international law. In *Behrami*, the Court noted both that 'the Convention cannot be interpreted and applied in a vacuum'[71] (sic) whilst at the same time recognising its own

[66] ibid, para 288.

[67] ibid, para 375.

[68] Cf Wessel (n 35) 6: 'In the face of the reality of these and perhaps future judgments in this field by regional or national courts, the Security Council will need to make this regime not only smart and targeted, but also develop its own comprehensive system for human rights protection'.

[69] Above (n 16) para 291.

[70] ibid, para 316.

[71] Above (n 59) para 122.

specific purpose as a 'constitutional instrument of European public order'.[72] The Strasbourg Court has seemingly grasped something that the Luxembourg Court has not; that it need not be a case of mutual exclusivity in the application of global and regional norms. Critics, of course, might rightly say that the European Court of Human Rights has so far only been able to achieve this by taking an interpretative—rather loose—approach to articles 25 and 103 of the UN Charter. For such critics, the House of Lords in *Al-Jedda* reveals the artificiality of such reconciliation. In turn, as noted above, *Al-Jedda* can itself be criticised for taking a restrictive understanding of article 103 UN Charter, with particular application to human rights norms.

The judgment in *Kadi* avoids direct investigation of article 103, but is arguably premised upon the assumption that as article 103 precludes human rights protection, it is reliant upon the EU to provide such guarantees. Nevertheless, as this note has suggested, a better approach all round might be if article 103 was not read in absolute terms, but rather one which reflects the constitutional limitations of its original scope, specifically recognizing the overriding human rights purposes of the United Nations. Whether, of course, such an interpretation would have induced the Luxembourg Court to have adopted a more integrationist view of international law is perhaps unlikely; it was not the interpretation of article 103 that resulted in the Court coming to the conclusion that it did, but rather the Court's view as to the EU's own particular position in the global legal order.

Moreover, the *Kadi* judgment also raises some interesting issues of fragmentation in approach. Regardless of whether the European Court of Justice was correct in its judgment as to the place of international legal norms within EU law, it nevertheless highlights a growing sense of divergence in opinion between EU and public international lawyers, especially in terms of our respective normative 'points of reference'—in the case of EU lawyers, the EU treaties, in the case of international lawyers, the UN Charter. While EU lawyers will continue to seek to assert the primacy of the EU treaties, international lawyers will point to the overarching framework in which they form but one part. To that extent, with such polarized starting positions, consensus between the two camps on the relationship between them continues to be unlikely.[73] Separately *Kadi* also raises an important dilemma for international lawyers, themselves. Though international lawyers instinctively mistrust anything that prejudices the global remit of international law, especially the UN Charter, which is often spoken of in constitutional terms, it would be somewhat perverse for international lawyers to demand human rights compliance by the UN Security Council and other key players in the so-called 'war on terror' but seek abstinence from regional judicial courts striving to ensure the same outcome.

Paul James Cardwell, Duncan French and Nigel White*

[72] *Bosphorus*, para 156 as quoted in *Behrami*, para 145, itself reliant upon *Loizidou v Turkey (preliminary objections)* (1995) para 75.

[73] This can perhaps explain why the three authors of this note, though sharing responsibility for its contents, do not necessarily agree on all aspects of the analysis.

* All of School of Law, University of Sheffield.

[18]

Human rights litigation and the 'war on terror'

Helen Duffy*

Helen Duffy is the Litigation Director of INTERIGHTS, the International Centre for the Legal Protection of Human Rights.

Abstract

The 'war on terror' has led to grave human rights violations and, in response, to a growing volume of human rights litigation. This article provides an overview of litigation that has unfolded in recent years in relation to issues such as arbitrary detention, torture and ill-treatment, extraordinary rendition, extraterritorial application of human rights norms and the creeping reach of the 'terrorism' label. These cases provide a prism through which are displayed key characteristics of the war on terror as it affects human rights, and enables us to begin to ask questions regarding the role of the courts and the impact of human rights litigation in this area.

On 12 June 2008 the Supreme Court of the United States decided that persons detained by the United States in Guantánamo Bay have the constitutional privilege of habeas corpus. The recognition that all detainees are entitled to this basic right, irrespective of their nationality, their designation as 'enemy combatants' or their offshore location, has been hailed as a victory for the rule of law. Jubilation is somewhat tempered by the fact that it took six years to decide that detainees are entitled to a protection that would normally guarantee judicial access within hours, days or maybe weeks.

* An early version of this paper was delivered as the Annual Public Lecture in International Law at the School of Law, London School of Economics, 11 October 2007. The author is very grateful to Silvia Borelli for research assistance and to Steven Watt, David Geer and Fabricio Guariglia for their helpful comments in the preparation of that speech. This article reflects the author's views only and not those of INTERIGHTS.

Whether you see the *Boumediene* judgment as a historic victory for justice or a reminder of its woeful failure, it tells a story. It provides a graphic illustration of how far executive violations of human rights have gone in the name of security, and of the nature of the judicial response: deferential and perhaps faltering at first, gradually ceding to a more invigorated role as a matter of last resort.

This judgment is only one part of a burgeoning mass of litigation, each component of which tells its own story. Cases vary as vastly in their goals – gaining access to information, challenging the legality of detention, preventing expulsion or deportation, securing acknowledgement of and compensation for wrongs, for example – as they do in their processes and outcomes. This article will present a necessarily brief survey of some of this practice of human rights litigation to date at the national, regional and international levels.[1]

An enquiry into current litigation practice can serve several purposes. First, it provides an insight into key human rights issues arising in the so-called 'global war on terror'. Looking at issues through cases necessarily gives a limited perspective: a case concerns a particular individual and particular sets of facts as assessed against the particular legal issues within the jurisdiction of the particular court. The number of affected individuals that make it to court is a tiny minority. But, taken together, the practice of litigation in relation to international terrorism over the past few years provides a prism through which, I believe, are displayed quite vividly some of the key characteristics of the global war on terror, its objective and modus operandi.

Second, the brief survey of litigation practice may provide a comparative framework for assessing the impact and limitations of that litigation itself, and the role of the courts in responding to the human rights challenges posed by the war on terror. It remains early days for any such assessment. The cycle of litigation takes time, particularly in the light of the challenges to bringing litigation in this field in the first place, some of which will be explored below, and relatively few cases have run their course. Certainly any assessment of the *impact* of litigation has to be seen through a long-term lens and anything like a meaningful audit of impact would have to wait perhaps another ten years. But the extent of recent developments suggests that it is timely to at least begin to enquire into practice to date and to ask questions regarding the role of the courts in this context.

I shall therefore look first at cases that have arisen post-9/11 addressing five groups of issues (which I believe are illustrative of key characteristics of the 'war on terror' as it affects human rights). These issues are arbitrary detention, extraterritorial application of human rights obligations, torture and related

1 This note focuses on select human rights cases against state violations brought before national or, to a lesser extent, regional and international human rights bodies. In many of the cases cited in this survey, INTERIGHTS was involved as representative or third party/*amicus curiae* intervener. It is noted that cases that serve human rights ends can take many other forms, from civil cases against corporations to criminal cases against individual members of intelligence agencies or – on the basis of universal jurisdiction – against high government officials. There are examples of such cases being brought in the relation to the GWOT but these are not addressed here.

Volume 90 Number 871 September 2008

safeguards, extraordinary rendition, and the spreading reach of the 'terrorist' label and notions of guilt by association. In the conclusion I shall return to the question of the role of the courts and the impact of human rights litigation.

Issue 1: Arbitrary detention

Guantánamo

Probably the most notorious issue, and certainly the one giving rise to the most voluminous litigation, is the Guantánamo anomaly. The facts related to the detention of hundreds of enemy aliens by US personnel in Guantánamo Bay need no introduction.

Detentions at Guantánamo have spurred a litany of litigation in US courts (as well as beyond),[2] focusing mainly on two issues: the right to habeas corpus and the lawfulness of trial by military commission. It is worth sketching out the development of these cases in US courts and the curious game of legal ping-pong that has been played out between the judicial and political branches in the past couple of years, culminating in the 2008 *Boumediene* judgment referred to above.

Round 1: in 2004 a series of cases made their way through US courts challenging the denial of the right of access of detainees to a court to challenge the designation of the individuals in question as 'enemy combatants' and the lawfulness of their detention.[3] This led to two judgments handed down in June 2004. In *Hamdi* v. *Rumsfeld*,[4] the Supreme Court held that US nationals had certain constitutional rights, including having 'a meaningful opportunity to contest the factual basis for that detention before a neutral decision-maker'. Justice Sandra Day O'Connor famously cautioned on the behalf of the Court that 'We have long since made clear that a state of war is not a blank check for the President when it comes to the rights of the Nation's citizens'.[5] This 2004 case was seen to represent an important marker of executive accountability, albeit in the limited cases where the detainees are US nationals.

2 As regards US responsibility under the American Declaration of the Rights and Duties of Man, see Inter-American Commission on Human Rights, Precautionary Measures in Guantánamo Bay, 13 March 2002. Another line of litigation has concerned the role of other states in transferring or failing to support nationals detained in Guantánamo: see, e.g., ECtHR, *Boumediene and others* v. *Bosnia and Herzegovina*, Application Nos. 38703/06, 40123/06, 43301/06, 43302/06, 2131/07 and 2141/07 found inadmissable by the ECtHR on 18 November 2008 before the European Court of Human Rights (ECHR = Convention), or England and Wales Court of Appeal, *R (Abbasi)* v. *Secretary of State for Foreign and Commonwealth Affairs*, [2002] EWCA Civ 1598.

3 Two of the three groups of cases concerned US nationals detained in the United States or outside, and the third (affecting the vast majority of detainees) concerned non-nationals detained beyond US soil. The first of these cases – *Padilla* v. *Rumsfeld*, 352 F.3d 695 (2d Cir. 2003) – is less relevant, as it concerned a US citizen who was ultimately transferred to the regular criminal justice system within the United States, charged with conspiracy and found guilty before a federal court.

4 US Supreme Court, *Yaser Esam Hamdi and Esam Fouad Hamdi as next friend of Yaser Esam Hamdi, Petitioners* v. *Donald H. Rumsfeld, Secretary of Defense, et al.*, 542 US 507 (2004) decided June 28 2004.

5 Ibid., 536.

In respect of the right of habeas corpus of the vast majority of detainees who were non-nationals detained outside the United States, in *Rasul & Ors* v. *Bush*[6] the Supreme Court took a far more cautious approach. It refrained from addressing the issue as a constitutional rights issue. But the Court found, by reference to a statute conferring jurisdiction on courts, that there was nothing to prevent the courts from exercising jurisdiction in these cases.

The government's response to these judgments is well known. As regards US nationals, one had already been released and the other was transferred to regular courts.[7] As regards the hundreds of non-nationals detained at Guantánamo, the response was quite different. First, the executive introduced the Combatant Status Review Tribunals and Administrative Review Boards in an apparent attempt to provide a habeas corpus substitute, despite these being non-judicial mechanisms that lacked basic procedural rights associated with the right of habeas corpus.[8] This provided cover for congressional follow-up with the Detainee Treatment Act 2005 (DTA), which, in addition to some positive provisions on treatment of detainees, responded to the judgment by making it explicit that there is *no* right of habeas corpus for Guantánamo detainees.

Round 2: this led to a second round at the Supreme Court in the form of *Hamdan* v. *Rumsfeld*.[9] The US government claimed that the DTA had stripped Hamdan of his right to habeas corpus. In its June 2006 judgment, the Court again refrained from addressing the question whether there was a constitutional right to habeas corpus that rendered the DTA's purported habeas corpus stripping unconstitutional. It found instead that the Act did not apply to Hamdan anyway, as his case was ongoing at the time the DTA was adopted.

Having determined that it had jurisdiction, the Court went on to find that basic due process guarantees contained in Common Article 3 of the Geneva Conventions, incorporated into US law by the Uniform Code of Military Justice (UCMJ)[10] statute, applied to all detainees. The decision that the military commissions were unlawful because they violated these basic provisions was an important and positive decision in terms of rights protection. It is noteworthy, though, that *Hamdan* is not framed in terms of 'individual rights', but as a separation of powers issue, addressing whether 'the President has acted in a way that exceeded [congressional] limits'.

6 US Supreme Court, *Shafiq Rasul, et al., Petitioners* v. *George W. Bush, President of the United States, et al.; Fawzi Khalid Abdullah Fahad al Odah, et al., Petitioners* v. *United States, et al.*, 542 US 466, decided June 28 2004.

7 See notes on *Padilla* and *Hamdi*, above notes 3 and 4.

8 For an analysis of the operation of the Combatant Status Review Tribunals, where detainees lack access to the evidence against them, see Mark Denbeaux et al., *No-Hearing Hearings: CSRT: The Modern Habeas Corpus?*, available at http://law.shu.edu/news/final_no_hearing_hearings_report.pdf (last visited 15 October 2008).

9 US Supreme Court, *Salim Ahmed Hamdan, Petitioner v. Donald H. Rumsfeld & Others*, 548 US 557 (2006).

10 Uniform Code of Military Justice, UCMJ, 64 Stat. 109, 10 USC ch.47.

Volume 90 Number 871 September 2008

Nonetheless, there had been a finding by the Supreme Court that the executive's conduct violated international and domestic law. The US government again faced the quandary of how to respond to this judicial slight. With the 2006 Military Commission Act, Congress responded in two ways. First, it determined that the relevant international law – the Geneva Conventions – could no longer be relied upon as a source of rights in habeas corpus or other civil proceedings against US personnel. Second, it provided that courts would not have jurisdiction to hear habeas corpus applications (or any other action) by any person determined to be an enemy combatant or awaiting such determination, thus extending the jurisdiction-stripping provisions of the DTA beyond Guantánamo to detentions anywhere.[11] Rather than a response that would seek to deal with the problem by bringing policy in line with law, the law was identified as the problem, and international sources of law and judicial oversight of them were removed.

Despite several Supreme Court judgments, the basic question of whether constitutional due process and habeas corpus protections apply to non-nationals detained outside US territory remained unanswered until June 2008.[12] With no further possibility of constitutional avoidance, in *Boumediene* v. *Bush*[13] the issue was finally resolved in the affirmative. The US Supreme Court ruled that 'enemy combatants' held by the United States at Guantánamo Bay have the right under the US Constitution to challenge their detention before regular courts. The Court also ruled that the procedures for review of the detainees' status under the 2005 Detainee Treatment Act were not an adequate and effective substitute for habeas corpus. It therefore declared unconstitutional section 7 of the 2006 Military Commissions Act, which denied habeas corpus to any detained foreign 'enemy combatant'.

The importance of this ruling should not be underestimated. Ultimately, the Supreme Court has addressed the issue of habeas corpus as the fundamental rights issue it is. It rejects artificial distinctions based on nationality or geographical location as relevant to determining the existence of rights and obligations.

11 MCA, s.7(1)(e):

(1) No court, justice, or judge shall have jurisdiction to hear or consider an application for a writ of habeas corpus filed by or on behalf of an alien detained by the United States who has been determined by the United States to have been properly detained as an enemy combatant or is awaiting such determination.

(2) Except as provided in paragraphs (2) and (3) of section 1005(e) of the Detainee Treatment Act of 2005 (10 USC 801 note), no court, justice, or judge shall have jurisdiction to hear or consider any other action against the United States or its agents relating to any aspect of the detention, transfer, treatment, trial, or conditions of confinement of an alien who is or was detained by the United States and has been determined by the United States to have been properly detained as an enemy combatant or is awaiting such determination.

12 Little clarity was provided by lower courts. In two cases – *Al Odah* and *Boumediene* – the district courts reached completely different outcomes and, on 20 February 2007, the DC Circuit Court of Appeals ruled 2–1 that the Guantánamo detainees have no constitutional right to habeas corpus review of their detentions in federal court.

13 US Supreme Court, *Lakhdar Boumediene, et al., Petitioners* v. *George W. Bush, President of the United States, et al.*, 553 US.

It represents the willingness of the judiciary to engage and fulfil their democratic mandate and reinforce the legal and constitutional limits on executive action. How the executive responds to those decisions will also be an important measure of the state of health of the rule of law and the separation of powers.[14] It will also determine what the ruling means in practice for the approximately 270 detainees remaining in Guantánamo Bay.

At the same time, the judgment itself was a close 5:4 decision, with some strident dissents that graphically demonstrate the extent of the antipathy of certain judges to step into what they see as issues of security properly for executive determination.[15] Of most concern, of course, is simply the time it has taken to reach this decision. Litigation is a time-consuming business, and due process of law and respect for the judicial function require that it be allowed to run its course. Undoubtedly, some gains have been made at each stage of this judicial marathon (as I shall return to when looking at the question of impact later). But one has to ask whether the judicial process has not been characterized by undue constitutional avoidance, as well as excessive judicial deference to the executive and congressional decision-making role, in the refusal to address the constitutional question at an earlier stage. Unfortunately, the political organs did not repay the democratic compliment and react to judicial suggestions about the need to bring policy into line with law.[16] Whether this was a miscalculation as to how the political branches would respond, or a strict approach to the judicial doctrine of constitutional avoidance, is open to question. But the somewhat anomalous result is a decision six years down the line that the right to habeas corpus applies, theoretically guaranteeing access to a court within hours or days of arrest and detention. One must question the extent to which this constitutes a meaningful a judicial response for this sort of emergency remedy.

The same day that the US Supreme Court handed down its judgment in *Boumediene* it also handed down *Munaf* v. *Geren*,[17] in which it acknowledged that persons detained in Iraq also have the right to habeas corpus. It found that in the Iraqi context it was Iraqi courts that should exercise jurisdiction, and it therefore denied the jurisdiction of US courts on that basis. But the case is significant in reinforcing the principle that the right of habeas corpus applies to persons detained by US personnel beyond US jurisdiction. This may become particularly important

14 While President Bush's immediate response to the judgment was equivocal, US President Barak Obama indicated shortly upon taking office that the Guantanamo facility would be closed. 'Obama plans executive order to close Guantanamo Bay' CNN on-line, 22 January 2009, http://edition.cnn.com/2009/POLITICS/01/21/guantanamo.hearings/index.html.

15 This was graphically demonstrated by the tone and content of some of the dissents, notably Scalia J's assertion of the 'disastrous conse-quences' of the majority judgment which he claimed 'will almost certainly cause more Ameri-cans to be killed'. *Boumediene*, above note 13, Dissenting Judgment of Scalia J, p. 2.

16 E.g., as noted above, Congress reacted to the *Hamdan* judgment by divesting the courts of jurisdiction and of 'inconvenient' sources of law, rather than taking the judicial lead and bringing policy into line with law.

17 *Munaf et al.* v. *Geren, Secretary of the Army, et al.*, Certiorari to the United States Court of Appeals for the District of Columbia circuit, No. 06–1666. Argued March 25, 2008 – Decided 12 June 2008.

Volume 90 Number 871 September 2008

in a context of increasing resort to Guantánamo 'alternatives' in the form of detention abroad.

Belmarsh

In 2004, parallel cases made their way through the English courts, resulting in the famous *A & Ors* derogation case before the House of Lords (Belmarsh judgment).[18] The case concerned the detention of non-UK nationals in Belmarsh prison on the basis of their suspected involvement in international terrorism, pursuant to the 2001 Anti-Terrorism, Crime and Security Act.[19] In order to allow such a measure, the United Kingdom had derogated from its obligations in respect of the right to liberty under Article 5 of the European Convention on Human Rights (ECHR).

The case raised different issues from those before US courts. The UK Act itself provided for regular independent review by the Special Immigration Appeals Commission, which is a court of law, albeit in the context of limited and controversial rules and procedures.[20] The right of habeas corpus was not, as such, in dispute in the United Kingdom, and the case that made its way to the House of Lords concerned the lawfulness of the derogation and of the detention itself.

When the matter went before the House of Lords – the supreme court of appeal in the United Kingdom – the court found that the United Kingdom's derogation from the European Convention on Human Rights to enable it to detain people on national security grounds, potentially indefinitely, was not valid. The majority deferred to the government's assessment of the existence of an 'emergency' justifying derogation. However, they found that the detention of non-nationals could not be justified as strictly required by that emergency. The judgment notes that 'If derogation is not strictly required in the case of one group [nationals], it cannot be strictly required in the case of the other group [non-nationals] that presents the same threat.'[21] The court therefore found a violation of

18 UK House of Lords Appellate Committee, *A and Others* v. *Secretary of State for the Home Department, X and another* v. *Secretary of State for the Home Department* [2004] UKHL 56 (A & Ors (Derogation)).

19 See sections 21–32 of the United Kingdom's Anti-terrorism, Crime and Security Act, 2001, which 'allow[s] the detention of those the Secretary of State has certified as threats to national security and who are suspected of being international terrorists where their removal is not possible at the present time. These provisions change the current law, which allows detention with a view to removal only where removal is a realistic option within a reasonable period of time … '.

20 Controversial rules related to, for example, access to counsel and to evidence. See, e.g., the report of the United Kingdom's Parliamentary Constitutional Affairs Committee 'The operation of the Special Immigration Appeals Commission (SIAC) and the use of Special Advocates', report of session 2004/5, HC 323-II, available at www.parliament.the-stationery-office.co.uk/pa/cm200405/cmselect/cmconst/323/323ii.pdf (last visited 15 October 2008). See also, e.g., 'Ian Macdonald QC resigns from SIAC', 1 November 2004, available at www.gardencourtchambers.co.uk/news/news_detail.cfm?iNewsID=268 (last visited 20 April 2008).

21 *A & Ors (Derogation)*, above note 17, Lord Bingham, para. 132: 'I would hold that the indefinite detention of foreign nationals without trial has not been shown to be strictly required, as the same threat from British nationals whom the government is unable or unwilling to prosecute is being met by other measures which do not require them to be detained indefinitely without trial. The distinction which the government seeks to draw between these two groups – British nationals and foreign nationals – raises an issue of discrimination. But, as the distinction is irrational, it goes to the heart of the issue about

the rights to liberty and to non-discrimination, provided for in law in the United Kingdom via Articles 5 and 14 of the ECHR.

The positive significance of this decision lies on many different levels. The first relates to the obvious importance of the strict approach to the protection of the right to liberty and the need for careful but challenging judicial oversight. Beyond that, the case did what much of debate and indeed litigation elsewhere – including the US litigation referred to above – had neglected to do, in signalling the centrality of the equality issue. This is particularly significant in a context of frequent reliance on divisions and distinctions based on nationality as well as other grounds as a basis for inferior treatment. While nationality does have some significance in the context of the application of certain aspects of international humanitarian law (IHL), it is a critical manifestation of the universality that underpins human rights law that nationals and non-nationals alike are protected.[22] The onus is on the state to demonstrate that discrimination is justified, which it was unable to do in this case.

The case is also constitutionally significant in its assessment of the proper judicial role and the limits of due judicial deference. In a powerful passage Lord Bingham famously rejects the Attorney General's submissions in this respect, noting,

> "I do not in particular accept the distinction which he drew between democratic institutions and the courts ... the function of independent judges ... [is] a cardinal feature of the modern democratic state, a cornerstone of the rule of law itself. The Attorney General is fully entitled to insist on the proper limits of judicial authority, but he is wrong to stigmatise judicial decision-making as in some way undemocratic."

Significant too was the executive's response. The UK government changed its law and practice in the light of the Belmarsh judgment. The derogation and offending legislation were withdrawn, and new legislation was adopted, providing, *inter alia*, for 'control orders' rather than imprisonment for persons suspected of involvement in international terrorism.[23]

proportionality also. It proceeds on the misconception that it is a sufficient answer to the question whether the derogation is strictly required that the two groups have different rights in the immigration context. So they do. But the derogation is from the right to liberty. The right to liberty is the same for each group. If derogation is not strictly required in the case of one group, it cannot be strictly required in the case of the other group that presents the same threat.'

22 Only in relation to certain rights in limited circumstances – notably relating to political life – are rights enjoyed only or to a greater degree by a state's own citizens. See, e.g., UN Human Rights Committee General Comment No. 15, The position of aliens under the Covenant [1986], in UN Doc. HRI/GEN/1/Rev.6 (2003), p. 140. Also note the IACHR comment in relation to Guantánamo detainees: '[t]he determination of a state's responsibility for violations of the international human rights of a particular individual turns not on the individual's nationality ... '. Inter-American Commission on Human Rights, Precautionary Measures in Guantánamo Bay, Cuba, 13 March 2002.

23 On control orders authorized by the Prevention of Terrorism Act 2005 and their operation, see the statement made by Tony McNulty, Minister for Security, Counter-Terrorism, Crime and Policing (The Rt Hon Tony McNulty) to Parliament: 'Control Orders Update (11 March 2008–10 June 2008)', 12 June 2008, available at http://security.homeoffice.gov.uk/news-publications/news-speeches/control-orders-update-0608 (last visited 15 October 2008). The Act authorized both derogating control orders,

Volume 90 Number 871 September 2008

These orders spurred their own controversy and their own litigation. The judgments handed down provide, among other things, an interesting analysis of what constitutes 'detention' as opposed to limits on freedom of movement, and the stage at which not only physical limits but also the degree of control over aspects of daily life might amount to unlawful detention.[24] The House of Lords found in one case that those orders that allowed for persons to be confined to specified areas for up to 18 hours a day and cut off from contact with the outside world amounted to detention by any other name, and required derogation from Article 5 of the ECHR. These cases also demonstrated the willingness of the courts to engage in and seek to grapple with the difficult issue of what balance is an acceptable one in a democratic society facing the challenge of international terrorism.

Issue 2: Limiting the applicability of treaty obligations: extraterritorial application and action pursuant to Security Council authorization

Extraterritoriality

The rationale behind the Guantánamo anomaly referred to above was that, due to its offshore location, the constitutional human rights obligations that normally apply on US soil would not apply there. As a constitutional matter, the fallacy of such a distinction has been clarified by the *Boumediene* and *Munaf* cases discussed above. As a matter of international human rights law, the proposition was always straightforwardly wrong. The complete control exercised by the United States over the part of Cuba where Guantánamo lies, as well as over the detainees themselves, meant that the United States exercised jurisdiction and control to satisfy the criteria for applicability of human rights treaties.[25] As the Inter-American

where the government recognized that derogation from the ECHR would be required, and non-derogating orders, where, in the government's view, it would not.

24 UK House of Lords, *Secretary of State for the Home Department (Appellant)* v. *JJ and others (FC) (Respondents)*, [2007] UKHL 45, decided 31 October 2007. On control order litigation in Australian courts, see High Court of Australia, *Thomas* v. *Mowbray* [2007] HCA 33, 2 August 2007, available at www.austlii.edu.au/au/cases/cth/HCA/2007/33.html (last visited 15 October 2008), where, in a 5:2 decision, the High Court of Australia upheld the constitutionality of a criminal anti-terror law under which a federal magistrate issued an interim control order.

25 Human rights bodies have long considered the extraterritorial application to depend on whether the state exercised 'effective control' abroad. See, e.g., International Court of Justice, *Legal Consequences of the Construction of a Wall in the Occupied Palestinian Territory*, Advisory Opinion, 9 July 2004, which, following earlier Human Rights Committee decisions, noted that it is unconscionable to permit states to do abroad what they are prohibited from doing at home. A stricter approach, at least as regards the ECHR, was apparent when the European Court of Human Rights suggested in the *Bankovic* v. *Belgium* case that control over territory, and not just control over individuals or situations by agents acting abroad, may be required for the Convention obligations to apply. See, e.g., Helen Duffy, *The War on Terror and the Framework of International Law*, Cambridge University Press, Cambridge, 2005, pp. 282–9, 332–7.

Commission on Human Rights observed when requesting that the United States adopt precautionary measures to protect the detainees (a request ultimately unheeded),'[t]he determination of a state's responsibility [for human rights violations] turns not on the individual's nationality or presence within a particular geographic area, but rather on whether, under the specific circumstances, that person fell within the state's authority and control.'[26]

While the Guantánamo anomaly is so stark as to provide an easy target, a narrow view of extraterritorial application is mirrored elsewhere, albeit in slightly less caricatured form. In a judgment of June 2007, in *Al-Skeini* v. *Secretary of State for Defence*,[27] the House of Lords ruled on the application of the ECHR to the conduct of British troops in Iraq. The case concerned six appellants, the first five of whom had been killed by UK 'patrols' in occupied Basra, for example while eating a family evening meal, during a raid on a family member's house or while driving a minibus. The sixth, Baha Mousa Baha, was tortured while in UK custody in Iraq. The object of the litigation was to compel the government to carry out an investigation into these violations as required by the ECHR, incorporated via the UK Human Rights Act.

At first the government argued that the ECHR did not apply to its actions in Iraq. In the course of litigation the government's position changed (providing an example of how the process of litigation can itself quite directly shape policy), and it argued that the ECHR did apply to persons in UK custody in Iraq but not to persons killed or injured on the streets of Basra.[28]

When the case made its way to the highest UK court, the House of Lords, the court accepted the government's view as regards the scope of application of the Convention. It found that while individuals killed or mistreated within UK 'custody' are entitled to the protection of the ECHR, those on the streets of Basra – including those directly shot or mistreated by UK soldiers patrolling streets – are not.

The strength of the *Al-Skeini* case lies in its confirmation that for individuals detained by UK authorities anywhere in the world, the ECHR, and the Human Rights Act giving effect to it in the United Kingdom, apply. Although the issues were somewhat different, this sentiment is replicated and reinforced by the recent finding, in *Munaf* v. *Geren*, of the US Supreme Court concerning due process rights applicable to US detainees in Iraq. This rejects the more restrictive approach argued by the authorities of the United States, and at an earlier stage, the United Kingdom, as to the non-applicability of international human rights treaties.

However, on this occasion the House of Lords may have adopted an unduly restrictive approach to human rights protection in rejecting the applicability

26 See IACHR Guantanamo Bay Precautionary Measures, above note 21.

27 UK House of Lords, *Al-Skeini* v. *Secretary of State for Defence*, [2007] UKHL 26, 13 June 2007.

28 At all stages the government denied the extraterritorial applicability of the Human Rights Act (as opposed to the ECHR). The government did not challenge the fact that, provided that the Convention and the UK Act were applicable, there existed an obligation to carry out an investigation and the case should go back to the divisional court for assessment of the facts.

of the European Convention beyond situations of detention. It rejected arguments that the relevant question related to the degree of control the state exercised over the situation, and whether there was in all the circumstances a sufficiently 'direct or immediate' link between the extraterritorial conduct and the alleged violation of individual rights.[29] It focused instead on what might be described as formalistic distinctions based on custody or not. The somewhat anomalous result is that an individual's ability to achieve redress depends on whether his abusers were courteous enough to arrest him beforehand, or whether his abuse occurred inside or outside prison walls. While the implications of this judgment remain to be seen, in *Al-Skeini* the House of Lords may have contributed to confusion in an already murky field.

A restrictive approach to extraterritoriality, and growing confusion in this area, has potentially important implications for accountability in the war on terror, a large part of which is being executed extraterritorially. Of course, states continue to be bound normatively by customary law and IHL. But, as this case shows, the extraterritorial application of human rights treaties is critically important in practice in a context where the application of human rights law in fact amounts to the only way of accessing a court of law and ultimately of securing a remedy.[30]

It remains to be seen whether this somewhat novel approach by the UK courts will be adopted elsewhere.[31] The Committee against Torture (CAT) has certainly made it clear that the Convention against Torture and Cruel, Inhuman and Degrading Treatment does apply extraterritorially, and has been implicitly critical of both the United Kingdom and United States for taking an approach limiting the Convention's applicability in Iraq or Afghanistan.[32] The CAT has stated, for example, that '[t]he State party should recognize and ensure that the provisions of the Convention expressed as applicable to "territory under the State party's jurisdiction" apply to, and are fully enjoyed, by all persons under the effective control of its authorities, of whichever type, wherever located in the world.'

29 For the NGO third-party intervention, including support for the 'direct or immediate' link, see www.interights.org.

30 As in the United Kingdom, human rights protections are often incorporated into domestic law. However, IHL violations lack an enforcement mechanism and, under CAT, neither the United States nor the United Kingdom has made the declaration required under Art. 22 to allow for individual petitions.

31 The *Al Skeini* case, above note 26, has been presented to the ECtHR.

32 See, e.g., Conclusions and recommendations of the Committee against Torture; United States of America, UN Doc. CAT/C/USA/CO/2, 25 July 2006: 'The State party should recognize and ensure that the provisions of the Convention expressed as applicable to "territory under the State party's jurisdiction" apply to, and are fully enjoyed, by all persons under the effective control of its authorities, of whichever type, wherever located in the world.' See also Conclusions and recommendations of the Committee against Torture; United Kingdom of Great Britain and Northern Ireland, Crown Dependencies and Overseas Territories, UN Doc. CAT/C/CR/33/3, 10 December 2004: 'The Committee expresses its concern at ... the State party's limited acceptance of the applicability of the Convention to the actions of its forces abroad, in particular its explanation that " those parts of the Convention which are applicable only in respect of territory under the jurisdiction of a State party cannot be applicable in relation to actions of the United Kingdom in Afghanistan and Iraq"; the Committee observes that the Convention protections extend to all territories under the jurisdiction of a State party and considers that this principle includes all areas under the de facto effective control of the State party's authorities.'

Just as *Al-Skeini* raised questions about the applicability of human rights treaty obligations extraterritorially, a more recent House of Lords case provoked questions about the impact of such obligations where the state acts under the apparent authority of a Security Council resolution. This issue arose in the case of *R (on the application of Al-Jedda)* v. *Secretary of State for Defence*, decided on 12 December 2007.[33] A cautious and arguably restrictive approach to human rights protection was again apparent.

The case concerned Iraqis detained by UK soldiers (acting as part of a UN force in Iraq) on terrorism charges. The first question the House of Lords addressed on appeal was whether the government was liable for the appellant's allegedly wrongful detention, as opposed to the United Nations being responsible on the basis that the impugned acts were attributable to the United Nations as a result of Security Council resolutions authorizing the Multinational Force in Iraq. The Lords found the question of fact to be whether the United Nations exercised effective control over UK actions, which it found not to be the case.[34] The court had no difficulty in distinguishing this mission from the Kosovo Force (KFOR), where more difficult issues of attribution arise.[35] Thus the allegedly wrongful conduct was attributable to the United Kingdom, not the United Nations.

The second question proved more problematic. The court asked itself whether the United Kingdom's obligations under the European Convention on Human Rights were qualified by those that arise under the UN Charter, particularly under relevant Security Council resolutions. All five Lords of Appeal found that the United Kingdom's obligations under the European Convention had to be limited by those due under the Charter. They therefore upheld the authority to detain individuals in Iraq on this basis. However, Lord Bingham found that while the United Kingdom had the authority to detain the appellant pursuant to Security Council resolutions, it must still 'ensure that the detainee's rights under Article 5 [of the European Convention] are not infringed to any greater extent than is inherent in such detention'.

The Court did not find, as the applicants had argued, that a distinction should be drawn between clear *obligations* under Security Council resolutions, and other activities that might be authorized by, or indeed broadly carried out pursuant to, such resolutions. Article 103 of the Charter undoubtedly provides that where there is a conflict between obligations under the Charter and treaty obligations, the former prevail. But if the judgment were to be understood as exempting the whole range of actions taken under Security Council resolutions from human rights obligations (or indeed those under IHL), the result could be a serious

33 UK House of Lords, *R (on the application of Al-Jedda)* v. *Secretary of State for Defence*, [2007] UKHL 58, Judgment of 12 December 2007.

34 As the Lords noted, the United Kingdom had never claimed before the case that the UN did exercise control over these operations.

35 The majority distinguished the admissibility decision of the Grand Chamber of the European Court of Human Rights in *Behrami* v. *France, Saramati* v. *France, Germany and Norway*, Application Nos. 71412/01 and 78166/01, May 2, 2007, which attributed the acts of KFOR to the United Nations and not to the individual countries that contributed forces to that mission.

Volume 90 Number 871 September 2008

protection gap. This is particularly so in the 'war against terrorism' context, where wide-ranging resolutions have called on far-reaching action against terrorism, but without clear definition as to either the action required or the nature of the terrorism against which it is directed.

Issue 3: Torture

Practices of torture and cruel, inhuman or degrading treatment have come to light in recent years with increasing regularity, as epitomized by (though far from limited to) scandals such as Abu Ghraib or Baghram. This has regrettably been coupled with attempts to redefine torture according to obscenely high thresholds of barbarity, to 'justify' it, *inter alia*, as a matter of 'executive privilege', or to undermine procedural safeguards associated with it. I shall highlight a couple of cases from the other side of the Atlantic that fall into the last category and illustrate attempts to erode, indirectly, the prohibition.

Deportation to torture or ill-treatment

The first set of cases, *Saadi* v. *Italy*[36] and *Ramzy* v. *Netherlands*[37] before the European Court of Human Rights (ECtHR), relate to the deportation of individuals to states where, the applicants allege, there is a real risk of their being subject to torture and ill-treatment. When the *Ramzy* case appeared before the Court, the Dutch government's case related, as many in Strasbourg do, to the difficult and not uncontroversial question of whether there was a real and personal risk to Mr Ramzy in Algeria. But several other governments, led by the United Kingdom, changed the face of the case by taking the unusual step of presenting a third-party intervention.[38] They argued that in the light of the growth of 'Islamist extremist terrorism' the Court should re-examine the relationship between protection from ill-treatment and 'national security' interests. In effect, they argued that, through introducing a 'balancing' test, national security could justify exposing persons to real and imminent risk of torture if those individuals were deemed by the government to represent a risk. Numerous international NGOs intervened, based on the absolute nature of the *non-refoulement* rule (the ban on forcible return), and the standard for assessing risk.[39]

36 ECtHR, *Saadi* v. *Italy*, Appl. No. 37201/06, Judgment of 28 February 2008.

37 ECtHR, *Ramzy* v. *the Netherlands*, Appl. No. 25424/05, pending, available at www.echr.coe.int/eng/press/2005/oct/applicationlodgedramzyvnetherlands.htm (last visited 16 October 2008).

38 The intervention was presented by the governments of Lithuania, Latvia, Portugal and the United Kingdom. See the 'refining' and limiting of the UK government position to cruel and inhuman treatment in the Parliamentary Joint Committee on Human Rights Thirty Second report, Session 2005-6, available at www.publications.parliament.uk/pa/jt200506/jtselect/jtrights/278/27808.htm (last visited 15 October 2008).

39 For the intervention in the *Ramzy* case submitted on behalf of several international NGOs, see www.interights.org.

When the *Saadi* case then came before the court addressing similar issues – Mr Saadi claimed that he would be at risk of torture and ill-treatment in Tunisia, where mistreatment of alleged terrorists is well documented – the UK government again seized its opportunity to argue in favour of the 'balancing' test on the same terms as it had in Ramzy. The *Saadi* case leapfrogged the Ramzy case, which is still pending at the time of writing, and the Grand Chamber of the Court handed down judgment on 28 February 2008.

In a unanimous judgment the European Court remained resolute in upholding the approach established by its earlier decisions and followed by other international courts and bodies. The judgment reaffirmed that the prohibition on transfer of individuals to countries where they face a real risk of torture or other ill-treatment is part of the absolute prohibition on torture. The Court was emphatic in recognizing the difficulties states face in countering terrorism, but categorical in its rebuke of the notion that there are exceptions to the absolute nature of the prohibition of torture or ill-treatment or any room for balancing:

> States face immense difficulties in modern times in protecting their communities from terrorist violence. It cannot therefore underestimate the scale of the danger of terrorism today and the threat it presents to the community. That must not, however, call into question the absolute nature of Article 3 [of the European Convention, prohibiting torture and other ill-treatment].

Although they were unsuccessful, the very fact that governments made these interventions, despite the odds of success being seriously stacked against them (in the light of clear and on-point jurisprudence from the Court itself,[40] quite apart from any of the principles at stake), is telling. It arguably reveals a shift in the approach to rights protection by certain states at least, and a questioning and undermining of even the most sacrosanct human rights protections. The resolute rejection of this approach by the European Court is an example of the important role of the courts in reaffirming fundamental principles.

A & Ors: admissibility of torture evidence

A second issue related to safeguards against torture, which has arisen in several states in the context of the fight against international terrorism in recent years, is the reliance on, and admissibility of, evidence obtained through torture and ill-treatment.

Again in the United Kingdom, the issue played out in the case of *A and Others* v. *Secretary of State for the Home Department* (*No. 2*).[41] The case concerned the admissibility, before the UK Special Immigration Appeals Commission, of

40 See, most notably, ECtHR, *Chahal* v. *United Kingdom*, ECtHR Reports 1996-V, no. 22, Judgment of 15 November 1996.

41 UK House of Lords, *A* v. *Secretary of State for the Home Department* (SSHD) (No. 2) [2005] UKHL 71, Judgment of 9 December 2005.

evidence that may have been obtained through torture by foreign states. The UK government advanced the argument – anomalous perhaps, yet accepted by the Court of Appeal – that evidence obtained through torture at the hand of a UK official is inadmissible, whereas evidence obtained through torture at the hand of foreign officials, for whom the United Kingdom is not responsible, is admissible.

In its judgment of 8 December 2005, the House of Lords rejected this rationale, finding that torture is torture no matter who does it, and that such evidence can never be admitted in legal proceedings. It also noted the link between the safeguards against torture and the incidence of torture, finding that the state 'cannot condemn torture while making use of the mute confession obtained through torture, because the effect is to encourage torture'.[42]

The judgment is a strong reassertion of principle, seeing the admissibility of evidence not only as linked to fair trial issues but also as an inherent aspect of the positive obligations around the torture prohibition itself. It is worth flagging, however, that the judgment is somewhat more limited in other respects. First, while clear on the principle of inadmissibility, it is less clear – and the court was more cautious – on how the rule would operate in practice. The court found that evidence is inadmissible where the tribunal had 'established' on balance of probabilities that it had been obtained under torture. If that is not 'established' – as presumably happens not infrequently in view of the opacity and uncertainty surrounding intelligence – but there remained a real risk that such was the case, the court found that evidence could be admitted but afforded less weight.[43]

Second, the court focused on the issue of admissibility in 'proceedings', but indicated what may be an overly sweeping inclination to accept the lawfulness of the use of torture evidence for other purposes, such as arrest, search or detention. The difficult and sensitive issue of the extent of obligations, if any, of states not to rely on, solicit or trade in evidence obtained through torture outside the courtroom remains unclear.

Issue 4: Extraordinary rendition

Among the most innovative and the most shocking of the many violations to which the war on terror has given rise is the practice of 'extraordinary rendition'. Reliable reports are increasing of the kidnapping and secret transfer of individuals without any process of law to various locations and/or to third states for what has been referred to as detention or torture by proxy.[44] This is straightforwardly a violation

42 Ibid., p. 30 citing McNally JA.

43 In contrast to the majority finding, compare the test proposed by Lord Bingham, according to which evidence should be regarded as inadmissible if the executive had been unable to show that it was not obtained by torture. Ibid., paras. 54–56.

44 See, e.g., Council of Europe Committee on Legal Affairs and Human Rights, Rapporteur Mr Dick Marty, Alleged secret detentions in Council of Europe member states, Information Memorandum II, AS/Jur (2006) 03 rev, 22 January 2006, available at http://assembly.coe.int/CommitteeDocs/2006/20060124_Jdoc032006_E.pdf (last visited 15 October 2008).

of many human rights, on account not only of its eventual purpose – torture, arbitrary detention or other serious violation – but also due to the procedural arbitrariness that attends it and, most insidiously, the effect of removing the person from the protection of law and withholding information from that person and his or her family. The latter characteristic has led to this practice being described as enforced disappearance.[45]

As is perhaps obvious, rendition litigation poses particular challenges for litigators, which can euphemistically be grouped as 'access' issues of various types: access to victims, to evidence and to courts. First and most obviously, the cases often concern disappeared persons. Despite the excellent monitoring work done by NGOs, journalists and investigators, for the most part we do not know who or where the victims are, at least not at the point when they most need protection. While jurisdictions vary, the ability to bring 'public interest' cases without identified victims is extremely limited. Access to information or evidence is inevitably extremely challenging, given the clandestine nature of operations, but made even harder by what has been described as a systematic cover-up to preclude such access.[46] The third group of access issues relates to effective access to courts. In the rare situation where a person emerges and is willing to put his or her head above the parapet again despite past abuses, the state secrets' doctrine is liable to have the case thrown out.

This was the experience of Khalid el-Masri, whose case provides graphic insight into both the practice of extraordinary rendition and the extent of the secrecy and challenges to litigation in this area.[47] El-Masri is a German citizen who was arrested by Macedonian border officials in December 2003, apparently because he has the same name as the alleged mentor of the al-Qaeda Hamburg cell and on suspicion that his passport was a forgery. After three weeks he was handed over to the US Central Intelligence Agency (CIA) and flown to Baghdad and then to 'the salt pit', a covert CIA interrogation centre in Afghanistan. He was held for 14 months, allegedly mistreated and prevented from communicating with anyone outside the detention facility, including his family and the German government. Along the way it became apparent to his captors that his passport was genuine and that he had nothing to do with the other el-Masri, so he was finally set free in May 2004. Instead of the grovelling apology and help in re-establishing his life one might expect in such circumstances, he was released at night on a desolate road in Albania.

When questioned in Germany over the el-Masri affair, the US Defence Secretary Condoleezza Rice stated, 'I believe this will be handled in the proper

45 See, e.g., Elaine Sciolino, 'Spanish judge tells US Guantánamo is an insult', *International Herald Tribune*, 4 June 2006, available at www.iht.com/articles/2006/06/04/news/gitmo.php (last visited 16 October 2008).

46 See Committee on Legal Affairs and Human Rights, Information Memorandum II, above note 43.

47 Information on the case is available at www.aclu.org/safefree/torture/29868res20070524.html (last visited 15 October 2008).

courts here in Germany and if necessary in American courts as well'. In fact, when a lawsuit *was* brought before a US court, the government invoked the so-called 'state secrets' privilege, arguing that the 'entire aim of the case is to establish state secrets'. The case was dismissed in its entirety by the US District Court, upheld by the US Court of Appeals. In October 2007, the Supreme Court decided, without giving reasons, to refuse to review the case.[48] This is not a case in which courts settled on (or even considered) excluding particular documents, evidence or sources, holding parts of the hearing in camera, or taking other special measures. It is simply the end of the line for justice in US courts for el-Masri. The wholesale vacation of proceedings alleging government misconduct, on the basis of the government's own assessment that those proceedings might per se damage national security, is anathema to justice and a striking illustration of the extent of secrecy in this area.

The *el-Masri* case and others like it[49] have been taken up elsewhere, but attempts to secure justice continue to falter. Arrest warrants were issued by a German court in January 2007. But the German Justice Minister subsequently announced that, as the United States had made it clear that it would not co-operate, the German authorities would therefore not be pursuing a formal request for the extradition of the 13 CIA agents involved in el-Masri's abduction.[50] In a parallel development, Italian courts too have issued arrest warrants in respect of another CIA rendition, Abu Omar, who was kidnapped by the CIA while living in Italy, taken to Egypt and allegedly tortured there. Interestingly, however, the Italian government has also raised state secrets concerns before the Constitutional Court, and criminal proceedings have been suspended pending the decision.[51]

One of the striking characteristics of rendition is its transnational nature, involving multiple state agents who together share direct and indirect responsibility. It is therefore important that, through litigation and other measures, attempts are underway to hold a range of states to account separately for assisting rendition or facilitating or failing to prevent it on their own territory.[52]

48 In the US Supreme Court, *El-Masri* v. *United States*, Case No. 06-1613, petition for a writ of certiorari denied 9 October 2007. In the US District Court for the Eastern District of Virginia, *El-Masri* v. *Tenet*, Case 1:05-cv-01417-TSE-TRJ, order granting US motion to dismiss granted May 12, 2006. For details of the petition lodged before the Inter-American Commission on Human Rights, see www.aclu.org/pdfs/safefree/elmasri_iachr_20080409.pdf (last visited 15 October 2008).

49 See also, e.g., the case of Maher Arar, a Syrian-born Canadian detained in the United States and transferred to torture in Syria. 'Torture and accountability', *International Herald Tribune*, 19 November 2007.

50 See, e.g., Jeannie Shawl, 'US rejects German bid for extraction of CIA agents in el-Masri rendition', Associated Press via Jurist Legal News & Research, 22 September 2007, available at http://jurist.law.pitt.edu/paperchase/2007/09/us-rejects-germany-bid-for-extradition.php (last visited 16 October 2008).

51 'Italy indicts 31 linked to CIA rendition case', *International Herald Tribune*, 15 February 2007, available at www.iht.com/articles/ap/2007/02/16/europe/EU-GEN-Italy-CIA-Kidnap.php (last visited 16 October 2008).

52 As regards the *el-Masri* case specifically, calls for an effective investigation into the involvement of Macedonian officials have been reiterated. See, e.g., ICJ E-Bulletin on Counterterrorism & Human Rights, 'FYR Macedonia: UN experts call for Macedonian investigation in El-Masri case', No. 24, June 2008, available at www.icj.org/IMG/E-Bulletin_June08.pdf (last visited 15 October 2008): 'In April and

One such example is the case of Boumediene and Ors v. Bosnia before the European Court of Human Rights. The case concerns Bosnians of Algerian descent held in Bosnia after 9/11 at the behest of the United States, eventually released by Bosnian courts for lack of evidence against them, and immediately then arrested by US authorities (apparently with some collusion from their Bosnian Counterparts) and transferred to Guantanamo Bay. In addition to the now famous proceedings in US courts,[53] this case has also gone before the ECtHR in a challenge against the Bosnian state for its part in the process.[54]

One of the questions arising is the nature and content of a state's ongoing obligations when it transfers or facilitates the transfer of an individual to a situation where there is a real risk of serious human rights violations. One of the issues that the Court itself has highlighted as a key consideration in the case is the extent to which Bosnia is obliged to make diplomatic representations on behalf of individuals to ensure their rights are not violated following transfer.[55]

Rendition cases are also beginning to unfold in Africa.[56] Reports allege, for example, the involvement of Kenyan authorities, at US behest, in the rendition of Somali and Kenyan nationals to Somalia and, in some cases, to Guantánamo Bay. It will be important to see what measure of justice is afforded in fora outside the United States. Clearly, rendition litigation promises to be a growth area, as cases seek to play their role in prising open the facts and pursuing justice against a range of international players in this most challenging of areas.

May, the UN Committee against Torture and the Human Rights Committee expressed concerns about the investigations carried out by the Former Republic of Macedonia in the abduction and ill-treatment of Mr Khaled El-Masri when held by CIA agents in secret detention. The Committees advised the Macedonian government to undertake a new and thorough investigation and the Human Rights Committee recommended that it should consider awarding him compensation'. Human Rights Committee, Ninety-second session, Consideration of Reports Submitted By States Parties Under Article 40 of the Covenant: Concluding Observations Of The Human Committee: The Former Yugoslav Republic Of Macedonia, 17 April 2008, available at www.icj.org/IMG/HRC_Macedonia.pdf (last visited 15 October 2008).

53 When these individuals took proceedings in US courts challenging the lawfulness of their transfer and detention, it was at first held that the Military Commission Act prevented them from raising any claim in a US court, until this was overturned by the Supreme Court's June 2008 judgment.

54 Wilmer Hale, 'Guantanamo claims before EU Court of Human Rights', 14 March 2008, available at www.haledorr.com/about/news/newsDetail.aspx?news=1134 (last visited 15 October 2008). For the third-party intervention by INTERIGHTS and the ICJ, see www.interights.org. *Boumidiene and Others v. Bosnia and Herzogovina*, Applications nos. 38703/06 et al, decided 18 November 2008. One of the questions arising was the nature and content of a state's ongoing obligations following transfer of an individual to a situation where there is a real risk of serious human rights violations. However, the Court found the case manifestly ill-founded and inadmissible on the grounds that, on the facts, Bosnia and Herzegovina was taking all possible steps to the present date to protect the basic rights of the applicants.

55 See Applications 38703/06 et al, supra n.54, para 67.

56 See, e.g., Daniel Auma, 'US rendition on trial in Africa', Spero News, 25 September 2007, available at www.speroforum.com/site/article.asp?id=11196 (last visited 15 October 2008); see also Human Rights Watch, '*Why Am I Still Here?*': *The Horn of Africa Renditions and the Fate of the Missing*, September 2008, available at http://hrw.org/reports/2008/eastafrica1008/ (last visited 15 October 2008). A case on rendition of Kenyan nationals, for instance, is at the time of writing, before Kenyan courts.

Volume 90 Number 871 September 2008

Issue 5: The 'terrorism' label and its implications for alleged terrorists and others associated with them

The 'terrorism' label has been applied liberally since 9/11, without clarity as to its scope (the term being undefined or ill-defined), often without due process, and with serious consequences for those thus branded or others associated with them.

Perhaps the most obvious manifestation of this phenomenon are the various terrorism 'lists' established at national, regional and (under the Security Council's watchful eye) international level. While systems and safeguards vary, the problem with these lists is often the lack of transparency around the reasons for inclusion in them, and the lack of meaningful opportunity to challenge such inclusion. Little by little, litigation is seeking to call governments to account for decisions made in this respect, and to provide a degree of judicial oversight at least to temper an otherwise opaque and arbitrary practice.

Some success has been had by litigants before the European Court of Justice (ECJ). In 2006 the Court held that individuals associated with a banned organization had the right to reasons for their listing, to effective judicial protection and to be heard.[57] Although disputed by the respondent state, the ECJ confirmed that while the common EU position that led to the listing in the first place could not be reviewed by the Court, the decision to include a particular organization on the list could. This robust approach was recently maintained by the Grand Chamber of the ECJ in respect of listings authorized by the Security Council.[58] Similar issues are currently pending before the European Court of Human Rights, which might be expected to follow the human rights-friendly approach of the ECJ.

In 2008 a parallel case, challenging domestic listing procedures, made its way through UK courts. On 7 May, the UK Court of Appeal upheld a decision of the Proscribed Organisations Appeal Commission requiring the removal of an Iranian opposition group from its blacklist of terror organizations.[59] The case illustrates the willingness of the courts, assessing in detail the facts and evidence available, to challenge the Secretary of State's determination that the organization was concerned in terrorism. The Court was satisfied that the organization was no longer engaged in violence, and it confirmed that proscription could not be justified on the basis that an organization had been engaged in violence and might at a future date reacquire the capacity and intent to so engage.

57 European Court of Justice, *Organisation des Modjahedines du peuple d'Iran* v. *Council of the European Union, United Kingdom of Great Britain and Northern Ireland*, Case T-228/02, Judgment of The Court of First Instance (Second Chamber), 12 December 2006.

58 Kadi and Yusef were unsuccessful in challenges at first instance: European Court of Justice, Case T-306/01 *Yusuf and Al Barakaat International Foundation* v. *Council and Commission*, [2005] ECR II-3533, 21 September 2005, para. 73 (*Yusuf*); and Case T-315/01, *Kadi* v. *Council and Commission*, [2005] ECR II-3649, 21 September 2005 (*Kadi*). However, the challenges were won on appeal: Cases C-402/05 P and C-415/05 P, Judgment of Grand Chamber on 3 September 2008, available at http://curia.europa.eu/jurisp/cgi-bin/form.pl?lang=EN&Submit=rechercher&numaff=C-402/05 (last visited 15 October 2008). OMIC case distinguished them because they involved the direct imposition of Security Council resolutions.

59 England and Wales Court of Appeal, *Secretary of State for the Home Department* v. *Lord Alton of Liverpool and Others*, [2008] EWCA Civ 443, Judgment of 7 May 2008.

The terrorism label can have far-reaching consequences not only for the alleged terrorists themselves, but for others associated with them. One illustration is found in a case currently being litigated in the ECtHR on behalf of the family of the killed Chechen leader Aslan Maskhadov.[60] Laws in the Russian Federation that were applied in this case stipulate that if persons deemed to be terrorists are killed by the state in the course of counter-terrorist operations, their bodies will not be returned to their families. This draconian measure targets families who are deeply affected by being unable to duly observe a mourning period, pay their last respects and bury their family member in accordance with Islamic religious requirements, which according to their religious tradition may ultimately lead to the deceased being denied access to heaven. While there is no meaningful relationship between the prevention of terrorism and such a measure, it is justified by reference to the deterrence of terrorism. This case, which has been declared admissible by the ECtHR, provides an example of the blanket use of the 'terrorist' label to justify otherwise unacceptable special forms of treatment, and to punish those 'associated' with persons accused of ill-defined acts of terrorism.

A positive example of courts curbing the creeping effect of the notion of guilt by association arose in an Australian case of 2007 – *Haneef* v. *Minister for Immigration and Citizenship* (*Federal Court of Australia*).[61] The case concerned Mohamed Haneef, whose visa was revoked by Australian authorities on the grounds that he was the second cousin of one of the men who had crashed a car into Glasgow airport's terminal building, had stayed in the same hostel and, on leaving the country, had left him his mobile phone.

In the Australian courts the authorities argued that any form of 'association' (family or other) with persons accused of this sort of criminal activity was enough to fail the 'character test' laid down in Australian immigration law. The judgment rejected this contention and provided a fitting rebuke to the spreading notion of guilt by association and the dangers of it. The judge questioned whether he might also fall within the category of person having associated with terrorists, given former professional association as a barrister. He held that, for the law to apply, the 'association' must itself be of a criminal rather than of a family or innocent nature.

I shall end this survey of cases by citing the observations of the government of Botswana in a case pending before the African Commission on Human and Peoples Rights:

> We wish to recall here the bombings that occurred in London, Madrid and the 2001 events in NY and more recently Egypt. It is against this background that

60 ECtHR, *Kusama Yazedovna Maskhadova and Others* v. *Russia*, Application No. 18071/05, Decision as to Admissibility, 8 July 2008. INTERIGHTS represents the applicants, the family of deceased Chechen leader Aslan Maskhadov. The case has been declared admissible. INTERIGHTS, Maskhadov Press Release, 1 October 2007, available at www.interights.org/view-document/index.htm?id=209 (last visited 15 October 2008).

61 Federal Court of Australia, *Haneef* v. *Minister for Immigration and Citizenship*, [2007] FCA 1273, 21 August 2007.

Volume 90 Number 871 September 2008

> Botswana reminds the Commission that the declaration of Mr Good as a prohibited immigrant was made 'in the interests of peace, stability and national security' ... We have given examples of traumatic results that occur once there is a lapse in dealing with national security issues ... If the President visualizes a threat to national security, it is wrong for him to wait for the threat to materialize into a national disaster. It is right to state that decisions whether something is or is not in the interest of national security are not a matter for any organ other than the executive.[62]

One might assume that this case concerned terrorism. In fact it concerns a professor deported for criticizing presidential succession in Botswana. The facts could not be much further removed from the terrorism context. Yet this case exemplifies the extent to which national security, the global terrorist threat and the exceptionalism of the war on terror are being relied upon to set aside human rights in contexts that have nothing conceivably to do with international terrorism.

Concluding observations

The human rights picture

I said at the beginning of this article that litigation can serve to highlight key human rights issues. The case developments described above illustrate, in my view, some of these key characteristics of the war on terror as it impacts on human rights.

An overarching point is that, leaving aside military aspirations, the main policy aim being pursued after 9/11 was intelligence gathering. It was not and is not about justice in the legal sense, certainly not about criminal responsibility. While there may be many reasons contributing to this, it is suggested that this is consistent with and borne out by the dearth of criminal prosecutions of high-level al-Qaeda terrorist suspects. There have been more Supreme Court judgments on whether Guantánamo detainees have rights than there have been trials by military commission or otherwise. The first military commission judgment handed down, on 6 August 2008, convicts Osama Bin Laden's driver for providing support for known terrorists and sentences him to 66 months' imprisonment, of which he has already served 61.[63] Seven years on, experience does not point to a massive

62 The government cites the decision of the Supreme Court of Botswana, the highest judicial authority in Botswana, in *Kenneth Good* v. *Attorney General*, Civil Appeal No. 28/2005. An application to the African Commission on Human and Peoples' Rights was submitted by Interights on 10 October 2007 and was pending at the time of writing. The brief for the applicant is obtainable from www.interights.org.

63 'Bin Laden Driver Sentenced to a Short Term', William Glaberson, *New York Times*, 8 August 2008.

global criminal justice campaign resulting in the investigation and prosecution of high-level suspects, although undoubtedly many have been either killed or detained and interrogated without charge.

Second, the cases illustrate that the means to achieve that intelligence has involved violations of the most sacred human rights norms, notably torture and arbitrary detention.

Third, to the extent that states may not themselves have engaged in torture, there has been widespread practice of playing fast and loose with safeguards *against* torture that are part of the prohibition thereof and essential to give it meaningful effect. The decision by some states to challenge the basic rules on *non-refoulement* before the European Court of Human Rights illustrates this point.

Fourth, unprincipled distinctions have emerged recurrently. This may be between nationals and non-nationals, as illustrated by widespread justification of arbitrary detention of non-nationals. It may be between standards that officials are expected to meet at home, and those considered applicable abroad, as highlighted by the approach of certain states, and the restrictive judgment referred to on the extra-territoriality issue. Or it may be evident in a 'hands off' approach to torture whereby distinctions are drawn between what states themselves do, and what they facilitate or encourage at the hand of others, as noted in the case concerning torture evidence, for example.

Fifth, and most insidious perhaps, has been the move from illegality to extra-legality – the practice of removing individuals from the protection of the law altogether, epitomized by rendition and disappearance that have been the subject of various litigation initiatives.

Finally, there is the 'creeping reach' of measures and approaches that are originally justified exceptionally in the context of international terrorism and national security. The 'terrorism' and 'national security' labels have been relied upon to erode standards beyond those exceptional circumstances, to affect persons loosely associated with persons loosely implicated in loosely defined acts of terrorism. The result is that genuine exigencies of the global fight against international terrorism are being brought to bear as a pretext for violations far beyond the terrorism context.

The role of the courts and the impact of human rights litigation

It is clear is that in recent years, across diverse systems, there has been a burgeoning of human rights litigation. That has reinforced the critical role for the courts in human rights protection. Caution is due in trying to draw conclusions from such wide-ranging practice, addressing different issues in diverse systems. But I will offer a few tentative observations on how we might begin to think about the practice of human rights litigation in this field to date and its potential impact.

In many cases the judiciary has shown its reluctance to make determinations that may impact on security, refusing, for example, to question executive assessments of the existence of an emergency. But when particular practices

Volume 90 Number 871 September 2008

have come under scrutiny, the courts in diverse systems have often and increasingly proved themselves willing – in some cases promptly, in other cases after painstaking process and only as a matter of genuine last resort – to criticize the legitimacy, necessity or proportionality of particular measures.

While experience has been both positive and negative, I shall suggest the following ways in which litigation may have had, or in some cases may yet have, a positive effect.

First, simply taking a human rights violation to court frames the issue as a matter of law, not only of politics. As such it reasserts the principle of legality and the rule of law in the highly politicized discourse around terrorism and security. Critically, these cases indicate, to varying degrees, the existence of a check on executive action. This is seen in reminders that 'a state of war is not a blank check for the President' or by the willingness of courts in cases such as *Belmarsh* or *Haneef* to subject to close scrutiny the determination of what was necessary for national security. As a rebuke to the executive when it has failed in its role as primary protector of rights, this can be critical in reasserting the democratic credentials of the system, which are often lost through the illegitimacy of the conduct impugned.

Judgments have often, to quite varying degrees, been conservative and characterized by judicial deference to political branches. One may ask whether the US Supreme Court could and should have decided whether detainees have the basic right to habeas corpus when the matter first came before it in 2004. At what price in terms of judicial efficiency in the administration of justice – and protection of individuals – came the virtue of judicial restraint? But so far as jurisprudence reflects and deliberates on the thorny issue of the role of courts in determining such matters, and on the relationship between political branches and the judiciary, it may ultimately contribute to and enrich our understanding of the separation of powers and the democratic judicial function.

Second, litigation can also serve as a catalyst to change law or practice. In some cases, such as the changes in law and policy following the *Belmarsh* judgment, the causal effect is fairly clear. In others, it is difficult to tell to what extent, if at all, the irritant effect of litigation contributed to shifts in practice, such as the return of UK nationals from Guantánamo following unsuccessful litigation seeking to obligate the state to intervene on their behalf.[64] The course of litigation often itself exposes particular policies and practices, and may lead states to clarify their own policies or articulation of them.[65]

Judgments may themselves develop or clarify the law through jurisprudence or, as is often the case in the context of the war on terror, they may simply serve to reinforce established principles that have increasingly been cast in doubt,

64 *Abbasi* case, above note 2.

65 See, e.g., the *Al-Skeini* case, above note 26, in which the UK government shifted its position as regards the applicability of the ECHR to individuals detained by UK officials in Iraq and allegedly tortured in detention.

as in the *Saadi* judgment.[66] The challenge in many of the cases highlighted has been to hold ground rather than to advance the protection of human rights as such, in other words to win back and keep winning gains that were made years ago, that were thought secure but rendered vulnerable in the course of the war on terror.

Sometimes courts serve as democracy alerters whereby the interplay between judicial and political branches is such that a signal from the former can be a catalyst to a more proactive approach by the latter. Persuasive judicial messages can also be sent transnationally, as seen, for example, in the unusually robust judicial rebuke of the system of Guantánamo Bay detentions by the English Court of Appeals in the *Abbasi* case.[67]

Cases can themselves play an important role in securing access to information and in prising open facts, sometimes in face of a wall of state secrecy. Litigation may have this as its goal – such as cases in the United Kingdom pursuing access to military files,[68] FOIA (Freedom of Information Act) litigation in the United States which has had a measure of success[69] and Canadian litigation where the government was compelled to produce information or evidence in relation to proceedings in another state[70] – or this may be a by-product of the process. This unearthing of information is particularly critical in areas such as rendition, characterized by a concerted cover-up. At a minimum litigation draws out government positions – as seen, for example, in the shift in positions of the UK government in the course of the *al Skeini* case – as they engage as parties and clarify or adjust their positions in the course of litigation.

Litigation of the sort referred to also opens legal systems to the cross-fertilization of ideas from other systems as international and comparative perspectives are brought to bear, notably through *amicus* interventions. Guantánamo litigation in the United States has been perhaps the most massive piece of international human rights litigation ever, if judged at least by the unprecedented level and nature of interventions before the Supreme Court.[71]

Ultimately, the impact of litigation on human rights issues generally lies in its gradual contribution to social change. There has, for example, been a shift in

66 This works both ways and can also weaken or confuse the framework of rights protection, as is suggested may have been the outcome of the *Al-Skeini* case, for example.

67 *R (Abbasi)* v. *Secretary of State for Foreign and Commonwealth Affairs*, [2003] UKHRR 76, where the English Court of Appeal criticized the system of Guantanamo detentions in unusually strident terms.

68 John Aston, 'Lawyers in Basra death case win access to files', *Independent*, 4 October 2007.

69 See, e.g., US District Court for the Southern District of New York, *Associated Press* v. *United States Department of Defense*, 498 F. Supp. 2d 707 (SDNY, 2007), and US Court of Appeals, DC Circuit, *Center for National Security Studies* v. *Dep't of Justice*, 331 F.3d 918 (DC Cir. 2003) (cert denied, 540 US 1104 (2004)).

70 Supreme Court of Canada, *Canada (Justice)* v. *Khadr*, 2008 SCC 28, 23 May 2008. On 23 May 2008, the Canadian Supreme Court ruled that the government had violated Canada's Constitution and its international human rights obligations by transmitting to US official information resulting from Canadian officials' interviews of Omar Kadhr at the Guantánamo Bay detention centre. The Court took the unusual step of ordering Canadian officials to allow Mr Kadhr access to records of his interrogations with Canadian agents, for use in preparing his defence before the Guantánamo Military Commission.

71 *Amicus* interventions appeared from such diverse quarters as British Lords as well as Israeli military lawyers.

Volume 90 Number 871 September 2008

public opinion (national and international) on Guantánamo, and arguably litigation may have been an important contributor. What is undoubtedly true is that litigation has to be understood not in isolation but as one small piece of a much bigger and more complex puzzle.

Finally, and perhaps most importantly, real cases serve to tell the victims' stories. They provide often graphic illustrations of what euphemisms such as 'extraordinary rendition' and 'enhanced interrogation techniques' mean to human beings like you or me. Judgments validate those stories and experiences. One of the essential characteristics of the 'war on terror' has been the attempt to put certain people beyond the reach of the law. Litigation can be a tool, as one English judge put it, not for transferring power from the executive to the judiciary, but for transferring power from the executive to the individual.[72] If any particular case can bring an individual back into the legal framework, and reassert the individual as a rights-bearer and human being, then perhaps that is impact enough.

72 Dame Mary Arden has stated that 'the decision in the A case should not be misinterpreted as a transfer of power from the executive to the judiciary. The position is that the judiciary now has the important task of reviewing executive action against the benchmark of human rights. Thus, the transfer of power is not to the judiciary but to the individual'. (2005) 121 LQR at pp. 623–4, in A. T. H. Smith, 'Balancing liberty and security? A legal analysis of United Kingdom anti-terrorist legislation', *European Journal on Criminal Policy and Research*, 13 (2007), pp. 73–83, DOI 10.1007/s10610-007-9035-6.

[19]

Al Qaeda, Terrorism, and Military Commissions

Ruth Wedgewood

It is now more than an academic question whether one should regard terrorism as crime or as war. The attacks mounted by the Al Qaeda organization on September 11, 2001, were of unprecedented scale, heretofore seen only in wartime, killing three thousand people in a few hours' time. Most victims were civilians, and most were Americans, yet the dead included people from eighty-seven countries. Had the emergency evacuation of the World Trade Center towers not run efficiently, as many as twenty-five thousand more might have died.

The psychological sense that this was an act of war is founded on the extraordinary destructiveness of the act. In the past, even terrorism has evinced an implicit set of expectations—using violence to intimidate or gain publicity, targeting civilians so as to undermine the confidence placed in organized authority, but generally stopping short of this irrational magnitude of destruction. Only nihilism might seem to explain a scale of wreckage that serves no programmatic demands or political ambition.

[101] Geneva Convention No. IV, *supra* note 71, Art. 147, leads to the same result.

[102] 18 U.S.C. §2441 (2000).

[*] Legal Officer (international law), Office of the Prosecutor, International Criminal Tribunal for the Former Yugoslavia. The views expressed are solely those of the author and are not attributable to the United Nations, the ICTY, or the Office of the Prosecutor.

In a sense, Al Qaeda's real target was globalization itself—the willing premise that borders no longer matter, and that distinctions between alien and citizen status might gradually be erased. The free flow of goods and people across national boundaries can facilitate economic growth and intellectual exchange, but also permits more sinister commerce. So, too, the real target might seem to be liberalism, since Al Qaeda's enterprise exploits freedom's core values. Our delight in free association, privacy, and a multiethnic social fabric, and a stalwart sense that government should leave us alone were exploited by a violent jihad that corrupted the humanistic traditions of Islam.

Al Qaeda's published doctrine maintains that there are no innocent civilians in Western society, and this tenet leads it to the gravest of international crimes. In warfare, the principle of distinction requires that civilians never be singled out as targets. Yet Al Qaeda deliberately timed its hijackings to attack the World Trade Center in New York City during the morning rush hour when the office towers would be teeming with workers. Al Qaeda also acted as a piratical group that feigned civilian status, condemned by the laws of war as banditry and sabotage.

The American response to the Al Qaeda attacks looks like a war as well. The air campaign in Afghanistan has dropped thousands of tons of ordnance. American special forces entered Afghanistan to work alongside Afghan troops from the Northern and Eastern Alliance. The American use of force was endorsed in binding resolutions of the United Nations Security Council; the Council declared unanimously that an armed attack had occurred on American soil, within the meaning of Article 51, and that the United States had the right to use armed force in self-defense.[1] Its recognition of a profound threat to international peace and security also brought the Council to announce a rigorous new regime in which states are forbidden to give any aid, assistance, or asylum to the perpetrators of international terrorism.[2] The North Atlantic Treaty Organization declared (for the first time in the history of the security pact) that the "acts of barbarism" if "directed from abroad" amounted to an armed attack against a member state and called upon members to render assistance.[3]

The prosecution of the war in Afghanistan has now succeeded in displacing the Taliban regime, and permitted the creation of a transitional government in Kabul. Most Al Qaeda fighters in Afghanistan have fled across the border or been killed. More than four hundred combatants captured from the ranks of Al Qaeda and senior Taliban have been turned over to American custody. Over two hundred detainees have been flown to Guantánamo Bay, Cuba, and others will apparently follow.

The question addressed in the presidential order of November 13, 2001, is thus at hand. What should be done with members of Al Qaeda once they are in our hands? Should they be detained, and if so, on what basis? Should they be tried, and if so, in what court?

In the 1990s, when we cornered an Al Qaeda member, the preferred avenue was to mount a federal criminal trial in district court, charging terrorism and murder under American federal statutes. Detention of an Al Qaeda member as an enemy combatant was not contemplated. Rather, restraint on Al Qaeda's freedom of action was sought only where intelligence reports could be fleshed out by trial-quality evidence, with proof beyond a reasonable doubt. Otherwise, we stayed our hand. The most startling example was the White House's reported decision to turn down an offer by Sudan in the spring of 1996 to deliver Osama bin Laden into American or Saudi custody.[4] The doubt was that we might not convict him in a federal court. Apparently, no one contemplated that we could hold him as a combatant in an ongoing conflict, for the paradigm of crime had not yet admitted the pertinence of the norms of

[1] SC Res. 1368 (Sept. 12, 2001), 40 ILM 1277 (2001); SC Res. 1373 (Sept. 28, 2001), 40 ILM at 1278.

[2] SC Res. 1373, *supra* note 1, paras. 1–2.

[3] NATO Press Release (2001)124, Statement by the North Atlantic Council (Sept. 12, 2001), 40 ILM 1267 (2001).

[4] Ruth Wedgwood, *The Law at War: How Osama Slipped Away,* NAT'L INTEREST, Winter 2001/02, at 69.

war. Bin Laden then departed for Afghanistan, where his training camps have tutored thousands of mujahedin in the skills of combat and terror. The Saudi exile also continued to build his network of compartmentalized underground cells in Europe, Asia, and North America.

In an intellectual shift, the Bush order announced that the paradigm of war fit the case after all. Al Qaeda's campaign throughout the 1990s against American targets amounted to a war. In recitation, this may seem more obvious now. The cumulative chain of events is quite striking—the 1992 attempt to kill American troops in Aden on the way to Somalia; the 1993 ambush of American army rangers in Mogadishu; the 1993 truck bombing of the World Trade Center by conspirators who later announced that they had intended to topple the towers; the 1995 bombing of the Riyadh training center in Saudi Arabia; the 1996 bombing of the Khobar Towers American barracks in Saudi Arabia (five weeks after bin Laden was permitted to leave Sudan); the 1998 destruction of two American embassies in East Africa; and the 2000 bombing of the U.S.S. *Cole*, in a Yemeni harbor. The innumerable other threats against American embassies and offices around the world; the plot to down ten American airliners over the Pacific and to bomb the Lincoln and Holland Tunnels in New York, as well as the United Nations; the smuggling of explosive materials across the Canadian border for a planned millennium attack at Los Angeles Airport; and finally, the attacks on the Pentagon and the World Trade Center—were taken to constitute a coherent campaign rather than the isolated acts of individuals. Al Qaeda's open ambition to acquire a nuclear device has made the metaphor of war even more compelling.

The current debate on how one should respond to the acts committed by Al Qaeda may have profound operational consequences, and consequences for our culture. One can plausibly argue that the fabric of American liberalism and democracy would be irreparably coarsened if government proves unable to provide a reasonable guarantee of life and safety to its citizens. It is difficult to prove a negative, but certainly the prior effort to investigate Al Qaeda through the criminal justice channels of grand jury and trial was not sufficient to deter or intercept the later attacks.

Good faith suggestions have issued from several quarters that any trials against Al Qaeda members should take place in federal court or an ad hoc international tribunal. Some cases may be suitable for such modalities. But in the middle of a grave conflict with an efficient and undeterrable adversary, military commissions may be the most practicable course.

In federal court, for example, there is no method of protecting sensitive intelligence intercepts required as proof. The 1980 Classified Information Procedures Act permits some predictability in trials where sensitive information is at stake.[5] The accused's lawyers must notify the government if they wish to present classified information in their defense case. To a limited extent, generic descriptions may be substituted for particular data, and the government can seek a protective order to forbid the further disclosure of classified information that is not entered into evidence at trial. But ultimately, the presentation of proof remains entirely open to the public. Any intelligence used as proof against a defendant must, by definition, also be revealed to state or nonstate adversaries who care to listen.

Second is the problem of evidence. The rules governing the admission of evidence—what can be placed before a jury for consideration in fact-finding—are strict and unchangeable in federal criminal trials. In general, only eyewitness testimony can be heard, even where testimony of one degree's farther remove may have significant probative value. This high hurdle for what can be presented reflects a historical distrust of the jury's ability to weigh evidence, and is far less characteristic of continental legal systems and international courts. It poses a less daunting obstacle in an ordinary domestic trial because every citizen is pre-

[5] Classified Information Procedures Act, Pub. L. No. 96-456, 94 Stat. 2025 (1980) (codified as amended at 18 U.S.C. app. 696, §1 (2000)), *as amended by* Pub. L. No. 106-567, tit. VI, §607, 114 Stat. 2855 (2000).

sumed willing to obey the order of the court to give evidence. But in legal action against a terrorist group violent, skilled in countersurveillance, and compartmentalized, there may be no such ready reserve of available witnesses. It has been widely reported that Osama bin Laden telephoned his mother in Syria shortly before September 11 to warn her that a major event was imminent, and that he would be out of touch for some time. If the mother confided to a close friend about her son's warning, still one could not call the friend to give testimony, for technically it would be hearsay.

Similarly, federal court rules governing physical objects and documentary evidence found in searches may exclude probative evidence. The so-called exclusionary rule keeps from the fact finder any evidence found to have been taken in an illegal search by federal authorities (except where the search was pursuant to a warrant and the law was unclear at the time). The exclusionary rule has many strong proponents in ordinary circumstances, because it creates an incentive system for the proper execution of searches by government agents. In wartime, where accuracy in fact-finding is needed to prevent acts of terrorism, this rule finds a less obvious place. So, too, the usual rules on chain of custody and authentication may be difficult to meet for objects obtained in a battlefield environment, where many witnesses are scattered, deceased, or uncooperative. Consider, for example, the computer hard drives found by an American reporter in a market in Afghanistan, evidently scavenged from an abandoned Al Qaeda office and loaded with Al Qaeda memoranda.[6] The order of November 13 would allow a military commission to consider all forms of evidence that a reasonable person would find probative, and in this more latitudinarian rule, will create a broader record for evaluation by the fact finder.

Third is the problem of security. In ordinary times, the safety of the jury, judges, and prosecutor is beyond question. In prosecutions of Al Qaeda, the physical integrity of the trial is difficult to sustain. Guards with automatic weapons now protect the front doors of the federal courthouse at Foley Square in Manhattan. The federal judges who handled Al Qaeda cases during the 1990s have been provided with twenty-four-hour protection by special teams of federal marshals, rotated at short intervals for freshness, and they will probably require such protection for the rest of their lives. No such protection is available for juries, who are summoned to sit as a duty of citizenship, rather than as volunteers. In the aftermath of the first World Trade Center bombing case, Al Qaeda carried out a mass killing abroad and left a written message stating that the killing was in retaliation for the actions of the federal trial judge. The courthouse in Manhattan is a mere six blocks from the site of the now-destroyed World Trade Center towers. Perhaps it is only coincidence that the World Trade Center attack of September 11 took place the day before defendants from the Al Qaeda embassy bombing case were originally due to be sentenced in federal court. Perhaps it is also only bad luck that a defendant in the embassy bombings crippled a guard in the metropolitan correctional center in an unexpected attack with a filed-off plastic comb serving as a knife, or that Al Qaeda prisoners in Afghanistan have mounted attacks against their guards even after their surrender was accepted. But in the aftermath of September 11, with the demonstration of Al Qaeda's appetite for violence, some find it difficult to fathom how the security of trials can be assured against the network's members.

The idea of international trials presents similar difficulties—whether through a new ad hoc chamber created by the Security Council or a permanent international criminal court. Even though the statute of the United Nations tribunal for the former Yugoslavia has been read to permit anonymous witnesses and might be similarly read or amended to mask the source of intelligence information, the very act of revealing intelligence information to international

[6] Alan Cullison & Andrew Higgins, *How Al Qaeda Agent Scouted Attack Sites in Israel and Egypt—Account on Kabul Computer Matches Travels of Reid, the Alleged Shoe-Bomber*, WALL ST. J., Jan. 16, 2002, at A1.

court personnel in the midst of a war would be problematic. Even before the international community sets to work on a code of judicial ethics for international judges, one can acknowledge that some international judicial personnel remain in contact with their home governments, and some may not maintain the standard of financial transparency expected of domestic judges. Sharing intelligence intercepts after a conflict is completed may be less prejudicial. But while a conflict is ongoing, it would be hazardous in the extreme to risk disclosing how bin Laden is tracked. The Al Qaeda leader has repeatedly changed communications systems, and timely surveillance remains essential to our ability to intercept fresh attacks. The criminal tribunals created by the UN Security Council for the former Yugoslavia and Rwanda have dealt with regional conflicts that were local, confined, and largely completed.

In addition, security would be hard to provide. The trial of the Pan Am Flight 103 bombing, held at Camp Zeist before Scottish judges, was staged with the consent of Libya, the suspected state sponsor of the terrorist acts. Even then the trial was moved to the safer setting of a mothballed American military base outside The Hague, and security preparations took months. The Hague is hardly remote from the threats of Al Qaeda that have interleaved European cities, including recent threats to bomb the airport in Strasbourg, France, the situs of European human rights law.

The claim for greater legitimacy through an international tribunal also founders on the facts of international politics. Should the tribunal include broad representation from Muslim countries, in order to enhance the acceptance of verdicts within the Muslim world? Few, if any, Arab or Muslim governments could nominate a judge without fearing reaction from their own militant sectors, and the fatwas of bin Laden have announced that any Muslim government cooperating against him is an apostate enemy. There is also the place of Israel. Bin Laden's 1998 declaration of war was against all Americans and all Jews. Thus, Israel might also wish to send a judge to an international tribunal. Yet the sad fact of the world is that few, if any, Muslim governments would allow their judges to sit alongside an Israeli judge. And within the regional politics of the UN system, Israelis are rarely nominated, much less elected, to significant international bodies. In addition, only one American judge would likely be seated on such a tribunal, and crucial trial chambers would lack any American voice.

The shared commitment to the ethical and legal norms sheltering civilians against deliberate attack can be demonstrated in other ways. One can admit into evidence the respected works of Muslim legal scholars who reiterate that the human lives of innocent civilians are an inappropriate object of attack in wartime. The multiethnic nature of American society itself, including the American military, also serves as a reminder that the honorable rules of warfare are not confined to any particular cultural group.

The president's proposal for military commissions to try Al Qaeda suspects conforms to international law and does not represent any usurpation of civilian jurisdiction. Indeed, military commissions have been the historic and traditional venue for the trial of war crimes. The Nuremberg trials of the Nazi leadership were organized by the Allies in 1945 to educate the German public and the world, and were held in a mixed military commission. Military commissions tried war crimes throughout Europe and the Far East at the conclusion of the world war, and considered the cases of approximately twenty-five hundred defendants. Military commissions have been used throughout the history of the American Republic. Instances include the Civil War trials of Confederate soldiers who shed their uniforms to attempt to commandeer civilian sailing ships, and a Confederate spy named Robert Kennedy who tried to burn New York City.[7] The recent suggestion of Professor George Fletcher that military commissions were deployed only for cases of spying and not for other war crimes[8]

[7] *See Ex parte* Quirin, 317 U.S. 1, 31 n.10(1942).

[8] George P. Fletcher, *War and the Constitution: Bush's Military Tribunals Haven't Got a Legal Leg to Stand On*, AM. PROSPECT, Jan. 1–14, 2002, at 26, *available at* <http://www.prospect.org/print/V13/1/fletcher-g.html>.

is belied by the trial of the commandant of the Andersonville prison camp at the conclusion of the Civil War.[9]

The role of military commissions has been recognized by the Supreme Court in case law stemming from World War II—including the 1942 trial of German saboteurs who landed on the shores of Long Island and Florida,[10] the trial of Japanese General Yamashita at the conclusion of the war in the Pacific in 1945,[11] and the trial of German citizens in China who passed intelligence information to the Japanese even after Germany surrendered.[12] Though the trial procedure of the German saboteurs case and the *Yamashita* trial may not fully accord with our modern sensibility, the same may be said of many civilian trials of the same era. Any suggestion that military tribunals will never acquit a defendant overlooks the outcome of the proceedings against the Germans in China, in which six defendants were acquitted by U.S. Army judges. The story of some of the trials may be more complicated than is recognized as well. The case of the German saboteurs was held in a closed courtroom in the Justice Department, with daily press briefings, in part to mask the role of George Dasch, a defecting saboteur. Dasch had reported the sabotage plot to the Federal Bureau of Investigation, and his family remained in wartime Germany vulnerable to retaliation. The trial of General Yamashita, commander of the Fourteenth Army Group in the Philippines, is famous in human rights jurisprudence for its enunciation of the principle of command responsibility, holding that a military commander has a duty to monitor and restrain the activities of his troops. The *Yamashita* principle may indeed be central to the prosecutions of Radovan Karadžić and Slobodan Milošević in the UN tribunal at The Hague. The short preparation time accorded to Yamashita's counsel, and the disregard of the general's claim that he was preoccupied with repelling the American advance and could not effectively control the Japanese Navy forces, do not change the fact that the earlier events of Nanking had put every Japanese commander on notice that close monitoring of troops was necessary.

The accepted use of a military venue for the trial of war crimes is confirmed by the Geneva Conventions. Article 84 of the Third Geneva Convention of 1949 instructs that "[a] prisoner of war shall be tried *only by a military court*, unless the existing laws of the Detaining Power expressly permit the civil courts to try a member of the armed forces of the Detaining Power in respect of the particular offense."[13] Only in 1996 did Congress create any general federal court jurisdiction to try international war crimes,[14] limiting the scope to grave breaches of the Geneva Conventions and violations of common Article 3 and the Hague rules.[15] Crimes under

[9] Accounts of the early history of American military commissions can be found in WILLIAM WINTHROP, MILITARY LAW AND PRECEDENTS (2d rev. ed. 1920), and WILLIAM BIRKHIMER, MILITARY GOVERNMENT AND MARTIAL LAW (1914). On the history of commissions generally, see also Madsen v. Kinsella, 343 U.S. 341 (1952); A. Wigfall Green, *The Military Commission*, 42 AJIL 832 (1948). See further the statement of Major General Enoch H. Crowder, judge advocate general, on revision of the Articles of War:

> There will be more instances in the future than in the past when the jurisdiction of courts-martial will overlap that of the war courts, and the question would arise whether Congress having vested jurisdiction by statute the common law of war jurisdiction was not ousted. I wish to make it perfectly plain by the new article [15] that in such cases the jurisdiction of the war court is concurrent.

S. REP. NO. 63-229, at 53, 98 (1912). On Article 15 of the Articles of War, see note 17 *infra*.

[10] *Ex parte* Quirin, 317 U.S. 1 (1942).

[11] *In re* Yamashita, 327 U.S. 1 (1946).

[12] Johnson v. Eisentrager, 339 U.S. 763 (1950).

[13] Convention Relative to the Treatment of Prisoners of War, Aug. 12, 1949, Art. 84, 6 UST 3316, 75 UNTS 135 [hereinafter Third Geneva Convention] (consented to by the United States Senate on July 6, 1955, with reservations) (emphasis added).

[14] 18 U.S.C. §2441 (2000) (as amended in 1996 and 1997).

[15] *Id.* §2441 (c). For the Hague rules, see Regulations Respecting the Laws and Customs of War on Land, *infra* note 27. Violations of the Land Mines Protocol (Protocol II), May 3, 1996, 35 ILM 1206 (1996), to the Convention on Conventional Weapons can also be prosecuted under the War Crimes Act. Only cases where an American national or member of the American armed forces is involved as perpetrator or victim fall within the statute's reach.

the customary law of war remain outside federal criminal jurisdiction. And by memorandum of agreement between the Department of Defense and the Department of Justice, despite the new statute, any current member of the American armed forces still "would be tried for a violation of the War Crimes Act in a military court."[16]

Indeed, the jurisdiction of military commissions has been set by the bounds of international law directly incorporated within American law. Under the Articles of War and the Uniform Code of Military Justice, the disciplinary offenses of persons in American military service have been handled through courts-martial, including offenses such as failing to report for duty or misbehavior of a sentinel. Over the last fifty years, the American system of courts-martial has come to more closely resemble civilian trials, for example, adopting the Federal Rules of Evidence and a version of the *Miranda* rule even more liberal than is used in civilian courts (by requiring a warning of the right to counsel as soon as a person is suspected of an offense).

But each time Congress has revised the rules for courts-martial, it has also confirmed the right of the president as commander in chief to convene military commissions for the enforcement of the law of war. Article 15 of the 1920 Articles of War, for example, states that "[t]he provisions of these articles conferring jurisdiction upon courts-martial shall not be construed as depriving military commissions . . . of concurrent jurisdiction in respect of offenders or offenses that by statute *or by the law of war* may be triable by such military commissions."[17] Similar language appears in the Uniform Code of Military Justice, passed by Congress in 1950 to replace the standing Articles of War.[18]

This statutory language acknowledges that the jurisdiction of military commissions is defined by the norms of the customary law of nations, namely, the law of war.[19] These provisions of the Articles of War and the Uniform Code of Military Justice are the fraternal twins, if you like, of the Alien Tort Claims Act, which also authorizes the incorporation of customary international law into United States law—a parallel noted by Chief Justice Stone in *Ex parte Quirin*.[20] (Some critics of *Filartiga*[21] may wish to reexamine their analysis in light of this direct Supreme Court authority.)

It is also wrong to suggest that military commissions can be convened only where there is a *de novo* statutory authorization—for Congress's language says that offenders and offenses can fall under a commission's purview either by statute or by the law of war. And lest there be scruple about the force of "old" statutes, it is worth noting that the legislative history of the 1996 War Crimes Act reiterates the grounding of commissions and their jurisdiction in the customary law of war.[22]

[16] Letter from Judith Miller, general counsel of the Department of Defense, to Congressman Bill McCollum (May 22, 1996), *reprinted in* H.R. REP. NO. 104-698, at 12, 13 (1996). *Compare id. with* Opinion of Attorney General James Speed, 11 Op. Att'y Gen. 297, 315 (1865) ("The civil courts have no more right to prevent the military, in time of war, from trying an offender against the laws of war than they have a right to interfere with or prevent a battle.").

[17] Articles of War, Art. 15, *in* Pub. L. No. 242, ch. 227, 41 Stat. 787, 790 (1920) (emphasis added).

[18] 10 U.S.C. §821 (2000), also cited in the preambular language of President Bush's order of November 13, 2001, 66 Fed. Reg. 57,833 (Nov. 16, 2001).

[19] *In re* Yamashita, 327 U.S. 1, 20 (1946) (stating that "[b]y thus recognizing military commissions in order to preserve their traditional jurisdiction over enemy combatants unimpaired by the Articles, Congress gave sanction, as we held in *Ex parte Quirin*, to any use of the military commission contemplated by the common law of war," and that "the [*Yamashita*] military commission . . . [was] convened . . . pursuant to the common law of war").

[20] 317 U.S. 1, 29 n.6 (1942). Congress, noted Chief Justice Stone in *Ex parte Quirin*, "had the choice of crystallizing in permanent form and in minute detail every offense against the law of war, or of adopting the system of common law applied by military tribunals so far as it should be recognized and deemed applicable by the courts. It chose the latter course." *Id.* at 29. *See also* Johnson v. Eisentrager, 339 U.S. 763, 786 (1950) (stating that "we have held in the *Quirin* and *Yamashita* cases . . . that the military commission is a lawful tribunal to adjudge enemy offenses against the laws of war"); *Ex parte* Vallandigham, 68 U.S. (1 Wall.) 249 (1863) ("[M]ilitary offenses which do not come within the statute must be tried and punished under the common law of war.").

[21] Filartiga v. Pena-Irala, 630 F.2d 876 (2d Cir. 1980).

[22] H.R. REP. NO. 104-698, *supra* note 16.

The absence of a formal declaration of war makes no difference, for as the 1949 Geneva Conventions note, the law of war applies in any international "state of armed conflict." The statutes for the Rwanda and Yugoslav war crimes tribunals, crafted by the UN Security Council, also establish that the "laws and customs of war" govern civil wars, where declarations of war are ordinarily lacking. Countries rarely "declare war" anymore, perhaps because of the strictures of the UN Charter concerning the use of force in self-defense.[23] Congress has plainly authorized the president's use of force against Al Qaeda and its Taliban hosts.[24]

Likewise, the Third Geneva Convention does not preclude military commissions in this war against terrorism. First, Washington is warranted in considering Al Qaeda irregulars to be "unlawful" or "unprivileged" combatants who do not qualify as prisoners of war and hence do not enjoy the full privileges of the Third Geneva Convention.[25] Al Qaeda has failed to fulfill four prerequisites of lawful belligerency. These require a responsible commander, a distinctive and visible insignia, the open bearing of arms, and general observance of the laws and customs of war.[26] It is also open to question whether an international terrorist group that does not fight for a sovereign state (but, rather, if anything dominates the state) can ever qualify as a lawful belligerent. Thus, the specification of trial procedures in the Third Geneva Convention would not be applicable as such to Al Qaeda, except arguably for the customary norm reflected in common Article 3 calling for a "regularly constituted court" and the "judicial guarantees . . . recognized as indispensable by civilized peoples."

The Taliban also fail to qualify as lawful combatants or prisoners of war, under the tests of the Third Geneva Convention. In particular, they have abetted Al Qaeda's flagrant violation of the laws of war, and this assistance was condemned by the Security Council in Resolution 1373. Any claim that the Taliban are a "regular army" exempted from these qualifying conditions stumbles on the explicit language of the precedent 1907 Hague Rules of Land Warfare[27] and the 1874 Brussels Declaration.[28] It would make little sense to exempt a supposed "army" from the requirement of distinguishing themselves from civilians and reciprocally obeying the laws of war. The *Commentary* to the Third Geneva Convention notes that these "material characteristics" are prerequisite to even qualifying as "armed forces" and "regular armed forces."[29]

[23] UN Charter Arts. 2(4), 51.

[24] Joint Resolution to Authorize the Use of United States Armed Forces Against Those Responsible for the Recent Attacks Launched Against the United States, Sept. 18, 2001, Pub. L. No. 107-40, 115 Stat. 224, *reprinted in* 40 ILM 1282 (2001). The resolution authorized the President's use of

> all necessary and appropriate force against those nations, organizations, or persons he determines planned, authorized, committed, or aided the terrorist attacks that occurred on September 11, 2001, or harbored such organizations or persons, in order to prevent any future acts of international terrorism against the United States by such nations, organizations or persons.

Id. §2(a).

[25] Ari Fleischer, White House Spokesman, Special White House Announcement Re: Application of Geneva Conventions in Afghanistan (Feb. 7, 2002), *available in* LEXIS, Legis Library, Fednew File; *see also* White House Fact Sheet: Status of Detainees at Guantanamo (Feb. 7, 2002), *at* <http://www.whitehouse.gov/news/releases/2002/02/>.

[26] Third Geneva Convention, *supra* note 13, Art. 4(A)(2).

[27] Regulations Respecting the Laws and Customs of War on Land, Art. 1, annex to Hague Convention [No. IV] Respecting the Laws and Customs of War on Land, Oct. 18, 1907, 36 Stat. 2277, 1 Bevans 631.

[28] Project of an International Declaration Concerning the Laws and Customs of War, Aug. 27, 1874, Art. 9, 65 BRIT. & FOREIGN ST. PAPERS 1005 (1873–74), *reprinted in* THE LAWS OF ARMED CONFLICTS 27 (Dietrich Schindler & Jiří Toman eds., 3d rev. ed. 1988).

[29] As the Commentary notes:

> These "regular armed forces" [under Third Geneva Convention Article 4(A)(3)] have all the material characteristics and all the attributes of armed forces in the sense of [Article 4(A)(1)]: they wear uniform[s], they have an organized hierarchy and they know and respect the laws and customs of war. The delegates to the 1949 Diplomatic Conference were therefore fully justified in considering that there was no need to specify for such armed forces the requirements stated in [Article 4(A)(2)].

INTERNATIONAL COMMITTEE OF THE RED CROSS, COMMENTARY: III GENEVA CONVENTION RELATIVE TO THE TREATMENT OF PRISONERS OF WAR 63 (Jean de Preux ed., 1960).

It is certainly relevant, as well, that the leader of the new interim government of Afghanistan, as the successor regime of the treaty party, has stated that he does not consider either Al Qaeda or the Taliban as qualified for prisoner-of-war status under the Geneva Convention.[30] This statement is of interest as a stipulation of their characteristics, and even as a waiver of any treaty claim that might be mounted on their behalf.

The criticism by some European allies may stem from their own decision to ratify the 1977 Additional Protocol I to the Geneva Conventions. This Protocol dilutes the requirements for lawful belligerency and prisoner-of-war status. But neither Afghanistan nor the United States has ratified Protocol I, and it is implausible to suggest that this sharply contested instrument has become customary law in all its parts.[31] Nevertheless, it should be noted that Protocol I itself apparently preserves the requirement that an armed group generally observe the laws of war in order to qualify as an "armed force."[32]

In any event, the implementing rules under the president's order of November 13 are likely to guarantee the full norms of fair trial set forth by the Third Geneva Convention, even for prisoners of war. The Convention does not forbid the weighing of hearsay evidence. Article 105 permits the detaining power to conduct portions of a trial "*in camera* in the interest of State security." And the Convention suggests in Article 106 that a right of petition from a sentence is a permissible alternative to a right of appeal.[33]

The implementing rules for the military commissions authorized by the president are still under consideration, as of this writing. The American Bar Association has supported the use of military commissions for the trial of Al Qaeda's violations of the law of war, subject to suitable safeguards, as has the United States attorney for the Southern District of New York who supervised the Al Qaeda terrorist trials in the 1990s.[34] Published reports on the draft rules suggest that they will indeed enunciate a presumption of innocence, require proof beyond a reasonable doubt, guarantee the right to full notice of charges and the right to call witnesses in defense, and ensure an effective right to counsel.[35] In addition, proceedings would be open except where the presentation of sensitive or classified evidence requires a limited clo-

[30] *Afghan Agrees with Bush on Prisoners*, N.Y. TIMES, Jan. 30, 2002, at A9.

[31] *Contra* Aryeh Neier, *The Military Tribunals on Trial*, N.Y. REV. BOOKS, Feb.14, 2002, at 11, *available at* <http://www.nybooks.com>.

[32] Protocol Additional to the Geneva Conventions of 12 August 1949, and Relating to the Protection of Victims of International Armed Conflicts, *opened for signature* Dec. 12, 1977, Art. 43(1), 1125 UNTS 3 ("armed forces shall be subject to an internal disciplinary system which, *inter alia*, shall enforce compliance with the rules of international law applicable in armed conflict"). One may distinguish between the moral vagrancy of an individual, per Article 44(2), and of an entire fighting force, per Article 43(1).

[33] The only places where the Third Geneva Convention may differ from the likely commission rules for the unlawful combatants of Al Qaeda is in the possible reading of Article 105 that a qualified prisoner of war can choose any counsel he pleases (a choice that may logically be constrained by the demands of security clearance), and by the suggestion of a "most favored combatant" clause in Articles 102 and 106 to the effect that the sentencing procedure and mode of review must be the same as that accorded to the soldiers of the detaining power for like offenses. The latter is complicated when one notes that courts-martial are not the only available mode of trial even of American soldiers for violations of the law of war—indeed, the punishment of war crimes is not codified in the Uniform Code of Military Justice. Military commissions have been used historically for the trial of American soldiers as well as enemy combatants.

[34] AMERICAN BAR ASSOCIATION, TASK FORCE ON TERRORISM AND THE LAW, REPORT AND RECOMMENDATIONS ON MILITARY COMMISSIONS (Jan. 4, 2002), *available at* <http://www.abanet.org>; Benjamin Weiser, *Ex-Prosecutor Wants Tribunals to Retain Liberties*, N.Y. TIMES, Jan. 8, 2002, at A13.

[35] The rules issued on March 21, 2002, are more forthcoming than most critics had expected, and guarantee, inter alia, the presumption of innocence, the right against self-incrimination, burden of proof on the government, the choice of civilian defense counsel to serve alongside military defense counsel, the right of cross-examination and presentation of proof by the defense, and proof beyond a reasonable doubt. In addition, there is a requirement of unanimity for any capital sentence, a right of petition to an appellate review panel with autonomous power to reverse any conviction, and participation of civilians on the review panel (though they will be nominally commissioned as officers during their service). U.S. Dep't of Defense, Military Commissions Order No. 1, Procedures for Trials by Military Commissions of Certain Non–United States Citizens in the War Against Terrorism (Mar. 21, 2002), *at* <http://www.defenselink.mil/news/Mar2002/d20020321ord.pdf>.

sure. In a liberal polity, one wishes to assure trial procedures that are as generous as possible, even amid the exigencies of a very real conflict.

Still, the problems of a different kind of war remain, especially for any trials that are convened in the middle of the battle. Some Al Qaeda actors may simply be held for the duration of an arduous conflict, as combatants captured in war, subject to administrative safeguards. Should criminal trials be held, we may wish to acknowledge that our familiar habits from civilian courts and United Nations tribunals are not the only models of fairness. The humanitarian law of war and the law of armed conflict are equally a part of international law, framed to meet the unsought circumstances of states that must protect the safety of their citizens.

RUTH WEDGWOOD*

[20]

The Case Against Military Commissions

Harold Hongju Koh

In January 2002, Zacarias Moussaoui, a French national of Moroccan descent, pleaded not guilty in Virginia federal court to six counts of conspiring to commit acts of international terrorism in connection with the September 11 attacks on the Pentagon and the World Trade Center.[1] In other times, it would have seemed unremarkable for someone charged with conspiring to murder American citizens and destroy American property on American soil to be tried in a U.S. civilian court. More than two centuries ago, Article I, Section 8, Clause 10 of the United States Constitution granted Congress the power to "define and punish Piracies, Felonies committed on the High Seas, and Offenses against the Law of Nations," a power that Congress immediately exercised by criminalizing piracy, the eighteenth-century version of modern terrorism.[2] Since then, Congress has criminalized numerous other international offenses.[3] In recent decades, United States courts have decided criminal cases convicting international hijackers, terrorists, and drug smugglers,[4] as well as a string of well-publicized civil lawsuits adjudicating gross human rights violations.[5] Most pertinent, federal prosecutors have successfully tried and convicted in U.S. courts numerous members of Al Qaeda, the very terrorist group charged with planning the September 11 attacks, for earlier attacks on the World Trade Center and the U.S. embassies in Tanzania and Kenya.[6]

Had only three or three hundred died on September 11, no one would have suggested that their murderers be tried anywhere but in U.S. civilian courts. This history made even more surprising President Bush's military order (Military Order), issued on November 13, 2001, with-

* Of the Board of Editors.

[1] Brooke A. Masters, *Invoking Allah, Terror Suspect Enters No Plea: U.S. Judge in Alexandria Schedules October Trial*, WASH. POST, Jan. 3, 2002, at A1.

[2] Act of Apr. 30, 1790, ch. 9, §8, 1 Stat. 112, 113–14.

[3] *See, e.g.*, 18 U.S.C. §1201 (aircraft sabotage and kidnapping act), §1203 (criminalizing hostage taking), §831 (theft of nuclear materials) (2000).

[4] *See, e.g.*, United States v. McVeigh, 9 Fed. Appx. 980 (10th Cir. 2001), 2001 U.S. App. LEXIS 11804 (unpublished); United States v. Noriega, 683 F.Supp. 1373 (S.D. Fla. 1988) (trying Panamanian leader who was apprehended by U.S. Special Forces after extended military operations).

[5] *See, e.g.*, Kadic v. Karadzic, 70 F.3d 232, 238 (2d Cir. 1995), *cert. denied*, 518 U.S. 1005 (1996); *In re* Estate of Marcos, 25 F.3d 1467, 1472–76 (9th Cir. 1994), *cert. denied*, 513 U.S. 1126 (1995); Filartiga v. Pena-Irala, 630 F.2d 876 (2d Cir. 1980). *See generally* Harold Hongju Koh, *Transnational Public Law Litigation*, 100 YALE L.J. 2347 (1991) (reviewing litigation trend).

[6] *See* Charisse Jones, *Four Guilty in U.S. Embassy Attacks: Two Bombings in Africa Killed 224*, USA TODAY, May 30, 2001, at 1A; Martha T. Moore, *Bomb Verdicts Are 2nd Victory for Government*, USA TODAY, Nov. 13, 1997, at 3A. Under the Classified Information Procedures Act, U.S. prosecutors have regularly used special pretrial procedures in these cases to protect classified information. 18 U.S.C. app. 696, §1 (2000). *See generally* Richard P. Salgado, *Government Secrets, Fair Trials, and the Classified Information Procedures Act*, 98 YALE L.J. 427 (1988) (describing practice under the Act); Bill Keller, *Trials and Tribulations*, N.Y. TIMES, Dec. 15, 2001, at A31 ("Over the past eight years the U.S. attorney [for the Southern District of New York] . . . has successfully prosecuted 26 jihad conspirators, in six major trials and some minor ones.").

out congressional authorization or consultation, which declared that "[t]o protect the United States and its citizens, . . . *it is necessary for* (noncitizen suspects designated by the president under the order) . . . *to be tried for violations of the laws of war and other applicable laws by military tribunals.*"[7] It came as no surprise, however, that the Military Order quickly attracted intense criticism from constitutional and international lawyers.[8] That response has triggered a legal process of narrowing the order that seems likely to continue until the first commission cases are brought.[9]

Nevertheless, the practical question remains: given the exigencies created by the events of September 11, why should the United States not have the option of trying suspected terrorists before military commissions? Two simple answers: First, the Military Order undermines the United States' perceived commitment to the rule of law and national confidence in U.S. judicial institutions at precisely the time when that commitment and confidence are most needed. Second, by failing to deliver justice that the world at large will find credible, the Military Order undermines the U.S. ability to lead an international campaign against terrorism under a rule-of-law banner.

I. How Commissions Fail

Undermining the Rule of Law

The Military Order's specific legal deficiencies have received extensive commentary and are cogently summarized in a recent letter to the chair of the Senate Committee on the Judiciary signed by more than seven hundred American law professors.[10] On its face, the order authorizes the Department of Defense to dispense with the basic procedural guarantees required by the Bill of Rights, the International Covenant on Civil and Political Rights (ICCPR), and the

[7] Military Order, Detention, Treatment, and Trial of Certain Non-Citizens in the War Against Terrorism §1 (e) (Nov. 13, 2001), 66 Fed. Reg. 57,833 (Nov. 16, 2001) [hereinafter Military Order] (emphasis added). The Military Order provides: (1) that "it is not practicable to apply in military commissions under this order the principles of law and the rules of evidence generally recognized in the trial of criminal cases in the United States district courts"; (2) that trials need not be open; (3) that conviction and sentencing shall be "only upon the concurrence of two-thirds of the members of the commission"; and (4) that defendants "shall not be privileged to seek any remedy or maintain any proceeding, directly or indirectly," in any U.S., foreign, or international court. *Id.* §§1 (f), 4(c) (4), 4(c) (6)–(7), 7(b) (2).

[8] *See* George Lardner, Jr., *On Left and Right, Concern Over Anti-Terrorism Moves: Administration Actions Threaten Civil Liberties, Critics Say*, WASH. POST, Nov. 16, 2001, at A40.

[9] The president's legal counsel subsequently asserted that the order "covers only foreign enemy war criminals" who are chargeable "with offenses against the international laws of war"; that the order "does not require that any trial, or even portions of a trial, be conducted in secret"; that "[e]veryone tried before a military commission will know the charges against him, be represented by qualified counsel and be allowed to present a defense"; and that "anyone arrested, detained or tried in the United States by a military commission will be able to challenge the lawfulness of the commission's jurisdiction through a habeas corpus proceeding in a federal court." Alberto R. Gonzales, *Martial Justice, Full and Fair*, N.Y. TIMES, Nov. 30, 2001, at A27. While the regulations issued by the Department of Defense after this essay was written (U.S. Dep't of Defense, Military Commissions Order No. 1, Procedures for Trials by Military Commissions of Certain Non–United States Citizens in the War Against Terrorism (Mar. 21, 2002), *at*<http://www.defenselink.mil/news/Mar2002/d20020321ord.pdf>) respond to the heated criticism of the Military Order by providing more courtlike guarantees, they pointedly omit any opportunity for judicial review before a civilian court. The irony, as I suggest in the text, is that proceedings before these commissions will now be likely to suffer from many of the inefficiencies associated with judicial proceedings, but without garnering in return the global respect that genuine, credible judicial proceedings are accorded.

[10] Letter from Law Professors and Lawyers to the Honorable Patrick J. Leahy (Dec. 5, 2001), *at* <http://www.yale.edu/lawweb/liman/letterleahy.pdf> [hereinafter Law Professors' Letter]. Those law professors (including this author) called "the untested institutions contemplated by the Order . . . legally deficient, unnecessary, and unwise." In particular, they argued that the order violates separation of powers, "does not comport with either constitutional or international standards of due process," and "allows the Executive to violate the United States' binding treaty obligations." For devastating critiques of the Military Order under American constitutional law, see, for example, Neal K. Katyal & Laurence H. Tribe, *Waging War, Deciding Guilt: Trying the Military Tribunals*, 111 YALE L.J. 1259 (2002) (arguing that order is unconstitutional on its face); George P. Fletcher, *War and the Constitution: Bush's Military Tribunals Haven't Got a Legal Leg to Stand On*, AM. PROSPECT, Jan. 1–14, 2002, at 26.

Third Geneva Convention of 1949.[11] Insofar as any of these guarantees—which include the presumption of innocence, the rights to be informed of charges and to equal treatment before the courts, public hearings, independent and impartial decision makers, the rights to speedy trial, confrontation, and counsel of one's own choosing, the privilege against self-incrimination, and review by a higher tribunal according to law—are subject to suspension in time of emergency, the Bush administration has taken no formal steps to enable it to derogate from them.[12] By omitting these guarantees, the Military Order violates binding U.S. treaty commitments under both the ICCPR and the Third Geneva Convention.[13]

Fundamentally, the Military Order undermines the constitutional principle of separation of powers. For under the order, the president directs his subordinates to create military commissions, to determine who shall be tried before them, and to choose the finders of fact, law, and guilt. However detailed its rules and procedures may be, a military commission is not an independent court, and its commissioners are not genuinely independent decision makers. Historically, a military commission is neither a court nor a tribunal, but "an advisory board of officers, convened for the purpose of informing the conscience of the commanding officer, in cases where he might act for himself if he chose."[14] Commissioners are not independent judges, but usually military officers who are ultimately answerable to the secretary of defense and the president, who prosecute the cases.[15] "Such blending of functions in one branch of the Government," Justice Black recognized, "is the objectionable thing which the draftsmen of the Constitution endeavored to prevent by providing for the separation of governmental powers."[16]

Admittedly, in *Ex parte Quirin*, a pressured Supreme Court upheld the use of World War II military commissions, reasoning that Nazi saboteurs who had entered the United States

[11] U.S. CONST. amends. V, VI, VIII; International Covenant on Civil and Political Rights, Dec. 16, 1966, Art. 14, 999 UNTS 171 [hereinafter ICCPR]; Convention Relative to the Treatment of Prisoners of War, Aug. 12, 1949, Arts. 4–5, 6 UST 3316, 75 UNTS 135 [hereinafter Third Geneva Convention]; *see also* Joan Fitzpatrick, *Jurisdiction of Military Commissions and the Ambiguous War on Terrorism*, 96 AJIL 345 (2002); Daryl A. Mundis, *The Use of Military Commissions to Prosecute Individuals Accused of Terrorist Acts*, 96 AJIL 320 (2002) (both finding inconsistencies between administration's position and international standards).

[12] *See Ex parte* Milligan, 71 U.S. (4 Wall.) 2, 120–21 (1866) (stating that the U.S. Constitution is a "law for rulers and people, equally in war and in peace, . . . at all times, and under all circumstances. No doctrine, involving more pernicious consequences, was ever invented by the wit of man than that any of its provisions can be suspended during any of the great exigencies of government."). In any event, the Bush administration has taken none of the requisite steps to declare a state of emergency warranting derogation from its ICCPR obligations. *See also* The Administration of Justice and the Human Rights of Detainees: Question of Human Rights and States of Emergency, UN Doc. E/CN.4/Sub.2/1997/19, para. 111 (1997) ("[M]easures adopted by a Government to combat terrorism should not affect the exercise of the fundamental rights set forth in the Covenant . . . . Regarding article 14 [fair trial requirements], the [Human Rights] Committee said that no derogation whatsoever from any of its provisions was possible.").

[13] Law Professors' Letter, *supra* note 10 (stating that the ICCPR "obligates States Parties to protect the due process rights of all persons subject to any criminal proceeding" and that the Third Geneva Convention "requires that every prisoner of war have a meaningful right to appeal a sentence or a conviction. Under Article VI of the Constitution, these obligations are the 'supreme Law of the Land' and cannot be superseded by a unilateral presidential order.").

[14] *Milligan*, 71 U.S. at 47 (quoting David Dudley Field's Supreme Court argument). Military commissioners are even less independent than court-martial judges, who operate under the statutory protections of the Uniform Code of Military Justice. Yet as Justice Black noted in *Reid v. Covert*, 354 U.S. 1, 36 (1957) (plurality opinion), even "[c]onceding to military personnel that high degree of honesty and sense of justice which nearly all of them undoubtedly have, the members of a court-martial, in the nature of things, do not and cannot have the independence of jurors drawn from the general public or of civilian judges."

[15] Even when sitting American judges have served on military commissions, their independence has been compromised because they act as appointees of the executive branch capable of being fired or ordered to decide particular cases in particular ways. *See* ROBERT M. COVER, OWEN M. FISS, & JUDITH RESNIK, PROCEDURE 1343–45 (1988) (describing "United States Court for Berlin," an "Article II court" established in 1979 under authority of the U.S. high commissioner for Germany and presided over by Herbert Stern, a sitting Article III judge: "After that suit was filed in Berlin, the United States Ambassador . . . instructed the judge on how he was to decide the case; the ambassador ordered Judge Stern either to dismiss the case or to resign his commission.").

[16] *Reid*, 354 U.S. at 39.

clandestinely were "unlawful belligerents," having forfeited their prisoner-of-war status by removing their uniforms, surreptitiously entering the United States, and committing acts of sabotage.[17] But *Quirin* nowhere gave the president carte blanche unilaterally to create an alternative military system of criminal justice for suspicious aliens captured abroad.[18] Nor did *Quirin* authorize the president unilaterally to shift all cases involving war crimes by detained noncitizens into military commissions.[19] In *Quirin*, Congress had formally declared war, which it has not done here, and had specifically authorized the use of military commissions in its Articles of War.[20] In any event, it seriously disserves the long-term interests of the United States—whose nonuniformed intelligence and military personnel will conduct extensive armed activities abroad in the months ahead—to assert that any captive who can be labeled an "unlawful combatant" should be denied prisoner-of-war status under the Geneva Conventions, and hence subjected to trial for "war crimes" before military commissions.[21]

These specific legal deficiencies stand atop a much broader rule-of-law concern. International law permits the United States to redress the unprovoked killing of thousands on September 11, 2001, by itself engaging in an armed attack upon the Al Qaeda perpetrators. But should those culprits be captured, the United States must try, not lynch, them to promote four legal values higher than vengeance: holding them *accountable* for their crimes against humanity; *telling the world the truth* about those crimes; reaffirming that such acts violate all *norms* of civilized society; and demonstrating that law-abiding societies, unlike

[17] 317 U.S. 1 (1942). *Quirin* was itself an embarrassing "tale of . . . a prosecution designed to obtain the death penalty; . . . a rush to judgment, [and] an agonizing effort to justify a *fait accompli*." David J. Danelski, *The Saboteurs' Case*, 1 J. S.CT. HIST. 61, 61 (1996). Justice Douglas later recalled the procedure in *Quirin*, which announced a result with an opinion following later, as "extremely undesirable"; Justice Frankfurter, as "not a happy precedent." Justice Black's law clerk argued that "if the judges are to run a court of law and not a butcher shop, the reasons for killing a man should be expressed before he is dead; otherwise the proceedings are purely military and not for courts at all." *Id.* at 80; *accord* Robert E. Cushman, Ex parte Quirin et al.—*The Nazi Saboteur Case*, 28 CORNELL L.Q. 54 (1942) (recounting rush to judgment).

[18] Fifteen years after *Quirin*, Justice Black reiterated that "[e]very extension of military jurisdiction," including, presumably, the assertion of military jurisdiction over alien war crimes, "is an encroachment on the jurisdiction of the civil courts, and, more important, acts as a deprivation of the right to jury trial and of other treasured constitutional protections." *Reid*, 354 U.S. at 21.

[19] Far from endorsing such a broad divestiture of civilian jurisdiction over war crimes, Congress in 1996 enacted the War Crimes Act, which plainly envisioned that persons inside or outside the United States who commit certain statutory "war crimes" should be punished before the extant, functioning U.S. courts. War Crimes Act, 18 U.S.C. §2441 (2000); *accord Reid*, 354 U.S. at 41 (Frankfurter, J., concurring in the result) ("The normal method of trial of federal offenses under the Constitution is in a civilian tribunal. Trial of offenses by way of court-martial, with all the characteristics of its procedure so different from the forms and safeguards of procedure in the conventional courts, is an exercise of exceptional jurisdiction . . . ").

[20] *Quirin* carefully specified that "[i]t is unnecessary for present purposes to determine to what extent the President as Commander in Chief has constitutional power to create military commissions *without the support of Congressional legislation*." 317 U.S. at 29 (emphasis added). The Act of Congress passed immediately after September 11 does not authorize the adjudication by military commissions of past acts by apprehended terrorists. It only authorizes the president to use "force" against persons involved in the September 11 attacks so as to prevent future harm to the United States. Authorization for Use of Military Force, Pub. L. No. 107-40, 115 Stat. 224 (2001).

[21] *Accord* William Glaberson, *Critics' Attack on Tribunals Turns to Law Among Nations*, N.Y. TIMES, Dec. 26, 2001, at B1 (citing international lawyers who argue that Military Order conflicts with the Geneva Conventions' guarantees of procedural rights to prisoners of war). Significantly, the first two reported American casualties in Afghanistan were a nonuniformed CIA agent killed at a prison riot and a Special Forces officer ambushed while investigating civilian deaths. John Diamond & Liz Sly, *Enemy Ambush Kills U.S. Soldier; Surrender Talks Continue near Omar's Hideout*, CHICAGO TRIB., Jan. 5, 2002, at 1, *available in* LEXIS, News Library, Majpap File. Under the broad definition now asserted by the Bush administration, both deceased Americans could have been labeled "unlawful combatants" potentially triable before military tribunals. This concern makes even more troubling the White House's recent, blanket determination that although the Geneva Conventions apply to Taliban detainees (but not Al Qaeda), anyone who fought for the Taliban violated the laws of war and thus cannot claim prisoner-of-war status. White House Fact Sheet, Status of Detainees at Guantanamo (Feb. 7, 2002), *at* <http://www.whitehouse.gov/news/releases/2002/02>. A correct application of the Geneva Conventions would have required that all detainees in U.S. custody be presumed to be prisoners of war until each had his status individually determined by the "competent tribunal" required by Article 5 of the Third Geneva Convention, *supra* note 11. Thus, the president's announced decision to apply the Geneva Conventions to Taliban detainees should have required him to defer to a competent tribunal's individualized determinations as to whether particular detainees are entitled to prisoner-of-war status, not allowed him to make his own blanket determination that all detainees are per se unlawful combatants.

terrorists, *respect human rights* by channeling retribution into criminal punishment for even the most heinous outlaws.

The Military Order undermines each of these values. First, military commissions create the impression of kangaroo courts, not legitimate mechanisms of accountability. Second, rather than openly announcing the truth, commissions tend to hide the very facts and principles the United States now seeks to announce to the world. Third, because military tribunals in Burma, Colombia, Egypt, Peru, Turkey, and elsewhere have been perceived as granting judgments based on politics, not legal norms, the United States Department of State has regularly pressed to have cases involving U.S. citizens heard in civilian courts in those countries.[22]

Those who promote military commissions have been misled by the *O. J. Simpson* fiasco to conclude that standing American courts—whether civilian courts or military courts-martial—are somehow incapable of rendering full, fair, and expeditious justice in such cases. One might understand a country's resorting to a military commission when no currently functioning court could fairly and efficiently try the case. But over the centuries, the U.S. judicial system has amply demonstrated its ability to adapt to new, complex problems in criminal and civil law. Why should the United States try suspects in military commissions without congressional authorization when its own federal courts have fairly and openly tried and convicted Al Qaeda members? Perversely, the Military Order threatens national confidence in existing legal institutions and principles just when that confidence is already badly shaken by horrific terrorist attacks. Despite those attacks, both the presidency and Congress have continued to function, yet the order implicitly assumes that the third branch, comprising existing civilian and military courts, can no longer handle the very cases it dealt with just before the attacks occurred.[23]

Fourth and finally, military commissions provide ad hoc justice, hence uncertain protection for defendants' rights. Although the Defense Department's regulations implementing the order reportedly provide greater protections for the accused, unlike the Bill of Rights, the Federal Rules of Criminal Procedure, or the Uniform Code of Military Justice, those regulations cannot guarantee those rights, as they are subject to change at the president's will.[24] The absence of binding legal protection for the accused's human rights will become particularly acute should military commissions be convened at the United States Naval Base at Guantánamo Bay, Cuba, where scores of the detainees have been transferred.[25] In 1994, when large numbers of Cuban boat people were held on Guantánamo, the U.S. Court of Appeals for the Eleventh Circuit rendered the extraordinarily broad (and strongly contested) ruling that "these [alien detainees on Guantánamo] are without legal rights that are cognizable in

[22] When Peru, for example, branded Lori Berenson, an American citizen, a "terrorist," the United States properly protested that her "trial" was not held in open civilian court with full rights of legal defense, in accordance with international judicial norms. *See* U.S. DEP'T OF STATE, *Peru, in* 1999 COUNTRY REPORTS ON HUMAN RIGHTS PRACTICES, *available at* <http://www.state.gov/www/global/human_rights/1999_hrp_report/peru.html>.

[23] Attorney General John Ashcroft's own public defense of the Military Order before Congress was stunning in its dismissiveness about the capacity of United States judges and federal prosecutors (whose nominations he oversees) to try terrorist suspects fairly and expeditiously under existing judicial procedures. *See* Lane, *supra* note 10 (quoting testimony of Attorney General John Ashcroft, Senate Committee on the Judiciary, Dec. 6, 2001 ("Are we supposed to read [terror suspects] their Miranda rights, hire a flamboyant defense lawyer, bring them back to the United States to create a new cable network of 'Osama TV,' provide a worldwide platform for propaganda?")).

[24] *Cf. Ex parte* Milligan, 71 U.S. (4 Wall.) 2, 119 (1866) ("By the protection of the law human rights are secured; withdraw that protection, and they are at the mercy of wicked rulers, or the clamor of an excited people."). Under the so-called *Charming Betsy* principle, U.S. courts have regularly restrained proposed executive action within the bounds of international legal obligations. Murray v. The Schooner Charming Betsy, 6 U.S. (2 Cranch) 64, 118 (1804) (Marshall, C.J.). *See generally* Ralph G. Steinhardt, *The Role of International Law as a Canon of Domestic Statutory Construction*, 43 VAND. L. REV. 1103 (1990). To the extent that both the Third Geneva Convention and the ICCPR represent customary international law, fidelity to binding international obligations should require that the open-ended language of the Military Order be construed to require the procedural guarantees required by those instruments.

[25] Katharine Q. Seelye, *Troops Arrive at Base in Cuba to Build Jails*, N.Y. TIMES, Jan. 7, 2002, at A8 (Defense Secretary "Rumsfeld said he had not ruled out holding such tribunals at Guantánamo Bay").

the courts of the United States."[26] Read literally, the panel's holding would permit American officials deliberately to starve the alien detainees, to subject them to forced sterilizations, or to discriminate against them on the basis of their religion or skin color. Yet given the persistent U.S. criticism of Communist Cuba for violating the rights of its prisoners over the past forty years, it would be supremely ironic if the United States now created its own rights-free zone for alien detainees on that part of Cuba under American jurisdiction.[27]

Undermining Moral Leadership

The use of military commissions potentially endangers Americans overseas by undermining the U.S. government's ability to protest effectively when other countries use such tribunals. But just as troubling, espousing military commissions undermines U.S. moral leadership abroad when that leadership is needed the most.[28] The United States regularly takes other countries to task for military proceedings that violate basic civil rights. How, then, can the United States be surprised when its European allies refuse to extradite captured terrorist suspects to U.S. military justice?[29] When the Chinese or Russians try Uighur or Chechen Muslims as terrorists in military courts, U.S. diplomats protest vigorously and the world condemns those tribunals as anti-Muslim. How, then, can the United States object when other countries choose to treat U.S. military commissions the same way?

To win a global war against terrorism, nations that lay claim to moral rectitude and fidelity to the rule of law must not only apply, but also be universally seen to be applying, *credible justice.* Credible justice for international crimes demands tribunals that are fair and impartial *both in fact and in appearance.* By their very nature, military tribunals fail this test. Even if, through tinkering, the Defense Department's regulations could ensure that military commissions will operate more fairly in fact, they will never be perceived as fair by those skeptical of their political purpose, namely, the very Muslim nations whose continuing support the United States needs to maintain its durable coalition against terrorism. Ironically, the more the Defense Department tries to address the perceived unfairness of military tribunals by making them more "courtlike"—more transparent, with more procedural protections, more independent decision makers, and more input into their design by the legislative branch—the more these modifications will eliminate the supposed "practical" advantages of having military tribunals in the first place, yet without dispelling the fatal global perception of unfairness.

II. THE WAY FORWARD

Against this background, how should the United States pursue international justice in the months ahead? To ensure that the international community perceives that those convicted

[26] Cuban Am. Bar Ass'n v. Christopher, 43 F.3d 1412, 1430 (11th Cir. 1995). The Eleventh Circuit's broad ruling in the Cuban case would effectively treat alien detainees on Guantánamo as human beings without human rights. That ruling conflicted, however, with earlier decisions by the Second Circuit and a Brooklyn federal court involving Haitian refugees on Guantánamo. Haitian Ctrs. Council, Inc. v. McNary, 969 F. 2d 1326 (2d Cir. 1992), *vacated as moot on other grounds,* 113 S.Ct. 3028 (1993) (finding substantial likelihood that alien detainees on Guantánamo do have due process rights); Haitian Ctrs. Council v. McNary, 823 F.Supp. 1028, 1042 (E.D.N.Y. 1993), *vacated by settlement* (finding the same on the merits after a full bench trial). I should disclose that I served as counsel of record for both the Haitian and the Cuban refugees in the Guantánamo cases discussed here.

[27] *Cf.* Harold Hongju Koh, *America's Offshore Refugee Camps,* 29 RICHMOND L. REV. 139, 140–41 (1994) ("[T]he United States government has consistently asserted—and some courts have agreed—that these offshore locations constitute 'rights-free zones,' where [alien detainees] lack any legal rights cognizable under U.S. law and American [lawyers] lack First Amendment rights to communicate with them.").

[28] *See UN Human Rights Expert Concerned over Military Order Signed by United States President,* UN NEWSLETTER (United Nations Information Centre New Delhi) (Nov. 24, 2001), *at* <http://www.unic.org.in> (urgent appeal of UN Special Rapporteur for the Independence of the Judiciary Param Cumaraswamy, calling Military Order regrettable for "the wrong signals it sent, not only in the United States, but around the world").

[29] *See, e.g.,* Sam Dillon with Donald G. McNeil, Jr., *Spain Sets Hurdle for Extraditions,* N.Y. TIMES, Nov. 24, 2001, at A1 (suggesting that Spain will not extradite its suspects to U.S. military tribunal).

for the September 11 attacks will receive fair and impartial justice, the United States should send suspects only to standing tribunals that have demonstrated their capacity to dispense such justice in the past.

While I have long supported international adjudication, I am skeptical about the international community's ability to overcome existing political obstacles and create a fair international tribunal quickly.[30] International tribunals make the most sense when there is no functioning municipal court that could fairly and efficiently try the case, as happened in the former Yugoslavia and Rwanda. But even if the United States government were to support such a tribunal here (which it seems unlikely to do), at least two other permanent members of the Security Council—Russia and China—would probably withhold their consent from any body that might pursue trials of Chechen or Uighur rebels whom they have labeled as domestic "terrorists." Recent history shows that building new international tribunals from scratch is slow and expensive and requires arduous negotiations.[31] Although proponents claim that an international tribunal would be more likely to be viewed as impartial than a U.S. court, it is unclear why an ad hoc tribunal created for the express purpose of trying the September 11 terrorists and their supporters would find greater acceptance throughout the Muslim world than the judgments of a civilian court system that has been in place for more than two centuries. Finally, those who believe that an international tribunal with Muslim judges would ensure "Muslim buy-in" into the international adjudicatory process should recall that the last United Nations gathering before September 11 was the World Conference Against Racism, in which several Islamic countries sought to use the forum to pursue their political grievances against Israel.[32] Many of the same countries would doubtless use their diplomatic clout to argue that any UN tribunal to try terrorists should also try Israeli officials who bore no connection to the September 11 attacks, an alternative that potential Western signatories to the tribunal would surely reject. We should not conclude, therefore, that only international tribunals can grant meaningful justice for international crimes. Absent extant, functioning international tribunals, the most credible justice will be delivered by time-tested domestic judicial institutions, such as the United States' Article III courts and courts-martial.

In surveying its justice options, the United States should carefully distinguish between its most pressing concern—redressing and preventing the murder of Americans on American soil—and much broader efforts to support the creation of an enduring post-Taliban system of justice in Afghanistan. International justice demands a clear and simple division of labor: American prosecutors and judges should try crimes committed against Americans on American soil, while experienced UN and international lawyers should address crimes committed against Afghans on Afghan soil.

Cases primarily involving crimes in Afghanistan—whether committed by the Taliban or the Northern Alliance—will be best addressed by rebuilding the judicial system of Afghanistan itself, a task that, like the rebuilding of the Sierra Leonean, East Timorese, Bosnian, and Kosovar legal systems, will require substantial and sustained international and UN input.[33]

[30] Some distinguished scholars have argued that such cases should be heard before an international tribunal, preferably one on which both American and Muslim judges sit. *See, e.g.*, Anne-Marie Slaughter, *Al Qaeda Should Be Tried Before the World*, N.Y. TIMES, Nov. 17, 2001, at A23. *But see* Michael J. Matheson, *U.S. Military Commissions: One of Several Options*, 96 AJIL 354 (2002) (reviewing practical reasons why it remains unlikely that such a tribunal will be created).

[31] For example, the Sierra Leonean tribunal has yet to hear any cases several years after the mass killings there, and a war crimes tribunal for Cambodia has yet to be set up more than twenty-five years after the operative events. *See* Seth Mydans, *Khmer Rouge Trials Won't Be Fair, Critics Say*, N.Y. TIMES, Feb. 10, 2002, §1, at 12.

[32] *See* Ellis Cose, *Silver Linings from a Summit*, NEWSWEEK, Sept. 17, 2001, at 40.

[33] The precise shape of the Afghan judicial system remains to be determined. I have no objection, for example, to an Afghan tribunal that would combine domestic and international elements, such as the Sierra Leonean tribunal created under UN auspices is designed to do. Whatever happens, United Nations transitional support and involvement will be critically necessary to stabilize the postconflict environment of Afghanistan, to promote the Bonn process of building a representative post-Taliban government, and to address justice, accountability, and truth telling about past human rights abuses by all parties to the Afghan conflict. This part of the judicial problem,

However heinous the offenses of Afghan war criminals against other Afghan citizens may be, they have little to do with the United States, and should not be adjudicated by American courts or courts-martial that have little interest or expertise in the decades-old Afghan conflict. Egregious Afghan violators such as Mullah Omar and his close deputies should be given treatment similar to that given brutal rebel leader Foday Sankoh of Sierra Leone: namely, arrest, humanitarian treatment in custody, permanent exclusion from further governmental activity, no amnesty for war crimes or crimes against humanity, and eventual trial before the emerging Afghan judicial system.[34] Wherever possible, third-party combatants should be sent back to the country of their nationality to face national punishment, with assurances that their trials will strictly observe international due process standards.

Under this strategy, the U.S. government should send only those cases involving defendants (such as leading Al Qaeda members) who are charged with or suspected of murdering or plotting to murder American citizens on American soil to American civilian courts for criminal trials by seasoned federal prosecutors. Since three Al Qaeda suspects—Zacarias Moussaoui, the "American Taliban" John Walker Lindh, and the "sneaker bomber" Richard Reid—have already been charged before U.S. civilian courts, I see no need to charge any future defendants before untested and suspect military commissions.[35]

In sum, the battle against global terrorism requires credible justice, which military commissions cannot provide. Credible international tribunals can provide credible justice but may be difficult to create under the current political circumstances. That leaves standing civilian courts or courts-martial that operate under preexisting and transparent rules. Sweeping all "unlawful combatants" who have committed "war crimes" into untested, unwise, and legally deficient U.S. military commissions will invite hostile foreign governments reciprocally to "try" and execute captured nonuniformed American personnel before similar tribunals. If the United States wants to show the world its commitment to the very rule of law that the terrorists sought to undermine, it should take this opportunity to demonstrate that American courts can give universal justice.

HAROLD HONGJU KOH*

however, differs little from that faced in Bosnia, East Timor, Kosovo, and Sierra Leone, where the United States similarly supported multilateral military operations that eventually secured a war-torn territory for a new, more democratic government. What makes this military struggle distinctive—and the element that engages U.S. judicial jurisdiction—is that this conflict was triggered by the massive September 11 attacks that killed thousands of American and other civilians on American soil.

[34] While I agree with much of Professor Matheson's sensible analysis, I disagree with his suggestion that persons who commit violations of the law of armed conflict on the battlefield of Afghanistan but have no provable connection to the September 11 attacks should be tried before U.S. military commissions. Instead, I share his alternative view: that "[e]ven for these persons, the alternative of trial . . . by any suitable Afghan tribunals should be considered." Matheson, *supra* note 30, at 358.

[35] My colleague Professor Wedgwood speculates that federal court trials of Al Qaeda suspects will jeopardize classified information, limit available evidence, and endanger the security of judges and jurors. Ruth Wedgwood, *Al Qaeda, Terrorism, and Military Commissions*, 96 AJIL 328 (2002). Having dealt regularly with classified materials and federal trials during stints at both the State and Justice Departments, I find these claims vastly overstated. As one journalist has noted, during twenty-six successful federal prosecutions of jihad supporters over the past eight years, "[n]either the Justice Department nor prosecutors in New York could recall for me a single specific instance when national security was actually compromised during the trials in New York." Keller, *supra* note 6. Nor is it clear why the potential excludability of some evidence should cripple prosecutors, given the huge volume of evidence that will be amassed in what has regularly been called the largest criminal investigation in history. And although extra security measures should doubtless be taken to ensure the safety of juries, judges, and prosecutors, such measures have been taken routinely in the past, not just in Al Qaeda cases, but also in numerous cases involving organized crime, drug kingpins, and the like. In any event, it now seems clear that the Justice Department has not deemed any of these concerns sufficiently serious to militate against charging Moussaoui, Reid, and Walker in federal court. The Justice Department's indictment practice so far thus casts serious doubt on Professor Wedgwood's claim that "military commissions may be the most practicable course" for trials against Al Qaeda members. Wedgwood, *supra*, at 330.

* Of the Board of Editors.

Part VIII
An Emerging Framework?

[21]

The Emergence of Terrorism as a Distinct Category of International Law

DANIEL MOECKLI*

A considerable body of international norms, institutions, and procedures specifically designed to deal with terrorism has emerged over the last few years. This body of international law increasingly bears the characteristics of a "special regime." At the same time, legal scholars have started to treat terrorism as a "branch" of international law in its own right, both in terms of research and teaching. This article argues that the emergence of a distinct category of terrorism law is due to reasons that are very different from those that account for the general trend towards the fragmentation and compartmentalization of international law. It is primarily the result of political pressure by certain powerful states to establish, at the international level, a separate legal system for terrorism that mirrors their own domestic special regimes, so as to give expression to the "international community's" sense of outrage at terrorist acts, stigmatize the perpetrators, and reassure the public. As these objectives can only be achieved if those who fall under the anti-terrorism regime are singled out for particularly harsh treatment, the special treatment model inevitably undermines the fundamental principle that all human beings deserve equal protection of the law.

SUMMARY

---

* University of Zurich, Switzerland. Email: daniel.moeckli@rwi.uzh.ch. I presented a much earlier version of this paper at the International Law Association (British Branch) Spring Conference in London in March 2006 and would like to thank the participants for their constructive criticism and helpful feedback. I am also grateful to Robert McCorquodale, Sangeeta Shah, and Sandy Sivakumaran for their insightful comments on a previous draft of this article. Anna Hardy provided excellent research assistance.

[T]errorism is not a discrete topic of international law with its own substantive legal norms.

Rosalyn Higgins, 1997[1]

There is no category of the "law of terrorism" and the problems must be characterized in accordance with the applicable sectors of public international law: jurisdiction, international criminal justice, State responsibility, and so forth.

Ian Brownlie, 2003[2]

INTRODUCTION

In recent years, and especially since the terrorist attacks of September 11, 2001, a substantial set of international norms, procedures, and institutions relating to terrorism has emerged. Arguably, this body of international law on terrorism, which continues to grow at a frantic pace, increasingly bears the characteristics of a "special regime," *i.e.*, an interrelated cluster of primary and secondary rules on a limited problem. At the same time, legal scholars have started to treat the subject of terrorism as a "branch" of international law in its own right. These developments are eroding Rosalyn Higgins' and Ian Brownlie's claim that terrorism is not a discrete "topic" or "category" of international law, at least if these terms are understood, as they generally are,[3] as umbrella terms encompassing the notions of legal "regime" and academic "branch." Terrorism law, it seems, is going through the same process as human rights law, trade law, space law, or environmental law in earlier years.[4]

1. Rosalyn Higgins, *The General International Law of Terrorism*, *in* TERRORISM AND INTERNATIONAL LAW 13, 13–14 (Rosalyn Higgins & Maurice Flory eds., 1997).

2. IAN BROWNLIE, PRINCIPLES OF PUBLIC INTERNATIONAL LAW 745 (7th ed. 2008).

3. *See, e.g.*, Robert Jennings, *International Law*, *in* 7 ENCYCLOPEDIA OF PUBLIC INTERNATIONAL LAW 278, 288 ff (1984).

4. *See generally, e.g.*, Brett Frischmann, *A Dynamic Institutional Theory of International Law*, 51 BUFF. L. REV. 679 (2003) (discussing trade law and environmental law regimes); Jo M. Pasqualucci,

However, it is not the primary purpose of this article to give a definitive answer to the rather academic question of whether terrorism law has now indeed turned into a separate category of international law. I am more interested in the reasons for, and the implications of, the emergence of terrorism as an increasingly significant and distinct subject area of international law. Considering that "la question de la fragmentation du droit international constitue par excellence le débat doctrinal à l'ère de la globalisation,"[5] relatively little attention has been paid to the fact that the materialization of new sub-systems of international law is not always triggered by the same factors and, accordingly, may have widely divergent implications. There are, in other words, very different types of fragmentation. The reasons why a category of terrorism law is emerging are completely different from those behind such categories as trade law or space law, and this development therefore raises very peculiar concerns.

Part I is an overview of the rapidly growing body of international law specifically designed to deal with terrorism and will highlight some features that suggest that this body of law now constitutes a special regime. Part II will demonstrate that since September 11, legal academia has not only given unprecedented attention to the subject of terrorism but has also started to treat it as a separate branch of international law. Part III will explore the reasons for the emergence of terrorism as a separate category of international law. Finally, Part IV will briefly sketch why this development matters: what is at stake in the debate about the distinctness of terrorism?

I. THE GROWING BODY OF LAW ON TERRORISM: A SPECIAL REGIME?

The phenomenon of the fragmentation of international law refers to the increased emergence in recent years of special regimes or sub-systems within the international legal system. International relations scholars define regimes as "sets of implicit or explicit principles, norms, rules, and decision-making procedures around which actors' expectations converge in a given area of international relations."[6] This notion of regime can be combined with H.L.A. Hart's definition of a legal system as a union of primary and secondary rules[7] to arrive at a definition of regime that can be usefully applied in the international law context. Accordingly, the chairman of the International Law Commission's ("ILC") Study Group on Fragmentation of International Law, Martti Koskenniemi, has defined the term regime as follows:

> [L]egal rules appear in clusters that contain not only rules laying down substantive rights, duties and powers (primary rules) but also rules that

Advisory Practice of the Inter-American Court of Human Rights, 38 STAN. J. INT'L L. 241 (2002) (discussing the emergence of international human rights law as a separate branch of public international law).

5. Pierre-Marie Dupuy, *Un Débat Doctrinal à l'Ere de la Globalisation: Sur la Fragmentation du Droit International*, 1 EUR. J. LEGAL STUD. 1, 1 (2007) ("The question of the fragmentation of international law constitutes the leading doctrinal debate in the era of globalization.").

6. Stephen D. Krasner, *Structural Causes and Regime Consequences: Regimes as Intervening Variables*, *in* INTERNATIONAL REGIMES 1, 2 (Stephen D. Krasner ed., 1983). *See also* ANDREAS HASENCLEVER, PETER MAYER & VOLKER RITTBERGER, THEORIES OF INTERNATIONAL REGIMES 8–22 (1997) (discussing conceptual issues inherent in defining international regimes).

7. H.L.A. HART, THE CONCEPT OF LAW 79–99 (2d ed. 1994).

> have to do with the administration of primary rules (secondary rules). Such clusters[,] freely following from international relations, [may be] termed *regimes*. A regime is a union of rules laying down particular rights, duties and powers and rules having to do with the administration of such rules, including in particular rules for reacting to breaches.[8]

The final report of the ILC Study Group similarly defines a (special) regime as "any interrelated cluster (set, regime, subsystem) of rules on a limited problem together with the rules for the creation, interpretation, application, modification, or termination—in a word, administration—of those rules."[9] Such special regimes may enjoy varying degrees of autonomy from general international law, and regimes with a high degree of autonomy have sometimes been referred to as "self-contained regimes."[10] The Study Group report, however, rejects this term as "a misnomer," since "[n]o legal regime is isolated from general international law," and it is "doubtful whether such isolation is even possible."[11] Instead, the report suggests the general use of the term "special regime."[12]

Can the increasingly significant cluster of international norms and procedures pertaining to terrorism be described as a special regime within the terms set out above? To answer this question I first examine the growing body of primary rules, rules creating a set of duties, rights, and powers, relating to terrorism. Next, I examine the corresponding cluster of secondary rules, rules that have to do with the administration and enforcement of the primary rules on terrorism.

A. *Primary Rules*

The vast majority of states have committed themselves to take a number of measures specifically designed to counter terrorism. Starting with the 1963 Convention on Offences and Certain Other Acts Committed on Board Aircraft, thirteen widely ratified international treaties[13] have been concluded to address specific manifestations of terrorism, such as the hijacking of planes or hostage taking.[14] This specialized body of primary rules on terrorism obliges states parties to

---

8. MARTTI KOSKENNIEMI, INT'L L. COMMISSION, STUDY GROUP ON FRAGMENTATION, FRAGMENTATION OF INTERNATIONAL LAW 8–9 (2003), *available at* http://untreaty.un.org/ilc/sessions/55/fragmentation_outline.pdf.

9. United Nations Int'l. L. Comm'n, *Fragmentation of International Law: Difficulties Arising from the Diversification and Expansion of International Law: Report of the Study Group of the International Law Commission*, para. 152, U.N. Doc. A/CN.4/L.682 (Apr. 13, 2006) [hereinafter *Report on Fragmentation*].

10. United States Diplomatic and Consular Staff in Tehran (U.S. v. Iran), 1980 I.C.J. 3, 40 (May 24). *See also* Bruno Simma & Dirk Pulkowski, *Of Planets and the Universe: Self-contained Regimes in International Law*, 17 EUR. J. INT'L L. 483 (2006); Bruno Simma, *Self-Contained Regimes*, 16 NETH. Y.B. INT'L L. 111, 115 (1985).

11. *Report on Fragmentation*, *supra* note 9, para. 193. *See also id.* para. 152 (drawing conclusions of the treatment of "self-contained" regimes by the International Law Commission in the context of State responsibility).

12. *Id.* para. 152.

13. BEN SAUL, DEFINING TERRORISM IN INTERNATIONAL LAW 134 (2006).

14. Convention on the Marking of Plastic Explosives for the Purposes of Detection, Mar. 1, 1991, 2122 U.N.T.S. 359; Protocol for the Suppression of Unlawful Acts of Violence at Airports Serving International Civil Aviation, Supplementary to the Convention for the Suppression of Unlawful Acts Against the Safety of Civil Aviation, Feb. 24, 1988, 1589 U.N.T.S. 474; Convention for the Suppression of Unlawful Acts

prohibit in domestic law the specified acts and to either extradite or prosecute (*aut dedere aut judicare*) all alleged offenders.[15]

In 1972 the United Nations General Assembly, which in previous years had referred to terrorist acts only incidentally,[16] started to address terrorism as a discrete subject.[17] It has since adopted several resolutions that call on states to combat terrorism,[18] including the 1994 Declaration on Measures to Eliminate International Terrorism, which has been reiterated in many later resolutions.[19] Furthermore, in 1996 the Assembly set up a committee to develop "a comprehensive legal framework of conventions dealing with international terrorism."[20] This Ad Hoc Committee on Terrorism has elaborated a draft Comprehensive Convention on International Terrorism, intending to supplement the existing anti-terrorism conventions.[21] In 2006, the Assembly unanimously adopted the U.N. Global Counter-Terrorism Strategy, in which the member states resolved to undertake a number of concrete steps to prevent and combat terrorism.[22]

Similarly, the U.N. Security Council, which had originally limited itself to addressing particular terrorist acts, has, in recent years and especially since September 11, started to impose measures against terrorism as such. For instance, the Council has called on states to work together to prevent and suppress all terrorist

against the Safety of Maritime Navigation, Mar. 10, 1988, 1678 U.N.T.S. 221; Protocol for the Suppression of Unlawful Acts Against the Safety of Fixed Platforms Located on the Continental Shelf, Mar. 10, 1988, 1678 U.N.T.S. 304; Convention on the Physical Protection of Nuclear Material, Mar. 3, 1980, 1456 U.N.T.S. 124; International Convention against the Taking of Hostages, Dec. 17, 1979, 1316 U.N.T.S. 205; Convention on the Prevention and Punishment of Crimes Against Internationally Protected Persons, Including Diplomatic Agents, Dec. 14, 1973, 1035 U.N.T.S. 167; Convention for the Suppression of Unlawful Acts against the Safety of Civil Aviation, Sept. 23, 1971, 974 U.N.T.S. 177; Convention for the Suppression of Unlawful Seizure of Aircraft, Dec. 16, 1970, 860 U.N.T.S. 105; Convention on Offences and Certain Other Acts Committed on Board Aircraft, Sept. 14, 1963, 704 U.N.T.S. 219; International Convention for the Suppression of Acts of Nuclear Terrorism, G.A. Res. 59/290, U.N. Doc. A/RES/59/290 (Apr. 13, 2005); International Convention for the Suppression of the Financing of Terrorism, G.A. Res. 54/109, U.N. Doc. A/RES/54/109 (Dec. 9, 1999); International Convention for the Suppression of Terrorist Bombings, G.A. Res. 52/164, U.N. Doc. A/RES/52/653 (Dec. 15, 1997).

15. *Id.*

16. *See* Declaration on Principles of International Law Concerning Friendly Relations and Co-operation Among States in Accordance with the Charter of the United Nations, annexed to G.A. Res. 2625 (XXV), U.N. Doc. A/1883 (Oct. 24, 1970) (stating every State's duty to refrain from organizing, participating, or acquiescing in any acts of civil strife or terrorism in another State); Declaration on the Inadmissibility of Intervention in the Domestic Affairs of States and the Protection of their Independence and Sovereignty, annexed to G.A. Res. 2131 (XX), U.N. Doc A/1408 (Dec. 21, 1965) (stating that no State shall incite terrorist activities for the purpose of regime change).

17. *See* G.A. Res. 3034 (XXVII), U.N. Doc. A/2114 (Dec. 18, 1972). In this resolution, adopted shortly after the attack at the Munich Olympics, the General Assembly, "[d]eeply perturbed over acts of international terrorism which are occurring with increasing frequency," invited states to become parties to the existing anti-terrorism conventions and to "take all appropriate measures at the national level with a view to the speedy and final elimination of the problem."

18. *See* SAUL, *supra* note 13, at 198–213 (listing various U.N. resolutions adopted since the 1960's).

19. Declaration on Measures to Eliminate International Terrorism, G.A. Res. 49/60, UN Doc. A/RES/49/60 (Dec. 9, 1994).

20. G.A. Res. 51/210, para. 9, U.N. Doc. A/RES/51/210 (Dec. 17, 1996).

21. *See* Draft Convention on International Terrorism: Working Document Submitted by India, UN Doc. A/C6/55/1 (Aug. 28, 2000) (containing original text of the draft convention); G. A., Report of the Ad Hoc Committee Established by G.A. Resolution 51/210: Sixth Session (Jan. 28–Feb. 1, 2002), UN Doc. A/57/37. The convention has not yet progressed further than the drafting stage.

22. G.A. Res. 60/288, U.N. Doc. A/RES/60/288 (Sept. 8, 2006).

acts,[23] to become parties to the relevant international conventions relating to terrorism,[24] and to adopt the draft Comprehensive Convention on International Terrorism.[25] Furthermore, deviating from its normal practice of taking action only against state entities, it has established a unique system of sanctions against individuals and groups allegedly involved in international terrorism. In a string of resolutions all adopted under Chapter VII of the U.N. Charter and thus legally binding, the Security Council has required states to take measures against individuals and entities associated with Al Qaeda, Osama bin Laden, and the Taliban.[26] In particular, states must freeze funds and other financial assets or economic resources of designated individuals and entities; impose travel bans on them; and prevent the supply, sale, and transfer of arms and related materials to them.[27]

The most significant Security Council measure adopted against terrorism is Resolution 1373 of September 28, 2001.[28] This resolution, also adopted under Chapter VII of the U.N. Charter, requires member states to create a legal and institutional framework to prevent and suppress the financing, preparation, and commission of terrorist acts and to cooperate with other states in this effort. In particular, states must (1) ensure that "terrorist acts are established as serious criminal offences in domestic laws and regulations and that the punishment duly reflects the seriousness of such terrorist acts;"[29] (2) put in place effective border controls and ensure that asylum-seekers who are involved in terrorism are not granted refugee status;[30] and (3) deny financial support and safe haven to terrorists.[31] Resolution 1373 has been described as "one of the most comprehensive and far-reaching resolutions adopted in the history of the Security Council."[32] It is groundbreaking in that it was adopted not in response to a specific conflict or to a situation in a particular country but in response to the abstract phenomenon of international terrorism.[33] Accordingly, it imposes on all states a set of detailed obligations, to combat this phenomenon, a body of rules with general application. In

23. *E.g.*, S.C. Res. 1566, paras. 2–3, U.N. Doc. S/RES/1566 (Oct. 8, 2004); S.C. Res. 1368, U.N. Doc. S/RES/1368 (Sept. 12, 2001); S.C. Res. 1269, U.N. Doc. S/RES/1269 (Oct. 15, 1999).

24. S.C. Res. 1566, para. 4, U.N. Doc. S/RES/1566 (Oct. 8, 2004); S.C. Res. 1373, para. 3(d), U.N. Doc. S/RES/1373 (Sept. 28, 2001).

25. S.C. Res. 1566, para. 5, U.N. Doc. S/RES/1566 (Oct. 8, 2004).

26. S.C Res. 1735, U.N. Doc. S/RES/1735 (Dec. 22, 2006); S.C. Res. 1617, U.N. Doc. S/RES/1617 (Jul. 29, 2005); S.C. Res. 1526, U.N. Doc. S/RES/1526 (Jan. 20, 2004); S.C. Res. 1455, U.N. Doc. S/RES/1455 (Jan. 17, 2003); S.C. Res. 1390, U.N. Doc. S/RES/1390 (Jan. 28, 2002); S.C. Res. 1333, U.N. Doc. S/RES/1333 (Dec. 19, 2000); S.C. Res. 1267, U.N. Doc. S/RES/1267 (Oct. 15, 1999).

27. S.C. Res. 1333, U.N. Doc. S/RES/1333 (Dec. 19, 2000); S.C. Res. 1267, U.N. Doc. S/RES/1267 (Oct. 15, 1999).

28. S.C. Res. 1373, U.N. Doc. S/RES/1373 (Sept. 28, 2001).

29. *Id.* para. 2(e).

30. *Id.* paras. 2(g), 3(f).

31. *Id.* paras. 2(c), 2(d).

32. Curtis A. Ward, *Building Capacity to Combat International Terrorism: The Role of the United Nations Security Council*, 8 J. CONFLICT & SEC. L. 289, 298 (2003).

33. Preambulary paragraph three of S.C. Res. 1373 declares that "any act of international terrorism" constitutes a threat to peace and security. On this point, *see* Jurij Daniel Aston, *Die Bekämpfung abstrakter Gefahren für den Weltfrieden durch legislative Massnahmen des Sicherheitsrats—Resolution 1373 (2001) im Kontext*, 62 ZEITSCHRIFT FÜR AUSLÄNDISCHES ÖFFENTLICHES RECHT UND VÖLKERRECHT 257 (2002); Jane E. Stromseth, *The Security Council's Counter-Terrorism Role: Continuity and Innovation*, 97 AM. SOC'Y INT'L L. PROC. 41 (2003). (stating that the resolution was "in response to the more global threat to peace and security posed by terrorism.").

this sense, it can be described as legislative in nature.[34] The list of measures that states must adopt against terrorism was further expanded in 2004 and 2005 by Resolution 1540, which obliges states to prevent non-state actors, in particular terrorist groups, from acquiring weapons of mass destruction,[35] and by Resolution 1624, which calls on states to prohibit by law incitement to commit terrorist acts.[36] Thus, in the anti-terrorism field the Security Council has assumed a comprehensive law-making function.[37]

A substantial body of primary rules on terrorism exists not only at the U.N. but also at the regional level. In most regions legislative frameworks to combat terrorism were already in place before September 11.[38] After that date, many regional organizations adopted new declarations, plans of action, and, in some instances, treaties. The European Union (EU) adopted a range of measures designed to enhance its anti-terrorism capabilities after September 11,[39] the most important of which is the Framework Decision on Combating Terrorism.[40] This Framework Decision lists a number of acts that member states must deem "terrorist offences" in their jurisdictions, and it establishes minimum sentences for these offences.[41] In this way, it requires member states to harmonize their domestic criminal laws in relation to the definition and punishment of terrorist offenses. The Inter-American Convention Against Terrorism, which was passed by the Organization of American States (OAS) in 2002 and entered into force in 2003, was the first international treaty on this subject after the September 11 attacks. It requires states parties to take measures to prevent the financing of terrorism, enhance cooperation in anti-terrorism law enforcement, and afford one another greater mutual legal assistance in terrorism matters.[42] In 2003, the Council of Europe

34. Matthew Happold, *Security Council Resolution 1373 and the Constitution of the United Nations*, 16 LEIDEN J. INT'L L. 593 (2003); Eric Rosand, *The Security Council as "Global Legislator": Ultra Vires or Ultra Innovative?*, 28 FORDHAM INT'L L.J. 542 (2005); Paul C. Szasz, *The Security Council Starts Legislating*, 96 AM. J. INT'L L. 901 (2002); Stefan Talmon, *The Security Council as World Legislature*, 99 AM. J. INT'L L. 175 (2005).

35. S.C. Res. 1540, U.N. Doc. S/RES/1540 (Apr. 28, 2004).

36. S.C. Res. 1624, para. 1(c), U.N. Doc. S/RES/1624 (Sept. 14, 2005).

37. *See* Andrea Bianchi, *Assessing the Effectiveness of the UN Security Council's Anti-terrorism Measures: The Quest for Legitimacy and Cohesion*, 17 EUR. J. INT'L L. 881 (2006) (stating that no convincing argument against the Security Council's law-making powers has been made).

38. The regional treaties concluded before that date include the following: OAU Convention on the Prevention and Combating of Terrorism, July 14, 1999; Convention of the Organization of the Islamic Conference on Combating International Terrorism, July 1, 1999; Treaty on Cooperation among States Members of the Commonwealth of Independent States in Combating Terrorism, June 4, 1999; Arab Convention for the Suppression of Terrorism, Apr. 22, 1998; SAARC Regional Convention on Suppression of Terrorism, Nov. 4, 1987; European Convention on the Suppression of Terrorism, Jan. 27, 1977, EUROP. T.S. No. 090; OAS Convention to Prevent and Punish Acts of Terrorism Taking the Form of Crimes against Persons and Related Extortion that are of International Significance, Feb. 2, 1971, 27 U.S.T. 3949, 1438 U.N.T.S. 194.

39. For overviews, *see* Jörg Monar, *Die EU und die Herausforderung des internationalen Terrorismus: Handlungsgrundlagen, Fortschritte und Defizite*, *in* HERAUSFORDERUNG TERRORISMUS: DIE ZUKUNFT DER SICHERHEIT 136 (Werner Weidenfeld ed., 2004); Jörg Monar, *Common Threat and Common Response? The European Union's Counter-Terrorism Strategy and its Problems*, 42 GOV'T & OPPOSITION 292 (2007); Steve Peers, *EU Responses to Terrorism*, 52 INT'L & COMP. L.Q. 227 (2003).

40. Council Decision 2002/475, 2002 O.J. (L164) (EU).

41. *Id.* arts. 1(1), 4.

42. Inter-American Convention against Terrorism arts. 4, 8, 9, June 3, 2002, 42 I.L.M. 19.

adopted a protocol that amended the European Convention on the Suppression of Terrorism by extending the list of offenses that are not to be regarded as political offenses preventing extradition.[43] This was followed, in 2005, by a convention designed to contribute to the prevention of terrorism.[44] Regional instruments have also been passed by the African Union (AU),[45] the South Asian Association for Regional Cooperation (SAARC),[46] the Association of Southeast Asian Nations (ASEAN),[47] the Organization of the Islamic Conference (OIC),[48] the Organisation for Security and Cooperation in Europe (OSCE),[49] and the Commonwealth of Nations.[50] These instruments, mainly intended to enhance cooperation in anti-terrorism matters, contain various specific measures that member states must adopt to combat terrorism.

Whereas these primary norms have been specifically laid down in anti-terrorism treaties and instruments, other terrorism-related aspects of international law appear to be in the process of reshaping, with the content and scope of the respective norms still unclear and contentious. For example, it has been claimed that the terrorist attacks of September 11 and the reaction they provoked have resulted in a change in the law on the use of force. Some states and authors argue that the law on self-defense has been, or needs to be, adapted to the specific capabilities and objectives of today's terrorists. They argue in particular that the right of self-defense against terrorism now covers the use of force "to preempt emerging threats."[51] Similarly, as far as the *jus in bello* is concerned, some have claimed that the fight against terrorism

43. Protocol Amending the European Convention on the Suppression of Terrorism, May 15, 2003, EUROP. T.S. NO. 190.

44. Convention on the Prevention of Terrorism, May 16, 2005, EUROP. T.S. NO. 196.

45. Protocol to the OAU Convention on the Prevention and Combating of Terrorism, July 8, 2004, *available at* http://www.africa-union.org/root/au/Documents/Treaties/treaties.htm; African Union [AU], *Plan of Action of the African Union High-Level Inter-Governmental Meeting on the Prevention and Combating of Terrorism in Africa*, AU Doc. Mtg/HLIG/Conv.Terror/Plan.(I) (Sept. 14, 2002).

46. Additional Protocol to the SAARC Regional Convention on Suppression of Terrorism, Jan. 6, 2004, *available at* http://www.saarc-sec.org/data/summit12/additionalprotocolterrorism.pdf.

47. ASEAN Convention on Counter-Terrorism, Jan. 13, 2007, *available at* http://www.aseansec.org/19250.htm; Ass'n of Southeast Asian Nations [ASEAN], *ASEAN Declaration on Joint Action to Counter Terrorism*, (Nov. 5, 2001), *available at* http://www.aseansec.org/5620.htm.

48. Org. of the Islamic Conference [OIC], *Kuala Lumpur Declaration on International Terrorism* (Apr. 3, 2002), *available at* http://www.oic-oci.org/english/conf/fm/11_extraordinary/declaration.htm.

49. Org. for Security and Co-Operation in Eur. [OSCE], *Decision No. 1 on Combating Terrorism*, OSCE Doc. MC(9).DEC/1 (Dec. 4, 2001), *available at* http://www.osce.org/item/2229.html; OSCE, *Bucharest Plan of Action for Combating Terrorism*, OSCE Doc. MC(9).DEC/1 Annex (Dec. 4, 2001) *available at* http://www.osce.org/item/851.html; *OSCE Charter on Preventing and Combating Terrorism*, OSCE Doc. MC(10).JOUR/2 (Dec. 7, 2002), *available at* http://www.osce.org/item/1654.html.

50. COMMONWEALTH OF NATIONS, REPORT OF THE COMMONWEALTH COMMITTEE ON TERRORISM (CCT): COMMONWEALTH PLAN OF ACTION (2001), *available at* http://www.thecommonwealth.org/document/181889/34293/35144/35145/report_of_the_commonwealth_committee_on_terrorism.htm.

51. THE NAT'L SEC. COUNCIL, THE NATIONAL SECURITY STRATEGY OF THE UNITED STATES OF AMERICA 6, 15 (2002). *See also* Ruth Wedgwood, *The Fall of Saddam Hussein: Security Council Mandates and Preemptive Self-Defense*, 97 AM. J. INT'L L. 576, 582–83 (2003) (arguing that traditional doctrines are no longer reliable and "one must consider acting against terrorist *capability* before it is employed."); John Yoo, *Using Force*, 71 U. CHI. L. REV. 729, 729–30 (2004) (contending that the "consensus academic view on self-defense . . . which was largely borrowed from the criminal law, makes little sense . . . [in] the international context."). For a critical assessment, *see* Michael Bothe, *Terrorism and the Legality of Pre-Emptive Force*, 14 EUR. J. INT'L L. 227 (2003) (claiming that the National Security Strategy "constitute[s] an unacceptable expansion of the right of anticipatory self-defence.").

is "a new kind of war"[52] "not envisaged when the Geneva Convention was signed in 1949"[53] and requires "a new approach . . . towards captured terrorists," which renders obsolete some of the general rules of international humanitarian law.[54] Finally, some authors have called for the creation of a discrete international crime of terrorism,[55] while others argue that such a prohibition of terrorism as a distinct category of international crimes has already become part of customary international law.[56]

B. Secondary Rules

The primary rules on terrorism described in the previous section are supported by a special set of secondary rules, rules that have to do with the administration of the primary law. In particular, these rules provide for the powers of specialized bodies to create, modify, apply, and enforce the primary rules.

At the U.N. level, the General Assembly has established the Ad Hoc Committee on Terrorism to develop new primary norms on terrorism.[57] The Security Council, for its part, has created a host of subsidiary bodies to monitor and enforce states' compliance with its different resolutions on terrorism. These committees coordinate their work and cooperate closely.[58] In 1999, Resolution 1267 established a committee known as "The Al-Qaida and Taliban Sanctions Committee," which maintains the consolidated list of individuals and entities associated with Al Qaeda, Osama bin Laden, and the Taliban, and oversees the implementation of sanction measures against them.[59] U.N. member states are obliged to inform the committee on the actions taken to implement the sanctions regime.[60] The Analytical Support and Sanctions Monitoring Team, which is composed of independent experts appointed by the Secretary-General, supports the committee.[61]

The most important special enforcement mechanism is the Counter-Terrorism Committee (CTC). Established by the Security Council shortly after the events of September 11, it is charged with monitoring implementation of the detailed and far-

52. Memorandum from Alberto Gonzales, White House Counsel, to George W. Bush, President of the U.S., Decision Re Application of the Geneva Convention on Prisoners of War to the Conflict With Al Qaeda and the Taliban (Jan. 25, 2002), *available at* http://www.washingtonpost.com/wp-srv/politics/documents/cheney/gonzales_addington_memo_jan252001.pdf [hereinafter Jan. 2002 Gonzales Memorandum].

53. Ari Fleischer, White House Press Secretary, Statement by the Press Secretary on the Geneva Convention (May 7, 2003), *available at* http://www.whitehouse.gov/news/releases/2003/05/20030507-18.html.

54. Jan. 2002 Gonzales Memorandum, *supra* note 52.

55. SAUL, *supra* note 13, at 27.

56. Antonio Cassese, *Terrorism as an International Crime*, *in* ENFORCING INTERNATIONAL LAW NORMS AGAINST TERRORISM 213, 213–225 (Andrea Bianchi ed., 2004).

57. G.A. Res. 51/210, *supra* note 20, para. 9.

58. *See, e.g.*, S.C. Res. 1617, paras. 12–13, U.N. Doc. S/RES/1617 (July 29, 2005).

59. S.C. Res. 1333, para. 16, U.N. Doc. S/RES/1333 (Dec. 19, 2000); S.C. Res. 1267, para. 6, U.N. Doc. S/RES/1267 (Oct. 15, 1999).

60. S.C. Res. 1617, paras. 10–12, U.N. Doc. S/RES/1617 (July 19, 2005); S.C. Res. 1455, paras. 5–6, U.N. Doc. S/RES/1455 (Jan. 17, 2003).

61. S.C. Res. 1617, *supra* note 58, paras. 19–20; S.C. Res. 1363, paras. 4–5, U.N. Doc. S/RES/1363 (July 30, 2001).

reaching obligations of Resolution 1373.[62] Based on states' reports on the steps taken to comply with the requirements of the resolution, the CTC assesses their compliance and may ask them to submit further information.[63] In 2004, the Security Council also set up the Counter-Terrorism Committee Executive Directorate (CTED), a body of experts assisting the CTC.[64] The CTED carries out visits to states, particularly to monitor the adoption by states of an adequate executive machinery to implement their anti-terrorism legislation.[65]

The U.N. established two additional bodies related to counter-terrorism in 2004. The 1540 Committee monitors member states' compliance with Resolution 1540, which aims to prevent the proliferation of weapons of mass destruction to non-state actors, including terrorist groups.[66] States are required to report on the steps they have taken to implement the resolution, an obligation that the Security Council reinforced in Resolution 1673.[67] In Resolution 1566, the Security Council established a working group to recommend "practical measures to be imposed upon individuals, groups or entities involved in or associated with terrorist activities, other than those designated by the Al-Qaida [and] Taliban Sanctions Committee."[68]

Special procedures relating to the creation and enforcement of the primary law on terrorism also exist at the regional level. For example, the OAS has established the Inter-American Committee Against Terrorism (CICTE), which coordinates regional efforts by enhancing exchange of information, assisting states in drafting counter-terrorism legislation, and improving border cooperation and travel document security measures.[69] In 2001, the Council of Europe set up the Multidisciplinary Group on International Action against Terrorism (GMT), a governmental committee of experts tasked with identifying priorities of action by the Council of Europe and reviewing its international instruments.[70] The GMT prepared the Protocol Amending the European Convention on the Suppression of Terrorism.[71] In 2003, the Council of Europe created a Committee of Experts on Terrorism (CODEXTER).[72] This body, responsible for coordinating the Council's

62. S.C. Res. 1373, para. 6, U.N. Doc. S/RES/1373 (Sept. 28, 2001).

63. United Nations Econ. & Soc. Council [ECOSOC], United Nations High Comm'r for Human Rights, Report of the United Nations High Commissioner for Human Rights and Follow-up to the World Conference on Human Rights, paras. 6–9 annex, U.N. Doc. E/CN.4/2002/18 (Feb. 27, 2002), *available at* http://daccess-ods.un.org/access.nsf/Get?Open&DS=E/CN.4/2002/18&Lang=E (Proposals for "Further Guidance" for the submission of reports pursuant to Paragraph 6 of Security Council Resolution 1373 (2001)).

64. S.C. Res. 1535, paras. 2–3, U.N. Doc. S/RES/1535 (Mar. 26, 2004).

65. *See* Counter Terrorism Comm. [CTC], *Framework Document for CTC Visits to States in Order to Enhance the Monitoring of the Implementation of Resolution 1373 (2001)*, paras. II(1)–(4) (Mar. 9, 2005), *available at* http://www.un.org/sc/ctc/documents/frameworkdocument.htm. (defining the four main objectives of CTED State visits as: the analysis of States' implementation of Resolution 1373 obligations, analysis of the capacity to implement 1373 obligations, identifying areas of needed technical assistance, and the recommendation of steps to be taken for full implementation of Resolution 1373).

66. S.C. Res. 1540, para. 1, U.N. Doc. S/RES/1540 (Apr. 28, 2004).

67. S.C. Res. 1673, para. 2, U.N. Doc. S/RES/1673 (Apr. 27, 2006).

68. S.C. Res. 1566, para. 9, U.N. Doc. S/RES/1566 (Oct. 8, 2004).

69. G.A. Res. 1650, OAS Doc. AG/RES 1650 (XXIX-O/99) (June 7, 1999).

70. Council of Eur., Human Rights and Legal Affairs, The Multidisciplinary Group on International Action Against Terrorism (GMT), http://www.coe.int/t/e/legal_affairs/legal_co-operation/fight_against_terrorism/3_codexter/The_GMT/.

71. *Id.*; Protocol Amending the European Convention on the Suppression of Terrorism, *opened for signature* May 15, 2003, EUROP. T.S. NO. 190.

72. Council of Europe: Human Rights and Legal Affairs, Committee of Experts on Terrorism

counter-terrorist activities, prepared the draft of the Council of Europe Convention on the Prevention of Terrorism. Similarly, the OSCE has established the Action Against Terrorism Unit, a focal point for the coordination of counter-terrorism initiatives.[73] The OIC has set up a ministerial-level body, the Committee on International Terrorism with the mandate to strengthen OIC cooperation in the counter-terrorism field and to implement the OIC Convention on Combating International Terrorism.[74]

In addition to founding these specialized bodies engaged in the creation and enforcement of primary rules on terrorism, there is also a trend towards establishing distinct international judicial structures to deal with terrorist crimes. In 1998, the Security Council mandated the creation of the Lockerbie court,[75] a specially convened Scottish court sitting in the Netherlands that tried the two Libyan nationals accused of the bombing of Pan Am flight 103 over Lockerbie.[76] After the attacks of September 11, some scholars suggested the establishment of a similar international tribunal to try those involved in the attacks or even suspected international terrorists in general.[77] More recently, in 2007 the Security Council set up a special international tribunal to try those responsible for the terrorist bombing that killed, among others, the former Lebanese Prime Minister Rafiq Hariri and subsequent connected terrorist attacks.[78] This Special Tribunal for Lebanon, which will sit in the Netherlands, has jurisdiction over crimes of terrorism and illicit association as well as offences against life and personal integrity as defined under Lebanese law.[79] It will be the first international tribunal with a subject-matter jurisdiction framed exclusively with reference to domestic law.[80]

C. *A Special Regime?*

In summary, a considerable body of norms, institutions, and mechanisms specifically designed to deal with terrorism has emerged over the last few years and

(CODEXTER), http://www.coe.int/t/e/legal_affairs/legal_co-operation/fight_against_terrorism/3_CODEXTER/.

73. OSCE, *Decision No. 1 on Combating Terrorism*, *supra* note 49; OSCE, *Bucharest Plan of Action for Combating Terrorism*, *supra* note 49.

74. OIC, *Kuala Lumpur Declaration on International Terrorism*, *supra* note 48, para. 1.

75. S.C. Res. 1192, U.N. Doc. S/RES/1192 (Aug. 27, 1998).

76. *See* Her Majesty's Advocate v. Megrahi, No. 1475/99, (H.C.J. at Camp Zeist 2001) (Scot.), *available at* http://www.scotcourts.gov.uk/opinions/opinion%20no%203.html; *see also* Megrahi v. Her Majesty's Advocate, No. C104/01, (H.C.J. Appeal Ct. 2002) (Scot.), *available at* http://www.scotcourts.gov.uk/opinions/KIRK1307.html (for the appeal decision).

77. KEN GUDE, CTR. FOR AM. PROGRESS, AFTER GUANTANAMO: A SPECIAL TRIBUNAL FOR INTERNATIONAL TERRORIST SUSPECTS 8 (2006), *available at* http://www.americanprogress.org/kf/AFTER%20GUANTANAMO%20REPORT.PDF; Leila Sadat, *International Court Should Try Defendants*, ST. LOUIS POST DISPATCH, November 18, 2001; Anne-Marie Slaughter, *Al Qaeda Should Be Tried Before the World*, N.Y. TIMES, Nov. 17, 2001, at 23; Anne-Marie Slaughter, *Terrorism and Justice: An International Tribunal Comprising US and Islamic Judiciary Should Be Set Up to Try Terrorists*, FIN. TIMES, Oct. 12, 2001.

78. S.C. Res. 1757, Art. 1, U.N. Doc. S/RES/1757 (May 30, 2007).

79. *Id.* art. 2.

80. *See* Nidal Nabil Jurdi, *The Subject-Matter Jurisdiction of the Special Tribunal for Lebanon*, 5 J. INT'L CRIM. JUST. 1125, 1125 (2007) (explaining that the tribunal is *sui generis* in "its sole dependence on domestic substantive crimes.").

continues to grow. This body has the most important characteristics of a special legal regime: it appears as an interrelated cluster of primary rules on a limited problem, namely terrorism, together with rules for the administration of those primary rules. The set of rules and procedures relating to terrorism that has been established by the U.N. Security Council could even be described as unique in the international legal system. In an unprecedented move, the Security Council has required states to impose sanctions against individuals and groups, rather than other states.[81] Additionally, in what is arguably its first resolution of a legislative nature, the Council has imposed a detailed set of obligations on states to combat international terrorism.[82] This set of duties, or, in Hart's terms,[83] primary rules relating to the particular subject matter of terrorism is supported by a range of secondary rules that create a web of specialized monitoring mechanisms with extraordinary enforcement tools at their disposal.

In addition to the anti-terrorism regime established by the Security Council, there are various other primary and secondary rules on terrorism, including international and regional anti-terrorism treaties, alleged special norms in the law of armed conflict and international criminal law, international and regional bodies and mechanisms engaged in the creation and enforcement of anti-terrorism instruments, and special international tribunals. That these different sets of norms and mechanisms could also be described as separate regimes themselves does not necessarily preclude the existence of one international anti-terrorism regime. In human rights law, for example, one also speaks of "the international human rights regime,"[84] even though this regime in fact consists of a web of different international and regional sub-regimes.

II. ACADEMIC TREATMENT: A SEPARATE BRANCH?

To consider whether terrorism law is emerging as a separate topic or category of international law, it is also important to look at the way legal scholars have treated terrorism, as it is often the academic world that first divides a subject such as international law into different branches in order "to arrange [it] in a comprehensible (and teachable) manner."[85] In wider academia, terrorism has evolved into an increasingly important subject in its own right after September 11, with its own journals, conferences, and courses.[86] Reflecting this general trend, legal scholars have given unprecedented attention to the law of terrorism and have started to treat it as a discrete branch, both as far as research and teaching is concerned.

In the last few years, legal writing on different aspects of terrorism and counter-terrorism has mushroomed; a plethora of books and articles on terrorism and international law have been published and chapters on terrorism have been added to

81. *See supra* note 26.

82. *See supra* notes 23–35 and accompanying text.

83. *See* HART, *supra* note 7, at 95.

84. *See, e.g.*, MANFRED NOWAK, INTRODUCTION TO THE INTERNATIONAL HUMAN RIGHTS REGIME (Verena Tomasik trans., Christopher Cassetta ed., Martinus Nijhoff Publishers 2003).

85. *See* Peter Malanczuk, *Space Law as a Branch of International Law*, *in* DIVERSITY IN SECONDARY RULES AND THE UNITY OF INTERNATIONAL LAW 143, 146 (L.A.N.M. Barnhoorn & K.C. Wellens eds., 1995).

86. Avishag Gordon, *Terrorism as an Academic Subject after 9/11: Searching the Internet Reveals a Stockholm Syndrome Trend*, 28 STUD. IN CONFLICT & TERRORISM 45 (2005).

international law textbooks.[87] The Library of Congress Subject Headings, accepted as the worldwide standard for subject heading classifications, lists "Terrorism" and "War on Terrorism 2001" as separate main subjects.[88] A search of the catalogues of the major law libraries reveals that there are very substantial holdings under these headings. At the time of writing, the Yale Law School library catalogue, for example, lists 362 books under "Terrorism" and 235 books under "War on Terrorism 2001."[89] International law bibliographies and other legal research tools now regularly include a separate heading for "Terrorism," often as a sub-category of international law or as a sub-sub-category of international criminal law. In "Public International Law," the current bibliography of books and articles compiled by the Max Planck Institute in Heidelberg, "Terrorism" is listed as a sub-category of "International Criminal Law."[90] At the time of writing, there are 1,674 titles under that heading, more than 1,500 of which were published after 2001. In comparison, under "Refugees and Asylum" there are 1,192 entries, under "Air Law" 98, and under "Diplomatic Relations" 96.[91] The Peace Palace Library maintains a regularly updated bibliography on "Terrorism and International Law" that consists of more than 6,000 articles and books.[92] Electronic databases also frequently include separate sections on terrorism: Westlaw International lists Homeland Security, including Homeland Security and Anti-Terrorism, as a separate practice area; the Electronic Information System for International Law (EISIL) lists Terrorism as a sub-category of International Criminal Law;[93] JURIST has a webpage devoted to Terrorism Law & Policy;[94] and FindLaw provides Special Coverage on the War on Terrorism.[95] Finally, there are now very few international law conferences that do not have a panel specifically devoted to terrorism.[96]

It is not only legal research that reflects this trend. Also as far as teaching is concerned, terrorism law has become a significant, and increasingly separate, branch of international law. Prior to 2001, terrorism had to some extent been part of the curriculum in international relations and political science programs, but not of that

87. *E.g.*, ANTONIO CASSESE, INTERNATIONAL LAW (2d ed. 2005); HENRY J. STEINER, PHILIP ALSTON & RYAN GOODMAN, INTERNATIONAL HUMAN RIGHTS IN CONTEXT: LAW, POLITICS, MORALS (3d ed. 2008); CHRISTINE GRAY, INTERNATIONAL LAW AND THE USE OF FORCE (2d ed. 2004).

88. Library of Congress: Cataloging Distribution Service, http://www.loc.gov/cds/lcsh.html (last visited Oct. 17, 2008); Library of Congress Authorities, http://authorities.loc.gov/ (last visited Feb. 4, 2009).

89. Yale Law School, Morris Library Catalogue, http://morris.law.yale.edu (last visited Feb. 12, 2009).

90. Max Planck Institute for Comparative Public Law and International Law, Public International Law, http://www.mpil.de/ww/en/publ/library/catalogues_databases/doc_of_articles/pil.cfm (last visited Feb. 12, 2009).

91. *Id.* (last visited Feb. 12, 2009).

92. Peace Palace Library, Bibliographies, http://www.ppl.nl/content.php?webpage=bibliographies (follow "Bibliography on terrorism and international law" hyperlink) (last visited Feb. 12, 2009).

93. Electronic Information System for International Law, http://www.eisil.org/ (last visited Oct. 17, 2008).

94. JURIST Legal Intelligence, http://jurist.law.pitt.edu/terrorism.htm (last visited Oct. 17, 2008).

95. FindLaw Legal News, http://news.findlaw.com/legalnews/us/terrorism/ (last visited Oct. 17, 2008).

96. *See* The 2007 American Society of International Law Conference, www.asil.org/events/am07/agenda.html (offering three panel discussions related to terrorism and international law); The 2005 ESIL Forum, http://www.esil-sedi.eu/english/pdf/ESIL_2005_Forum_Programme.pdf (featuring a workshop on human rights and terrorism with three papers) (all last visited Oct. 17, 2008); and The 2004 European Society of International Law (ESIL) conference, http://www.esil-sedi.eu/english/florence_agora_papers.html (featuring two paper presentations on terrorism and international law).

of law schools.[97] Today, 35 out of the top 40 U.S. law schools[98] offer at least one, and in many cases several, courses on terrorism and the law.[99] Most of these courses focus on the international law dimensions of terrorism and counter-terrorism and have titles such as "International Law and Terrorism,"[100] "The War Against Terrorism and the Rule of Law,"[101] or "Guantánamo, Law, and the War on Terror."[102] Law schools in Europe and other parts of the world have similarly started to make terrorism a distinct component of their curricula. Courses dealing with the international legal aspects of terrorism are offered by at least sixteen British academic institutions[103] as well as by universities in different regions of the world, including, for example, Australia,[104] Austria,[105] Canada,[106] Chile,[107] China,[108] Germany,[109] Hungary,[110] Ireland,[111] New Zealand,[112] Spain,[113] Sweden,[114] and

97. *See* John F. Murphy, *International Legal Education*, 37 INT'L LAW. 623, 628 (2003) (noting that several law schools added courses on terrorism in response to student interest following the events of September 11, 2001, and providing a list of such schools).

98. U.S. News and World Report, America's Best Graduate Schools 2009, Best Law Schools (Ranked in 2008), http://grad-schools.usnews.rankingsandreviews.com/grad/law/search (last visited Oct. 17, 2008).

99. They include the law schools of the following universities: Yale University, Harvard University, Stanford University, New York University, Columbia University, University of Chicago, University of Pennsylvania, University of Michigan, Duke University, University of Virginia, Northwestern University, Cornell University, Georgetown University, University of Texas, UCLA, University of Southern California, Vanderbilt University, Washington University, Boston University, University of Minnesota, George Washington University, University of Iowa, Fordham University, University of Illinois, Boston College, University of Notre Dame, University of Washington, College of William and Mary, George Mason University, Indiana University, University of California (Hastings), University of Georgia, University of Maryland, University of North Carolina, and Wake Forest University. (The full list with links to the respective course descriptions is available from the author).

100. University of Michigan Law School, http://cgi2.www.law.umich.edu/_ClassSchedule/aboutCourse.asp?crse_id=041522 (last visited Oct. 17, 2008).

101. Yale University Law School, http://www.yale.edu/bulletin/html/law/course.html (last visited Oct. 17, 2008).

102. Stanford University Law School, http://www.law.stanford.edu/program/courses/details/309/Guant%C3%A1namo%2C%20Law%2C%20and%20the%20War%20on%20Terror/ (last visited Oct. 17, 2008).

103. University of Aberdeen, University of Birmingham, University of Central Lancashire, University of Dundee, University of East London, King's College London, University of Lancaster, University of Leeds, London School of Economics, University of Manchester, University of Newcastle, University of Nottingham, Nottingham Trent University, University of Reading, University of St. Andrews, and University of Southampton.

104. Monash University: "Terrorism and Human Rights," http://www.monash.edu.au/pubs/handbooks/units/LAW7320.html (last visited Oct. 18, 2008).

105. University of Vienna: "Terrorism and the Use of Force," http://public.univie.ac.at/fileadmin/user_upload/legal_studies/courses/Zemanek-Terrorism_and_the_Use_of_ForceNEU.pdf (last visited Oct. 18, 2008).

106. University of Toronto: "Comparative Anti-Terrorism and National Security Law," http://www.law.utoronto.ca/students_content.asp?docNo=1190&itemPath=2/16/0/0/0&cType=coursespg (last visited Oct. 18, 2008).

107. Universidad Católica de Chile: "Derecho Internacional de la Guerra después del 11 de Septiembre de 2001 y la Guerra de Iraq," http://cursos.puc.cl/catalogo/programas/dei237.pdf (last visited Oct. 18, 2008).

108. University of Hong Kong, Faculty of Law: "Religious Movements: Peace, Nationalism and Terrorism," http://www.hku.hk/student/all/uregcourse/pdf2003/ba.pdf (last visited Oct. 18, 2008).

109. Universität Münster: "Rechtsfragen der Bekämpfung des Internationalen Terrorismus," http://www.jura.uni-muenster.de/go/organisation/institute/oeffentliches-recht/vr/studieren/veranstaltungen-sose.html (last visited Oct. 18, 2008).

Switzerland.[115] Although the existence of an academic branch is not established simply by considering course offerings, these are a further indication of the trend towards treatment of terrorism as a separate branch of international law.

III. REASONS: WHY IS TERRORISM EMERGING AS A DISTINCT CATEGORY OF INTERNATIONAL LAW?

The emergence of a new category of international law may be caused by different reasons. Even within one special legal regime, the creation of different sub-regimes may be prompted by differing factors. The specific considerations behind the establishment of an international anti-terrorism regime such as that under Resolution 1373, for example, are not necessarily the same as those behind the establishment of a special international tribunal to deal with terrorist offenses. And the reasons why legal academia starts to treat a subject area such as terrorism as a distinct branch of international law might be different yet again. Nevertheless, there are a number of common concerns that underlie the creation of all the new special norms, institutions, and mechanisms pertaining to terrorism described above. It is on these generic rationales for the special treatment of terrorism that I want to focus. These rationales, I will argue, are very different from those behind the emergence of other categories of international law.

Generally, the most important reason for the emergence of a new category of international law is that a new social problem or phenomenon materializes, requiring regulation at the international level.[116] As the ILC Study Group explained, fragmentation "reflects the rapid expansion of international legal activity into various new fields,"[117] as "[n]ew types of specialized law ... seek to respond to new technical and functional requirements."[118] Typical examples of such "new" areas of international law include international environmental law[119] and space law.[120] The

110. Central European University: "Inside and Outside the Rule of Law: Guantánamo Bay and Other Legal Black Holes," http://web.ceu.hu/downloads/admissions_bulletin_2007_2008.pdf (last visited Oct. 18, 2008).

111. National University of Ireland, Galway: "Counter-Terrorism and Human Rights," http://www.nuigalway.ie/human_rights/documents/Course%20Docs/SoEmeregencyCounterTerror%20syllabus%2007-08.doc (last visited Oct. 18, 2008); University of Cork: "Terrorism, Dissonance and Criminal Justice" http://www.ucc.ie/en/lawsite/postgrad/llmgeneral/llm_modules/#d.en.11063 (last visited Oct. 18, 2008).

112. University of Wellington: "International Law and the Use of Extraordinary Renditions and Other Methods of Irregular Rendition in the Fight Against Terrorism," http://www.victoria.ac.nz/home/study/postgrad/publications/law-pg-07.pdf (last visited Oct. 18, 2008).

113. Universidad Rey Juan Carlos: "Terrorismo Internacional, Democracia y Derechos Humanos," http://www.fcjs.urjc.es/Doctorado/pdf/curso03.pdf (last visited Oct. 18, 2008).

114. University of Växjö: "Terrorism," http://www.vxu.se/english/education/2007_2008/aut_2007_fullsem/rv3401/ (last visited Oct. 18, 2008).

115. Universität Bern: "Terrorismusbekämpfung durch Strafrecht," http://evub.unibe.ch/pievub/?KursID=2285232&KursNr=WN115&UeberschriftID=378171&page=detail (last visited Oct. 18, 2008).

116. *See* Report on Fragmentation, *supra* note 9, paras. 7–9, 20.

117. *Id.* para. 14.

118. *Id.* para. 15.

119. *See* Malgosia Fitzmaurice, *International Environmental Law as a Special Field*, *in* DIVERSITY IN SECONDARY RULES AND THE UNITY OF INTERNATIONAL LAW 181, 182–83 (L.A.N.M. Barnhoorn & K.C.

recent creation of an international anti-terrorism regime is often explained and justified on the same basis. As the argument goes, the sort of international terrorist networks that were behind the September 11 attacks are an unprecedented phenomenon and existing legal systems do not offer adequate instruments to deal with it.[121] Contemporary international terrorism does not fit easily within existing categories of international law.[122] The fight against it is "a new kind of war,"[123] and innovative international mechanisms for cooperation and enforcement are needed to bring states to effectively combat this phenomenon.[124] According to this account, the new body of law fills a gap in the international legal system, or at least creates "a more context-sensitive . . . regulation of a matter than what is offered under the general law."[125]

Yet the explanation that the new regulatory measures are a response to the unprecedented nature of international terrorism as a social phenomenon is unconvincing. In fact, international terrorism dates back a long time, as do international efforts to combat it. What could be termed the first international conference on terrorism, as well as a first move toward increased cooperation between the police forces of different states, was held as early as 1898.[126] The conference was a reaction to the terrorist attacks that rocked Europe and the United States at that time and were seen as the deeds of an international anarchist organization.[127] By the turn of the twentieth century, terrorism was at the top of the global political agenda.[128] Acts of international terrorism again started to become frequent in the 1960s and 1970s, in turn triggering renewed global counter-terrorism efforts.[129] As far as the more specific threat from Islamist terrorism is concerned, Islamist terrorist networks have been operating for many years, as illustrated, for example, by the World Trade Center bombing in 1993.[130] Hence, the situation is hardly comparable to the case of space law or international environmental law; the social problem that the new body of terrorism law is purportedly addressing is anything but new.

A second, closely related, factor for the emergence of new categories of law is linked to the requirements of legal practice. In technical legal areas, professionals

Wellens eds., 1995); Catherine Redgwell, *International Environmental Law*, *in* INTERNATIONAL LAW 657, 657–61 (Malcolm D. Evans ed., 2006).

120. Malanczuk, *supra* note 85, at 144–46.

121. Ruth Wedgwood, *Countering Catastrophic Terrorism: An American View*, *in* ENFORCING INTERNATIONAL LAW NORMS AGAINST TERRORISM 103, 103–04, 109–11 (Andrea Bianchi ed., 2004).

122. Christopher Greenwood, *International Law and the "War against Terrorism"*, 78 INT'L AFF. 301, 301 (2002).

123. Jan. 2002 Gonzales Memorandum, *supra* note 52, at 2.

124. Eric Rosand, *The UN-Led Multilateral Institutional Response to Jihadist Terrorism: Is a Global Counterterrorism Body Needed?*, 11 J. CONFLICT & SEC. L. 399, 399, 405–06 (2006).

125. Report on Fragmentation, *supra* note 9, para. 186.

126. Richard Bach Jensen, *The International Anti-Anarchist Conference of 1898 and the Origins of Interpol*, 16 J. CONTEMP. HIST. 323, 323 (1981); Rick Coolsaet, *The Business of Terror: Anarchist Outrages*, LE MONDE DIPLOMATIQUE, Sept. 2004, *available at* http://mondediplo.com/2004/09/03anarchists.

127. Jensen, *supra* note 126; Coolsaet, *supra* note 126.

128. David C. Rapoport, *The Four Waves of Rebel Terror and September 11*, *in* THE NEW GLOBAL TERRORISM: CHARACTERISTICS, CAUSES, CONTROLS 36, 36–40, 46 (Charles W. Kegley ed., 2003).

129. *See* CONOR GEARTY, TERROR 53–64 (1991) (describing various terrorist activities beginning in the 1970s); BRUCE HOFFMAN, INSIDE TERRORISM 67–86 (1998) (describing the internationalization of terrorism).

130. JASON BURKE, AL-QAEDA: CASTING A SHADOW OF TERROR 93–100 (2003).

active in those areas (judges, panel members, government lawyers, counsel, academics, etc.) acquire special expertise which, over time, may become a requirement to practice in such branches of law. Thus, the technicality of a subject matter generally entails a high degree of specialization, often with expert bodies needed to adjudicate disputes. Trade law is perhaps the most evident example of such a specialized branch of international law, where the requirements of technical legal expertise have led to the formation of a distinct professional culture over the years.[131] Terrorism, however, cannot be seen as falling within this category. From the point of view of legal practice, terrorism is just an area of criminal law like many others; no special knowledge or expertise is needed to litigate or adjudicate terrorism cases.

Instead, the emergence of an anti-terrorism regime at the international level is mainly a reflection of a parallel development at the *national* level. Following September 11, many influential states have expanded their domestic capabilities to combat terrorism through the adoption of special anti-terrorism laws and the creation of specialized mechanisms and institutions, including tribunals and law enforcement agencies.[132] This can be seen as part of a wider trend whereby criminal justice systems increasingly rely on special powers to deal with "special" crimes and risks.[133] Rather than being inevitable for practical legal reasons, this special treatment approach is largely prompted by political pressures: special criminal laws are typically "passed amidst great public outrage in the wake of sensational crimes of violence" and "designed to be expressive, cathartic actions, undertaken to denounce the crime and reassure the public."[134] "Law-making [thus] becomes a matter of retaliatory gestures," relegating the question of whether the new measures are practicable and effective to the background.[135] This particularly applies in the case of terrorism. Since political violence is seen as an especially serious danger that potentially undermines the political, economic, and social structures of the state, it reacts more resolutely to terrorism than other forms of crime, and seeks to attach a special stigma to it.

This symbolic function underlies virtually all anti-terrorism regimes and mirrors the symbolic nature of the type of violence that these regimes are designed to counter. The military commission system in the United States,[136] for example, was

131. For the particular case of international economic arbitration, *see* Catherine A. Rogers, *The Vocation of the International Arbitrator*, 20 AM. U. INT'L. L. REV. 957, 958–59 (2005).

132. Examples include the U.S. Uniting and Strengthening America by Providing Appropriate Tools Required to Intercept and Obstruct Terrorism (USA PATRIOT) Act of 2001, Pub. L. No. 107-56, §§ 101–1016, 115 Stat. 272, 272–402 (2001) (codified as amended in scattered sections of 8, 15, 18, 22, 31, 42, 49, and 50 U.S.C.); the British Anti-Terrorism, Crime and Security Act (ATCSA), 2001, 49 Eliz. 2, c. 24 (Eng.); the German Gesetz zur Bekämpfung des internationalen Terrorismus, Jan. 9, 2002, BGBl. I at 361 (F.R.G.); and the Indian Prevention of Terrorism Act (POTA) 2002, No. 15, Acts of Parliament, 2002. For a good overview, *see generally* GLOBAL ANTI-TERRORISM LAW AND POLICY (Victor V. Ramraj et al. eds., 2005).

133. Clive Walker, *Terrorism and Criminal Justice: Past, Present and Future*, CRIM. L. REV. 311, 325 (2004).

134. DAVID GARLAND, THE CULTURE OF CONTROL: CRIME AND SOCIAL ORDER IN CONTEMPORARY SOCIETY 133 (2001). *See also* Kent Roach, *The Criminal Law and Terrorism*, *in* GLOBAL ANTI-TERRORISM LAW AND POLICY, *supra* note 132, at 129, 131–35 (noting examples in the U.S., U.K., and Indonesia).

135. GARLAND, *supra* note 134, at 134.

136. Military Commissions Act of 2006, Pub. L. No. 109-366, 120 Stat. 2600 (codified at 10 U.S.C. §§ 948(a)–950(w) and scattered sections of 10, 18, 28, and 42 U.S.C.).

not created because there is a lack of suitable fora for the trial of suspected terrorists. From the point of view of practicability, civilian courts and ordinary courts-martial are, as they have demonstrated on many occasions, perfectly capable of trying terrorist suspects.[137] Instead, the creation of these special tribunals reflects the belief that international terrorists deserve exceptional treatment as enemies rather than ordinary criminals: trial by military commission primarily serves a symbolic, stigmatizing function.[138] There is not a gap in the existing system, but rather discontent with it; the ordinary courts are seen as too meek to deal with the exceptional danger posed by contemporary international terrorists[139] and, as one supporter of the military commissions puts it, to "wholly satisfy our sense of their evil acts."[140]

The perception that terrorist attacks require a resolute state response in the form of exceptional legislative measures has led some of the most powerful states to press for the establishment of a parallel special anti-terrorism regime at the international level. The pre-2001 anti-terrorism treaties were adopted mostly in reaction to particularly shocking terrorist incidents,[141] and the same approach of giving expression to the "international community's" sense of outrage and condemnation accounts for the post-September 11 anti-terrorism measures. This fits the general pattern, observed by a number of authors, that international law is mainly developed in reaction to "triggering events,"[142] "incidents,"[143] or "crises."[144] The problem with this crisis management approach and its focus on particular events is

137. U.S. Federal Courts, applying ordinary procedures, convicted 253 persons for "terrorism or terrorism-related [crimes] with an international connection" in the time between September 11, 2001 and May 2006. Deputy Attorney General Paul J. McNulty, U.S. Department of Justice, Remarks at the American Enterprise Institute (May 24, 2006), http://www.justice.gov/archive/dag/speeches/2006/dag_speech_060524.html (last visited Feb. 5, 2009).

138. President Bush has claimed that those tried before the military commissions "are more than criminal suspects. They are unlawful combatants who seek to destroy our country and our way of life." Mike Allen & Susan Schmidt, *Bush Defends Secret Tribunals for Terrorism Suspects*, WASH. POST, Nov. 30, 2001, *available at* http://www.law.uchicago.edu/tribunals/docs/wp_13001.pdf. Similarly, Kenneth Anderson has argued that because of their fundamental opposition to the targeted state and society, contemporary terrorists should be treated as enemies rather than criminals; the civilian courts were the wrong forum not only for practical reasons but also for conceptual reasons. Kenneth Anderson, *What to Do with Bin Laden and Al Qaeda Terrorists?: A Qualified Defense of Military Commissions and United States Policy on Detainees at Guantanamo Bay Naval Base*, 25 HARV. J. L. & PUB. POL'Y 591, 609–11, 632–34 (2002).

139. *See* Harold H. Koh, *The Case against Military Commissions*, 96 AM. J. INT'L L. 337, 341 (2002) (arguing that those who promote military commissions "have been misled by the *O.J. Simpson* fiasco to conclude that standing American courts . . . are somehow incapable of rendering full, fair, and expeditious justice in such cases" and retorting that "the U.S. judicial system has amply demonstrated its ability to adapt to new, complex problems"); Frédéric Mégret, *Justice in Times of Violence*, 14 EUR. J. INT'L L. 327, 335 (2003) (claiming the support for commissions "reflects a conservative impatience with the ordinary judicial system, characterized as overly meek").

140. Anderson, *supra* note 138, at 633.

141. SAUL, *supra* note 13, at 130–31.

142. Michael Bothe, *The Historical Evolution of International Humanitarian Law, International Human Rights Law, Refugee Law and International Criminal Law*, *in* KRISENSICHERUNG UND HUMANITÄRER SCHUTZ – CRISIS MANAGEMENT AND HUMANITARIAN PROTECTION 37 (Horst Fischer et al. eds., 2004).

143. W. Michael Reisman, *International Incidents: Introduction to a New Genre in the Study of International Law*, 10 YALE J. INT'L L. 1, 1 (1984–1985).

144. Hilary Charlesworth, *International Law: A Discipline of Crisis*, 65 MOD. L. REV. 377, 377 (2002) (examining "the way that international lawyers tend to focus on crises for the development of international law.").

that it entails the creation of issue-related special regimes that rest on truncated understandings of events.[145] Reactive international law reform occurring quickly after terrorist acts tends to proceed without a thorough analysis of why the terrorists succeeded, or even of who they are,[146] and results in ill-considered and ineffective measures that simply borrow from domestic anti-terrorism policies.[147]

The centerpiece of the U.N. special anti-terrorism regime, Security Council Resolution 1373, for example, was passed in the immediate aftermath of September 11. The two main pillars of the resolution, suppression of the financing of terrorism and the use of immigration law as an anti-terrorism tool, reflect the central elements underlying the domestic anti-terrorism policies of most Western states,[148] including the United States, which sponsored the resolution.[149] In the face of huge political pressure on the governments of all states to show a swift and strong reaction to the terrorist attacks, the resolution was approved with hardly any recorded debate in a formal meeting that took five minutes,[150] despite introducing exceptionally far-reaching obligations. This is all the more striking given that it is highly questionable whether the terrorist financing and immigration measures required by the resolution are an effective means of preventing terrorism or, even, whether they relate in any way to regulatory deficiencies exposed by the September 11 attacks.[151] After a thorough review of the measures introduced by Resolution 1373, Kent Roach concluded that "[t]he Security Council, like domestic bodies struggling to do something to reassure the public, engaged in a form of bricolage."[152]

Similarly, Resolution 1624 was the result of pressure by the British government to target speech associated with terrorism, reflecting its own domestic anti-terrorism strategy adopted in the wake of the London bombings of July 7, 2005. Immediately after the bombings, the Home Secretary and the Prime Minister announced new legislation criminalizing indirect incitement to commit terrorist acts, including condoning and glorifying terrorism.[153] A respective draft bill, which eventually became the Terrorism Act 2006, was then put forward on September 13, 2005.[154] The

145. *Id.* at 382.

146. *See, e.g.*, Therese O'Donnell, *Naming and Shaming: The Sorry Tale of Security Council Resolution 1530 (2004)*, 17 EUR. J. INT'L L. 945 (2006) (discussing the hasty drafting of Security Council Resolution 1530 in response to the 2003 Madrid bombings).

147. Roach, *supra* note 134, at 131–32.

148. *See, e.g.*, Anti-Terrorism, Crime, and Security Act, 2001, c. 24, §§ 1–16, 21–36, sched. 1 (Eng.); Gesetz zur Bekämpfung des internationalen Terrorismus, Jan. 9, 2002, BGBl. I at 361, Arts. 1–3, 11–16 (F.R.G.); Anti-terrorism Act, 2001 S.C., ch. 41, §§ 47–75, 83–86, 105–11 (Can.).

149. *See* USA PATRIOT Act, Pub. L. No. 107-56, §§ 301–77, 401–28, 115 Stat. 272 (2001) (codified as amended in scattered sections of 8, 15, 18, 22, 31, 42, 49, and 50 U.S.C.); Hale E. Sheppard, *U.S. Actions to Freeze Assets of Terrorism: Manifest and Latent Implications for Latin America*, 17 AM. U. INT'L L. REV. 625, 628 (2002).

150. U.N. Security Council (U.N. SCOR), 56th Sess., 4385th mtg. at 2, U.N. Doc. S/PV.4385 (Sept. 28, 2001).

151. *See* Kent Roach, *Sources and Trends in Post-9/11 Anti-terrorism Laws*, *in* SECURITY AND HUMAN RIGHTS 227, 230–41 (Benjamin J. Goold and Liora Lazarus eds., 2007); Bianchi, *supra* note 37, at 892–903, 914–15.

152. Roach, *supra* note 151, at 234–35.

153. 436 PARL. DEB., H.C. (6th ser.) (2005) 1254; Tony Blair, Prime Minister's Press Conference (Aug. 5, 2005), http://www.number10.gov.uk/Page8041 (last visited Feb. 5, 2009).

154. Draft of Terrorism Bill, (Sept. 13, 2005), *available at* www.statewatch.org/news/2005/sep/terror-bill.pdf.

following day, the Security Council adopted the text of Resolution 1624 as tabled by the United Kingdom, calling on states to prohibit by law incitement to commit terrorist acts.[155] In the debate in the Security Council, the British Prime Minister promoted the resolution on the basis that the root cause of terrorism was "a doctrine of fanaticism." Therefore, not just the methods of terrorism had to be combated, "but also the terrorists' motivation, twisted reasoning and wretched excuses for terror."[156] Yet there is no evidence that prohibitions of speech such as criminalizing the glorification of terrorism that go beyond already existing laws against incitement of crimes and racial hatred help prevent acts of terrorism.[157]

Nor can the creation of the special sanctions regime against terrorist suspects be characterized as a reaction to a new social problem that would fill a gap in the international legal system. There are many other forms of organized crime that could be countered with financial sanctions, yet no one has pointed to the lack of a respective U.N. sanctions system as a gap in the law. Only in the case of terrorism has a sanctions regime been established. This fact demonstrates that the states represented on the Security Council view terrorism as a special form of crime requiring a resolute international response through the adoption of especially stringent measures. These highly political and symbolic considerations seem also to have played a crucial role in the passage of Resolution 1566.[158] This resolution, which established a Working Group to review the U.N. terrorist sanctions system, was passed in response to the Beslan school hostage crisis and consequent pressure by the Russian Federation to expand the scope of sanctions beyond the Taliban and Al Qaeda.[159]

Finally, similar rationales underlie proposals for the further extension of the international anti-terrorism regime, such as the Comprehensive Convention on International Terrorism. The High-level Panel on Threats, Challenges and Change, established by the U.N. Secretary-General, has admitted that there is no lack of legal regulation that would need to be addressed through the adoption of such a convention: "Legally, virtually all forms of terrorism are prohibited by one of [twelve] international counter-terrorism conventions, international customary law, the Geneva Conventions or the Rome Statutes."[160] Rather, according to the panel, the lack of a comprehensive convention is "not so much a legal question as a political one,"[161] since such a convention would send "an unequivocal message that terrorism is never an acceptable tactic."[162] In other words, the justification for the special regime is not that international terrorism is a new social phenomenon requiring adjustments at the legal level, but rather that it is such an exceptional threat it

155. S.C. Res. 1624, U.N. Doc. S/RES/1624 (Sept. 14, 2005); U.N. SCOR, 60th Sess., 5261st mtg. at 4, U.N. Doc. S/PV.5261 (Sept. 14, 2005).

156. UN SCOR, *supra* note 155, at 10.

157. Roach, *supra* note 151, at 245–49.

158. S.C. Res. 1566, *supra* note 68.

159. *See* U.N. SCOR, 59th Sess., 5053d mtg. at 3, U.N. Doc. S/PV.5053 (Oct. 8, 2004) (containing comments from the Russian Federation's representative emphasizing the "unprecedented escalation of international terrorism," urging more decisive action by SCOR, and thanking his colleagues for the passage of Resolution 1566).

160. Chairman of the High-level Panel on Threats, Challenges and Change, *A More Secure World: Our Shared Responsibility: Report of the High-level Panel on Threats, Challenges and Change*, para. 159, *delivered to the General Assembly*, U.N. Doc. A/59/565 (Dec. 2, 2004).

161. *Id.*

162. *Id.* para. 157.

necessitates some form of symbolic and particularly resolute response by the state community. The same reasoning underlies calls for the creation of a discrete international crime of terrorism. Ben Saul, for example, supports a distinct terrorism offense on the basis that "[t]he expressive function of the criminal law cannot be overstated; a conviction for *political* violence sends a symbolic message that certain kinds of violence, *as such*, cannot be tolerated, and reinforces the ethical values of the political community."[163]

To conclude, whereas other categories of international law have emerged as a reaction to the need for rules that are specifically tailored to a new social phenomenon or for actors and bodies with special expertise, the *raison d'être* of the distinct category of terrorism law is very different. What is special about international terrorism is the fact that states perceive it as a particularly dangerous form of violence that threatens their existence and thus necessitates the stigmatization of the perpetrators and reassurance of the public through the adoption of exceptional counter-measures. This has led certain states to exert political pressure to create an international anti-terrorism regime that mirrors the special regimes they have established at the national level—regimes that provide for exceptional powers to deal with conduct defined as terrorism, in deviance from the general criminal law. In this sense, the emergence of the international anti-terrorism regime is a reflection of the fragmentation and specialization of domestic criminal justice systems. At the same time, it is the result of a hegemonic move by certain states. By claiming that the international anti-terrorism regime embodies the interests of the "international community", they attempt to formulate their particular interests in universal terms and to have their special interests identified with the general interest.[164] Thereby, they not only give their domestic counter-terrorism policies a global reach, but also imbue them with international legitimacy.[165]

IV. IMPLICATIONS: WHY DOES IT MATTER?

Even though international terrorism might not be a new phenomenon, it is undoubtedly true that this particular form of crime presents a major challenge to the community of states. Surely, this justifies its special treatment in international law? What is wrong with sending out a clear signal that terrorism will not be tolerated? Is it not a good thing to stigmatize terrorists and reassure the public through the adoption of special counter-measures? And why would the phenomenon of international terrorism and the myriad legal responses it has provoked not deserve to be treated as an academic branch in its own right? Why, in short, does all of the above matter?

---

163. SAUL, *supra* note 13, at 39 (emphasis in original).

164. *See* Pierre Klein, *Les problèmes soulevés par la référence à la "communauté internationale" comme facteur de légitimité*, *in* DROIT, LÉGITIMATION ET POLITIQUE EXTERIEURE: L'EUROPE ET LA GUERRE DU KOSOVO 261, 263 (Olivier Corten & Barbara Delcourt eds., 2000) (discussing the situation in Kosovo, and providing examples of States, organizations, and other entities that advanced the idea of an "international community" in order to legitimize their own interests); Martti Koskenniemi, *International Law and Hegemony: A Reconfiguration*, 17 CAMBRIDGE REV. INT'L AFF. 197, 198 (2004) (discussing international law as a hegemonic technique).

165. For the example of Spain, *see* O'Donnell, *supra* note 146, at 955 ("Official acknowledgement of Spain's imperilment imbued Spanish domestic counter-terrorism measures, both existing and potential, with international legitimacy.").

It matters, first, because the crisis management and special treatment approach, which is mainly advanced through Security Council action, concentrates the attention of international law on a phenomenon that is primarily of concern to a number of powerful states, while at the same time marginalizing issues of structural justice that affect the everyday lives of the vast majority of the world's population.[166] A thorough exploration of this fundamental and complex issue is beyond the scope of this article. Instead, I will focus on the second, more limited, implication: namely, that the emergence of a special body of law on terrorism has led to a radical change in the legal discourse on terrorism—a change that has been reinforced by the academic treatment of the subject as a distinct branch of international law.

The traditional approach of international lawyers to terrorism, epitomized by the quotations at the beginning this article, was to treat it as one contemporary social phenomenon among many and to investigate how international law applied to this particular phenomenon. Today, this approach has been reversed. Treating terrorism as an autonomous subject involves a focus on what is distinct about terrorism as compared to other political or social phenomena. Under the special treatment model, the starting point of any legal analysis of terrorism is that what is offered by general international law is inadequate to deal with this exceptional phenomenon, and so special rules, bodies, and mechanisms—a fresh legal approach—are required.[167] The result is a self-perpetuating circle of assertions of the exceptional nature of contemporary international terrorism and the need for a resolute legal response in the form of unprecedented special measures. Despite its claim to "freshness," this kind of discourse is in fact impoverished. Constantly devised and revised in response to particular terrorist attacks, it focuses on swift legal amendments without thorough consideration of the practical need for them or their effectiveness, and obscures the possibility of applying general principles and rules of international law. The crisis model of international law, as Hilary Charlesworth perceptively observed, "leads us to rediscover an issue constantly and to analyse it without building on past scholarship."[168]

How this new approach to terrorism tends to obscure the possibility of applying the *lex generalis* is illustrated, for example, by the Council of Europe Guidelines on Human Rights and the Fight against Terrorism, adopted in 2002.[169] The guidelines have been widely, and rightly, lauded for making it clear that the fight against terrorism must conform to basic standards of human rights law.[170] But at the same time it is striking that they merely restate what, prior to the emergence of the special treatment model, was obvious and did not need stating. For example, the guidelines stress that terrorist suspects should be brought promptly before a judge upon arrest,

166. *See* Charlesworth, *supra* note 144, at 391–92 (discussing the day-to-day effects of "poverty, discrimination and violence" on the majority of the world's population).

167. *See* Spencer J. Crona & Neal A. Richardson, *Justice for War Criminals of Invisible Armies: A New Legal and Military Approach to Terrorism*, 21 OKLA. CITY U. L. REV. 349, 349–350 (1996) (expounding on the steps necessary for developing a new approach to terrorism); Jan. 2002 Gonzales Memorandum, *supra* note 52.

168. Charlesworth, *supra* note 144, at 384 (citing remarks of Philip Alston, ANZSIL/ASIL joint meeting, Canberra (June 29, 2000)).

169. DIRECTORATE GEN. OF HUMAN RIGHTS, COUNCIL OF EUR., GUIDELINES ON HUMAN RIGHTS AND THE FIGHT AGAINST TERRORISM, ADOPTED BY THE COMMITTEE OF MINISTERS ON 11 JULY 2002, at 44 (2002) *available at* http://www.coe.int/T/E/Human_rights/h-inf(2002)8eng.pdf [hereinafter GUIDELINES ON HUMAN RIGHTS].

170. *See, e.g.*, C. A. Gearty, *Terrorism and Human Rights*, 1 EUR. HUMAN RTS. L. REV. 1, 1 (2005).

that they have the right to a fair trial before an independent and impartial tribunal, that they must be treated with due respect for human dignity, and that they should not be tortured.[171] Only in the light of the general trend towards special treatment of terrorism is it understandable why the Council of Europe ends up pointing out the obvious. Like all other special norms pertaining to terrorism, the guidelines seem to be based on the assumption that counter-terrorism is a distinctly separate field of criminal justice. As a consequence, it becomes necessary to state that the general rules in the form of basic human rights standards are still applicable. If it is, in the words of Pierre-Marie Dupuy, "la cohérence, et donc l'unité de l'ordre juridique international qui donnent leur signification aux normes et aux institutions,"[172] the special treatment model, by narrowing thinking to what is "within the box," contributes to confusion over the meaning and the applicability of norms.

The coherence and unity of international law is not an end in and of itself. Its significance has been described by the ILC Study Group as follows: "[c]oherence is valued positively owing to the connection it has with predictability and legal security. Moreover, only a coherent legal system treats legal subjects equally."[173] It is, in my view, the second aspect—only mentioned as a side-note in the ILC report—which is the crucial function of the coherence of international law. Already Kant understood that only a legal system based on formal, general, universally applicable norms can guarantee equality.[174] This insight is also central to the theories of modern liberal thinkers, such as Ronald Dworkin, whose principle of equal concern implies the "political virtue of integrity," requiring the state to act on a single, coherent set of principles of justice and fairness.[175] Critical scholars, such as the Frankfurt-school jurist Franz Neumann, have equally highlighted the link between the coherence and generality of the law on the one hand and the universalistic idea of legal equality on the other; situation-specific state action is antithetical to this idea.[176] More recently, Martti Koskenniemi has pointed out with regard to international law, "the form of law . . . [affirms] . . . the principle that the conditions applying to the treatment of any one member of the community must apply to every other member as well."[177]

From this perspective, the creation of a kind of shadow legal system for terrorism, accompanied by the emergence of a respective academic branch, not only threatens the coherence and unity of international law but also implicitly attacks the principle that every legal subject deserves to be treated with equal respect and concern. Since the main purposes of the special treatment model—whose principal

171. GUIDELINES ON HUMAN RIGHTS, *supra* note 169, §§ IV, VII, IX, XI.

172. Dupuy, *supra* note 5, at 13.

173. *Report on Fragmentation, supra* note 9, para. 491.

174. *See* IMMANUEL KANT, GROUNDWORK OF THE METAPHYSICS OF MORALS 13–14 (James W. Ellington trans., Hackett Publ'g 1981) (1785).

175. RONALD DWORKIN, LAW'S EMPIRE 164–67, 176–224 (1986).

176. FRANZ NEUMANN, THE RULE OF LAW: POLITICAL THEORY AND THE LEGAL SYSTEM IN MODERN SOCIETY 256–57 (1986); FRANZ NEUMANN, THE DEMOCRATIC AND THE AUTHORITARIAN STATE: ESSAYS IN POLITICAL AND LEGAL THEORY 42 (Herbert Marcuse ed., 1957). *See also* WILLIAM E. SCHEUERMAN, BETWEEN THE NORM AND THE EXCEPTION: THE FRANKFURT SCHOOL AND THE RULE OF LAW 104 (1994) ("When the state abandons cogent general law in favor of situation-specific action, capitalism gains the upper hand over the fragile, constantly threatened aspirations of the liberal political tradition.").

177. Martti Koskenniemi, *What Is International Law For?*, *in* INTERNATIONAL LAW 57, 70 (Malcolm D. Evans ed., 2006).

driving force is the Security Council with its web of anti-terrorism norms and bodies—are condemnation, stigmatization, and reassurance, those subject to the anti-terrorism regime are inevitably singled out for particularly harsh treatment. Not only are separate legal categories of conduct created but also different levels of protection: the category of people that falls under the special regime is seen as undeserving of the same level of protection of the law as everyone else. This premise underlies virtually all norms and mechanisms that make up the contemporary special anti-terrorism regime, turning the (suspected) terrorist into what the pirate was in previous times: the "enemy of mankind," the pariah of the international community.[178]

The terrorist sanctions regime imposed by the Security Council, for instance, provides far less protection to those affected by the sanctions than is generally available under national and international law, in particular depriving them of the rights to a fair hearing and a judicial remedy.[179] This inferior level of due process protection has been justified on the basis that the Security Council's sanctions resolutions, by virtue of Article 103 of the U.N. Charter, prevail over every other obligation of states under domestic or international law, including obligations under human rights treaties.[180] The same reduced protection is evident in the 1373 regime. Resolution 1373 obliges states to adopt numerous, very far-reaching measures against terrorism, but lacks any reference to their obligations under international law to respect the basic human rights of individuals affected by these measures.[181] This omission is compounded by the fact that the mandate of the CTC does not include reviewing anti-terrorism measures for their compliance with international human rights standard; accordingly, its first years of activity have been marked by an almost complete disregard for human rights issues.[182] Similarly, Security Council Resolution

178. *See* GERRY SIMPSON, LAW, WAR AND CRIME: WAR CRIMES TRIALS AND THE REINVENTION OF INTERNATIONAL LAW 159–77 (2007); Malvina Halberstam, *Terrorism on the High Seas: The Achille Lauro, Piracy and the IMO Convention on Maritime Safety*, 82 AM. J. INT'L. L. 269 (1988).

179. Erika de Wet & André Nollkaemper, *Review of Security Council Decisions by National Courts*, 45 GERMAN YBK INT'L L. 166, 166 (2002). *See* Council of Europe, *The European Convention on Human Rights, Due Process and United Nations Security Council Counter-Terrorism Sanctions* (Feb. 6, 2006) (*prepared by* Iain Cameron), http://www.coe.int/t/e/legal_affairs/legal_co-operation/public_international_law/Texts_&_Documents/2006/I.%20Cameron%20Report%2006.pdf; U.N. Office of Legal Affairs, Office of the Legal Counsel, *Targeted Sanctions and Due Process* (Mar. 20, 2006) (*prepared by* Bardo Fassbender), *available at* www.un.org/law/counsel/Fassbender_study.pdf; Bianchi, *supra* note 37, at 903–10; Elin Miller, *The Use of Targeted Sanctions in the Fight against Terrorism – What about Human Rights?*, 97 AM. SOC'Y INT'L L. PROC. 46, 48 (2003).

180. *See* Case T-306/01, Yusuf and Al Barakaat Int'l Found. v. Council of the E.U. and the Comm'n of the Eur. Cmties., 2005 E.C.R. II-3533 ("According to Article 103 of the Charter of the United Nations, '[i]n the event of a conflict between the obligations of the Members of the United Nations under the present Charter and their obligations under any other international agreement, their obligations under the present Charter shall prevail.'"); Case T-315/01, Kadi v. Council of the E.U. and the Comm'n of the Eur. Cmties., 2005 E.C.R. II-3649. These decisions were later overturned by the European Court of Justice. Joined Cases C-402/05 P and C-415/05 P, *Yassin Abdullah Kadi and Al Barakaat International Foundation v Council of the E.U. and Comm'n of the Eur. Cmties* (ECJ Judgment), Sept. 3, 2008, available at http://curia.europa.eu/en/content/juris/index.htm (last visited Feb. 12, 2009).

181. Only in January 2003, in a resolution *not* adopted under Chapter VII of the UN Charter, did the Security Council make clear that "[s]tates must ensure that any measure taken to combat terrorism comply with all their obligations under international law." S.C. Res. 1456, para. 6, UN Doc. S/RES/1456 (Jan. 20, 2003).

182. *See* U.N. Econ. & Soc. Council [ECOSOC], Comm'n on Human Rights, *Report of the Special Rapporteur on the Promotion and Protection of Human Rights and Fundamental Freedoms While Countering Terrorism*, paras. 51–63, UN Doc. E/CN.4/2006/98, (Dec. 28, 2005); E.J. Flynn, *The Security*

1624, by calling on states to "[p]rohibit by law *incitement* to commit a *terrorist act*" without defining either term,[183] may help to legitimate exceptionally vague and far-reaching restrictions on the freedom of political expression.[184] As a final example, the claim that the Geneva Conventions are outdated and new legal categories, such as that of the "enemy combatant," are needed,[185] aims to deny suspected terrorists the guarantees that are normally available to those captured during armed conflict under the general rules of international humanitarian law as well as the protections enjoyed by those who are charged with a criminal offense.[186] Thus, while the special treatment model may not place the terrorist beyond the law,[187] it does turn him or her into a stigmatized figure without the full protection of the law.

Of course, this is not the only instance where international law serves the purpose of stigmatization. For example, certain forms of crime, including crimes against humanity and genocide, are treated as international crimes to which a special stigma is attached, as they "particularly shock the collective conscience."[188] However, what makes these crimes particularly shocking and deserving of stigmatization is the nature of the act: the fact that they are committed as part of a widespread or systematic violation of basic human rights.[189] In contrast, in the case of terrorism, the reason for the special treatment is the nature of the actor: the fact that he or she pursues political or ideological goals. This is made explicit, for example, in the European Commission's proposal for the Framework Decision to Combat Terrorism: "Most terrorist acts are basically ordinary offences which become terrorist offences because of the motivations of the offender. If the motivation is to alter seriously or to destroy the fundamental principles and pillars of the state, intimidating people, there is a terrorist offence."[190] What is stigmatized is not the crime itself but the perpetrator's motivation.

Inherent in this focus on the actor and their motivation is a tendency to direct the stigmatizing effect of the special anti-terrorism regime against a certain category of people: those who, because of their nationality, ethnicity, national origin, religion, or other personal characteristics, are seen as potentially sympathetic to the respective political or ideological cause. In other words, the creation of an

---

Council's Counter-Terrorism Committee and Human Rights, 7 HUM. RTS. L. REV. 371, 377 (2007); HUMAN RIGHTS WATCH, HEAR NO EVIL, SEE NO EVIL: THE UN SECURITY COUNCIL'S APPROACH TO HUMAN RIGHTS VIOLATIONS IN THE GLOBAL COUNTER-TERRORISM EFFORT 6–7 (2004), *available at* http://www.hrw.org/backgrounder/un/2004/un0804/un0804.pdf.

183. S.C. Res. 1624, para. 1(a), UN Doc. S/RES/1624 (Sept. 14, 2005) (emphases added).

184. Roach, *supra* note 151, at 247–49.

185. Hamdi v. Rumsfeld, 542 U.S. 507, 516 (2004); Jan. 2002 Gonzales Memorandum, *supra* note 52. *See* Jordan Paust, *War and Enemy Status after 9/11: Attacks on the Laws of War*, 28 YALE J. INT'L L. 325, 325–26 (2003).

186. Daniel Moeckli, *The US Supreme Court's 'Enemy Combatant' Decisions: A 'Major Victory for the Rule of Law'?*, 10 J. CONFLICT & SEC. L. 75, 77–79 (2005).

187. *See* Fleur Johns, *Guantánamo Bay and the Annihilation of the Exception*, 16 EUR. J. INT'L L. 613, 617 (2005).

188. Prosecutor v. Kambanda, Case No. ICTR 97-23-S, Judgment and Sentence, para. 14 (Sept. 4, 1998).

189. Rome Statute of the International Criminal Court, art. 7.1, July 17, 1998, 2187 U.N.T.S. 3 ("For the purpose of this Statute, 'crime against humanity' means any of the following acts when committed as part of a widespread or systematic attack").

190. *Commission Proposal for a Council Framework Decision on Combating Terrorism*, at 6, COM (2001) 521 final (Sept. 19, 2001).

alternative legal system for terrorism inevitably carries with it the danger of discrimination.[191] The treatment of terrorism as a separate category of international law should therefore not only be resisted by those who are concerned about the coherence and unity of the international legal system—those who believe that this unity can be an end in itself—it should also be opposed by those who are concerned about the fundamental principle that all human beings deserve equal protection of the law. It is this bedrock of the international human rights system[192] that is ultimately at stake in the debate about the proper place of terrorism in international law.

CONCLUSION

Various authors have considered the positive and negative impacts that the fragmentation of international law may have on the international legal system. On the positive side, specialized and tailored regulation may better accommodate the special needs of the particular subject matter, which, in turn, may lead states to better comply with international law.[193] Similarly, institutional fragmentation, i.e., the proliferation of implementation organs, may improve the efficiency of the international legal system by "generating a more refined and precise system of interpretation of norms."[194] On the negative side, whereas the coherence of the international legal system contributes to its intelligibility and efficiency,[195] fragmentation increases the opportunities for frictions and contradictions between different special regimes, thus undermining predictability and legal certainty.[196] In addition, fragmentation is dangerous from a "political" perspective: since any special regime can be rejected by states, fragmentation may lead to an *à la carte* approach to international law that could ultimately threaten its very existence.[197]

Yet the fragmentation of international law is not a unitary phenomenon whose overall benefits could be balanced against its drawbacks. Instead, there are different forms of fragmentation. Different reasons lead to the emergence of different special regimes and respective academic branches, and these developments accordingly raise different concerns. This is evidenced by the creation of the international anti-terrorism regime and the emergence of an academic branch of terrorism law. The *raison d'être* of this category of international law is very different from that of other international legal categories, as it primarily relates to a perceived need for stigmatization and reassurance through the creation of an international anti-terrorism regime that mirrors special regimes established at the domestic level. The

191. DANIEL MOECKLI, HUMAN RIGHTS AND NON-DISCRIMINATION IN THE "WAR ON TERROR" 56 (2008).

192. *See, e.g.*, International Covenant on Civil and Political Rights, art. 26, Dec. 16, 1966, 999 U.N.T.S. 171; Universal Declaration of Human Rights, G.A. Res. 217A, art. 7, U.N. GAOR, 3d Sess., 1st plen. mtg., U.N. Doc. A/810 (Dec. 12, 1948).

193. Gerhard Hafner, *Pros and Cons Ensuing from Fragmentation of International Law*, 25 MICH. J. INT'L L. 849, 859 (2004).

194. Pierre-Marie Dupuy, *The Danger of Fragmentation or Unification of the International Legal System and the International Court of Justice*, 31 NYU J. INT'L L. & POL. 791, 796 (1999); *see also* Georges Abi-Saab, *Fragmentation or Unification: Some Concluding Remarks*, 31 NYU J. INT'L L. & POL. 919, 925–26 (1999).

195. Dupuy, *supra* note 5, at 13–14.

196. Hafner, *supra* note 193, at 856–58.

197. Dupuy, *supra* note 5, at 14–15.

problem with this development is not, as with other types of fragmentation, that special regimes may be rejected by states. Since the international anti-terrorism regime is built around binding Security Council resolutions and backed up by the political pressure of powerful (Western) states, there is no opt-out possibility. Nor is it merely a technical problem, threatening legal security and efficiency. The real concern raised by the emergence of terrorism as a distinct category of international law is that it undermines the principle that every legal subject deserves to be treated with equal respect and dignity.

In one respect, however, the emergence of terrorism law is characteristic of the general trend towards the fragmentation and compartmentalization of international law. Martti Koskenniemi and Päivi Leino have convincingly argued that these developments "arise as effects of politics and not as technical mistakes or unfortunate side-effects of some global logic."[198] When Koskenniemi and Leino refer to "politics," they have the hegemonic struggle between different international implementation organs in mind.[199] The emergence of the international anti-terrorism regime is equally the consequence of political pressures, albeit of a different sort: it is the result of a hegemonic attempt by certain states to impose a global approach to countering terrorism that mirrors their own domestic anti-terrorism policies.

198. Martti Koskenniemi & Päivi Leino, *Fragmentation of International Law? Postmodern Anxieties*, 15 LEIDEN J. INT'L L. 553, 561 (2002).

199. *Id.* at 562.

[22]

The UN-Led Multilateral Institutional Response to Jihadist Terrorism: Is a Global Counterterrorism Body Needed?

Eric Rosand*

Abstract

This article first briefly outlines the current terrorist threat posed by militant Islamist radical terrorism and the complexity and evolving nature of threat. It highlights the lack of consensus in academic and policy communities regarding the underlying causes of this terrorism. It them posits that the overarching challenge in the next few years will be to maintain the broad-based international co-operation in the fight against terrorism that has existed since 11 September 2001, which is essential to address the threat effectively. Elements of this challenge include dispelling the notion that the US-led counterterrorism effort is targeting Islam and keeping the global South engaged. Durable, effective and flexible mechanisms are needed at the global, regional and national levels to ensure that multifaceted, holistic strategies are developed and implemented to address these issues. The article then outlines the current capacity of multilateral institutions to contribute to the fight against terrorism. The performance of the main UN counterterrorism bodies – led by the Security Council's different counterterrorism entities – as well as some of the key regional and functional ones, this article concludes, has been uneven. Different organisations have developed counterterrorism programs and units, but these have emerged from political reactions rather than strategic decisions with corresponding achievable technical objectives. The duplication of efforts, overlapping mandates and lack of co-ordination at the international, regional and sub-regional levels have limited the different bodies' overall contribution to the global non-military counterterrorism

*Eric Rosand is a Senior Fellow at the Center on Global Counter-Terrorism Cooperation in New York, NY. E-mail: erosand@globalct.com. He previously served in the Office of the Counterterrorism Coordinator at the US Department of State and as the Deputy Legal Counselor at the US Mission to the UN in New York. This article draws and builds upon a monograph on the role of multilateral institutions in the fight against terrorism, Eric Rosand & Alistair Millar, *Allied Against Terrorism: What's Needed to Strengthen Worldwide Commitment* (2006).

effort and have left many of the world's vulnerabilities to terrorism unaddressed. This article concludes that maintaining international co-operation and the focus on capacity-building and other non-military counterterrorism measures, as well as the need to address the proliferation of counterterrorism bodies, highlights the need for an effective multilateral body at the center of the effort. The UN Security Council's Counter-Terrorism Committee was supposed to be this body, but it has been unable to fulfill its broad mandate effectively. The article details the limitations of the current UN Security Council-led approach and the inherent, political, administrative and budgetary challenges of operating within the UN system that would make it difficult to co-ordinate global capacity-building efforts effectively. While it proposes a possible short-term improvement – the consolidation of the different parts of the Security Council counterterrorism program into as single body – in the end, it argues that a new international body dedicated to counterterrorism outside of, but perhaps related in some way to, the UN may be needed.

1. The Threat

A historic tendency has been overtaken because of the emergence of al-Qaeda and the global Jihadist threat that it represents. States have traditionally considered other states' internal problems with violent political opponents who resort to terrorist violence as their own domestic problems. There is now broad recognition, even amongst the most powerful of countries, that all states are potential targets of terrorism and no state or even group of states can fight that threat on its own and that mechanisms for effective co-ordination and co-operation are needed at the national, regional and global levels.[1] Many countries can suffer from the economic impact of a major attack or even a threatened attack. An Australian Government white paper on terrorism makes this point clear: 'the transnational impact of the threat means that a country does not have to experience a direct terrorist attack on its soil to suffer from the effects of terrorism.' A country with weak governance or financial infrastructure corrupted and exploited by terrorists may have devastating implications for countries on the other side of the world and economic repercussions for the entire world economy.[2]

1 Numerous leaders have made this point, including Philippines President Arroyo, who, speaking at the August 2006 ASEAN Leaders Summit, stated that '[w]e cannot deal with the [terrorist] threats alone. We must work with other countries and international institutions if we are determined to successfully address and eliminate them', 6 August 2006, <http://archive.gulfnews.com/articles/06/08/13/10059705.html>; Kofi Annan, who has noted that 'terrorism is a threat to all States, to all people, which can strike anytime, anywhere', Secretary General's Global Strategy for Fighting Terrorism, 11 March 2005, <http://www.un.org/News/Press/docs/2005/sgsm9757.doc.htm>; and US President George W. Bush has remarked, 'The global threat of terrorism requires a global response', The White House, 'President Bush Discusses Progress in the War on Terror', Oak Ridge National Laboratory, Oak Ridge, Tennessee, 12 July 2004.

2 Australian Department of Foreign Affairs and Trade, 'Australian Paper: Experiences in Combating Transnational Terrorism'. Available at <http://www.dfat.gov.au/globalissues/combating_transnational_terrorism.html#_ftn1>.

Since 9/11, an unprecedented global counterterrorism campaign has resulted in the death or capture of much of the al-Qaeda leadership. As a formal hierarchical network, today al-Qaeda is a shell of the organisation it once was. Years of offensive military operations against it and its leadership and other efforts to disrupt its operations have significantly degraded al-Qaeda's capacity to centrally orchestrate large-scale attacks. The result is a wider, more disparate and dispersed movement, in many ways just as or more dangerous, still capable of operationally directing and inspiring large-scale terrorist violence worldwide. Although there is no consensus among experts as to just how decentralised the movement is, there is broad agreement that its members are bent on inflicting unprecedented destruction, going beyond the scale of achieving limited political aims like terrorist groups of the past. There is also little dispute that al-Qaeda has spawned successor groups and inspired movements and individuals that share its messianic goals and destructive means. Unlike during the Cold War, when like-minded allies could focus on protecting centres of military and industrial capacity, it is now the least governed, most lawless places that are either breeding grounds or potential breeding grounds for terrorists who, as the example of September 11 showed, are motivated by a palpable sense of Western vulnerability. This new breed of terror networks frequently has no affiliation to sovereign nations and operates across religious or national boundaries. To respond to this threat, counterterrorism efforts must deliberately cut across the cultural, ethnic, regional and religious divides that terrorists seek to exploit.[3]

Yet, the threat is not just coming from the ungoverned spaces on the globe, as the bombings in both Madrid and London as well as the murder of Dutch artist Theo van Gogh by a young Dutch militant have revealed. There is a growing group of what the Center on Strategic and International Studies' Daniel Benjamin has referred to as self-starter, 'home-grown' terrorists who may have very little connection to al-Qaeda or other pre-existing groups but have been won over by the ideas of Osama bin Laden and his followers.[4] Self-recruited and often self-trained, they have relied on the Internet, operating without external support or instructions from what might remain of an al-Qaeda hierarchy to carry out deadly attacks.[5]

3 Anthony Cordesman, 'The Lessons of International Cooperation in Counterterrorism', address to the RUSI Conference on Transnational Terrorism 'A Global Approach', 18 January 2006.

4 Daniel Benjamin, Senior Fellow, Center for Strategic and International Studies, Testimony before the Senate Foreign Relations Committee, 'The Changing Face of Terror – A Post 9–11 Assessment', 13 June 2006. Available at <http://www.senate.gov/~foreign/testimony/2006/BenjaminTestimony060613.pdf>.

5 Rik Coolsaet, 'Jihadi Terrorism – Where Do We Stand?', Second IRRI (Belgian Royal Institute for International Relations) Conference on International Terrorism, 13 February 2006. Available at <http://irri-kiib.be/speechnotes/06/060213-jihad.terr/coolsaet.htm>.

There is no consensus as to what is the direct cause of the existence and spread of Jihadist terrorism. For example, in a BBC interview two days after the London Underground bombings, British Prime Minister Tony Blair stated that it is crucial to address terrorism's 'underlying causes', which he identified as poverty, lack of democracy and the Middle East conflict.[6] Yet, if the prime minister were correct, the terrorist phenomenon would be different than the one that actually exists. Despite poverty being widespread, most of the world's poorest societies have not produced terrorist organisations, particularly not ones with an international scope. A Norwegian Institute of International Affairs panel of leading terrorism experts found that there is only a weak and indirect relationship between poverty and terrorism.[7] Similarly, most countries lack democracy; and it is far from clear that democracy is the goal of most terrorist organisations.[8] On the contrary, few would dispute that the US-led invasion and the various missteps that have characterised the occupation of Iraq have been directly responsible for the rise in Jihadist violence in that part of the world.

The policy and academic communities do, however, appear to share a common understanding of some of the conditions that attract individuals to this brand of extremism. As the Secretary General stated in his April 2006 report, Uniting against Terrorism, 'terrorist acts do not occur in a social or political vacuum'. According to the Secretary General, these 'conditions conducive to exploitation by terrorists' include extremist ideologies and dehumanisation of victims, violent conflict, poor governance, lack of civil rights and human rights abuse, religious and ethnic discrimination, political exclusion and socio-economic marginalisation.[9] Even the United States, which had long been reluctant to acknowledge that certain societal factors can lead people to embrace rather than spurn terrorism, now agrees: addressing these 'underlying conditions' is now one of three prongs of its counterterrorism strategy (with the other two being the removal of terrorist leaders and the denial of physical and virtual safe haven).[10]

Given the complexity and evolving nature of the threat, as well as the diversity of conditions that make the soil fertile for terrorist recruitment and radicalisation, combating international terrorism requires a comprehensive, multifaceted response at the global, regional and local levels. To be effective,

6 Tony Blair, 9 July 2005. Available at <http://news.bbc.co.uk/1/hi/uk_politics/4666311.stm>.

7 Norwegian Institute of International Affairs, *Root Causes of Terrorism* (2002). Available at <http://www.nupi.no/IPS/filestore/Root_Causes_report.pdf>.

8 Don Radlauer, 'The London Bombings and "the Root Causes" of Terrorism', Institute for Counter-Terrorism, 10 July 2005. Available at <http://www.ict.org.il/editorials/editorialdet.cfm?editorialid=1>.

9 Report of the Secretary General, 'Uniting Against Terrorism: Recommendations for a Global Counter-Terrorism Strategy', 27 April 2006, at paras. 8 and 20–38.

10 Henry A. Crumpton, United States Coordinator for Counterterrorism, 'Remarks at the Royal United Services Institute Conference on Transnational Terrorism', London, England, 16 January 2006. Available at <http://www.state.gov/s/ct/rls/rm/2006/59987.htm>.

responses must be enduring and sustainable and must include a significant non-military component. Worldwide co-ordination is essential to ensure the cross-border co-operation necessary to track funding, disrupt planning and prevent future attacks as well as to investigate, capture and prosecute terrorists and their supporters, should those preventive efforts fail. It is also needed to develop and implement strategies for addressing the above-mentioned 'underlying conditions' and, in doing so, create a positive narrative to counter the hatred and violence that the Jihadists are so eager to spread.

Multilateral institutions can make meaningful contributions to the global campaign against terrorism, including by promoting worldwide co-ordination and co-operation in various aspects of the non-military counterterrorism effort, but in some cases they can also impede progress. As will be discussed below, the UN-led multilateral institutional response to terrorism has produced mixed results. In addition, there continues to be a shortage of serious thinking being done on how to improve the response. On the one hand, the role of such bodies is almost an afterthought in the writings of the vast majority of counterterrorism experts, who focus on bilateral or informal international co-operative efforts and generally lack a full appreciation of the workings of these institutions and the comparative advantages they might have in the fight against terrorism. On the other hand, UN or international organisation specialists generally lack the necessary background on the evolving terrorist threat and strategies for addressing it to be able to contribute much in the way of meaningful or creative ideas on the counterterrorism role of multilateral bodies.

2. The Challenge of Sustaining International Co-operation

The overarching challenge in the next few years will be to maintain the broad-based international co-operation in the fight against terrorism that has existed since 11 September 2001 and is essential to address the threat effectively. To the extent that the global counterterrorism campaign succeeds in crippling al-Qaeda's global network and its ability to conduct massive attacks or leads to further decentralisation of al-Qaeda, with self-starter and self-recruiting cells and individuals, the more difficult it will be to maintain the international coalition. It is worth recalling that there is no common definition at the UN of terrorism that extends beyond Osama bin Laden, the Taliban, al-Qaeda and its followers or offspring. There is no consensus among States as to who is or is not a terrorist as the debates surrounding Hamas, Hezbollah, the Chechneyan separatists and the East Turkestan Liberation Organisation attest.

As part of this challenge, the global North will need to dispel the growing scepticism and distrust among Muslims around the globe that the US-led counterterrorism effort is targeting Islam. It will need to recognise that, as Jessica Stern, a counterterrorism expert at Harvard University, has recently reminded us, 'the tools required in the long run to win the war are neither bombs nor torture chambers. They are ideas and stories that counter the terrorist narrative -- and draw potential recruits away from the lure of jihad'.[11] The ability to maintain and hopefully strengthen international co-operation in the fight against terrorism will also depend on developing strategies and programmes at the global, regional and local level that can address the ever changing terrorist tactics. For example, terrorist groups are becoming more sophisticated in their use of technology, particularly the Internet and the media. To highlight the growing problem, Gabriel Weimann, author of *Terror on the Internet*, estimated the number of terrorist websites to be around 4,800, up from around 20 in 1998 and growing at a faster rate than other segments of the Internet.[12]

To the extent that the threat continues to become decentralised, with a growing 'patchwork of homegrown networks,' with local conditions being the main driving force behind terrorist activities, greater attention will need to be paid to addressing the conditions that are providing fertile soil for radicalisation and recruitment in communities in Europe and elsewhere. Yet, effective strategies have yet to be developed at the international, or for that matter local, level for tackling many of these social and political conditions. This is partly because many of them, for example, local conflicts, religious extremism, human rights abuse, lack of political freedoms, touch upon highly sensitive issues on which it is difficult to achieve consensus on the most effective approaches for addressing them. As a result, 'international counterterrorism cooperation has been least successful where it matters most'.[13]

Another aspect of the broad challenge of maintaining international co-operation is keeping the global South engaged. For many developing countries, counterterrorism is seen largely as a Western priority, although cities in the global South have been victimised by terrorist attacks much more often than those in the North.[14] This perception is likely to increase the more decentralised al-Qaeda becomes, the more the 'self-starter' terrorist cells begin to dominate the landscape and the more often population centres in the global North are victimised. For the global South, the higher priorities are the battles against poverty, underdevelopment, HIV/AIDs and malaria. Relatively few countries have the necessary legal, administrative and regulatory capacities to freeze terrorists' assets, monitor the formal and informal banking systems, prevent the travel of designated individuals, deny safe haven to terrorists and their supporters and suppress the recruitment and military supply of terrorist groups. Many face

11 Jessica Stern, 'Jihad – A Global Fad', *Boston Globe*, 1 August 2006.

12 See <http://www.technologyreview.com/read_article.aspx?ch=specialsections&sc=social&id=16566> and <http://www.voanews.com/english/archive/2006-05/Terrorism2006-05-03-voa74.cfm>.

13 Rik Coolsaet, 'Jihadi Terrorism – Where Do We Stand?', Second IRRI Conference on International Terrorism, 13 February 2006, p. 7. Available at <http://www.irri-kiib.be/speechnotes/06/060213-jihad.terr/coolsaet.htm>.

14 *Ibid.*, p. 5.

deficiencies in their operational and administrative capacity for combating terrorism but may lack the resources and/or political will to take the necessary steps to address these gaps. This lack of capacity is particularly troubling because terrorists have proven adept at exploiting such gaps to fund, organise, equip and train their recruits, carry out their attacks and hide from arrest. In the end, given the global and fast-moving nature of the terrorist threat, the international community's ability to deal effectively with it will only be as strong as the globe's weakest link. Thus, building capacity of all States, including those in the often vulnerable global South must remain a priority.

Two elements of an effective long-term strategy to sustain the global South's commitment to strengthen their counterterrorism capabilities are (1) a more effectively co-ordinated international technical assistance effort, so that the States lacking both capacity and means are matched with the appropriate technical assistance in a timely manner, and (2) a clearer and more widely disseminated message as to the benefits that will accrue from enhanced counterterrorism capacities.

With respect to the latter, creating more effective law enforcement capabilities – including through the training of judges, prosecutors, intelligence officials and police; improving border, immigration and customs controls; regulating banks and financial institutions and strengthening security at ports and border crossings – will do much more than simply improve counterterrorism capacity; these improvements would parallel the steps increasingly recognised among aid donors and recipients as essential to economic development and the expansion of social and economic opportunity. Trade and investment depend on stable government and the rule of law. The G8 Leaders acknowledged this linkage in the G8's first-ever statement on strengthening the UN's counterterrorism programme, recognising that enhanced counterterrorism capacity 'will have far-reaching benefits. It will reduce the likelihood of conflict and social unrest and contribute to increased foreign investment, good governance and long-term development'.[15]

More than five years after the horrific events of 11 September 2001, it is increasingly clear that this will likely be a decades-long struggle. The longer the threat continues, the more sophisticated and adaptable the terrorists and the more complex the strategy for combating terrorism become. What started out as a predominantly military response to the attacks on the World Trade Center and the Pentagon has now morphed and broadened into one that focuses much more on the non-military aspects of counterterrorism, with greater emphasis now being placed on capacity building and addressing the societal and political conditions that can spawn terrorists. Thus, more then ever, durable, effective

15 G8 Statement on Strengthening the UN's Counter-Terrorism Programme, St. Petersburg, Russia, 16 July 2006, para 4. Available at <http://www.g7.utoronto.ca/summit/2006stpetersburg/counterterrorism-un.html>.

and flexible mechanisms are needed at the global, regional and national levels to ensure that the multifaceted, holistic strategies are in fact implemented.

3. The Capacity of Multilateral Institutions to Contribute to the Fight against Terrorism

Given the greater emphasis being placed on the role of non-military measures in the fight against terrorism and the broad recognition that sustained international co-operation at all levels remains a necessary component of the effort, multilateral institutions are well-placed to make a meaningful contribution.

Yet, as the brief overview of the main UN counterterrorism bodies, as well as some of the key regional and functional ones, will show, their performance has been uneven. Different international and regional bodies have developed counter-terrorism programmes and units, but these have emerged from political reactions rather than strategic decisions with corresponding achievable technical objectives. This has led to a general lack of sustained attention from politicians and senior government officials. In turn, it has failed to inspire the confidence of national technical experts, who often see the work of a growing number of committees as paper-producing machines, having little measurable impact on the enemy. This view is confirmed by the duplication of efforts, overlapping mandates and lack of co-ordination at the international, regional and sub-regional levels – all of which have limited the different bodies' overall contribution to the global non-military counterterrorism effort and have left many of the world's vulnerabilities to terrorism unaddressed.

A. United Nations

The UN has struggled since its inception with how to formulate an effective response to terrorism. On the one hand, using its norm-setting authority, it has provided a solid international legal framework for combating terrorism – via the adoption of thirteen terrorism-related treaties adopted by the General Assembly and UN agencies and a number of legally binding resolutions adopted by the Security Council – thus often reinforcing the efforts of the United States and other countries outside of the UN. On the other hand, it has been unable to reach agreement on a definition of terrorism that outlaws all indiscriminate attacks against civilians. A further defining feature of the UN's counterterrorism effort has been its reactive nature, adopting declarations or treaties or establishing committees or programmes in response to individual attacks, without developing a coherent and co-ordinated response. Because of its largely piecemeal approach, today more than twenty different parts of the UN system deal with terrorism in one form or another, with the Security Council and its four separate counterterrorism-related bodies and three staff bodies now at the centre of this effort.[16]

(i) General Assembly

Although the General Assembly has contributed a handful of important international counterterrorism treaties, it is most well-known in the counterterrorism world for what it has not contributed, namely a definition of terrorism. The global body has been divided on this question since it first took up the issue of terrorism in 1972. This ongoing failure is evidenced by the still unsuccessful efforts of the Ad Hoc Committee to conclude a comprehensive convention on international terrorism, with differences surrounding the definition of terrorism continuing to impede progress. Two major outstanding issues remain. The first is the proposed exclusion from the scope of the convention for the activities of state military forces. The second is the continuing Organisation of the Islamic Conference demand for inclusion of language that would distinguish between terrorist acts and the activities of national liberation movements and 'peoples struggling against foreign occupation'. Despite momentum generated at different times by the September 11 attacks and by the convening of heads of state at the 2005 World Summit, which declared the concluding of the convention to be a priority, the talks remain stalled.

The General Assembly's inability to reach agreement on a definition of terrorism after nearly thirty-five years of discussions in one form or another – with the unfortunate continuing relevance of the phrase 'one man's terrorist is another man's freedom fighter' – has limited the impact of its counterterrorism efforts. Ongoing conflicts in the Middle East, the Kashmir dispute and the difficulty UN Member States seem to have keeping political issues away from the negotiation of a technical, law enforcement instrument mean that we are unlikely to see a breakthrough any time soon.

16 In addition to the General Assembly and Security Council and its subsidiary bodies, the other parts of the UN involved in counterterrorism-related issues include: the Department of Peacekeeping Operations, the Department of Political Affairs, the Department of Public Information, the Department for Disarmament Affairs, the Department of Safety and Security, the International Atomic Energy Agency, the International Civil Aviation Organisation, the International Maritime Organisation, the International Monetary Fund, Interpol, the Office on Drugs and Crime, the Office of the High Commissioner for Human Rights, the Office of Legal Affairs, the Organisation for the Prohibition of Chemical Weapons, United Nations Development Programme, United Nations Educational, Scientific and Cultural Organisation, the World Customs Organisation, the World Bank, the World Health Organisation, the Special Rapporteur on the Promotion and Protection of Human Rights While Countering Terrorism and the three Security Council staff bodies: the Counter-Terrorism Committee Executive Directorate, the Al-Qaida and Taliban Sanctions Committee Analytical Support and Sanctions Monitoring Team and the 1540 Committee's Group of Experts.

(ii) The Security Council

Until 9/11, the Security Council shied away from addressing the challenge of terrorism on a global scale. Although it had adopted resolutions in response to discrete acts of terrorism, for example, in response to the bombing of Pan Am flight 103 and the bombings of the US Embassies in Kenya and Tanzania, its deep involvement in the UN's counterterrorism effort, commencing with Resolution 1373, is a new development. For years before 9/11, the general topic of international terrorism was largely considered a General Assembly issue.[17] This reluctance to consider terrorism was due to a number of factors, among them was the Cold War deadlock in the Security Council and the related North–South divide, which prevented the Council from condemning some of the most heinous terrorist attacks, including the killings of Israeli athletes at the 1972 Munich Olympics. In addition, before the emergence of al-Qaeda, terrorism was considered primarily to be associated with local and regional conflicts, and terrorists thought to define themselves and their field of operations primarily in local rather than global terms. Now, following the attacks on the World Trade Centre and with al-Qaeda and other Jihadist groups operating around the globe, few would dispute that terrorism constitutes one of the most dangerous threats to *international* peace and security. Thus, the Security Council is now leading the UN counterterrorism effort, with its Counter-Terrorism Committee (CTC) at the centre of a programme consisting of several diffuse Security Council subsidiary bodies and other UN entities.

The Security Council created its four counterterrorism-related bodies, using the authority under article 29 of the UN Charter, which allows the Council to establish subsidiary bodies to enable it to function properly. Each body comprises all fifteen Members of the Council and is modelled on the country-specific sanctions committees the Council created over the years to monitor States' implementation of different Council sanctions regimes. The general rule has been that each body is chaired by an Ambassador, usually selected among the elected Members of the Council, whose Mission is in charge of co-ordinating the committee's work. States are generally called on to report to the relevant committee on issues related to its mandate and a team of independent experts hired by the UN Secretariat as consultants, but with the consent of the committee Members, who analyse the reports and provide guidance to its parent body. The bodies all operate by consensus, generally meet in private and report periodically to the Security Council. Before 9/11, the Council had used its article 29 authority to create committees to give particular focus to a continuing threat emanating from a specific country or region. By contrast, each of the counterterrorism bodies was given a global mandate to focus on global threats that have no end in sight.

17 Kendall W. Stiles, 'The Power of Procedure and the Procedures of the Powerful: Anti-Terror Law in the United Nations', (2006) 43(1) *Journal of Peace Research* 39–40.

The Counter-Terrorism Committee

The CTC has received priority attention and resources as the 'center of global efforts to fight terrorism'.[18] The committee has been tasked with monitoring, assessing and facilitating implementation of Resolution 1373 by States. This ground-breaking resolution imposed sweeping legal obligations on UN Member States, creating an unprecedented campaign of co-operative law enforcement measures to combat global terrorist threats. It goes beyond the existing counter-terrorism treaties, which bind only those who have voluntarily become parties to them by creating uniform global obligations.[19] The resolution requires every country, among other things, to freeze the financial assets of terrorists and their supporters, deny travel or safe haven for terrorists, prevent terrorist recruitment and weapons supply and co-operate with other countries in information sharing and criminal prosecution. The CTC's mandate includes 'explor[ing] ways in which States can be assisted by working with international, regional and sub-regional organizations to promote best-practices' and to encourage synergies among technical assistance programmes.[20] The CTC's first chair, Sir Jeremy Greenstock of the United Kingdom, described the CTC as 'a switchboard, a catalyst and a driver of other institutions to do their work in a globally coordinated way'.[21] Its essential functions remain twofold: to determine States' capacity to comply with their obligations under Resolution 1373 and to ensure that potential donors have sufficient information to provide technical assistance that will address the most urgent needs in a timely and sustainable manner.

In its first five years, the CTC has achieved a record of accomplishment in three key areas. First, it has helped to sustain political awareness of the importance of non-military measures against terrorism, through the adoption by

18 United Nations Secretary General Kofi Annan, Statement at Ministerial Level Meeting of the UN Security Council. See United Nations Security Council, *High-level Meeting of the Security Council: Combating Terrorism*, S/PV.4688, New York, 20 January 2003.

19 The Council's adoption of Resolution 1373 (and 1540) has been questioned and criticised by some States as falling outside its mandate. The Council, they argue, was not intended to act as a 'global legislator'. They fear that such action could disrupt the balance of power between the Council and the General Assembly as set forth in the UN Charter. Moreover, they assert that having the Council, a fifteen-Member body not accountable to the other UN organs, impose obligations on all 191 Members, threatens to weaken one of the cornerstones of traditional international law, namely, the principle that international law is based on the consent of States. Others, however, argue that the UN Charter has evolved to allow the Council to act as a 'global legislator' under certain circumstances and that the Council needs to be able to use this tool to address effectively, within the State-centred UN Charter system in which it operates, the threats posed by non-state terrorists and terrorist groups. For an in-depth discussion of the Security Council's 'legislative' role, see Stephen Talmon, 'Note and Comment: The Security Council as World Legislature', (2005) 99 *AJIL* 175; and Eric Rosand, 'The Security Council as "Global Legislator": Ultra Vires or Ultra Innovative', (2005) 28 *Ford ILJ* 542.

20 United Nations Security Council, SC Res. 1377 (2001), S/RES/1377, New York, 12 November 2001.

21 Quoted in United Nations Information Service, 'Vienna Symposium on Terrorism Adds More Momentum to Global Fight Against Terrorism', *United Nations Office on Drugs and Crime*, UNIS/CP/413, Vienna, 6 June 2002.

States of new or the improved implementation, of existing international counter-terrorism instruments and the development and implementation of counter-terrorism action plans. Second, it has played an important role in ensuring that Member State compliance with reporting requirements has been far greater than for any previous Security Council mandate (all 191 UN Member States have, at a minimum, submitted first-round reports explaining their efforts to implement Resolution 1373). The CTC has received and reviewed more than 600 reports from Member States and is thus conducting the first worldwide audit of counterterrorism capacities.[22] Third, the CTC has become a significant element of the worldwide campaign against terrorism by laying the groundwork for effective needs assessments and the co-ordination of capacity-building efforts. It is encouraging States and regional, sub-regional and functional organisations to co-ordinate and improve their counterterrorism efforts, with a view to helping their Members implement the Security Council-imposed counterterrorism obligations and/or join and implement the international conventions and protocols related to terrorism.

The CTC's progress in all three areas can be attributed in large part to its focus on the less controversial aspects of counterterrorism. Although Resolution 1373 imposes a series of legal obligations on all States, it does not attempt to define terrorism or identify specific terrorists, leaving such determinations up to individual Member States. Rather, in addition to the legal obligations it imposes, Resolution 1373 directs Member States to afford one another the greatest measure of assistance in tracking terrorists and investigating terrorist acts. States are urged to intensify and facilitate the exchange of information on matters related to travel, communications and arms trafficking among terrorists, but there has been no mention of any punitive action for States that do not comply with the resolution. Accordingly, the CTC has concentrated on incentives, trying to help States build capacity, with the aim of serving as a 'switchboard' between donors and States lacking capacity.

The Counter-Terrorism Executive Directorate

With the establishment of the Counter-Terrorism Executive Directorate (CTED) in March 2004, the Council sought to provide the CTC with a much needed, larger, more permanent and professional support unit. In doing so, the Council sought to enhance the CTC's ability to fulfil its broad mandate as a capacity-building body by providing it additional resources to work with States and relevant organisations. After lengthy delays due principally to the cumbersome UN budget and personnel processes, the CTED became fully staffed in the fall of 2005, more than

22 According to the CTC's seventeenth work programme, as of 30 September 2005, it had received 613 reports from UN Member States. This includes first reports from all 191 States, 169 second reports, 130 third reports, 101 fourth reports, and twenty-two fifth reports. See Counter-Terrorism Committee, 'CTC Programme of Work'. Available online at the United Nations <http://www.un.org/Docs/sc/committees/1373/programme_of_work.html> (accessed 7 December 2005).

eighteen months after it was created. It is currently preparing technical assistance needs assessments and conducting site visits in an effort to determine the areas in which States need the most help. To date, nearly one hundred needs assessments have been prepared, of which some seventy are being partially shared with donors.[23] It conducted site visits to five countries during 2005, with some twelve more scheduled to follow in 2006. A fully staffed CTED should enable the CTC more expeditiously to solicit and respond to follow-up reports from States and to play a better co-ordinating role among the different international, regional and sub-regional organisations contributing to the counterterrorism effort.

Building and sustaining more effective UN counterterrorism effort, however, requires more than a larger staff. It also requires more effective strategies and programmes, and it remains to be seen whether the CTED will help the CTC develop and implement them.

The Non-Proliferation Committee

Motivated partly by a heightened sensitivity to nuclear security after the revelations in February 2004 of the nuclear black market run by Pakistani scientist A.Q. Khan and following the precedent of Resolution 1373, the Council adopted Resolution 1540 in April 2004, requiring all States to take a series of legislative and regulatory steps to prevent weapons of mass destruction (WMD) and their means of delivery from getting into the hands of terrorists. The CTC's capacity-building and co-ordination-focused approach was the model for the Council when it established the 1540 Committee – with a mandate of two years – to monitor States' efforts to implement their 1540 obligations.[24] In addition, the Council established a group of eight independent experts to support the committee's work. The committee got off to a slow start because of the presence of a particularly obstructive non-permanent Council Member, which rotated off the Security Council and thus the Committee at the end of 2004. Reporting to the committee has lagged, partly because of reporting fatigue among countries burdened with an ever-increasing number of requirements.[25] The committee has developed an elaborate matrix, however, which identifies the different steps States should take to implement fully the provisions of the resolution and indicates what additional steps still need to be taken. The committee has reviewed and sent a copy of the matrix to all 124 States that submitted first-round reports thus far. As for the facilitation of technical assistance, the committee is in the

23 The needs assessments contain two parts. The first consists of an analysis of the particular State's efforts to implement Resolution 1373. The second consists of a list of priority areas where the CTED believes the particular State needs technical assistance to enable it to implement the resolution fully. Currently, only the latter part is shared – only with the State's consent – with relevant donors.

24 On 27 April 2006, the Security Council adopted Resolution 1673 to extend the committee's mandate for a second two-year term.

25 As of October 2005, the committee has received reports from 124 States, i.e. some two-thirds of the UN Membership.

early stages of developing its policies in this area. If the development of policies in the other Security Council subsidiary bodies is any guide, this is expected to be a bureaucratic and time-consuming process. The committee's group of experts has so far resisted Security Council calls for greater co-ordination and co-operation with the other Security Council counterterrorism-related staff bodies, citing the WMD (rather than terrorism) focus of the 1540 Committee.

Al-Qaeda/Taliban Sanctions Committee

Although originally established as part of the Security Council's strategy to address the terrorist threat posed by Taliban-controlled Afghanistan, the mandate of the 1267 Committee (which has since become known as the al-Qaeda and Taliban Sanctions Committee) was expanded following 11 September 2001, to deal with the global al-Qaeda threat. Thus, it now monitors the implementation of financial, travel and arms sanctions against al-Qaeda, the Taliban, Osama bin Laden and their associates. As part of its response to the events of September 11, the council required all states to impose these measures on the individuals and entities listed by the committee, which manages and updates the list. To assist the committee with its work, the council established an eight-person Analytical Support and Sanctions Monitoring Team (Monitoring Team) to 'collate, assess, monitor, and report on' steps being taken to implement and enforce the sanctions measures against those on the list and to recommend new measures to address the evolving al-Qaeda threat.

Today, there are more than four hundred names on the committee's list, the vast majority of which were submitted by the United States in the aftermath of September 11 either alone or in conjunction with other UN member states. In the weeks following that day, according to one Security Council diplomat, 'there was enormous good will and a willingness to take on trust any name the U.S. submitted'.[26] During this period, the creation of the list was based largely on political trust, with the committee having no particular guidelines or standards for states to follow in proposing names. Since then, the committee has adopted such guidelines, putting minimum evidentiary standards for submitting names and a transparent listing process into place to help ensure that due process and other human rights standards are respected. Yet, concerns about the committee's lack of due process continue to dominate discussions regarding its work, with the procedures for listing and delisting proving to be contentious.

Maintaining support for the committee's work and implementation of the sanctions remain high priorities in the global counterterrorism effort. Such support, however, according to council watchers, seems to be eroding because of these due process concerns.[27] The committee continues to try to strike the right

26 Christopher Cooper, 'Shunned in Sweden: How the Drive to Block Funds for Terrorism Entangled Mr. Aden', *Wall Street Journal*, 6 May 2002.

27 'The 1267 (Al-Qaeda/Taliban) Committee and the 1540 (WMD) Sanctions Committee', *Security Council Report*, Update Report no. 5, 16 January 2006.

balance between its European members, which generally favour greater transparency and providing those on the list with more rights, including possibly allowing them to approach the committee directly, and other, less forward-leaning members. Even with the mounting controversy surrounding the process (or lack thereof) for adding and removing names from the list, however, it does still serve as the primary vehicle by which states are empowered to freeze the assets of suspected al-Qaeda and Taliban members. Whereas countries may be reluctant to freeze the assets of an entity simply because the United States or another powerful country suspects it of having ties to al-Qaeda, they have an obligation under international law to do so if that entity is included on the committee's list.[28]

With respect to state implementation of the sanctions themselves, the record is mixed.[29] As the reports of the Monitoring Team have revealed, the travel ban and arms embargo have produced few tangible results. The asset-freeze requirement, as mentioned above, has proved valuable in helping internationalise the policy of freezing terrorist assets.[30] However, despite the success, albeit limited, of the asset freeze, the UN Secretary General's High Level Panel on Threats, Challenges and Change, the Secretary General himself and world leaders at the 2005 World Summit noted that too often the UN-imposed sanctions are not implemented and more must be done to ensure that they are. Rather than a lack of political commitment from states, the Monitoring Team has found a lack of legislative and operational capacity to be the major impediment to implementation.

1566 Working Group

The Security Council's response to the seizure of approximately 1,200 hostages and the death of hundreds of children at a school in Beslan, Russia, was emblematic of its broader efforts to address the terrorist threat. The desire to

28 Moreover, more than forty have still not reported to the committee on steps they are taking to implement the sanctions, as called for by the Security Council in January 2003.

29 For a critical analysis of the work of the Al-Qaida and Taliban Sanctions Committee, see Eric Rosand, 'Current Developments: The Security Council's Efforts to Monitor the Implementation of Al-Qaida/Taliban Sanctions', (2004) 98 *AJIL* 745.

30 As of January 2005, states were reported to have seized or frozen $147 million in assets belonging to 435 individuals and groups linked to al-Qaeda or the Taliban. In October 2005, the list included 140 individuals associated with the Taliban and 182 people and 117 businesses or groups linked to al-Qaeda. This number is somewhat misleading for a number of reasons. First, between 11 September 2001 and the end of 2001 alone, $112 million in alleged terrorist funds had been frozen (Chantal de Jonge Oudraat, 'Combating Terrorism', *The Washington Quarterly* [Autumn 2003]). Second, in the two years after that, only $24 million was frozen. Unspecified 'recently published US Treasury report' cited in UN Security Council doc. S/2003/1070, 2 December 2003, 12, fn. c. Little if any of the $24 million were linked to individuals or entities listed on the al-Qaeda and Taliban Sanction Committee's list (UN doc. S/2003/1070, 36). Finally, according to a 2002 independent US expert panel on terrorist finance, 'the frequently cited total amount of terrorist-related assets blocked overstates the amount of money taken from al-Qaida and its supporters specifically, and undoubtedly represents only a small fraction of total funds available to that terrorist organization' [Maurice Greenberg, William F. Wechsler, and Lee S. Wolosky, *Terrorist Financing: Independent Task Force Report* (2002) 20].

satisfy short-term political objectives of one or more council members overcame the need to develop a coherent council-led UN counterterrorism programme.

The Russian Federation, using the council's robust response to September 11 as its benchmark, pushed the council to adopt its strongest condemnation to date of attacks against civilians in Resolution 1566. Many council members, some of which had been victimised by terrorism, wanted to show their solidarity with the Russians and thus were eager to accommodate the Russian proposals, which had little support on their merits. Despite recognising that the council's three existing terrorism-related committees were having difficulty co-ordinating and that the council's counterterrorism programme needed to be rationalised, the council agreed to establish yet another terrorism-related committee, the working group established by Resolution 1566 (2004). The council provided the working group with a mandate (1) to consider practical measures to be imposed upon individuals, groups or entities involved in or associated with terrorist activities, other than those on the al-Qaeda/Taliban consolidated list, and (2) to look into the possibility of creating an international fund for the victims of terrorism. Many individual council members objected both to the notion of an expanded UN list of terrorists absent a UN definition of terrorism and to the idea of an international fund for terrorist victims.

Predictably, the differences among council members that were subsumed during the negotiations of Resolution 1566 surfaced during the meetings of the working group, which has rarely met and, not surprisingly, has been unable to reach consensus on any meaningful recommendations. Thus, for example, discussions on whether and how to expand the list beyond al-Qaeda and the Taliban got nowhere, running into the same roadblocks that have prevented the General Assembly from agreeing on a global definition of terrorism. This impasse served as a further reminder of the difficulties the UN will face trying to maintain international counterterrorism co-operation against groups other than al-Qaeda or its associates.

With a combined budget of $13–14 million and some thirty-six experts, the largely under-resourced mechanisms the council established to prod and encourage states to implement its counterterrorism framework were generally part of the council's reaction to particular terrorist attacks, at which times the politics of the moment trumped the need to develop an effective and coherent council counterterrorism programme. Despite pockets of success, the council has failed to develop a coherent and effective counterterrorism programme capable of implementing the far-reaching legal mandate it gave itself in this area and thus has been unable to co-ordinate global counterterrorism capacity-building efforts effectively.

(iii) UN Office on Drugs and Crime

A number of other UN agencies have become involved in providing counterterrorism-related assistance and training to states. The most significant element of this assistance programme is carried out by the UN Office on Drugs and Crime (UNODC), located in Vienna. Its Terrorism Prevention Branch (TPB) and Global Programme against Money Laundering (GPML) provide States with legislative drafting and other technical assistance and have expanded their respective programmes since 11 September 2001. The former focuses on helping States ratify and implement the thirteen international conventions and protocols related to terrorism and the latter on helping States implement the Terrorist Financing Convention and the Financial Action Task Force's (FATF) special recommendations on money laundering and terrorist financing. With staff and consultants stationed in regional offices and country offices around the globe, it has been able to co-ordinate quite closely with regional organisations, including by co-hosting legislative drafting workshops in different regions.

(iv) UN efforts to strengthen and streamline its counterterrorism programme

Since the events of 11 September 2001, the UN's counterterrorism programme has expanded considerably. It is no longer limited to condemning discrete terrorist acts and setting normative and legal standards but now includes monitoring of states' efforts to meet these standards and working with states to improve their capacity to fight terrorism. The locus of the UN's efforts has thus shifted away from the General Assembly to the Security Council's intergovernmental bodies and the five UN staff bodies (three Security Council bodies and two UNODC staff bodies).

There is a growing concern among UN members about the effectiveness of the UN's counterterrorism initiatives and the lack of co-ordination among its different components, particularly the Security Council committees and staff bodies. For example, in 2004, Costa Rica and Switzerland called for the establishment of a UN High Commissioner for terrorism to co-ordinate the growing number of UN counterterrorism initiatives. The proposal was motivated in part by a desire among non–Security Council members to shift the focus of the UN counterterrorism effort back to the more inclusive General Assembly by having the General Assembly take control of the currently council-led counterterrorism programme, in particular its staff bodies. In the end, the five permanent members of the council objected to it for just that reason, despite acknowledging that the UN effort could be improved.

Reflecting the broad dissatisfaction with the UN's counterterrorism programme, both the leaders at the UN World Summit and the 60th General Assembly requested the Secretary General to prepare a report with recommendations on how to enhance the UN effort.[31] The Secretary General's report, *Uniting Against Terrorism*, urged states to focus their efforts on the concrete, practical contributions that the different parts of the UN system can make in the

31 *Op. cit.*, fn. 9, UN doc. A/60825.

counterterrorism effort and on improving co-ordination and co-operation among the twenty-three different parts of the system currently engaged in this effort. The report emphasised the role that the UN can play in helping countries strengthen their counterterrorism capacities, both by identifying and by helping close gaps. The Secretary General also argued for the development of a more holistic, inclusive UN approach to counterterrorism, seeking to deepen the co-ordination between the Security Council's security-focused counterterrorism programme and the parts of the UN system that deal with development, human rights, education and peacekeeping – issues which are connected to one or more of the underlying societal and political underlying conditions that may contribute to terrorism.

The General Assembly started considering the Secretary General's recommendations in May 2006, with a view to develop its own counterterrorism strategy. Not surprisingly, given the global body's track record in dealing with terrorism-related issues, and the difficulties in getting different parts of the UN system to co-operate and co-ordinate to address cross-cutting issues effectively, the General Assembly has made little progress to date. It got bogged down with the same political issues that have prevented it from reaching agreement on a definition of terrorism. On the former, the United States, the EU, Japan and the rest of the global North have favoured the Secretary General's pragmatic approach. Yet, many in the global South, including nearly every member of the Organisation of Islamic Conferences (OIC), has sought to have any General Assembly strategy make an explicit distinction between terrorism and 'freedom fighters' and to recognise foreign occupation as a root cause of terrorism. Some OIC members sought to use this exercise to downplay the significance of the Security Council's contribution to the global counterterrorism campaign, with the Egyptian Permanent Representative going so far as to call for the deletion of all references to Security Council resolutions and accompanying mandates. Furthermore, some States cite the lack of a UN definition as a reason for not implementing their existing UN counterterrorism obligations, whether imposed by the Security Council or undertaken voluntarily because of joining the international conventions and protocols related to terrorism.

On the latter, some UN Members pushed back against the Secretary General's call for the United Nations Development Programme (UNDP) 'to integrat[e] concerns about terrorism into democratic governance programming', fearing that such integration might unduly politicise the UNDP's more traditional development projects.[32] This concern has also been voiced by the UNDP staff itself.

In the end, although unable to endorse many of the Secretary General's recommendations, the General Assembly was able to reach agreement on a rather anodyne, but consensus, strategy that largely repeats previous commitments

32 *Op. cit.*, fn. 9, para. 34.

made by one UN body or another but may provide a framework for enhancing the UN system's counterterrorism efforts.[33]

B. Regional/Functional Bodies

Although the UN has sought to assume the leading role in the post-September 11, 2001, multilateral effort, other intergovernmental bodies have joined what has become a growth industry, with more and more counterterrorism programmes being initiated at different levels and in different substantive areas. Regional organisations such as the Asia-Pacific Economic Co-operation (APEC), the African Union (AU) and the Organisation of American States (OAS) have adopted strong political counterterrorism declarations and action plans and/or established dedicated counterterrorism units within their secretariats to work with their members in building capacity. Functional international organisations such as the International Civil Aviation Organisation (ICAO), the International Maritime Organisation (IMO), the International Monetary Fund and the World Customs Organisation (WCO), to name just a few, have also added a counterterrorism component to their work. Some have adopted counterterrorism-related best practices, codes or standards and/or provided training and other forms of counterterrorism technical assistance. Some regional bodies have succeeded in getting their members to implement the technical standards developed by the functional institutions. This has generally occurred, however, only where there is a strong donor presence among the membership, for example APEC (Australia, Canada, Japan and USA), OAS (Canada and USA) and Organization for Security and Cooperation in Europe (OSCE) (EU, Canada and US). In these bodies, donors have funded technical assistance programmes to help the less-developed members implement the relevant standards or best practices.

In addition to the above-mentioned, more formal entities, informal intergovernmental bodies such as the thirty-three member FATF and the G8 have sought to become involved in the global counterterrorism effort. The G8's Lyon-Roma Anti-Crime and Terrorism Group, which consists of a series of sub-groups staffed by experts from each of the G8 capitals meeting several times annually, has developed counterterrorism standards and best practices on a wide variety of topics. Because participation in the Group and its sub-groups is informal and flexible enough to allow the participation of a wide assortment of experts according to different subjects, the G8 is often able to produce concrete results, for example counterterrorism standards or best practices, more quickly than

33 Associated Press, 'U.N. General Assembly adopts counter-terrorism strategy', *International Herald Tribune*, 9 September 2006. Available at <http://www.iht.com/articles/ap/2006/09/08/news/UN_GEN_UN_Counter_Terrorism.php>.

more formal multilateral bodies.[34] Because of the G8's limited membership, however, it lacks broad legitimacy among members of the global South. Although the G8 has had some success exporting its work for adoption or endorsement by some of the functional organisations such as ICAO and/or certain regional bodies where there is a G8 Member present, it has generally had much less success in getting regional bodies where there is no such presence, for example Africa, the Middle East and South Asia.

To complement its standard setting work, in 2003, the G8 created the Counter-Terrorism Action Group (CTAG), to co-ordinate the delivery of global counter-terrorism assistance in close co-ordination with the CTC. Yet, the CTAG, like the G8 itself, is an ad hoc political mechanism with no permanent secretariat, and thus, it has had difficulty sustaining momentum from one year to the next. Furthermore, it lacks the legitimacy in the global South to enable it to assume a role in co-ordinating global multilateral, non-military counterterrorism efforts. As a result, it has yet to deliver the results G8 Leaders had hoped for when it was established at the G8 summit in Evian, France.

The FATF, which was created by the then G7 in 1989 and which has strict membership criteria, has developed a set of recommendations in the fields of money laundering and terrorist financing that are widely accepted as the global standards in these areas. Although consisting of only thirty-three members, to broaden its appeal and the legitimacy of its work, FATF has helped establish FATF-style regional bodies (FSRBs) in all regions, including Africa and the Middle East. Each of the more than 150 States, which are now members of one of the FSRBs, are thus politically committed to implementing the FATF's standard-setting work.[35]

Although improved regional and functional responses should be applauded, most of the bodies are toiling on small pieces of territory or within a narrow field. This piecemeal approach has left swaths of territory (e.g. the Middle East and North Africa, Sub-Saharan Africa, South Asia and former Soviet states) and substantive functional areas (e.g. terrorist safe haven, travel and misuse of the Internet and other media) not covered by an effective multilateral body. It is in these areas where the terrorist threat may be the greatest, with states often lacking the capacity – for example appropriate legal and intelligence infrastructures and land, port and airport security – to confront the threat posed by home-grown terrorist groups and/or recruited radical Islamists. Partly due to a

34 For example, at the June 2004 G8 Summit, the G8 adopted the Secure and Facilitated International Travel Initiative (SAFTI), which included twenty-eight forward-leaning projects in multiple areas of travel security, including ensuring safe and efficient movement of passengers and cargo, enhancing travel document security and interoperability, information exchange, security co-operation and MANPADS threat reduction. Less than two years later, work on nearly all of the projects has been completed, and many have already been exported to broader international bodies such as ICAO.

35 For a detailed description of FATF's current mandate, see <http://www.fatf-gafi.org/dataoecd/14/60/36309648.pdf>.

lack of a robust technical assistance programme, regional bodies in Africa and the Middle East have generally not had much success in prodding their members to take the steps necessary to upgrade their counterterrorism capacities. The result is that the goal of developing a seamless counterterrorism web remains incomplete. The challenge is to find ways to get multilateral bodies in Africa and the Middle East, and their members, to become more active in this area.

As within the UN, the plethora of counterterrorism programmes outside it has led to overlapping mandates and lack of co-ordination and information sharing among the different organisations as well as gaps in regional and thematic coverage. This in turn has led to a growing need and calls for greater co-operation and co-ordination among the organisations to create more synergy and minimise duplication of effort. For more than four years, the CTC has sought to assume the global co-ordinating role among organisations involved in counterterrorism. Yet, apart from the convening of four international meetings that brought together representatives of more than sixty international, regional and subregional organisations as well as encouraging increased counterterrorism efforts by all organisations, the CTC has not made a significant or enduring contribution in this area. The CTC has not been able to develop close and responsive relationships with many of these organisations, which has led to difficulties in co-operating to bring technical assistance to states in need.

4. The Need for a More Effective International Co-ordinating Mechanism

Maintaining both the international co-operation that has characterised the post-September 11, 2001, campaign against terrorism and the focus on capacity building and other non-military measures in this campaign, as well as the need to address the proliferation of counterterrorism bodies, highlights the need for an effective multilateral body at the centre of the effort.

The CTC was supposed to be this body. It has produced some modest successes in increasing awareness of the global nature of the terrorist threat and compiling useful information from the hundreds of country reports that have been submitted. The CTC, however, has not been able to play an effective co-ordinating role among states and organisations and has not effectively co-ordinated global capacity-building efforts to help ensure that the priority gaps are filled. Neither the CTC nor its CTED have the resources to provide any assistance. Thus, even if the CTC can effectively determine the most urgent gaps to be filled, which still remains a big if, it must rely on donors to come forward to deliver the necessary aid. In fact, the CTC has no authority over even the counterterrorism assistance providers within the UN system such as the UNODC's TPB and GPML and has had difficulties getting the other parts of the Council's counterterrorism programme to co-operate with it. Furthermore, purely political bodies such as the CTC and its sister council subsidiary bodies are ill-suited to the task of implementing the technical aspects of the mandates given to them by the Security Council. The most straightforward uncontroversial matters, such as facilitating technical assistance between consenting donors and recipients, have a tendency to get bound up in red tape and side-tracked by seemingly endless political discussions.

Moreover, the proliferation of Security Council counterterrorism programmes and initiatives has produced overlapping mandates, turf battles, duplication of work, multiple and sometimes confusing reporting requirements for states and continuing tension between the Security Council and the UN Secretariat. In general, information sharing and other forms of co-operation between and among these groups have been inadequate and often redundant, which has inhibited the overall council effort.

In short, if the current arrangement continues, the CTC, as well as the other Council counterterrorism bodies will probably find it more and more difficult to maintain co-operation from the broader UN Membership. This particularly goes for countries from the global South, which will continue to grow increasingly frustrated with a set of Council bodies that place a growing number of demands on under-resourced bureaucracies, without being able to provide them anything tangible, for example technical assistance, in return. In addition, the lack of co-ordination and co-operation among the different regional and functional institutions, which are central to create a seamless counterterrorism web, would continue. Moreover, little progress will probably be made in developing a more holistic UN response to terrorism, as UNDP, UNESCO and other parts of the UN system that focus on some of the 'underlying conditions' that can lead to terrorism would continue to balk at deepening their co-operation with the Security Council's CTC for fear that their work might become unduly politicised. Perhaps most importantly, simply maintaining the *status quo* will both lend support to the growing number of people who question whether the UN is capable of making a meaningful contribution to address twenty-first-century global threats and hinder efforts to enhance the role of multilateral institutions in the fight against terrorism.

A. Possible Short-Term Fix

With the largest UN counterterrorism staff body's (the CTED) mandate set to expire at the end of 2007, rather than simply renew its mandate as would be the norm in the UN, the Security Council could take a somewhat bold step and consolidate its multiple counterterrorism-related bodies into a single entity to make the Council's programme more coherent and effective. The Secretary General has recently recommended that the council consider this.[36] Consolidation would improve the situation somewhat and need not consume significant time and energy. It could be pursued in the short term while states give careful consideration to the question of what is needed to create an effective multilateral body capable of playing a central role in global capacity-building and other non-military counterterrorism efforts.

In addition to two options for consolidating the various council bodies – one limited to its staff bodies and one combining the committees themselves into a single Member State body – a third could include bringing the experts in the UNODC's TPB and GPML into the fold.[37] Any steps involving either of the UNODC programmes would require a decision of the General Assembly, the body with oversight over those offices.

Any of these steps could be carried out in conjunction with two other reforms, which would enhance the council's efforts and build support from non-council member states, particularly the smaller ones: the consolidation of the multiple reporting requirements into a single requirement and consolidated country visits by the various groups of experts. States would submit one report to the council, on a periodic basis, that contains efforts to implement all of the Security Council-imposed counterterrorism mandates. By addressing the reporting fatigue complaint head-on in this way, the council would eliminate a reason (or excuse) more and more states are giving for not co-operating fully with the various counterterrorism-related bodies.[38]

B. *Limitations of the UN Security Council-Led Approach*

Even a more unified UN counterterrorism programme, however, would run up against the inherent political, administrative and budgetary challenges of

36 'Mandating and Delivering: Analysis and Recommendations to Facilitate the Review of Mandates', A/60/733, Report of Secretary General of the United Nations, New York, 30 March 2006, paras. 122–123.

37 The 2005 Gingrich/Mitchell Task Force on UN Reform, finding the UN Security Council-led counterterrorism programme poorly co-ordinated, recommended that some of these options be explored. It highlighted the problem of lack of co-ordination in the UN counterterrorism programme: 'Among the solutions that should be explored are mandating closer coordination among the committees (including reducing unnecessary duplication in Member States' reports), combining their staffs and combining the committees themselves'. *American Interests on UN Reform: Report of the Task Force on the United Nations* (Washington, D.C.: United States Institute of Peace, 2005), 78. The United States has even suggested that such a consolidation might be necessary. See 'Statement by Nicholas Rostow, General Counsel, on the Work of the 1267 Committee, in the Security Council, July 20, 2005', USUN Press Release no. 136 (05), <http://www.un.int/usa/05_136.htm>.

38 In addition, as recently confirmed by the Japanese Permanent Representative to the UN, consolidated site visits would enhance the effectiveness of the dialogue between the various council counterterrorism mechanisms and government officials and improve the information gathering and sharing. The 'rationalization of visits would [also] relieve the burden on visited states'. See statement by Japan (Kenzo Oshima) at the 30 May 2006, Security Council meeting to discuss the council's counterterrorism programme. A summary of the meeting is available online at <http://www.un.org/News/Press/docs/2006/sc8730.doc.htm>.

operating within the UN system that would make it difficult to co-ordinate global capacity-building efforts effectively. For example, even if one were to combine Security Council and UNODC counterterrorism staff and resources, you would have only some fifty to sixty experts, with an annual budget of around $16–20 million. These are not sufficient to allow the UN to fulfil its broad counterterrorism mandate. To highlight this point: the International Atomic Energy Agency (IAEA) – the world's central intergovernmental forum for scientific and technical co-operation in the nuclear field, working to verify that safeguarded nuclear material and activities are not used for military purposes – has a staff of some 2,200 people (with more than half of them technical experts) and an annual budget of some $268 million.[39]

Second, because the funding for the Security Council's counterterrorism programmes comes from the regular UN budget, it is subject to the politics of the Fifth Committee, the main committee of the General Assembly responsible for administration and budgetary matters. It must compete in this committee with other important programmes for limited resources.[40] Given the different, and at times competing, priorities of the global North and South and the Fifth Committee practice of reaching consensus on the budget, it is unlikely that the counterterrorism programme could ever be allocated the resources needed to succeed so long as it is funded out of the UN regular budget and perceived as a Security Council-led exercise.[41]

Third, the decision-making processes of the Security Council CTCs have also presented serious challenges. The practice of taking all decisions by consensus has significantly impeded their ability to take action in a timely fashion and at times diluted their work. To maintain its relevance and effectiveness, the leading multilateral counterterrorism body needs to be able to act quickly and decisively on matters that are often technical in nature and does not need to get bogged down in seemingly endless political debates. This is particularly so given the often fast-paced transformations in the global security environment.

The same consensus-based practice has made it difficult for any of the Security Council counterterrorism-related bodies to identify non-performers ('name

39 For information about the IAEA's budget and staff, see the IAEA's website: <http://www.iaea.org/About/budget.html> and <http://www.iaea.org/About/staff.html>.

40 Of those counterterrorism-related bodies, only the UNODC/TPB and GPML accept voluntary contributions. Voluntary contributions are a major source of funding for most other UN organisations and programmes such as the IAEA, UNDP and the UN Environmental Programme.

41 The total 2005 budget for the Security Council counterterrorism programmes was $12.5 million; for the Al-Qaida and Taliban Monitoring Team, $3,559,300; for the CTED, $6,888,300 and for the 1540 Committee group of experts, $1,794,900. See 'Questions Relating to the Programme Budget for the Biennium 2004–2005'; 'Estimates in Respect of Special Political Missions, Good Offices and Other Political Initiatives Authorized by the General Assembly and/or the Security Council', A/59/534/Add.1. United Nations General Assembly, New York, 23 November 2004. The TPB's budget for 2005 was $3.5 million, with $1 million coming out of the UN regular budget and the rest coming from voluntary contributions and the GPML's for 2005 was $3.2 million in voluntary contributions.

and shame') or even to agree on a set of standards against which to measure performance. The consensus approach has meant that the political and legal power of the different Security Council resolutions on terrorism adopted under Chapter VII of the UN Charter, which authorises the Council to impose far-reaching legal obligations and sanctions on States, and the subsidiary bodies that were created using this same authority are significantly weakened.

Fourth, the council is generally focused on responding to specific, time-limited threats to international peace and security. Thus, it responds quickly and forcefully to a discrete terrorist incident, meeting at night or on the weekend to adopt the necessary resolution or presidential statement. It has found it difficult, however, to sustain the momentum of its long-term counterterrorism capacity-building programme and the multitude of tasks that are involved.

Fifth, the UN's comparative advantage in the field of counterterrorism lies in capacity building and standard setting, both of which have a significant technical component. Yet, because the UN's work in this area is overseen by the Security Council and its subsidiary bodies, this effort has been and will continue to be heavily (and perhaps unnecessarily) politicised, with delegations often interjecting tendentious political issues, thus slowing down the legal and technical work. Thus, when the Security Council is in the throes of a contentious negotiation outside the purview of its counterterrorism-related committees, the differences of views and even animosities among certain delegations can spill over into these bodies.[42]

The problem of overpoliticisation of technical issues is exacerbated by the fact that the representatives on the CTC and other Security Council counterterrorism-related bodies are usually political officers (regular diplomats or generalists), often with little or no background in the technical field of counterterrorism. As a result, rather than focusing on concrete country, regional or thematic issues, the bodies, in particular the CTC, have tended to become unnecessarily consumed in negotiating process-oriented papers and focusing on the political rather than the technical aspects of a particular issue. This is in contrast to technical organisations such as the IAEA, the Organisation for the Prohibition of Chemical Weapons (OPCW), Interpol and ICAO, where member state delegations generally include domestic experts in the relevant field.[43]

Finally, the principal UN organs in New York, including the Security Council and its subsidiary bodies, are often devotees of precedent, determined to follow established precedents and fearful of setting new ones, which often results in an excess of caution and a fear of trying anything new. This fear of setting a

42 This occurred in the latter part of 2005, for example when the council was seized with the assassination of former Lebanese Prime Minister Rafic Hariri.

43 For example, the US delegation to the IAEA includes representatives from the Department of Energy, its delegation to the ICAO includes representatives from the Federal Aviation Administration and its delegation to the World Customs Organisation includes representatives from the Department of Homeland Security.

precedent for other council work prolonged the negotiations that led to the establishment of the CTED, a somewhat unique UN body that is both part of the Secretariat and reports to the Security Council. It has also been partly responsible for the CTC's reluctance to reach out to the development and human rights communities, including non-governmental organisations in those areas. Given the rapidly evolving nature of the terrorist threat, it is important that the body that is supposed to be co-ordinating the multilateral, non-military counterterrorism effort has the operating flexibility it needs to adjust to the threat and make decisions without having to worry about establishing a precedent that might not be welcomed in non-terrorism contexts. Neither the CTC nor any of the other council counterterrorism-related bodies currently has this luxury.

C. *A Possible Long-Term Solution: The Establishment of a Global Counterterrorism Body*

Monitoring the implementation of states' counterterrorism obligations and helping States develop their counterterrorism capacities requires a long-term and unwavering commitment – one that will not diminish as memories of the most recent horrific terrorist attack fade or if the Security Council is seized with specific threats to international peace and security that require its urgent attention. Given the importance and long-term nature of the task, and the abovementioned political and institutional limitations of working within the UN, a new international body dedicated to counterterrorism outside of, but perhaps related in some way to, the UN is probably needed.

Whether directly connected to the United Nations or as a stand-alone entity, a dedicated counterterrorism organisation could take over the work of the existing Security Council counterterrorism-related bodies, particularly the CTC, plus UNODC. This new organisation could focus and build upon their work.[44] Moreover, it would work to monitor implementation of current and future UN conventions and other instruments against terrorism. Freed from the limitations of the UN political bodies, it could more effectively perform the tasks currently being performed by them. The counterterrorism-related work of organisations in the broader UN family need not be affected, except insofar as a new global body would enhance the co-operation and co-ordination among them. Some States might initially balk at transferring the responsibilities for monitoring the implementation of Security Council counterterrorism obligations to a new, non-council body for fear that such a body would not be as powerful as those under the Security Council, lacking as it would the council's enforcement capacity. For reasons explained above, however, none of the council's counterterrorism bodies are able to make use of the council's authority and influence. For example, they are unlikely ever to identify non-performers, let alone be able to

44 Presumably, this could only be done via a decision of the Security Council.

refer a country to the council for enforcement action. While there would be a number of benefits from no longer being part of the council, the new organisation could also retain some link to it, for example the authority to refer states to it for remedial action. Thus, no real loss of power or authority needs result from such a transfer.

There would be a number of benefits that would accrue from creating a dedicated, global counterterrorism body. For example, first, it could take a more comprehensive approach to combating terrorism, in part by ensuring more rigorous analysis of states' capacities, identification of what states' priorities should be and a more proactive approach to working with states and organisations. This enhanced analysis and action could be used to address states' lack of capacity and difficulties in implementing the myriad counterterrorism-related obligations in a more effective manner, reducing the current overlap of the expert assessments being done by both UN and non-UN bodies and more efficiently utilising limited resources.

Second, it could carry out its mandate free from the limitations that bog down the current UN effort. For instance, if provided the necessary operational capacity, human and financial resources and appropriate array of technical expertise, it could conduct credible and comprehensive assessments of the counterterrorism capacity of states and ensure that those that lack the capacity are linked up with available assistance.

Third, it could help shoulder the capacity-building and training burden currently undertaken by a handful of states and organisations. In the area of terrorist financing, for example the United States, because of diminishing resources due to the heavy costs of training Iraqi and Afghan officials, focuses its technical assistance efforts on some twenty priority countries it believes are the most vulnerable. A global body could focus on those countries that are not priority countries for the United States or the other major donors (e.g. the European Union or the CTAG).

Fourth, a global body with broad North-South support could take the lead in working with those countries in which the major donors lack the necessary access and leverage to push for the enhancement of counterterrorism capacity. Assuming that it had regional offices, these could be used as platforms for capacity-building efforts such as training programmes at the regional level. Using this type of framework for training would be particularly valuable in regions where a US or other Western capacity-building effort might not be welcomed. This approach, as opposed to bilateral training programmes, would also be valuable as it would bring together officials from a group of countries in a region or sub-region and allow them to develop relationships essential to promote law enforcement and other co-operation.

Fifth, a specialised body could co-ordinate with regional and functional organisations to conduct on-the-ground assessments and provide legislative drafting and infrastructural development assistance. Effectively co-ordinating the counterterrorism efforts of international, regional and sub-regional organisations requires sufficient staff and resources to convene meetings and workshops of domestic counterterrorism experts to exchange information, share best practices and report on challenges being faced in the fight against terrorism. The global body could perform the important function of working with regional organisations to help them establish priorities and develop programmes and projects.

Sixth, in addition to sharing information regarding regional counterterrorism initiatives, the global body could serve as a central authority to facilitate the sharing of evidence among domestic judicial authorities, mutual legal assistance among prosecutorial authorities and the implementation of extradition requests. Finally, this new body could examine existing and new ways for law enforcement and judicial authorities to co-operate more effectively.

Seventh, a global, dedicated counterterrorism organisation would not only be able to carry out more effectively and efficiently the tasks currently being performed by the existing UN bodies; it could also undertake additional tasks. It could develop a system to measure states' performance and encourage donors to require states to meet certain minimum standards to be eligible for various forms of non-counterterrorism-related assistance. A permanent global counterterrorism body could address the most topical and emerging terrorism issues – such as incitement, bio-terrorism, cyber-terrorism and terrorism and the media – which do not fit naturally within the purview of any existing multilateral fora. A larger, more expert global organisation could also be mandated to propagate counterterrorism methodologies and technologies. A new entity could help to follow trends, as the World Health Organisation (WHO) does with regard to potential epidemics, to develop global solutions to global problems. The most common procedure to address such changes today is for the General Assembly to discuss them and/or the Security Council to either establish a new subsidiary body to deal with an issue or, as in the case of terrorist incitement, refer it to the CTC.

The numerous international bodies that have been created in the past fifty years to address security and other global issues offer a range of models to look to when forming a multilateral counterterrorism organisation. They fit broadly into three categories: a treaty-based body (e.g. IAEA or OPCW), an informal, political body (e.g. Wassenaar Arrangement or FATF) or a UN programme (e.g. UNDP or UN High Commissioner for Refugees). Given the *sui generis* nature of a global counterterrorism organisation, a new body would probably draw upon elements from many, if not all, of these models.

As a first step to establish a new entity, an international process involving a broad range of stakeholders from both the global North and South should be convened outside of the unduly politicised UN setting to discuss the pros and cons of the various possibilities, with a view to recommend the elements of each that should be included in a global counterterrorism body and what the mandate of such an entity should be. Regardless of which model is chosen, any body needs to attract broad support from a cross-section of countries to obtain the financial and political support necessary for long-term viability and legitimacy. In addition, it needs to be designed to help ensure an effective and long-lasting mechanism exists both to co-ordinate the delivery of counterterrorism capacity-building assistance to the global South and develop a more holistic and representative counterterrorism programme than the current Security Council-led one, which is too narrow in its focus.

Name Index

For Product Safety Concerns and Information please contact our EU representative GPSR@taylorandfrancis.com Taylor & Francis Verlag GmbH, Kaufingerstraße 24, 80331 München, Germany

Batch number: 10726294

Printed by Printforce, the Netherlands